The American Film History Reader

What do we talk or write about when we discuss American film history? The answer is predictably complex and elusive. *The American Film History Reader* acknowledges and accommodates this complexity by showcasing a range of historical writing demonstrating that when we reflect upon film history we, by necessity, talk and write about a lot of different things.

The American Film History Reader provides a selective history of American cinema and offers an introduction to historiographic practice in relation to American moviemaking and moviegoing.

The Reader is composed of eighteen essays organized into six thematic sections:

- Industrial Practice
- Technology
- Reception
- Films and Filmmakers
- Censorship and Regulation
- Stardom

Appreciating that methods and materials change over time, this structure allows the editors to showcase a breadth of historiographic approaches and a range of research materials within each section. Each essay acts as a point of entry into a history that accounts for the essential and inherent commercial, experiential, social, and cultural aspects of the medium.

All eighteen essays are individually introduced by the editors, who provide additional context and suggestions for further reading, making it an ideal resource for students of film studies and particularly for students taking courses on film history.

Jon Lewis is Professor of Film Studies at Oregon State University and the former editor of *Cinema Journal*. He has published nine books, including *Whom God Wishes to Destroy . . . Francis Coppola and the New Hollywood* (1997) and *Hollywood v. Hard Core: How the Struggle over Censorship Saved the Modern Film Industry* (2002).

Eric Smoodin is Professor of American Studies at the University of California, Davis. He has authored several books, including an analysis of *Snow White and the Seven Dwarfs* (2012) and *Regarding Frank Capra: Audience, Celebrity, and American Film Studies, 1930–1960* (2004).

"Lewis and Smoodin have assembled an absolutely essential reader for scholars and students of American film history. Structured around eighteen key essays, the book is far more than a survey of important films; it is, most importantly, a compelling reminder that any film history should reflect a spectrum of historiographic methods."
Timothy Corrigan, *Director of Cinema Studies, University of Pennsylvania*

"Lewis and Smoodin – the scholarly equivalent of a star-powered Hollywood double-act – have brilliantly assembled a collection of essays that enable readers to examine both the history of American film and the changing historiographic practices that address that commercial art form. I can think of no better guides, and the book they have produced will rightly become integral to the ways we teach American film history."
Lee Grieveson, *Director of the Graduate Programme in Film Studies, University College London*

The American Film History Reader

Edited by

Jon Lewis and Eric Smoodin

Routledge
Taylor & Francis Group
LONDON AND NEW YORK

First published 2015
by Routledge
2 Park Square, Milton Park, Abingdon, Oxon, OX14 4RN

and by Routledge
711 Third Avenue, New York, NY 10017

Routledge is an imprint of the Taylor & Francis Group, an informa business

British Library Cataloguing in Publication Data
A catalogue record for this book is available from the British Library

Library of Congress Cataloging in Publication Data
The American film history reader / edited by Jon Lewis and Eric Smoodin.
pages cm
Includes bibliographical references and index.
1. Motion pictures–United States–History–20th century. 2. Motion picture industry–United States–History–20th century. I. Lewis, Jon, 1955- editor. II. Smoodin, Eric Loren, editor.
PN1993.5.U6A865 2015
791.430973–dc23
2014021158

ISBN: 978-0-415-70621-6 (hbk)
ISBN: 978-0-415-70688-9 (pbk)

Typeset in Perpetua and Bell Gothic
by RefineCatch Limited, Bungay, Suffolk

Printed and bound in the United States of America by
Edwards Brothers Malloy on sustainably sourced paper

Contents

Figures

Acknowledgements

The following essays have been reproduced with kind permission. Every effort has been made to contact copyright-holders. Please advise the publisher of any errors or omissions, and these will be corrected in subsequent editions.

1. Oxford University Press for permission to reprint Edward Buscombe, "Notes on Columbia Pictures Corporation 1926–41," *Screen*, 16:3 (Autumn 1975), pp. 65–82. Copyright © 1975, John Logie Baird Centre and Oxford University Press.
2. Thomas Schatz for kind permission to reprint "Warner Bros.: Power Plays and Prestige," in *The Genius of the System* (New York: Pantheon, 1988), pp. 199–227.
3. University of Minnesota Press for permission to reprint Danae Clark, "Labor and Film Narrative," in *Negotiating Hollywood: The Cultural Politics of Actors' Labor* (Minnesota, 1995), pp. 82–117.
4. Charles Barr, "CinemaScope: Before and After," *Film Quarterly*, 16:4 (Summer, 1963), pp. 4–24. Copyright © 1963, The Regents of the University of California.
5. Barry Salt, "Film Style and Technology in the Thirties", *Film Quarterly*, vol. 30, No. 1 (Autumn, 1976), pp. 19–32. Copyright © 1976, The Regents of the University of California.
6. Kristen Whissel, "Tales of Upward Mobility," *Film Quarterly*, 59:4 (Summer 2006), pp. 23–34. Copyright © 2006, The Regents of the University of California.
7. "The Souls of Black Folk in the Age of Mechanical Reproduction: Black Newspaper Criticism and the Early Cinema, 1909–16," in *Returning the Gaze*, Anna Everett, pp. 12–58. Copyright © 2001, Duke University Press. All rights reserved. Republished by permission of the copyright holder. www.dukeupress.edu
8. Kathryn Fuller-Seeley, "Dish Night at the Movies: Exhibitor Promotions and Female Audiences During the Great Depression," in *Looking Past the Screen*, Jon Lewis, Eric Smoodin, Eds., pp. 246–75. Copyright © 2007, Duke University Press. All rights reserved. Republished by permission of the copyright © holder. www.dukeupress.edu

9. Oxford University Press for permission to reprint Eric Smoodin, "This Business of America: Fan Mail, Film Reception and *Meet John Doe*," *Screen*, 37:2 (1996), pp. 111–28 Copyright © 1996, John Logie Baird Centre and Oxford University Press
10. "Howard Hawks" by Molly Haskell. Originally published in *Cinema: A Critical Dictionary.* Copyright © 1980 by Molly Haskell. Reprinted by permission of Georges Borchardt, Inc., on behalf of the author.
11. Judith Mayne, "Female Authorship Reconsidered" in *The Woman at the Keyhole: Feminism and Women's Cinema*, pp. 89–123. Copyright © 1990, Indiana University Press. Reprinted with permission of Indiana University Press.
12. From "Papering the Cracks: Fantasy and Ideology in the Reagan Era," *Hollywood from Vietnam to Reagan* by Robin Wood. Copyright © 1986, Columbia University Press. Reprinted with permission of the publisher.
13. University of Texas Press for permission to reprint Lea Jacobs, "The Censorship of *Blonde Venus*: Textual Analysis and Historical Method," *Cinema Journal*, 27:3 (1988), pp. 21–31.
14. From "Classical Hollywood Cinema: The World According to Joseph I. Breen," in *Pre-Code Hollywood* by Thomas Doherty. Copyright © 1999, Columbia University Press. Reprinted with permission of the publisher.
15. University of Texas Press for permission to reprint Jon Lewis, "We Do Not Ask You to Condone This: How the Blacklist Saved Hollywood," *Cinema Journal*, 39:2 (2000), pp. 3–30.
16. "A Star is Born: The Transnational Success of *The Cheat* and Its Race and Gender Politics," in *Sessue Hayakawa*, Daisuke Miyao, pp. 21–49. Copyright © 2007, Duke University Press. All right reserved. Republished by permission of the copyright holder. www.dukeupress.edu
17. University of Texas Press for permission to reprint Miriam Hansen, "Pleasure, Ambivalence, Identification: Valentino and Female Spectatorship," *Cinema Journal*, 25:4 (1986), pp. 6–32.
18. Oxford University Press for permission to reprint Jackie Stacey, "Hollywood Memories," *Screen*, 35:4 (Winter, 1994), pp. 317–35. Copyright © 1994, John Logie Baird Centre and Oxford University Press.

Jon Lewis and Eric Smoodin

INTRODUCTION

What do we talk or write about when we talk and write about American film history? The answer is predictably complex and elusive, because there is a lot to talk and write about, because the medium as it has evolved over more than a century in the United States encompasses the textual, the industrial, and the social. This *American Film History Reader* acknowledges and accommodates this complex and elusive task by showcasing a range of historical writing, sampling a variety of answers to this fundamental question. When we talk or write about film history, we by necessity talk and write about a lot of different things.

The project of this book is twofold: (1) to provide the reader with a selective history of American cinema; and (2) to provide an introduction to historiographic practice as it relates to American moviemaking and moviegoing. The book is composed of eighteen essays organized into six parts focusing on: Industrial Practice, Technology, Reception, Films and Filmmakers, Censorship and Regulation, and Stardom. Appreciating that methods and materials change over time, this structure allows us to showcase a breadth of historiographic approaches and a range of research materials within each of these six parts. Each essay is a point of entry into a history that necessarily accounts for the essential and inherent commercial, experiential, social, and cultural aspects of the medium. This thematic structure organizes essays that are to an extent chronological as we are keenly interested in the evolution or trajectory of work within each of the six schools of film history we have chosen to highlight in this book.

The selection process within each part heading was difficult; and no doubt different editors might well have made some different choices. The task of choosing just three essays from the extensive historical work in each category resulted in selections not, or not just of work with a canonical significance, but rather, or also, work that presents an apparent trajectory within each of these approaches. Each essay is introduced separately and specifically and for each of our choices we provide suggestions for additional reading chosen rather carefully from work we could easily have selected instead.

We are interested in schools of film history – schools focusing in different ways on political economy, textuality, scientific and technological innovation, audience reception, industrial intention. And we are interested in the different ways different historians work within these categories . . . how, over time, the study of industry, technology, reception, *auteurism*, content or workforce regulation, and celebrity has evolved within film studies.

Again, we should note that a comprehensive project is quite beyond the scope of this book. Our goal is not to create a set of canonical readings or writings but instead to offer film studies scholars and students as well as general readers a manageable set of texts that together introduce how an American film history might be written, how it might be studied, taking into account a range of concerns, sources, socio-political arguments closely examined and ably discussed by eighteen influential film historians.

As this book suggests, there is no single unique and perfect approach. Movies in America merge the commercial and the artistic, the industrial and the creative. To talk about one half of this duality, this paradox, requires some accounting of the other. Cinema in the U.S. is mechanically and/or technologically reproduced. It is by artistic and commercial intention promoted, distributed, and exhibited as a mass medium with a profound, significant effect on its mass audience. What and how we talk about movies ranges from close readings of individual and representative texts to broader social, cultural, economic, and political concerns. There's the notion of movies and me, movies and you, movies and America, movies and the global audience and marketplace. This *American Film History Reader* introduces such a complex historical conversation with an eye on encouraging further reading, further conversation.

The parts can be taken separately as specific interventions into an historical study or taken together as a complex interdisciplinary approach to a history that cannot be so simply told. Each part has its own inherent history and trajectory, its own seminal or central texts, its own unique materials and methods. What follows is an introduction to each of the six interventions, each of the six schools of American film history we showcase in this book.

Industrial Practice

The first film course at an American university dates to 1915, the year D.W. Griffith's *Birth of a Nation* was released nationwide. The class was offered through Columbia University extended education and focused on the "photoplay" as a literary genre. The course was taught by university faculty and local theatre and film professionals and given its extension status it was something of a hybrid, at once an academic course (in literary studies) and a trade school skills class (like auto repair). A second early experiment in university film studies came over a decade later at Harvard – a business of film course taught by a who's who of early industry players: Adolph Zukor, Cecil B. DeMille, Marcus Loew, William Fox, Jack Warner, Sam Katz, Robert Cochrane and Louis B. Mayer. These two early forays into film education took a while to take root at universities nationwide, but they nonetheless revealed a fundamental tension in teaching and writing film history: whether to focus on films as works of art or as products of a commercial enterprise.[1]

Early historical accountings of the film industry – Leo Rosten's *Hollywood: The Movie Colony, The Movie Makers*; Hortense Powdermaker's *Hollywood: The Dream Factory*; Roy Pickard's *The Hollywood Studios*; and Ethan Mordden's *The Hollywood Studios* – betrayed a fascination with studio Hollywood as a subculture, and did little to show how looking at the system of filmmaking might enable a close reading of specific movies made at the studios.[2] More sophisticated investigations into the structure and process of studio filmmaking followed: Douglas Gomery's *The Hollywood Studio System*; Tino Balio's edited collection *The American Film Industry*; and Gorham Kindem's anthology *The American Movie Industry: The Business of Motion Pictures*.[3] These books presented more complex and comprehensive histories of the studio system that still continued to insist on a distinction between the study of industry economies and textual analysis.

The first systematic study of the relationship between mode of production and film style was certainly David Bordwell, Janet Staiger, and Kristin Thompson's work on classical Hollywood.[4] Their notion that film style (what was discussed in film studies classes, many of which were offered by English Departments at the time) might be rooted in business practice (which rather distinguished film from the other arts), foregrounded Thomas Schatz's *The Genius of the System: Hollywood Filmmaking in the Studio Era*, which provided a second important bridge, this time between industry studies and *auteurism*.[5] Schatz audaciously complicated the notion of authorship to include collaborations between artists and businessmen, filmmakers and studio executives and producers.

Studio history was also of interest to the cultural historians Robert Sklar in *Movie-Made America: A Cultural History of the Movies* and Garth Jowett in *Film: The Democratic Art: A Social History of the American Film*. Both authors contextualized industrial production with regard to the social and political effects of motion pictures.[6]

Today, industry histories rather abound in film studies and cover a wide range of topics. There are histories of movie labor (Danae Clark's *Negotiating Hollywood: The Politics of Actors' Labor*), movie advertising and promotion (Justin Wyatt's *High Concept: Movies and Marketing in Hollywood*), movies and racial politics (Jesse Algernon Rhines' *Black Film/White Money*), movies and global capitalism (Toby Miller, Nitin Govil, John McMurria, and Richard Maxwell's *Global Hollywood*).[7] The focus on industry has come to inform other approaches, especially *auteurism*: Jon Lewis' study of Francis Coppola's Zoetrope project for example and Thomas Elsaesser's essays on blockbusters and the "new economy Hollywood."[8] Key to these newer industry histories is an awareness of the fundamental dialectic of film study: that movies are at once art and commerce and an affirmation that one cannot be fully understood independent of the other.

Technology

Technology studies has a long history as a significant genre of film writing. At least as far back as the World War One era, those studies typically appeared in trade journals, and were written by film professionals for their colleagues. For the next thirty or forty years, *The Motion Picture Projectionist, The Journal of the Society of Motion Picture Engineers*, and *American Cinematographer*, among others, were the places to find information and analysis on a variety of subjects directly related to the technologies of cinema; color or 3D cinematography or stereophonic sound.

In the film histories written during these same years, however, from around 1920 through the 1950s, technology came to be relegated to the margins or entirely absent. Terry Ramsaye's *A Million and One Nights*, from 1926, established the pattern. This history of the first thirty years of film was itself endorsed by Thomas Edison, one of the inventors of the motion picture camera, whose photograph appeared on the frontispiece. Ramsaye devoted the first quarter of the book to the machinery developed by Edison and others, and particularly to such cinematic precursors as Eadweard Muybridge and Étienne-Jules Marey, the high-speed photographers of the 1870s and 1880s. Then, however, technology dropped out of Ramsaye's story, replaced by studios, stars, and spectacle. Similarly, Benjamin Hampton's *History of the American Film Industry*, from 1931, touched only lightly upon the machinery that the industry used, in an opening section about Edison and other early inventors, and then at the end, with a discussion of the introduction of sound. Margaret Farrand Thorp, in *America at the Movies*, her 1939 examination, mostly ignored film technology altogether.[9]

With few exceptions, this was the state of things in American film studies for decades. The film stock, the lights, or the projector were understood to be of utmost significance during the very early period of film's existence. After that, however, the important story of film would be the development of the feature length movie, or the star system, or the changing status of the director, or the relationships between film and cultural context, with only the coming of sound technology in the late 1920s worthy of notice. During this time, the serious study of technology still could only be found in those trade journals devoted to spreading the news about mechanical developments.

By the 1950s and for the next thirty years or so, academic interest in film technology began to grow. All of the reasons for this shift remain unclear, but of particular importance would be a new publication, *The Hollywood Quarterly*, which first appeared in 1947. The *Quarterly* was designed as a place where scholars and practitioners might talk to each other and to a common readership. As a result, the journal published articles by such film and cultural historians as Theodor Adorno, Iris Barry, Siegfried Kracauer, and Georges Sadoul, as well as filmmakers talking about their craft: Chuck Jones and Norman McLaren on animation, or Edith Head on costume design.[10] This as much as anything marked the migration of technology studies into film studies, and when *The Hollywood Quarterly* became *Film Quarterly* in 1957, the journal kept publishing significant works about movie technology, including the two essays reprinted here by Charles Barr and Barry Salt.

In the 1970s and 1980s, scholars interested in the economic history of American film came to understand that technological advances often fueled industrial development and expansion. This period witnessed the scholarship of Douglas Gomery, for instance, about the influence on the international market of the coming of sound. In similar fashion, Bordwell, Staiger, and Thompson's foundational *Classical Hollywood Cinema* described motion picture technology – lighting, microphones, and cameras, for example – as fundamental to the development of the visual and narrative systems that governed American film at least from World War One until 1960.[11] Thus as it moved from margin to center, the study of technology has transformed our understanding of the place of research, design, and invention in the film industry, and our sense of the impact of the mechanical apparatus of cinema on the stories that we see on screen.

Reception

Questions about the audience have been central to film studies for at least a century. In the German context alone, Emilie Altenloh completed her *Sociology of the Cinema: The Audience* in 1914, while Hugo Munsterberg published one of the earliest, extended works of film theory, *The Photoplay: A Psychological Study*, in 1916.[12] Both works were marked by a detailed interest in spectatorship, in the case of the former a cataloging of preferences and habits among filmgoers, and in the latter a broad view of the medium's psychological effects on viewers.

For many years, when American film scholars studied the audience, their efforts were marked by the analytical, quantitative method of Altenloh. As we move through Robert and Helen Merrell Lynd's 1929 study of Muncie, Indiana, *Middletown*, to the Payne Fund Studies of the 1930s, to Margaret Farrand Thorp's *America at the Movies* from 1939, to Leo Handel's 1950 monograph *Hollywood Looks at Its Audience*, to David and Evelyn T. Riesman's 1952 essay, "Movies and Audiences," we can see many of the same inquiries and interests.[13] Scholars during this period sought to determine who, precisely, made up the audience, what those audiences wanted to see, when those audiences went to the movies and for what reasons, and how viewers might be affected by the movies they saw.

In a broad sense, as film studies became more firmly established as an academic discipline, as it moved closer and closer to literary studies, and as it came under the influence of 1950s French *auteur* theory, about the significance of the director, American scholars moved away from the more sociological concerns of previous decades. Indeed throughout the 1960s and 1970s, scholarship on audience invoked the spirit of Munsterberg far more than that of Altenloh, using Marxist, semiotic, and psychoanalytic approaches to imagine a more theoretical rather than empirical viewer, and to investigate the ideological and linguistic effects, among others, of the film text on an undifferentiated audience.

Over the last thirty or forty years, scholars have moved back to a more sociological, empirical study of audiences, but one always informed by the theoretical advances of the previous decades. Such scholars as Melvyn Stokes, Richard Maltby, Janet Staiger, Ruth Vasey, Gregory Waller, Annette Kuhn, and Catherine Jurca, as well as those represented in this volume, opened new inquiries into historically specific audience studies.[14] These scholars have shown us that film audiences must, on the one hand, be thought of in international terms and on the other as a vast number of small audiences, separated by age or class or race or gender or location. And these audiences have understood movies, and have enjoyed them or been displeased by them, in varied ways, and in ways that films and filmmakers could never fully control.

These new audience studies, marked by a sense of the complexity of audiences and by the ways filmgoers and films interact with various institutions and leisure activities, owe a great deal to the expansion since the 1980s in the available materials for studying film viewing. Holdings at the Academy of Motion Picture Arts and Sciences in Los Angeles, at the New York Public Library, at such universities as UCLA, the University of Southern California, and Wesleyan

University, as well as the federal Freedom of Information Act provide extensive evidence relating to the film audience. As a result, we can understand the intricacies of the history of spectatorship as never before, and appreciate the varied relationships between film text and film viewer.

Films and Filmmakers

The *auteur* theory, which focuses on films and their filmmakers, holds a crucial, albeit controversial position in cine-historiography. For many serious film scholars today, *auteurism* is regarded as a necessary and necessarily flawed first step away from historical models drawn from the social sciences (especially sociology and psychology, as discussed above) and towards a methodology more akin to art and literary history, a brief stop, so to speak, en route to an historical method that focuses less on the effect of movies and more on the films and filmmakers themselves.

The *auteur* theory first emerged in postwar France, rooted in the reactionary politics of a handful of young film journalists (François Truffaut, Jean-Luc Godard, Eric Rohmer, and Claude Chabrol) and their venerable editor André Bazin at the film magazine, *Cahiers du Cinéma*. The *auteur* theory that they promoted was pure provocation; it celebrated the American cinema at the expense of the French tradition, and argued, somewhat paradoxically for a "politique des auteurs," the notion that despite a commercial, collaborative system rigged to obscure authorship, the key to appreciating and understanding American cinema involved a necessary identification of the American movie director as the principal if not sole author of his or her films.[15]

Auteurism spread to England (where critics for the magazine *Movie* embraced the notion of the director as *auteur*) and to the United States where the film critic Andrew Sarris systematized and historicized American cinema according to certain filmmakers and their films. In doing so, Sarris insisted upon a basic, crucial assumption: that films are works of art – it is astonishing that as late as 1968 that was still an argument that needed to be made – and that films (good and bad, big and small, commercial and independent) are made by individual artists of varying abilities and significance. In his groundbreaking *The American Cinema: Directors and Directions, 1929–1968*, Sarris created an elaborate and highly impressionistic scheme for the wide range in quality he observed in American moviemaking, ranking directors and their films.[16] Transcendent artists like Chaplin and Welles occupied "The Pantheon." Well-known directors with inflated reputations prompted inclusion in a chapter titled "Less than Meets the Eye." Especially important to Sarris, and this he got from the French *auteurists*, was the rescue of under-rated directors who labored in relative obscurity during their careers. While Sarris' accounting was based mostly upon astute, close textual analysis, his work nonetheless veered into journalistic subjectivity and his persistent bickering with Pauline Kael, the film reviewer at the *New Yorker*, mired his critical analysis in unproductive discussions of taste. Moreover, affections at the time among the literary community for the ahistorical New Criticism relegated Sarris' work to outlier status among the cognoscenti.

What eventually cemented the importance of the *auteur* theory in the historiography of film in the U.S. is its role in the evolution of film studies at universities after the Second World War. As film studies evolved into a viable discipline, it did so because the *auteur* theory, flawed as it may have been, implied a fundamental connection to already established historical methods in established disciplines: art and literary history. In art history, it was the convention at the time to teach the great works of the great artists. In literature classes, the Great Books tradition persisted. The insistence on authorship – that despite the commercial enterprise out of which American films are produced, there might nonetheless be a tradition of great films and great filmmakers (just as there was a tradition of great works of art and artists, great books and writers) – eased the transition of film studies into the established liberal arts curriculum.

Much as the historical traditions in film are more nuanced today, the organization of material for the purposes of teaching or writing history often betrays a continued celebration of the best and the brightest, great artists and their works of art. As such, *auteur* critics and historians have more recently used the films and filmmakers approach to explore a range of other topics: a semiotics of cinema (Peter Wollen's *Signs and Meaning in the Cinema*), issues of gender and sexuality (Molly Haskell's *From Reverence to Rape*, for example, as well as Judith Mayne's work on the filmmaker Dorothy Arzner), cultural and political history (Andrew Britton's "Blissing Out: The Politics of Reaganite Entertainment (1986)" and Robin Wood's *Hollywood from Vietnam to Reagan*).[17] What distinguishes the *auteur* approach today is its versatility, that a close look at films and filmmakers might be a starting point for a study of genre, gender and sexuality, politics and culture, industry and technology.

Censorship and Regulation

Content censorship has been a fact of life for filmmaking and filmgoing in the U.S. since the advent of the medium. The challenge for American film studios has never been whether or not to censor, but instead a matter of finding a practical way to *use* censorship. On the one hand, content regulation addressed civic concerns about the effect of the medium on the mass audience but on the other the practice was necessarily incorporated into studio operations from film production through public relations. The goal of the 1930 Production Code, for example, was not only to establish a fundamental moral guidebook, but also to assure the free flow of movies through the marketplace, which at the time was complicated by local censorship boards as well as religious and progressive grassroots organizations. The 1968 Voluntary Movie Rating System bypassed morality altogether (except with regard to hard core pornography) and was instead designed to classify a newly diverse range of productions (films rated: G, M, and R – later G, PG, PG-13, R, and NC-17), again to be assured free and fair trade in the marketplace.

There are a number of historical studies that focus on the effect of censorship on movies and moviemaking (Frank Miller's *Censored Hollywood: Sex, Sin and Violence on Screen* and Gerald Gardner's *The Censorship Papers: Movie Censorship Letters from the Hays Office, 1934–1968*) and/or the significance of content censorship to American cultural history (Frances Couvares' edited collection *Movie Censorship and American Culture*; Gregory Black's *Hollywood Censored: Morality Codes, Catholics and the Movies*; Thomas Doherty's *Pre-Code Hollywood: Sex, Immorality and Insurrection in American Culture;* and Charles Lyon's *The New Censors: Movies and the Culture Wars*).[18] These cultural studies regard the complex social contract forged between the studios and a mass culture at once fascinated by and more than a little leery of the power of the moving image. Larger questions regarding the cultural significance of institutionalized censorship in general (Marjorie Heins' *Not in Front of the Children: Indecency, Censorship and the Innocence of Youth*)[19] and/or works that focus on judicial questions regarding obscenity and pornography round out the more socio-politically inflected work on the subject.[20]

Eschewing the public debate about morality, some historians of censorship have focused instead on industry organization and operation: Lea Jacobs' *The Wages of Sin: Censorship and the Fallen Woman Film, 1928–1942*; Matthew Bernstein's edited collection *Controlling Hollywood: Censorship and Regulation in the Studio Era*; Thomas Doherty's *Hollywood's Censor: Joseph I. Breen and the Production Code Administration* and Kevin Sandler's *The Naked Truth: Why Hollywood Doesn't Make X-Rated Movies.*[21] This body of historical work rather overlaps with industry or studio history and regards content regulation as a matter of studio policy and procedure, industry organization and operation, mode of production and censorship's impact upon film form or style.

For historians, content censorship is the most studied mode of industry self-regulation. But there are other forms of industry supervision and management worth studying: the studio workforce, for example. Content censorship and work-force regulation are inextricably related. Movie censorship was first instituted industrywide by the Motion Picture Producers and Distributors Association (MPPDA), then headed by Will Hays, following a series of movie star scandals.[22] The connections between workforce regulation and content censorship were especially significant during the Hollywood blacklist when politically progressive speech in movie screenplays was treated much the same as speech expressed in "questionable" political affiliations and union memberships.[23]

The very formation of the studio system involved a fundamental regulation of a creative and artisanal workforce. The Fordist system streamlined and standardized production, and workers were by necessity tied to option contracts that guaranteed exclusivity and exploitation. Unionization was as much a reaction to the inevitable collapse of the studio system as it was a reflection of a dynamic opposition between an industry committed to using regulation for public relations and a progressive workforce committed to a free and fair marketplace, a stake in industry profits, and the freedom to work on whatever project one chooses.[24]

Stardom

The movie star has fascinated film scholars since the beginning of the star system in the early 1900s. Around 1908 or 1910, film studios realized the importance of their performers, who went from being uncredited and unpublicized to being scrutinized by millions of fans and celebrated by the film industry. Historians often identify Florence Lawrence as the first movie star, with her persona carefully constructed by the various film studios that employed her. By 1915, Vachel Lindsay, in his book, *The Art of the Moving Picture*, extolled "the pale Lillian Gish" in Griffith's *Enoch Arden* (1911), and also told readers about one of the other great female stars of the day and the kind of film she makes; "we know the Mary Pickford mood," whether the actress portrays "a doll, a village belle, or a church angel."[25]

Lindsay, of course, was a poet, and his writing about movies showed a poet's sensibility. Even with less aesthetic aspiration, though, scholars for many years concentrated on the individual star, like Gish or Pickford. In the 1930s and the Payne Fund Studies, which examined the effects of movies on children and adolescents, American researchers worried about the onscreen impact of John Gilbert or Clark Gable, for example, and whether they might be able to convince young girls to forget all sense of moral propriety. Around this time, scholars also took an interest in the star system in general, often disparagingly, as they examined an industrial system that worked to commodify celebrity on a large scale. Paul Rotha, for instance, in his encyclopedic *The Film Till Now*, from 1930, castigated the Hollywood film studios when he wrote, about the late 1910s and early 1920s, that "the American cinema began to succumb to the personality process, resulting in the tyrannical reign of the star-system," and that the movie companies "decided to recapture the attention of the public by the wholesale exploitation of stars."[26]

In France, which we tend to mythologize as a bastion of the cult of the director, the 1972 publication of sociologist Edgar Morin's *Les Stars* helped galvanize modern star scholarship.[27] Since then, in British and American-based film studies, the work of Richard Dyer and Christine Gledhill has been instrumental in bringing greater and greater sophistication to star studies.[28] As a result, the historical analysis of movie stars has become a significant aspect of film studies, as we examine the ways that movie audiences have understood stars at various times, or the ways that stars might be used to organize the visual and narrative logic of films, or how they take part in a broad range of cultural production and activity, for instance fashion, music, or politics. From Vachel Lindsay to the present day, the movie star has served as one of the most important ways for us to understand many of the pleasures we take in cinema, and also to assess the American film industry and the ways it provides those pleasures to a global audience.

Notes

1 For a comprehensive history of university film education, see: Dana Polan, *Scenes of Instruction: The Beginnings of U.S. Film Education* (Berkeley: University of California Press, 2007). Also relevant here: *Inventing Film Studies*, edited by Lee Grieveson and Haidee Wasson (Durham, NC: Duke University Press, 2008).

2 Leo Rosten, *Hollywood: The Movie Colony, The Movie Makers* (NY: Arno Press, 1941); Hortense Powdermaker, *Hollywood: The Dream Factory* (NY: Little, Brown, 1950); Roy Pickard, *The Hollywood Studios* (London: Frederick Muller, 1978) and Ethan Mordden, *The Hollywood Studios* (NY: Knopf, 1987).

3 Douglas Gomery, *The Hollywood Studio System* (NY: St. Martins, 1986); *The American Film Industry*, edited by Tino Balio (Madison: University of Wisconsin Press, 1985); *The American Movie Industry: The Business of Motion Pictures*, edited by Gorham Kindem (Carbondale: University of Illinois Press, 1982)

4 David Bordwell, Janet Staiger, and Kristin Thompson, *The Classical Hollywood Cinema: Film Style and Mode of Production to 1960* (NY: Columbia University Press, 1985).

5 Thomas Schatz, *The Genius of the System: Hollywood Filmmaking in the Studio Era* (NY: Henry Holt, 1988).

6 Robert Sklar, *Movie-Made America: A Cultural History of the Movies* (NY: Vintage, 1975) and Garth Jowett, *Film: The Democratic Art: A Social History of the American Film* (Boston: Little Brown, 1976).

7 Danae Clark, *Negotiating Hollywood: The Politics of Actors' Labor* (Minneapolis: University of Minnesota Press, 1995); Justin Wyatt's *High Concept: Movies and Marketing in Hollywood* (Austin: University of Texas Press, 1994); Jesse Algernon Rhines, *Black Film/White Money* (New Brunswick, NJ: Rutgers University Press, 1996); Toby Miller, Nitin Govil, John McMurria, and Richard Maxwell's *Global Hollywood* (London: BFI, 2002).

8 Jon Lewis, *Whom God Wishes to Destroy . . . Francis Coppola and the New Hollywood* (Durham, NC: Duke University Press, 1996); Thomas Elsaesser, "Auteur Cinema and the New Economy of Hollywood," and "Auteurism Today: Signature Products, Concept-Authors and Access for All: *Avatar*," in *The Persistence of Hollywood* (NY: Routledge, 2012).

9 Terry Ramsaye, *A Million and One Nights: A History of the Motion Picture Through 1925* (New York: Simon and Schuster, 1926); Benjamin Hampton, *History of the American Film Industry* (New York: Covici, Friede, 1931); Margaret Farrand Thorp, *America at the Movies* (New Haven: Yale University Press 1939).

10 T.W. Adorno, "How to Look at Television," *The Quarterly of Film, Radio, and Television*, Volume 8, Number 3 (Spring, 1954), pp. 213–35 (in 1951, *Hollywood Quarterly* was renamed *The Quarterly of Film, Radio, and Television*); Iris Barry, "Why Wait for Posterity?" *Hollywood Quarterly*, Volume 1, Number 2 (January, 1946), pp. 131–37; Siegfried Kracauer, "Jean Vigo," *Hollywood Quarterly*, Volume 2, Number 3 (April, 1947), pp. 261–63; Georges Sadoul, "The Postwar French Cinema," *Hollywood Quarterly*, Volume 4, Number 3 (Spring, 1950), pp. 233–44; Chuck Jones, "Music and the Animated Cartoon," *Hollywood Quarterly*, Volume 1, Number 4 (July, 1946), pp. 364–70; Norman McLaren, "Notes on Animated Sound," *The Quarterly of Film, Radio, and Television*, Volume 7, Number 3 (Spring, 1953), pp. 223–29; Edith Head, "A Costume Problem: From Shot to Stage to Screen," *Hollywood Quarterly*, Volume 2, Number 1 (October, 1946), p. 44.

11 Douglas Gomery, "Economic Struggle and Hollywood Imperialism: Europe Converts to Sound." *Yale French Studies*, 60 (1980), pp. 80–93; David Bordwell, Janet Staiger, and Kristin Thompson, *The Classical Hollywood Cinema: Film Style & Mode of Production to 1960* (New York: Columbia University Press, 1985).

12 Emilie Altenloh, *A Sociology of the Cinema: The Audience*, (1914), Kathleen Cross, translator, *Screen*, Volume 42, Number 3 (Autumn 2001), pp. 249–93; Hugo Münsterberg, *The Photoplay: A Psychological Study* (New York: D. Appleton and Company, 1916).

13 Robert Lynd and Helen Merrell Lynd, *Middletown* (New York: Harcourt, Brace, and World, 1929); various volumes in the Payne Fund Studies, research conducted between 1929 and 1932, and published throughout the 1930s; Margaret Farrand Thorp, *America at the Movies* (New Haven: Yale University Press, 1939); Leo A. Handel, *Hollywood Looks at Its Audience* (Urbana: The University of Illinois Press, 1950); David A. Riesman and Evelyn T. Riesman. "Movies and Audiences," *American Quarterly*, Volume 4, Number 3 (Fall 1952), pp. 195–202.

14 Melvyn Stokes and Richard Maltby, eds., *American Movie Audiences: From the Turn of the Century to the Early Sound Era* (London: British Film Institute, 1999); Janet Staiger, *Interpreting Films: Studies in the Historical Reception of American Cinema* (Princeton: Princeton University Press, 1992); Ruth Vasey, *The World According to Hollywood, 1918–1939* (Madison: University of Wisconsin Press, 1997); Gregory Waller, *Main Street Amusements: Movies and Commercial Entertainment in a Southern City, 1896–1930* (Washington, DC: Smithsonian Institution Press, 1995); Annette Kuhn, *Dreaming of Fred and Ginger: Cinema and Cultural Memory* (New York: New York University Press, 2002); Catherine Jurca, *Hollywood 1938: Motion Pictures' Greatest Year* (Berkeley: University of California Press, 2012).

15 André Bazin, "La politique des auteurs," in *The French New Wave: Critical Landmarks*, edited by Peter Graham (London: BFI, 1968), pp. 130–48.

16 Andrew Sarris, *The American Cinema: Directors and Directions, 1929–68* (NY: Dutton, 1968).

17 Peter Wollen, *Signs and Meaning in the Cinema* (Bloomington: Indiana University Press, 1972); Molly Haskell, *From Reverence to Rape: The Treatment of Women in Movies* (NY: New English Library, 1974); Judith Mayne, *Directed by Dorothy Arzner* (London: John Wiley, 1995) and *The Woman at the Keyhole: Feminism and Women's*

Cinema (Bloomington: Indiana University Press, 1990); Andrew Britton, "Blissing Out: The Politics of Reaganite Entertainment (1986)," *Movie*, 31/32 (1987), pp. 1–42; and Robin Wood, *Hollywood from Vietnam to Reagan* (NY: Columbia University Press, 1986).

18 *Movie Censorship and American Culture*, edited by Frances Couvares (Washington, DC: Smithsonian Press, 1996); Gregory Black's *Hollywood Censored: Morality Codes, Catholics and the Movies* (NY: Cambridge University Press, 1994); Thomas Doherty's *Pre-Code Hollywood: Sex, Immorality and Insurrection in American Culture* (NY: Columbia University Press, 1999) and Charles Lyon's *The New Censors: Movies and the Culture Wars* (Philadelphia: Temple University Press, 1997). See also: Frank Walsh, *Sin and Censorship: The Catholic Church and Motion Picture Censorship* (New Haven: Yale University Press, 1996); Kevin Brownlow, *Behind the Mask of Innocence: Sex, Violence, Prejudice, Crime: Films of Social Conscience in the Silent Era* (NY: Knopf, 1990).

19 Marjorie Heins, *Not in Front of the Children: "Indecency," Censorship and the Innocence of Youth* (NY: Hill and Wang, 2001).

20 See: Jon Lewis, *Hollywood v. Hard Core: How the Struggle over Censorship Saved the Modern Film Industry* (NY: NYU Press, 2000).

21 Lea Jacobs' *The Wages of Sin: Censorship and the Fallen Woman Film, 1928–1942* (Berkeley: University of California Press, 1997); Matthew Bernstein's edited collection *Controlling Hollywood: Censorship and Regulation in the Studio Era* (New Brunswick, NJ: Rutgers University Press, 1999); Thomas Doherty's *Hollywood's Censor: Joseph I. Breen and the Production Code Administration* (NY: Columbia University Press, 1997) and Kevin Sandler's *The Naked Truth: Why Hollywood Doesn't Make X-Rated Movies* (New Brunswick: Rutgers University Press, 2007).

22 See: Richard deCordova, *Picture Personalities: The Emergence of the Star System in America* (Urbana: University of Illinois press, 1990).

23 See: Larry Ceplair and Steven Englund, *The Inquisition in Hollywood: Politics in the Film Community, 1930–1960* (NY: Anchor Press, 1980), pp. 441–44; *Tender Comrades: A Backstory of the Hollywood Blacklist*, edited by Patrick McGilligan and Paul Buhle (NY: St. Martins, 1997) and Victor Navasky, *Naming Names* (NY: Hill and Wang, 2003).

24 See: Danae Clark, *Negotiating Hollywood: The Cultural Politics of Actors' Labor* (Minneapolis: University of Minnesota Press, 1995); Gerald Horne, *Class Struggle in Hollywood, 1930–1950: Moguls, Mobsters, Stars, Reds and Trade Unionists* (Austin: University of Texas Press, 2001) and Saverio Giovacchini, *Hollywood Modernism: Film and Politics in the Age of the New Deal* (Philadelphia: Temple University Press, 2001).

25 Vachel Lindsay, *The Art of the Moving Picture* (New York: The MacMillan Company, 1915), pp. 24, 26–27.

26 Paul Rotha, *The Film Till Now: A Survey of World Cinema* (London: Jonathan Cape, 1930), p. 129.

27 Edgar Morin, *Les Stars* (Paris: Éditions du Seuil, 1972).

28 Richard Dyer, *Stars* (London: British Film Institute, 1979); Christine Gledhill, ed., *Stardom: Industry of Desire* (London: Routledge, 1991).

PART I

Industrial Practice

Chapter 1

Edward Buscombe

NOTES ON COLUMBIA PICTURES CORPORATION 1926–41 (1975)

Editors' Introduction

In this 1975 essay, Edward Buscombe introduces an historical methodology integrating industry history with close reading. Such a methodology affirms the fundamental and unique dichotomy of the medium; that the object of study is at once a work of art and a piece of merchandise, a creative *and* a commercial/industrial product. Buscombe argues that it is critically unproductive to separate these two aspects of the cinema and in doing so he posits a radically new cine-sociology focused less on the impact of films on audiences and more on Hollywood as an institution "with its own history, specific practices, economic relationships, and technological and other material constraints."

Buscombe's decision to focus on Columbia Pictures in the 1930s is particularly canny here: how, he asks, can we read, or more accurately *re-read* Frank Capra's films for the studio – *Mr. Deeds Goes to Town, Mr. Smith Goes to Washington,* and *You Can't Take it with You* – taking into account the company's formation in the 1920s, its initial identity as a Poverty Row production house and its slow emergence as a mini-major, its anti-establishment reputation, and its relative financial independence. How, Buscombe asks, might we apprehend Capra's populism, his stories about everyday Americans pitted against an intractable power structure, as the product of a studio that was positioned within the industry in much the same way, a studio that saw itself in the 1930s as "the little guy." The political and social effect of Capra's films, then, can be fully appreciated and understood only when we have taken into account the complexities of the studio and the system that produced them.

Suggested Reading

Tino Balio, *Grand Design: Hollywood as a Modern Business Enterprise, 1930–1939* (Berkeley: University of California Press, 1993); Douglas Gomery, "Writing the History of the American Film Industry: Warner Bros. and Sound," *Screen,* 17:1 (1976), pp. 40–53; Thomas Schatz, *The Genius of the System: Hollywood Filmmaking in the Studio Era* (NY: Pantheon, 1988).

I

THE FILM INDUSTRY, THE CINEMA. How are these terms related in film criticism? *The film industry* describes an economic system, a way (or ways) of organising the structure of production, distribution, and consumption. Historically such organisation has, in Britain and America, conformed to the usual pattern of capitalist activity; film can be seen as an industry like any other. It has passed from the primitive stage of small-scale entrepreneurial activity to the formation of large-scale monopolies, securing their position by vertical integration, spreading from production into distribution and exhibition. Since the war the industry has, like other forms of business, developed towards diversification and the formation of multinational corporations. In other respects too film has developed like other industries. Production in particular has been based on a division of labour, of a fairly extreme kind. From early days the industry has employed the techniques of mass advertising, and it has required the injection of huge sums of capital, resulting in turn in the passing of control of the industry from its original owners and from the primary producers.

In film criticism, then, the term *film industry* implies a way of looking at film which minimises its differences from other forms of economic activity; a way which is of course predominantly that of those who actually own the industry. Its characteristic descriptions are sufficiently indicative of a perspective: *the trade, marketing, exploitation, a package, product.*

The cinema suggests something else. While the term might, notionally, encompass the industry, the pull is surely in a different direction. *The cinema* implies film as art. As Raymond Williams has shown with convincing detail in *Culture and Society*, the opposition between art and industry has a long history in our culture. The division between the two is experienced everywhere as deep, but nowhere deeper than in film. On the one hand, we are given to understand, is the industry, churning out product for financial gain. On the other are artists, creating enduring works of personal expression or comment on life and society. Such an opposition has taken different forms at different times. Sometimes it has been geographical. In America there was Hollywood, the industrial system par excellence. In Europe (usually excluding Britain, apart from its documentaries) there were artists: Renoir, Dreyer, Bergman, Antonioni, etc. Later the auteur theory, as applied to American cinema, changed the emphasis. Though Hollywood was still an industry, through diligent critical work some artists could be winnowed from the chaff, artists who against the odds managed by luck, cunning, or sheer genius to overcome the system, the industry. The auteur theory, whatever its "theory" may have been, did not in practice abolish the distinction between art and industry; it merely shifted the line of demarcation.

One might suppose that a little common sense would tell us that such a distinction is nonsense, that all film is both industry *and* art, in some sense. Even the lowest, most despised products (choose your own examples) are made with some kind of art. Do they not share the same language as the acknowledged masterpieces: do they not tell a story, try to affect the spectators' emotions? They may do it more or less effectively, but isn't this a difference of degree, not of kind? Conversely, in the making of the most spiritual and sublime films grubby bank notes change hands. The film stock on which the masterpiece is recorded may come from the same batch used to shoot the potboiler on the adjoining stage.

Yet proof that the mutual exclusion of art and industry operates at a level too deep to be affected by mere common sense can be found not only in the dominant critical attitudes but in the organisation of social institutions. To give an example close to home: the British Film Institute (BFI) was set up, as its Memorandum of Association states, "to encourage the development of the art of the film." At the same time it is stated that the BFI is permitted neither "to control nor attempt to interfere with purely trade matters." Art not only can but must be divorced from industry. And the split is preserved even in the structure of government.

Whereas the BFI is administered by the Department of Education and Science, the film industry comes under the Department of Trade and Industry. Thus the opposition art/industry has to be seen not merely as a mistake in film criticism which can be easily rectified by a more careful look at the facts but as the result of a whole practice of thinking, talking, writing, and disseminating inscribed in institutions like the BFI, those parts of the education system that handle film, plus also exhibition/viewing practice—the art-house circuit and its audience(s)—the immaterial thought both reflecting and being part of this apparatus; in short, as part of an ideology.

The main concern here, however, is not with the origins of such an opposition but with its consequence for film criticism. This may be baldly stated: there has been scarcely any serious attempt to think the relationship between art and industry with regard to films produced in what have historically been for us the two most important film-making countries, namely, Great Britain and the United States. Criticism has been devoted not to relating them but to separating them out, and in practice this has meant that critics have concentrated on the beauties and mysteries of art and left the industry, presumably a tougher plant, to take care of itself. Study of the industry might require knowledge of, say, economics or of how films are actually made, knowledge which critics have not been expected to acquire. The main effort of criticism, therefore, has gone into the study of film texts viewed as autonomous, self-sufficient entities or, occasionally, as reflections of society, but certainly not as reflections of the industry which produced them, unless they are being dismissed as rubbish. Even recent work deriving from structuralism and concerned to open up the text, to deconstruct it, has tended to take the film as given and has ignored questions of how the organisation of a film text might relate to the organisation of an industry or to specific working practices.

It is in respect of Hollywood, the largest field of activity in both film-making and criticism, that the lack of a history of the industry is most glaring. Of course there is a certain amount of information around. Statistics have occasionally been assembled (a number of government and trade reports on Hollywood in the 1930s are listed in the notes of Leo C. Rosten's *Hollywood: The Movie Colony, The Movie Makers*, a book which has some useful material on this period). There are one or two books, again on the 1930s, which assemble some facts about the economics of the industry (for example, F. D. Klingender and Stuart Legg, *The Money behind the Screen*, and Mae D. Huettig, *Economic Control of the Motion Picture Industry*). But of course they don't attempt to make any connections between the economics and the actual films produced. There is also the ragbag of publicity releases, inaccurate box-office returns, and general gossip which makes up the trade press (*Film Daily, Motion Picture Herald, Variety, Hollywood Reporter*, etc.). To this may be added a host of biographies (or ghosted autobiographies) of prominent industry figures, of which *Hollywood Rajah*, by Bosley Crowther (on Louis B. Mayer), and *King Cohn*, by Bob Thomas (on Harry Cohn) are representative examples. Little that is useful can be gleaned from such works, which mostly string together collections of anecdotes about the "great men." On such questions as the financial structures within which they were obliged to operate or the actual working methods of their studios they are for the most part silent. Of studio histories, properly speaking, there are none, with the possible exception of Richard Schickel's book *The Disney Version*, which is hampered by Schickel's failure to get any cooperation from the Disney studio itself—a fact, of course, that is not without its significance, since it indicates the difficulties of this kind of work.

Indeed, the neglect of industry history is not only a consequence of critical attitudes and priorities which have abandoned the field to those whose interest does not go beyond personalities. It is also the result of very real practical problems. The fact is that the history of the American film industry is extremely difficult to write, because many of the basic materials that would be needed are simply not available. The statistics are incomplete and unreliable. The trade press presents only the acceptable face of the business, even when one can get access to it (the BFI Library, virtually the only collection of such periodicals in Britain, has no run of *Variety*, though there are plans to acquire one). The biographies, and studio histories, where they exist at all (for example, Bosley Crowther's *Lion's Share*, on MGM), are based largely on reminiscences. Concrete documented evidence in the form, say, of studio memoranda, accounts, and other records, is almost totally lacking. If such records still exist they are mostly locked away in studio vaults. And the history of technological development in Hollywood has still to be written. Lastly, the films themselves; such prints as have been preserved are often impossible to see. The situation is little different from that which exists in relation to the history of the Elizabethan stage, with this exception, that infinitely less method and application have gone into researching it.

The result is that when Hollywood has been written about, its industrial dimension has been ignored. Much of the writing has been based on an idea of history as one damned thing after another. Even such a prestigious work as Lewis Jacobs's *Rise of the American Film* scarcely rises above this, most sections being simply annotated film lists. The only principle to compete has been auteurism, which leaves film history at the stage which history proper reached in the nineteenth century when Carlyle defined it as the lives of great men. Deliberate attempts to get away from auteurism, such as Colin McArthur's *Underworld USA* (on the crime film) and Jim Kitses's *Horizons West* (on the western) are ultimately broken-backed books. Genres may be related to aspects of American history, but in the end it is the auteurs who dominate the account.

Some recent, more promising directions have been pursued. Patrick Ogle's work on deep-focus (*Screen*, v. 13, n. 1) and that of John Ellis and Charles Barr on Ealing Studios (*Screen*, v. 15, nn. 1–2, v. 16, n. 1) have from different perspectives tried to make connections between films and the nature of the industry which produced them. *The Velvet Light Trap* has brought to light valuable material on the studio system, though the use that has been made of it has often been disappointing. But the gaps in our knowledge are still enormous.

II

One consequence of the existence of such gaps has been that attempts to relate Hollywood films to the society which produced them have simply by-passed the industry altogether. The result has been a series of short circuits. Hollywood films are seen as merely reflecting society. On the one hand is society, seen as a collection of facts, attitudes, psychological patterns, or whatever. On the other are the films, where one sees such facts, attitudes, etc., mirrored. Though it may be conceded that the mirror sometimes distorts, insofar as there is a theory behind such a view it is a naively realist one, and indeed how could it be otherwise? If there is no conception of Hollywood as an industry with its own history, specific practices, economic relationships, and technological and other material constraints, if film is seen as something that somehow mysteriously appears and having appeared is simply there, fixed and given, then how is one to understand the nature of any mediation? To confine ourselves again to the period of the 1930s, a book such as Andrew Bergman's *We're in the Money* devotes a mere four pages to "A Note on the Movie Industry and the Depression," which ends thus: "The preliminaries completed, we proceed to the black and white footage itself." And in the black-and-white footage the social comment can simply be read off as if the films were so many sociologists' reports. Here is an admittedly rather extreme example: "Tod Browning's 1932 MGM film, *Freaks*, had a cast made up of pinheads, human torsos, midgets, and dwarfs, like nothing ever in the movies. And what more stunted a year than 1932 for such a film?" (p. 168).

One might expect that more specifically Marxist attempts to relate Hollywood to American society would display a little more rigour and subtlety. Bourgeois cultural theories, with their assumptions about the values of artistic freedom and personal expression, are obviously ill equipped to deal with a medium so conditioned by money, technology, and organisational structures. Books such as Bergman's, which dispense with most of that theory (though never completely, for some auteurs, such as Capra and Vidor, make an appearance), seem to have no theory at all to replace it. Marxism, on the other hand, proposes a sophisticated understanding of the relations between society, a system of production, and the actual product. Yet such Marxist models as have been put forward for understanding Hollywood have suffered from a crudity which has had the effect of deadening further thought. The crudest model of all is that encapsulated in Godard's phrase *Nixon-Paramount*. The model implied in such a phrase has had obvious attractions for the political avant-garde and indeed contains some truth. But the truth contained in such vulgar Marxism is so vague and general as to have scarcely any use at all. Ideological products such as films are seen as directly caused by the nature of the economic base of society. A capitalist system produces capitalist films, and that is all there is to it. Alternatively—but the slight sophistication is scarcely a modification—the products of Hollywood are bourgeois and capitalist because the particular industry which produces them is capitalist. And the more specific the model becomes, the more its crudity is exposed. Thus in the first section of the *Cahiers du Cinéma* text on *Young Mr. Lincoln* (translated in *Screen*, v. 13, n. 3), we are told that since Hollywood is involved with big business, its ideology is not just a generally capitalist one. It supports the more reactionary wing of the political spectrum, represented by the Republican Party.

The *Cahiers* text is only one example of a desire to show not only that Hollywood is a part of bourgeois ideology in general but that some Hollywood films are intended to carry a specific and reactionary message which has a direct reference to a particular political situation. Another example of such over-politicisation comes in a recent issue of *Jump Cut*, n. 4, Nov.-Dec. 1974, which contains an interpretation of *King Kong* as an anti-Roosevelt tract. The article conveniently states its premises in a footnote:

> This article is built round two suppositions. First, that all huge business corporations (such as RKO) are conservative Republican unless demonstrated otherwise, and that their products (like *King Kong*) will reinforce their interests instead of betraying them. Second, that the auteur theory in its standard application is not a germane approach when dealing with a political film, especially under the tight studio control of the 1930's. A political film would only be allowed release if its philosophy was in line with that of the studio which made it. Therefore, RKO studio will be regarded as the true "auteur" of *King Kong*, despite the innumerable personal touches of its artistic crew.

Although the phrase *unless demonstrated otherwise* indicates that the author, Gerald Peary, is aware of the dangers of oversimple generalisations, his assumptions still seem open to two major objections. First, is it not possible that even in Hollywood (not noted perhaps for its political sophistication) there were in the 1930s people who could see that the survival of capitalism (and hence of their huge corporations) was not necessarily synonymous with the victory of the Republican Party, especially a Republican Party so discredited as the one which had been led to electoral disaster and intellectual bankruptcy by Herbert Hoover? Second, what exactly *are* the interests of such corporations? In the long term, obviously, the survival of a system which allowed them to make profits. But in the short term surely it was those profits themselves. Is it to be assumed that studio executives saw the possibility of profits in attacking a leader who had so recently demonstrated his popularity at the polls (especially among the cinema going section of the public)? Or should we assume that the political commitment of the studio executives overcame their dedication to profits?

It seems unlikely, but our ignorance about Hollywood generally and about the particular organisation of RKO is such that we cannot answer these questions. Precisely for this reason we ought to beware of assuming any answers. Even if we do assume, with the authors in *Cahiers* and *Jump Cut*, that a studio is owned by big business and that one of its products promotes the political and hence economic interests of the company (I say apparently because the actual interpretation of the films seems open to question), it does not necessarily follow that the political meaning is the direct result of who owns the studio. Post hoc is not *propter hoc*.

The lack of any detailed knowledge of industry history, then, suggests caution on the question of the political orientation of Hollywood in the 1930s. First, is it true that the film industry was controlled by big business? And is this the same as the Republican Party (there was business influence among the Democrats too)? Second, if it is true, can one assume a direct effect on the ideology of Hollywood films? Even the term *ideology* seems to pose a problem here. It is one thing to argue that, using the term in its classical Marxist sense (or as refined by Althusser) to mean a general worldview or structure of thought situated primarily below the conscious level, Hollywood films are ideological expressions of bourgeois society. It is quite another to argue that they support a specific set of political attitudes. Bourgeois society is more than simply the Republican Party. And in any case Marxist theory claims only that ideological products are determined in the last instance by the economic relations existing at the base of society. The arguments about *Young Mr. Lincoln* and *King Kong* appear to assume that facts about who controls the film industry can provide a sufficient explanation of a film's ideology, ignoring the dimension of the institutional structures which may intervene between the economic base and the final product. Without a knowledge of these structures one cannot say that these films are *not* propaganda; but if they were intended as such, as the *Cahiers* and *Jump Cut* articles imply, it is a strange sort of propaganda, which requires an ingenious interpretation thirty or forty years later to make its point. Surely it would have to be demonstrated that such a reading was available to an audience at the time.

III

These problems were thrown into relief by a viewing some time ago of *American Madness*, directed for Columbia in 1932 by Frank Capra. The story of the film concerns Dickson, the manager of a small-town bank (played by Walter Huston). The directors of the bank are financiers of the old school (pre-Keynesians), dedicated to tight money policies, which they pursue ruthlessly and selfishly. Dickson, however, has a different view of what the function of a bank should be. He believes that money should be put to work to create jobs and opportunities. His policy is to lend to small businessmen, trusting in his own assessment of their good intentions rather than in the security they can offer. His beliefs are put to the test when a run on the bank occurs; the run is stopped and his faith in his clients vindicated when the little people he has helped rally round to deposit money and so restore confidence in the bank.

The programme note which accompanied the screening of the film at the National Film Theatre suggested that the character of Dickson might have been based on A. H. Giannini, a California banker who was influential in Columbia's affairs in the 1930s. Such a suggestion raises one immediate difficulty, in that it seems to assume that the apparent, or manifest, meaning of the film is the only one, and ignores the possibility that the latent meaning may be quite different. The film might be about other things besides banking. It excludes, that is, the possibility of analysing the film along the lines of the *Young Mr. Lincoln* text, which finds that despite the film's apparent project of supporting the Republican cause in the 1940 presidential election, the "real" meaning of the film undermines this. (The problem of such readings, despite their obvious attractions, is that it is never explained how in practice the subversive meaning of the film becomes available to the people to whom it might be some use, i.e., the working class.) Nevertheless, the suggestion seemed worth following up because of the possibility that it might throw some light on the question of Hollywood's relation to politics in the 1930s and on the nature of the production system generally. And this might in turn tell us something about Capra's films.

Robert Mundy, in a review of Capra's autobiography in the American *Cinema* (v. 7, n. 1, Fall 1971, p. 56), speculates on how it was that Capra was able to make films which so closely embodied his personal ideas. He suggests two reasons: firstly, that Capra was working for a small studio where freedom was greater, and secondly, that Capra's vision "was unusually consonant with the vision of America which Hollywood purveyed with such commercial success in the 1930s. Ideologically his films were rarely at odds with the image of life which the studios believed the public wanted to see." Mundy avoids the facile assumptions that Capra was "in touch" with America and that his films arise out of some special relationship to the people and the mood of the time. Instead, he suggests that his work is an expression of the point of view of his *studio*. He concludes, however, that we need to know more: "A persuasive history of Columbia in the 1930s [is] needed before an informed critical account of Capra's work can be written." Quite. The problem is to know where to start, given the problems of such research outlined above. Mr. Giannini seemed to offer a way in.

He is referred to in a number of books about Hollywood, but as far as I know never more than in passing, as a prominent Californian banker who was involved in movie financing. In several of the references there is a curious uncertainty about his initials. Sometimes he is called A. P. Giannini, sometimes A. H. Thus Philip French in his "informal" history of the Hollywood tycoons, *The Movie Moguls*, mentions him on page 25: "In fact the first banker to take the cinema seriously was the Californian A. P. Giannini, the son of an Italian immigrant, whose Bank of Italy (later renamed the Bank of America) has played an important part in movie finance since before the first world war." On page 79 we read: "A H Giannini, the influential movie financier whose Bank of Italy had a special claim on Hollywood consciences of whatever religious denomination."

The mystery of A. H. or A. P. was only cleared up when I looked up Giannini in the *National Cyclopædia of American Biography*. It appears that there were two of them. (Obviously I am not the first person since Mr. Giannini pére to be aware of this fact, but it seems as though Philip French was not when he wrote his book. Of such confusions is film history made.) It's worth giving some details of their careers, since they are relevant to Capra's film. A. H. and A. P. (or to give them their full names, Attilio Henry and Amadeo Peter) were brothers. Both their parents were natives of Italy; their father had been a hotel keeper but had come to California to try farming. Amadeo was born in 1870 and his brother four years later. The older brother had gone to work at the age of twelve in his stepfather's firm of wholesale commission agents in San Francisco, and while still in his twenties he formed the Columbus Savings and Loan Society. In 1904 he founded the Bank of Italy. Giannini's bank was at the time of a novel kind. Branches were set up in small towns across the country to attract the savings of the man in the street, and Giannini even started savings schemes in schools. His bank specialised in making loans to small businesses with minimal collateral and introduced the practice of lending money for house purchase repayable in monthly instalments. He appears to have been a man of some determination and imagination; during the great San

Francisco earthquake and fire of 1906, Giannini was the first to reopen his bank, setting up his desk on the waterfront while the fire still raged. By 1930 he had built up his banking interests to the point where the holding company, the Transamerica Corporation, was the largest of its kind in the world, with assets of $1,000 million. Giannini's unorthodox methods did not endear him to more conservative financiers on Wall Street; particularly deplorable was his policy of encouraging wide public ownership of his corporation and of assisting his employees to become stockholders through profit-sharing schemes.

His brother Attilio (sometimes called Dr. Giannini, though he abandoned medicine when made vice-president of his brother's Bank of Italy) was involved in various movie companies between the world wars. In 1920 he lent Chaplin half a million dollars to make *The Kid*. In 1936 he became president and chairman of the Board of United Artists, and though he resigned from this position in 1938 he retained an influential position in the film industry by virtue of his place on the voting trust which controlled Universal Pictures. He was also involved with several so-called independent production companies such as Selznick International Pictures and Lesser-Lubitsch. It's worth pointing out that none of these organisations possessed large chains of movie theatres. It was the tangible assets of real estate which tempted the Wall Street banks into movie finance in the 1920s. Giannini does at least seem to have been more interested in making pictures.

Giannini's main importance for present purposes in his role in Columbia. The company was originally formed in 1920 as CBC, the letters standing for the names of the three men who set it up: Harry Cohn, Joe Brandt, and Harry's brother Jack. All of them had previously worked for Carl Laemmle at Universal. Attilio Giannini lent them $100,000 to get started. In 1924 the company changed its name to Columbia Pictures Corporation (possibly an echo of the Columbus Savings and Loan Society?). Giannini continued to be closely involved. Although in 1929 the studio decided to establish stock on the New York exchange, 96 per cent of the voting stock was concentrated in the hands of a voting trust. In 1932 Joe Brandt was bought out by Harry Cohn (after Jack Cohn had attempted to enlist Giannini's support in a coup against his brother), and thereafter the voting trust which controlled the company consisted of the two Cohns and Giannini. Unlike most studios at this time Columbia had no debts to the New York investment banks and instead was run as a family business.

Giannini's position was therefore a powerful one. Unfortunately one has no actual knowledge of how he used it. All that can be done is to suggest what his influence might have been given the kind of background from which he and his brother came. The Gianninis were quite separate from the New York banking establishment. Not only was theirs a different kind of business (deposit as opposed to investment banking), involving them with different kinds of clients; they were Catholics (unlike the Rockefellers and Morgans), they were second-generation immigrants, they came from the other side of the country, and their social attitudes were, as far as one can tell, less patrician. A. P.'s entry in the *National Cyclopædia* says that he "has ever been known as a friend of the poor and struggling" and if ever a banker could be so described it seems likely that he was. Not surprisingly, therefore, he supported the Banking Act introduced by Roosevelt in 1935 because, he said, he preferred a measure of government control to domination of the banks by the Wall Street establishment. In 1936 he actively supported Roosevelt's campaign for a second term, at a time when Wall Street considered FDR as no better than a Communist. It seems reasonable to assume that his brother shared his liberal views.

The Gianninis might, then, be seen as a kind of contradiction in terms: populist bankers. The populists of the nineteenth century had regarded bankers as the physical embodiment of all that was evil, and believed that the agricultural problems of the Mid-West were largely caused by a conspiracy of monopolists on Wall Street keeping interest rates up and farm prices down. (Amadeo Giannini was, we are told, greatly interested in agricultural progress.)

The little man, the populists contended, stood no chance against those who commanded such resources and used them for selfish purposes. But the Gianninis believed in deliberately aiding such small businessmen and farmers who got no help from Wall Street. In this respect they are in line with the policies of the New Deal, which attempted to get big business under some kind of government control while at the same time trying to raise farm prices and help small firms and individuals by encouraging banks to make loans, by refinancing mortgages, and so on.

This too is Dickson's policy in *American Madness* and it seems plausible that the character is indeed based on Dr. Giannini. The question then is, What do we make of it? A simple and tempting theory might be constructed: Capra's film doesn't so much capture what "people" were thinking at the time as represent the thinking of a New Dealer on the voting trust controlling Columbia. Such a theory certainly has its attractions. Firstly, it provides a corrective to the crude assumption that Hollywood = big business = the Republican Party. Secondly, other Capra films such as *Mr. Deeds Goes to Town, Mr. Smith Goes to Washington*, and *You Can't Take It with You* also embody the populism that was a powerful element in the New Deal. Thirdly, the situation of Columbia itself, quite apart from the beliefs of those in control, might well be seen as impelling it towards the New Deal coalition of anti-establishment forces. Despite the Academy Awards Capra collected for the studio in the 1930s it never entirely freed itself from its Poverty Row origins. Although the company bought its own studio in 1926 and in 1929 set up a national distribution organisation, at the beginning of the 1930s Columbia was still producing less than thirty features a year (to MGM's forty-three), and most of these were destined for the lower half of a double bill. Output increased steadily during the decade, but the studio was never in the same league as the majors. In 1935, for example, the total volume of business of Loew's, the parent company of MGM, was $85 million; Columbia's was $16 million. Thus Loew's had nearly 22 per cent of the total volume of business of the industry, Columbia only 4 per cent. And despite the characteristically violent swings in the film industry each year from profit to loss and back again, these relative percentages did not change for the rest of the decade. The reason why Columbia was unable to increase its share of business is that, unlike the major studios, it had no chain of theatres of its own which could serve as a secure outlet for its product. All the money it made came from the sale of its own pictures to theatres owned by other studios. MGM and the other majors could, and frequently did, recoup losses on their own films by profits on the exhibition of other companies' output.

But a potential advantage of this relative weakness was that Columbia preserved its financial independence. It had not had to borrow heavily from the banks to finance the acquisition of theatre chains, and as a result the studio was still in the control of the men who founded it, the two Cohns and Giannini. Its independence of Wall Street meant that it might well become the focus of anti-establishment forces, and that if it did it had the freedom to make films which reflected that, always providing of course that it could sell them to the theatres.

But caution is necessary even before trying to test out such a thesis. Capra in his autobiography devotes several pages to recording how charmed he was by Roosevelt's personality; yet, he says, this only made him "almost a Democrat." One might suppose that Capra, a first-generation immigrant, an Italian Catholic born in Sicily, was a natural Democrat. But the political content of his films, while embodying support for the underdog, does not attach itself to any party. His belief in the people goes hand in hand with a classically populist distrust of *all* their leaders. And other tendencies in his films, such as a pervasive anti-intellectualism and a hostility to central government, are certainly not characteristic of the New Deal.

Nevertheless there is a kind of radicalism in his films which would certainly not have commended itself to the fiercely Republican Louis B. Mayer, for example, and it therefore seems worth pursuing the thesis that Columbia might have been a focus for Roosevelt sympathisers. Harry Cohn, who controlled the production side of the company throughout the period, appears to have had no interest in politics at all. It is true that he visited Mussolini in 1933 after Columbia had released a complimentary documentary entitled *Mussolini Speaks*. But Cohn seems to have been more impressed with the intimidating lay-out of the dictator's office than with his politics. When he returned to Hollywood he rearranged his own office in imitation. Capra remarked in an interview at the National Film Theatre that Cohn didn't care what the politics of his studio's films were. His concern was with their money-making potential, which he estimated with a "foolproof device. . . . . If my fanny squirms it's bad. If my fanny doesn't squirm it's good. It's as simple as that" (quoted in *King Cohn*, p. 142). If Giannini had wanted the studio to take a pro-New-Deal stance, then it seems as though Cohn would have had no particular objections.

The only way of testing whether there was such a policy, in default of any access to whatever records of the company may still exist, is to look at the films that Columbia made during the period and to find out what one can about the people who made them. It's at this point that the sheer physical difficulties of this kind of work intrude. Taking the period 1926–41, from just before the introduction of sound to a year or so after Capra left Columbia (an arbitrary choice, but less arbitrary than some, and one which corresponds very roughly to the period of the Depression and the consequent New Deal, as far as World War II), Columbia, despite being one of the smaller studios, made on my calculations 627 feature films. (The figure may not be exact because the *Film Daily Year Book*, from which the calculation is made, lists the films of each year twice—once under each studio and once in alphabetical order for the whole industry. Titles appearing in one list don't always appear in the other.) To make those films the company employed 67 different producers, 171 directors, and 269 writers. (The figure for writers is from 1928; they are not credited in the *Year Book* before that date.) By writers is meant those credited with a screenplay. Authors of the original stories from which the films were made might amount to another two or three hundred people. There are also fifteen people whose names appear at one time or another as directors of the company, Columbia Pictures Corporation.

These are the people within the organisation whose position would have allowed them to influence the political content of the films. One might wish to argue that everyone—actors, cameramen, designers, right down to the studio policemen—had some kind of influence, however small. Melvyn Douglas, for example, who acted in many films for Columbia in the 1930s, was active in liberal causes. I have excluded these workers from consideration mainly because, given the nature of the production process, as far as one understands it, and the rigid division of labour, their control over the political content (if any) of a film would have been less. Actors didn't make up their own lines. In any case one has to stop somewhere, and it's not too easy to find out who the studio policemen were.

One is thus faced with a preliminary list of 522 people; to be precise, it is slightly less because the division of labour was not absolute and some writers directed or vice versa. But there is not much overlapping, and the total must be around 500 (this for one small studio during a mere fifteen years of its fifty-year existence). The BFI Library has a card index system which allows one to check whether the library has entries on individuals in books, in periodicals, or on microfiche. I accordingly looked up everyone who worked on more than the occasional film. Very few of these names appear in the index and when they do it is often merely a reference to a tiny cutting in *Variety* recording the person's death and giving a person/short list of the films worked on. (This is not a criticism of the state of the library but of the state of film history.)

A few things do emerge. Columbia seems to have been, in the higher echelons, a tight-knit community (one precondition perhaps of a consistent policy). One of the producers was

Ralph Cohn, the son of Jack. Everett Riskin, another producer, was the older brother of Robert, who wrote several of Capra's screenplays. Sam Briskin, general manager of the studio in the early 1930s and executive in charge of production from 1938 to 1942, was the brother-in-law of Abe Schneider, treasurer of the company for most of this period. Briskin's brother, Irving, was another producer at Columbia. Yet this doesn't tell us much about an industry where the pull of family relationships was always strong and where "the son-in-law also rises" was a standard joke.

On the political affiliations of the vast majority, I found no information at all, nor even any information on their lives which would permit a guess. Some very few wrote books or had books written about them, but with the exception of Cohn and Capra their careers were peripheral to Columbia. A few more have been the subject of articles in film magazines, and from these one can glean scraps of information. Richard Maibaum, who wrote a few scripts for the studio, was the author of some anti-lynching and anti-Nazi plays before coming to Hollywood. Dore Schary, whose Democrat sympathies were well known, was also a writer at Columbia in the 1930s. So, very occasionally, were Donald Ogden Stewart, associated with left wing causes at the time, and Edward Chodorov, involved with committees for refugees from Spain and Germany and later more or less black-listed. But this scarcely amounts to much. Stewart, after all, wrote a lot of scripts for MGM.

More significant, at first sight, than the presence of liberals, is the fact that exactly half of the Hollywood Ten were actually employed at Columbia during the 1930s, namely, Edward Dmytryk, Dalton Trumbo, Herbert Biberman, John Howard Lawson, and Lester Cole. But a concerted Communist effort at the studio is hardly likely. Only Dmytryk worked there more than occasionally, and he during his time as a contract director was making routine B-feature films (musicals, horror pictures, thrillers) which, one must assume, offered little scope for the kind of social comment Dmytryk later put into *Crossfire*. There were one or two other Communists working at Columbia who testified before the House Un-American Activities Committee four years after the 1947 hearings which sent the Ten to jail. Paul Jarrico, who wrote for Columbia the screenplays of *No Time to Marry* (1938) and *The Face behind the Mask* (1941), was called before the committee in 1951 but refused to testify and pleaded the Fifth Amendment. Another called before the committee in 1951 was Sidney Buchman. One of Harry Cohn's favourite writers, Buchman specialised in comedy. Among his credits for Columbia are *Whom the Gods Destroy* (1934); *I'll Love You Always, Love Me Forever, She Married Her Boss* (1935); *The King Steps Out, Theodora Goes Wild, Adventure in Manhattan, The Music Goes Round* (1936); *Holiday* (1938); *Mr. Smith Goes to Washington* (1939); *The Howards of Virginia* (1940); and *Here Comes Mr. Jordan* (1941). Buchman admitted that he had been in the Communist Party from 1938 to 1945, but refused to supply the committee with the list of names of other members it required and was cited for contempt. He was found guilty and given a one-year suspended sentence and a $150 fine.

Buchman clearly occupied an influential position at Columbia. He was a producer as well as a writer and was associated with some of Columbia's greatest successes in the late 1930s and early 1940s. But if *Mr. Smith* is satirical about Washington life, it retains an unswerving, even touching, faith in American political institutions, and it is difficult to see that Buchman's membership of the Communist Party had any great effect on what he wrote. Indeed many of his associates appear to have been surprised to learn that he was a Communist.

It may be that a more detailed search through such records as are available would turn up some decisive evidence. But on what has been presented so far it seems unlikely that, Dr. Giannini notwithstanding, there was any deliberate policy of favouritism to the New Deal or left causes. The same conclusion seems likely to follow from the films. Here again one is attempting generalisations based on woefully inadequate knowledge, because, apart from those directed by Capra, I have seen very few of the films Columbia made during the period. Nevertheless some impressions can be gained from looking at the records. In the late 1920s and early 1930s the staples of the studio's output were adventure and action films, comedies often mildly risqué, and the occasional exposé (one of Jack Cohn's first successes at Universal was to convince Carl Laemmle of the box office potential of *Traffic in Souls*, a sensationalist feature on the white slave trade). Westerns and thrillers made up the rest of the production schedule. Of course titles can be misleading, but a list of the films produced in 1928 probably gives a fair indication of at least the type of films being made:

> *That Certain Thing, The Wife's Relations, Lady Raffles, So This Is Love, Woman's Way, Sporting Age, Matinee Idol, Desert Bride, Broadway Daddies, After the Storm, Golf Widows, Modern Mothers, Name the Woman, Ransom, Way of the Strong, Beware of Blondes, Say It with Sables, Virgin Lips, Scarlet Lady, Court Martial, Runaway Girls, Streets of Illusion, Sinners' Parade, Driftwood, Stool Pigeon, The Power of the Press, Nothing to Wear, Submarine, The Apache, The Lone Wolf's Daughter, Restless Youth, The Sideshow.*

Besides Capra, directors working regularly for Columbia at this time included the veteran director of serials George B. Seitz (*The Perils of Pauline*), and Erle Kenton, another veteran who had been in pictures since 1914. The policy, one guesses, was one of efficient professionalism dedicated to getting the most out of Columbia's meagre resources. Not only did Columbia make less films; it also spent less on each production than the major studios. (Few of its films at this time ran more than seventy minutes.) This would seem to leave little room for the carefully considered personal statements of the kind Capra aspired to later in the 1930s. This is not to say that there was no possibility of social or political comment, however, as the history of Warner's at the same time shows.

After Capra's astonishing success with *It Happened One Night* in 1934, which won Columbia its first Oscars and enormously increased the studio's prestige, pictures of the earlier type were supplemented by the occasional more expensive production. Though Columbia had contract players of its own (for example, Jack Holt and Ralph Bellamy or, in westerns, Buck Jones and Charles Starrett), they could not compare in box-office appeal with the stars of bigger studios. Columbia could not afford the budgets which having bigger stars would have entailed. On the other hand it could never break into the big time without them. Harry Cohn's solution to this vicious circle was to invite successful directors from other studios to make occasional pictures for Columbia, pictures which would be given larger than usual budgets and which would have stars borrowed from other studios. Careful planning permitted short production schedules and kept costs down to what Columbia could afford. Capra too was given increasingly larger budgets and outside stars. Thus a number of big-name directors came to work at Columbia during the later 1930s, often tempted by the offer of being allowed to produce their own films. Among the titles produced at Columbia during the period after *It Happened One Night* were:

> 1934: *20th Century* (dir. Howard Hawks, with John Barrymore and Carole Lombard), *The Captain Hates the Sea* (dir. Lewis Milestone, with Victor McLaglen and John Gilbert); 1935: *The Whole Town's Talking* (dir. John Ford, with Edward G. Robinson), *She Married Her Boss* (dir. Gregory La Cava, with Claudette Colbert), *She Couldn't Take It* (dir. Tay Garnett, with George Raft and Joan Bennett), *Crime and Punishment* (dir. Josef von Sternberg, with Peter Lorre); 1936: *Theodora Goes Wild* (dir. Richard Boleslavski, with Irene Dunne); 1937: *The Awful Truth* (dir. Leo McCarey, with Cary Grant and Irene Dunne); 1938: *Holiday* (dir. George Cukor, with Cary Grant and Katherine Hepburn); 1939:

Let Us Live (dir. John Brahm, with Maureen O'Sullivan and Henry Fonda), *Only Angels Have Wings* (dir. Howard Hawks, with Cary Grant, Thomas Mitchell, and Richard Barthelmess), *Golden Boy* (dir. Rouben Mamoulian, with Barbara Stanwyck and Adolphe Menjou); 1940: *His Girl Friday* (dir. Howard Hawks, with Cary Grant and Rosalind Russell), *The Howards of Virginia* (dir. Frank Lloyd, with Cary Grant), *Angels over Broadway* (dir. Ben Hecht and Lee Garmes, with Douglas Fairbanks Jr.), *Arizona* (dir. Wesley Ruggles, with William Holden); 1941: *Penny Serenade* (dir. George Stevens, with Cary Grant and Irene Dunne), *Texas* (dir. George Marshall, with William Holden, Glenn Ford, and Claire Trevor), *You Belong to Me* (dir. Wesley Ruggles, with Barbara Stanwyck and Henry Fonda), *The Men in Her Life* (dir. Gregory Ratoff, with Loretta Young).

But despite this sprinkling of prestige productions the basic recipe remained much the same as before. There were lots of low-budget westerns (a dozen or so in 1940) directed by Lambert Hillyer, a veteran of the Columbia lot, or Joseph H. Lewis, and starring Bill Elliott or Charles Starrett. The studio made several series: a number of films based on Blondie, the cartoon character, the Lone Wolf series of thrillers, an Ellery Queen mystery series, and so on. There were light comedies from Alexander Hall, more light comedies and musicals from Walter Lang, and plenty of crime films (a few titles at random from 1938: *Women in Prison, When G-Men Step In, Penitentiary, Highway Patrol, Reformatory, Convicted, I Am the Law, Juvenile Court, Smashing the Spy Ring*).

What is one to conclude from what emerges of Columbia's production policy in this period? Aware that a viewing of all the films might prove one wrong, it could be said that there is no evidence of Columbia's deliberately following a line favourable to the New Deal. Of course it could be objected that a similar scanning of the titles of Warner Brothers films of the same time would fail to reveal what an actual viewing of the films shows—a detectable if not pronounced leaning towards Rooseveltian attitudes. But this much seems likely: the policy of bringing in outside stars and directors (and writers too) for big-budget productions would have worked against the continuity required for a deliberate political policy. Whereas at Warners a nucleus of stars, writers, producers, and directors was built up capable of producing pictures that fused the thrills of crime with social comment, at Columbia the occasional film (such as *A Man's Castle*, directed by Frank Borzage in 1933) which took the Depression as its subject was a one-off, with the exception of Capra. And it does seem as though Capra *was* an exception. As far as one can tell, the directors who did not have his freedom at the studio did not follow him in the direction of social comment, and neither did directors brought in from outside with a similar amount of freedom. And Capra's films, after all, despite his standing within the studio, are only a tiny proportion of all the films Columbia made in the 1930s.

If one can say that the presence of Giannini on the trust controlling Columbia did not lead to films predominantly favourable to the New Deal, then can one not also throw doubt on the assumption that control of a studio by interests favourable to the Republican Party led to films (such as *Young Mr. Lincoln* and *King Kong*) designed to make propaganda for that party? No one would argue that there was a total lack of correlation between ownership and the content of films. No studio in the 1930s would have tolerated outright Communist movies, or anything very close to that. (Nor for that matter would a fascist film have stood any chance of being made.) But within these parameters, considerable diversity was possible—a diversity, moreover, which it is dangerous to reduce by the simple expedient of labelling all the films as bourgeois. The difference in political attitudes between, say, *The Good Earth* (MGM, 1937) and *The Grapes of Wrath* (20th Century-Fox, 1940)—two films with not totally dissimilar subjects—are not negligible and relate to real political and social events of the time. But they cannot be explained simply in terms of who owned the studios or in terms only of social attitudes at the time. Any explanation would require that a number of factors be taken into account, and not least of these would be the exact nature of the institutions which produced them.

The history of the American film industry, then, forms a kind of missing link in attempts, Marxist and otherwise, to make connections between films and society. As we have seen, many of the materials needed to forge that link are missing, which is why the title of this essay, "Notes on Columbia Pictures Corporation 1926–41," is intended to imply more than the customary academic modesty. The problems of producing such a history are both practical and the result of a massive ideological prejudice, and I am aware that the information I have produced on Columbia in the 1930s amounts to very little in the way of real knowledge. But this information has been the result of a few hours in the library, not of a large-scale research programme. If one considers how much has been learned, for example, about British labour history in the nineteenth century, the possibilities for further research do not seem hopeless. As a subject it would appear equally as unpromising as the history of the film industry. Apart from newspapers there are few written sources and the people involved are all dead. The history therefore has to a great extent to be reconstructed from the material objects which survive: buildings, institutional structures, the customs and practices of a people. But full-time academics and research students have been working in the field for years. The study of the history of the American film industry has scarcely begun.

Note

From *Screen* 16:3 (Autumn 1975), 65–82. Reprinted with permission of the author and *Screen*.

Chapter 2

Thomas Schatz

WARNER BROS.: POWER PLAYS AND PRESTIGE (1988)

Editors' Introduction

Thomas Schatz's notion of "the genius of the system," a term borrowed from André Bazin, provided a strategic undermining of the *auteur* model, celebrating instead a collaborative system that systematically organized the division of labor on and off the set. While the *auteurist* model was built upon the notion of an industry thwarting creativity in favor of corporate interests, Schatz outlined how the very structure and operation of the Hollywood studio system affected a productive balance between the two. In this essay on Warner Bros., Schatz explores the relationship between the studio moguls Harry and Jack Warner and their head of production, Darryl Zanuck. Key to their collaboration was Zanuck's evocation of a gritty realist "house style," a style necessitated by the moguls' cheapskate budgets and the peculiar talents of the studio's un-pretty contract actors James Cagney, Paul Muni, and Edward G. Robinson. Two films model "the genius of the system" at Warner's in the Zanuck era: *I Am a Fugitive from a Chain Gang* (a film based on a story serialized in 1931 in the pulp magazine *True Detective Mysteries*) and *42nd Street,* a hybrid film composed of a backstage drama captured in the house style and a musical revue that banked on the prodigious talents of opulent choreographer Busby Berkeley. The former title, Schatz argues, "tells us something about the usual interplay of technique, thematics, and production design in Warners pictures. It also tells us something about the interplay of narrative economy and cost-efficiency." *42nd Street,* he posits, was a more complex beast, if only because it was two films in one. But it too showcased "the balance of Warners' economic and creative forces." Proof of Schatz's argument here isn't found simply or only in Zanuck's success at Warners, but in the studio's success without him (after his ouster in 1933) and his later success at Fox, where he collaborated in the creation of a very different, but nonetheless economically and creatively successful house style.

Suggested Reading

Tino Balio, *The American Film Industry* (Madison: University of Wisconsin Press,

1976); David Bordwell, Janet Staiger, and Kristin Thompson, *The Classical Hollywood Cinema: Film Style and Mode of Production to 1960* (NY: Columbia University Press, 1985); and Douglas Gomery, *The Hollywood Studio System: A History* (London: British Film Industry, 2008).

THE PROSPECT OF *Jezebel* or any other Warners picture worrying an independent prestige-level producer like David O. Selznick would have been unthinkable five years earlier. But *Jezebel* was a far cry from the hell-bent urban crime dramas that Warners cranked out during Darryl Zanuck's regime, and Warners itself was a very different studio. It was Zanuck's departure, in fact, that first signaled a series of changes for the studio in the mid-1930s—changes in production and management operations, in economic conditions and market strategy, and ultimately, in Warners' house style. After the Zanuck era, Warners underwent a decentralization of creative and administrative control, much the same as MGM did in 1933. Schenck and Mayer eliminated the role of central producer altogether at Metro, but the Warners had neither the resources nor the corps of producers to go that route. Instead they initiated a supervisory system under Hal B. Wallis, a longtime Warners employee who had been Zanuck's executive assistant for the past three years.

The first sign of Wallis's upgraded executive status came even before Zanuck left. On March 19, 1933, while Zanuck and Harry Warner were battling over 50 percent pay cuts for all studio employees, Wallis's salary was raised from $900 to $1,100 per week. Then on June 14, 1933, three months to the day after Zanuck's abrupt resignation, Wallis signed a new contract giving him a salary of $1,750 weekly and defining his duties as being "of an executive and/or administrative character in connection with the supervision and general overseeing of production." So Wallis clearly was Warners' new production chief, though at a salary well below the $5,000 per week Zanuck had been earning. And in a business where paychecks were a barometer of power and authority as well as success, the disparity was significant. Wallis would oversee studio operations, but he was by no means a central producer à la Zanuck. In the mold of Paramount "mill foreman" Ben Schulberg, Wallis was a company man whose strengths were administrative, and he relied on his writers and supervisors for creative input. By late 1933 every Warners picture was assigned a supervisor, many of whom were culled from the screenwriting ranks. Some writer-producers like Robert Lord and Robert Presnell had been supervising informally for some time, and these "hyphenates" were the key creative personnel and the highest-paid supervisors on the lot; Lord earned $1,750 and Presnell $1,000 per week in late 1933. The lowest-paid supervisors were straight middle-management types like Henry Blanke at $500 and Lou Edelmen at $300. But whatever their writing skills, Warners supervisors oversaw script development as well as production, and then helped prepare a rough cut before passing the project back to Wallis and Jack Warner.

These changes on the Warners lot were not immediately evident on the screen. In fact, judging from Warners' output in 1933 and 1934, it was almost as if Zanuck had never left. The studio turned out a steady supply of efficient and predictable products—backstage musicals and urban melodramas, action pictures and crime films "torn from the day's headlines" that typified Warners' early-thirties style. But even in a backstage musical like *Dames* or a crime saga like *Bordertown*, we can glimpse changes in the production and management process. Both pictures were under Wallis's administrative control and were supervised by Robert Lord, who was to oversee script development and monitor actual production. There were problems on both pictures, though, reflecting not only the difficulty of shifting to a supervisory system but also the consequences of dispersing authority into the creative ranks.

Dames was initiated in August 1933, some six weeks after the release of *Gold Diggers of 1933*,

Warners' biggest hit of the year. The Warners wanted a follow-up, so Wallis put Robert Lord to work on a story idea with choreographer and dance director Busby Berkeley, who was suddenly the hottest thing in Hollywood. Lord brainstormed with Berkeley, and the two came up with a story idea and title, which Wallis relayed back to Jack Warner. Wallis told Warner to "register the title *Dames*," and told him that the picture would be "done with a stage background, with Dick Powell in mind as the dance director patterned after Busby Berkeley and Ruby Keeler as one of the girls in the chorus." Wallis put Lord and screenwriter Tom Buckingham on the project, and by early October the two had a script draft and a new title, "Stage Struck"—neither of which Wallis liked. Wallis decided to bring in another writer-producer, James Seymour, who had coscripted *42nd Street* and *Gold Diggers of 1933*. Wallis gave Seymour specific instructions to reprise his earlier hits, and the result was a story about a struggling songwriter who falls for a chorine, which Seymour described to Wallis as derivative of *Gold Diggers* but "much more up to date," with a female lead "tailor-made for Keeler." Wallis was satisfied and sent the project into preproduction, with Seymour supervising and Archie Mayo assigned to direct. Mayo was the first of three directors for *Dames*, and the fact is that any number of Warners directors could have handled the "book" portion of the picture. But only Berkeley could have done the choreography and musical direction.

Busby Berkeley was a rare commodity at Warners, a specialist and true visionary amid a corps of interchangeable directors. He signed a new seven-year contract in February 1934 that identified him as a director, but Berkeley's work was so specialized and distinctive—and commercially successful—that he was given a remarkable degree of authority. He conceived, designed, choreographed, directed, and even edited the musical numbers himself. The elaborate sets and costumes in his musical numbers, the fluid camera work and dramatic angles, the clarity and precision of the images themselves—all were uncommon qualities in Warners' pictures. They were even exceptional in the musicals themselves, setting off the numbers from the rest of the picture, creating a tension between story and music, between reality and artifice. Despite this tension there was a curious integrity and coherence to these Warners musicals, since Berkeley's densely populated numbers and his penchant for reducing human forms to machinelike, syncopated displays complemented the offstage sagas of struggling songwriters and anonymous chorines working together to survive the Depression.

There was a logic of excess to Berkeley's work, which Wallis both appreciated and continually fought to keep in check. Berkeley had his own unit for the musical numbers on *Dames*, as he'd had on *42nd Street* and *Gold Diggers*, and it operated outside of any supervisor's purview. Berkeley had virtually complete creative control, with Wallis repeatedly pulling rank to keep him in line. Wallis overruled Berkeley's casting decisions and insisted that Berkeley never cast without consulting him. He nixed Berkeley's idea for a "pussy song," arguing that "we are accused of obscenity in our pictures enough as it is without reason, and besides there is no use besmirching the name of Berkeley with filth." Wallis's greatest concern, though, was Berkeley's casual disregard for the budget in his production numbers. The "I Only Have Eyes for You" number, for example, was budgeted for thirty-six performers and a set cost of $15,000. But by the time he was ready to start shooting, Berkeley wanted 250 chorines and a $50,000 set. "We have been warned not to have this kind of number in the picture," Wallis informed Berkeley before set construction for the scene began, "and I, personally, will not approve anything of this kind."

There were no such problems with director Ray Enright, a model of Warners efficiency who took over the picture only a week before shooting began. By then Robert Lord was back on *Dames* supervising the Enright unit, with Wallis screening their footage in his home each evening on a projection system installed by the studio. But still Berkeley remained the dominant creative force, cutting and scoring the musical numbers and advising Wallis on the rest of the picture. When Jack Warner screened the film and decided that a certain production number needed to be redone, Berkeley staged, directed, and edited the scene. Although Wallis demanded to see the number rehearsed before it was shot, the number was Berkeley's. So was the picture itself, in large measure, which Wallis acknowledged in a postproduction memo concerning the credits and billing: "The title *Dames* is to be followed by the name of the director and Busby Berkeley in equal-size type." *Dames* was in final cut by mid-July, and it opened on August 16 at New York City's Strand theater.

On the following day back at Burbank, *Bordertown* went into production. That project was equally illuminating in terms of Warners' changing management and production operations, though for altogether different reasons. The primary reason was Paul Muni, who was without question the most powerful star at Warners in the mid-1930s. Back in June 1933, just after Zanuck's departure, Jack Warner signed Muni to a two-year, eight-picture deal, paying him $50,000 per picture and allowing concessions that were given to no other star on the lot. These included approval of story, role, and script; billing as sole star, both on-screen and in all advertising; loan-outs only on consent, with story and role approval, and at a fifty-fifty split with Warners on any salary overage; and permission for Muni "to render his services as he sees fit upon the legitimate stage" between film projects. The only previous Warners star who had enjoyed that kind of authority was George Arliss, who followed Zanuck to Twentieth that same summer of 1933. The Warners figured they had an even better bet in Paul Muni, who had just hit in *Scarface* and *I Am a Fugitive from a Chain Gang*. They saw Muni as a hybrid of Cagney and Arliss, part surly tough guy and part cultured stage star.

Muni himself initiated *Bordertown* when he sent Carroll Graham's novel to Wallis in March 1934. The story centered on a Mexican lawyer who, blinded by both the American success ethic and a wanton Anglo seductress, forsakes his own people and degenerates into a murderous criminal. Wallis sent the novel to Jack Warner, who liked its possibilities as a crime saga and approved its purchase for $5,000. Wallis put Edward Chodorov on script development, instructing him to "give the character as much motivation and sympathy for the things he does as possible," to accommodate Muni. Two weeks later Chodorov submitted a treatment that, he told Wallis, provided "complete justification for the initial murders" committed by the hero, although "after this he emerges as a completely cold Little Caesar."

Chodorov's invocation of Edward G. Robinson's legendary gangster-hero might have pleased Wallis and Warner, but it could not have come at a less opportune time. Two weeks later, on April 11, 1934, while Chodorov was working on the screenplay for *Bordertown*, the Catholic Church officially announced the formation of the Legion of Decency. The Legion was created by the nation's bishops expressly to battle "indecent and immoral pictures, and those which glorify crime or criminals." The chief weapon was abstention. A Catholic was expected to pledge not only to avoid "pictures that are dangerous to my moral life," but also "to stay away altogether from places of amusement which show them as a matter of policy." This all went largely unnoticed at Warners—until Cardinal Dougherty of Philadelphia ordered a boycott of all movie theaters. There were boycotts against specific films in other cities like Boston and St. Louis, but only in Philadelphia was there a general boycott against all movies and theaters. There were some 800,000 Catholics in Philadelphia, but well over a million people of all denominations participated in the boycott. In fact, *Newsweek* magazine reported in early July that the movement had spread well beyond the Catholic constituency, and "no less than 65,000,000—half the population of the country—were under official church pressure to boycott indecent and un-Christian films."

The Warners had gotten their start in Pittsburgh with a string of nickelodeons, and by the mid-1930s they controlled the entire state of Pennsylvania. Out of 152 affiliated theaters in the state, 140 were Warners', including almost all the first-run houses in Pittsburgh and Philadelphia. So the boycott got the Warners' attention, and it got the MPPDA's as well. It was during the boycott that the Production Code Administration was created and Joe Breen was installed as president. The code would be enforced beginning July 15, 1934. No script could go into production without PCA approval; no film could be released without a PCA seal. For the time being the Catholic bishops were appeased—and both the Legion and the PCA were now permanent fixtures of the movie industry. So the heat was off the theaters, but it was on in Hollywood. And for the time being, at least, the studios were more than willing to submit to the PCA. Hollywood could scarcely deal with a widespread theater boycott, and there were also veiled threats of government censorship. If Breen's self-censorship outfit could forestall those external threats and maintain more favorable public relations, the studios would learn to live with it.

As it turned out, *Dames* and *Bordertown* were two of the first Warners pictures to require PCA approval. There were a few minor problems on *Dames*—a reference to bribery and a brief suggestion of nudity in a silhouette shot—but these were cleared up easily enough. On July 19, Jack Warner received a letter from Breen informing him that "the version we saw this morning in your projection room of your production *Dames* is acceptable under the provisions of the Production Code." *Bordertown* was a different story, however. By early July Chodorov had taken it through two script drafts, both of which were savaged by the PCA. "The general background of the story is very low toned," wrote Breen to Warner, "with practically no compensating moral values." Breen was particularly concerned about the "sympathetic" Muni character, who lives "in adultery" with a prostitute and "becomes a murderer, gambler, and crook, always trying to 'go American.' " He also expressed dismay that "the race distinctions between Mexican and American" might offend "our southern neighbors." Breen advised Warner that "it would be difficult, if not impossible, to produce a picture from this script which would meet the requirements of the Production Code."

It was clear that wholesale revisions were in order, so Wallis brought in a new writing team under Robert Lord's supervision. Lord came through, and the massive rewrites not only gutted *Bordertown* but set a pattern for future compromises with the Breen office and marked an overnight transformation of Warners' crime sagas. Muni's character was watered down from a "completely cold Little Caesar" to a well-intentioned but hot-tempered lawyer whose only crime is punching out a rival attorney during a trial. He is disbarred and winds up running a seedy casino across the border—which puts Muni on the margins of society but scarcely in the gangster class. And rather than take up with an Anglo prostitute, in this version Muni spurns the advances of the casino owner's libidinous wife. To remove the obvious impediment, she kills her husband, and this murder leads to a climactic trial and, eventually, to the hero's redemptive return, at the behest of his mother and a neighborhood priest, to his own Hispanic people. Lord had a new script ready in three weeks that Wallis sent to the PCA. After a personal meeting between Wallis and Breen on August 10, Jack Warner was informed that there were "no definite Code violations" in the script, although numerous "details" needed to be "cleared up." That meant Wallis could schedule the shoot, and he sent word to director Archie Mayo that production would start the following week.

It also meant that Jack Warner finally had to decide on a female lead. Muni wanted Carole Lombard, but Warner was leaning toward Bette Davis. The gifted, headstrong Davis was at a turning point in her career in August 1934. After two and a half years at Warners, Davis had done sixteen films and had bitched nonstop about her roles, her work load, and her pay, which by then was $750 per week. Back in February 1934 Warner had decided to placate her—and get her off his case—by loaning her to RKO to play the cockney prostitute in an adaptation of Somerset Maugham's *Of Human Bondage*. It was an inspired bit of casting, and in that RKO picture Davis, at age twenty-six, first displayed the nature and range of her talent. While the RKO picture was in postproduction, she went back to Warners and more second-rate roles. She played a home-wrecking secretary in *Housewife* and then was assigned a supporting role (as secretary Della Street) in a low-budget Perry Mason thriller, *The Case of the Howling Dog*. Davis refused to report, and Jack Warner promptly suspended her. Two weeks later RKO released *Of Human Bondage*, which changed Jack Warner's attitude rather quickly. The response to the picture was such that Davis, as *The Los Angeles Times* put it, was "welcomed back into the fold with embarrassing effusion." Jack Warner's first effusive gesture was to give her the part of the adulterous Marie in *Bordertown*.

Bordertown, scheduled for six weeks and budgeted at $343,000, went into production on August 17. The shoot went well, though there was a mild flap over Davis's performance at one point that indicated the limits of Wallis's authority over—and his understanding of—the filmmaking process. Some three weeks into the shoot, Wallis sent a memo to Archie Mayo after seeing the dailies of a scene that was to appear toward the end of the picture. "I don't like the way you played Bette Davis at all in the scene in the construction set," said Wallis. "It's about time she's starting to crack . . . [yet] she plays it like Alice in Wonderland." Wallis instructed Mayo to retake the scene "and make it in a more emotional-hysterical way." He even specified what camera angle and setups would have to be redone.

Lord sent a return memo that same day. "I emphatically disagree with your criticism," he said. "I think Archie has directed the scene perfectly. At least, he has directed the scene as I, who wrote it, intended it to be directed." Lord reminded Wallis that they were shooting out of continuity and explained how carefully he and Mayo were setting up Davis's "growing insanity." Lord reasoned that "if we start Miss Davis cracking up and screaming too early, we will have absolutely nothing left for her in the later clinching scenes." Wallis let the scene stand, and once the film took shape during postproduction, it was clear that Lord had been right. Several successful previews confirmed that Warners had another hit in the works, one that would require only minimal retakes if they could get past the PCA. Breen himself came to the studio on November 11, 1934, and reported to Jack Warner later that day that the picture merited Code approval.

Bordertown was released in January 1935, the first of many crime pictures by Warners that year—pictures like *G-Men, Special Agent*, and *Dr. Socrates*. These, too, were vintage Warners in terms of technique, budget, and narrative economy, but they also had been sanitized to accommodate the PCA. Clearly, the hard-edged antisocial type popularized by Cagney and Robinson and Muni had quite literally been outlawed by the Breen office, and so had his "low-toned" background and amoral world view.

The type would undoubtedly have faded from Warners' repertoire even without Breen's encouragement, given the improving economic climate at Warners in 1935 and the generally upbeat mood in the industry and nation at large. After losing over $20 million in 1932–33, Warners suffered losses of only $2.5 million in 1934 and Harry Warner fully expected to turn a profit in 1935. This was the year in fact when Warner planned to start competing with MGM, Paramount, and Fox on their own terms. That meant prestige productions, which hadn't been on Warners' agenda since the 1920s, but the studio was now ready to go that route. Not only had Warners adjusted its management and production operations in 1933 after Zanuck's departure, but it also initiated a series of deals that were key to a first-run strategy. The most important of these were the $40,000 purchase of Hervey Allen's bestselling historical romance, *Anthony Adverse*, and a two-year pact with free-lance director and two-time Oscar winner Frank Borzage, calling for six "Frank Borzage Productions" that were to be, in the words of his contract, "of the highest type and character as is practicable, having due regard to the efficient and economic operations of [Warners'] business." In fall 1934 Warners signed German stage legend Max Reinhardt "in connection with the directing, staging, creating, and producing of *A Midsummer Night's Dream*," which he had staged the previous summer at the Hollywood Bowl. Warners was willing to spend a million dollars on a film version and bill it as "A Max Reinhardt

Production." Later in 1934, Warners cut what was without question the most important deal in its climb to prestige status, a deal with William Randolph Hearst.

The decade-long partnership between MGM and Cosmopolitan Pictures had soured in recent years, as Marion Davies's appeal waned and she kept losing roles to Norma Shearer that Hearst wanted for her. So the newspaper czar and *ersatz* independent producer decided to leave MGM, and he did so with characteristic flair. In November 1934 he cut a twelve-picture deal with Warners; he also cut Davies's elaborate two-story bungalow into three sections and had it moved from Culver City to Burbank. Warner Bros. agreed to finance, produce, and distribute the twelve "Cosmopolitan Productions," four of which would star Davies. Warners would retain "full charge of production and the sole and absolute power and control over all matters in connection therewith." After recovering its production and distribution costs, Warners would split all profits evenly with Cosmopolitan. A major benefit of the deal for Warners was access to Hearst's publishing empire as a source of story material and publicity. The contract promised Warners "lists and manuscripts of all stories appearing or about to appear in the Hearst newspapers, *Cosmopolitan* magazine, *Good Housekeeping, Harper's Bazaar*, and other magazines published by William Randolph Hearst." The contract also stated that "Cosmopolitan will cause to be published in newspapers controlled by William Randolph Hearst, without expense to [Warner Bros.], adequate advertisement and publicity in connection with . . . the promotion of Cosmopolitan productions."

The Warners did not expect much from Davies, and indeed her four pictures for them closed out her career. But they expected quite a bit more from Hearst, thanks to his publications and also his leverage with first-run exhibitors, developed over the past decade at MGM. Warners tested those expectations only weeks after the Hearst deal by initiating two ambitious Cosmopolitan projects, *Captain Blood* and *The Story of Louis Pasteur*, two "costume pictures" geared to the same prestige market for which they had produced *Midsummer Night's Dream* and *Anthony Adverse*. Historical epics, swashbucklers, and biopics were undergoing a full-scale revival in the mid-1930s, particularly through the efforts of two Warners alumni, Darryl Zanuck and George Arliss. The two did *Voltaire* just before leaving Warners, and then at Twentieth Century Pictures they scored with two other biopics: *The House of Rothschild* in 1934 and *Cardinal Richelieu* in 1935. Along with these high-minded Arliss vehicles, Twentieth also turned out several epic romances like *The Affairs of Cellini, Clive of India*, and *Les Misérables*—history with a measure of sex, swordplay, and the old Zanuck hokum.

Warners followed the same dual trajectory of history and hokum in 1935 with *The Story of Louis Pasteur* and *Captain Blood. Pasteur* clearly was modeled after the Arliss biopics; it was another solemn celebration of a European Great Man and champion of enlightenment, modern science, and liberal humanism. Muni took readily to the genre. Like Arliss, he had been trained in theater and he never let anyone forget it. Both on and off the screen, he was given to histrionic excess, long-winded tirades, and an inflated sense of his own status as an artist and social crusader. The biopic provided an ideal idiom for those conceits, and Warners was obliged to indulge Muni since he had story and role approval. But Wallis minimized the risk by capping *Pasteur*'s budget at $330,000.

Warners had fewer reservations about its swashbuckler, *Captain Blood*, even without the likes of Muni cast in the lead. Based on a 1922 best-seller by Rafael Sabatini, the story was a heady blend of action, romance, and European politics, and Jack Warner wanted someone in the Douglas Fairbanks style for the surgeon-turned-pirate, Peter Blood. But Warner and Wallis had trouble finding anyone with Fairbanks's rare amalgam of charm, athleticism, and sex appeal. They had considered Fredric March for the title role, but signed him instead to play the more cerebral and subdued Anthony Adverse. Ronald Colman was considered for the part, as was Robert Donat, but Warner eventually decided to look closer to home, and he came up with Errol Flynn. Still in his mid-twenties and with no real acting experience,

Flynn had the face, the physique, and the general élan for the role—and for major stardom as well. Flynn won over the Warners brass with his first screen test for *Blood*, and when he tested opposite nineteen-year-old Olivia de Havilland in late March 1935, the costars were set. The Flynn–De Havilland chemistry was unmistakable, though a bit incongruous, with De Havilland's subdued charm and virginal innocence offsetting Flynn's overt sexuality and dashing, reckless personality. At times, due to her maternal aura as well as his endearing childishness, she seemed more like Flynn's mother than his lover.

Captain Blood was in production by late summer, with a budget of $1.2 million and steadily rising expectations on the lot. Writer Casey Robinson stayed on the shoot to adjust the dialogue and accentuate the action for Flynn, and director Michael Curtiz learned to rely less on Flynn's acting skills than on his mere screen presence. Preview audiences were enthusiastic, so Warners rushed *Captain Blood* into a holiday release. It opened in New York at the Strand on Christmas day, ten weeks after *A Midsummer Night's Dream*. Both movies did well commercially and critically to confirm Warners' changing market strategy. Both also received an Oscar nomination for best picture, and *A Midsummer Night's Dream* made the National Board of Review's top ten—a first for Warners since *I Am a Fugitive* back in 1932.

The Reinhardt project was very much an isolated case, giving Warners' credibility a boost but scarcely providing a platform for any future projects. *Captain Blood* was quite another matter. In Errol Flynn Warners seemed to have found a possible successor to Douglas Fairbanks, at a time when no one else in Hollywood seemed able to take up Fairbanks's cutlass. The studio renewed Flynn's option and increased his salary to $750—a paltry figure compared to Muni's or Cagney's salary, but five times what Flynn had been making a year earlier. Wallis and Curtiz initiated another Flynn–De Havilland vehicle, *The Charge of the Light Brigade*, solidifying its commitment to the costarring team and to the costume epic, with its peculiar blend of history and legend, of action and romance. Flynn was at the narrative epicenter of those fantasies, which Jack Warner affirmed with successive pay hikes. Flynn's option was picked up in November 1936, just after the release of *Light Brigade*, giving him $800 weekly. By December the picture was a hit and Warners was preparing its biggest Flynn epic yet, *The Adventures of Robin Hood*. In a grandiose gesture, Jack Warner "tore up" Flynn's contract and signed him to a long-term deal starting in February 1937 at $2,250 per week. Meanwhile De Havilland was learning that Warners was still very much a man's world. She was set to play Maid Marian opposite Flynn's Robin Hood, but her $500-per-week contract of April 1936 remained intact.

If prestige were defined only in terms of excess and box-office performance, then the Flynn blockbusters certainly qualified. But the term also implied critical acclaim and top Oscars, and that brand of prestige was supplied by the Muni biopics. In 1936 *The Story of Louis Pasteur* ranked higher than any recent Warners release in the polls of both the *Film Daily* and the prestigious National Board of Review. Muni also won an Academy Award for best actor, giving Warners its first major Oscar since 1929–30, when Arliss won for *Disraeli*. In 1937 *The Life of Emile Zola* did even better than *Pasteur*, both critically and commercially, and finally brought Warners a best-picture Oscar, culminating its climb to prestige status. But Warners Bros. was an institutional creature of habit, and once the costume epics and biopics took hold so did the studio's reflex to standardize and economize. However risky and innovative *Captain Blood* and *Pasteur* may have been in 1935, within two years both types of movies were hardening into formulas, into standard operating procedures at the studio and standardized products in the marketplace.

That process was facilitated by Warners' supervisory system, which was beginning to look like a unit-production operation in 1937. That was the year, in fact, that Warners' supervisors began getting "associate producer" credit on-screen. Predictably, Warners' units

Figure 2.1 Director Michael Curtiz with two of Warners' newest and brightest stars in the mid-thirties, Olivia de Havilland and Errol Flynn, on the set of *The Charge of the Light Brigade* (1936)

tended to center on the studio's star-genre combinations, invariably involving a top staff director as well as a contract player—as with the Flynn–De Havilland epics directed by Michael Curtiz, the Berkeley musicals with Dick Powell, and the Cagney crime dramas directed by Lloyd Bacon. Warners' most efficient and most accomplished production team was the biopic unit, whose key personnel were Muni, supervisor Henry Blanke, director William Dieterle, and cinematographer Tony Gaudio. There was always a certain tension between innovation and standardization in unit production, which was especially acute with prestige pictures because they were, by definition, the studio's most distinctive and inventive products. It was this factor, more than the play of personalities or the economic stakes involved, that made biopic production at Warners such a complex and embattled process. The making of *Zola*, coming in the wake of *Pasteur's* success, provides an ideal glimpse of this process at Warners.

The Life of Emile Zola was initiated early in 1936. At the time Muni was on loan to RKO, but Blanke, Dieterle, and Gaudio were actively reformulating *Pasteur*'s success with a Great Woman biopic, *The White Angel*, starring Kay Francis as Florence Nightingale. Meanwhile literary agent Heinz Herald came to Blanke with a story about the French novelist Emile Zola's heroic defense of Alfred Dreyfus, a military officer victimized by the bureaucratic ineptitude and ingrained anti-Semitism of France's judiciary and military systems during the 1890s. Blanke and Muni both liked the idea, so Wallis, the executive producer on the biopics, assigned Herald and another German expatriate, Geza Herczeg, to develop it further. In June Herald and Herczeg submitted an eighteen-page treatment entitled "Emile Zola: The Conscience of Humanity," whose opening two-page precis made it clear that "the Dreyfus affair" was the heart of the story, and that Zola's earlier literary career would be the "back-story." It also was clear that this project was designed along the lines of *Pasteur*. "Pasteur fought bacteria, while Zola opposed lies," wrote Herald and Herczeg in the opening pitch.

"Like Pasteur, who had to face obstacles, Zola had to suffer from defamation, prison, flight, and deportation." What's more, Zola "decided quite by himself to be a crusader of truth and be crucified." They closed with Zola's own proclamation that "the Truth is on the march and nothing can stop it," a notion that they felt had "never been more timely than today."

Wallis passed the treatment on to Jack Warner, who then got story approval from Muni; Warner agreed to pay the authors $3,000 for the treatment and another $10,000 for a continuity script. By November, they had completed a two-hundred-page draft, which staff writer Norman Reilly Raine transformed into a "revised temporary" during the following month. Meanwhile Wallis worked with various department heads on scheduling, budgeting, and the initial production design process. Blanke supervised final script preparation, which meant juggling input from the three writers as well as from Wallis, Muni, and Dieterle, each of whom had his own conception of the project. In early February a "script final" was ready, and ten days later Wallis circulated an estimated budget of $699,000—over twice the cost of *Pasteur* but only half what Warners was spending on Flynn's pictures. The above-the-line costs were remarkably low: $37,000 for story and script, $32,000 for Dieterle, $12,000 for Blanke, and a flat fee of $50,000 for Muni. At another major the above-the-line costs on a top star-genre picture comprised one-third to one-half of the budget, but Warners was able to keep that portion of the budget to about one-fifth on *Zola*.

Wallis's role in the process was primarily administrative and Jack Warner's involvement was only marginal—during the initiation and final approval of the picture. As on most Warner productions, Jack Warner handled property acquisition for *Zola* and then saw little of the project until it was ready for preview. But while there was little contact between Warner and Wallis on the picture, there was heavy interaction at the next juncture in the hierarchy of authority. Wallis and Blanke's working relationship was one of continual struggle and negotiation, the two men virtually embodying and acting out the studio's contrary impulses for standardization and innovation. While Wallis was inclined simply to reformulate *Pasteur*, Blanke—more than Dieterle or Muni or anyone else involved—fought for what he considered the integrity of the project. He and Wallis battled over every phase of the production, from casting and costume design to camera work and performances and even the title of the film.

It became obvious early on that Wallis's sense of history extended only as far back as Muni's last picture. Blanke understood the logic of reworking *Pasteur*, but he wanted a more authentic re-creation of the actual Zola-Dreyfus episode. The two first flared over Muni's makeup. *Zola* was Muni's third straight historical drama (including the RKO loan-out) in which he played a bearded Frenchman. In a November 1936 memo to Wallis, Blanke said "our greatest problem on this production" was keeping Muni's appearance "as different from Pasteur as possible." Wallis disagreed, arguing that Muni's box-office clout was not to be compromised for the sake of historical accuracy. This conflict came to a head in February, just before production began, when Blanke had makeup specialist Perc Westmore use "additional flesh compositions" in recreating Zola's facial appearance. After seeing the makeup tests, Wallis feared they would "lose the Muni personality." Countermanding Blanke's instructions, Wallis told Westmore to "make [Muni] up for the character so far as hair and beard is concerned and still retain for the audience the impression that Paul Muni is playing the part." Blanke acquiesced, but soon he and Wallis were haggling over the female lead. Wallis wanted Josephine Hutchinson cast as the woman behind the Great Man. Blanke objected, reminding Wallis that "she played the wife of Pasteur in a picture laid in France in the same period as *Zola*." Wallis insisted on exploiting Hutchinson's residual box-office appeal, and the two finally compromised; Hutchinson was cast in a minor but important role as Dreyfus's wife.

The most severe preproduction hassle between Wallis and Blanke involved costume design. Wallis assigned Milo Anderson, who had done the costumes for *Pasteur* with only minimal attention to authenticity and detail. Blanke wanted *Zola* to display "more of the genuine touch of the period," and Wallis agreed to let Blanke bring in another designer, Ali Hubert. But Wallis then rescinded his approval on the recommendation of studio manager T. C. "Tenny" Wright, who was trying to keep costs down. In a rage, Blanke told Wallis "to talk with Mr. Warner and see that I may be relieved of my duties" if Hubert was taken off the picture. "We [supervisors] get little enough credit for what we are doing," lamented Blanke, "but one likes to have at least the feeling that one is responsible for the quality and good taste of some of the pictures, even if nobody else knows about it." Wallis backed off, and Hubert served as technical adviser and shared costume designer credit with Milo Anderson on *Zola*.

Shooting began in March, scheduled for forty-two days, with Dieterle and company working as quickly as they had on *Pasteur*. During the first week Dieterle and Gaudio averaged just under twenty setups per day, generating a remarkable 29′30″ of finished footage. They sustained that pace, slowing only for the now-legendary courtroom scene that culminated in Zola's impassioned plea for social justice. Dieterle shot Muni's tour de force in a single six-minute take in which Muni addressed the camera, which was situated in the jury box. Wallis sent congratulations to Dieterle and Muni after he saw the dailies, but he doubted that the scene would work as a single take. Wallis suggested that Dieterle shoot more "coverage" of the crowd and also that he "protect himself with a tight two-shot" of Muni and another character to facilitate editing. But Blanke supervised a rough cut of the scene and he felt that it played perfectly. "I would consider it a waste of money to shoot any more of this," Blanke told Wallis, reasoning that crowd scenes were costly and difficult to shoot. Besides, the shots were unnecessary since "the main characters in the courtroom and their actions are so fascinating that you can hardly cut away from them." And about Muni's speech, Blanke simply stated, "We did not figure on spoiling it by intercutting with anything else."

While Blanke readily played on Wallis's frugality when it served his own purposes, he was severely critical when it compromised the quality of the project. Like most Warners pictures, *Zola* was shot out of sequence. Among the last scenes to be shot were those depicting Zola's early development as a writer and his friendship with painter Paul Cézanne. In a daily exchange of memos in early April, Wallis and Blanke debated the merits of Ben Weldon's performance as Cézanne. Wallis admitted that he cast Weldon "to save money," but still he felt the performance was satisfactory. Blanke insisted that neither the performance nor the cut scenes were working and the picture would open on a decidedly weak note. Wallis finally relented and on April 17, Vladimir Sokoloff was brought in and the Cézanne scenes were reshot in a single week. Those retakes pushed *Zola* ten days over schedule, with the picture closing on May 10. By then Blanke and Wallis had reached another compromise, this one involving the title, and again the key issue was whether to adhere to the norms set by *Pasteur*. Wallis had been holding out for "The Story of Emile Zola," while Blanke lobbied for various alternatives: "The Truth Is on the March," "I Accuse," "Destiny," and others. In late April Wallis and the Warners finally agreed on "The Life of Emile Zola"—a curious decision since little of Zola's life was actually depicted in the film.

During postproduction Wallis's involvement was minimal. He spent two days going over the rough cut, dictating ideas for tightening and polishing scenes, and later he suggested cuts to accommodate Joe Breen and the PCA. (The picture managed to tell the Dreyfus story without the word *Jew* ever being uttered, although Dieterle did highlight the anti-Semitism issue with a bit of telltale camera work, pulling in for a close-up on the word when it appeared on a military document.) By late June *Zola* was close to a final cut and was previewed, without Max Steiner's score, at Warners' theater in Hollywood. The preview went well, and most of July was devoted to scoring. *The Life of Emile Zola* premiered on August 11, 1937, and was an immediate sensation. A week later Harry, Jack, and Abe Warner took full-page ads in various

Los Angeles papers, offering congratulations "to Mr. Muni and his fellow players, to director William Dieterle, to the writers, to the nameless and numberless studio workers and technicians who gave their share in its shaping. They, and they alone, own the glory of having created a masterpiece." Two of the workers who remained nameless—not just here but in the countless rave reviews of *Zola*—were Hal Wallis and Henry Blanke. Their enforced, embattled collaboration was crucial to the picture's creation and its success, but they scarcely expected recognition. Indeed, the critical raves and box-office revenues were reward enough. *Zola* did exceptional business, it was named the year's best picture by the Academy and *Film Daily*, and it placed second in the National Board of Review's annual poll.

While Warners' star-genre units were solidifying in the mid- to late-1930s, another very different kind of unit production emerged at the studio. The prestige pictures and other A-class features made up only half of Warners' output of sixty pictures per year. To supplement them and to keep the entire Warners system operating at full capacity, the studio relied on the newly organized Foy unit. Bryan "Brynie" Foy had started in vaudeville, breaking into movies as producer-director of vaudeville shorts at Warner's Vitagraph studio in New York in the 1920s. Having achieved sudden and unexpected notoriety when he did Warners' first all-talking feature, *The Lights of New York*, in 1927, he was directing low-budget features in Hollywood by the early 1930s, and by 1935 he'd become the studio's B-movie specialist on a salary of $750 per week. In 1936 Warners doubled his salary and put him in charge of all B-movie production, which totaled twenty-nine releases in 1936 and thirty in 1937.

The Foy unit's function, in essence, was to keep Warners' facilities, personnel, and second-rate talent operating at top efficiency while supplying a steady flow of low-cost product. Warners' B pictures gave costars and featured players from the A ranks like Ann Dvorak or Barton MacLane an opportunity to star, and they were directed by the likes of B. Reeves Eason, Nick Grinde, and William McGann, who also did second-unit work on A-class

Figure 2.2 The nucleus of Warners' biopic unit: director William Dieterle, star Paul Muni, executive producer Hal Wallis, and unit producer Henry Blanke

features. Even the scripts for many of Foy's productions were recruited from the A ranks. Two 1932 hits, *Tiger Shark* and *Five Star Final*, for instance, were redone in 1936 as B pictures under the titles *Bengal Tiger* and *The Voice of Life*. Schedules ranged from fifteen to twenty-five days and budgets from $50,000 to $125,000; pre- and postproduction ran three to four weeks. Executive input was minimal. Since few of the pictures were star vehicles or based on presold properties, Jack Warner was rarely involved before the final cut. Wallis monitored each production, but the process was so mechanical that it required little real input. Thus Foy had considerable authority, although it was over a process of assembly-line moviemaking. But Warners had the most productive and efficient B-picture unit among the majors, and Foy was well paid for his success. His weekly paycheck was up to $2,000 by 1938, putting him on a par with those associate producers who supervised only a half-dozen projects per annum.

With the prestige productions settling into a regulated process and Foy's B-picture unit going strong, there was a marked return in 1937 to Warners' tradition of efficient filmmaking. But even as things leveled off, Warners was clearly operating on a higher plane. *The Life of Emile Zola* was the hit of the year, the 1937 profits were nearly $6 million—twice the 1936 take—and *Fortune* magazine closed out the year with a piece on Warners' "ten-year zoom . . . from the rank of outsider to the biggest thing in show business." That "zoom" was attributed to Warners' system, to its executive corps and its production operation rather than to any "producing genius." The company "used to have one of those in Darryl Zanuck," said *Fortune*, but he "has never been officially replaced." Now production operations were "in the hands of a jocose penny watcher, Jack Warner, his methodical assistant, Hal Wallis, and a half-dozen almost anonymous supervisors." Jack was described as the "supreme head of Warner Bros. production," though *Fortune* suggested that he "would not be Harry's brother if he did not look upon the making of movies like any other kind of factory production, requiring discipline and order rather than temperament and talent."

There was a certain truth to that viewpoint, since Warners was a well-regulated studio and a classic top-down operation, with power descending through its executives and into the filmmaking ranks. But Warners was scarcely a smooth-running "factory" whose recent surge was accomplished without its share of "temperament and talent." Those qualities were rarely flashed by its directors, who were indeed a disciplined lot in an era when the producer-director was emerging as an important filmmaking force. Mervyn LeRoy had tried vaulting to that privileged status in 1936–37, when Harry Warner gave him his own independent unit. The result was four overblown failures and LeRoy's abrupt segue to MGM. Once LeRoy left, the only director who worked regularly at Warners in the late 1930s with any real administrative and creative authority was free-lancer Howard Hawks. He invariably signed one- and two-picture deals that paid him well and gave him much greater control than any of Warners' staff directors. For instance on a 1936 project, *Ceiling Zero*, Hawks got $6,000 per week and contractual rights to "collaborate" during both the scripting and the editing of the picture, which was billed as a "Howard Hawks Production."

Ceiling Zero was even more illuminating in terms of its star's authority. In fact, Warners' stars were the most talented and temperamental individuals on the lot throughout the 1930s. *Ceiling Zero* was made to placate James Cagney, who was locked in a bitter dispute with Jack Warner and Hal Wallis over casting and project quality. Cagney wanted more "serious" dramatic projects and an occasional musical, and he was not satisfied with the likes of *Ceiling Zero*—which critic Otis Ferguson called "the best of all airplane pictures" but Cagney dismissed as just another action yarn. Cagney was dead serious, and he was willing to bolt Warners to prove it. In 1936 he successfully sued for release from his $4,500-per-week contract, contending that Warners' vehicles were not commensurate with his standing in the industry. Cagney had the contractual leverage and the box-office clout to defy Warners, and he encouraged other Warners stars to follow suit. Several tried, but without Cagney's success—not that any of them really expected to succeed. Bette Davis, George Brent, Kay Francis, Ann Dvorak, and others fought Warners in the courts during the 1930s, less in hopes of defeating the studio than of gaining some degree of control over their careers.

Cagney's battles with Warners were well publicized, but Bette Davis's were equally intense and even more significant, not only in terms of her career but of the studio's house style as well. Cagney's victory over Warners was a hollow one; within two years he was back making the same kind of pictures he had sued the company to avoid. Davis, meanwhile, battled the entrenched Warners system and traditional male ethos, managing somehow to reshape her screen image into a star persona that was as powerful and provocative—and distinctly feminine—as any in the industry. Her struggles with Jack Warner extended throughout her eighteen-year tenure at Warners, from 1931 to 1948. But the most dramatic and important skirmishes were in the mid-to late-1930s, culminating in the production of *Jezebel*.

The release of *Bordertown* in January 1935 bolstered the image that Davis established a few month earlier in *Of Human Bondage*—the image of an intense, ruthless, sexually aggressive woman who relied on her will and wits to get what she wanted. But Warner and Wallis failed to exploit these qualities, casting Davis in a second-rate woman's picture and then two routine crime thrillers after *Bordertown*. Not until late 1935 was she given roles that she could really work with: an alcoholic, self-destructive actress in *Dangerous*, and a naive love-struck waitress in *The Petrified Forest*. *Dangerous* was released in December while Davis was doing *The Petrified Forest*, and though it brought her an Oscar nomination it scarcely improved her stature at the studio. Her next assignment was in *Satan Met a Lady*, a cut-rate version of Dashiell Hammett's *The Maltese Falcon*. Davis found both the part and the picture unacceptable and she refused to report. A suspension changed her mind and she did the picture—her sixth that year and the twenty-third for Warners in four years. Her next assignment was *Golden Arrow*, in a role so weak that Kay Francis had taken a suspension to avoid it, and when production closed in February 1936 Davis resolved not to start another picture without a new contract and the assurance of better roles.

This was not an unreasonable endeavor, considering Warners' move to prestige production and Davis's own market value, which climbed even higher in late February 1936 when she captured the best actress Oscar for *Dangerous*. In early March, two weeks after finishing *Golden Arrow* and only days after the Academy Awards ceremony, Davis was offered the lead in RKO's *Mary, Queen of Scots*. Set to direct was John Ford, who had just won best director and best picture for *The Informer*. Davis desperately wanted the role, but when Jack Warner received a memo on RKO's request to borrow Davis, he simply returned it with "Not interested" scrawled across the bottom. That was the last straw; Davis resolved to stay out of pictures altogether until her status at the studio changed. She took a six-week "layoff"—a leave without pay, though not a suspension. She went back East, where she was big news after the recent Oscar, and through the press she lambasted Hollywood's power brokers. "Film Bosses 'Headache' to Bette Davis," blared *The Evening Journal*, wherein she openly castigated Warners and declared she would not return for retakes on *Golden Arrow*. That same date (March 25, 1936) the *World Telegram* ran a banner headline. " 'They'd Make All the Women Wed the Men,' Cries Bette Davis." This time she took on the studio's willing submission to the Breen office.

While Davis was in New York, her agent sent Warners a list of her contract demands. She wanted a new contract on these terms: five years, with salaries escalating from $100,000 to $220,000 per year (she was then earning $64,000 per year); a maximum of four pictures annually; star or costar billing with her name above the title and in type size equal to that of her costar; the services of either Tony Gaudio, Sol Polito, or Ernie Haller on camera; three

Figure 2.3 A key event in Bette Davis's career—and in her ongoing battles with Jack Warner—was her 1935 Academy Award. Davis is pictured here with Victor McLaglen, who won the Oscar for best actor that same year

months' consecutive vacation each year with the right to do one outside picture. Davis refused to start another picture without the new pact, and she was promptly suspended. That led to weeks and then months of negotiation. By midsummer Davis was offered $2,000 per week and a vague promise of better roles, but still she held out. In mid-August, she sailed to England to work for an independent company, Toeplitz Productions. Warners sued to prevent Davis from signing, and the case was tried in London in October 1936. Warners prevailed, although its British attorney voiced his surprise at the outcome. He agreed that the studio "should have the right to suspend" and also "to discontinue payment of salary." But he suggested that "there should be a limit to the period which the Producer can add on to the existing period of the contract"—that is, the time that can be tacked on to actors' contracts when they refused to perform, thus preventing them from sitting out and becoming "free agents."

Davis accepted the judgment and took a different tack. She went after Warner through his attorneys, who conveyed to Warner that after the trial Davis "was very subdued and in a much more chastened spirit," and that she would return to work without any "modifications" of her existing contract. At the close of this report, though, several "requests, as mere suggestions," were relayed, intended for "the mutual benefit of [Davis] and the Company." The studio's attorneys then began pleading Davis's case, reiterating her earlier demands for Jack's "sympathetic consideration" and even suggesting that the studio cover her court costs. Warner held firm but he got the message; Davis might have lost this skirmish, but the war would go on. And Warner himself, having been without his top actress for nearly a year, was ready to compromise. He already had set several routine Davis projects in motion, beginning with *Marked Woman*, a crime thriller. But he also bought Davis a property that he knew she wanted, one that featured a difficult role he now believed she could pull off. Davis expressed her appreciation to Warner in a handwritten note in January 1937. "I am thrilled to death about *Jezebel*," she wrote. "I think it can be as great, if not greater, than *Gone with the Wind*—thank you for buying it."

David Selznick's two-year "Search for Scarlett" was just getting under way in early 1937, and Bette Davis was a leading contender for the part. There was no real chance of her playing Scarlett O'Hara, since her improving market value only reinforced Warners' opposition to her doing any outside work. Still Davis coveted the role, and what with her Oscar, the lawsuit, and the best-selling status of Margaret Mitchell's novel, Warner was inclined to give it to her—or to give her a reasonable facsimile in *Jezebel*, a play by Owen Davis that had run on Broadway in 1933–34. The story was set in the Old South and centered on Julie Marston, a spoiled southern belle whose headstrong behavior costs her the love of a young Yankee banker. After he breaks their engagement and leaves New Orleans, Julie realizes her loss and connives to get him back, even after he weds someone else. A yellow fever epidemic gives her her chance: though the two seem destined to a tragic end, it finally unites Julie with her beloved after he contracts the disease.

Actually, Warners had almost bought *Jezebel* for Bette Davis back in 1935. But there were misgivings about the property, which Wallis's assistant Walter MacEwen summarized in a February 1935 memo. No doubt the story "would provide a good role for Bette Davis," said MacEwen, "who could play the spots off the part of a little bitch of an aristocratic southern girl." But he doubted whether "a picture built solely around her in an unsympathetic role would be so well liked." MacEwen suggested "a touch of the good old regeneration through suffering," which would make her character "a wiser and more palatable person after the final fade-out." Wallis concurred, but a succession of writers and supervisors failed to work out a suitable adaptation, and in March 1935 Wallis decided against buying the property.

The stakes obviously had changed since then, and in January 1937 Warner bought the rights to *Jezebel* for $12,000. The story problems remained, however, though this time around Wallis hoped to resolve them by placing more emphasis on Julie's suffering after her fiancé's departure. Another parade of writers, directors, and supervisors tried and failed to make the story work. Their sentiments were best expressed by Edmund Goulding, a writer-director who came to Warners from MGM and had just directed Davis and Henry Fonda in *That Certain Woman*. In a July 1937 memo to Wallis, Goulding said he found the "background and characters" of the play "intriguing," and he felt that it was "quite possible to put a vivid picture upon the screen." But he was convinced the project was doomed because, with or without the plague and the redemptive finale, "the picture can only tell the story of the triumph of bitchery."

Another six weeks of script revisions only reinforced that estimation, and in late August Warner and Wallis began looking outside the studio for help. They decided on William Wyler, a director under contract to independent producer Sam Goldwyn. Still in his mid-thirties, Wyler had come a long way since his apprentice years directing shorts and five-reel westerns for Universal. He had recently handled such A-class Goldwyn projects as *These Three* and *Dodsworth*. He had two dozen features to his credit over the last decade, and he also had gained a reputation as a capable script doctor. Warner signed him to write and direct for fifteen weeks at $6,250 per week, with instructions that *Jezebel* be ready to shoot by late October. Wyler came aboard on September 6, 1937, and between rewrite sessions with Abem Finkel and Clements Ripley (who eventually received screen credit), he worked on preproduction with associate producer Henry Blanke and various department heads. A "final draft screenplay" was approved on October 13, the same day Jack Warner closed a deal with independent producer Walter Wanger, getting the fast-rising Henry Fonda in a straight swap for Joan Blondell. A start date of October 25 was set, with a seven-week shooting schedule and a preliminary budget of $783,508.

Wyler knew when he started shooting that the script still needed work, but his and Fonda's upcoming commitments and Warner's production schedule demanded that he start production in late October. Wallis kept Finkel and Ripley on the project for rewrites, but Wyler had someone else in mind. John Huston was then a much traveled thirty-year-old writer, actor, painter, and former prizefighter, just off a theater stint in Chicago. He had worked for Universal in the early 1930s, where he met Wyler, and he decided in 1937 to take another shot at movie writing. He reworked his short story, "Three Men and a Girl," as a movie treatment. "I then called Willie Wyler," Huston later recollected, "asked him to put me up for a while, took a plane to California, and sold the treatment to Warner Brothers for $5,000, with a contract . . . to write the screenplay."

Warners signed Huston on September 18, 1937, and while Huston was staying with Wyler the two began talking about *Jezebel*. Wyler was impressed with Huston's ideas and when production opened in late October, he asked Wallis to put Huston on the picture. Three days later Wallis sent a memo to Blanke explaining that Huston was "to sort of represent [Wyler] in collaboration with the writers and yourself." He added that Wyler "knows Huston personally, spends a great deal of time with him, and will see him at night, and he maintains that Huston knows exactly his feeling and thoughts about the script, and his views on the last half of it."

Bette Davis also was getting to know Wyler personally and seeing him at night. The two became lovers soon after Wyler arrived on the lot, and the affair brought an end to Davis's troubled marriage to band-leader Ham Nelson. Wyler and Huston worked evenings throughout the shoot, with heavy input from Davis, rewriting the script, polishing the dialogue, and blocking out each day's camera setups. Thus Davis helped shape the project and John Huston got a crash course in film-making and in the politics of sex and power in Hollywood. Warners tolerated the affair and the unconventional writing setup, since neither threatened the project's development—on the contrary, both seemed to enhance it.

Wyler's shooting of *Jezebel* was another matter. From the opening weeks of production, his deliberate and seemingly excessive methods caused concern. "Possibly Wyler likes to see those big numbers on the slate," wrote Wallis to Blanke early in the shoot, "and maybe we could arrange to have them start with number 6 on each take; then it wouldn't take so long to get up to 9 or 10." By late November Wallis had lost his sense of humor, and unit manager Bob Fellows was sounding the alarm almost daily. Appended to Fellows's production report of November 24, for example, were these comments: "To date Wyler has averaged a little better than two [script] pages per day for twenty-five days. . . . I do not believe anyone is aware of just how slow Mr. Wyler is. Company delayed from 9:00 A.M. to 11:30 A.M. changing script and rehearsing new scene with Miss Davis and Mr. Fonda. Picture is nine days behind schedule."

Like any production manager, Fellows was basically an efficiency expert, and he was used to operating with staff directors like Mike Curtiz or William Dieterle, who followed the shooting script, put their actors through their paces, and brought pictures in on time and under budget. Wyler, conversely, freely reworked the script, and often called for one take after another without saying a word to the performers about what he wanted done differently. He also designed intricate camera setups and elaborate movements, often using long takes, reframing, and deep-focus shooting to involve several planes of action in a given shot. This demanded heavy rehearsal and meticulous work by both cast and crew—demands that were altogether new to most Warners personnel.

Figure 2.4 William Wyler, seated at left, directing Bette Davis in *Jezebel*. Credit: Warner Bros/ First National/Kobal Collection/Crail, Schuyler

Soon both Wallis and studio manager Tenny Wright were badgering Blanke about the time and money Wyler was costing the studio. A memo in early January about the previous day's shoot typified Wallis's attitude as the picture fell further behind schedule: "The first [take] was excellent, yet he took it sixteen times. Doesn't this man know that we have close-ups to break up a scene of this kind? . . . What the hell is the matter with him anyhow—is he absolutely daffy?" Wallis's anger was fueled by the fact that he could do little besides fire off memos to Blanke, who as associate producer was to represent the interests of the front office but without alienating the director or disrupting the project. Blanke was equally frustrated. This was no unit production, and an outside director like Wyler was not about to adjust his working methods at the behest of a mere supervisor.

Even with the delays and the escalating costs, Wyler's authority over the shoot was never directly challenged. There was a suggestion in mid-December that William Dieterle be brought in to make sure the scenes with Fonda were completed before December 17, when Wanger needed him back, but Bette Davis refused to work with anyone but Wyler on the production, so the issue was dropped. Wyler did manage to close Fonda by the seventeenth, but by mid-January Wyler was so far behind schedule that John Huston was tapped to direct a scene in which one of Davis's suitors and the younger brother of her former fiancé fight a duel. The sequence was shot "on location" at the Warners ranch and marked Huston's directoral debut some three years before *The Maltese Falcon*, his first credited work as a Warners director.

This was another violation of the studio's standard operating procedure; Huston was, after all, an untried director and fledgling writer who had been under contract for only a few months. But Warner and Wallis permitted such violations since they didn't want to upset their temperamental star or her director, who clearly was getting from Davis the performance of her career. Her Julie Marston struck the perfect balance of bitchery and captivating charm, of euphoria and barely subdued hysteria, evoking both sympathy and grating irritation. It was equally evident as the rough cut came together how important Wyler's skills as a director were to the picture and to Davis's performance. Warner and Wallis were not used to making such distinctions, since their factory-oriented system required that staff directors be more adept as technicians and traffic cops than as narrative artists. But Wyler's direction was bringing Julie Marston to life, shaping the viewer's conception of both character and story. This involved more than simply lighting and shot composition, although Wyler and cinematographer Ernie Haller did capture Davis's physical beauty as no previous Warners filmmakers had. Even more important was Wyler's ability, through camera work and cutting, to situate Julie as the governing sensibility of the story. Through the calculated use of point-of-view shots, reaction shots, glance-object cutting, and shot/reverse-shot exchanges, Wyler orchestrated the viewer's identification with and sympathy for Julie, which were so essential if the story was to "play."

Wyler's artistry cost Warners both time and money; the *Jezebel* budget climbed from $783,000 to $1,073,000 as the project fell some five weeks behind its seven-week schedule, finally closing on January 17. The extent of Wyler's "inefficiency," at least by Warners' standards, was most evident in the daily production reports. Consider these figures from a single week of shooting on both *Zola* and *Jezebel* (see Table 2.1).

Table 2.1

THE LIFE OF EMILE ZOLA (Dieterle, 1937)				
3/15/37	4 scenes	16 setups	37 takes	3:00
3/16	10	25	58	5:50
3/17	3	22	44	4:05
3/18	21	23	47	3:45
3/19	3	31	52	6:50
JEZEBEL (Wyler, 1938)				
11/1/37	5 scenes	4 setups	25 takes	1:45
11/2	1	8	57	0:20
11/3	2	6	43	1:25
11/4	3	4	36	1:50
11/5	3	14	69	2:05

In the early 1930s, LeRoy set the standard of productivity at Warners, and his working methods had been a key to its house style as well—he was a master at translating on-set efficiency into narrative economy. LeRoy had left, but staff directors like Lloyd Bacon and William Dieterle still cranked out films at nearly the same rate. Note Dieterle's pace on *The Life of Emile Zola*, a period piece featuring Warners' highest-paid star shot in eight weeks on a budget of $699,000. And note too its connections with the traditional Warners style. Its elliptical story developed at a frantic pace, replete with montages and ellipses, yet the overall pacing was countered in individual scenes by the minimal camera work and cutting. Dieterle usually framed the action in medium or medium-long shots, cutting to close-ups, reactions shots, or point-of-view shots only when absolutely necessary—which was not often, given his pacing and Muni's stage-bound performance. Thus *Zola* had much the same feel as Warners' earlier crime sagas, despite obvious social and thematic distinctions.

The same was true of *Marked Woman*, the Davis crime thriller that Lloyd Bacon directed earlier in 1937. The story elicits sympathy for Davis's heroine, an amoral hustler who goes straight when mobsters kill her innocent sister, but neither her performance nor Bacon's direction draw the viewer into the narrative or lift the picture above the ranks of a routine Warners thriller. Its performances, production values, and narrative structure seem altogether primitive compared to those of *Jezebel*, which was paced much more evenly and deliberately—never as frantic and elliptical as *Zola* or *Marked Woman* in its transitions, and never as ponderous in its dramatic sequences. And perhaps most important, to watch *Jezebel* was to be wedded to Julie Marston's consciousness, to adopt her way of seeing and perverse logic in making sense of her world and her plight.

A hit both commercially and critically after its March 1938 release, *Jezebel* brought Davis another Oscar and solidified Warners' commitment to quality women's pictures. Suddenly the "female Jimmy Cagney" rap and the urban crime thrillers were behind her, and Davis starred over the next few years in some of the greatest melodramas in Hollywood's history, including *The Sisters, Dark Victory, The Old Maid, All This and Heaven Too, The Letter, The Great Lie, The Little Foxes*, and *Now Voyager*. Each of those roles was a variation on the contradictory Julie Marston, with Davis cast either as an emasculating shrew or as a charming innocent. Davis had fought for the Marston role, and Warners, to its credit, went with it once *Jezebel* hit. The process of struggle and negotiation was fairly dramatic in Davis's case, since the transformation of her screen persona went against the studio's traditional male ethos—an ethos that dominated not only its screen fare but its executive offices as well. But in fact Warners' other top stars were undergoing much the same process in the late 1930s and with similar results. The Warners were learning that prestige filmmaking meant giving more power to top contract talent and allowing wider variation in the studio's basic star-genre formulas.

The lesson came hard, particularly for Jack, but the results were altogether positive. Davis, Flynn, and Cagney made the exhibitors' 1939 top-ten poll, and in 1939–40 Warners turned out a succession of pictures that displayed a remarkable penchant for variation and reformulation. Flynn scored yet again as the heroic Brit in *The Sea Hawk*, but also as an American westerner in *Dodge City* and *Santa Fe Trail*. Cagney reprised his gangster persona in *The Roaring Twenties* but also hit in a war picture, *The Fighting 69th*, and in a screwball comedy with Bette Davis, *The Bride Came C.O.D.* Robinson parodied his gangster persona in *Brother Orchid*, and, after Paul Muni left the studio, he took over the biopic with *Confessions of a Nazi Spy, Dr. Ehrlich's Magic Bullet*, and *A Dispatch from Reuters*. Marking a high point for Warners at decade's end, these and other hits proved that the studio could turn out first-rate pictures and compete consistently with Metro, Paramount, and Fox. They also marked a period of equilibrium, when the studio struck an ideal balance between efficiency and excess, convention and innovation, administrative constraint and creative freedom. They proved that Warners, after two decades of struggle, had come of age.

Chapter 3

Danae Clark

LABOR AND FILM NARRATIVE (1995)

Editors' Introduction

In her book *Negotiating Hollywood: The Cultural Politics of Actors' Labor*, Danae Clark opens with a clear and concise disclaimer: "This book is not about stars." Indeed, her goal is to break with the tradition of focusing on "the actor as object." In "Labor and Film Narrative," the final chapter in the book, Clark focuses on the gap between the actual conditions of actors' labor and the representation of those conditions in a variety of studio discourses, including promotional material and popular movies. Such an approach to the meaning and function of the film text breaks with the more formalist tendencies of "close reading" in favor of a notion of movies as commodities. Appropriating a Marxist approach, Clark examines "the subjective and discursive dimensions of actors' labor within the productive domain of industrial relations."

The historical focus on 1933 in this chapter is significant as it coincides with one of President Franklin D. Roosevelt's bolder New Deal moves, the introduction of the National Recovery Administration (NRA), meant to foster improved cooperation between labor and management, provide for fair and safe working conditions, and most controversially for collective bargaining for an organized workforce. A minor scene early in the Warner Bros. feature *42nd Street* convincingly sets up Clark's contextual reading. A stage star peruses an equity contract (the contract itself is remarkably shown on screen) and quips "It's the biggest contract I've ever signed." We see her producer eye her legs, a first indication of the star as commodity. But more telling, Clark argues, is the later depiction of the moral implications of such well-compensated labor. The star is a spoiled brat. The chorus girl, whose far more exploitive contract we never see, is by contrast a team player. The film provides the frame for an understanding of industry labor relations and given the film's popularity, the studio's labor discourse is not only a textual matter but as well a larger context for labor relations in general at the time.

Suggested Reading

Richard Dyer, *Stars* (London: BFI, 1979); Barry King, "Articulating Stardom," *Screen*, 26:5, pp. 27–50; David Prindle, *The Politics of Glamour: Ideology and Democracy in the Screen Actors Guild* (Madison: University of Wisconsin Press, 1988).

FILM STUDIES SEEMS INCOMPLETE without the study of films. Since much of the recent critical work within film studies has been preoccupied with the notion of "text," and with obtaining a semiotic, psychoanalytic, or poststructuralist understanding of textuality, the Hollywood film has been a privileged object of study. Within cultural studies, however, this form of textual analysis has been placed into question. As Richard Johnson notes, textual analysis remains an important current within cultural studies, but the text is only a *means* to an end. It is "no longer studied for its own sake . . . but rather for the subjective or cultural forms which it realises and makes available."[1]

In the context of studying actors' labor and subjectivity, the film text has not assumed primacy for perhaps obvious reasons. That is, in my attempt to break star studies' fetishistic attachment to the actor as object, a certain distance from the film text has been necessary. But even here, the film text takes on an important role. As Tom Gunning argues:

> There are important tasks of film history, such as the establishment of studio policies and the economics of the industry that need not refer to individual films in any textual specificity. But analysis of the individual film provides a sort of laboratory for testing the relation between history and theory. It is at the level of the specific film that theory and history converge.[2]

Thus, by juxtaposing a single film against the "rationality of a system," historical analysis can reveal the "complex transaction that takes place between text and context."[3]

The importance of filmic analysis becomes clearer in the context of labor and subjectivity when film is viewed not as a text, but as a commodity. For as Marx argued so insistently, "All commodities are only definite quantities of congealed labour-time."[4] The social relations of capitalist production, he says, are embodied in the commodity and can be traced, in the final analysis, back to the commodity-form. According to Martyn J. Lee, "The real significance of the commodity, then, rests upon the fact that it tends to reflect the whole social organization of capitalism at any historical and geographical point in its development."[5] Having explored in previous chapters* the subjective and discursive dimensions of actors' labor within the productive domain of industrial relations, I will now, in the final analysis, subject the commodity-form to a theoretical and historical test. For, if Marx is right, these social relations have been embodied in the textual terrain of the film commodity, and labor policies and labor discourses can be revealed through a textual analysis of films.

One problem, however, is that the commodity is never fixed and cannot be coherently defined. Like the notion of text, the notion of commodity must be opened up to include various contextual aspects of commodification. Hollywood, in other words, produces many commodities, including film publicity and, of course, the film star. The film text as commodity therefore accrues a number of "encrustations" (to borrow Tony Bennett and Janet Woollacott's term) that must be analyzed in its conjuncture.[6] Film publicity in particular assumes a critical role in transforming the use value of the film commodity into exchange value through a manipulation of the symbolic aspect of commodity signs. What follows is thus an attempt to analyze the encrustations of commodification, especially the role of film publicity, in relation to several film shorts and two feature-length presentations, *42nd Street* and *Morning Glory*, that were produced during the NRA period in Hollywood.

NRA Publicity

One of the ways that industry could show support for President Roosevelt's national recovery program was to use the NIRA Blue Eagle insignia in its advertising and publicity. This practice benefited industry in return since consumers were encouraged to patronize businesses and buy products (from Macy's department store to Marchand's castille soap) that displayed the Blue Eagle. In addition, use of the Blue Eagle functioned as a ready form of "goodwill advertising." According to Stuart Ewen, advertisers had worked throughout the 1920s to transform the image of the soulless corporation into a bastion of public concern. "While daily life was projected as a flux of disastrous and unpredictable events," corporations were presented with "a nurturing image of permanence which . . . def[ied] the upheavals of day to day existence" and provided security for the consumer.[7] The economic instability of the Depression era, combined with the promises of the Roosevelt administration, thus provided fertile ground for goodwill advertising. Through such advertising, industry posed as the sympathetic friend to the "little fellow," and reassured the public of its commitment to putting America back to work.

The major film studios capitalized upon the goodwill opportunities made possible by the NRA in the hopes that they could reverse the downward trend in movie attendance and film production.[8] The idea of using the Blue Eagle for publicity first occurred in July of 1933, a time when the film industry was busy developing its Code of Fair Competition. According to a report in *Variety*, the studios decided "to hang the NIRA insignia over the box office and to use it generally in advertising and exploitation." Industry leaders felt that by advertising the NIRA and displaying the Blue Eagle they would not only be "the first to tell the public that [they were] for higher wages and fewer hours," but they would also gain "an extra $10 paid in at the box office for every dollar paid out under the Roosevelt movement."[9]

Even before the Blue Eagle insignia was created, however, studio publicity departments had appropriated the language and events of the NRA for their image enhancement. As early as March 1933, Warner Bros. studio employed the "theme" of Roosevelt's bank holiday to announce its spring lineup of films and to assure the public that Warner Bros. would not fall short of its commitment to quality production in the face of a national crisis. "No Shutdown—No Letdown—but A SHOWDOWN in the war against depression!" proclaims the ad (Figure 3.1). "Whether you're a Democrat or a Republican you'll endorse—WARNER BROS.' 10-WEEK RECONSTRUCTION PROGRAM."[10] The accompanying illustration of a fist being pounded into an open palm suggests that Warner Bros. meant "business." Embedded in this discourse of entertainment, however, is a complete revision of the role that Warner Bros. and the other major studios played during the banking crisis. In response to a possible shutdown in the film industry, studios imposed an eight-week salary waiver, not a "10-week reconstruction period." And, while Warner Bros. claims "more consecutive star strength than ha[d] been massed in any other period" of the studio's history, the furor over the salary waiver was causing actors to strengthen their own ranks in opposition to the studios. In keeping with its goodwill objective, however, it is important for the ad to leave the impression that Warner Bros., its stars, the public, and the Roosevelt administration are unified by their common goals for national recovery.

Later on, the studios developed "a national campaign along Greater Movie Season lines," which used the NRA as its nucleus for advertising and publicity. One MGM advertisement from this campaign (Figure 3.2) uses the NRA Code hearings as a theme to promote its patriotism and commitment to public service.[11] The photograph at the top of the ad purportedly represents an assembly of NRA Code administrators and their audience during Code

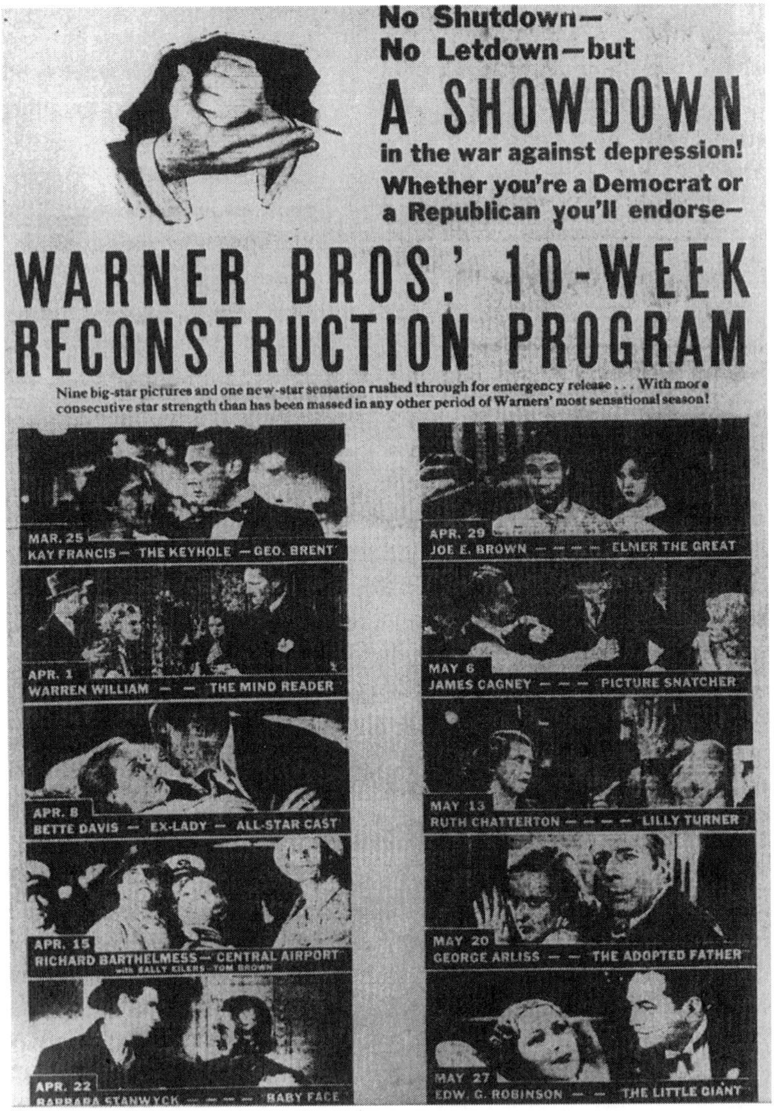

Figure 3.1 Warner Bros. "10 Week Reconstruction Program" advert, reproduced from *Variety*, March 21, 1933

deliberations. Addressing this assembly, Leo the Lion proclaims that "QUALITY cannot be coded!" The implication is that the real business of the film industry—the production of quality entertainment—cannot be legislated by the NRA Code; it can only be created by MGM and its stars. But, like the Warner Bros.' ad, MGM claims "star power" for itself while stars are rendered as passive subjects, graphically and literally embedded within the studio. The Blue Eagle symbol in the lower righthand corner suggests that this "unity" between stars and the MGM name has earned the NIRA stamp of approval.

Some Hollywood employees objected to the studios' use of the NIRA insignia. Members of the International Alliance of Theatrical Stage Employees (IATSE), for example, sent a telegram to President Roosevelt and NIRA administrator General Hugh S. Johnson stating that "the producers [were] using the emblems, or their equivalent, in advertising and publicity . . . at the same time [they were] conducting a campaign to destroy the principle of collective bargaining."[12] They pointed out that, in blatant disregard of NRA guidelines, sound technicians were required to work "unusually long hours" and were denied arbitration on grievances. In other instances, studio executives were criticized for interpreting NRA guidelines in ways that conveniently suited their own interests. The head office at Universal studios, for example, argued at one point that it was unpatriotic to pay employees for meals and overtime: "If our employees remain overtime and put in vouchers for supper money, it will defeat the purpose of the President's agreement."[13]

This memo was criticized for ignoring the studio's role in forcing employees to work overtime and for implying that employees deliberately conspired against the NRA's "shorter hours, more workers" policy. Even those studios that voluntarily fed employees were not exempt from criticism. For whether the NRA was used as an excuse to cut expenses or as a reason to showcase studios' "generosity" to the press, as employee groups contended, the studios were criticized for perceiving the matter of feeding the underemployed as charity and not as a contractual responsibility.

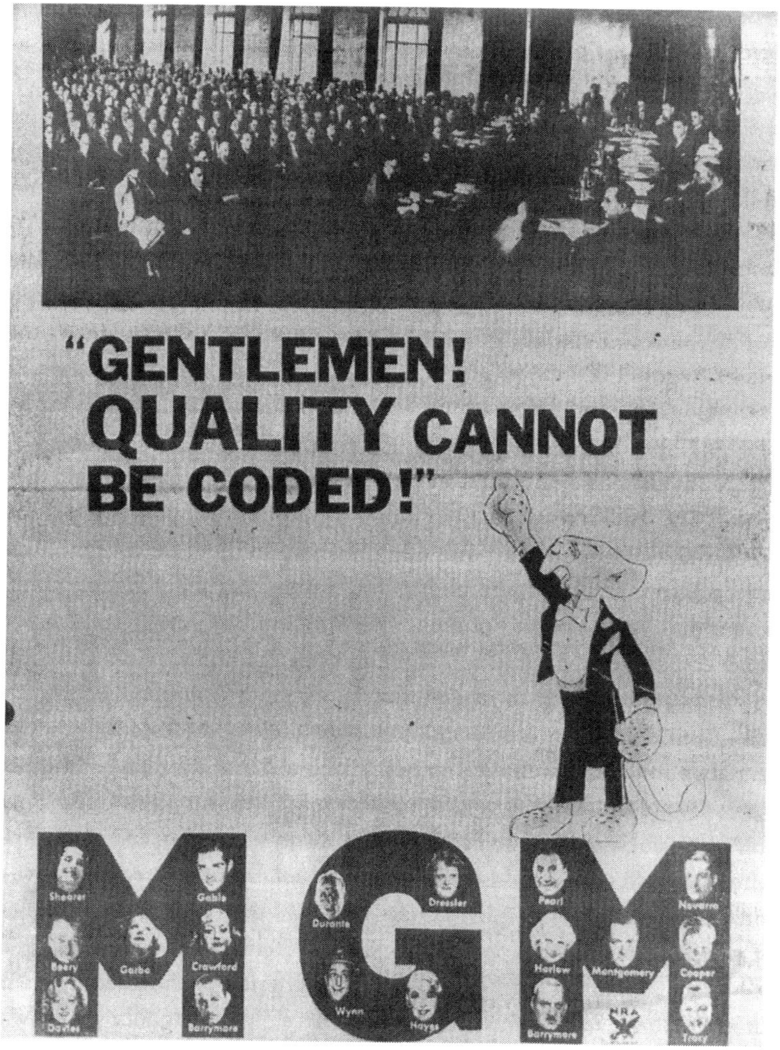

Figure 3.2 MGM "Quality cannot be coded!" advert, reproduced from *Variety*, October 3, 1933

Attempts to prohibit producers from using the Blue Eagle for publicity purposes, however, were unsuccessful. In fact, at the same time that the IATSE submitted its complaint, Harry Warner was seeking approval from General Johnson to produce an NRA screen trailer for theatrical release.[14] To be titled simply *The New Deal*, the film short was designed "to stimulate public interest in the Recovery Program."[15] Within a few weeks, the other major studios had produced their own versions of NRA shorts, and by the end of August 1,000 copies of the eight films were promised exhibition in 8,000 theaters for a total of 64,000 individual showings nationwide.[16] The films (scheduled for an eight-week run beginning September 10) were distributed by the National Screen Service at no charge to the participating theaters.[17] The studios relied on their minor stars or contract players to fill the NRA film roles, but, unlike with other Hollywood films, the stars received little publicity and were not used as box office draws. Subsuming actors within the overall rhetoric of their "We Do Our Part" campaign, studios rather emphasized the content of the films or the fact of the films' existence.

It would be wrong to suggest that, by virtue of their presence in such films, these actors were ideological dupes who merely acquiesced to producers' labor policies. It would be equally wrong to assert that these and other actors did not in some way share the producers' fervent support of the NRA. As American citizens concerned about the nation's economy, and as workers who had much to gain from the NRA's labor policies, actors regularly sponsored and participated in activities that supported the NRA or its principles of community and worker solidarity. The difference between actors' and producers' support of the NRA lay in their differing public visibility, their differing power to mobilize the resources necessary to produce their own positions, and the differing degree of institutional legitimacy accompanying these positions. Both parties, for example, marched in the massive NRA parade in New York City in September 1933. Whereas the Actors' Equity contingent was fairly small and relatively undistinguishable from other groups, the major studios used the opportunity to create a spectacle of entertainment. According to a report in the *New York Times*:

> The Metro-Goldywn-Mayer section created a mild sensation by releasing three large baskets full of pigeons. The Paramount girls, in blue dancing costumes, were impersonating blue eagles and had to keep their arms outspread, like wings.[18]

The Paramount girls most likely experienced some ambivalence about their role in the parade. While they may have been happy for the opportunity to support the NRA and to boost their career potential, they may also have had some complaints about the working conditions. (Even the *New York Times* noted that they "looked tired.") The studios, meanwhile, represented Hollywood as a discursively unified community, an institutional position that eclipsed any separate concerns held by actors who marched for the NRA.

The studios further capitalized on their productive capacities to establish closer connections with the Roosevelt administration. In the case of the NRA film shorts, the studios volunteered to produce the films for the government's NRA Propaganda Division and to absorb the production costs. Outwardly, this film campaign contradicted the studios' standing policy regarding the use of film for propagandistic purposes. According to the 1932 MPPDA Annual Report:

> The function of motion pictures is to ENTERTAIN. This we must keep before us at all times and we must realize constantly the fatality of ever permitting our concern with social values to lead us into the realm of *propaganda*.[19]

It seems, however, that "propaganda" was another one of those slippery terms employed by the studios according to convenience. In this case, "propaganda" was relegated to those discursive representations that conflicted with national policy. Propaganda was not called propaganda when it was good business and when it garnered the support of government officials who agreed to protect the industry's monopolistic practices. According to John C. Flinn, in charge of the film activities of NRA publicity, the motion picture industry "acquitted itself admirably in the patriotic and important tasks undertaken under [the] supervision [of the NRA Propaganda Division]."[20]

Although the industry's NRA film campaign may have ignored the MPPDA's report regarding propaganda (or interpreted the term in a specifically convenient way), it upheld the notion that the primary function of motion pictures is to entertain. Though the NRA films were part of a propaganda campaign, they were produced not as documentaries, as one might expect, but as classical realist narratives or entertainment spectacles. MGM's contribution, for example, featured Jimmy Durante singing a humorous rendition of "Give Me a Job" in a film short bearing the same title. Other films or "dramatic featurettes" drew from the romantic comedy or domestic comedy genre. One example of this, the Fox film *Mother's Helper*, is described by *Variety* as follows:

> El Brendel tries to explain in a Weber and Fieldian manner how his working only 40 hours weekly will give another man employment. When his wife, Zasu Pitts, wants to know if the NRA affects housewives, Brendel explains he has attended to that and brings in the hot looking Esther Muir, explaining that in the future she'll take care of half of Miss Pitts' wifely duties. Miss Pitts conks Brendel for the fade out.[21]

Within a generic tradition of personalizing social issues, the gender politics of the NRA period are made more palatable (i.e., entertaining) for audience consumption. Within the studios, however, female employees were especially hard hit by the NRA's "shorter hours and more workers" policy. In May of 1933, several thousand female employees, mostly secretaries and stenographers, signed petitions against a bill proposed by the California legislature that would limit the work of all women in the state to an eight-hour day. The major studios also objected to the bill, arguing that the film industry was not like other industries, and that "the emergency nature of much of the studios' vital activities," such as those found in the story department (which employed 1,000–1,500 women), required special consideration.[22] According to a report in *Variety*, however, the studios later praised the passage of the bill because the reduction of work hours for female secretaries and stenographers allowed them more time to concentrate on "domestic bliss" and food preparation for their husbands, thus making everything "hotsy-totsy, thanks to the indigo spreadeagle over the hearth."[23]

Warner Bros.' film short, *The Road Is Open Again*, adopted a more serious tone toward NRA events. According to *Variety*'s description of the film:

> [Dick] Powell is a young composer trying to write music for an NRA song. Visions of Lincoln, Washington and Wilson appear over the piano to advise him. Each tells of his efforts to guide America and admit that President Roosevelt is on the right track.
>
> Powell, through their inspiration, writes the number, "The Road Is Open Again." He sings a verse and its chorus, steps to the front of the curtain and invites the audience to join him.
>
> [The p]icture dissolves into a series of industrial scenes throughout the country with the chorus of the song superimposed on the scenes.[24]

As the most blatantly propagandistic film of the NRA film series, the Warner Bros.' contribution acquired the look and feel of a paid political announcement for the Roosevelt administration. (*Variety* even predicted that the film's "stirring march" would become the theme song of the NRA.) At the same time, the film and its title song served as a form of goodwill advertising that asserted the studio's own economic optimism and authority. Thus, in its sponsorship of the ad/film, Warner Bros. not only displayed its support for the NRA, but celebrated the studio's role in leading the nation to recovery.

Though the NRA films confronted public concerns and offered corporate reassurance in the guise of patriotic entertainment, they were only a temporary and blatant form of propaganda aimed at winning public approval. The more subtle and more profitable means of maintaining public support was achieved through the studios' feature-length films, because these films remained the primary source of contact between fans and the industry and provided the basis of continuity for the production-consumption cycle. While most of these commercial films were of little relevance to the current conditions of crisis, they nonetheless offered a kind of reassurance. Through their sensational plots, elaborate sets, and star attractions, feature films packaged public fantasies and promulgated the discourse of entertainment necessary to studio survival. There were several films released in 1933, however, that directly commented on national affairs or that indirectly voiced the studios' corporate policies. Using the events of the NRA period to reinforce the Hollywood ideology of entertainment, these fictional narratives also provided studios with a powerful outlet for voicing their views of labor, enabling them to shift public attention away from actor–producer conflicts and to rewrite labor issues into a discourse of entertainment.

42nd Street

The best-known feature films of the NRA period that actually incorporated the Depression or the NRA as themes are the Warner Bros. musicals *42nd Street, Gold Diggers of 1933*, and *Footlight Parade*. These films have received a great deal of scholarly attention, partly because the first two films of this trilogy were top-grossing films for Warner Bros., and, according to some, helped to reinstate the musical as a respectable and profitable genre.[25] Film scholars have examined these films for their gritty realism, their escapism (attributed primarily to Busby Berkeley's production numbers), or their spirit of cooperation with Roosevelt's New Deal.[26] In his article "Some Warners Musicals and the Spirit of the New Deal," Mark Roth argues that the musicals are "essentially political" because their purpose is "to come to terms with the questioning of the American Dream and to reaffirm faith in that ideal."[27] However, as films that claimed to inaugurate a "New Deal in Entertainment," the full implication of their political force can only be understood by examining how their restoration of the American Dream was beneficial to the Hollywood image—and studio labor policies. For these musicals are not simply films about the NRA; they are films about the acting profession.

42nd Street, the first of these musicals released in 1933, was preceded by an extravagant promotional tour. On February 21, a troupe of chorus girls and several of Warner Bros.' top stars (Bebe Daniels, James Cagney, Dick Powell, and Joe E. Brown) boarded a train in Los Angeles. The train, called the Better Times Special, stopped at several key cities (Denver, Kansas City, Chicago) on its trek eastward before arriving in Washington, D.C., for Roosevelt's inauguration on March 4; the group's final destination was 42nd Street, New York.[28] The promotional tour was made possible through the cooperation of General Electric, which saw the tour as a good opportunity to advertise its own products:

> The outside of the train [was] leafed in gold and silver with a constant electric sign burning the legend "Better Times" and announcing the Warner picture and the G.E. equipment contained therein.[29]

As the parent organization of RCA and NBC, GE was in a position to authorize hookups between local radio affiliates and the train's broadcast facilities. At each stop, the Better Times' radio broadcast songs by Dick Powell while it advertised GE products, the Warner Bros. film, and the NRA spirit of optimism. During the day, the stars were transported to GE showrooms to demonstrate appliances, and, in the evenings, they appeared at local theaters for premieres of *42nd Street*.[30] In what *Variety* called "one of the juiciest exploitation tie-ups known [to Hollywood],"[31] actors thus served as living advertisements for the studio's products and discourses of entertainment. But within the fictional narrative of *42nd Street*, the presence of actors took on an added significance. Here, actors provided Warner Bros. with an opportunity to comment upon actors' labor and subject positioning within the studio system.

The plot of *42nd Street* is simple. Set as a backstage musical, the story revolves around "puttin' on a show." When the star of the show breaks her ankle, a determined young novice learns the dance numbers and becomes an overnight success. But against the backdrop of this simple plot, *42nd Street* establishes an authoritative commentary on actors' labor. The mechanism for beginning this commentary occurs after the opening montage sequence of New York's theater district as the camera settles on a close-up of an Actors' Equity contract (Figure 3.3). It reads:

> Jones and Barry, Theatrical Producers, hereby engage Dorothy Brock to star in their musical production *Pretty Lady* . . .

What is interesting about this shot is that a display of the contract is not necessary as a plot element; that is, viewers do not need to *see* the document in order to pick up information essential to the plot. Yet, given its privileged position and prominence after the film's preface, the Equity contract serves as the source of conflict that sets the narrative into motion. Actors' labor becomes condensed into the Equity contract as an overdetermined and isolated sign that signifies a site of tension between actors and producers. The task of the narrative, then, is to find a resolution to this conflict. By using a "genuine Equity contract" (as called for in the script) the film makes the threat of organized labor more visible, and increases the possibility that viewers will sympathize with the terms of narrative closure.

In addition to representing actors' labor in general, the contract specifically represents the Actors' Equity union, an organization that had caused considerable problems for Hollywood management since its arrival in 1919. Though the union was divested of bargaining power in 1927 when the Academy was formed, Equity still maintained a noticeable presence in Hollywood (screen actors who worked in the theater necessarily retained membership, and many others never bothered to sever their ties with the union), and studios continued to be wary of its influence. In the film *42nd Street*, however, Equity's eradication from Hollywood is finally achieved. Producers return the union to its "proper" origin by associating Equity with the theater. This movement has the advantage of displacing actor–producer conflicts from Hollywood onto the New York stage, and of allowing the film to present an interpretation of actors' unions that is disassociated from inequitable labor practices in Hollywood. Viewers were thus encouraged to identify with an ideology of labor that was distanced from, yet integral to, Hollywood.

Management literally has its hands and eyes on actors' contracts from the beginning of *42nd Street* as *Pretty Lady*'s producer, millionaire Abner Dillon (Guy Kibbee), holds the

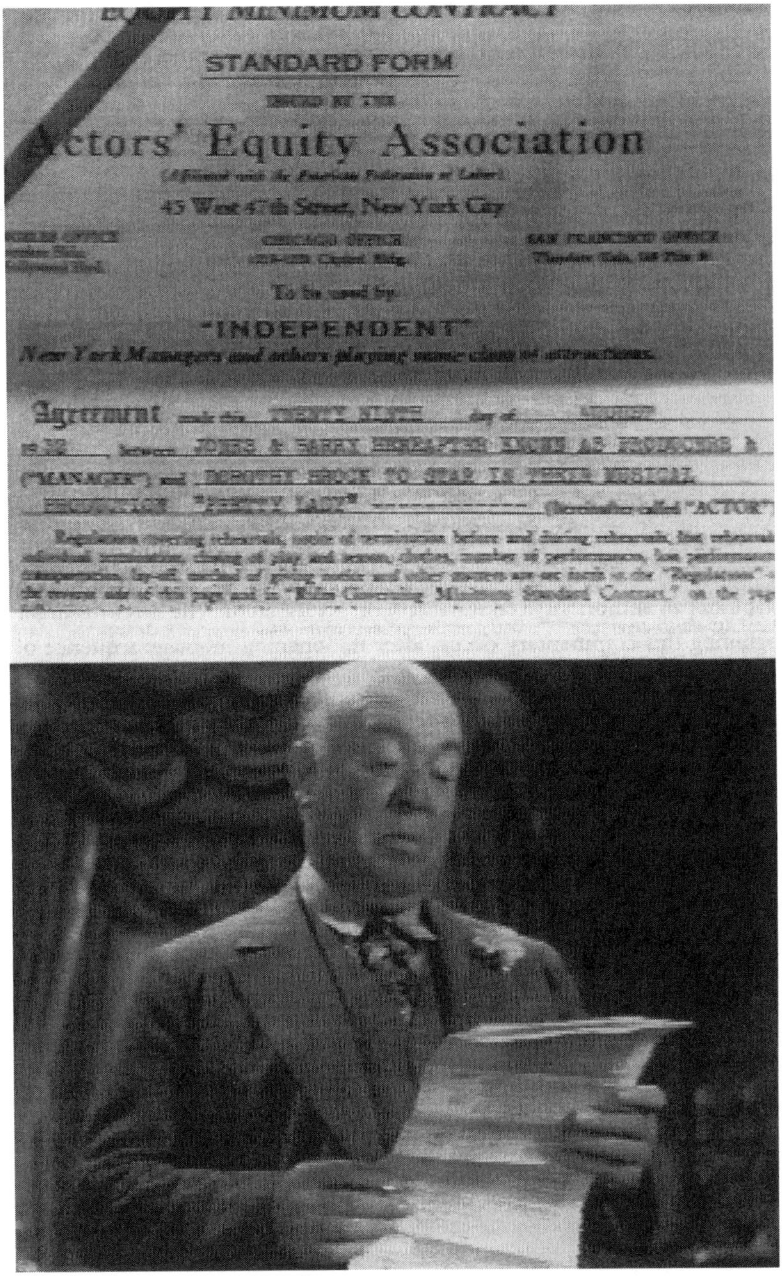

Figure 3.3 Producer Abner Dillon (Guy Kibbee) inspects an Actors' Equity Association contract in *42nd Street* (1933)

contract up for inspection (Figure 3.3). Management's point of view (and, thus, the desired point of view for the audience) is established through a shot–reverse shot technique that focuses first on a close-up of the Equity contract, then cuts to a medium shot of Dillon holding the contract. This perspective is reinforced orally through voice continuity. During the close-up we hear Dillon's voice-over: "Well, of course, I'm not a lawyer. I'm in the kiddie car business." But as the film cuts to the shot of him holding the contract, Dillon is shown speaking: "I don't know much about contracts, but this looks good to me." As Dillon speaks the final clause of his statement, the camera cuts to a close-up of a woman's legs (shown in mirror reflection). It is clear that what "looks good" to the producer is not the contract, but the legs of Dorothy Brock (Bebe Daniels), the show's star. This association discredits the terms of the contract by substituting the star's sexuality for the legal document. As such, the cutaway defines the nature of contracts as payment for a fetish object rather than as procurement of an actor's labor.

A publicity still for *42nd Street* (Figure 3.4) offers an interesting comparison to the scene that occurred in the film release. In the still photograph, both "characters" are more or less facing the camera, and we do not see the contract exclusively from the producer's point of view. Indeed, the actor, not the producer, is in possession of the contract, and the latter is positioned behind and to the side of the former to see the contract from her visual perspective. While there may be sexual overtones to this photo, the producer is also not directly fetishizing some aspect of the actor's body through the sexual gaze. The different positioning of the characters in relation to the contract thus creates a more harmonious representation of labor relations. I doubt, however, that this was the purpose of the publicity photo. It was common practice for publicity stills to be taken on the production sets by studio photographers (who may or may not have known the plot of the film) and not copied from the films themselves. Moreover, since the point of such publicity was to display the starring actors (and not a single, minor actor), it is not surprising that top-billed Bebe Daniels is present in the still. This comparison, however, only underscores the significance of the shot–reverse shot sequence used in the film. Although the harmonious relations in the publicity photo deemphasize the contract (a viewer may not even realize that the object Kibbee and Daniels are looking at is a contract), the foregrounding of the Equity contract in narrative form sets the stage for actor–producer conflict.

Dorothy Brock's response to Dillon ("It's the biggest contract *I've* ever signed—thanks to *you*, Mr. Dillon.") immediately places the actor and producer at cross-purposes since the star defines her relation to the contract primarily in terms of salary. Yet, the coyness of her response—as she peeks over the top of a *New Yorker* magazine, then slips him a knowing (though slightly disgusted) smile—indicates that she has achieved her role and contract through sexual manipulation and thus is implicated in Dillon's understanding of the contract

Figure 3.4 Dorothy Brock (Bebe Daniels) and Abner Dillon (Guy Kibbee) in *42nd Street* (1933)

as a sexual agreement. Later on, then, when the star withdraws her sexual attention, Dillon's threat of dismissal is presented as a justified action. In an interesting and effective conflation of discourses, labor–management conflicts are collapsed into gender politics, and the sexual contact between male producer and female star is shown to be more binding than the union contract. In the final analysis, the union contract means nothing more than the producer's definition of it. The film furthermore suggests that actors are better off without one. For when novice Peggy Sawyer (Ruby Keeler) replaces the star, she does not sign an Equity contract. Grateful for the chance to become a star, and willing to do whatever management requests, the success of the nonunion actor far outshines that of the union star.

In *42nd Street*, union contracts obviously carry moral implications. Dorothy Brock, the only actor (i.e., character) in the film to sign a contract, is depicted as petty, gold-digging, and sexually suspect. She is concerned only with salary and status, not with the welfare of others or the success of the show. Peggy Sawyer, by contrast, is sexually pure and uninterested in money. Her only desire is to get her chance on Broadway; she leaves all decisions regarding salary and performance to management, implicitly trusting that she will be well cared for. Sawyer was not the sort of actor who would turn the industry into a "cheap racket" as feared by Academy spokesman Lester Cowan. Nor would this type of actor be likely to sabotage the public relations efforts of the Hays Office. It is no coincidence, then, that this cooperative and obedient character was represented as the more desirable actor to audiences.

Audience identification with the Sawyer character was further reinforced through the wholesome star image of Ruby Keeler. Far from being a sex goddess, Keeler was perceived as an innocent, working-class girl with high morals, lots of enthusiasm, and only average talent. According to Rocco Fumento,

> There's something so very vulnerable about her, so moronically endearing in her klutziness while she earnestly looks down at her feet as she clumps her way up Forty-second Street . . . But women liked her . . . Old men wanted to protect her (and her incredible innocence) . . . young men wanted to embrace and make her their wife, *never* their mistress . . . and to boys stumbling into puberty she was an angel, a first infatuation . . . a madonna of the musicals.[32]

This image of wholesomeness was exploited in the studio publicity surrounding the Warners' musical trilogy. Advance features sent to theaters, for example, sported headlines such as "Ruby Keeler Just an Old-Fashioned Sweet Girl" and "Ruby Keeler, Millionairess Is as Timid as an Extra." In press kit interviews, Keeler was modest, playing down her theatrical abilities and playing up her homespun qualities.[33] According to a report in *Variety*, Keeler refused to continue production on *Footlight Parade* until the studio provided her with a less revealing costume: "Keeler claimed that she could not do her dance properly, and that she was more interested in giving a satisfactory performance than in supplying s. a. [sex appeal] to picture fans."[34] Though Keeler could have been penalized for her rebellion, Warner Bros. undoubtedly did not want to place the studio's commitment to morality into question, and thus immediately honored her request.

The studio's concern over maintaining a morally acceptable image had also led them to take certain precautions in preparation for the *42nd Street* Better Times publicity tour. They were particularly concerned about how the public might perceive the twelve young women of the chorus troupe who would be traveling across the country in mixed company. According to an interoffice memo,

> The trip in itself is . . . one which may result in unfavorable criticism of the company in the event anything of a serious nature should happen to anyone [*sic*]

> of these young girls, and it is needless for me [R. J. Obringer] to impress upon you the necessity of strict discipline.[35]

In an attempt to avoid any problems, Warner Bros. included a clause in the chorines' contracts that required them to "promptly and faithfully" comply with the "especially strict rules" set down for the purpose of the tour:

> It will be particularly required that all persons upon such tour . . . shall conduct themselves with special regard to *public convention and morals* and that no action which will tend to degrade Artist or the tour, will bring either Artist or any member of such tour into public hatred, contempt, scorn or ridicule, or which will tend to shock, insult or offend public morals or decency, or prejudice the Producer or the motion picture industry in general, will be tolerated.[36]

Failure to comply with these terms (which remained necessarily vague) was cited as sufficient cause for termination.

Although the chorus girl contracts for the film production of *42nd Street* did not include a morality clause, Warner Bros. still felt compelled to promote the idea that the studio cared about its employees' moral welfare. According to a press kit article credited to the *Brooklyn Daily Eagle*, the chorus girls in *42nd Street*

> were put on a strict diet, a stricter exercise routine, and an even stricter mode of living. To save their beauteous legs, they were provided with roller skates, on which to glide from their stage to the restaurant. Too, they all live under one roof; must be in bed by 9 o'clock, must be up at 7. Nor is that all. For on the way to and from the studio, the gals are chaperoned by a corps of husky studio policemen.[37]

This connection between morality and strict discipline became an implicit part of every actor's agreement with a studio. Even when morality clauses were not included, every contract stipulated that the artist would perform services "in a conscientious and painstaking manner and in accordance with the reasonable instructions of the producer [and] the reasonable studio rules and regulations of the producer."[38] The notion of what was "reasonable" was, of course, the source of conflict between actors and producers.

According to a Screen Actors Guild retrospective report, actors at this time were faced with unreasonable demands due to unregulated hours and working conditions:

> Actors were required to work almost every Saturday night and often into the early hours of Sunday morning. If a studio closed for a holiday during the week, the actor often would be required to work the following Sunday without pay to make up for the holiday. Meal periods came at the producers' convenience, not necessarily to meet the human needs of the actor.
>
> There was seldom any 12-hour rest period between work calls. Actors often worked well past midnight and then were ordered to report back for work at 7 a.m. Actors were not paid for overtime and no premium was paid for work on Saturdays, Sundays and holidays nor for night work.[39]

During the filming of *42nd Street*, "Daily Production and Progress Reports" indicate that actors (and other employees) were indeed asked to work overtime (including Sundays), and were not always given a twelve-hour rest period between work calls, even though these practices violated the terms of their contracts. During a two-day dress rehearsal for one of the Busby Berkeley numbers, for example, the cast worked seventeen to eighteen hours per day (10:00 a.m. to 2:30 a.m. and 9:00 a.m. to 2:50 a.m.) with only a six-and-a-half-hour rest period in between. Thus, contrary to Warner Bros. publicity, chorus girls were not in bed every night by the wholesome hour of 9:00.

This type of situation is duplicated in the narrative of *42nd Street*. Director Julian Marsh (Warner Baxter) keeps the cast members well into the night during a grueling dress rehearsal for *Pretty Lady*. When the actors become tired and inattentive, he yells: "Not one of you leaves this stage tonight until I get what I want." One elderly actor does leave after fainting, but the others remain until Marsh is satisfied with their performance. Another time, when Peggy Sawyer faints during a rehearsal, Marsh orders the actors to resume their positions. "This is a rehearsal," he says, "not a rest cure!" According to a report by the Chorus Equity division of the Actors' Equity Association, chorus girls at this time worked up to ninety hours per week and were paid below regular wages, if anything at all, for rehearsals. Having little or no money to eat (or no time to eat if the director failed to call a lunch break) would easily have caused a girl like Peggy Sawyer to faint from exhaustion.[40] In the case of *42nd Street*, however, the director was not violating any contractual agreements, because the film implies that only the star of the show has signed a contract. Marsh's actions are further motivated and exonerated by his ill health and poor financial condition; although nearing collapse, he pushes himself and the actors to produce a successful show.

Occasionally, the actors are cynical, or even critical, about their working conditions, as in the following exchange:

> —They [the rehearsals] just about kill these youngsters . . . and for what?
> —For thirty-five a week—when you can get it!

Indeed, though some theater managers claimed that chorines earned $40 a week and over, statistics compiled by Chorus Equity showed that "the remuneration in most instances was not more than $25 a week."[41] The quoted remarks remained a form of resistance that had little potency, however, in terms of changing working conditions. Because the actors were otherwise portrayed as lazy, insolent, temperamental, untalented, or sufficiently lacking in intelligence, these verbal resistances served as comic one-liners that diffused labor–management tensions and implied that the actors were not to be taken seriously. According to the moral logic of *42nd Street*, the major reason the show became a hit was the director's unrelenting vision and dedication. This idea is reinforced in the final scene through an ironic twist. After the show, as Marsh leans wearily against a fire escape in the alley, he listens to the remarks of people coming out of the theater and hears them praise everyone but himself. ("I can't see that Marsh did a thing." "It's simply having the right cast—that's all!") The implication, however, is that the director deserves all the credit; he was the one who transformed these feckless players into a productive and obedient group of entertainers.

Ultimately, the key to the film's morality is an ideology of labor that combines individual initiative with collective subordination. In his article on Warners' musicals, Mark Roth finds these two notions contradictory, arguing that the film's Horatio Alger version of the American Dream—in which the myth that individual initiative, hard work, and luck lead to ultimate success—is contradicted by the film's production numbers (and its resolution), in which we see many individuals subordinated to the will of a single person—the director.[42] But, contrary to Roth's argument, both individual initiative and collective subordination were essential to reinforcing an ideology of stardom that served management goals. Individual initiative promoted the idea of mobility within the star system hierarchy. When individual initiative was perceived as "hard work," actors low in the hierarchy (like Peggy Sawyer) might be rewarded with an opportunity to move upward; but when individual initiative was perceived by management as a temperamental display or selfish demand, stars (like Dorothy Brock) could be threatened with dismissal or downward mobility. Contained within the myth of individual success, then, is the notion of subordination. Studios merely extended this notion to the sphere of collective work: actors were expected to collectively serve management's (moral) goals instead of forming (immoral) collective bargaining units to protect their own interests.

Although *42nd Street* was conceived, developed, and produced in 1932, before the NRA even existed, Warner Bros. capitalized on the occasion of Roosevelt's inauguration and the popularity of the NRA for the film's release in March 1933. Within this context the film's portrayal of actors served to strengthen studio labor discourse. Through their dedication to the collective production of the show, actors come to represent the collective spirit of the New Deal. This allegorical shift allows the film to ignore or displace the specific problems of actors. In other words, *42nd Street* is no longer a film about actors struggling to survive in their profession, but a film about American citizens struggling toward national recovery. Through this redefinition, the film successfully diverts attention away from actor–producer conflicts while implicitly encouraging viewers to sympathize with management's ideology of labor. As in the NRA film shorts, actors' labor thus becomes subsumed under a collective, industrial discourse that sought unproblematic and profitable solutions to quality entertainment and national recovery.

Though *42nd Street* was the third top moneymaker of the year for Warner Bros., the studio did not feel obliged to share the fruits of collective effort. On the contrary, the studio's profits were accumulated at a time when it sought to curtail actors' wages even more by imposing, and trying to extend, its eight-week salary waiver. Guy Kibbee, who played the lecherous, bumbling producer in *42nd Street*, protested against this situation. In a letter to Warner Bros. studio he argues that, in view of the fact that the producers "refused to comply with the terms and conditions set forth in the Emergency Bulletin" by choosing to extend the salary waiver period beyond the agreed upon eight-week period, he no longer considers himself legally bound to his signature on the salary waiver form and therefore demands that Warner Bros. compensate him for the period of the salary waiver as per his original contract.[43] Kibbee's letter was sent a few days after he received notice from Warner Bros. that the studio had decided to exercise its right to lay him off for a period of three weeks without pay. The studio justified its action by citing the paragraph regarding noncontinuous employment in Kibbee's contract dated May 16, 1931 (the same contract that Kibbee refers to), but its letter does not mention the salary waiver period or Warner Bros.' obligation to honor the original terms of said contract as regards salary.[44]

Some of the *42nd Street* actors posed no problems for Warner Bros. management. As Thomas Schatz has pointed out, Dick Powell was not only well suited to "Warners more economical and genre-based approach to production," but was willing "to work more often and for lower salaries" and to let the studio shape his screen roles.[45] Powell's participation in both the Warners' NRA film short and the *42nd Street* promotional train tour supports the idea that he was amenable to the studio's broader publicity goals as well. His dance partner in the musical trilogy, Ruby Keeler, also fit well into Warner Bros.' publicity scheme. The studio played up the fact that, after a successful career on Broadway, Keeler was getting her "big break" in motion pictures, and thus her story was not unlike that of Peggy Sawyer in *42nd Street*. In one publicity article, for example, Keeler is quoted as saying that landing the lead role in *42nd Street* was a stroke of "luck" and that she felt as timid in her first film as Sawyer did in her first stage production.[46] One difference between Keeler and Sawyer, however, is that the former signed a multiyear contract that guaranteed substantial yearly increases in salary.

While Warner Bros. may have tried to exploit certain connections between the film and its actors, aspects of labor–management conflict within the industry were rewritten or made invisible by the film's narrative discourse about labor. It is ironic, for example, that Bebe Daniels plays the role of a prima donna who has a contract dispute with her producer, because several months prior to the filming of *42nd Street* Daniels was engaged in a lengthy contract dispute with Warner Bros. Daniels refused as many as eight stories from Warners on the basis that they were unsuitable and that the studio had not given her "the proper opportunity to prove her drawing power."[47] She finally took it upon herself to submit a story for consideration, but Warners refused to produce it on her terms (which included choice of director and final approval of the dialogue). For several months Warners and Daniels's agents made compromises and counteroffers. Because both parties wanted to sever the contractual arrangement, the issue was no longer which picture she would play in but how she could finish out the terms of her contract. In an affidavit regarding Bebe Daniels, Darryl F. Zanuck concluded that Warner Bros. "had conscientiously endeavored to compromise with her and she had stalled until [they] were over a barrel."[48] In the end, Daniels managed to get a contract that was, for the most part, on her terms.

George Brent, the actor who portrayed Dorothy Brock's boyfriend in *42nd Street*, became engaged in a lengthy contract dispute with Warner Bros. several months after the film's release, but he was not as fortunate as Bebe Daniels. Brent's refusal to report to the set of a movie for which he was scheduled resulted in his suspension. Warner Bros. also sent a letter disclosing Brent's action to nine different studios and to the Association of Motion Picture Producers.[49] While this letter put Brent into a bind by informing other studios that he was not a free agent and not available to sign elsewhere, it also was meant to protect Warner Bros. against star raiding. Warners was a leader against star raiding, at one time even calling a special meeting of the Hays organization to investigate the alleged raiding practices of 20th Century studio.[50] Meanwhile, screen actors were fighting against the producers' anti–star raiding provision of the NRA Code, a document whose process of conflict and negotiation tells a very different narrative of actor–producer relations than that found in *42nd Street*.

As Jane Feuer notes, "The musical turns its self-reflective technique to its own purposes," oscillating between demystification and remythicization to reproduce "the myth of entertainment."[51] The backstage musical, in particular, purports to foreground the secrets of its making by providing viewers with a behind-the-scenes look at the production process. But this demystifying technique only sets the stage for a revisionist discourse whereby the film mythologizes the economic and stylistic forces of production—including the role that labor plays in this process. Thus, when Warner Bros foregrounds the acting profession and its working conditions in its backstage musicals, actors' labor becomes subject to commentary and reformulation. This strategy allows for a double reinforcement of the studio's version of labor discourse by promoting management's point of view while simultaneously discounting or silencing alternative points of view from actors.

I do not wish to imply that the Screen Actors Guild version of labor–management relations describes the "real" situation and that the studios created a "false" version of labor through their publicity and film narratives. Hollywood discourses of entertainment were certainly real enough to actors and affected actors' labor in concrete ways. The point is that in the discursive struggle over the meaning of actors' labor, studio management had a more advantageous position from which to speak. The studio additionally benefited from the films' widespread distribution, which guaranteed that the public would have much greater access to the films than to information that would have challenged the studio's position on labor–management relations. In light of these factors, and given the immense popularity of the films, it appears that audiences accepted, at least on some level, the studio's version of labor discourse.

Morning Glory

The Warners' musicals did not singlehandedly rewrite actors' labor into a discourse of entertainment during the NRA period; they merely stand out because their representations of the acting profession had direct tie-ins with economic and political events. Other films of this period promulgated the familiar discourse about stardom and complemented the studios' public relations efforts on other fronts. One example is *Morning Glory* (1933), a top-grossing RKO picture described by one critic as "*42nd Street* without music, dancing or Ruby Keeler."[52] Katharine Hepburn plays the lead role of Eva Lovelace, a stagestruck young woman from Vermont who goes to Broadway to fulfill her destiny as a great actress. When her "natural talent" is not immediately recognized, the actress perseveres; even when she is penniless and homeless, Lovelace retains an undying (if not naive) faith in the theater and in herself. This dedication and reverence toward acting become the key to her success as she finally is rewarded with a chance in a major Broadway production.

Unlike *42nd Street, Morning Glory* is not so much about collective subordination as it is about individual initiative and artistry. This tribute to individualism is established in the opening scene as Lovelace enters a theater lobby and stands in awe before the portraits of great stage actors such as Sarah Bernhardt, Ethel Barrymore, and John Drew. Lovelace's own budding greatness is revealed through her subsequent encounters with Rita Vernon (Mary Duncan), an actor who has just landed the lead role in the comedy production *Blue Skies*. Like Dorothy Brock and Peggy Sawyer in *42nd Street*, Vernon and Lovelace represent two types of actors with two different attitudes toward their work. Vernon is the stereotypic gum-snapping, peroxided chorus girl who has made it to the top through her streetwise (i.e., sexual) manipulations (Figure 3.5). Vernon is a careerist, not an artist; she is concerned primarily with status and money, and acting appears to be a glamorous means to achieve these ends. By contrast, Lovelace has naturally colored hair along with her natural talent (Figure 3.6); she is an artist whose passion is reserved for the stage. By setting up such a distinct comparison between these two actors, the narrative must resolve the conflict they embody. The turning point comes when Vernon demands a contract.

The only reason Vernon agreed to play the lead in *Blue Skies* is that her producer, Louis Easton (Adolphe Menjou), promised her that she could have her choice of plays thereafter.

Figure 3.5 Louis Easton (Adolphe Menjou) and Rita Vernon (Mary Duncan) in *Morning Glory* (1933)

Figure 3.6 Joseph Sheridan (Douglas Fairbanks, Jr.) and Eva Lovelace (Katharine Hepburn) in *Morning Glory* (1933)

The play she chooses is *The Golden Bough*, a dramatic piece that she feels will allow her to develop the image of a serious actress. But on opening night, fifteen minutes before curtain time, Vernon confronts Easton with contract demands. We learn that for four years Vernon has never had a contract; instead, actor and producer had a verbal agreement whereby she would be "reasonable," Easton would "do the right thing," and they would "take each other's word." Vernon reminds Easton that while she has never "talked salary," she has made a fortune for him. In addition, "being reasonable" has meant that Vernon never asked for what she *really* wanted—until now. Vernon makes several demands. She wants her name in electric lights; a run-of-the-play contract for *The Golden Bough* in New York and on the road; $1,500 a week; half the show's profits; and a percentage of the motion picture rights.

Vernon feels confident that Easton will agree to her demands, since she has placed him in a tough spot. But Easton responds with anger, threatening to report Vernon to the Actors' Equity Association and asserting that he will make certain she never works again. However, when Vernon says that she will not appear on opening night, he fears that his entire investment in the show will be lost if he refuses to meet her terms. Just as Easton is prepared to give in, playwright Joseph Sheridan (Douglas Fairbanks, Jr.) urges him to take a chance on the understudy. The understudy, of course, is Eva Lovelace, who, unbeknownst to Easton, had been hired by Sheridan for the part. Easton agrees to give the novice a chance and reports back to Vernon: "Since you've decided to act in this most *unprofessional* manner . . . I've decided to let you do exactly as you please." Vernon's exit simultaneously marks her eradication from the play/film and the producer's victory in the contract dispute.

Lovelace is a success in the play, but the film audience does not witness her performance. In fact, aside from a few brief shots that indicate that Lovelace has taken interim jobs in variety shows, *Morning Glory* never represents the actors at work. Unlike *42nd Street*, which must portray actors at work in order to make the connection to Americans working toward economic recovery, *Morning Glory* abolishes any notion of actors as laborers. This construction allows the film to explore the artistic side of the acting profession while separating labor from art. The film still places actors in a subordinate position, however. As the film suggests, actors who perceive the acting profession as a spiritual or artistic calling do not question labor practices or demand (better) contracts. Artistry is furthermore linked to morality in the eyes of producers. Vernon, a mediocre talent with questionable moral habits (drinking, sexual propositioning), is finally dismissed when she attempts to define herself as a worker. Although the film intimates that Lovelace and Easton have a sexual encounter (he takes advantage of her at a party when she is drunk), she retains her moral sensibilities by defining herself in nonthreatening terms as an artist. The key to moral relations between actors and producers is thus a matter of who is initiating what and who plays the subordinate role.

After her performance on opening night, Lovelace's one desire is to make Easton proud of her—a desire complicated by the fact that she has fallen in love with him. But Easton puts her new role in perspective by explaining that she is now under his *professional* wing:

> —It's going to be difficult, my dear, because I'm a difficult task master and I'm likely to make a pest of myself. But you're too valuable to ever get out of my sight. . . . That's why you're coming to my office tomorrow and signing a contract to play this part as long as the public wants to see you in it.

Easton is no longer threatened by the idea of a contract once he is able to initiate it on his own terms. Although a contract was not "necessary" before, it now establishes a (task) master–slave relationship that allows Easton to protect his investment. (Easton refers to Lovelace as "the most valuable piece of theatrical property I have ever owned.") The contract is not intended to protect the actor's investment of labor, nor is it designed according to NRA guidelines concerned with protecting actors as a group.

When a producer has the power to grant (or refuse) contracts according to his own convenience and terms, actors are divested of collective bargaining power. It is interesting that, like *42nd Street*, the narrative of *Morning Glory* recognizes the existence of Actors' Equity but attributes very little power to it. In this case, Easton ironically assumes that the actors' union will protect *him* from temperamental actors and that he has the power—and the right—to intervene between an actor and her union. But while Easton goes so far as to threaten Vernon with retaliation from the Equity union, it is unclear on what grounds Easton feels the union could logically retaliate. Perhaps because Vernon had cooperated with the producer and forfeited an Equity contract for four years, she would somehow be ineligible for union membership in good standing. More likely, if Vernon was already an Equity member and was working without a contract, she could automatically be suspended from the union for undermining its objectives. Equity regulations stated that "an Equity member may play only in companies where every member is a member of Equity in good standing."[53] The union felt that stardom, especially, involved certain responsibilities as well as privileges. If stars had "any hand at any time in breaking down the conditions of the standard contracts they [would] be haled before the Equity Council."[54]

As the Equity policies suggest, a union-minded actor would be concerned with the treatment and fate of other actors in a show. Lovelace, however, never asks what happens to Rita Vernon. Easton has successfully divided the two actors from each other and prevented any contact that might cause them (and other performers in the show) to work together against his interests. Lovelace also does not question her own fate. After her successful debut, a seasoned actor warns her that she could become a "morning glory" ("a flower that fades before the sun is very high"), but Lovelace responds that she is not afraid of fleeting stardom. Lovelace thus accepts an ideological discourse of stardom that insists that even the most gifted artists must subordinate their talent to a producer-dominated structure of labor with no guarantee of job security or control over their image. According to a fan magazine's assessment of the situation for screen actors: "Idolatry today, Isolation Tomorrow. That's the Dangerous Paths [*sic*] of Hollywood Glory."[55]

Morning Glory represents the star system as a heartless but immutable structure in which individual artistry breeds competition among actors, and success is often determined by an actor's degree of cooperation with producers. Actors experience problems when they are unable to cope with the system, when they expect too much from it (e.g., Rita Vernon), or when events in their personal lives conflict with their professional goals. For example, when Lovelace finally falls in love with Sheridan, the playwright, she realizes that she must learn to juggle a career and a family life. The film's depiction of the difficulties encountered in the acting profession are not enough, however, to undermine the romanticization of stardom. Though Lovelace occasionally goes without food or income in her struggle to reach the top, she nonetheless becomes a star. The moral of the story appears to be that if one has talent and is dedicated enough, one will achieve one's destiny. How long one remains a star is immaterial.

Hollywood studios sent this same type of mixed signal to young hopefuls trying to enter the acting profession. Though studios discouraged young girls from the Midwest from traveling to Hollywood in hopes of landing a screen test and being discovered, the rags-to-riches narratives found repeatedly in fan magazines and films such as *42nd Street* and *Morning Glory* reinforced a discourse of stardom that seemed to place success within the reach of starry-eyed novices. A typical example is the article "Extra Girl Gets Her First Close-up!" in which writers for *The Hollywood Reporter* imagine what Jean Harlow must have been thinking before her big moment arrived:

> Suppose—oh, just suppose, it doesn't cost anything—suppose she could get a close-up today!
>
> The thought warmed her. She had summoned it into mental existence hundreds of times, just for the sake of that warming tingle which came in its wake. After all, it wasn't IMPOSSIBLE! It DOES happen to extra girls—well, not regularly but frequently enough to justify the perennial visualization of its glorious possibility.[56]

But this discourse, which was essential to a romanticized construct of the acting profession that divorced artistry from labor, and glamour from hard work, was also creating a problem of overcrowding and unemployment in Hollywood.

During the spring and summer of 1933, as the number of screen extras skyrocketed and the number of job opportunities shrank, the studios tried to do something about this problem. In one case, the Hays Office warned publicists for the Chicago World's Fair that they would be in trouble if the "Hollywood exhibit [was] found responsible for any addition to the West Coast's unemployment situation." The warning came after the Hays Office discovered that some of the Fair's publicity copy was promising "beautiful Chicago girls and handsome youths" career opportunities in Hollywood. According to the producers' association, "Unofficial screen tests and picture popularity contests, with that free ride to Hollywood, long ago were condemned by the picture industry."[57] The producers' response to the situation, however, may have had more to do with the fact that the World's Fair publicists had acted in an unauthorized capacity. For, as subsequent accounts in *Variety* indicate, the studios had not altogether ceased the practice of holding contests.

In October of 1933, the number of Hollywood potentials increased dramatically when Paramount held its "Panther Woman and Search for Beauty Contests and its much publicized hunt for an 'Alice in Wonderland.' " Problems arose because three hundred of the contest entrants decided to stick around and prove to studio officials that they should have been the winners. In addition, says *Variety*, "Metro [w]asn't help[ing] the stay-away-from-Hollywood cause much by its national tour of a mobile talent testing studio."[58] The major studios justified these measures as part of an organized drive to find new talent that could be developed into star material. They felt new faces were needed to replace the fading box office names and to alleviate the load of current box office stars, whom the studios were overworking in order to protect stories.[59]

The studios' strategy was to sign a large number of people to contracts for three to six months with options, and see if anyone panned out. They figured that "if one or two potential stars [could] be developed from the batch, it would be worth the effort."[60] The studios also revived the talent school system, which provided aspiring actors with a nominal weekly income, some on-the-job training, and, for those who were lucky enough after three months, an opportunity for bit work or feature roles.[61] Many of those who were not chosen to continue, however, remained in Hollywood and tried to get work as extras as they waited for their lucky break from some more observant director or producer. Thus, while studio practices promised to produce a star or two, they otherwise contributed to the growing unemployment situation in Hollywood.

Given the stiff competition for jobs, the opportunities for unknowns were minimal. Statistics based on actor employment figures from May 1932 to April 1933 indicated that of the 9,830 registered principal and bit players hoping to gain a steady livelihood as actors, only 1,102 (nearly a 10-to-1 ratio) had jobs during this period.[62] This ratio was much worse for extras. Of the 18,000 extras registered with the Central Casting Bureau, only an average of 550 were employed by the studios on any given day; most extras were lucky to get eleven or twelve full days of work each year.[63] The influx of new people into Hollywood's extra labor supply also made employment more difficult for existing actors, especially "old-timers" from the silents who had been let go by the majors and relegated to casual employment. In August of 1933, the Academy of Motion Pictures tried to intervene in this situation by compiling and distributing a list of old-timers who were to receive "first call for extra parts," but it could not guarantee employment for these actors.[64]

In the face of the Academy's efforts to alleviate the extra situation in Hollywood, the studios' talent searches and contests were not only wasteful of human resources, they were irresponsible and negligent. Just before the studios stepped up their talent searches, the Academy's Standing Committee on Extras released its report citing the growing unemployment and sweatshop treatment of screen extras. The findings were presented at the NRA Code hearings and formed the basis of many of the provisions protecting extras' labor in the final NRA Code. During the Academy's investigation, a number of ideas for handling or restructuring the situation also emerged. One plan required "all persons entering Hollywood with the intent of pursuing an extra career" to make their desires known immediately to the Central Casting Bureau. The Bureau would in turn refer each applicant to a "carefully selected talent picking committee." If this committee decided that the applicant demonstrated ample qualifications, he or she would be "officially awarded" the title of performer or extra.[65] This idea had the advantage of funneling people through the star system from the ground floor up and thus, like the talent schools, allowing the studios to maintain better control over the careers of emerging actors. One problem with this system, of course, is that few people came to Hollywood with the dream of becoming an extra. Most of those in the extra ranks ended up there by default, either by failing to achieve a high-ranking status or through downward mobility in the star system.

Contrary to the discourse of stardom found in films such as *Morning Glory*, talent was not necessarily the key ingredient to an actor's success. Hiring and firing decisions were rooted more firmly in economics. During this period, for example, the major studios were signing contract players at an almost unprecedented rate. During one week in September of 1933, more than two hundred actors were signed. *Variety* explained that this situation was due partly to the studios' anticipation of increased production and the need not to be caught waiting for desired players to finish out freelance engagements. The major angle, however, was "the feeling that inflation was just around the corner [and] that would mean upped salaries to meet the new conditions."[66] The recent wave of talent searches and beauty contests shared this same impetus. Though these practices were costly, both in terms of their operation and the aftereffect of unemployment, they were economically beneficial in the long run because they provided studio managers with a means by which to introduce new actors into the star system at lower salaries.

Decisions not to renew silent film actors had likewise been based less on the actors' talent than on the studios' desire to increase box office receipts—in this case, by associating new faces with a new technology. According to an article in *Screen Book*, the aesthetic and technological revolution brought on by the talking picture demanded a new standard of beauty. The old style, epitomized by the "cold immobility" of silent screen stars, was replaced by a modern standard of beauty based on inner warmth, grace of motion, and, above all, personality.[67] Accordingly, this new form of beauty generated an expressiveness and desirability that obviated the need for "talent" in its traditional sense and thus minimized the discursive role of talent in defining what the screen actor should be.

The relationship between talent and beauty nonetheless remained a slippery one that was complicated by differing discourses of stardom perpetuated in Hollywood and on Broadway. In their contests and "talent" searches, for example, the Hollywood studios tended to privilege beauty as a marketable commodity. According to *Variety*,

> It's practically a pushover to get a screen test for a girl who has looks, but for an actress who doesn't appear so hot in person or in a still picture, it remains as tough as ever.
>
> When the agent has a prospect with plenty of talent, but lacking in looks in her street appearance, he has to talk himself out of wind to get attention [from a studio].[68]

Discourses of talent had greater ties to the legitimate stage (as evidenced by *Morning Glory's* homage to the artistry of great stage actors). By the early 1930s, however, slightly more than two-thirds of the actors under contract with major studios had begun their careers on the stage.[69] This crossover encouraged the integration of star discourses at the same time it provided a form of legitimation for screen acting. Thus, although the studios may have looked initially to beauty for star material, the addition of talent legitimated and gave depth to the spectacle of beauty.

Morning Glory effectively connects these discourses of stage and screen by exploiting the star image of Katharine Hepburn. On one hand, Hepburn's image fit uneasily between the discourses of talent and beauty. According to one account, the question of how to "put Hepburn over" initially gave Hollywood press agents a headache: "She fit into no known pattern for a movie star. But she was too smart to become another glamour girl."[70] As this story implies, however, part of Hepburn's success was due to the way her image combined, yet held in tension, notions of talent and beauty. This tension was put to good use by publicists, who, by separating out different aspects of her image for different venues, could exploit the range of Hepburn's image. A publicity still for *Morning Glory*, for example, represents Hepburn as a Hollywood siren, while the film narrative accentuates her talent. The film further capitalizes on the connection between Hepburn and the character she plays. Hepburn herself had achieved some success in the theater before turning to motion pictures. The film suggests that Eva Lovelace will follow this same trend, because the play she is starring in has motion picture rights attached to it.

By foregrounding discourses of talent in its narrative, *Morning Glory* not only legitimizes the acting profession; it diverts attention away from the conditions of labor in Hollywood.

Like *42nd Street, Morning Glory* displaces its narratives of stardom onto Broadway. But it also plays down the economic and political aspects of acting by highlighting a romanticized notion of talent and personal sacrifice. The film's brief glimpses into Eva Lovelace's life as an extra, for example, suggest that it is a humiliating, but temporary, period she must endure until she gets her lucky break. The "extra" thus figures discursively as a point of origin in a personalized narrative of upward mobility that hides certain ongoing professional realities for an entire rank of performers. Like the six extras who played the parts of "actors looking for work" during the coffee shop scene of *Morning Glory*, most of these performers remain nameless, receiving no acknowledgment of their work in the film credits. Their history in the acting profession is a fragmented, discontinuous (and often anonymous) narrative that leads nowhere, leaving behind only an accumulation of facts and anecdotes regarding extras' working conditions.

According to the report submitted by the Academy's Standing Committee on Extras, there appeared to be an unwritten policy "to keep wages down to the lowest level and to take advantage of the distress of unemployed players."[71] During the Depression, wages for extras had gone down an average of 20 percent. Whereas an average call netted $9.00 in 1930, it was reduced to $7.48 in 1932, and, by 1933, wages of $2.00 were not unheard of. Many formerly well known actors were working as extras for $3.00 per call.[72] Wages for extras varied also because the roles for extras were not categorized in any consistent manner. An extra named Hugh Lester became so confused by this situation that he wrote a letter to the Screen Actors Guild magazine, *The Screen Player*.

> How come I only get seven-five-oh for being a ship's steward, and a lot of other guys get ten for bein' ship's officers? My uniform was just as snappy as theirs was, and God knows I worked just as hard. . . .
>
> A couple of weeks ago, I worked for Paramount. I was a spectator at a night club, in good-looking summer street clothes (Macintosh, forty bucks). My check was for seven-five-oh. Some mugg made a holler and we got a two-fifty adjustment. Now, that was fine, but about four days later I was a pedestrian in the same good-looking summer street clothes and only got a five for my trouble. It was a lot easier bein' a spectator at a night club, even if the floor show was lousy, than it was bein' a pedestrian. How come a spectator rates higher than a pedestrian?
>
> Here's something else I want to know. Why did I get fifteen bucks for bein' a waiter, and four other guys only got seven-five-oh? They made a squawk, but it didn't get them anywhere. I kept my mouth closed, as I figured maybe someone made a mistake and gave me the fifteen thinkin' I was twins.[73]

Production notes for *Morning Glory* indicate this same variance in wages. In one scene, for example, the nine atmosphere players received anywhere between $10.00 and $35.00. Extras playing pedestrians received $7.50 for the day while "actors looking for work" received only $5.00. Actors used for two scenes—a day scene requiring "smart winter clothes" and a night scene requiring "full formal evening dress"—received $10.00. Yet other actors who were used for only one scene requiring formal evening dress received between $10.00 and $25.00.

Extras in Hollywood were subject to a number of abuses as well. In one case, a director "forced an extra player to turn his back to the camera while the director spoke lines into the mike that should have been said by the extra player."[74] By doing so he saved his studio the difference between $7.50 and $25.00. In another case, extras hired to play a crowd scene were asked to wear a hat and topcoat and to bring along a second pair of these items. When they arrived on the set they were ordered to put the extra clothing on dummies to help fill the background. No additional wages were given for these efforts.[75] By 1935 the Screen Actors Guild was so distressed by the treatment of extras that it ran a feature in its magazine titled "Are Extras People?" The story recounts some rather serious physical abuse of extras:

> Forty women received the call to report at 5:30 P.M. to the set for "Riff Raff" which J. Walter Ruben was directing for Metro-Goldwyn-Mayer. The call from Central Casting Corp. had specified "light rain." . . . The set worked twelve hours until 5:30 A.M., and each woman received a check-and-a-half—$11.25. Lunch was not called until twelve midnight—six-and-one-half hours after the extras reported to the set.
>
> A few minutes after 10:00 P.M., the women were ordered into the rain for the first time. The set was equipped with overhead sprinklers, three fire hoses, and three wind machines. The latter created such a terrific gale that a number of women were forcibly knocked down and bruised in each take. One woman was knocked unconscious while another who took the full force of the stream of water from the hose on her back, was paralyzed from her hips down for several hours. Four women were temporarily blinded when the water hit them full force in the eyes.[76]

According to the SAG, no law prevented such abuse of actors. Although the California law restricting the employment of women to eight hours a day might have otherwise averted the foregoing situation, studios found loopholes that allowed them to sidestep the law. A portion of the Industrial Welfare Commission Order No. 16-A stated:

> No employer shall employ or suffer or permit any woman extra receiving a wage of $15.00 or under per day or a wage of $65.00 or under per week to be employed more than eight hours in any one day of twenty-four hours, except that *in the case of emergency* women may be employed in excess of eight hours.[77]

Studios sidestepped the financial provision of the law by paying just over the legal limit; a common wage for chorus girls, for example, was $66.00 per week. They also manipulated the provision that allowed for extras to work overtime. According to the SAG, the problem with Order No. 16-A arose because it did not define the term "emergency." Thus, when studios were running behind schedule on their film production, they simply called an emergency. During a ten-month period in 1935, the Guild learned that there had been an "emergency" almost every day at one or more of the major studios, causing anywhere between five women extras and two hundred women extras to work from two to eight hours overtime (see Table 3.1).

The SAG had been researching and monitoring the working conditions of actors since its inception, but it was often the job of actors on the set to police the day-to-day actions of producers. Aside from demanding overtime pay and comparable wages for comparable work, extras balked against the use of nonprofessional actors for extra roles. During the filming of *College Holiday* in Santa Barbara, for example, a group of women extras put a stop to the hiring of rich debutantes who wanted the "thrill" of working in pictures: "Get rid of those society girls and give those jobs to legitimate extras, or we'll walk out—and every star in the cast goes with us!" they warned.[78] Since their demand was backed by Jack Benny, George Burns, and Gracie Allen, the studios relented and replaced the local thrill seekers with professionals.

Much of the available information concerning abuses of actors (especially extras) was recorded after 1933—after the formation of the Screen Actors Guild and after the passage of

Table 3.1 Women extras overtime on major studio sets (January 1, 1935, to October 15, 1935)

Studio	*No. cases*	*¼ checks*	*½ checks*	*¾ checks*	*Full checks*	*No. directors*
Columbia Pictures Corp.	12	8	4	. . .	. . .	6
Fox Film Corp. Studio[a]	40	21	14	4	[b]	13
Metro-Goldwyn-Mayer Studio	49	41	3	5	. . .	18
Paramount Studio	28	17	10	1	. . .	10
RKO-Radio Pictures Studio	49	29	10	3	[c, d]	20
United Artists Studio[e]	11	7	1	2	1	4
Universal Studios	16	13	. . .	2	. . .	6
Warner Bros.-First National Studio	50	33	12	3	2	15

[a] Includes one Twentieth Century-Fox.
[b] For 17 hours, extras received one ¾ check. Another ¼ check was received by each woman, as an adjustment.
[c] Eighty-five women forced to remain on the set for 17 hours.
[d] Under director Stevens for six days from September 9 to September 14, extras received from ¼ to ¾ checks every day.
[e] Includes Samuel Goldwyn, Inc., Edward Small Productions, and Twentieth Century Pictures.
The above figures are based on fewer than 12 women members of the Junior Guild.

the movie industry's NRA Code of Fair Competition. NRA labor policies, in other words, did not prevent abuses from occurring. Studios violated these policies whenever it suited them, and, until 1935, they even ignored the Guild's legal right to represent actors in collective bargaining situations. In their hands the NRA thus became a discursive tool that effectively shielded the public from these facts. The studios' goodwill advertising, propaganda films, and overall public relations efforts created an image of industrial unity and national concern. The feature-length entertainment films additionally provided studios with a means to rewrite labor–management conflict in Hollywood *(42nd Street)* or to foreground discourses of stardom that diverted attention away from such conflict *(Morning Glory).*

Morning Glory achieved widespread popularity, grossing $65,000 in only the first four days of its release.[79] Audience attention was focused especially on Katharine Hepburn, a rising star at RKO who would later win the Academy Award for best actress for her portrayal of Eva Lovelace. It is perhaps fitting that in the most tumultuous year of actor–producer relations in Hollywood's history, the Academy would present one of its prestigious awards to someone for her portrayal of an actor who characterized the discourse of entertainment and ideology of stardom that was so profitable to studio management. Although there were members within the Academy who were concerned about protecting actors through such means as the Standing Committee on Extras, the Academy was still an organization that was controlled by producers and that functioned as a powerful discursive machine on their behalf. As tokens of the movie industry's appreciation of film excellence, the Academy Awards seem harmless enough. But they stand as a symbolic gesture of the producers' vested interest in diverting our attention away from the struggles that have constituted the institution of stardom.

Notes

1 Richard Johnson, "What Is Cultural Studies Anyway?" *Social Text* 6.1 (1987): 62.
2 Tom Gunning, "Film History and Film Analysis: The Individual Film in the Course of Time," *Wide Angle* 12.3 (1990): 6.

3 Ibid., 14.
4 Karl Marx, *Capital*, vol. 1, trans. Ben Fowkes (New York: Vintage, 1977): 130.
5 Martyn J. Lee, *Consumer Culture Reborn* (London: Routledge, 1993): 119.
* This refers to Danae Clark, *Negotiating Hollywood: The Cultural Politics of Actors' Labor* (Minnesota: University of Minnesota Press, 1995).
6 Tony Bennett and Janet Woollacott, *Bond and Beyond* (London: Macmillan, 1987): 189.
7 Stuart Ewen, *Captains of Consciousness* (New York: McGraw-Hill, 1976): 100.
8 "Studio Prod. Is 75% Normal," *Variety* (1 August 1933): 5.
9 "Want to Be First for Roosevelt," *Variety* (25 June 1933): 7.
10 This Warner Bros. advertisement appeared in *Variety* (21 March 1933): 15.
11 This MGM advertisement appeared in *Variety* (3 October 1933): 28.
12 "Strike Unions Squawk to President," *Variety* (1 August 1933): 5.
13 "Unpatriotic to Pay for Meals, Overtime," *Variety* (8 August 1933): 1. See also, "Up for Extras," *Variety* (2 May 1933): 2; Eric L. Ergenbright, "All Over the Hollywood Lot," *Screen Book* (December 1933): 28.
14 "Harry Warner as NIRA Propagandist," *Variety* (1 August 1933): 5.
15 "Warner's Semi-official 'New Deal' NRA Short," *Variety* (1 August 1933): 1.
16 "64,000 Showings per NRA Short Scheduled," *Variety* (29 August 1933): 3.
17 "Eight NRA Films Made; One Release a Week," *Motion Picture Herald* (16 September 1933): 22.
18 "250,000 March under the Blue Eagle in the City's Greatest Demonstration," *New York Times* (14 September 1933): 3.
19 Motion Picture Producers and Distributors Association Annual Report (11 April 1932): 24.
20 "Eight NRA Films Made," 22.
21 "Film Shorts for NRA Shown," *Variety* (5 September 1933): 4.
22 "Femme Film Workers Protest to Legislature against 8-Hr. Day," *Variety* (2 May 1933): 2.
23 "No Blue Eagle Blues," *Variety* (29 August 1933): 2.
24 "Film Shorts for NRA Shown," 4. *The New Deal*, the original title proposed by Warner Bros., did not become part of this NRA series.
25 Andrew Bergman, *We're in the Money* (New York: Harper & Row, 1971): 64.
26 For example, see John Belton, "The Backstage Musical," *Movie* 24 (1977): 36–43; Bergman, *We're in the Money*; Rocco Fumento, "Those Berkeley and Astaire-Rogers Depression Musicals: Two Different Worlds," *American Classic Screen* 5.4 (1981): 15–18; Mark Roth, "Some Warners Musicals and the Spirit of the New Deal," in *Genre: The Musical*, ed. Rick Altman (London: Routledge & Kegan Paul, 1981): 41–56. For a feminist analysis, see Paula Rabinowitz, "Commodity Fetishism: Women in *Gold Diggers of 1933*," *Film Reader* 5 (1982): 141–49.
27 Roth, "Some Warners Musicals," 45.
28 "WB Sets High Figure for '42nd St.' if RKO Wants Special Train Angle," *Variety* (14 February 1933): 7.
29 Ibid.
30 Charles Eckert, "The Carole Lombard in Macy's Window," *Quarterly Review of Film Studies* 3.1 (1978): 3.
31 "WB Sets High Figure," 7.
32 Rocco Fumento, ed., "Introduction: From Bastards and Bitches to Heros and Heroines," in *42nd Street*. Wisconsin/Warner Bros. Screenplay Series (Madison: University of Wisconsin Press, 1980): 35.
33 Warner Bros. Archives, press kit, University of Southern California, Los Angeles.
34 "Ruby Keeler Would Dance, Not Hand Out S. A. in WB's 'Footlight Parade,' " *Variety* (25 July 1933): 2.
35 Warner Bros. Archives, memo from R. J. Obringer to Mr. Sully (18 February 1933).
36 Contract of Virginia Dabney (18 February 1933).
37 Warner Bros. Archives, press kit.
38 Contract of Ginger Rogers (15 September 1932).
39 "The Guild's Heritage," Screen Actors Guild pamphlet, n.d.
40 "Chorus Girls Toil 86 Hours for $25 Week, Hearing Told," *Motion Picture Herald* (16 September 1933): 21. Also see "Are Extras People?" *Screen Guilds' Magazine* (November 1935): 25.
41 "Chorus Girls Toil 86 Hours," 21.
42 Roth, "Some Warners Musicals," 45.
43 Warner Bros. Archives, letter from Guy B. Kibbee to Warner Bros. Pictures, Inc., n.d.
44 Warner Bros. Archives, letter from Warner Bros. Pictures, Inc., to Guy Kibbee (15 April 1933). Although the two letters obviously refer to the same contract, Kibbee dates the contract March 16, 1931 and Warners dates it May 16, 1931.

45 Thomas Schatz, " 'A Triumph of Bitchery': Warner Bros., Bette Davis and *Jezebel," Wide Angle* 10.1 (1988): 18.

46 Warner Bros. Archives, press kit.

47 Warner Bros. Archives, letter from Frank Joyce to Jack Warner (11 February 1932).

48 Warner Bros. Archives, affidavit re: Bebe Daniels (21 April 1932).

49 Warner Bros. Archives, letter from Warner Bros. Pictures, Inc., to Fox Film Corporation; Metro-Goldwyn-Mayer Corp.; RKO Studios, Inc.; Columbia Pictures, Corp.; United Artists Studios; Universal Pictures Corporation; Samuel Goldwyn Inc. Ltd.; Paramount Productions, Inc.; Tiffany Productions of Calif. Ind. Ltd.; Mr. Fred Beetson, Assn. of Motion Picture Producers (30 October 1933).

50 See "Zanuck's Raiding Mess," *Variety* (13 June 1933): 5, 43; "Harry Warner Says Battle Is Now On," *Variety* (27 June 1933): 5.

51 Jane Feuer, "The Self-Reflective Musical and the Myth of Entertainment," in *Genre: The Musical*, ed. Rick Altman, 159, 162.

52 Alvin H. Marill, *Katharine Hepburn* (New York: Galahad, 1973): 26.

53 "Dos and Don'ts for Equity Members," *Equity* (June 1933): 19.

54 "Stars Have Responsibilities as well as Privileges," *Equity* (May 1933): 18.

55 Lew Garvey, "Fleeting Fame," *Screen Book* (November 1933): 30.

56 Tichi Wilkerson and Marcia Borie, "Extra Girl Gets Her First Close-up," *The Hollywood Reporter: The Golden Years* (New York: Coward-McCann, 1984): 61.

57 "Unemployment Fear from H'Wood-at-Fair," *Variety* (23 May 1933): 6.

58 "Peeved Beaut Contest Losers Storm H'wood with Gate-Crashing Wiles," *Variety* (3 October 1933): 3.

59 "Hungry Need for New Film Faces, Every Studio on Talent Hunt," *Variety* (10 October 1933): 3; "Talent Famine, and No Kiddin'," *Variety* (5 December 1933): 1.

60 "Studios Revive School System," *Variety* (10 October 1933): 3.

61 "Actors' Chances Put at 10 to 1," *Variety* (9 May 1933): 7.

62 "Coast Bums Not 'Extras,' " *Variety* (15 August 1933): 3.

63 Ibid.

64 "Oldtimers Topping Studios' 1st Call List," *Variety* (1 August 1933): 1.

65 "Coast Bums Not 'Extras,' " 3.

66 "Sign over 200 Pic Players, Inflation?" *Variety* (19 September 1933): 2.

67 Jay B. Chapman, "Hollywood's New Beauty Standards," *Screen Book* (August 1933): 11–13.

68 "Looks, Not Talent, Still Gets Tests," *Variety* (26 September 1933): 2.

69 "Footlite Talent Tops Active List," *Variety* (19 September 1933): 1.

70 Constance McCormick Collection, University of Southern California, Los Angeles.

71 "Sweat Shop Charge of Penny-Ante Pay Takes Extras' Plight to Code," *Variety* (12 September 1933): 7.

72 Ibid.

73 "The Letter Box," *Screen Player* (June 1934): 20–21.

74 "A Jeer," *Screen Player* (June 1934): 13.

75 "Cheers and Jeers," *Screen Player* (March 1934): 7.

76 "Are Extras People?" *Screen Guilds' Magazine* (November 1935): 3.

77 Ibid.

78 "Shop Talk," *Screen Guilds' Magazine* (October 1936): 3.

79 This information is taken from a *Morning Glory* advertisement, *Variety* (22 August 1933): 32.

PART II

Technology

Chapter 4

Charles Barr

CINEMASCOPE: BEFORE AND AFTER (1963)

Editors' Introduction

For decades, film practitioners had written about technology in professional journals, for an audience of their colleagues. During the same period, however, from the 1910s until the early 1960s, technology studies seemed less well adapted to the prevailing sociological and aesthetic interests of most film scholars. Charles Barr's 1963 essay helps mark the arrival of technology studies to film studies, and signals the importance of producing theories and histories of film technology. Barr explains the various widescreen formats, and in particular CinemaScope, but with an eye towards placing new aspect ratios within debates about film aesthetics, and in particular the preferred uses of the film frame. Barr establishes a different historical model for considering cinema, as he moves away from the typical silent/sound dichotomy while proposing a new one, pre- and post-widescreen. But Barr's writing is also fully entrenched in its own historical moment. As a result, he emphasizes the literary equivalents to widescreen – in Nabokov or Hardy or other great novelists. Moreover the figures who seem to preside over the entire argument are Sergei Eisenstein and André Bazin, both so important to film theorists in the 1960s. They represent opposite ends of the spectrum in terms of the plasticity of the image and concerns over cinematic realism, with Barr firmly in the Bazin camp, and so aligning widescreen formats with Bazin's aesthetic preferences. Barr's concerns here form a link to the nuts and bolts considerations of technology of previous decades, and so much work from the last 25 years on the coming of recorded sound to cinema, and John Belton's scholarship on Barr's subject, the impact of widescreen on film form, film narrative, and film viewing.

Suggested Reading

Kenneth MacGowan, "The Wide Screen of Yesterday and Tomorrow," *The Quarterly Review of Film Radio and Television*, 11:3 (Spring 1957), pp. 217–41; John Belton, *Widescreen Cinema* (Harvard University Press, 1992).

"Imagine Lauren Bacall on a couch—and 64 feet long!" a producer was reported to have crowed, upon the introduction of CinemaScope. Since then, CinemaScope and its widescreen relatives have received an almost uniformly bad press, from critics, directors, and cameramen alike. Yet year by year more films are made in wide screen. It has seemed time, therefore, for a considerable reassessment. One of the valuable contributions of the new generation of English critics (in "Movie" and in "Motion," where an early version of this article appeared) has been their recognition of the special potentialities of the larger formats. No one, however, has previously related these to questions of playing and cutting style, and to general questions of film conception and method, with the thoroughness, precision, and suggestiveness demanded by the important issues at stake.

CINEMASCOPE WAS INTRODUCED BY 20th Century-Fox in 1953. It confused a lot of people, and has continued to do so. It was assumed that its value was purely a sensational one, that it was self-evidently "inartistic," and that once the novelty wore off the companies would be forced to drop it as abruptly as they had dropped 3-D, Hollywood's previous answer to the Television Menace. A decade later, however, the CinemaScope revolution is a fait accompli. Not only are a large proportion of Hollywood films in CinemaScope or similar processes, but other countries too make Scope films in increasing numbers. Most theaters have been adapted for Scope projection without changing the old pattern of exhibition, as it had been forecast they would have to. CinemaScope scarcely makes an impact any longer for its own sake: most of the really big pictures today are made on 70mm film or in Cinerama. It is even possible now to be disappointed when a blockbuster (*The Guns of Navarone, The Longest Day*) is "only" in CinemaScope.

I will assume that the technical details are familiar.[1] Since Fox hold the rights to CinemaScope itself, other companies have preferred to develop their own variants, some of which use different methods, and are arguably superior, but which are similar in essentials, with an aspect ratio (height to width) of 1:2.35. All of these can be classed together, as indeed they usually are, as "CinemaScope" or just as "Scope."

CinemaScope has had a more general, indirect influence: although non-Scope productions still use 35mm nonanamorphic film, very few of them are still designed for projection in the old 1:1.33 ratio. Instead, the top and bottom are masked off, and the image thrown over a wider area. This ratio is, it seems, becoming settled at 1:1.85. Thus all films, with the occasional foreign-language exception, are now widescreen films; this format will clearly share, in a minor way, some of the characteristics of CinemaScope, and normally when I talk of the effects of the "CinemaScope" ratio this can be taken to mean something like "Scope; and even more so the 70mm systems; and to a lesser extent the wide screen."

The commercial survival of CinemaScope has disconcerted critics, especially English-speaking ones. So far as I can see, all of them had condemned it from the start as a medium for anything other than the spectacular and the trivial. Its shape was apparently wrong for "serious" or "intimate" drama, for the kind of film and the kind of effects which a sensitive director aims at. Now CinemaScope was, obviously, a commercial innovation designed purely to save the finances of Fox, whose executives were evasive and hypocritical in their pretense that they were doing this for Art's sake. Most of the early Scope films were indeed crude. Fox was enlightened neither in choice of subjects nor of directors: among those who made the first of these films were Koster, Dunne, Johnson, Dmytryk, and Negulesco. However, since then a great number of serious and/or intimate films have been made in Scope, too many to catalogue, and too many for it to be worth remarking on any longer, when each comes out. The early ones included *A Star Is Born* (Cukor), *East of Eden* (Kazan) and

River of No Return (Preminger); then, among others, all Truffaut's features; *La Dolce Vita, The Island, Trials of Oscar Wilde, Lola, Lola Montes, Rebel Without a Cause, Bitter Victory, Tarnished Angels, Man of the West, The Tall Men, Some Came Running, The Courtship of Eddie's Father* . . . not forgetting *L'Année Dernière à Marienbad* and, on 70mm film, *Lawrence of Arabia* and *Exodus*.

The cycle of events has been very close to that which followed the introduction of sound. That too was a commercial move, designed to save Warner Brothers, and it led to a comparable, temporary chaos. Most commentators were misled into thinking that sound must be in itself inartistic, and a betrayal of "pure" cinema, but gradually it became accepted as a useful development, and one could say that Scope too is coming, tacitly, to be accepted, because there is really no alternative. In *Sight and Sound*, Autumn, 1961, editor Penelope Houston confesses in a coy parenthesis, "How many of us, for instance, would hold to the views we first expressed about CinemaScope?" The fact remains that few critics have made more than a token change of view, or show any sign of having learnt from their miscalculation; it is this after all that matters, and not the result of a counting of heads, which might perhaps reveal that CinemaScope, after being outlawed for ten years like a nationalist leader in Africa, has finally been recognized at Headquarters.

The point is this: the rejection of CinemaScope was, and is, based on certain familiar, but in fact highly disputable, assumptions, the fundamental one being that the film image consists of a *frame* into which a number of things are successively *fitted*, and that a film is made by sticking such images together in a creative way. The old 1:1.33 ratio screen was compatible with this aesthetic, and the CinemaScope screen is not, but instead of considering afresh whether these preconceptions were valid the critics simply used them to make an a priori condemnation of a format which is, one admits, manifestly unsuitable for "framing" things.

One can call this the "traditional" aesthetic: it is the one which is found in books. It puts the emphasis on framing, the close-up, camera angles, and montage. Montage is only the French word for editing, and is clearly indispensable to any director; the difference is that here this stage is made into the crucial one in a process which consists of selecting details and "showing them one by one" (Pudovkin in *Film Technique*).

I believe this aesthetic was always misguided, at least in the dogmatic form in which it was applied, and that the most valuable and forward-looking films at any time have been made to some extent outside it. Ideally, Scope could have been the occasion for its ceremonial abandonment. It was no longer workable, but then it was no longer necessary. It is a

Figure 4.1 Early CinemaScope: *East of Eden*. (The still is printed in full CinemaScope proportions.)

hangover from the silent cinema, but people still try to muddle through using it as an implicit basis for their judgment even of Scope films: it is not surprising if they can't cope. You still get films evaluated according to whether the "set-ups" are "imaginative" or not, and a film which uses long takes and few close-ups is liable to be dismissed automatically as unfilmic or as visually dull. Any summary of the development of style is bound to be schematic, but if one bears in mind that there can be no clear-cut division between sound and silent, and between post- and pre-Scope, I think it is useful to go back and estimate how this "traditional" aesthetic was established, and became ingrained.

There were four main factors:

(1) The image was narrow and unaccompanied by sound; it was therefore difficult to make a full impact within a single shot, and without cutting. Naturally, this objection applies less and less after the introduction of, in turn, the moving camera, sound, composition in depth, and CinemaScope.

The film was a new and bewildering medium; this aesthetic made it easy to assimilate to the pattern of other arts, notably painting and literature:

(2) It played down the film's basis in "reality," which was felt to be incompatible with art.

(3) It took the shot as a "unit," like the ideogram or the word: this made it more easily manageable and gave it the prestige of a "language" of its own.[2]

Finally, (4) it was formulated and applied chiefly by certain Russian directors; theirs is one kind of film, and of temperament, which it really suits.

These points merge into one another, and need to be elaborated more fully.

The first films were straightforward records of everyday reality. As such, they gave audiences a big thrill. Lumière set up his camera to take a scene in a single, static shot: workers leaving a factory, a train entering a station, a family eating out of doors, etc. The spectators' first instinct was to scramble out of the way of the approaching train, and in the background of the shot of the family eating *(Bébé Mange sa Soupe)* they noticed the detail of leaves blowing in the wind, and called out excitedly.

However, once the novelty of such shots wore off, it became apparent that the impact of a single image was limited. You do not, in fact, get a very strong sense of actuality from a narrow, silent image; it is too much of an abstraction, the picture too remote. For the same reason, there is not much scope for the integration of background detail. It was difficult to cover a scene of any complexity, as film-makers discovered when they began to extend their range and to tell stories. Few of them thought to move the camera, or to move and group people with any precision, within the frame. The usual solution would be to photograph the action in long shot, in order to get it all in, or to huddle actors and décor unrealistically close together. Then came montage, and the close-up, and this was of course a great advance. But although Griffith is associated with their development, he was already very skillful in controlling, when appropriate, all the elements of a scene within the same shot; indeed, the most striking thing today about *Birth of a Nation* is the number of scenes which are played in a remarkably modern, integral style (for instance: the scenes in the hospital; at the Camerons' home; in Lincoln's office). To judge from the few films of his that I have seen, and particularly *The Coward* (1915), Thomas Ince was working in the same way.

Meanwhile, however, pundits had decided that the film could not be art if it confined itself to recording "reality," and they extended this to mean that an uncut piece of film was nothing, that montage was all. Now "reality" is a word which has to be handled carefully. Nabokov nicely describes it as "one of the few words which mean nothing without quotes."

Both the still and the movie camera make a record of "reality" in the sense that they record, objectively, what is put in front of them. As Helmut Gernsheim (*Creative Photography*, 1960) expresses it: "The camera intercepts images, the paintbrush reconstructs them." This

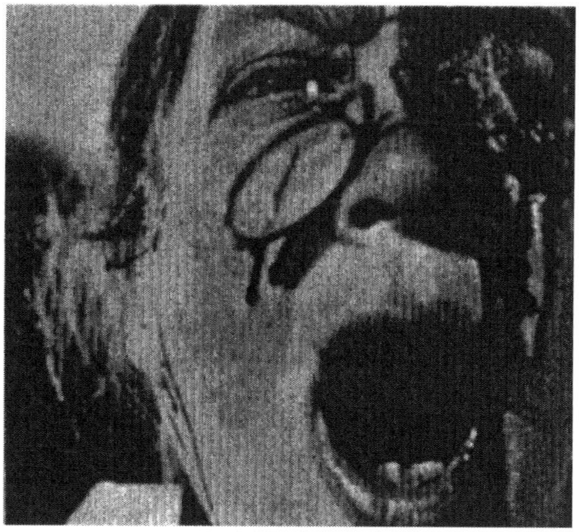

Figure 4.2 The old format: an isolated close-up filling the entire screen

worried theorists from the start. No other art presented this problem, and no other art, furthermore, had ever been suddenly invented like this, rootless, instead of evolving slowly, and evolving a function as it did so. A decision had to be made. One interpretation was this: the camera records reality, but reality is not art, therefore photography cannot be art. And later: the cinema cannot be art. The second interpretation arises from this and is complementary to it: agreed, reality is not art, but we improve upon it by treating it in a creative way. In practice, this meant getting as far away as possible from objectivity, and it produced, in the first decades of photography, some quite ludicrous results, prints being posed and processed and stuck together in a form of "montage" in such a way as to be indistinguishable from painting. The "masterpieces" of this art look grotesque today, and I think warn us against dismissing as irrelevant the objective basis of the cinema. Gernsheim (*op. cit.*) puts this phase into perspective: "The mistaken ambition to compete with painting drove a minority to artificial picture-making alien to the nature of photography . . . to appreciate photography requires above all understanding of the qualities and limitations peculiar to it."

This is what André Bazin—the Gernsheim of the cinema—means when he says "Les virtualités esthétiques de la photographie résident dans la révélation du réel." In this essay[3] Bazin makes a far more useful analysis of the nature of film and its implications for film style, than Kracauer does in the whole of his book.

The film image is taken direct from "reality" and the spectator perceives and "recognizes" it direct; there is no intermediate process as there is when the writer "translates" his material into words which are in turn translated back by the imagination of the reader. This is a major difference which conditions the whole of the respective media, and the attempt to draw literal analogies between the two (for instance between the word and the shot) is as much of a dead end as the attempt to assimilate photography to the rules of painting.

However, to say that the camera records "reality" is not to advocate that the cinema should remain at the level of Lumière. The experience of seeing even a film like *Exodus*, which is about the furthest the cinema has gone in the direction of "reality"—70mm film, long static takes, complete surface authenticity—is not something we get each day when we go out into the street. It is *a* reality, organized by the director; and in any case a record of reality is not the same thing as reality itself. The director selects or stages his "reality," and photographs it; we perceive the image, on the screen, in the course of the film. This process *in itself* means that the experience belongs to the "imaginative" as opposed to the "actual" life to use the categories distinguished by the art critic Roger Fry (*An Essay in Aesthetics*, 1909). Fry was talking about differences in our perception of life and of paintings, but the distinction applies equally to film, and he did in fact cite the examples of the elementary newsreel-type films of his time to illustrate how even a "transparent" recording of an everyday scene was perceived in a radically different way from actuality. This distinction, which is basic to our responses to any art, is summed up thus by I. A. Richards (*Principles of Literary Criticism*): "In ordinary life a thousand considerations prohibit for most of us any complete working-out of our response; the range and complexity of the impulse-systems involved is less; the need for action, the comparative uncertainty and vagueness of the situation, the intrusion of accidental irrelevancies, inconvenient temporal spacing—the action being too slow or too fast—all these obscure the issue and prevent the full development of the experience. But in the "imaginative experience" these obstacles are removed. . . . As a chemist's balance to a grocer's scales, so is the mind in the imaginative moment to the mind engaged in ordinary intercourse or in practical affairs."

The crucial point is that in the cinema this distinction operates *before* the montage stage, and independently of it.

Art does indeed involve organization, but this is just as possible within a complex image as in a montage sequence: it can in many ways be more subtle. I will analyze these possibilities more specifically later on. For a number of reasons, as I say, they had not been explored very fully in the early days of the cinema. The cutting together of separate shots is a more obviously "creative" method, and a more straightforward one.

Even if it's true, as I think it is, that those who first imagined and developed the cinematograph thought in terms of a *total* illusion, with sound, color and depth[4] and that the restricted form it temporarily took was in this sense accidental, it is still possible to see the history of the cinema as a nicely arranged series of advances, each one coming when directors, and audiences, were ready for it. First they learned to cope with the camera alone, then gradually with more and more of the ingredients of reality: they could hardly have controlled all of them at once, from the start, without practice or precedent, any more than primitive musicians would have been able to cope immediately with a symphony orchestra—or audiences to respond to it. The greater density of the sound-Scope-color image requires a more precise control than the simple "unit" image does. One has to ascend by stages. The idea of predetermined advance should not be applied too rigidly, for the immediate instrument of each advance has after all been financial pressure, and Warners' crisis, and therefore their introduction of the sound film, could have come a few years earlier or later; similarly with Fox and the introduction of CinemaScope. But this does not make the whole thing fortuitous, as Macgowan seems to imply when he says that we might easily have had Todd-AO thirty years ago, at the same time as sound, only support was withheld. The cinema evolves by a form of Natural Selection: technicians and financiers provide the "mutations," and their survival depends upon whether they can be usefully assimilated at the time.

Often when "use of CinemaScope" is picked out by a critic it indicates an obtrusive style, with the director striving to "compensate" for the openness of the frame, or indulging in flashy compositional effects—as in, say, Kurosawa's *The Hidden Fortress*, or *Vera-Cruz*, the first half-hour of which Robert Aldrich makes into an absolute orgy of formalism, composing frames within frames, and blocking up the sides of the image with rocks, trees, etc. In general, what they say about the camera makes a good working rule for Scope: if you notice it, it's bad. Or, more reasonably: you don't have to notice it for it to be good. This is not to forbid the critic the phrase "use of Scope," which may be useful to avoid periphrasis, provided that it's not made into a criterion in itself, unrelated to the work as a whole.

In their book *Hitchcock*, Chabrol and Rohmer mention that in CinemaScope "the extreme edges of the screen are virtually unusable": that the edges are by no means useless, but that they will not be used for the placing of details meaningful for their own sake.

While the chief advantage of Scope is, as they maintain, its opening-up of the frame, the greater sense it gives us of a continuous space—and this is where it relates to the film they are discussing here, namely *Rope*—this is a slight over-simplification. Sometimes people can be placed at the extreme edges for perfectly legitimate effect: as in *The Tall Men* (Walsh, 1955): Jane Russell and Clark Gable play a long, intimate scene together; it ends in a fight, and they retire sulking to opposite corners of the room—and of the Scope frame, leaving a great gulf between them. A different effect: near the end of *The True Story of Jesse James* (Nicholas Ray, 1957) Jesse decides to retire: he goes out into the garden to play with his children: a green and white image, Jesse on the right: a man walks past, glimpsed on the extreme left of the frame, and calls out a greeting: the strong "horizontal" effect here reinforces the feeling of a new freedom. In *Spartacus* Kubrick uses a similar technique for the shots of Crassus and his entourage visiting the training camp; the contrast between this openness and the cooped-up images showing the gladiators' existence helps express the general contrast between luxury and oppression.

But it is not only the horizontal line which is emphasized in CinemaScope (this was implied by critics who concentrated on the *shape* of the frame qua shape—as though it were the frame of a painting—and concluded that the format was suitable only for showing/ framing horizontal things like crocodiles and processions). The more open the frame, the greater the impression of depth: the image is more vivid, and involves us more directly. The most striking effect in Cinerama is the roller-coaster shot, which gives us a very strong sensation of movement forward. Even though at the crucial moment we may be focussing only on the very center of the image, i.e., the area of track directly in front of the roller-coaster—an area, in fact, no larger than the standard frame—the rest of the image is not useless. We may not be conscious of what exactly is there, but we are marginally aware of the objects and the space on either side. It is this peripheral vision which orients us and makes the experience so vivid. Similar effects were tried in the early films in Todd-AO (roller-coaster; train ride) and CinemaScope (the shots from the nose of the plane in *How to Marry a Millionaire*). In Scope the involvement is less strong, but it is still considerable: so are its implications. Although the

Figure 4.3 Relationships within the CinemaScope image: a scene from Kazan's *Wild River*

shots quoted aim at nothing more than a circus effect, *physical* sensation of this kind can be dramatically useful (elementary form-and-content). This power was there even in the 1:1.33 image, but for the most part (after Lumière's train) remained latent. But there are classic examples of movement in this plane in Renoir's *Partie de Campagne*: the long-held shot at the end, taken from the stern of the boat being rowed home; rain on the water: an overwhelming sense of nostalgia conveyed by the movement. And in Wyler's *The Best Years of Our Lives*, the shots from the nose of the plane in which the three servicemen are returning home. The movement gives us a direct insight into their sensations and through this into "what it is like" generally for them.

Scope automatically gives images like these more "weight," and it also of course enhances the effect of lateral movement.

In *Rebel Without a Cause* (Ray, 1956) a shot of extraordinary beauty comes after the first twenty minutes of the film, during which the surroundings have been uniformly cramped and depressing, the images physically cluttered-up and dominated by blacks and browns. Now, James Dean is about to set out for school; he looks out of the window. He recognizes a girl (Natalie Wood) walking past in the distance. Cut to the first day/exterior shot, the first bright one, the first "horizontal" one. A close shot of Natalie Wood, in a light-green cardigan, against a background of green bushes. As she walks the camera moves laterally with her. This makes a direct, sensual impression which gives us an insight into Dean's experience, while at the same time remaining completely natural and unforced. On the small screen, such an image could not conceivably have had a comparable weight.

One of the climaxes of *Jesse James* is Jesse's revenge killing of a farmer. This is important to the story because it ruins Jesse's chance of an amnesty, and it is equally important to the understanding of his character in that it illustrates his pride, and his thoughtlessness. The crucial shot here has the farmer ploughing his land. Jesse rides up behind him, stops, and lifts his rifle. The man starts to run but Jesse keeps with him. The camera tracks back with them holding this composition—the farmer in the foreground, running into camera, Jesse inexorably behind, aiming—until finally Jesse shoots him dead. This is over in a moment but has a hypnotic, almost a slow-motion impact, which again is the result of the greater physical involvement achieved by Scope, its more vivid sense of space. The impact is direct, and there is no need to emphasize it by putting it into literal slow-motion, or making a significant "pattern."

Rudolf Arnheim, in *Film as Art*, claims that any such sensation of depth will be undesirable: compositional patterns which in the more abstract image would come across as being deliberate will, if the image is more vivid, seem natural, even accidental, so that the spectator may fail to note their symbolic force.[5]

From this point of view, an even more relevant Scope scene is this one from *River of No Return*, analyzed by V. F. Perkins in *Movie* 2. I think the narrative is clear enough from his description:

"As Harry lifts Kay from the raft, she drops the bundle which contains most of her 'things' into the water. Kay's gradual loss of the physical tokens of her way of life has great symbolic significance. But Preminger is not over-impressed. The bundle simply floats away off-screen while Harry brings Kay ashore. It would be wrong to describe this as understatement. The symbolism is in the event, not in the visual pattern, so the director presents the action clearly and leaves the interpretation to the spectator."

Arnheim would no doubt regard this as a reductio ad absurdum. His attitude, which is shared, deep down, by most critics, is based on his phobia of using the camera as a "recording machine" (reality is not art). It further reflects an unwillingness to leave the spectator any freedom to interpret action or behavior, or, to make connections. This concept of "freedom" has been distorted as much as that of "reality." It's taken to be absurd that a director should allow a viewer any freedom of interpretation, for he may then notice things that he isn't meant to, or fail to notice things that he should; he may get the wrong point altogether. This is in line with the idea that the test of a good film is whether it "makes statements."

Now in this scene from *River of No Return*, the spectator is "free" to notice the bundle, and, when he does so, free to interpret it as significant. But there is nothing random about the shot. The detail is placed in the background of the shot, and integrated naturally, so that we have to make a positive act of interpreting, of "reading," the shot. The act of interpreting the visual field—and through that the action—is in itself valuable. The significance of the detail is not announced, it is allowed to speak for itself. An alert spectator will notice the bundle, and "follow" it as it floats off screen.

The traditional method would be to make its significance unmistakable by cutting in close-ups. In this case we would gather that the bundle is meaningful *because* it is picked out for us. In Preminger's film, the process is reversed: we pick it out *because* it is meaningful. The emphasis arises organically out of the whole action; it is not imposed.

"The symbolism is in the event, not in the visual pattern." Before Scope, it was difficult to show the "event" lucidly, with each detail given its appropriate weight. It wasn't impossible: many Renoir films, as well as Mizoguchi's *Ugetsu Monogatari*, are superlative examples of the "opening-up" of the 1:1.33 frame to achieve this kind of fluidity. But on the whole the tendency was to split up the event into its component parts, and to impose, whether deliberately or not, a "visual pattern," a pattern of montage and/or of obtrusively "composed" images. And a *visual* pattern involves a pattern of motivation, a pattern of significance, which in certain films is appropriate, but is more often damagingly crude.

At this stage one can hardly avoid talking of "participation," which is another much-abused word. Everyone agrees, in principle, that art should not so much state as reveal, and that we should not just register its meaning but understand it. Our experience of a work should involve active participation more than passive assimilation.

The Russians, in their theoretical work, appropriated this idea, and applied it in a somewhat outrageous way; but critics, even intelligent ones, have continued to accept what they said. The confusion rests on a misunderstanding of the relation between film and the other arts, notably literature. Eisenstein said that "participation" took place in the association of successive images (as in the association of juxtaposed images in poetry)—that it depended purely on montage. In *October* he had intercut shots of Kerensky with ironic titles, and then with shots of a peacock preening itself. These images in themselves are fairly neutral, but the spectator fuses them together freely, he "participates," and arrives at an "intellectual decision" at the expense of Kerensky. In *Strike* we are shown, alternately, shots of workmen being massacred and of bulls being slaughtered: again, the two sets of images are independent of each other and we have to make the imaginative link between the two. Commenting recently on passages like these, an English critic said, "Thus Eisenstein's 'intellectual cinema' proves itself a superior means of communication by demanding the co-operation of the spectator in consideration of the conflicting ideologies that Eisenstein chose to convey."

This seems to me so much solemn nonsense. The whole is more than the sum of its parts; but then the whole is *always* more than the sum of its parts. The spectator "interprets" but there is no genuine freedom of association. A montage link of this kind reminds one of the children's puzzle which consists of a series of numbered dots: when they are joined together correctly, the outline of an animal appears. We participate in solving these, but only in a mechanical way, and there is only one correct solution. The very last thing Eisenstein really wants us to do is to evaluate for ourselves, or even experience for ourselves, what we are shown. He does not show us heroic actions—which we can recognize or judge to be heroic—he shows actions (not even that, but only *bits* of actions) and tells us that they are heroic (or alternatively brutal). Vakoulintchouk, in *Potemkin*, is "defined" by the shots which are intercut with shots of his dead body: close-ups of weeping women, sympathetic titles. Similarly we are *told* how to react to Kerensky and to the killing of the workmen—told obliquely, it is true, by a form of visual code, but still told; nothing is in any useful sense communicated. It is revealing that the whole meaning of these films can be reversed, as happened apparently in places with *Potemkin*, by merely re-arranging certain shots and titles, just as one can reverse the meaning of a slogan by replacing one name with another. (This would be inconceivable with *Birth of a Nation*.)

What is in question is not Eisenstein's artistry, within his chosen field, but rather the way his technique has been rationalized, by him and by others, and a universal validity claimed for it. The style is appropriate to what he was aiming to do, namely to make propaganda. He was not interested (in the silent films) in characterization or in shades of meaning, nor did he want to leave the spectator any freedom of response. The struggle of authority against revolution, and of Old against New, is one of Black and White. Andrew Sarris, in an excellent article on Rossellini in the *New York Film Bulletin*, contrasts this extreme montage style—"Eisenstein's conceptual editing extracts a truth from the collision of two mechanistic forces in history"—with "Rossellini's visual conception of a unified cosmos undivided by the conceptual detail of montage," and he implies one should accept each on its own terms. I think it's legitimate to say that, even if the style reflects the vision accurately, the vision is crude, and the style, although powerful, crude likewise. The words Eisenstein and his contemporaries use in describing it are significant: impact, collision, clash, the juxtaposition of "concepts"; the approach is essentially a rhetorical one. What is obvious anyway from this is that Eisenstein is a special case, that few directors see things his way, and that few subjects are amenable to this treatment. Drama is not normally reducible to concepts, clashes and collisions. (This is quite apart from the implications of the change to the sound film, after which the technique becomes still less relevant.)

People complain sometimes that Eisenstein's methods of intellectual and ideological montage have been forgotten, as have the associative techniques of Pudovkin's *Mother*, and

Figure 4.4 The management of action in the wide open spaces: Sam Peckinpah's *Ride the High Country*

imply that directors today must be deficient in imagination: but insofar as they reject these techniques they are more subtle. And a field where they do notably survive is that of the filmed commercial. The product may not in itself look very special (a "dead object") but it takes on associations when intercut with a smiling mother holding a smiling baby. The montage-unit style no doubt sells products, and puts over propaganda, more effectively than would a more fluid one, and there are other films too for which it is perfectly appropriate: educational work, certain documentaries, anything which aims to put over a message concisely. One would not advocate CinemaScope for these.

Jean Mitry, in his interesting book *Eisenstein* criticizes him for at times indulging in arbitrary symbolism (the slaughterhouse in *Strike*), but he accepts Eisenstein's analogies between the interpretation of film and poetic images: the film-maker juxtaposing unrelated images by montage is like the poet juxtaposing words. But the reader genuinely "participates" in the associations he makes from the words, in building them up into a fused whole: words are allusive whereas the film image is concrete. Film images follow each other in rigid sequence, which we cannot vary; the interaction of words is much more flexible. The more one goes into the differences between word and shot, and between the literary and filmic sequences of description, the more shaky do all the analogies made by the Russians seem.

There is no literary equivalent for "getting things in the same shot." This seems never to have struck them. Both Eisenstein and Pudovkin made laborious comparisons between the word or ideogram and the individual shot, and between the sentence and the montage-sequence. This seems fantastically naïve. How else can you translate "the cat sat on the mat" into film except in a single shot? Disciples tend to admit that these theories went a bit far—after all, they never went quite so far in their films—but without realizing that the rest of their aesthetic, which sounds more plausible, is in fact equally shaky, and for similar reasons.

For instance: a writer has to describe details successively, even though they may exist together. In this case he will aim, by his description, to evoke a "total" simultaneous reality in the reader's mind. Because of the indirect, allusive quality of language this is not really a handicap. Thackeray, in his *Irish Sketchbook*, gives a description of a mountain scene, evoking it by a series of details and of comparisons; he adds, "Printer's ink cannot give these wonderful hues, and *the reader will make his picture at his leisure*" (my italics). But the film image is direct, it *shows* things.

In *Lolita* (the book) there is a scene which, had it been presented without comment, might have seemed a perfect vindication of the rules laid down by Pudovkin in *Film Technique*, in that it consists of a series of details, which Nabokov describes successively, and which Pudovkin would have filmed successively ("showing them one by one, just as we would describe them in separate sequence in literary work"). It is the scene of the death of Humbert's wife: "I rushed out. The far side of our steep little street presented a peculiar sight. . . . *I have to put the impact of an instantaneous vision into a sequence of words; their physical accumulation on the page impairs the actual flash, the sharp unity of impression*. Rug-heap, old-man doll, Miss O's nurse running with a rustle back to the screened porch . . ." (my italics).

It's naïve to suppose that even the most fragmented lines—"ships, towers, domes, theatres and temples lie/open unto the fields and to the sky"—can be given an exact cinematic equivalent by a montage of ships, towers, domes, and so on. Eisenstein makes much of the fragmentary narrative of Dickens; this is fair enough in that a change of scene would correspond to a cut in film, but it does not hold for the *texture* of a narrative. Thomas Hardy makes a useful reference here, and at the risk of seeming repetitive I'd like to consider some passages from his novels.

Often he will introduce a character by, as it were, discovering him within a landscape. Being a writer, he describes things one by one, but they all contribute to the creation of a broad, total environment. His protagonists emerge from this, and are in turn absorbed into it; they are never detached; we retain a mental picture of them as a part of it. The film equivalent is to *show* them as a part of it, to engulf them in it. Boetticher's *Ride Lonesome* and Ray's *The Savage Innocents* are two films which portray people dominated by, almost defined by, their natural environment, and this connection is perfectly conveyed in their first images. In *Ride Lonesome*, the camera is held on a shot of a vast plain, stretching away to mountains in the distance; then it tilts down slowly and we become aware of a rider coming toward us from deep among the rocks below. *The Savage Innocents* has a long, empty snow-scape: the camera is still: a sledge enters frame left, deep within the shot, and is drawn gradually toward us. One can contrast this with the opening of *Scott of the Antarctic*: a montage of snow vistas, evocative music. We look *at* the scene instead of being involved in it, as we are in *The Savage Innocents*; and we accept, intellectually, for the purposes of the narrative, that the characters are there, instead of genuinely feeling it. Both Boetticher's and Ray's films are in Scope, and this helps enormously: it increases the involvement of the spectator and the physical integration of the characters.

It might be said that these are "landscape" films, that Scope is suitable for them but not for more confined drama. But the same principles hold; the dichotomy often expressed between interior and exterior drama is a false one.

Consider this passage from *Tess of the d'Urbervilles*. On her wedding night, Tess confesses to her husband about the child she had by Alec:

"Her narrative had ended; even its reassertions and secondary explanations were done. Tess's voice throughout had hardly risen higher than its opening tone; there had been no exculpatory phrase of any kind, and she had not wept.

"But the complexion even of external things seemed to suffer transmutation as her announcement proceeded. The fire in the grate looked impish—demoniacally funny, as if it did not care in the least about her strait. The fender grinned idly, as if it too did not care. The light from the water-bottle was merely engaged in a chromatic problem. All material objects around announced their irresponsibility with terrible iteration. And yet nothing had changed since the moments when he had been kissing her; or rather, nothing in the substance of things. But the essence of things had changed."

The Russians, again, might interpret this their own way: fragmentation, subjectivity, justifying a similar technique for film. But in film everything is concrete. Film shows the

Figure 4.5 From Ray's *Bitter Victory*

Figure 4.6 The open image: Preminger's *Exodus*

substance, it cannot *show* the essence, but it can *suggest* the essence by *showing* the substance. It suggests inner reality by showing outer reality with the greatest possible intensity. The writer has to build up a scene by description and allusion: images and metaphors, however fanciful, can help to strengthen our *objective* picture of the scene, whereas if transposed to film they would distract, and distort (imagine a close-up of the fender, grinning idly). For filming this passage from *Tess* I can't imagine a better method than to keep both of them in the frame the whole time, with the "material objects" around and between them, and to have her explanation, and then his silence, and reactions, in a single take, without any overt emphasis from the camera. Ideally, in CinemaScope, which makes the surroundings more palpable, and enables you to get close to one or both of the characters without shutting out the rest of the scene. The more precisely the camera charts the substance of things, the external movement of words, expressions, gestures, the more subtly can it express the internal movement: the essence of things.

Such a sequence would be condemned a priori by Arnheim ("immobile recording machine") and by Eisenstein, who laid down that *any* scene where a transition in feeling was observed, without a cut, was "theatrical." Need one point out that you can get a far greater control, on film, of all the elements of the scene, and of how each spectator sees them? And that the division of change into before and after can often be crudely mechanical? There could be no more eloquent illustration of this danger than the scene which Eisenstein holds up as an example of how to handle such a change in feeling: the cream-separator episode from the *The General Line*.

A great comfort to upholders of the "traditional" aesthetic has always been the Kuleshov/Pudovkin experiment (three neutral CUs of an actor, Mosjoukine, intercut with three different shots, to give the impression of three different emotions). This was felt to define the cinema for all time, and to establish that its essence was montage. If the same effect was difficult to achieve with sound, and then CinemaScope, that must prove that they were a bad thing. I do not honestly think that the effect on spectators of these sequences, presented as Pudovkin relates, can have been quite so overwhelming as he claims (is there any evidence, I wonder, that the experiment was done, and does not represent wishful thinking?), but one can accept that they do, up to a point, work: we understand what is being depicted, we complete the equations. Later experiments by psychologists have confirmed that one expression abstracted from its context looks very much like another. But this can far more reasonably be seen, I think, as an argument for not abstracting it in the first place.

The experiment illustrates that each act of perception automatically conditions succeeding ones; this is something which applies continuously, to life as well as to art, and which any intelligent artist will have taken into account in working out a style—not, however, to the extent of making it the cornerstone of his method. Pudovkin here reminds one of the bakers who first extract the nourishing parts of the flour, process it, and then put some back as "extra goodness": the result may be eatable, but it is hardly the only way to make bread, and one can criticize it for being unnecessary and "synthetic." Indeed one could extend the culinary analogy and say that the experience put over by the traditional aesthetic is essentially a *predigested* one. These two epithets have in ordinary usage a literal meaning and, by extension, a metaphorical one, applied pejoratively; the same correlation is valid here.

Writers like Manvell, Reisz, and Lindgren (all of whom base their aesthetic more or less closely on the Russians') advocate a method which gives us a *digest* of what we might see, in real life, if we were experiencing a given scene. Lindgren, in *The Art of the Film*, goes into this in most detail. He makes the usual comparisons with literary fragmentation, and then between what we see in life and in films. Sometimes we consciously see things as a whole, in their interrelationship (general shot). Sometimes we look round (pan) or walk (tracking shot). Normally we focus on one thing at a time (close-up or close-shot) and we look from one thing to another (cutting). Now it should be clear that the correspondence is by no means exact. In a film we sit facing the same direction all the time, looking at a screen which is set at a finite distance. In life we are oriented in our surroundings and our perception of them is continuous—continuous in time and space. But Lindgren claims that "in so far as the film is photographic and reproduces movement, it can give us a lifelike semblance of what we see; in so far as it employs editing, it can exactly [sic] reproduce the *manner* in which we see it."

At any time we see "central" things and "marginal" things; of the latter we may be aware, or half-aware, or they may serve merely to orient us. The traditional aesthetic separates out the central things: the marginal ones it either omits as inessential and distracting, or intercuts in close shot—in which case they are no longer marginal but central.

So an alternative method, a more strictly realistic one, which Lindgren and company pass over, is to present a complex image organized in such a way that we are induced to interpret it for ourselves. This is where genuine participation comes in, as in the sequence quoted from *River of No Return*.

Manvell (*The Film and the Public*) writes that "the comparatively narrow bounds of the normal screen shape sharpen perception by closing it in, giving the director full control of every detail which the audience should perceive." Conversely in CinemaScope "the sharpened perception of the normal film will be lost." In his aesthetic, we either see a thing or we don't. If a detail is important, the director singles it out for us; if there is a symbol or a meaningful connection to be noted, the director again does it for us, emphasizing it by close-ups. (Cf. Eisenstein's criticism of Dovshenko's *Earth*, on the grounds that he had not made the symbolism explicit enough—i.e., he had not brought the symbolic detail into close-up but had left it integrated, so that it might appear accidental.) We do not have to bother about noticing it for ourselves, or estimating whether it is significant. On the other hand when the image is complex we *have* to be alert to interpret it and the details within it. The difference between the Preminger method cited from *River of No Return* and the explicit close-up/montage style which he could have used, but didn't, corresponds to the difference between reading the meaning for ourselves and having it spelled out for us.[6]

"I don't think CinemaScope is a good medium. It's good only for showing great masses of movement. For other things, it's distracting, it's hard to focus attention, and it's very difficult to cut. Some people just go ahead and cut it and let people's eyes jump around and find what they want to find. It's very hard for an audience to focus—they have too much to look at—they can't see the whole thing." (Howard Hawks in an interview with Peter Bogdanovich.)

This is the danger; it was more worrying at the introduction of Scope, when audiences did apparently have to get used to "exploring" the more open image, but this I think was temporary. If a Scope image is decently organized the eyes will not just "jump around and find what they want to find," purely at random—they can be led to focus on detail, and to look from one thing to another within the frame with the emphasis which the director intends: that is, if the spectator is alert. Hawks may not like Scope (he had an apparently traumatic experience using it for *Land of the Pharaohs*, perhaps his worst film), but he approves of the 1:1.85 screen, and his style has always been one which allows the spectator freedom; in this sense he does not need Scope. One of the best of all examples of the alternative style to Lindgren's is from his *Hatari!* (wide screen). General shot of a bedroom: right of frame, in bed, waiting for her supper, Elsa Martinelli (back to camera); on the bed, John Wayne. Centre of frame, background, a tame cheetah. Left of frame, enter Red Buttons, carrying a tray; he trips over the cheetah's tail and the supper lands on Wayne, Martinelli, and the floor. Typically, Hawks takes this (exceedingly funny) scene in one static shot. It is done with a beautiful directness and lucidity, and without any of the usual look-this-is-funny comedy emphasis. The scene exists autonomously, action and reaction being integrated: Martinelli suddenly collapses with the giggles but we can only just see her at the edge of the frame. The nicest thing of all is the cheetah's reaction. He is obviously quite bewildered by the whole episode. We can see him in the background, looking up in pained manner at Red Buttons, and Hawks leaves him there, fading out the scene after a brief moment. Contrast the almost invariable procedure in other films for handling animal performers: that of extracting a certain laugh by cutting in their cute reactions in close-up. We are left "free" to interpret the scene visually, and this means we are free to respond. Our responses are not "signposted" by successive close-ups—foot tripping over tail, result, various reactions. No single reading of the scene is imposed. One could put it another way: the scene, as directed, is at once more subtle and more *authentic*. The reason why animals' reactions are normally cut in separately is not only that they thus get a surer laugh but that it's difficult to direct an animal so that it genuinely does what it is represented to be doing. It is sometimes held to be the chief glory of the cinema that you can, by montage, "create" an event like this which never happened. But the result (leaving aside certain kinds of film where the convention obviously allows this) is mechanical.[7]

The same applies in a less obvious way to other details of action and acting. It is much easier to put together a complex scene synthetically out of separate details—especially when you have an incompetent actor, or a child—than to organize and film the scene in its integrity. But you sacrifice the possibility of real conviction, of real subtlety.

The advantage of Scope over even the wide screen of *Hatari!* is that it enables complex scenes to be covered even more naturally: detail can be integrated, and therefore perceived, in a still more realistic way. If I had to sum up its implications I would say that it gives a greater range for *gradation of emphasis*. George Kaplan wrote in *Scene* that "there is no room for subtlety on 70mm film"; on the contrary, there is twice as much room, as is clear both from arithmetic and from *Exodus*. The 1:1.33 screen is too much of an abstraction, compared with the way we normally see things, to admit easily the detail which can only be really effective if it is perceived *qua* casual detail. There are innumerable applications of this (the whole question of significant imagery is affected by it): one quite common one is the scene where two people talk, and a third watches, or just appears in the background unobtrusively—he might be a person who is relevant to the others in some way, or who is affected by what they say, and it useful for us to be "reminded" of his presence. The simple cutaway shot coarsens the effect by being too obvious a directorial aside (Look who's watching) and on the smaller screen it's difficult to play off foreground and background within the frame: the detail tends to look too obviously planted. The frame is so closed-in that any detail which is placed there *must* be deliberate—at some level we both feel this and know it intellectually.[8] Greater flexibility was achieved long before Scope by certain directors using depth of focus and the moving camera (one of whose main advantages, as Dai Vaughan pointed out in *Definition* 1, is that it allows points to be made literally "in passing"). Scope as always does not create a new method, it encourages, and refines, an old one. The most beautiful example of this "gradation of emphasis" point is I think *The Courtship of Eddie's Father*; others include *The True Story of Jesse James, Ride the High Country* (all Scope) and *Exodus* (70mm). This is not something which can be isolated from the excellence of the films as a whole, nor can it be satisfactorily documented—one just has to sit in front of the films and see how space and décor and relationships are organized, and the eye led from one point to another within the image; how connections are made, and characters introduced, not being "added on" to the rest of the context but developing *out of* it.

Few of the films like these which I'd regard as being the richest of all are liked by critics; to praise Ray, Preminger, Hawks, or Minnelli makes one liable to the charge of subscribing to a "cult," a common defense mechanism which enables critics to avoid any challenge to their preconceptions. While it's possible, of course, to reject any of these films in the last analysis, I think the disagreement is more basic than this. Mainstream critics have been conditioned to recognize only a style based on montage and the close-up, and on "signposting" of effects, as valid, and may be in effect physically unable to respond to a film which requires an active interpretation on every level. I mean by this that, as we become more sophisticated and get more familiar with ideas and concepts, we tend to interpret films in literary terms, and our visual acuteness atrophies. Norman Fruchter, conducting a Film Appreciation course for unsophisticated teenagers, found that "the cadets' visual responses were far more acute than anyone might have given them credit for. I had to watch a film at least three times to see as much as they caught in a single viewing. They rarely missed detail. . . ." (*Sight and Sound*, Autumn, 1962). Now the traditional aesthetic allows for, and encourages, our more sophisticated tendencies by, as I described, "predigesting" a scene and serving it up in separate units, each one of which we can read like a sign. Critics who are conditioned by this will keep on (consciously or subconsciously) trying to separate out the "subject" of each shot, the "content" of each sequence, even when the film is made in a denser and more fluid style which does not admit this kind of treatment. They resent, or more commonly fail to understand, directors who give them too much work to do, and they naturally resent CinemaScope, which automatically makes for a more open, complex image.

The specific objections made to CinemaScope now, I hope, fall into place: they are really no objections at all. Sidney Lumet in an interview (*Film Quarterly*, Winter, 1960) was asked about the new screen processes and answered "I think they're ridiculous, I think they're pointless, I think they're typical Hollywood products. And typical Hollywood mentality, because the essence of any dramatic piece is people, and it is symptomatic that Hollywood finds a way of photographing people directly opposite to the way they are built. CinemaScope makes no sense until people are fatter than they are taller."

This is about as logical as to say that a book should be the shape of what it's about. If the screen is to correspond exactly to the human build then we should have vertical CinemaScope. If to the human face, it should be square (if not oval), and the most common criticism of Scope was, indeed, that it made the close-up impossible: it no longer "fits" the screen. As Gavin Lambert said, "A face squashed across a concave screen is clearly an unedifying prospect." (In CinemaScope, unlike Cinerama, the screen is seldom noticeably curved, and clearly the objective is more to the dimensions than to the curvature itself.)

Figure 4.7 From Boetticher's *Ride Lonesome*

The argument is effectively a circular one. I think one can sum up the development of the close-up roughly like this: the natural subject for the film is man-in-a-situation. But the frame was too narrow for this to be shown comfortably: also, it was difficult to organize from scratch, without some experience of the cinema and what could be done with it. So man-in-situation came to be conveyed by man + situation: close-up of a face, intercut with shots defining his experience and/or surroundings.

Certain film-makers welcomed this because it was more manageable and also more clearly "creative." At the same time, the process was rejected by others as being mechanical. One can look at this first from the point of view of actor and director. There is a loss of spontaneity, which is reflected in the film. "If you isolate a detail, that means that you have to take it up again from cold, to resuscitate the emotion" (Vincente Minnelli). "The close-up in the cinema is essentially a reconstruction, something pre-fabricated, carefully worked up" (Jean Renoir).

This in turn affects the spectator, who has to take on trust the connection between the close-up and the rest of the scene; man + situation tends to become a formula, a cruder digest of a reality which is continuous and complex. "If I were to throw in ten more details, everything in my films would suddenly become extremely clear. But those ten details are just what I don't want to add. Nothing could be easier than to take a close-up; I don't take any, lest I be tempted to use them" (Roberto Rossellini).

Directors like these worked out a more integral style presenting man-*in*-situation. This involved compensating for the narrowness of the frame by moving the camera laterally and composing the scene in depth. If the actors were brought close to the camera they would fill the screen, and blot out the background; therefore they were seldom brought close. This style is associated mainly with Renoir, who in 1938 wrote: "The more I advance in my craft, the more I feel it necessary to have the scene set in depth in relation to the screen; and the less can I stand actors placed carefully before the camera, as if they were posing for their photograph. It suits me rather to set my actors freely at different distances from the camera, to make them move about." This can be traced back to *Boudu Sauvé des Eaux* (1932) and even to his silent films; and there are others in the 'thirties like Hawks and Ophuls who, while not applying any formal principle of composition in depth, concentrate on the organization of the space within the image, and avoid the detached close-up—see especially *The Criminal Code* and *Liebelei*. These, together with *Boudu*, make up a marvelous trio of early sound films, which if one relied upon historians one would scarcely know existed, for according to most theories they oughtn't to.

The most spectacular application of these ideas is undoubtedly Antonioni's *Le Amiche* (made in 1955 but in the 1:1.33 ratio), of which he said: "I wanted to show my characters in their context, not to separate them, by montage, from their daily environment. You will find no cross-cutting whatever in *Le Amiche*: this technique expresses nothing." There are no close-ups in this film, and the average length of shot is 30 seconds, which is a lot. Antonioni realizes, and demonstrates, that the interaction of people with each other and with their surroundings is much more subtly expressed by showing them simultaneously. To dissociate them by montage tends to dissociate them altogether. The difference is not one of degree but of kind.

How does this relate to CinemaScope? Many of the directors who thus "anticipate" it do not in fact use it; partly this is chance, partly that they can get along without. But while I would not quite agree with the magazine *Présence du Cinéma*, which states that everything is automatically better in Scope, I think that, other things being equal, Scope refines this style. The director can now afford to bring a character closer to the lens without shutting out the context, and this flexibility is useful. He can have two faces in close shot together, instead of having to cut from one to the other, or to squeeze them in unnaturally close together. (Antonioni, although he has not worked in Scope, has taken advantage of the 1:1.85 screen in this way. Ian Cameron discusses this apropos of *L'Avventura* in *Film Quarterly*, Fall, 1962).

In CinemaScope the close-up, so far from being impossible, is for the first time fully acceptable: it *cannot* be a mechanical, all-purpose CU like the one of Mosjoukine, and it cannot be detached, it must include a genuine and not just a token background. I say "cannot": at least, if it is done this way, it is patently absurd. The image is too open, its space too palpable, to accommodate the "dead object" and give it spurious life. A lifeless film is twice as lifeless in Scope, as certain directors continue to demonstrate by building up scenes in the cutting-room out of the most perfunctory of component-shots. The most grotesque example is *The Lion*, but *The Left Hand of God, The Barbarian and the Geisha, Bus Stop*, and *The Deep Blue Sea* are also instructively inept. (I don't suggest that Scope *makes* them bad; they would have been anyway, but Scope shows them up more clearly. Over-all, and with certain clear exceptions like the didactic and the animated film, Scope makes the bad film worse and the good film better: it should gradually separate the sheep among directors from the goats.)

Look at the Scope close-up, as before, from both angles, how it is shot, and how we see it. If it is to pass, it must be analytic rather than synthetic: instead of taking an insert CU,

Figure 4.8 The circus in Ophuls' *Lola Montès*

then, against a neutral background, the director will have to recreate the ambience of the whole, and this helps the actor. The actor at the same time is freer to move within the frame, and thus within his surroundings, instead of being "placed carefully before the camera". Mariette Hartley, the girl in *Ride the High Country*, stands at the window of her house, talking to a boy: Scope close-up: she moves around nervously while she talks, and the director (Sam Peckinpah) doesn't have to worry about keeping her fixed to any chalk-marks because there is room enough within the frame; the effect is marvelously spontaneous.

Kazan's *Wild River* (about the evacuation of a remote community by the Tennessee Valley Authority) is a film where environment, and its effect on different people, is as significant as in *Le Amiche* and *The Magnificent Ambersons*. Because it is in Scope it doesn't matter that it is full of close-ups and crosscut sequences. Antonioni's reservations no longer apply; Kazan can concentrate on a single face without dissociating it from its context and "dislocating" the spectator.

Finally, a not unusual CinemaScope scene (from Ray's *Bitter Victory*) which contradicts most of the facile generalizations about Scope, made alike by those against and those in favor. The three main characters sit around a table, talking. The atmosphere is important—a military club in Africa, during the war, a nervous, falsely cheerful environment. The scene is taken in a series of full or medium close-ups, each of the three in turn, as they talk, sometimes two together. The normal theoretical attitude is that this would be fine on the old-ratio screen but clumsy if not impossible in Scope. If anything, the reverse is true, and it works brilliantly *because* it is in Scope: the cutting does not disorient us, the close-ups do not wholly isolate the characters, we know where we are all through. At the edges of the frame there is décor and space and perhaps some casual detail; thus when the camera is on one of the men, Richard Burton, we can see a couple dancing, and an Arab guard, and a general background of the room; we are completely situated at each moment, and accept the scene as real, while getting the full concentration on each face which Ray intends. So far from distracting this awareness of environment and of the characters' relation in space is necessary.

In talking about the close-ups in *Bitter Victory* I am talking about the montage. The two have always been lumped together, by people condemning Scope ("the close-up and montage become impossible") and by those welcoming it ("but montage and the close-up are not essential anyway"); the implications of Scope are identical for both. Montage is at once less necessary and more acceptable. Bazin and Roger Leenhardt, two of the few who approved of Scope from the start, imagined it would come to eliminate cutting within a sequence, and that this was no bad thing, but fortunately the medium is more flexible: some directors cut more in Scope, some less. There is no need to fragment reality, but there is less harm in fragmenting it because the different bits can be fitted together more satisfactorily.

If one likes Scope and the 70mm systems it would at first sight seem natural to welcome Cinerama unreservedly on aesthetic grounds, though not on economic.

It is still at a fairly primitive stage. The old distraction of the three-panel effect is still with us, but no doubt this and other flaws will be eliminated just as certain early flaws in the CinemaScope process (poor color reproduction, lack of clarity, horizon-bending) have been. There is even talk of a new single-camera process.

All the formal necessities of Scope apply, only more so. A detached CU is not just ugly, it is impossible. Bill Daniels, one of the cameramen on *How the West Was Won*, said of it: "It's a magnificent process, but frightening. You have three cameras grouped together, embracing 143 degrees. Your lens has an extremely wide angle. In a close-up, the camera is right up against the subject, only three feet away, and even that gets him to the hips."

Because of this width, synthetic montage is almost impossible too. A given shot will be covering so much of the action that the only cuts can be to a reverse angle, or to another view of the same scene (though for obvious reasons multicamera shooting is impossible) or to a different scene altogether. An actor finds it difficult to move out of frame, but has instead to move to an inconspicuous corner and continue acting.

So Cinerama guarantees an integral style. My reservations about it may, I suppose, be caused by imperfections which will in time be sorted out, or by the same form of timidity which I condemned in earlier critics' reactions to sound and CinemaScope. But it seems to me that the admirable dreams of the film pioneers who saw, in their imagination, "a total, integral representation of reality . . . a perfect illusion of the outside world, with sound, color and depth" (Bazin's summary) are not going to be fulfilled simply by continuing to extend the Cinerama method.

Cinerama does not project its image onto the squared-off wall opposite the audience, as other wide-screen systems do (only in certain Todd-AO theatres is the screen significantly curved); instead, it wraps the image around in front of them. If one sits in a front seat and looks at the center of the image, one can't see anything but screen, and one can turn almost full left and full right and still be *facing* the screen. The bigger and more "realistic" screens get, the more will this be true, and it is confusing because it is too close to our perception of life: it demands an equivalent control over distances, which is impossible as yet. There is no problem, in principle or in practice, over giving the impression of a confined space in CinemaScope (think of *Les Amants, Bitter Victory, Les 400 Coups*); but to fill the curved Cinerama screen with a group of people does not give the impression of being hemmed in by people, the effect is rather of being surrounded by people at some distance away. The space within the scene automatically becomes expanded (again, if one sits close) to at least the dimensions of the front arc of the auditorium itself. The cameras, being at the center of an arc, instead of remaining outside the scene, can "interrupt" it. This means that a character can't look, or move, straight across from one side of the scene to the other, because this would entail going "across" the camera, and thus "across" the audience. Daniels explains that "an actor on the right or left cannot look directly at an actor at the center (if that's what the script calls for); if he does, he will look, on the screen, as if he is looking out front. This is because he is, of course, being photographed by a different camera at a different angle."

Cinerama is halfway between the traditional flat screen and an "all-around" cinema where the spectators are enclosed in a hemisphere of image. It is often assumed that this would be the ultimate in realism, but in fact there would still be this incongruous volume of space within the auditorium, a no-man's-land where the director and crew stood, surrounded by outward-looking cameras, and where, in turn, the audience now sit and look out from. I haven't any experience of this, not having been at the Brussels Fair, nor at the 1900 exhibition in Paris of Cinéorama,[9] which surrounded the audience with views taken from a balloon, projected onto a circular screen of circumference 333 feet. But the problem would seem to be: how to show the balloon itself, and the people in it. It's like a planetarium, where you can

Figure 4.9 *How the West Was Won*—proportions of Cinerama

reproduce perfectly the distant view, the night sky and the horizon all round, but could hardly put the audience *in* a house, or project close objects like over-hanging trees. The audience is too completely oriented to adjust to the distortion inherent in the means of projection.

No one could deny that planetaria, the various encircling 'Ramas, and Cinerama itself, achieve their spectacular effects admirably, but it seems doubtful whether even the relatively modest Cinerama is a good medium for story-telling. Todd-AO and the other 70mm systems can be almost as stunning in physical impact, they eliminate distortions, are easier to control and more natural to look at. This seems the nearest we will get, under present technology, to a "total cinema."

It seems a pity to abandon the question here, and one can take it that theorists, and businessmen, will continue the quest for total cinema.

The problem is to devise some way of surrounding each individual in the audience with a *total* visual world, in the same way that it's possible to surround him with a total aural one. A radio play can give a satisfactory total representation of what we would hear in reality. Our visual perceptions are more complex than our aural ones, and are more closely bound up with the other factors in our experience. We can *imagine* a total visual reality, in reading a book or hearing a play, but even in a Circlorama-type cinema we are still at the center of our *own* reality—the people next to us, the ground beneath us, the space between us and the screen . . . so it's impossible to "submit" ourselves entirely to total cinema as we can to total radio.

This would need an entirely revolutionary technique, one which could engulf each spectator in a total new world substituted for his "real" one. A form of controlled, waking dream. It is what René Barjavel, in a fascinating book written in 1945, *Le Cinéma Total*, seems to envisage. He talks of a cinema transmitted by "waves" or "impulses." He gives no technical explanation, taking it for granted that They will invent it. More recently Arthur C. Clarke (in *Profiles of the Future*, pp. 191–192) seems also to take into account the possibility of some such process. I have not the faintest idea whether, or when, or how, this would be feasible, but possibly the increasing power of mind over matter, and mind over mind, could culminate in this.

Notes

1 The best historical survey is that given by Kenneth Macgowan in the earlier incarnation of this magazine, *The Quarterly of Film, Radio and Television,* Winter, 1956.

2 "In the silent cinema, montage had a precise meaning, because it represented language. From the silent cinema we have inherited this myth of montage, though it has lost most of its meaning."—Roberto Rossellini.

3 *Ontology of the Photographic Image*, translated by Hugh Gray in *Film Quarterly*, Summer, 1960.

4 Cf. Bazin's essay "The Myth of Total Cinema," also published in the first volume of *Qu'est-ce que le Cinéma?*

5 Arnheim also wrote, and I am not making it up: "Silent laughter is often more effective than if the sound is actually heard. The gaping of the open mouth gives a vivid, highly artistic interpretation of the phenomenon 'laughter.' If, however, the sound is also heard, the opening of the mouth appears obvious and its value as a means of expression is almost entirely lost." But I don't know that this argument against sound is any more unconvincing than that against Scope—the logic is identical.

6 Cf. also in *Citizen Kane* Welles's extremely subtle handling of the Rosebud/snowglass paperweight imagery, which he often leaves naturally in the background of the shot for us to notice, and to make the connections. Pages could be written on this.

7 Bazin analyzed this issue—the existence of which no one before him seems to have realized—in another definitive essay, "*Montage Interdit*" [in *Qu'est-ce que le Cinéma?*].

8 In Antonioni's *Il Grido* there is a shot taken from inside a house: a woman goes out of the door and walks away. The door stays slightly ajar and through this very narrow aperture we continue to see her

walking, in a dead straight line away from the camera. This is a far too neat continued effect, and audiences groan. It is too good to be true that she should have walked along exactly the one line which would have kept her visible. On the other hand if the aperture had been wider, she would have been "free" to deviate, and even if she had in fact taken precisely the same path the shot would have been more acceptable—not in spite of but *because* of the "frame" of the door "fitting" her less well. I don't think it is fanciful to compare the door that frames her with the frame of the film image in general.

9 A Russian all-round cinema, the Circlorama, is due to open in London during May.

Chapter 5

Barry Salt

FILM STYLE AND TECHNOLOGY IN THE THIRTIES (1976)

Editors' Introduction

Just as we have "great man" histories, so too do we have histories marked by "great technology." American-based film studies has no shortage of analyses of the introduction of sound in the late 1920s, or the major studios' slower adoption, beginning in the 1930s, of Technicolor and other color processes, or the widescreen systems of the 1950s. Barry Salt, however, has produced a history, and a historical model for understanding, much subtler technological shifts in American cinema. In "Film Style and Technology in the Thirties," Salt has produced an historiographical catalog of shifts in lenses, shifts in film stock, shifts in lighting, and shifts in cameras, none of them absolutely determining film style, but all of them having some impact on how movies looked and sounded. Salt's work helps us to understand, for instance, that while tracking shots were possible in the early sound era (think of *Applause*, from 1929), tracking became much more plausible, and so more common, with the development of large camera cranes and camera blimps. As a result, the early-1930s artsiness of a director like Georg Wilhelm Pabst or Lewis Milestone became everyday practice for the more workmanlike studio directors later in the decade. In providing this history of technology and style, Salt also has extended our sense of the film studies archive. Salt meticulously studies the films themselves, for average shot length or looking for soft focus close-ups. But he also studies the journals of film professionals, for example *The American Cinematographer* and *The Journal of the Society of Motion Picture Engineers*. Salt's work has had a significant impact on the practices of film studies, from the wide-ranging work of David Bordwell, Janet Staiger, and Kristin Thompson, who detail the technological histories of American movies in *The Classical Hollywood Cinema*, to the more focused work of Ben Brewster, who examined shot construction and length in *Traffic in Souls* in order to understand the narrative possibilities of the early silent feature film. Of course, technology is not destiny for Salt. But he has shown the profound stylistic and narrative impact of technological innovations that most often had gone unnoticed by earlier generations of film historians.

Suggested Reading

Ben Brewster, "*Traffic in Souls*: An Experiment in Feature-Length Narrative Construction," *Cinema Journal*, 31:1 (Fall, 1991), pp. 37–56; David Bordwell, Janet Staiger, and Kristin Thompson, *The Classical Hollywood Cinema: Film Style & Mode of Production to 1960* (New York: Columbia University Press, 1985); Barry Salt, *Film Style and Technology: History and Analysis* (London: Starwood, 1983).

NOW THAT SOME INTEREST has arisen in the history of the influence of film technology on the forms of films, there has been an unfortunate tendency to exaggerate its importance, whereas in truth it appears that, as far as the more interesting aspects of movies are concerned, technology acts more as a loose pressure on what is done rather than a rigid constraint. For instance, one can connect the move towards faster cutting in the middle thirties with the introduction of "rubber numbering" (or "edge numbering") of the cutting copies of the sound and picture tracks, but an opposite tendency towards longer takes, which began at the end of the thirties, seems to be independent of any of the technical developments of the period. And a complex train of events involving aspects of sound recording and film stock development relate to the rise of background projection and total studio shooting that so distinguishes the later thirties from the early thirties.

So in this article these matters, and also other aspects of the general movement of the formal stylistic features in the mainstream cinema of the thirties, are considered in relation to the technological developments of the period. The emphasis is strongly on American practice, but the state of European developments is mentioned from time to time. The analytical approach to film style used here has already been demonstrated more fully in some respects in *Film Quarterly*, Vol. 28, No. 1, and since then extended somewhat, and the general attitude taken is that it is impossible to establish what is interesting about a particular film unless one knows the norms holding in general for other films of the same kind made at the same time and place. Ignoring this principle has led people to describe features of particular films as remarkable, when they are in fact quite commonplace in the context of their period, and although this error is much more common with early cinema, one instance in connection with sound editing can be mentioned here.

At the beginning of the thirties editors were beginning to realize the importance of what might be called the "dialogue cutting point" for making weak (i.e., smooth, un-noticeable) cuts when cutting from one speaker to another in a scene. In general the weakest cut from a speaker to the shot of his listener, who is about to reply in the succeeding shot, will be made while the last syllable of the last word of the speech is still being spoken. Some editors cut at the very end of the last syllable, which is almost equally acceptable, but virtually none cut in the middle of the pause between the two speeches, or just at the beginning of the reply. (Some uncertainty about this point is still visible in Capra's *Platinum Blonde*—1931.) Of course deviations from this point can be made for reasons of emphasis and expression in general, most notably cutting to a listener's reaction in the middle of a speech. Curiously enough this principle has never been written down in books on editing technique, and presumably it is passed on to apprentice assistants at the editor's knee, but in any case it should be immediately obvious to any would-be editor from watching a couple of films. But in a recent article by Raymond Bellour on *The Big Sleep* in *Screen*, Vol. 15, No. 4, p. 17, several lines are spent in discussing one instance of this standard dialogue cutting point as though it were something unique and remarkable rather than the usual thing.

The picture of the technology situation has been put together from information obtained from complete runs of *The American Cinematographer* and *The Journal of the Society of Motion*

Picture Engineers, together with *The Cinematographic Annual*, Vols. 1 and 2 (American Society of Cinematographers, Hollywood 1930 and 1931), *Recording Sound for Motion Pictures* (ed. Lester Cowan, McGraw-Hill, 1931) and *Motion Picture Sound Engineering* (Research Council of A.M.P.A.S., Hollywood, 1938). Some several hundred films of the period have been considered in the light of this information, and also of the present author's film-making experience at the professional level, principally as a cameraman, but extending a little way into most other areas.

Depth of Field and Other Photographic Variables Influencing the Film Image

Depth of field (often erroneously called depth of focus) is one of the central factors controlling the appearance of the film image, and it is really necessary to get a clear understanding of the way it is related to other variable factors if one is to appreciate the interconnections between the visual qualities of movies and film technology. The four central quantities whose variations are strictly connected with one another are Depth of Field, Lens Aperture, Focal Length of Lens, and Lens Focus.

Depth of Field is the range of distance in front of the camera lens inside which objects produce sharp images *as seen on the cinema screen* when the film is finally projected. The boundaries of this range of sharp focus are rather approximate, as objects just outside it are only slightly unsharp, and the casual glance at the cinema screen may not reveal this. The range of sharp focus as it appears on the ground-glass screen of a camera view-finding system is not necessarily the same as that on the cinema screen, though usually close to it.

Lens Aperture is the size of the variable opening in the iris diaphragm built into the middle of the lens. Its size is measured in "f numbers" or "stops," and these f numbers are inversely related to the actual diameter of the lens diaphragm opening. The basic series off numbers runs f 1, f 1.4, f 2, f 2.8, f 4, f 5.6, f 8, f 11, f 16, f 22, f 32. Each of these f numbers are said to differ from the next one by "one stop," and going from one to the next either halves or doubles the amount of light passing through the lens to the film. Intermediate f numbers are also possible, and tend to occur in the specification of the maximum aperture of a lens. The exposure is controlled by changing the amount of light falling on the scene and/or changing the lens aperture so that just the amount of light gets through the lens as appropriate to the film stock being used. "Faster" film stocks require less light through the lens than "slow" stocks, and so give the cameraman the option of decreasing the light level on the set or leaving it the same and reducing the lens aperture, which can increase depth of field (see below).

Focal Length of a lens is the distance behind its "optical center" of the plane in which the image of an infinitely distant object is formed. The "angle of view" of a camera lens is inversely proportional to its focal length, so short focal length lenses have a wide angle of view, and are colloquially referred to as wide-angle lenses, and long focal length lenses, some of which also have "tele-photo" type construction, have a narrow angle of view.

There is no definite criterion for what constitutes a "standard lens," though some fairly recent experimental work suggests that for the Academy frame focal lengths between 35mm and 40mm give most viewers a feeling of correct perspective. Before World War I some cameramen regarded even a 75mm lens as standard, though in the twenties all came to agree on 50mm as standard. This more or less continued to be the case through the thirties, but by the late forties there were many who had come to regard 35mm focal length as standard. Widescreen projection in the fifties continued the trend, but also introduced complexities which it would be out of place to discuss here.

Lens Focus is of course the distance at which the lens focus is set to produce the very sharpest images of objects.

Now the value of any one of these quantities is determined by the values of the other three, but it is usual to consider the effect on the depth of field of holding two of them fixed and varying the third. The results are nowadays set down in depth of field tables, but these did not exist in the thirties, and cameramen then had to rely on experience to predict the depth of field that would appear on the screen. So, given that the other two factors are constant, depth of field increases with: (i) Increase of distance at which the lens focus is set—up to a certain point called the hyperfocal distance; this variation is of no help in achieving "deep focus." (ii) Decrease of focal length of lens—that is, moving to wider angles of lens, which at the same time introduces perspective distortion. (iii) Reduction of lens aperture. This requires the use of faster film stock and/or increase of light levels on the set. To reduce the aperture by one stop requires a doubling of the light level, and as is well known, this in turn doubles the already considerable electricity consumption of the studio. But if one was prepared to pay the price it was possible, even in the early twenties, to raise the light level on studio sets to the point where considerable depth of field was obtained even with the slow (approximately 20 ASA) film of that time. An isolated instance of this occurs in von Stroheim's *Foolish Wives* (1921), where in a few scenes the interiors have been lit to match the level of the sunlit exteriors visible through doors, etc., and consequently the lens aperture is about f 5.6 or f 8, and sharp focus is carried from Medium Shot to Very Long Shot. This is not deep focus in the post-Toland sense, but it is on the way there, and it could have been pushed further by doubling up the arc lights used, and by using a wider angle lens, if there had been a specific desire to increase depth of field further, instead of this result having been achieved accidentally in pursuit of other ends.

Film Stock and Processing

At the beginning of the thirties the most commonly used negative stock continued to be Eastman Kodak panchromatic negative of the type introduced in 1928, but similar negative materials were also available from Agfa, Dupont, and Pathé. All these had slow emulsions that were used as though they had a speed of around 20 ASA in present-day terms, although there was no film speed rating system in use at that time. The faster Agfa negative which was already available, and the Eastman Supersensitive Negative which became available in 1931, were not in general use in Hollywood, except for filming the odd largish-scale night exterior. The principal reason for these negatives not being used to secure either lower light levels on the sets, or alternatively greater depth of field in the photography, was that they had noticeably greater graininess (as faster film stock usually does) and hence gave poorer defintion in the image. So photography on interiors continued to be at maximum aperture (f 2–f 2.8).

New improved duplicating negative and positive stocks were made available by Kodak in 1930 and 1933 respectively, and these were directly connected with the developments in optical printing which will be discussed below. Most important also for special effects was Eastman Background Negative introduced in 1933 in response to Hollywood's desire to employ more background projection. This negative had very fine grain, and made it possible to obtain shots whose graininess would not be evident when projected onto the new giant background projection screens. In this case the demand very definitely produced the technical development, which is not usually the case, but the causal chain can be traced back even further to the exigencies of sound recording at this period.

In 1934 Agfa-Ansco introduced their 32 ASA Superpan negative to the American market, and the next year Kodak riposted with Super X which was approximately 40 ASA. These new faster stocks had better definition than their predecessors, but the decisive innovations occurred in 1938, when Eastman Kodak introduced Plus X and Super XX with speeds equivalent to 80 ASA and 160 ASA respectively, and Agfa introduced Supreme and Ultrapan (64 ASA and 120 ASA). Of these new materials, Plus X immediately proved the most successful, for it gave definition comparable to the earlier slow stock for the first time, and in fact the vast majority of Hollywood features were shot with it for many years onwards. But in the later thirties the extra two stops of speed Plus X gave were never used to stop down by that amount from the usual maximum lens aperture, and so secure increased depth of field. On the contrary, the switch to Plux X was mainly used to economize on the light levels on the sets.[1]

However not quite all the speed advantage of the new stocks was absorbed in this way. To a certain extent they were over-exposed rather than being used with the light level intended for a given aperture. This over-exposure was compensated for by giving the negative reduced development, and this resulted in a flatter print, i.e., there were more middle greys in the image, and less true blacks and whites. MGM and RKO were the studios which went furthest in this direction, and all in all this practice was responsible for the distinctive pearly-grey look of many late thirties films when compared with the more contrasty films of the early thirties.

Lighting in the Early Nineteen-thirties

The principal lighting on studio sets during the twenties had been provided by arc lights, but these produced a humming noise when operating, and this made them useless for synchronous sound filming. By the beginning of 1930 electrical circuits to silence the hum had been devised and produced, but in most studios in that year their use was extremely limited, and most of the coverage for synch-sound shots continued to be achieved with the less intense, but silent, tungsten light sources. However Fox had already returned to the principal use of arc sources, and the result was the slightly sharper shadow and modelling to be observed in their films of that year, when compared with those from other studios.

In 1931 all studios had returned to the free use of arcs when convenient, but the majority (80%) of lights used continued to be various types of tungsten light. This was no doubt in part to realize the worth of the investment already made in these incandescent lighting units, but also in part because cameramen had come to appreciate the unique qualities of lighting that could be achieved with some of them. This was particularly true of the various kinds of floodlights with hemispherical metal reflectors containing tungsten bulbs of up to 1 kW, which gave a much softer light than any arc floodlight. Indeed in general the light from tungsten source lighting units was softer than that from equivalent units with arc sources, and when used for figure lighting they produced attractive soft-edged shadows on the face. Some cameramen took more advantage of these possibilities than others, but Victor Milner can stand as an example of those who exploited the softness of tungsten light extensively in such films as *Ladies Man* (1931), where the key lighting is done with tungsten floodlights even in Long Shot, and the cast shadows as well as the modelling shadows are as soft as can be achieved, short of using the type of "soft light" unit only available in recent decades. Milner persisted with this approach, in the lighting of closer shots at least, for the rest of his career.

Some Things Done by Cameraman James Wong Howe

In general it is not possible to isolate a consistent individual recognizable style in the work of even the best cameramen; there is no obvious connection between the strong chiaroscuro look of *Murders in the Rue Morgue* and the rather pedestrian mid-key look of *Back Street*, both photographed by Karl Freund for Universal in 1932. Nevertheless there are numerous occasions when individual cameramen achieve strikingly original results, and in the early thirties James Wong Howe stands out in this respect.

In this period James Wong Howe tried out the possibilities of using a fairly wide-angle lens (25mm) in various unusual ways. In ordinary Hollywood practice this lens was only rarely used, when the constrictions of an awkward set prevented a Long Shot being obtained in any other way, but Wong Howe used a 25mm lens on *Transatlantic* (1931) specifically to secure increased depth of field. The result was far from being deep focus in the modern, post-Toland sense, which strictly speaking means sharpness of focus from Big Close Up to Long Shot; the range achieved by Wong Howe was only from five feet to 30 feet, which is from Medium Shot to Long Shot with a 25mm lens. (These figures mean that the aperture used was approximately f 4, and the light levels would have been little more than those usual at this period.)

Less well known is that Wong Howe used a 25mm lens to get the close shots in *Viva Villa!* (1934) and also used long focal length lenses to shoot the massed battle scenes, an exceptional inversion of the usual procedures at that time.

Finally, *The Power and the Glory* (William K. Howard, 1933) contains a piece of exceptional lighting in the scenes in the tycoon's office, where Wong Howe somehow managed to duplicate exactly the fall of diffuse north light coming from windows to one side only. There is no back light or light from any other angle, and the effect is exactly what it would be in the real situation, or if using modern "soft lights" in the window positions. Ignoring a few instances involving close shots of people in other films at other times, this is the only instance the author has noted of anything before recent years that could reasonably be called "north lighting" applied to a studio scene.

It would appear that James Wong Howe was not encouraged in such individual efforts, as he did not do anything very unconventional again till the fifties; and indeed in general the later thirties and early forties were a period of conformism in all respects in films made everywhere. Directors who had a taste for experiment like William K. Howard were also not encouraged.

Lighting in the Late Thirties

The important development in lighting practice in the latter part of the thirties was the introduction of a new range of spotlights with Fresnel lenses. For the first time it was possible to have large diameter lenses (up to three feet) close in front of a powerful light source, either arc or tungsten, as well as a parabolic mirror behind the source. The efficiency of the source and its controllability were vastly increased, and these units have remained standard from that date to the present. The range available extended all the way from 500 watt tungsten spots to the biggest arc spotlights, and all had a beam spread that could be adjusted handily from 8 to 40 degrees, with a soft edge over a few degrees where the intensity fell off very rapidly to zero.

Even more completely than previously the main lighting of scenes in Hollywood movies was now executed with spotlights, and floodlighting was restricted to a certain amount of general fill lighting on sets or close-ups.

But the new Fresnel spots were slow to arrive in Europe, and even in the late thirties the main lighting of shots continued to be done with floodlights. The unavailability of big arc spots for extra figure lighting on location is quite obvious in Carné's *Quai des Brumes* (1938) and in Claude Renoir's work for his uncle, for instance. Of course satisfactory results could be obtained on the generally smaller European sets with floodlights, and indeed the look of the lighting was in the strict sense of the term more naturalistic than the American approach, but the point is just that European cameramen could not have produced exactly that Hollywood style if they had wanted to. The position in Britain was as usual intermediate.

There, with the somewhat superior equipment available, George Périnal was able to create the apotheosis of the European style in a series of Korda productions that he lit in the late thirties. The way of the best European film lighting since about 1913 had been to light the set and actors as one unit, and to apply no separate light (or very little) to produce special modelling on the actors. Périnal managed to combine an elegantly simple disposition of the major shadows on the set with glossy treatment of the figures at the appropriate moments. This creation of simple large geometrical shapes in the solid black shadows cast on the background of shots means that Périnal's lighting is probably the only work in the late thirties that can be attributed to its author without prior sight of a film's credits.

Throughout the later thirties in Hollywood photography continued to be conducted at, or near, maximum aperture and in general the faster stocks were not used to achieve smaller apertures and hence greater depth of field. This was also true of European practices. (For the last time, there is *no* true "deep focus" in Renoir's films, just staging in depth, sometimes beyond the limits of sharp focus.)

Camera Lenses

At the beginning of the thirties lenses with focal lengths from 25mm upwards were available as before, and were used, and the usual maximum aperture of wide-angle and standard lenses was around f 2.5, though the Taylor-Hobson series had a maximum aperture of f 2. The importance of the maximum aperture of the lenses commonly used, apart from its relation to depth of field as already indicated, stems from the continuing desire of film-makers to use lens diffusion ("soft focus") in varying degrees throughout films. It does not seem to be generally known that the aesthetic convention of "soft focus" in cinematography stems from its use in still photography in the early years of this century. By 1914 still cameras with special "soft focus" lenses were being mass-produced for amateur use, and around 1915 "soft focus" Close-Ups began to appear in American movies. (But *not* those of D. W. Griffith.) The extensive use of lens diffusion, especially but not only in close-ups, had become common by 1925, and since lens diffusion, whether it is carried out with gauzes, vaseline plates, or specially made lenses, is most effective at maximum lens aperture, so photography at, or near, maximum lens aperture had become usual by that time.

The practice of maximum aperture photography thus has nothing to do with the introduction of panchromatic film a year or two later, contrary to what is often claimed in discussions of the development of deep-focus cinematography. The further reduction in depth of field visible in early sound films is largely due to quite another cause. The simultaneous use of several camera booths in filming scenes on many sound films made in 1928, 1929, and to some extent into 1930, forced the use of longer focal length lenses to get tighter-frame, apparently closer shots than was the case both before and after. For instance, in the years mentioned a Medium Shot would quite probably be taken with a 75mm lens rather than the usual 50mm lens, and consequently the depth of field was even further reduced, becoming so shallow that everything but the actor was conspicuously out of focus. With the appearance of blimped cameras it was of course once more possible to get the camera, fitted with any lens, as close as one liked to the actors, so the extreme of shallowness of field disappeared again.

As a further complication, around 1929 and 1930 there was a minor school of thought in the studios which considered that lens diffusion should be dropped entirely as the "realism" added by synchronous sound demanded that everything in the image be sharply visible. This idea had a limited and passing influence, but may have been responsible for such peculiarities as the absence of lens diffusion throughout all the close shots of King Vidor's *Hallelujah* (1929), and nearly all other shots too, but on a couple of Very Long Shots heavy diffusion is used—remarkable inversion of the standard procedures.

Once into the thirties, sets were being designed on the assumption that the Long Shots would be taken with a 40mm lens. For closer shots a 50mm lens was once more the usual choice, and of course for Close-Ups something like 75mm.

In 1932 the Taylor-Hobson "Varo" variable focal length lens became available, and had occasional limited use in Hollywood for a few years. (The term "zoom lens" had not yet been coined.) The focal length of this lens could be continuously varied between 40mm and 120mm, with a possible maximum aperture of f 5.6. Apart from the rather small maximum aperture, the drawback of this lens was the fact that the focus was fixed at the hyperfocal distance, and closer objects had to be focussed by putting supplementary lenses in front of the front element, so focus-pulling in the middle of the shot was impossible. A further drawback was that the lens casing was a large and heavy oblong metal box about half the size of the body of a Mitchell camera. Zoom shots made with the Varo lens can be seen in the street scene opening of *Love Me Tonight* (Mamoulian, 1932) and also in the stag-hunting scene. It was also used in a number of other films at this time, but hardly ever in later years, although it continued to be available, and the last use I have detected was in a montage sequence of *Private Worlds* (LaCava, 1935).

Cameras

In 1930 Warners were the only studio still using the "ice-box" type of sound-proof booth containing both camera and operator for sound filming, and from 1931 all the studios were using Mitchell NC cameras in blimps of their own various hand-made designs. So although Warners had fitted some of their booths with wheels, as had other studios during 1929, there was still during 1930 at that studio a strict limitation on the use of panning simultaneously with tracking, a limitation that no longer obtained elsewhere. (Cameras inside sound-proof booths were naturally limited by the size of the booth window to pans of about 30 degrees on either side of the forward direction, whereas both unblimped and blimped cameras can obviously be pointed in any direction while the dolly they are mounted on is being tracked along.)

The prototype Mitchell BNC was produced in 1934, but this camera was not put into series production till 1938. However Gregg Toland acquired and used one of the prototypes years before it was put on sale, but with no visible effect on the style of his camerawork at this point. In 1935 another silent camera was designed for Twentieth Century-Fox, and in 1939 several were produced for the sole use of that studio, but further production was prevented by the precision engineering requirements of World War II. Both the Fox camera and the Mitchell BNC were slightly easier than earlier cameras to get into extreme positions, and slightly easier to use in general, but this really had little significance as far as studio filming was concerned. What *was* important was that synch-sound shooting with lenses of wider angle than 25mm was now possible. (Blimped cameras had been restricted to using lenses of focal length longer than 25mm) However the effect of this was not to be realized till the forties.

Camera Supports and Camera Mobility

Most of the major studios had acquired large camera cranes in imitation of Universal, and small cranes with a rise and fall of several feet appeared at Paramount in 1933, and at other studios shortly after. Naturally the improvised steerable dollies which were already in use for sound shooting continued to be used. On these the blimped camera was mounted on a heavy-duty tripod whose feet were fastened to the dolly platform. The pan and tilt head used under the blimped cameras was of the heavy spring-loaded friction type controlled with a pan bar, just like the still existing Mitchell and Vinten types. In 1930 Mole-Richardson had produced a large cradle geared head like the current types, having much faster and smoother pan and tilt movements than the small silent-period geared heads, but for some unknown reason this was not used till the end of the thirties.

Although tracking shots with synch-sound appear in a number of films made in 1929, for instance *The Saturday Night Kid* and *The Virginian*, not to mention the well-publicized instance of *Applause*, it must be realized that these are all instances of *parallel* tracking shots, in which the camera moves on a straight path with the actors, and without any large panning movements, for of course the camera and operator were inside wheeled booths, as already mentioned. However there were some films made in 1928 and 1929 which do show free panning and tilting on tracking shots; films such as *Hearts in Dixie* (1928) and *Chinatown Nights* (Wellman, 1929). But in these cases the shots in question were taken with an unblimped wild camera, and the sound laid under the shot in the editing. In fact the latter film appears to be a rare case of an entirely post-synchronized Hollywood film made in 1929.

Once the blimped cameras were on friction heads and dollies, the way was open to a complete continuation of the extensive use of the mobile camera that had characterized the work of many directors at the end of the silent period. At the beginning of the thirties obvious names like Pabst and Milestone spring to mind, but this very conscious trend spread to many directors, including newcomers like George Cukor and John Cromwell (as commented on by the latter at the National Film Theatre, London, in 1974).

The prototype of a small, extremely maneuverable dolly was used on Milestone's *The Front Page* in 1931, and this dolly was put into series production in 1932 as the Bell & Howell "Rotambulator." It had a camera mounting that could rise and fall beside a central column, and this column was fixed in turn to a circular base about three feet in diameter. There were three small wheels around the circumference of the base, two at the front with fixed direction, and one at the back that was steerable. This arrangement permitted very tight turns to be executed, and the Rotambulator's maneuverability (but not its stability) approached that of present crab dollies. The effect of its use can be seen in the press room scenes of *The Front Page*.

The Hollywood extreme of the "long take with mobile camera" style can be represented by John Stahl's *Back Street* (1932), which with an Average Shot Length (A.S.L.) of 23 seconds inevitably includes a fair number of takes that are minutes long. (The roughly Poisson-type distribution of shot lengths in mainstream feature films enables one to know very roughly how many shots there will be of any given length in a movie once one knows the A.S.L. and the total duration of the film (see *Film Quarterly*, Vol. 28 No. 1, 1974).

In the instance quoted, and in others as Pabst's *Kameradschaft*, this style tends to be associated with a push towards naturalism in other dimensions of the medium such as dialogue and acting. The connection is not absolute, as witness the rather stylized acting in Renoir's *Boudu Sauvé des Eaux* (1932), which has an A.S.L. of 15 seconds, but nothing much in the way of tracking shots.

None of the dollies or cranes that became available in this period permitted minimum lens heights much below three feet, and ultra-low camera angles continued to require special time-consuming measures; nevertheless they continue to make their appearance in a few films such as *Doorway to Hell* (Archie Mayo, 1930) and others, the inspiration presumably being various European films such as *Battleship Potemkin* which had arrived in America right at the end of the twenties. Unmotivated high angle shots are slightly more frequent, though still not common in non-musical films. A good place to study the use of these, and other, expressivist or "expressionist" devices at the Hollywood extreme of the expressivist-naturalist spectrum is *The Bat Whispers* (Roland West, 1931).

Background Projection

From 1930 the earlier travelling matte systems (Williams and Dunning processes) for combining live-action foreground scenes with separately filmed live-action background scenes were abandoned entirely, and replaced with background projection. In this latter process a previously filmed background scene is projected in the studio onto a large translucent screen from behind, while the actors are filmed from the front of it, acting against the image on the screen to produce a combined image giving the illusion that they are actually in the location shown in the background. The very first background projection screens were made of ground glass, and were limited in height to several feet. They were also prone to show a "hot-spot"; that is, the part of the image near their center photographed brighter than the parts at the edges. Attempts to use other materials to make large screens had other drawbacks, as can be seen in *The Dawn Patrol* (1930). Here very large screens, presumably made of some thin white cloth, were used in the final ground scenes showing the bombing of the German factory. The image of the distant parts of the bombed factory back projected onto the screen are partially obscured with an all-over wash of white, either from the screen material itself, or from flare in the optical system of the projector. The result is a glaringly unconvincing mismatch between the background and the actors and parts of set built in front of the screen. Earlier in the film close shots of pilots in aeroplanes made in front of smaller back projection screens are satisfactory because the effect is less marked, and also because one expects aerial haze to wash out the background in the real situation being mimicked.

Because of these flaws, background projection was limited to showing things like the passing street through the back window of cars, where small screen size does not matter, until a new cellulose screen material and redesign of the optics of background projectors in 1932 made possible satisfactory projection on screens as big as 17 feet by 23 feet.

The new possibilities of background projection after that date can be studied with advantage in *King Kong* (1933), where all the combination of animated models with live action is achieved by background projection, often with the new large screens, though it would appear that the new fine grain background negative stock was not available when the film was shot. (It must be emphasized that in this film some of the combination of actions in *different* parts of the frame is achieved with the much older fixed matte procedures. Also in one or two shots the silhouettes of birds flying past are made by simple superimposition.)

As a result of the unavailability of good background projection during the early thirties, many films continued to include synch-sound location dialogue sequences, some of them quite lengthy, whereas after 1933 such scenes are very rare. Naturally the point about shooting what purport to be exterior dialogue scenes in front of the background projection screen is that it gives total control over the environment—lighting, weather, and background noise—and hence more efficient production. The reduction of background noise was particularly important given the microphones available in the thirties.

Optical Printing

Optical (or projection) printers involve the frame-by-frame projection of an already shot film through a system of lenses and the frame-by-frame refilming of all or part of the projected image with an accurately aligned camera. In the twenties there were one or two specialist firms in Hollywood that had their own hand-built optical printers, to which the studios sometimes contracted out special effects, but the lack of satisfactory duplicating negative and positive stocks restricted the use of such printers. When duplicating negative and positive film with fine grain and low contrastiness become available at the beginning of the thirties, this permitted combinations of shots to be made in optical printers and then re-copied with hardly any noticeable deterioration in quality, which had not been the case before. Series-built optical printers were made and sold by such firms as DePue from 1930, and with these, or others constructed by their own technicians, the studios set up their own optical printing departments. Immediately such effects as front titles printed over live action at the beginning of films started to appear, followed by the wipe as a shot transition from 1931. (Various approximations to the wipe had been occasionally tried from 1918, but it was impossible to make an in-the-camera wipe accurately at every attempt.) The first wipes were straight-line replacement wipes with hard edges, but other shapes were flirted with, and the edge of the wipe line rapidly became slightly blurred. The availability of optical printers and duplicating stocks also encouraged the proliferation of "montage" sequences with a faster flow of shots than had been the case in the late twenties. In fact there was close to a qualitative change in the typical montage sequence: from a series of short shots linked by dissolves to a continuous series of dissolves end-to-end giving the effect of a continuously changing superimposition. Such an effect was of course impossible to create in the camera, as the late silent-period montage sequences were created.

In the late thirties there were virtually no new developments in this area in America; one should note only an imperfectly successful attempt at travelling mattes in the "Bojangles" scene of *Swing Time* (Stevens, 1936). In Europe optical printers came into use in 1934–35, but the montage sequence never became as widely used as in the United States, possibly partly because the studios tended to contract their processing out, and did not maintain their own optical effects departments, and hence the use of montage sequences was relatively more expensive.

The wipe continued to be used more and more to indicate a short time lapse, and its edge got more and more blurred.

Editing

The basic tool for sound editing had already been introduced at the beginning of sound film-making, and this was the multiple synchronizer just as we know it today in its unadorned form without track reading heads. Originally its purpose had been to keep the several simultaneous picture tracks obtained from multiple camera filming in synchronism with each other during editing, and hence finally with the sound-track disc, but by 1930 both multiple camera filming and sound on disc were abandoned. The synchronizer was then used just to manipulate the series of pairs of picture track and sound-on-film track, and keep them in synchronism during editing. This simple procedure gave no way of hearing the words on the soundtrack, was extremely inefficient, and was not conducive to scene dissection into a large number of shots.

But in 1930 the sound Moviola became available, and from 1931 the Average Shot Lengths in Hollywood films started to drop. The sound Moviola was a simple adaption of the silent Moviola, with a continuously moving sprocket drive pulling the sound-track film under a photoelectric sound head identical to that in a sound projector, the whole unit being mounted beside the standard Moviola picture head, and driven from it in synchronism by a rigid shaft drive. Basically the machine was the same as the present "Hollywood" Moviola, except that the picture was viewed through a magnifying lens, and not back-projected on to a tiny screen. The sound track could be moved slowly by hand under the sound head, and the exact position of any part of a sound identified.

The other development that facilitated the fast cutting (in both senses) of synch-sound shots occurred in 1932, with the introduction of "rubber numbering" (or "edge numbering") for sound and picture tracks. "Rubber numbers" are footage numbers stamped in ink down the outer edge of the picture and soundtrack for each shot. The numbers coincide at the points on the sound track and picture track where the corresponding image and its sound lie. After numbering has been carried out it is possible to shuffle about sections of picture and sound-track in the editing process with perfect freedom, secure in the knowledge that synchronism can be regained when necessary, purely "by the numbers."

As a result of the freedom provided by both these developments, the Average Shot Length in films of this period started to decrease in a way that can be exemplified by the work of William Wellman; *The Public Enemy* (1931) has an A.S.L. of 9 seconds, *Wild Boys of the Road* (1933) has an A.S.L. of 6.5 seconds, and Wellman stayed remarkably close to this latter figure for the rest of his career. Particular advantage of the possibility of speeding up the cutting rate was taken at the Warner Brothers Studio, and this effect can also be seen in Michael Curtiz's films, but the pressure was not absolute, as can be seen from the work of Mervyn Leroy who stayed with a slower speed (*Tugboat Annie*, 1933, A.S.L. 9 seconds) and some camera movement. (It is obviously difficult, though not impossible, to use camera movement in a large number of shots when the A.S.L. gets down to around 6 seconds.) The other extreme of cutting speed, which was commoner in 1930 than 1933, can be represented by John Stahl's *Only Yesterday* (1933), which has an A.S.L. of 14 seconds.

The trend towards faster cutting in many films in the middle thirties can be easily explained as a desire on the part of many people to return to the sort of cutting that had been usual in the majority of American silent films made in the late twenties, when Average Shot Lengths were usually down around 5 seconds. And once the restrictions on cutting sound had been removed by the sound Moviola and rubber numbering, they were free to return towards silent cutting speeds as far as the length of the average line of dialogue would let them. Then after some years of that sort of thing, many directors were ready for a new fashion which appeared, and which will now be discussed.

It was only in the middle thirties that the technical developments in editing procedures introduced prior to 1933 had their full effect. For the period 1934–1939 the mean Average Shot Length for Hollywood movies was around 8–9 seconds. (This figure has been derived from a fairly random collection of over 50 films. Although there are not enough results to make a year-by-year estimate of the mean figure, it is fairly clear that the minimum was achieved round 1935. This means that most directors were taking advantage of the ease of making a large number of cuts in a scene, but there was still a wide spread of characteristic Average Shot Lengths from director to director.) But by 1939 a new tendency in the opposite direction was just beginning to appear, a tendency towards long takes that only became fully developed in the forties.

To give some examples, George Cukor moved from A.S.L.s such as 17 sec. for *Dinner at Eight* (1933) to an A.S.L. of 10 sec. in 1935 for *Sylvia Scarlett*, and then back to long takes for *Holiday* (1938) (A.S.L. of 14 sec.) and *The Women* (1939) (A.S.L. of 13 sec.) and subsequent films. Obviously this sort of movement with the trend was the most common (e.g., Wyler, Hawks), but there were also a number of directors who stuck with what they were doing at the fast cutting end of the spectrum. For example, Curtiz had already arrived at an A.S.L. of around 7 seconds in the early thirties, and he continued right through with the later thirties and into the forties in the same way: *Charge of the Light Brigade*, (1936) has an A.S.L. of 7.5 sec. and *Dodge City* (1939) has an A.S.L. of 7 sec.

On the other hand it was possible to go against the tide, as John Stahl quite remarkably did. From an A.S.L. of 13 seconds in *Imitation of Life* in 1934 he went on to use even longer takes in *Magnificent Obsession* (1935) which has many shots some minutes long, and an Average Shot Length of 26 seconds. Even more remarkably, these long scenes are mostly carried out in "profile two-shot," with two performers facing each other, and there is very little staging in depth in the manner used in Europe by Renoir, and to a lesser extent Marcel Carné and others who used long takes. But none went to such lengths in this period as Stahl did. However by 1939 Stahl had retreated from this extreme position (*When Tomorrow Comes* has an A.S.L. of 14 seconds), and by the forties he was working near the norm for those years.

It might be thought that Average Shot Lengths are related to the genre of the films concerned, and not specific to the directors, but this is only so to an extremely limited extent. The only important cases so far discovered after checking several hundred are those of the musical, where if one includes the musical numbers in the count, there is a definite tendency for a director to use longer takes than he would otherwise. This conclusion is of course dependent on the assumption that the way the musical numbers were shot was controlled by the named director, which probably is not always the case. Another rare instance of the genre of a film dominating the way it is shot is that of the Tarzan films. Here the necessity of faking all the animal stuff ensured that the A.S.L. was always close to 4 seconds, from the thirties through to the fifties, regardless of who directed the films. Regular Tarzan directors such as Richard Thorpe never used such fast cutting on their later films.

On the other hand one finds consistency of Average Shot Length from comedies to dramas to action subjects in the work of directors such as Hawks and Wyler and so on throughout this (and other) periods.

Sound Recording

1930 saw the final triumph of sound-on-film recording; sound on disc was phased out. Starting at the beginning of the sound recording chain, we note that the microphones used continued to be of the "condenser" (capacitance) type. If several microphones were being used to record sound for a shot, their signals were mixed directly before being recorded photographically on the sound negative in the sound camera, in electrical synchronism with the film camera. The mixing of a set of film sound tracks subsequent to their intial recording to give a final combined recording was very rare at the beginning of the thirties; the extra film recording stage introduced a perceptible loss of quality. (This loss of sound quality can be studied in those Laurel and Hardy films from 1931–32 which have continuous background music mixed with the dialogue and effects.) Thus, although post-synchronization of voices to a film scene could be carried out from 1929, it was mostly not used in the early thirties, and location scenes involving dialogue were always shot with direct sound, which naturally ensured that both the voices *and* all the effects went into the right place. This was extremely difficult to do in one pass when post-synchronizing without re-mixing and re-recording.

In some location situations ultra-directional microphones were created by putting an ordinary microphone at the focus of a large (up to 6 ft.) parabolic metal reflector. In this way *fairly* good recordings could be obtained at 15 ft. or more from the actors. Since otherwise all the microphones in use were omnidirectional, picking up sounds equally whatever direction they came from, background noise could be a serious problem with location recording, and this was one of the pressures encouraging the change to the shooting of "exterior" dialogue scenes in the studio as soon as good background projection made this possible.

Throughout the thirties there were more or less continuous improvements in the performance of sound-on-film recording systems through attention to various aspects of their functioning: exposure and development control of the sound track negative, amplifier circuit improvements, mechanical refinements of the sound cameras and printers, and so on. But the really audible advance in the quality of recording was largely due to the track noise suppression techniques introduced in 1931.

By 1933 it was possible to mix a separately recorded music track with the synchronous dialogue track recording after the editing stage without audible loss of sound quality at the extra film recording stage, and from this point on "background music" came to be used more and more extensively. (Up to 1932 there was, roughly speaking, either dialogue *or* music on the sound track, but never both together unless they had been recorded simultaneously. Which they sometimes were.) As the kind of improvements already mentioned continued into the late thirties, including then the important introduction of "push-pull" double sound tracks in the RCA system, it became possible to do multiple-channel music recording on *One Hundred Men and a Girl* (Henry Koster, 1938) and other subsequent musical films.

Putting the situation in another way, there was now full freedom to assemble as complicated sound tracks as could be desired, going through several recording stages if that was necessary.

Technicolor

The Technicolor three-strip camera was to a certain extent modelled on the Mitchell, and was not all that much larger, except that the magazine was three times as wide to accommodate the three rolls of negative side by side. Unlike the Mitchell cameras there was no rack-over arrangement for rapid "through the lens" viewing of the image, and focusing had to be done entirely by the scale on the lens. The larger reliance on the supplementary viewfinder so caused may have produced a tendency to less precisely composed images in Technicolor when compared with the best black and white photography of the late thirties and forties.

Because of the prism block between the back element of the lens and the film gates, ordinary lenses could not be used in the Technicolor camera, and a special set was designed and made by Taylor-Hobson Ltd., but it included no wide angle or very long focal length lenses. Technicolor photography in the studio was carried out at, or near, maximum aperture by necessity, for in the initial period up to 1937 negatives were slower than twenties black-and-white negative, and the key-light level needed for correct exposure was very high. But in 1939 new negative stock was introduced (it was used on *Gone With the Wind*) and this stock was two to four times faster than the earlier material, being considered to have a speed equal to Super X (40 ASA). But even with this improvement, the speed of the film was not great enough, when taken in conjunction with the unavailability of wide-angle lenses for Technicolor cameras, to permit any sort of Toland-style deep-focus on Technicolor films made in the forties.

Flood lights were used rather more for Technicolor lighting than they were in the late thirties for black-and-white filming, which made for flatter lighting, and this fitted in with the usual desire of producers and the Technicolor organization to show as much color as possible in each image. The use of a fair amount of strong chiaroscuro, as in *The Garden of Allah* (1936), seems to have been discouraged, and on the other hand the strikingly modern simplicity of the lighting of *The Trail of the Lonesome Pine*, done by W. Howard Greene with only a few lights per scene, was not popular either.

A frequent feature of lighting for Technicolor, which persisted for decades, first appeared in *The Private Lives of Elizabeth and Essex* (1939) as lit by Sol Polito and W. Howard Greene. This was the practice of splashing areas of amber light and blue light on the backgrounds of "period" interior scenes without regard for any consistency with possible sources, the actors being lit with white light.

In 1937 the Technicolor process was capable of quite accurate reproduction of colours on natural exterior scenes, the true gauge of performance, as can be seen from original prints of *Ebb Tide*, for instance. Initially the system was extremely contrasty, roughly comparable in this respect to present (1976) broadcast-quality color video, the unfill-lighted shadows were solid black, and very bright areas such as white clouds had a tendency to burn out (i.e., become undifferentiated transparent areas on the positive print). However with the advent of the new camera negatives in 1939 this contrastiness was somewhat reduced. As far as faithfulness of color reproduction is concerned, it must be noted that for a couple of years, starting in 1937 and ending in 1939, it was the usual practice to make Technicolor prints with an overemphasis in the direction of orange, and such prints do not provide a true idea of the fidelity that the system was capable of at that time. (Further warning: A number of early Technicolor films such as *Becky Sharp* and *A Star Is Born* were later reissued in two-color Cinecolor prints, and these have very little relation at all to the color, definition, and contrast of the original prints.)

Because the light level on a background projection screen has to match the light level of the scene being filmed in front of it, the large light levels required for Technicolor before 1939 prevented the use of big BP screens, the upper limit being about ten feet. After 1939 the problem was minimized by the faster stock then available, and also by the development of triple background projectors at Paramount and Warners—the images from three projectors perfectly superimposed on one screen to give three times the screen brightness. But this restriction on background projection may have contributed to the large amount of location shooting in many of the Technicolor films of this period when compared with the usual practice in black-and-white filming in the late thirties.

Although the basic Technicolor camera was not much bigger and heavier than a Mitchell NC, the blimp for the Technicolor cameras was much bigger and heavier than the usual blimps made for Mitchell cameras. (Its dimensions were about two feet by three feet by three feet.) It might be speculated that this bulk and weight militated against using the larger number of camera set-ups that were required by the shorter end of the Hollywood A.S.L. range. Certainly Wellman's *A Star Is Born* (1937) has an A.S.L. of 9.5 seconds compared with his habitual 5 to 6 seconds, and Henry Hathaway, who also worked in the same range in his black-and-white films, went up to a slower cutting (A.S.L. of 7 seconds) in *The Trail of the Lonesome Pine*. It is doubtful if this effect extended to a pressure on those directors working near the mean Average Shot Length; Ford's *Drums Along the Mohawk* has an A.S.L. of 9.5 seconds, which is quite close enough to his usual black-and-white figure of 9 seconds.

Narrative Construction

The early thirties were a period when the brightest spirits were very active in trying out new devices for narrative construction in the mainstream sound cinema, and most of the instances are well known. Nevertheless for the sake of completeness we must mention such features as depend on the use and existence of a sound track as the internal monologue in Hitchcock's *Murder* (1930), the visual illustration of speeches continued on sound only in Fritz Lang's *M* (1931), the subjective camera sequence opening Mamoulian's *Dr. Jekyll and Mr. Hyde* (1932), and the jump cuts given continuity by dialogue continuing across them in Clair's *A Nous La Liberté* (1932). Less well known is the narration of *The Power and the Glory* (W. K. Howard, 1933) through a series of nonchronologically arranged flashbacks, and even more remarkably, in one flashback as the narrator quotes the dialogue used on the past occasion visually represented, his words coincide with the lip movements of the characters in the flashback so that he speaks their dialogue for them. Possibly the first occasion when the audience was addressed directly in a sound film was at the end of *Big Boy* (Alan Crosland, 1930), at which point the camera pulled back to reveal that what had seemed an ordinary film to that point was taking place on a theater stage. More importantly there are of course the asides to the audience in Lubitsch's *The Smiling Lieutenant* (1931) and *Love Me Tonight* (1932).

Finally one must also mention the use of zip pans as a transitional device to indicate time lapse in *The Trial of Vivian Ware* (William K. Howard, 1934).

The later thirties were the cinema's most restricted and restrictive period, and although as already indicated films continued to occupy a large range in most of the major formal dimensions of the medium, there was very little indeed going on at the innovative extremes. Even documentary films, which had to a certain extent taken the place of the by then nonexistent avant-garde, were rather timid in the main, and one cannot point to much more than the rhythmic sound-and-poetry tracks of Cavalcanti's *Coal Face* (1935) and its successors, and the peculiarities of Dziga-Vertov's *Three Songs about Lenin* (1934). In feature films Dovzhenko's *Aerograd* (1935), with its interjected choral songs illustrated on the picture track, springs to mind, but otherwise one is left with a very few individual cases such as the innovative games played with the medium in Sacha Guitry's *Roman d'un Tricheur* (1936).

Overall, one can say that the very general trend in the early thirties in mainstream cinema was back to the style of the last silent films, 1928 vintage, as soon as the various technological constraints on putting a film together were relieved. Having reached this point about 1934–35, new technical developments began to have some effect on film photography, and at the end of the thirties a new trend towards longer takes was just starting to emerge independently of any technological pressures—a trend that was to flourish in the forties.

Note

1 In 1937 typical values were 250–400 foot-candles for black and white filming and 800–1000 foot-candles for Technicolor, while in 1940 typical values were 75–150 foot-candles for black and white and 150–400 foot-candles for Technicolor.

Chapter 6

Kristen Whissel

TALES OF UPWARD MOBILITY (2006)

Editors' Introduction

Studies of film technology tend to follow at least one of two methods. There are those examinations of the development and implementation of technologies, for example Douglas Gomery's work on cinematic sound systems during the late 1920s and early 1930s, and the raft of contractual and patent agreements that went along with them. And then there are analyses, like Kristen Whissel's here, that detail the manner in which those new technologies affect film style and narrative. In her essay, Whissel does not propose that film technology fully informs and drives film style; there are, actually, far too many factors to consider, such as genre, studio, era, or star, for example. But it may well be true that there have been periods of technological overdetermination, when the machinery of filmmaking had an atypical impact on how films looked and sounded. Indeed, the introduction of recorded sound probably began one such period. And, as Whissel shows, so too did the introduction of various computer-generated technologies (CGI) in the late 1990s and early 2000s. Those movies that made full use of CGI, such as *The Matrix* series and the various *Lord of the Rings* movies shifted the usual visual plane of cinema from horizontal to vertical. Whissel charts the history of the vertical axis in cinema, from Harold Lloyd hanging on a clock in *Safety Last* (1923) to James Stewart in *Rear Window* (1954) to the big budget films of the 1970s, so that this "newer" view does not seem to spring fully grown from a special effects expert's computer in the 1990s. But the CGI movement from that period to the present has changed the ways that we see films and understand them, with Whissel showing us how to examine technology's impact on so many aspects of cinema, from production to representation to reception.

Suggested Reading

Douglas Gomery, "Economic Struggle and Hollywood Imperialism: Europe Converts to Sound," *Yale French Studies*, no. 60 (1980), pp. 80–93; Michelle Pierson, *Special Effects: Still in Search of Wonder* (New York: Columbia University Press, 2002); Alice

Maurice, " 'Cinema at its Source': Synchronizing Race and Sound in Early Talkies," *Camera Obscura*, 17 (1:49), 2002, pp. 1–71.

> So neither the horizontal nor the vertical proportion of the screen *alone* is ideal for it.
>
> *In actual fact, as we saw, in the forms of nature as in the forms of industry, and in the mutual encounter between these forms, we find the struggle, the conflict between both tendencies. And the screen, as a faithful mirror, not only of conflicts emotional and tragic, but equally of conflicts psychological and optically spatial, must be an appropriate battleground for the skirmishes of both these optical-by-view, but profoundly psychological-by-meaning, spatial tendencies on the part of the spectator.*
>
> (Sergei Eisenstein, "The Dynamic Square")[1]

FOLLOWING THE RELEASE OF *The Matrix* (1999, 2003) and *The Lord of the Rings* (2001, 2002, 2003) trilogies, *X-Men* and *X2* (2000, 2003), *Crouching Tiger, Hidden Dragon* (2000), and *Hero* (2002), it is safe to say that CGI technologies have given rise to a new generation of films that make increasing use of the screen's vertical axis. Drawing from cultural sources ranging from comic books and fantasy novels to the visual logics of video games and virtual reality, recent blockbusters deploy a broad range of digital special effects to create composite film bodies that effortlessly defy gravity or tragically succumb to its pull. In keeping with this tendency, these same films create breathtaking imaginary worlds defined by extreme heights and plunging depths whose stark verticality becomes the referential axis of many narrative conflicts. Such verticality is now pervasive enough to have become an important feature of popular cinema of the early twenty-first century and as such demands critical attention.

The following investigates what might be thought of as the spatial dialectics of contemporary cinema's vertical imagination—its tendency to map the violent collision of opposed forces onto a vertical axis marked by extreme highs and lows. Specifically, it approaches digitally enhanced verticality as a mode of cinematic representation designed to exploit to an unprecedented degree the visual pleasures of power and powerlessness.[2] Precisely because verticality automatically implies the intersection of two opposed forces—gravity and the force required to overcome it—it is an ideal technique for visualizing power. Verticality thereby facilitates a rather literal naturalization of culture in which the operation and effects of (social, economic, military) power are mapped onto the laws of space and time. Hence, in recent blockbuster films, vertically oriented bodies and objects imply a relation not just to the laws of physics but also to the spaces and times that define a fictional world's prevailing order. Vertical movement thereby gives dynamic, hyperkinetic expression to power and the individual's relation to it—defiant, transcendent, or subordinate.

This article will explore what recent (post-1996) blockbusters reveal about cinematic verticality and, in turn, what verticality can tell us about contemporary global cinema. While I will make reference to a number of popular films along the way, I will focus on *Titanic* (1997), *Hero, X-Men, The Matrix*, and *Crouching Tiger, Hidden Dragon*. Though the films under investigation here span a number of genres—including martial arts films, disaster films, comic-book adaptations, science-fiction films, action-adventure films, and fantasy films—and are produced in the U.S., Hong Kong, China, and Taiwan, they all share a number of characteristics linked to their insistent deployment of verticality.

To be sure, film history is replete with breathtaking falls and astonishing ascents enabled by historically available special effects, from Harold Lloyd's precarious climb up the side of a department store in *Safety Last!* (1923) to James Stewart's defenestration at the end of *Rear Window* (1954), and Slim Pickens' descent through the atmosphere astride a bomb in

Dr. Strange-love (1964). However, the blockbusters of the 1970s marked a turning point in the history of cinematic verticality; they deployed big-budget special effects to exploit the screen's vertical axis to a degree not seen before. While *The Poseidon Adventure* (1972) capsized an ocean liner and forced its protagonists to ascend through a series of inverted sets to find a way out through the ship's upended hull, *The Towering Inferno* (1974) turned the skyscraper into an upright labyrinth difficult to exit alive, and *King Kong* (1976) staged a battle between Kong and the NYPD on the top of the World Trade Center. Films like *Star Wars* (1977), *Superman* (1978), *Close Encounters of the Third Kind* (1979), and *E.T.* (1982) increasingly used models, miniatures, blue screens, and mattes to animate their characters' movements and desires along the screen's vertical axis, while *High Anxiety* (1977) parodied the use of the fall as a device for creating suspense in classical film.

The increasing exploitation of the screen's vertical axis continued through the 1980s and became significantly more pronounced with the development of digital special effects. In 1989, *The Abyss* used digital special effects to stage a deep-sea encounter with alien life forms: much of the film takes place on the edge of an underwater chasm plunging two-and-a-half miles to the ocean floor. In 1990, wire removal software created convincing images of bodies and matter in flight in *Back to the Future III*, while in 1993 Industrial Light and Magic's Digital Input Device animated the screen's vertical axis with towering photorealistic dinosaurs in *Jurassic Park*. In 1994, the infant protagonist of *Baby's Day Out* scaled the heights of Chicago's skyline thanks to composites that synthesized the baby's blue screen image with digitized photos of the cityscape.[3] Such developments reached a watershed in 1996, when the three top-grossing films of the year—*Independence Day, Twister* (both of which used new particle animation software), and *Mission: Impossible* (for which The Computer Film Company did digital compositing, paintwork, wire removal, and tracking)—suggested that digital technology's ability to polarize action along extreme spatial coordinates would continue to develop into the new millennium.

At its most basic level, the new digital verticality is a technique for activating polarized extremes. Its abstract spatial coordinates are those of the zenith and the nadir, and its favorite location is the precipice, regardless of setting. Since the early 1990s, skyscrapers, national monuments, elevator shafts, upended ocean liners, high towers, tall (and sometimes ambulatory) trees, mountaintops, hilltop cities, and chasms all function with equal efficiency to polarize conflict, to frame possible outcomes in terms of a devastating fall and/or a willfully insurgent rise. Even when action returns to terra firma and ordinary horizontality, digitally enhanced mises-en-scène activate the screen's vertical axis: pillared interiors, banners streaming down from high ceilings, drops of water falling in slow motion, and showers of brightly colored petals and bullet casings all indicate that actions and events will inevitably follow lines of ascent and descent, thereby compounding the thematic significance of vertical movement in these films.

In the process, verticality mobilizes various connotative meanings and feelings attached to ascent and descent. Upward mobility gives dynamic expression to feelings of soaring hope, joy, unbridled desire, and aspiration; it implies lightness, vitality, freedom, transcendence, defiance, and lofty ideals. In turn, falling and sinking give expression to dread, doom, and terror and are linked to heavy burdens, inertia, subordination, loss, and the void.[4] As a dynamic device for conveying the heightened emotions to which violent conflict gives rise, the new verticality draws heavily from 1950s Hollywood melodrama's use of expressionistic mise-en-scène, and takes the genre's association of staircases with rising and falling emotions to new extremes.[5] Not only has the scale of the vertical setting expanded exponentially with the development of CGI (to, say, elevator shafts spanning more than 100 floors, or the steep incline of a volcano), but so have the stakes: frequently a struggle for the survival of an entire city (*Spider-Man, X-Men, Godzilla* [1998]) or humanity itself (*The Matrix, The Lord of the*

Rings, The Day After Tomorrow [2004], *Armageddon* [1998], *Independence Day, Sky Captain and the World of Tomorrow* [2004], *The War of the Worlds* [2005]) is played out along spatial coordinates of extreme highs and lows. Because the new verticality vastly expands the terrain upon which (and with which) the cinema compels its protagonists to struggle, it logically favors the epic.

As the above suggests, verticality's link to gravity and the laws of space and time makes it an ideal aesthetic for dramatizing the individual's relationship to powerful historical forces. Horizontality, in this context, stands for temporal and historical continuity which, when ruptured by the upsurge or fall of a vertically articulated mass, creates a dynamized moment, a temporal-historical break that radically changes the course of events. In *Jurassic Park* the sudden and astonishing appearance of the massive T-Rex signals the violent resurrection of the evolutionary past and the foolhardiness of the park owner's plan, as Constance Balides describes it, to appropriate "historical time for profit on a grand scale."[6] In *The Day after Tomorrow*, a wall of water crashes into and submerges Manhattan to signal an irreversible shift in the international balance of power: the United States' economic and military supremacy comes to an end, initiating a new era in which it is dependent upon Mexico. In *Reign of Fire* (2002), *Deep Impact* (1998), *Armageddon*, and *Pearl Harbor* (2001), digitally rendered danger descends from above and threatens to bring human time itself to an end. Most recently, *The War of the Worlds* imagines the end of humanity through the apocalyptic arrival of alien forces from above and below: in an astonishing special-effects sequence, towering alien tripods erupt from deep beneath the earth's surface. The machines are themselves operated by creatures driven below ground by bolts of lightning that spike down violently from stormy skies above.

When verticality finds expression through the gravity-defying body of a protagonist, it often implies a crisis inseparable from his or her problematic relation to the historical, familial, and traditional past. Whereas a protagonist's upward vertical movement is frequently symbolic of a leap towards a new future, downward verticality is inseparable from the rapid approach of an inevitable end. In some of these films, the past is represented as a burden that constrains the protagonist's freedom precisely so that powerful social and political formations may carry on, unchanged, into the future (*Titanic, Crouching Tiger, Hidden Dragon*). In some cases, the past repeats itself and revives dark forces that promise to annihilate the protagonist in the not-so-distant future (*X-Men, The Fifth Element* [1997], *The Lord of the Rings* trilogy, *Minority Report* [2002], *Van Helsing*, and *Hellboy* [2004]). Conversely, in yet another group, historical continuity and a tangible relation to the past provide the conditions of possibility for an historical agency able to overcome forces whose power stems precisely from an ability to manipulate space and time at will (*The Matrix* trilogy, *Dark City* [1998]). Since extreme forms of vertical movement inevitably involve a violation of physical laws (which then often reassert themselves), vertically oriented bodies and narratives provide the ideal form for abstracting power and representing the struggles of the emergent against the dominant—a concept neatly conveyed by the title *Sky Captain and the World of Tomorrow*.

While the popularity of the blockbusters under consideration here can be explained in part by their presentation of astonishing digitally rendered spectacles, I would add that the "structure of feeling" invoked by verticality also causes them to resonate with contemporary audiences. Because verticality lends itself so well to the dynamic elaboration of conflict between opposed (historical, ideological, and natural) forces, it seems remarkably suitable for an era defined by economic polarization and new forms of political, religious, and military extremism, all of which seem to have had the effect (or so we are regularly told) of evacuating previously available middle grounds.[7] (The way that such global conflicts played out at the World Trade Center on September 11, 2001 only reinforced the link between verticality and the struggle for power in the popular imaginary.) Indeed, verticality allows these films simultaneously to acknowledge extremism, economic polarization, and thwarted upward mobility as significant aspects of their global audience's condition of existence, and to charge these crises with new visual pleasures. Even when they purport to represent actual historical events, these blockbusters feature mythological characters, breathtaking vertical terrains, and forms of embodiment—all of them more or less detached from any referent in the real world—onto which international audiences can map their conflicting identifications and emotional affiliations.[8] Precisely by defying verisimilitude, the new verticality lends these films a different sort of truth—a symbolic or emotional one that mediates present geopolitical reality.

This is not to say that previous eras have been free of either extremism or cinematic verticality. Indeed, verticality has been used to dramatize violent conflict since Flora Cameron was chased to the cliff's edge by Gus in *The Birth of a Nation* [1915]).[9] However, prior to the special-effects advances of the early 1990s, cinematic being-in-the-world remained for the most part anchored on a horizontal axis and terrestrial plane of existence, and verticality was used primarily to punctuate action and accent narrative climaxes and dramatic conflict. Recent blockbuster films exponentially extend and expand upon the cinema's ongoing exploitation of gravity's dramatic potential. Digital technologies have helped liberate many aspects of production from the laws of physics, allowing for much more pronounced and sustained exploitation of the screen's vertical axis. Hence, it seems that just as widescreen processes "created the functional grounds for a new film aesthetic based upon composition in width and depth" in the 1950s,[10] digital processes are currently giving rise to a new film aesthetic based on height and depth. As a result, verticality is no longer confined to hair-raising stunts and dramatic camera angles, but has become a cinematic mode that structures and coordinates setting, action, dialogue, and characterization along radical lines of ascent and descent. Now characters such as Gandalf in *The Lord of the Rings* plunge (followed by the "camera") thousands of feet without bodily injury, displacing the long fall's dramatic effect away from the body and onto narrative. Struggles between protagonists and antagonists hinge upon the degree to which each is able to defy or master the laws of physics, making extreme vertical settings—skyscrapers, deep chasms, mountain peaks—pervasive and imperative. The resulting spatialization of power and time allows the new verticality to map spatial transience onto historical transition and radical forms of mobility onto the possibilities and perils of change.

Gravity, Historical Inertia, and Inevitability

I want to begin with two extremely profitable films—*Titanic* and *Hero*[11]—that use verticality's spatial dialectics to represent mythologized historical pasts defined by the violent opposition of polarized (political, economic) extremes. By mapping complex struggles for power onto the laws of physics, verticality can make historical change a matter of inertia or inevitability. While *Titanic*'s verticality represents history as a body or force that will remain in motion along a specific trajectory unless displaced by another force, *Hero* uses verticality to make the outcome of imperial history as predictable as the operation of gravity itself. And while verticality loans some support to the "official" histories that these films appear to confirm (i.e., class conflict lies submerged in America's distant past; national greatness demands the violent suppression of internal dissent), its dual movement also accommodates contradictory interpretations.

We can begin with *Titanic*, which links its ship's forward propulsion to historical inertia and a sense that the early twentieth century was drifting blindly towards disaster. As many scholars have argued, *Titanic* depicts 1914 as a moment in American history defined by a rigid and punitive class-gender system in which a corrupt and decadent industrial patriarchy (modeled after European aristocracy) greedily pursued wealth and fame at the expense of others.[12] This world is remarkably polarized: there is no middle class (the ship offers only first- and third-class passage) and proper Victorian femininity (contrasted only by the French prostitutes in Jack's sketchbook) remains unchallenged by the New Woman. The ship's rigid segregation of classes by deck emphasizes two-tiered hierarchy and subordination from above. Aside from some minor grumblings about the tendency of first-class passengers to walk their dogs on the third-class deck, and the hushed explanation that women's choices are always difficult, acquiescence to a corrupt industrial patriarchy prevails among female and third-class passengers. Described as "a steamer so grand in scale and so luxurious in its appointments that its supremacy would never be challenged," the ship materializes both the decadent excesses of the industrial class and the arrogant presumption that it, like the *Titanic*, is unsinkable. Computer-generated tracking shots emphasize the ship's considerable length while wide shots display its smooth passage along the ocean's flat, expansive surface, linking the prevailing order with a seemingly endless horizontality. The film thereby turns the *Titanic* into an emblem of historical inertia: unless acted upon by another force, history will move in the direction of increasing imbalance of power between classes and genders.

Historical inertia is doubled by the inertia that seems to govern the fate of Rose Dewitt Bukater (Kate Winslet), whose impending marriage has been arranged purely for the profit of others: it will both enable her fiancé to come into his inheritance, and her mother to retain the upper-class lifestyle threatened by her late husband's debts. Marriage seems to reduce Rose to a mute object, incapable of action. A panning shot of the dining room at teatime shows other women gossiping animatedly about the wedding as Rose sits paralyzed, staring blankly ahead. Rose's voiceover explains: "I felt like I was standing at a great precipice with no one to pull me back, no one who cared or even noticed." Her later suicide attempt links her plight to a descent into a dark void. When asked why she tried to jump overboard, she explains: "It was everything: my whole world and the people in it. And the inertia of my life plunging ahead and me powerless to stop it." To extend the association of the bride with falling matter and social constraints with the force of gravity, Rose shows Jack (Leonardo DiCaprio) her engagement ring and he comments: "God, look at that thing: you would have gone straight to the bottom."

Verticality intervenes as a spectacular figure for temporal rupture and violent historical "break." Looming high above the ship's upper decks, an iceberg's sudden appearance reconfigures the ocean's topography by activating vertical space high above and deep below its surface: it punctures the ship's hull, rushing water into it from below, and showers chunks of ice onto the deck from above. This reorganization of linear space prepares the way for the astonishing special-effects shots of the ship's stern catapulting high up into the air, converting the *Titanic*'s unprecedented length into a terrifying precipice that spurs the fall of an unjust era. Gravity therefore acts as an historical corrective in this film: it violently undoes the flattened hierarchy of the ship's two-tiered class configuration by turning the first- and third-class decks into equivalent parallel lines aligned upright, side by side. Computer-generated long shots and point-of-view shots from the top of the upended stern show hundreds of (digital) passengers—transformed into mere objects by gravity—tumbling the length of ship to the icy waters far below. All fall to their deaths at the same speed regardless of class or rank as the ship's bow points to its new destination at the bottom of the ocean. Social determinism gives way to "mathematical certainties," and the indifferent laws of physics take control of the *Titanic*'s fate, emphasizing the idea that: "In the act of falling, history relentlessly marches on to its foregone conclusion."[13] Verticality further materializes the notion of an historical break as the ship cleaves in two before upending again and then plummeting down to the depths of the ocean floor.

That Rose's struggle for survival takes place at the stern is significant, for this site is associated with her earlier desire to give herself over to gravity and dissolution. The ship's sinking ultimately provokes her resistance to the force to which she earlier wished to succumb: she refuses to stay in the lifeboat (reserved for first-class passengers) that would preserve her identity and ends up quite literally on a new a precipice where, with Jack's help, she resists gravity's (previously alluring) pull. Verticality repeats and inverts the logic of Rose's attempted suicide: rather than escape an oppressive regime by jumping overboard, the oppressive regime is instead sent plunging into the depths of the ocean. Rose's temporary submersion ultimately dissolves oppressive social–familial ties and consigns Victorian femininity to an obscure past: kicking to the surface, she emerges from disaster as Rose Dawson, New Woman. By simultaneously resisting gravity and succumbing to its corrective forces, Rose bridges verticality's historical break to become the subject of a new history defined not by polarizations and inertia, but by middle grounds and hyperkinetic motion. While the frame narrative reveals that Rose went on to get married in the mid-West and has grown into old age as part of California's comfortable middle class, old photographs show a young Rose Dawson standing in front of a bi-plane and riding a horse in front of a roller coaster.

Critics have argued that Rose's transformation into a penniless third-class passenger who eventually rises to the middle class upholds the American ideology of upward economic mobility.[14] I agree, but would add that *Titanic* is equally concerned (as its special effects suggest) with downward mobility and that its focus upon descent simultaneously addresses a global audience for whom such myths of prosperity are untenable. Verticality is masterfully and profitably deployed in *Titanic* to charge downward mobility with unprecedented visual pleasure: not only are the most astonishing digital special effects reserved for the ship's near 90-degree inversion, but the latter facilitates a decline in Rose's social status that the film implies has only liberating consequences. Fantasies of potential and possibility are ultimately tied to a protagonist who wins by losing. Her ongoing determination to cast off the burdens of the society life she left behind is signaled when the elderly Rose tosses the Heart of the Ocean diamond into the sea—a moment that should remind us that she never was, in fact, lower-class. In contrast, Jack, who is the film's primary figure for irrepressible upward mobility, heroically slips beneath the ocean's surface. Even as the frame narrative makes the myth of upward mobility available to some audiences, the film's tendency to map mobility along a downward trajectory acknowledges that the middle class may indeed only be accessible from above. As *Titanic* suggests, verticality's spatial dialectics and dual movement allow it to mobilize extremes, elaborate struggles for and imbalances in power, and accommodate contradictory interpretations of each. In this way, verticality dramatizes and makes pleasurable the (spectatorial) position of being caught in the middle of violent conflict between polarized extremes, whatever its outcome.

Like *Titanic, Hero* represents historical shift through verticality in order to dramatize the spectacular end of an era. In this film, verticality finds its most stunning elaboration through the four assassins who attempt to end the bloody conquest of the region's warring kingdoms by the King of Qin (Daoming Chen). Digitally enhanced wire fighting mobilizes their bodies along an expanded vertical axis and works in tandem with a highly stylized mise-en-scène to map complex historical forces onto (spatially) polarized oppositions.

Hero is organized around three narratives that provide competing versions of the events that have brought the assassin Nameless (Jet Li) within ten paces, and hence striking distance, of the King. Within them, the assassins defy gravity in settings defined by high bookshelves, tall trees, mountains, desert rock formations, and cascading waterfalls, linking verticality to their obstruction of the King's plans for conquest. From the beginning, mise-en-scène supplements vertical motion to materialize the idea that history proceeds dialectically from the intersection of directionally opposed forces. When Nameless arrives at the King's court, horizontal and vertical lines clash to create a form of graphic montage within the frame. As he mounts the stairs to the palace, his upright figure cuts sharply against the lines of the broad staircase that span the entire width of the screen. Once inside, the interior of the Great Hall is even more starkly defined by linear conflict: in one shot taken from the King's point of view, Nameless's upright figure and the palace's pillars are dwarfed by horizontally aligned ceiling beams and rows of candles that dominate the frame and appear to exert pressure upon vertical elements from above and below. The visual dominance of horizontality in the opening scene is important, for *Hero* concludes with a funeral procession that celebrates the willing demise of forces of resistance. As the narrative unfolds, increasingly graceful images of downward mobility invest the assassins' surrender of power with elegiac beauty. In this respect, verticality aids in the aestheticization of acquiescence, and gravity's inescapable pull lends a sense of inevitability to past (and future) history and to the protagonist's heroic willingness to be leveled by the forward thrust of imperial "progress."

In the first, most fictional narrative, Nameless impersonates a prefect who defeats the King's enemies—Sky (Donnie Yen), Broken Sword (Tony Leung), and Flying Snow (Maggie Cheung)—by taking advantage of a love triangle that has bitterly divided the assassins. Here gravity-defiant insurgency is linked to heightened emotions and feuds fueled by jealousy and disloyalty. These connotations are most pronounced in the scene when Moon (Zhang Ziyi) fights Flying Snow to avenge her master's murder. Throughout the scene, rage fuels vertical mobility as the combatants whirl through the air like tornados, give chase over treetops, and dive from high up in the air towards grounded targets below. Throughout the fight, bright yellow leaves rain down upon the combatants, suggesting that the unbridled passions that propel them upwards will ultimately lead to their downfall. Indeed, when Flying Snow fatally wounds Moon, the trees and the falling leaves turn blood red. Mise-en-scène appears to mourn the futility of Moon's death, giving the impression that the natural world bleeds with her. At the end of the tale none but Nameless—the King's loyal prefect—is left standing. Though the King ultimately disproves this story, it serves the broader ideological function of allowing vertically articulated bodies to stand for the warring kingdoms that suffer needlessly by fighting amongst themselves, making unity through empire appear natural and necessary.

In the second tale, the King narrates events as he imagines they must have transpired, given his knowledge of the assassins' honorable character. The King correctly surmises that Nameless, too, is an assassin and assumes that unity of purpose among the assassins has allowed him to come within striking distance of the King's throne. In this version, verticality allows the King's admiration for the assassins' willingness to sacrifice themselves for their cause to be expressed through stunning images of descent. After picturing Flying Snow's heroic death during her staged battle with Nameless (as they fight, she exclaims: "I die willingly for our cause! Please make your move!"), the King imagines a subsequent, more spectacular fight between Nameless and Broken Sword. However, this one unfolds only in their minds as a tribute to Flying Snow, whose body lies nearby on a bier. The fight takes place on a lake, the surface of which mirrors the tree-covered mountains in the background, inverting the treetops and peaks so they point to the bottom of the frame. In some shots, only the reflection is visible in the frame, orienting mise-en-scène along a downward trajectory, while in others the frame is divided between the landscape and its mirror image, between competing images of ascent and descent that match the rising and falling action. The camera cuts between images of the fighters skipping across the surface of the water like birds taking flight and wide shots of them plunging headlong towards the lake, using the tips of their swords to rebound off the water's smooth surface. Here, ascent (and with it, insurgent power) is most beautiful when followed by images of descent that aestheticize the surrender to gravity and the loss of power. Not surprisingly, then, the King's imagination privileges and aestheticizes self-sacrifice and points towards the film's conclusion in which Nameless is given a hero's funeral after he sacrifices himself and his cause to the King's ostensibly higher goals of empire.

The third and final tale combines elements of the first two: the assassins are divided not by desire and jealousy but by conflicting political ideals. While Snow and Nameless still oppose the King (their families were killed by his army), Broken Sword embraces the vision of "Our Land" and the unification of the warring kingdoms through bloody conquest. Predictably, Broken Sword's decision to succumb to the forward march of progress follows the line of descent. In a flashback within the tale, he describes the fight in which he passed up the opportunity to assassinate the King. The fight unfolds in the Great Hall among long green banners that hang from the high ceiling and match the color of Broken Sword's clothing. Here, vertically articulated mise-en-scène aids wire fighting to give outward expression to Broken Sword's desire to relinquish his part in the struggle, and thereby helps map a shift in power. At a crucial moment, Broken Sword has the chance to cut the King's throat but ultimately pulls back. After the King realizes his life has been spared, a long shot shows the massive banners streaming gently to the floor on either side of the combatants. Opposed spatial coordinates of high and low are flattened as opposition gives way to acquiescence, allowing gravity to double for the inexorable force of China's (future) imperial history.

This force finds expression through the arrows that slice across the court when the King gives the order to execute Nameless, sacrificing him to the ideology of "Our Land." Having taken to heart Broken Sword's argument that only the King has the power to end suffering and "bring peace by uniting our land," Nameless also declines to assassinate the future Emperor and therefore forfeits his life. His execution concludes with an image that simultaneously documents the fall of oppositional power and aestheticizes its absence. The camera tracks along the Court Wall—now transformed by thousands of black arrows that protrude from a thick horizontal mass on its surface—until it reaches the empty, blank space where Nameless once stood. The negative space that gives shape to the assassin's absent upright figure perfectly emblematizes the ideology that national history always demands the noble self-erasure of insurgent forces which resist its forward movement and idealizes (self-) subordination to an oppressive regime.[15]

Walled Cities, Mountaintops, and the Force of Tradition

Crouching Tiger, Hidden Dragon, a *wu xia* film that undoubtedly helped prime *Hero*'s enthusiastic reception by Western audiences, uses digitally enhanced special effects to melodramatize a dynamic struggle for power by protagonists whose upward verticality is linked to insurgency against ongoing traditions and the past. As in *Hero*, resistance has deadly consequences and the film ends with a willing fall. At the opening of *Crouching Tiger*, each of the main characters is poised to break from the customs and institutions that define their lives. However, the past thwarts each attempt and asserts itself primarily through the obligations of duty and revenge, both of which preserve lines of power and maintain the past in the present.

Jen (Zhang Ziyi) is about to enter into an arranged marriage certain to advance her father's career and increase her family's power. Though she appears to be an obedient daughter, she is in fact, secretly, a powerful fighter trained by the notorious Jade Fox (Pei-Pei Cheng) and is in love with Lo (Chen Chang), an outlaw bandit. Jen wishes to lead a warrior's life, which she mistakenly believes is defined by freedom from duty to others. Li Mu Bai (Chow Yun Fat) wishes to quit his life as a warrior in order to spend it instead with Shu Lien (Michelle Yeoh), and she, too, contemplates forgetting her duty to honor the memory of her dead fiancé to be with Li Mu Bai. However, loyalty to his dead master (Yi) binds Li Mu Bai to the past. At the beginning of the film, he gives away the Green Destiny sword to escape the Giang Hu underworld, but, as he notes, "the cycle of bloodshed continues" as Jade Fox's arrival in Peking forces him to avenge his master's murder. In *Crouching Tiger*, vengeance maintains the past in the present by keeping one murder alive, so to speak, until another one consigns it to the past. Though Li Mu Bai kills Jade Fox, she slays him with the same poison she used to kill his master. Rather than free Li Mu Bai to pursue a new future, the act of vengeance gives the past the power to repeat itself and foreclose upon the future altogether. As in *Titanic* and *Hero*, the struggle for power between polarized forces takes place on an historical threshold, a moment of potential transition whose upheaval is figured through vertical movement.

Li Mu Bai and Jen are defined in part by their desire to jettison traditional duties to fathers and masters in favor of satisfying individual desire. They also imagine and long for a future that departs from the traditional order of things. In the first half of the film, Li Mu Bai plans to abandon his training altogether to be with Shu Lien, but in the second half, decides to return to Wudan to train a female disciple. In turn, Jen leaves behind the obligations of aristocratic femininity to roam freely as a rogue warrior unbound by any duty to others—even the consideration of others (Qing) that Shu Lien points out is necessary for survival. Indeed, Jen rejects the traditional female virtues of both Xie and Zhen (sexual purity), gives way to Yin (excessive sexual feeling), and fails to exhibit Li (propriety or conformity to accepted standards of social behavior).[16] Not surprisingly, Jen and Li Mu Bai are the film's primary and secondary agents of verticality. Ultimately, the film is ambivalent about any complete rejection of or acquiescence to the demands of the past, for both the fulfillment of traditional duties and rejection of them have disastrous consequences.

The first vertically oriented fight scene occurs immediately after Jen indicates to Shu Lien her desire to evade the confinement and subordination of her approaching arranged marriage. In an act of rebellion that will give her a material connection to the warrior life she desires, Jen steals the Green Destiny sword. Hearing the raised alarm, Shu Lien pursues Jen over peaked rooftops, giving the chase an undulating effect that choreographs their contrasting relation to the traditions and duties that bind present and future behavior to the past. As Christina Klein notes, whereas the dutiful Shu Lien acts as with the force of gravity throughout the scene, Jen defies gravity much as she desires to defy duty and tradition. Hence throughout the fight scene, Shu Lien counters each of Jen's vertical ascents: she knocks Jen out of the air by throwing bales of hay and pieces of brick at her; she steps on Jen's feet as Jen pushes off the ground to fly away; grabs her clothes before she soars out of reach; and scrambles up a wall to cut off Jen's ascent, demanding that she "Get down here!"[17]

Indeed, given her function as an anchor that works to keep the fight on solid ground, it is significant that throughout much of the film Shu Lien chooses to remain bound by tradition: she exemplifies filial piety to her dead father by successfully operating the security business he passed on to her (one client declares her an honor to her father's memory); she protects the interests and reputation of Sir Te (who regards her as a daughter) at all costs; and she explains that she and Li Mu Bai have forsaken their desire for one another to remain faithful to the memory of Meng Si Zhao, her fiancé and Li Mu Bai's blood brother. Rather than challenge patriarchy, her role as a warrior and security agent fulfills the principle of filial piety: she carries on her father's work in his absence.[18] If the digitally rendered walled city of Peking is an architectural manifestation of Jen's confinement by ongoing traditions and family histories far more powerful than she, then Shu Lien embodies the structural support of dutiful femininity on which tradition's continuity depends. Hence, throughout their first fight, tradition and duty—figured as the earth's gravitational pull—exercise themselves through Shu Lien, who acts as a counterweight to Jen's vertical flight.

We can compare the vertical action of this scene with the fight between Li Mu Bai and Jen atop the bamboo forest. In contrast with the rigid up-or-down verticality of the first fight (materialized in the walls and buildings of the city), the choreography of the fight in the forest is defined by the swaying flux of the bamboo trees that yield to the lightness and weight of the fighters' bodies. This pliant, bending verticality is a visual manifestation of Jen's wavering position, her suspension between courses of action: she may return to her parents and subordinate herself to tradition, become Li Mu Bai's disciple and subordinate herself to another tradition, or roam free as a masterless warrior. Whereas in the first fight scene Jen seems far more weightless than Shu Lien, in this scene Li Mu Bai floats and balances with far greater ease. Here the forest is an important element of verticality's mise-en-scène, for the trees provide a structural support for the weightless body that demands the masterful use of gravity as much as a transcendence or defiance of it. If gravity represents the force of tradition and the past, then Li Mu Bai's more powerful verticality derives in part from his connection to the traditions, training, and duties of Wudan. Hence he uses the rise and fall of the branches with far greater skill than Jen, who plunges halfway below the tree line when he shakes her from a branch. His greater utilization of gravity's force thereby implies that without some structural support from past tradition, without any master, the future is characterized by a perilous free-fall. Yet as an agent of verticality, he is also at odds with tradition. Indeed, at this point in the narrative, Li Mu Bai chases Jen into the treetops because he wishes simultaneously to carry on tradition and transform it by bringing a female disciple to Wudan Mountain.

In keeping with its ambivalence towards the new future each of the characters longs for, the film ends by suspending its protagonists between old worlds and new. As mentioned above, the past repeats itself in the present when Li Mu Bai is poisoned by Jade Fox (who thus kills off the future). Rather than using his last moments to meditate and enter heaven, Li Mu Bai chooses instead to remain a ghost, walking the earth by Shu Lien's side. This figurative suspension between two worlds, between heaven and earth, past life and future life, is visually expressed through the film's final image, as Jen jumps off Wudan Mountain. On the one hand, Jen's fall may be read as an elegiac image of an insurgent figure's fatal acquiescence to the laws of physics and hence to the laws that govern the social order she has so violently resisted. On the other, her fall might fulfill Lo's wish for them to return to the desert and a life unrestrained by family duty and class identity. Though the path has been cleared for Jen to live a life of freedom and autonomy, the film holds the future at bay, suspending the narrative and the spectator between opposing outcomes. Jen's descent through space emblematizes verticality's more general ability to accommodate ambivalence and the film's specific negotiation of—and refusal to resolve—the complicated relations between the past and the future, the desire for change and the insistent pull of tradition, and the struggle of emergent power against the dominant. *Crouching Tiger*'s concluding fall foregrounds the blockbuster's predictable refusal to pursue the outcome of verticality's spatial dialectics: rather than using its dynamic conflict between opposing powers to envision a radically new outcome, verticality ultimately remains suspended between potential outcomes or follows a downward trajectory towards an already-past, familiar future that confirms the present. In this way, verticality ultimately works not only to mobilize but also to accommodate the conflicting desires and demands of the blockbuster's broadly heterogeneous global audience.

Monumental Heights: Leaping Forward, and Looping Back

Like the *wu xia* film, comic-book films have provided an ideal outlet for the new verticality precisely because their source materials have always located their polarized struggles for power in bodies that effortlessly transcend the laws of physics.[19] Similar to the other films discussed here, *X-Men* locates violent conflict between polarized extremes on an historical threshold. Set in the not-too-distant future after radical genetic mutation has precipitated a break with the evolutionary past, the film opens with a voiceover that explains: "Mutation: it is the key to our evolution. It has enabled us to evolve from a single-celled organism into the dominant species on the planet. This process is slow, normally taking thousands and thousands of years. But every few hundred millennia, evolution leaps forward." This evolutionary leap is bodied forth by genetic mutants endowed with a broad variety of powers, ranging from omniscience and telekinesis, to control over magnetic fields and the weather. Radical mutation's rupture of evolutionary time is countered by the cyclical return of a horrifying historical past via the Mutant Registration Act, a piece of legislation that echoes both the Nazi propaganda of the past century and contemporary anti-homosexual propaganda (when Senator Kelly [Bruce Davison] debates the Registration Act, he insists that all mutants be outed, arguing: "I think the American people have the right to decide whether they want their children to be in school with mutants, to be taught by mutants").

X-Men begins with a prologue set in a Nazi concentration camp in Poland, positing a cyclical continuity between the dreadful past and the to-be-dreaded future. In the opening scene, the mutant powers of Eric/Magneto (Ian McKellan) emerge as a form of resistance to the violent and broad-scale fragmentation and annihilation of the Jewish family. Demonstrated in greater detail throughout the rest of the film, Magneto's powers make him the film's primary agent of verticality. When he kidnaps Rogue (Anna Paquin), he floats down the aisle of a passenger train and then suspends Wolverine (Hugh Jackman) several feet above the ground. When ordered to surrender by police, he instead levitates patrol cars high into the air and sends them crashing down onto other vehicles below. The expectation of fascism's return in the near future (he warns Charles Xavier [Patrick Stewart]—"Let them pass that law and they'll have you in chains with a number burned into your forehead") propels Magneto upward to monumental heights. Like the vertical chase sequences in *Dark City* and *Minority Report*, the X-Men's pursuit of Magneto follows an upward trajectory that maps conflict onto spatial extremes, and shifts in power onto bodies that rise and fall: they track him to the top of the Statue of Liberty, where he plans to turn the world's leaders, positioned vulnerably below on Ellis Island, into mutants. Magneto is thereby an extreme version of a figure whose power—defined as the mastery of space, time and matter and made visible through gravity-defiance—is the expression of a desire to transcend constraints placed upon the freedom of a demonized minority. However, Magneto's anti-fascism has become so extreme that it threatens humanity's survival. And so *X-Men* intensifies the spectatorial pleasure of being caught between violently opposed extremes by triangulating its power struggle and aligning audience identification with the X-Men, who struggle to thwart the efforts of both sides.

Magneto's ascent to the top of the Statue of Liberty is an attempt to prevent not just the return of the historical past in the shape of a second Holocaust, but to escape the weight of past family history as well. By Magneto's perverse logic, forcing an evolutionary leap forward in the bodies of the world's most powerful leaders will result in a new *mutant* family unity and continuity that will compensate for the annihilation of the Jewish family. When asked why he pursues his plans even though doing so requires the sacrifice of another mutant, he explains:

> Because there is no land of tolerance, there is no peace—not here or anywhere else. Women and children—whole families—destroyed simply because they were born different from those in power. Well after tonight, the world's powerful will be just like us. They will return home as brothers, as mutants. Our cause will be theirs. Your sacrifice will mean our survival.

Here, the "returning home" of the powerful as "brother mutants" promises to break the cyclical return of fascism. Magneto seems to be driven by the idea that once he manufactures another evolutionary leap forward, the scene of family fragmentation with which the film begins may never return again (from atop the Statue of Liberty he reasons: "Those people down there control our fate and the fate of every other mutant. Soon our fate will be their fate"). However, unknown to Magneto, his plan will first transport the powerful (and much of New York) into the genetic future but will then slowly liquefy them and return them all to a primordial ooze. Hence, rather than effecting a break from the past, his plan will instead result in a looping back, a return of humanity to its pre-historical origins. This evolutionary reversion is first represented by Senator Kelly's long fall from his cliff-top prison following his transformation by Magneto. After plunging to the ocean far below, the mutant Senator Kelly that emerges from the ocean resembles a jellyfish. Eventually, he is reduced to an entirely liquid state and splatters to the floor in a cascade of water.

When the X-Men ultimately thwart his plan, Magneto is captured and rendered powerless within a plastic prison. If within the film verticality maps the longing for a future unbound from the horrors of the past, then it also maps the inverse outcome of a return to the past. Gravity reasserts itself in direct proportion to the intensity of the desire to escape the historical and political constraints for which it stands. Verticality is not just a spatial or directional figure; rather, it is a figure for elaborating a flight from, or a return to, a former state—whether of the body, history, or narrative. Though Magneto drives towards a new future through upward verticality, such motion ultimately brings him full circle: in the end, he is imprisoned much as he was at the beginning of the film. Rather than provide clear resolution of its polarized conflict, the prison cell is a figure of narrative suspension: while it quite literally suspends Magneto over a dark void and forces a momentary cessation of hostilities, it also leaves the spectator poised between the narrative past of the trilogy's first installment and the narrative future towards which its concluding dialogue points (Magneto warns Xavier: "You know this plastic prison won't hold me for long").

Severed Pasts, and Skyscrapers

Science fiction's focus on the nature of time and its tendency to imagine worlds, technologies, and forms of embodiment that defy the laws of physics has made it another genre ideally suited to exploit the new verticality (prime examples include *Sky Captain and the World of Tomorrow, Dark City, The Fifth Element, I, Robot*, and *The War of the Worlds*). *The Matrix* is undoubtedly the film that most insistently ties vertically oriented action to the struggle for control over the laws of space and time. In it, humanity has been enslaved by a race of machines and exists in a state of suspended animation, as nothing more than a power source for artificially intelligent computers. Implicit and explicit in *The Matrix* is the idea that history operates according to horrifying cycles and ironic inversions: while images of the shackled Morpheus (Laurence Fishburne) link the current enslavement of mankind to the trans-Atlantic slave trade, humanity's mechanical subordination perverts modernity's equation of historical progress with technological development. Once freed from the matrix, Neo (Keanu Reeves) struggles to rescue humanity from machine-made, simulated space and time. In turn, this struggle has evolutionary overtones: while Agent Smith (Hugo Weaving) compares humans to dinosaurs and viruses, Neo (like Murdoch) will become the One precisely because he has somehow acquired the characteristics of his captors (Tank [Marcus Chong] refers to him as "a machine"). In turn, the film borrows and expands upon the vertically oriented action of the martial arts film to spatialize its protagonist's relation to time and power. Whereas Neo's powerlessness is emphasized through his fear of heights at the beginning of the film (he is first captured by Agent Smith when too frightened to climb the scaffolding to the top of the Metacortex building), his ascension to his position as the One is marked by his increasing ability to bend the laws of physics.

As in the other films discussed here, *The Matrix* does not use verticality simply for the sake of spectacle. Rather, verticality is the dynamic articulation of a desire to change the course of history, to precipitate a new future. Nearly all violent conflict with the Agents takes place along a vertical axis, from the opening scene when bullet-time sequences first display the spectacle of Trinity suspended in the air as she kicks her way out of a trap, to a later scene in which the rebels flee the hotel by sliding down through its interior walls. The spatialization of power is most evident in the scenes organized around Morpheus' rescue from the Agents, which begins with Neo and Trinity storming the lobby of a skyscraper and engaging in a shoot-out with security guards. The pillars that line the lobby materialize the film's broader theme of imprisonment and structure the vertical mise-en-scène and action of the fight sequence. As agents of verticality, Neo and Trinity create a downpour of falling shrapnel, objects, and bodies even as they defy gravity themselves. Fragments of marble and concrete, spent bullet casings, shards of glass, and water from a sprinkler system create a constant stream of downward motion that mimics the descent of binary codes seen falling across computer screens throughout the film. As other bodies drop, Neo and Trinity rise: in one of the rescue scene's many high-angle shots, they propel themselves to the top of the skyscraper by means of the cables of an elevator car they have sent plunging to the lobby, packed with explosives.

The bi-directional movement of this shot foregrounds the link between verticality and narratives of emergence. Neo's repeated defiance and bending of the matrix's machine-made gravity (he dodges bullets, runs up walls, dangles over a digitized bluescreen cityscape, and rescues Trinity as she falls from a downed helicopter) ultimately demonstrate that he is the One, who will bring about the potential liberation of humanity. Importantly, the film exploits the skyscraper to do so. While the jagged, burnt-out spikes of the real world's city skyline represent the end of human progress, the mirrored postmodern skyscrapers in the matrix represent an inversion of the principles according to which modern progress was measured. If the upward reach of the twentieth-century skyscraper implied the limitless potential of human endeavor, the simulated skyscrapers of the matrix imply humanity's backward slide, its reduction to nothing more than the energy given off by its biological processes. Hence the simulated skyscraper filled with workers lodged in tiny cubicles simply cloaks the real-world skyscrapers of the film's twenty-second century—the massive energy towers that reduce human history to the ahistorical temporality of thermodynamics. Like some of the other films discussed here, *The Matrix* has a somewhat inconclusive resolution. While *Crouching Tiger* ends with its protagonist's downward fall, *X-Men* with a figure of suspension, *The Matrix* ends with Neo promising a future revolution in voiceover, and soaring above the city skyline of the matrix. While we might link this open-endedness with the film's position as the first installment of a trilogy, it is worth noting that the trilogy itself ends not with a triumphant victory of human over machine, but with a truce between polarized forces.

Mythological and Technological Thresholds

That films defined by their spectacular use of CGI should be so concerned with historical thresholds is not surprising, particularly if we keep in mind the centrality of powerful new (and sometimes alien) technologies to the plots of so many recent blockbusters in which verticality is notable. For, as theorists and historians note, CGI synthesizes "old" and "new" media and frequently provokes critical speculations about the relation of the cinema's (digital) future to its (celluloid) past.[20] Indeed, the vertical bodies under consideration here are composites of old and new, of film and digital media—and visibly so. Though the harnesses and wires that keep the actors airborne can be erased from the digitized image, the visual effects of the actual force of gravity sometimes cannot. Unless compensated for by some other dynamic motion (kicking, running up a wall) occasionally these vertical bodies retain visible traces of their true condition in space: they, too, exist in a state of suspension between the upward pull of an invisible apparatus and the downward force of gravity. In such instances, gravity's visible trace corresponds, roughly, to the state of suspension in which these characters exist within their fictional worlds *as well as* within film history. Put differently, digital verticality's occasional lack of transparency foregrounds its association with the emergent.

Through flying and falling bodies, the new verticality makes visible the position occupied by computer-generated images within the recent past of commercial film history—poised at an historical threshold, between continuity with past tradition and a future defined by aesthetic and technological change.[21]

Notes

1 Sergei Eisenstein, "The Dynamic Square," in *S.M. Eisenstein: Selected Writings 1922–1934*, ed. Richard Taylor (Bloomington: Indiana University Press, 1988), 208. My thanks to Tom Gunning for this reference and for a productive conversation about an earlier version of this article at the 2003 Film and Literature Conference at Florida State University. I am also grateful to Linda Williams and Isaac Hager for their advice on revisions.

2 In *The Vatican to Vegas: A History of Special Effects* (New York: The New Press, 2004), Norman M. Klein persuasively argues that all special effects are, in one way or another, an articulation of power.

3 David Cook, *A History of Narrative Film*, 4th Edition (London: W.W. Norton & Company, 2004), 881–927.

4 For phenomenological analyses of verticality and horizontality, see Gaston Bachelard, *Air and Dreams: An Essay on the Imagination of Movement* (Dallas, TX: The Dallas Institute Publications, 2002) and Bernd Jaeger, "Horizontality and Verticality: A Phenomenological Exploration into Lived Space," *Duquesne Studies in Phenomenological Psychology*, vol. 1 (Pittsburgh, PA: Duquesne University Press, 1971), 212–35.

5 On the use of the staircase in melodramas, see Thomas Elsaesser, "Tales of Sound and Fury: Observations on the Family Melodrama," *Home Is Where the Heart Is: Studies in Melodrama and the Woman's Film*, ed. Christine Gledhill (London: BFI, 1987), 43–68.

6 Constance Balides, "Jurassic Post-Fordism: Tall Tales of Economics in the Theme Park," *Screen* 41, no. 2 (Summer 2000): 135.

7 I have in mind here a number of mass-mediated conflicts taking place in the past decade or so, including the Balkan wars of the 1990s, the suppression of student protests and the Tiananmen Square uprising in Beijing in 1989, the ongoing conflict between China and Taiwan, the rise of religious fundamentalism throughout the world, the recent unilateralism in U.S. foreign policy and George W. Bush's now-notorious declaration—"Either you are with us or you are against us," the polarization of electoral politics in the U.S. (red states vs. blue), the hyper-violent discourse on terror, and the increasing disparity between wealthy and poor nations and populations, thanks in part to the increasing power of multinational corporations.

8 Film scholars argue that this is a general tendency of the blockbuster. See especially Geoff King, *Spectacular Narratives: Hollywood in the Age of the Blockbuster* (New York: I.B. Tauris, 2000), Charles Acland, *Screen Traffic: Movies, Multiplexes, and Global Culture* (Durham, NC: Duke University Press, 2003).

9 Two notable works link verticality to historical change and conflict in previous eras. Zhang Zhen argues that 1930s martial arts films used "flying bodies" to express anxiety towards social and cultural changes precipitated by the emergence of technological modernity in China in "Bodies in the Air: The Magic of Science and the Fate of Early 'Martial Arts' Film in China," *Post Script* 20 (2001): 43–60. Ed Dimendberg argues that film noir represents the alienating effects of the American city's postwar verticality to express "longing for older horizontal forms and a reminder of the discomforts of the elevated city of capitalist commerce." *Film Noir and the Spaces of Modernity* (Cambridge, MA: Harvard University Press, 2004), 96.

10 Cook, 389.

11 *Titanic* made over $600 million and is the top-grossing film of all time. *Hero* made more than $217 million in China and more than $53 million in the USA.

12 See especially, Laurie Ouellette, "Ship of Dreams: Cross-Class Romance and the Cultural Fantasy of *Titanic*," and Adrienne Munich and Maura Spiegel, "Heart of the Ocean: Diamonds and Desire in *Titanic*," in *Titanic: Anatomy of a Blockbuster*, ed. Kevin S. Sandler and Gaylyn Studlar (New Brunswick, NJ: Rutgers University Press, 1999), 169–88 and 155–68.

13 Jaeger, 225.

14 See Ouellette, 169–88.

15 This aesthetic beauty of the film's images of self-sacrifice has led most reviewers to describe the film as an homage to pacifism. However, J. Hoberman argues: "*Hero*'s vast imperial sets and symmetrical tumult, its decorative dialectical montage and sanctimonious traditionalism, its glorification of ruthless leadership and self-sacrifice on the altar of national greatness, not to mention the sense that this might stoke the engine of political regeneration, are all redolent of fascinatin' fascism." "Man With No Name Tells Story of Heroics, Color Coordination," *The Village Voice* (August 23, 2004), http://www.villagevoice.com/film/0434,hoberman2,56140,20.html.

16 For a discussion and application of these Confucian principles to Chinese film, see Jenny Kowk Wah Lau, "*Ju Dou*: A Hermeneutical Reading of Cross-cultural Cinema," *Film Quarterly* 25, no. 2 (Winter 1991–2): 2–10.

17 Christina Klein, "*Crouching Tiger, Hidden Dragon*: A Diasporic Reading," *Cinema Journal* 43, no. 4 (summer 2002): 34.

18 For a discussion of unmarried daughters, female warriors, and their relation to tradition and modernity in Chinese cinema, see especially Chris Berry and Mary Farquhar, *China on Screen: Cinema and Nation* (forthcoming, Cambridge University Press).

19 On comic-book characters and flight, see Scott Bukatman, *Matters of Gravity: Special Effects and Supermen in the 20th Century* (Durham, NC: Duke University Press, 2003).

20 See especially Lev Manovich, *The Language of New Media* (Cambridge, MA: MIT Press, 2002); Michelle Pierson, *Special Effects: Still in Search of Wonder* (New York: Columbia University Press, 2002); and Philip Rosen, *Change Mummified: Cinema, Historicity, Theory* (Minneapolis: University of Minnesota Press, 2001), 301–50.

21 In his article "The Impact of Digital Technologies on Film Aesthetics," Michael Allen argues that the impact of digital technologies on celluloid film form has been "a combination of change and continuity over time." *The New Media Book*, ed. Dan Harries (London: BFI, 2002), 109.

PART III

Reception

Chapter 7

Anna Everett

THE SOULS OF BLACK FOLK IN THE AGE OF MECHANICAL REPRODUCTION: BLACK NEWSPAPER CRITICISM AND THE EARLY CINEMA, 1909–16 (2001)

Editors' Introduction

Over the last thirty years, film studies scholars have demonstrated the ways in which the American cinema, from its inception, depended on race and racial difference for narrative coherence. The work of Linda Williams, Fatimah Tobing-Rony, Jane Gaines, and Melvyn Stokes, among others, has been instrumental in this project. Other scholars, for instance Jacqueline Stewart and, in the present case, Anna Everett, have moved away from the film text, and have examined the implications of race on film reception. The history of reception studies in the United States has been the history of white audiences, and even those studies that refused the notion of a monolithic national audience have assumed that viewers were white. The Payne Fund Studies in the 1930s understood the child and adolescent viewer as unproblematically white (and concerned itself with effects even of films like *Birth of a Nation* on white viewers), while Margaret Farrand Thorp, in her pioneering *America at the Movies* (1939) acknowledged the importance of gender in viewing, but chose not to examine race. The work of Everett eliminates this blind spot in several ways. First, Everett's project is archaeological, as it unearths early-twentieth-century sources, from such African-American newspapers as the *New York Age* and the *Chicago Defender*. Second, this work performs the historiographic function of interpreting the responses of African-American critics to early cinema, and particularly to the racial politics of that cinema, and situating those responses within a diverse community of cultural commentators and an aesthetics of race and culture that was developing among African-American intellectuals. In practical, pedagogical terms, Everett's work gives teachers an answer to the students who might dismiss the racism of early cinema by saying that "Everyone felt that way back then." Everett has uncovered and analyzed the voices that objected to the racism of popular culture, and that led the fight to improve the racial politics of the film industry.

Suggested Reading

Jacqueline Stewart, *Migrating to the Movies: Cinema and Black Urban Modernity* (University of California, 2005); Linda Williams, *Playing the Race Card: Melodramas of Black and White from Uncle Tom to O.J. Simpson* (Princeton, 2002); Melvyn Stokes, *The Birth of a Nation: A History of "The Most Controversial Motion Picture of All Time"* (Oxford, 2007); Jane Gaines, *Fire and Desire: Mixed-Race Movies in the Silent Era* (Chicago, 2001); Mary Carbine, " 'The Finest Outside the Loop': Motion Picture Exhibition in Chicago's Black Metropolis, 1905–28," *Camera Obscura*, May 1990 (2:23), pp. 8–41.

> By means of its technical structure, the film has taken the physical shock effect out of the wrappers.
>
> (Walter Benjamin, *Work of Art*)

> While passing a moving picture theater . . . The writer was surprised to see . . . JOHN SMITH of PARIS, TEXAS, BURNED at the STAKE. HEAR HIS MOANS and GROANS. PRICE ONE CENT!
>
> (Lester Walton, *Degeneracy*)

> We seldom study the condition of the Negro today honestly and carefully. It is so much easier to assume that we know it all.
>
> (W. E. B. Du Bois, *Souls*)

THE AMERICAN CINEMA WAS born during the era Rayford Logan described as "the nadir" of the African American experience in post-Reconstruction America, from 1897 to 1917. African American film criticism was born likewise amid this political maelstrom, characterized by the nation's retrenchment from the goal of racial justice once advanced during Reconstruction. Emerging as it did within the late-nineteenth-century historical milieu marked by the 1897 *Plessey v. Ferguson* Supreme Court decision that inaugurated the sweeping system of "separate but equal" Jim Crow legislation, early American cinema at once reflected and influenced this fateful aspect of the nation's racial politics. From the outset, many of the era's one-reel films, such as American Mutascope and Biograph Company's (AMBCO) *Who Said Chicken* (1902), *The Gator and the Pickaninny* (1903), *While Strolling in the Park* (1904), *Kiss in the Dark* (1904), *The Misdirected Kiss* (1904), *A Bucket of Cream Ale* (1904), and *A Nigger in the Woodpile* (1904), yoked the cinema's earliest signifiers to the potent theatrical idiom of blackface minstrelsy. More important, since the cinematic apparatus was considered at one with other modern scientific instruments—namely, the microscope, thermometer, and telegraph (Winston 1993, 37), with their strong claims on "truth," "reality," and empirical verifiability—early cinematic narratives, often minstrel derivatives, were even more formidable in popularizing and reifying America's politics of white racial supremacy. Now the power of scientific inscription was put in the service of ultrareactionary race politics, as these early film shorts convey. At the same time, efforts to countermand this political blacklash against African Americans' sociocultural strivings must be recognized as a motivating factor in the rise of the critical discourse—inchoate as it may be—about the early cinema by African American literary figures, scholars, journalists, and cultural leaders.

Indeed, as effective as Jim Crow laws were in undermining any lingering ideals of racial equity between European and African American citizens in post-Reconstruction America (Janken 1993, 7), they became even more efficacious when aligned with America's ascendant institutions of mass culture. This separatist trend had clearly gained momentum in the mid- to late nineteenth century with the rise of antebellum minstrel theater, regarded by some observers as " 'the only true American drama' or an 'American National Opera' " (Toll 1974, v). In his book *Blacking Up: The Minstrel Show in Nineteenth Century America*, Robert Toll identifies blackface minstrelsy as the first national entertainment "shaped by and for the masses of average [white] Americans" (26). With the arrival of the motion picture industry, the kinds of distortions popularized by minstrelsy were taken up and promulgated by the new cinematic regime of representation.

Meanwhile, certain mainstream writers and theorists of the age entered into heated debate over the relative merits of these new mass arts in terms of "high" and "low" cultural norms and specificities, the dichotomy of art versus science, and the role of mimetic and nonrepresentational art in America's cultural institutions. In contrast, many turn-of-the-century African American cultural critics regarded the issues in less esoteric terms. For them, the advent of mass culture, especially the cinema, represented a fundamental transformation of the very nature of art itself. No longer was the matter a simple question of whether scientific innovations such as photography and film could be deemed worthy of the appellation "Art." More pressing for them was the potential of these new media to craft and legitimate even more destructive renderings of black life and culture. It is precisely this point that troubled the African American intellectuals writing about art and culture in America during this era, men such as the *New York Age*'s drama columnist Lester A. Walton, scholar and activist W.E.B. Du Bois, clergyman Adam Clayton Powell Sr., and minstrel performer George Walker, among many others. Moreover, in keeping with what Dolan Hubbard (1994) terms the "sermonic hermeneutics" of the African American "preacherly voice,"[1] these writers foregrounded the sociopolitical pragmatics of these new cultural forms and their impact on the newly self-reinvented black masses. Accordingly, these respected black leaders began to advance their own interpretive theories to explain the difficulties and potentialities of art's modernist transformation. From their often "messianic" writings, it becomes apparent that many of these black intellectuals understood clearly W.E.B. Du Bois's (1926) statement that "all art is propaganda and ever must be, despite the wailing of the purists" (514).

Taking the lead in articulating some important consequences of traditional cultural productions was the incomparable George Walker (1906). In an early instance of cultural critique, Walker's sage deliberations on blackface minstrelsy and its powerful naturalization of African Americans' racial subordination illustrate Du Bois's point well:

> Black faced white comedians used to make themselves look as ridiculous as they could when portraying a "darky" character. In their "make-up" they always had tremendously big red lips, and their costumes were frightfully exaggerated. The one fatal result of this to the colored performers was that they imitated the white performers in their [own] make-up as "darkies." *Nothing seemed more absurd than to see a colored man making himself ridiculous in order to portray himself.*
>
> (243; italics mine)

At once a celebrated cultural performer and astute critic, Walker, one-half of the world-renowned Williams and Walker black minstrel duo, experienced firsthand the difficulties of "double-consciousness' " incongruities. Walker well understood the absurdities inherent in the black minstrel's valiant attempt to reconcile the conflicting natures of his Eurocentric and Afrocentric cultural legacies. Even though Walker's essay "The Negro on the American Stage," published in 1906 by *Colored American Magazine,* is a specific analysis of the stage and thus is precinematic, its applicability to early film criticism is evident. Here, Walker's sophisticated critique of the African American minstrel's complicity in his own victimization, a complicity that aids and abets minstrelsy's anti-black rhetorics, is quite simply a brilliant instance of self-reflexivity. It is important to understand that Walker and partner Bert Williams established their minstrel act by rejecting the burnt-cork makeup convention instituted by white minstrels. Unfortunately, their reform efforts could go only so far. By articulating African Americans', indeed his own, conflicted participation in minstrelsy, a participation purchased at the exorbitant cost of negating more authentic black cultural expressions, Walker suggests clues whereby we might begin to appreciate the nascent cinema's powerful allure for early-twentieth-century African Americans.

Initially, the new entertainment medium seemed to promise an alternative to the limitations of black theatrical minstrelsy, so eloquently delineated by Walker. It is important to bear in mind, however, that this attenuated black theatricality flourished only as the national preoccupation with white minstrel shows waned (Toll 1974, 135). Notwithstanding the early cinema's predilection for crafting vituperous and dehumanizing caricatures of black life, the "nickelettes," as black minister Adam Clayton Powell Sr. referred to film exhibition houses in 1910, were immensely popular among the reconstituting African American communities on both sides of the Mason-Dixon line.[2] Against this backdrop, it is telling that the optimism and enthusiasm of the cinema's first black audiences rarely, if ever, corresponded to the brutal reality of the cinema's early racist narratives, of which Edison's *The Watermelon Patch* (1905), and AMBCO's *The Chicken Thief* (1904) are exemplars.[3] Put another way, turn-of-the-century African American spectators were seduced into a painfully unrequited and yet enduring love affair with the primitive cinema.

Figure 7.1 Advertisement for a black minstrel show displays the blackface caricatures that the Williams and Walker duo rejected. *Chicago Defender*, 1910

Figure 7.2 Preeminent black entertainer George W. Walker performing in sophisticated anti-minstrelsy garb, ca. 1900s. Courtesy of the Manuscripts, Archives, and Rare Books Division–Schomburg Center for Research in Black Culture, the New York Public Library, Astor, Lenox, and Tilden Foundations–Lester A. Walton Photograph Collection

Although some contemporary film historians have taken a second look at the earliest film literature in an effort to chronicle unofficial histories of European immigrants and other now-mainstream groups (Carbine 1990, 9), there still remains a conspicuous lack of concern for, and interest in, African Americans' literary contributions to American film history. To fill this void and to explore the love-hate dialectic suffusing the first African American cultural leaders' and spectators' interaction with the early cinema, it is necessary to recover the numerous black press articles and columns that were devoted to news of this technological innovation. In refocusing attention on the first decade of literary production by African Americans on the cinema, specifically from 1909 to 1916, we must first begin with the prolific doyen of early African American film criticism, the *New York Age*'s resident drama critic Lester A. Walton, and his contemporaries at the *Chicago Defender*, Sylvester Russell, Minnie Adams, Columbus Bragg, and Tony Langston.

Lester A. Walton and the Birth of Cinema's *Ecriture Noire*

For more than a decade, Lester A. Walton edited the *New York Age*'s popular entertainment page, which included music, stage, and film reviews. Until his 1920s promotion to managing editor of the newspaper and his subsequent return to stage theatrical management, Walton was the *New York Age*'s, and by extension most of black America's, cultural arbiter. In this capacity, he can be regarded as African America's first major mass-culture griot. Many features of Walton's penetrating analyses are recognizable today in such yet-to-be developed aspects of film study as genre criticism, narratology, spectatorship and reception, apparatus

Figure 7.3 Bert Williams and George Walker, the first black minstrels who refused the burnt-cork, blackface makeup tradition. Courtesy of the Manuscripts, Archives, and Rare Books Division–Schomburg Center for Research in Black Culture, the New York Public Library, Astor, Lenox, and Tilden Foundations—Lester A. Walton Photograph Collection

and textual analysis, and industry practices. It should also be pointed out that Walton's mixing of several of these critical approaches in a single essay does not represent a weakness in thematic unity as much as it underscores the cinema's interdisciplinarity. Additionally, his ever-vigilant gaze on the stages and screens of New York's theatrical establishments and his prolific literary output on the subject construct a historical and cultural blueprint for tracing African America's early tradition of responding to those early filmic narratives that Kay Sloan (1988) has dubbed "the loud silents." In effect, Walton used his public voice to "talk back," as bell hooks (1989) would term it, on behalf of the silenced mass of African Americans, a necessary act of opposition to the emerging hegemony of the country's nascent culture industries. " 'Talking back,' " hooks writes, "meant speaking as an equal to an authority figure. It meant daring to disagree and sometimes it just meant having an opinion" (hooks 1984, 5). Indeed, Walton had a number of audacious opinions that he dared to express in his weekly column, entitled "Music and the Stage." As a matter of course, Walton's critiques became increasingly fixated on cinematic objectifications of the black body.

Beginning with his 1909 essay "The Degeneracy of the Moving Picture Theatre," which followed a more customary theatrical review, and extending through the more complete discussions of the cinema that frequently commanded the entire column, Walton's talking back instigates the early cinema's first black writing. On 15 December 1910, for example, Walton addressed the ongoing battle for the souls of black folk being waged by the cinema and the church. On 23 February 1911, he covered the "Change Wrought by Motion Picture Craze"; on 5 June 1913, the column was devoted to "The Motion Picture Industry and the Negro"; in October of that year, it was "Motion Picture Concern Makes Film Ridiculing Race"; and in 1914 he wrote a column on African Americans and the push for representation on film censor boards in the Northeast, as well as "New Yorkers Have Gone 'Dippy' over the Movies." From his cultural pulpit at one of the most influential black newspapers of its day, Walton forged his column as a potent cultural force with which to talk back against what he saw as a tendency of "degeneracy" in America's emergent commercial cinema.

Walton's writings signify an early intervention in the new medium's ability to diminish and somehow displace the horror and national shame of black lynchings. His recourse to acts of literary defiance begins with his 5 August 1909 article for the *New York Age*, entitled "The Degeneracy of the Moving Picture Theatre." In this first critical essay on the cinema, Walton chafes at the P.T. Barnum promotional stratagem deployed by early movie theater establishments to lure unsuspecting film enthusiasts into venues aiming to profit from the spectacularization of this horrific aspect of African American pain and suffering:

> While passing a moving picture theatre on Sixth avenue several days ago, the writer was surprised to see a sign prominently displayed in front of the place bearing the following large print: JOHN SMITH of PARIS, TEXAS, BURNED at the STAKE. HEAR HIS MOANS and GROANS. PRICE ONE CENT! A crudely-painted picture of a colored man being burned at the stake completed the makeup of the offensive as well as repulsive-appearing sign. Judge the great surprise of the writer when two days later while walking down the Bowery a similar sign met his gaze, the same earnest appeal being made by the proprietor of the moving picture theatre to the public to walk in and *enjoy* [italics mine] the sight of a human being meeting death by burning, with the moans and groans thrown in for a penny. . . . The promoters of moving picture theatres make the assertion that their pictures are of an educational nature. . . . We would like to know where do the elements of education come in so far as the picture in question is concerned?
>
> (Walton 1909a)

Walton's righteous indignation at the ease with which early filmmakers hijacked the cinema's formal properties to aestheticize such "barbarism" (Walton's term) is certainly warranted. In recognizing the obvious racialized appeal of these shockingly desensitizing images to the film's implied white audience, Walton is correct to challenge the narrative intent of these loathsome and highly suggestive representations of black victimization in a society beset by routine racial conflagrations and deep-seated antagonisms.[4] Walton lucidly protests the cinematic effect in overpowering and ultimately supplanting an individual's moral thought processes during those heightened moments of spectatorial suturing and identification. His essay, in effect, demystifies the lynch film's incredibly seductive and affective powers to inhibit moral outrage even as it flaunts the film's ability to engender sociopolitical acquiescence. By suggesting further that the abhorrent lynching film will likely be exhibited in theaters across the nation, Walton warns against the very real and present dangers that mass communication of these incendiary images poses for the nation's divided body politic.

Decrying the moral bankruptcy informing the text of the theater's promotional placard, Walton makes clear his position that the scandal was not confined to the mere production and exhibition of these loathsome pictures. Consumption of them was equally ignoble in Walton's estimation because it meant "the planting of the seed of savagery in the breast of those whites who even in this enlightened day and time are not any too far from barbarism" if, indeed, their spectatorial pleasure could so easily be purchased by such wanton displays of barbarous violence.

Not content to leave his "sermonic hermeneutics" to revelation or exposé alone, in his preacherly mode, Walton then shifts to a prescriptive. In the article's conclusion, Walton issues a call to action (a call, incidentally, he repeats in subsequent articles). Having thus laid out the urgency of the situation, he implores ministers and lay readers alike to protest and, implicitly, to boycott such cinematic mendacity. Presciently, he ends with a caveat: "If, we do not start now to put an end to this insult to the race, expect to see more shocking pictures with the Negro as subject in the near future" (this quote has added saliency because the warning preceded the national protests of *The Birth of a Nation*). As his impassioned plea attests, Lester Walton refused to avert his gaze from the cinema's deliberate or unwitting vitiations of the shame and horrors of black lynchings, both literal and figurative. By refusing to mute his outrage over the commodification of black pain and suffering, Walton notified the commercial interests of the day that certainly he refused to participate in the conspiracy of silence and indifference that authorized the reduction of the lynched black body to the latest aesthetic feature in America's early cinema of attractions.

Apparently Walton's call for a moral rejection of such images did not go unheeded. So compelling was this article that certain white newspapers were moved or shamed into endorsing his position. Two weeks after the publication of his "Degeneracy" essay, Walton reported that his antilynching film commentary had struck a responsive chord in the larger community, evidenced by the essay's reprint in the white motion picture trade journal *Moving Picture News*. Walton and his readers must have felt a vindication of sorts when this white industry journal, during the height of the Jim Crow era, not only reprinted this African American criticism but included such sympathetic comments as "We would like to ask the writers and film makers to read [Walton's criticism] and let it burn into their consciences and cease giving offense to vast numbers of our population" (quoted in Walton 1909b). In addition to his critical interventionist approach to the new cinema, Walton's early film criticism was also characterized by a reformist propensity that enabled him to envision the cinema's dormant emancipatory potential.[5]

In the year following the "Degeneracy" article, Walton used his column to explore the growing tensions between the black church and the increasingly popular cinema. Exacerbating the controversy over what religious leaders saw as the secular erosion of the moral center of black life was the inability of the African American clerics to mount a united front in opposition to the major culprit in all this, the moving pictures. Positioned on one side of the hotly contested issue of whether moving picture theaters should be banned, with Godspeed, in the African American community were conservative ministers galvanizing support for a nationwide crusade against all moving picture establishments. On the other side stood clerics of a more moderate inclination. This group perceived the cinema as a relatively innocuous social outlet for the working masses, and even perhaps as a modern tool that might somehow be used for revitalizing the church itself. Endorsing this latter position, Walton nevertheless decided to submit the matter to his readers. In a mode that typifies the communal orientation of the black press at that time, Walton turned his column over to the Reverend Adam Clayton Powell Sr., "for the benefit of the readers of the *Age*, and for the Rev. Powell to tell, in his own words, 'why he is opposed to the church starting a crusade on the five and ten cent theaters' " (Walton 1910). In principle, it might appear that Walton should be predisposed in the opposite direction, especially with this article coming so soon after his own spirited campaign against cinematic sensationalism. According to this logic, Walton's support of the dissenting ministers might seem inconsistent. Although such a charge is understandable on the surface, a more probing review suggests that the two calls for censure operating here are sufficiently differentiated so as to make such a reduction or conflation of the two short-sighted. Whereas ministers Dr. Clair of Washington, D.C., and the Reverend E.W. Daniels of New York were agitating for a complete disavowal of all films and all movie theaters, Walton, even with his stage bias, judiciously confined his opposition only to those theaters exhibiting the repulsive lynch films.

Whereas Walton's articles from 1909 to 1910 outline his concerns with the micropolitics of the cinema's racial themes, his 1911 article entitled "Change Wrought by Motion Picture Craze" indicates his growing interest in the cinema's more far-reaching macropolitics of the racial discourse. At this time, he also begins to concentrate more on the institutional nature of cinema's encroachments on the entire entertainment establishment. In this column, Walton talks about the seemingly benign trend in Brooklyn and Manhattan theaters of abandoning their mainstays of musical comedy and dramatic plays in favor of the more popular vaudeville and the wildly successful motion pictures that, in many cases, accompanied them. But Walton's point is the imminent devastation these new entertainment policies could wreak on the newfound viability of the struggling African American theatrical establishments. Walton knew only too well how tenuous the present inroads African Americans had made on the so-called Great White Way were, and he put the case thus:

> The information [this entertainment shift] advanced did not occasion much of a flurry in theatrical circles over Brooklyn, being regarded merely as an incident in the meteoric career of the motion-picture business, which has had a marvelous growth in recent years—so much so that the entire theatrical map has undergone a decided change by its invasion. It is doubtful if there are many playgoers in Manhattan who are aware of the change of policy inaugurated by the management of the Court Street Theatre, and even so, they, too, do not attach much significance to the announcement. And yet, the desertion by the Court of musical comedy and drama for vaudeville and motion pictures means a great deal to one branch of the show business—the colored musical shows.
>
> (Walton 1911)

As one of the first generation of African American writers to earn a livelihood as a journalist specializing in the dramatic arts, Walton was not only in a unique position to read the proverbial handwriting on the wall; he also seems to have fully embraced his calling as the uniquely qualified and equipped messenger capable of deciphering these troubling new cultural codes. To be sure, Walton wanted his readers to understand the significance of the fact that the Court Theatre had "become inoculated with the motion-picture germ," as he described it. And here, as in most of Walton's rhetorical style, his linguistic choices demand a serious reckoning. His witty and accessible rhetorical style often veiled an assiduous and trenchant investigation: "For the past two seasons the Court Theatre has been the one bright and particular spot for colored shows. It has been the oasis of the local theatrical desert and the only popular-priced house in Greater New York that furnished financial encouragement to colored productions." In one of the few contemporaneous rationalizations of Bert Williams's Faustian decision to ally himself with the white minstrelsy establishment when he joined the Ziegfeld Company, Walton asserts: "That is the reason Bert Williams judiciously joined a white Broadway show, and early last season Cole and Johnson, seeing the hand writing on the wall, concluded not to take out a production. The situation is truly a trying one for colored shows."

Left unstated here is Walton's understanding of the trying time this transition betokened for his own newly established profession.

As was his usual practice, Walton appended to this analysis a related follow-up article reprinting relevant responses to a prior column. Many of the responses reprinted by Walton emanated from white writers and white establishments compelled to refute or reaffirm his searing critiques, as the earlier "Degeneracy" responses illustrate. In this case, however, the response was a letter from a white music publisher taking umbrage at Walton's charge of pervasive racist practices in the music publishing industry. The company involved was the Harry Von Tilzer Music Publishing Company. Although this particular reply concerned the music business, Walton's conjoining of the distinct scenarios establishes the necessary correlation between the racist practices underlying the transformation of the theater houses and this related music industry episode. Walton seems motivated to disclose the formidable pattern of racial exclusion endemic to all sectors of the white-controlled entertainment industry. He also had no compunction about taking on the white journalists whom Paul Laurence Dunbar would have considered "captious critics" (Dunbar 1913, 189) because of their ability to turn the racial problematic on its head by representing whites as the true victims of the nation's oppressive race-based policies.

In 1909 James Metcalfe, a white drama critic for *Life* magazine, wrote about racial matters and the cinema in a vein that resonates with current appeals to reverse discrimination and anti-affirmative action rhetoric. "It is a curious fact," Metcalf asserts, "that practically the Negro has more rights with respect of the theaters under the laws of New York than the white man has." In addition to reprinting Metcalfe's disingenuous argument in the 18 November 1909 column, Walton responds to the bogus claims and articulates well the deep-seated frustrations experienced by African Americans as true victims of American racism, whose oppression under Jim Crow laws was in little jeopardy of being inverted. Walton's effectiveness in literary contests of this sort hinges on a reprint strategy that permits the internal contradictions of opposing arguments to be self-disclosed, thereby bolstering his own contestations of specific points at issue. In this case, Walton had the easy task of countering Metcalfe's spurious claims that blacks somehow were privileged by a new law of equal access to New York theater seats. Walton reminds Metcalfe and *Age* readers, by quoting Metcalfe's own words, that there is always an available panacea for theater owners desiring to subvert the legal process: "[Where] Negroes have insured seats and insisted on their rights to be seated an ingenious solution has been found. . . . Under some pretext these representatives of the managers pick a row with the Negroes, create a disturbance, a policeman is called in and all hands are taken to the station house. The rest, of course, is easy." That Metcalfe willfully ignores society's de facto antiblack social contract that encourages such "easy" racist maneuvers is not the most important element of Walton's 18 November article. More to the point for Walton is society's refusal to recognize the Americanness of African Americans when the nation was experiencing a tidal wave of foreign immigration to its northern shores. Clearly, there was not the same difficulty of securing public accommodations for the nation's newly arriving European immigrants. Walton frames the national identity question in this way: "What is particularly galling to us is the thought that we who are native-born American citizens are discriminated against solely on account of color, and that an organized effort is being made to deprive us of rights and privileges to which we are justly entitled by law." Regarding the consensus by white theater managers that blacks should not insist on first-floor seats even during a performance of an African American show, Walton goes on to state: "The Negro race was [not] put on the earth to conform with every wish and desire of the Caucasian, and the fact that it was presumed that we were not wanted did not necessarily mean that we should not aspire to make an effort to realize our ambition" (1909c).

In 1912 Walton tuned his critical antennae toward the international response to the cinema's influence. In his 12 March column, Walton relays to his readership this bit of European news: "Moving picture shows are not only bringing about a new condition of affairs in the United States but in Europe, according to a [dispatch] to the *New York Sun* from Germany." In the reprinted *Sun* communiqué was a line that must surely have worried Walton's theater-loving heart: "At a meeting of actors and dramatists in Berlin, Ludwig Fulda said that in consequence of the competition of moving picture shows the 120 theatres in Germany would soon be hopelessly bankrupt." Though it may be true that Walton has excerpted this specific international communiqué because it echoes his own anxieties about the cinema's displacement of his beloved stage entertainments, the fact that he monitored, transmitted, and contextualized news of the global impact of the cinema is remarkable for that time period. Walton's recourse to this globalist strategy is not such an anomaly when viewed diachronically and in terms of the historic tradition of black letters. It is true, after all, that as Frederick Douglass and other former and fugitive slaves found an international audience for their antislavery messages, the American abolitionist movement gained momentum and increased support in progressive white communities in antebellum America. In this context, Walton's internationalist view falls within a historical continuum of audacious African American intellectual freedom fighting. Walton's reprinted *Sun* article goes on to add:

> There is a law in force now which restricts the cinematographs, and the managers and dramatists are looking for further legislation on this subject. The announcement that the new Royal Opera has granted the rights for the summer season to a Parisian film company has aroused angry protests.
>
> (Walton 1912a)

Given his past desire to curtail the cinema's destructive reach, Walton's ulterior motives seem justified, especially when counterposed to the cinema's threat to the future of African American theatricality in general, and its corresponding jeopardy to African American safety in particular, especially at this political moment in Jim Crow America. In his closing commentary, Walton underscores the seriousness of the cinematic threat by issuing a prophetic observation: "The majority of theatrical men confess that they do not see any prospects of the moving picture craze waning in popularity in the near future."

In 1949 Nicholas Vardac wrote *Stage to Screen, The Theatrical Origins of Early Film: David Garrick to D. W. Griffith*. In this book, Vardac traces what is now regarded as the early cinema's effort to borrow prestige from the legitimate stage by crafting early film dramas as filmed theater. With the evidence of Walton's discussion of the intense rivalry between the cinema and the stage during American cinema's formative years, there emerges a more complete picture of the origins of the "proscenium bias" that gave impetus to the early one-reelers, also known as filmed theater. Walton's detailing of the economic determinants responsible for the cinema's encroachments on the theater's audience base becomes an indispensable corollary to Vardac's subsequent work on the evolution of this cinematic aesthetic. Vardac begins his study by referencing the mutuality of influence occurring early on between the stage and screen: "Naturally, in these early years, the film and the stage were hardly differentiated from one another; the cinema frequently borrowed from the theatre, while the theatre, in an attempt to counter the new attraction, in its turn borrowed from the film" (xxvi). But in Walton's writings we are made privy to the more problematic dimensions of this "natural" evolutionary process outlined by Vardac. Contained in Walton's 5 March 1914 column, "New Yorkers Have Gone 'Dippy' over the Movies," is his lament over the cinema's "Broadway Invasion." This piece is remarkable for the glimpse it provides into the fierce internecine battles between theatrical luminaries such as David Belasco and Oscar Hammerstein over the cinema's rise to preeminence and the ultimate capitulation by Broadway to its powerful sway. Divulging the telling statistics of the phenomenal growth in the number of nickelodeons and picture palaces mushrooming throughout Greater New York (which the New York Bureau of Licenses tallied at about 950 to 1,000, with new additions daily), Walton clues us in to some of the fascinating facts behind these 1914 numbers:

> The greatly changed attitude of theatrical promoters toward the movies within the last twelve months has been interesting. Three or four years ago . . . representative theatrical managers, those who produced first-class attractions, turned up their noses at the motion picture industry and motion picture theatres, and this turning up of noses was more in a literal sense than figurative. But recently their olfactory organs quickly assumed a different angle. . . . David Belasco, the lessee, decided to sublet [The Republic] to a firm for the presentation of pictures. To this plan Oscar Hammerstein, the owner, vigorously demurred and sought to enjoin Mr. Belasco in the courts from carrying it out. The courts decided against Mr. Hammerstein. . . . And so the conquest of the movies goes merrily on. Additional surrenders are likely to be chronicled at any moment.
>
> (Walton 1914b)

On one level, Walton seems to relish the financial chaos inflicted by the cinema on the Great White Way; his message of comeuppance suggests a poetic justice in this state of affairs that ultimately compensates for the years of discrimination practiced against African American thespians, impresarios, and audiences. On another, he wants to pillory the powerful theater barons for their complicity in endangering the future of the legitimate theater. Overall, this article, with its nostalgic reminiscences of the great bygone days of Broadway and its stellar casts and productions, at once eulogizes those theaters that "succumbed to the hypnotizing influences of the movies" and attempts to blunt "the force of the shock sustained by the advent of the movies." Adding further complexity is Walton's own ambivalent response. Even as he despairs over the cinema's meteoric ascent, he demonstrates apparent pleasure at being able to report on the sensational "electrical display" of a new movie theater debuting with a film version of Alexander Dumas's *Three Musketeers* that "bedimmed the luster of the Vitagraph Theatre's electrical exhibition" just across the street. Significantly, this lengthy article is accompanied by a large lithograph image of the novelist Alexander Dumas, a writer of African descent with roots in the Caribbean. Walton's delight in seeing Dumas's name emblazoned in neon lights along Broadway must have diminished, temporarily, his apocalyptic view of the cinema's "invasion." For what other African diasporic writer's name had Walton seen so illuminated on the Great White Way?

The broadening of Walton's film criticism becomes more evident as he encompasses analyses of cinema news apart from "the familiar cry of drawing the Color Line" (1911) that so hobbled American entertainments. An example of this is Walton's commentary on the proliferation of "fake pictures" purporting to be of the *Titanic* disaster, which he titles "Ban on Titanic Moving Pictures." In this 2 May 1912 column, Walton excoriates the early film industry propensity to pander to "morbid curiosity" in the rush to supply "fake pictures . . . in connection with such an appalling disaster as the sinking of the *Titanic*."

> The sinking of the Titanic, accompanied by such a great loss of life, is too serious in character to be treated along cheap, melodramatic lines. Then even those who were not principals in this great sea tragedy, who secured their information

> through the newspapers, indulged in sufficient realism by reading the accounts of the sinking of the ship and drawing on their imagination. To see fake pictures was not necessary.
>
> (Walton 1912b)

Walton is incredulous when he acknowledges that "morbid curiosity, of course prompted some to spend their change to see a 'reproduction' of the great sea tragedy, *knowing, however, before entering that they would look at fake pictures*" (italics mine).

Here Walton communicates to his readers, in subtle fashion, that seeing a world represented in films is not always believing. He further informs them that "only a few days after it had been made known that the *Titanic* had gone down with hundreds on board several film concerns advertised that they could furnish pictures of the 'Sinking of the *Titanic*.' " This admonition to his constituency warns against being taken in by a cinematic ruse that trades on "morbid curiosity." More to the point, however, is Walton's understanding that the "willing suspension of disbelief" credo indeed authorizes such fantastic and often disingenuous cinematic claims to veracity. Walton's questioning of the limits of verisimilitude governing the enormously popular actuality films problematizes the veracity of filmic representation on the whole. Moreover, he indirectly challenges the presumed sanctity and irrefutability of the very principles of scientific inscription on which early film spectators uncritically based their mediated knowledge of the complex and often unknowable world that existed outside the narrow confines of their everyday lives. Besides noting how the fake *Titanic* pictures compromise the newsreels' privileged claims to verisimilitude, Walton also calls attention to other questionable examples of the actuality films' reliance on instances of "staged authenticity" (to borrow a phrase from Dean MacCannell).

Writing once again on the cinema in his 5 June 1913 column, Walton interrogates the role of the motion pictures "in properly presenting to the world at large the American Negro." Here Walton contrasts the Pathé Weekly newsreel depiction of black migrants from Memphis, Tennessee, moving to the nation's capital, with the newsreel's coverage of German peasants going to Sunday services. Pointing out the racial economy served by the filmmakers' conscious decision to inscribe this scene of black misery in the comedic vein, Walton observes:

> All the refugees in line were colored. Then the operator who took the pictures must have made up his mind to inject a bit of comedy. The spectacle of this long line of hungry, homeless men, women and children did not touch his sympathetic chord, nor did it awaken a feeling of sadness. . . . So he arranged three little black, half-starved pickannies in a row, sat a bowl of mush and a piece of bread before each and then waited to see the fun. Even a cultured grown-up person, when nearly famished, thinks but little of etiquette, and these youngsters did not disappoint the operator for the Pathé concern. . . . A negro woman was also put on exhibition.
>
> (Walton 1913b)

Walton then juxtaposes the documentary effect or naturalizing tendencies of the newsreel's comedic scenario of blackness to the more flattering travelogue footage signifying normative whiteness in the world of the German peasants:

> From the "comic" pictures the audience was taken abroad and the Kaiser of Germany figured in one scene. The peasants going to church on Sunday in one of the German towns was next shown, and as I gazed at the reproduction

> showing the German boys and girls making their way to church in large numbers, I wondered why it was that the Pathé people had seen fit to depict to the world the lowest type of the Negro—the ignorant, half-starved, homeless and deformed—while the peasantry of Germany was presented in Sunday clothes and at their best.
>
> (1913b)

Walton's Socratic irony in describing the racial binary oppositions this scene constructs is clarified in his cogent analysis of the ideological function of the abject images of blackness. To thwart this naturalizing of the first wave of the great black migration in terms of an undesirable social burden, Walton recalls the harm to African American sociopolitical advancement incurred by demeaning and pernicious stereotypes already circulating in America's polarized society. Although Walton does not address the fact that Pathé is predominantly a French film company, he is concerned with the global construction of racial difference that such juxtapositions of images advance. Consider this biting interrogative:

> Certain Negro stage types have been instrumental in making thousands of whites in this and in other countries believe us to be as a whole what we are not, and if the motion picture concerns continue to do as the Pathé people in showing the refugees at Memphis, or rather the colored refugees, the impression of the Negro in America will grow worse instead of better.
>
> (1913b)

When we situate this analysis in the context of the massive influx of new arrivals to the nation's northeastern industrial centers and the subsequent social and cultural vicissitudes it impelled, Walton's assessment takes on added significance. James Weldon Johnson's important study of the African American presence in New York from slavery through the Harlem Renaissance sheds further light on the sociopolitical stakes involved here. Originally published in 1930, Johnson's *Black Manhattan* (1968) census figures on the staggering number of Europe's first wave of Anglo-Saxon immigrants to New York, nearly four million by the turn of the century (45), provide the necessary background for a nuanced reading of Walton's discourse on the cinema's role in fomenting antiblack sentiments while at once fostering attitudes of tolerance for, and acceptance of, the first- and second-generation European immigrants. Even though Walton's critique of Pathé's newsreels predates the swell of the great migration of African Americans that ensued during and after World War I, it is clear that Walton's remarks do address the precipitous decline in the quality of life for black New Yorkers who "lost ground" as a result of their reduced competitiveness "in the wider fields of domestic service, common labor, and the so-called menial jobs" amid this cultural upheaval (Johnson 1968, 45). Through Walton's vigilant gaze we apprehend the contribution of these early cinematic images in authorizing society's tacit rules of interracial coexistence in turn-of-the-century New York. In "talking back" against this balkanization of racial prejudice directed at African Americans, he continues: "Even in the United States the white and colored citizens are living practically side by side, with the white citizens, in general, knowing very little about us." Additionally, Walton contends, "If the motion picture concerns are sincere in their desire to educate the masses, they ought to make pictures showing the better elements of the race, not the lowest" (1913b). As if to counteract Pathé's skewed cinematic portraiture of modern blackness, Walton printed a photo next to his article of an obviously refined, fair-skinned, middle-class black vaudeville performer named Ada Guiguesse. The photo suggests that if filmmakers would not present "pictures showing the better elements of the race," Walton certainly would.

Rather than leave this important matter up to white theatrical establishments profiting, in more ways than one, from such racially divisive film portrayals, Walton implores those "motion picture houses conducted by colored managers [to] make it their business to prevail upon the manufactures of motion picture films to present the Negro under more favorable conditions."

> The motion picture industry can wield an influence for good and serve as an educational medium in helping to solve the so-called Negro question if it will; but setting up to the world from time to time the very lowest types of the race, whether intentionally or unconsciously done is harmful.
>
> (1913b)

Here Walton demonstrates his profound understanding of the mediating function of films that prefigures later arguments against reflection theories of film and other media representations. As a member of a group most denied, as a matter of course, true cinematic reflections or mirrorings of its lived realities—even in actualities or newsreels—Walton knew firsthand how limited, though politically efficacious, claims to cinematic verisimilitude could be, especially in race matters. Moreover, it is evident that Walton understood films' incomparable ability to influence social attitudes on important issues of the day. In 1914 Walton begins his preemptive strikes against the unrelentingly demeaning portrayals of the race.

Walton's advocacy of African American representation on New York's Film Censor Board arises out of the study he made of black Chicago's parallel struggle. This 19 March

DRAMATICS

THE MOTION PICTURE INDUSTRY AND THE NEGRO

THE FLOOD REFUGEES.

(BY LESTER A. WALTON.)

WHAT part will the motion picture industry play in properly presenting to the world at large the American Negro?

This question flashed through my mind a few evenings ago while seated in a Harlem theatre looking at motion pictures which came under the heading of Pathe's Weekly. In this set of pictures important current happenings all over the world were produced for the edification of theatregoers, and the pictures, aside from being interesting, possessed some educational value.

Following the film showing President Wilson throwing the first ball at the opening game between New York and Washington at Washington, D. C., came a picture of flood refugees at Memphis, Tenn. All of the refugees in line were colored. Then the operator who took the pictures must have made up his mind to inject a bit of comedy. The spectacle of this long line of hungry, homeless men, women and children did not touch his sympathetic chord, nor did it awaken a feeling of sadness. Under these depressing conditions he was light of heart and wanted to laugh.

So he arranged three little black, half-starved pickaninnies in a row, set a bowl of mush and a piece of bread before each and then waited to see the fun. Even a cultured grown-up person, when nearly famished, thinks

ADA GUIGUESSE

In Vaudeville

TAYLOR AND "HIAWATHA"

FRANKLIN THEATRE

Figure 7.4 Refined black woman vaudevillian who displays "the better elements of the race" that Walton believed white motion picture firms put under erasure. *New York Age*, 1913

1914 article, entitled "Want Representation on Film Censor Board," not only advances this interventionist strategy but also denounces the culpability of negligent black entrepreneurs. "Severest criticism," he asserts, "should be directed at the colored people . . . who are not progressive enough to take advantage of the wonderful opportunities offered to make money in the amusement world" (1914a). Not one to turn a blind eye to the responsibility of intra-group critique, Walton is willing to lay partial blame for the dismal state of affairs at the feet of his own upwardly striving community. Instead of condoning a censuring of enterprising whites who endeavor to erect theaters for the black market, Walton instead seeks to prod African Americans along the same lines: "That white men are able to see the commercial possibilities existing among colored people [as avid film-goers] and colored men are not is a reflection on the business acumen of the latter." With that, Walton quotes the following statement provided by certain white theater promoters preparing to launch their black movie house in Norfolk. The remarks are telling:

> As you know, there is not a theater in the city that will seat a colored person, no matter how refined, anywhere except in the peanut gallery, where they are not only segregated to a disadvantage but are exposed to great danger in the case of fire. This theatre will obviate the necessity of colored people . . . subjecting themselves to "Jim Crow" conditions in order to see a decent theatrical production.
>
> (1914a)

To further provoke those "colored people fast asleep" and to awaken them as the cinematic revolution was gaining momentum, Walton adds yet another reprint, this time from

Figure 7.5 Lester Walton, ca. 1920s. Courtesy of the Manuscripts, Archives, and Rare Books Division–Schomburg Center for Research in Black Culture, the New York Public Library, Astor, Lenox, and Tilden Foundations–Lester A. Walton Photograph Collection

an article appearing in the 14 March 1914 edition of the *Philadelphia Bulletin*. The article details an ordeal suffered by a twenty-one-year-old African American woman arrested for her noncompliance with the segregation practices of a Philadelphia movie theater. When the young woman screamed as an usher tried to force her to a seat located in the rear of the theater, her screams caused a near stampede as other women in the theater bolted for the doors. The theater proprietors implored the judge to sentence the young woman to prison. Instead, he refused, and on discharging her, the judge suggested that she bring suit against the theater (Walton 1914a). Presumably Walton hoped to cause enough of a stir to galvanize the emergent black bourgeoisie to a proactive stance and thereby circumvent such common-place injustices. For Walton, this meant ushering in a new era of widespread black participation in the production, distribution, and exhibition of motion pictures. No doubt Walton's familiarity with the 1913 arrival of the Foster Photoplay Company of Chicago motivated his desire to see a viable black film industry emerge in New York and counter such systemic outrages. Walton wants to make it clear that until blacks themselves create the conditions for bringing about a more hospitable environment for black theatergoers (Carbine 1990, 9), such abuse, heaped daily on decent African American citizens whose only offense was attempting to indulge their movie fandom, would surely prevail.

By the end of the decade, Walton's concern with the interrelationship of the cinema and the nation's collective political unconscious had deepened. His last series of regular articles on the cinema for the *Age* appeared in 1919 and are representative. In his 15 March column, entitled "Stop German Opera; Un-American Film Allowed on Screen," Walton inculpates white America in its hypocrisy on matters concerning the public good. Written during America's involvement in the final stages of World War I, this article takes issue with white America's selective view of what constitutes political art. Occasioned by the violent protests of white servicemen against the performances of German operas in New York, Walton uses the situation to unveil the racist logic that permits whites to politicize the German operas as unacceptable "German propaganda" unfit for the wartime economy, and yet to depoliticize the blatant and unrelenting "un-American propaganda," as he puts it, in such films as Griffith's wildly popular opus *The Birth of a Nation*, among others.

> To colored Americans the campaign against German opera is a trivial matter compared to the un-American propaganda which upholds such vicious screen presentations as "The Birth of a Nation" and teaches the false doctrine of "All white men on top and all black men down." After all, aversion against German opera is a mere matter of sentiment; the anti-Negro propaganda strikes at the very roots of the fundamental principles of democracy.
>
> (Walton 1919a)

By couching his criticism in terms suggestive of the limits of American liberal humanism, an ethos that fails to include black humanity in its purview, Walton's strategy is twofold. First, he seems to be demanding an acknowledgment that African American lives are on the line in the fight for democracy against German imperialism. And Walton demonstrates that black soldiers, for all their patriotism, can expect no parallel rush to censor antiblack films. Second, he suggests the likelihood that this anti-German sentiment is a temporary, knee-jerk reaction merely projected on, and delimited to, the realm of art, as against the long-standing history of persecution of African Americans that pervades all spheres of American life, without benefit of future rescission. Although his relativizing of the dangers of intolerance in this piece creates another set of problematics, his larger aim to unmask the political unconscious of the nation regarding its racial myopia cannot be minimized.

In "World to Be Americanized by Such Films as 'Birth of a Nation,' " published on 7 June 1919, Walton continues his attack. In this instance, however, he forgoes the local for the global implications that stereotypical films pose. Again, he takes for his object the scrutiny of the highly celebrated text *The Birth of a Nation*. If nothing else, Walton's early example of a popular literature engagé must be seen as contesting and correcting errant notions about African Americans' passive engagement with the cinema's earliest discourses before *The Birth of a Nation*. As these early articles by Walton aptly demonstrate, African American cultural workers were not complacent with nor had they acquiesced to their historically prescribed places at the margins of early film criticism and literary development.

Leaving Walton's specialized discourse on the cinema, for the moment, we now turn to his contemporaries at the *Chicago Defender* and to the phenomenon of the cinema as front-page general news in the black press.

Sylvester Russell and the *Chicago Defender*'s Coterie of Critics

The *Chicago Defender*'s "Musical and Dramatic" column from 1910 to 1914 bore a structural and functional resemblance to its counterpart at the *New York Age*, though there were significant thematic and ideological differences. Unlike the *Age*, with its decade-long history of relatively consistent and evolving film criticism characterized by the tenacious probings of Lester Walton, the *Defender*'s early cinematic discourse is marked by a more sporadic and truncated engagement with the new medium. This was necessarily the situation during those early years at the *Defender*, due in large measure to its revolving door of theatrical critics. The *Defender*'s cadre of critics consisted of Sylvester Russell (the *Defender*'s self-styled "foremost dramatic critic"), Minnie Adams, Tony Langston, and Columbus Bragg. Another distinction separating the early film literature of these two major African American newspapers was each paper's ideological agenda regarding the merits of the cinema. The *Age*'s "Music and the Stage" column, under the philosophical guidance of Walton, took a generally dim view of the cinema as an apparatus for African American uplift or an agent for broader social change, even though Walton did agitate for the establishment of an autonomous African American cinema institution. In contrast, critics at the *Defender* tended toward the more optimistic view. This is perhaps because as early as 1905 Chicago could lay claim to operating the nation's first black-owned movie theater (Carbine 1990, 9). Given the magnitude of this achievement, it is easy to appreciate these critics' embrace of the new medium and the promise it represented.

The *Defender*'s earliest writings on the cinema were contributed by Sylvester Russell, whose 12 March 1910 column reveals that African American stage criticism was poised to enter its second decade, and that "it takes a very capable man in these days to handle it" (Russell 1910a). Of course, Minnie Adams's arrival as critic for the *Defender* complicates Russell's masculinist claim. By April of that year, Russell was making his own tepid overture to discoursing on the new celluloid art. For example, in his 9 April 1910 "Musical and Dramatic" column, Russell's enthusiastic, albeit scant, mention of the cinema amounts to little more than an acknowledgment that "the moving picture theater craze" had developed what he considered "a wonderful stampede among Negro and Yiddish theater goers" (1910b). That Russell's early musings on the cinema pale in comparison to Walton's is clear. Nevertheless, what Russell contributes is a revealing look at the theatrical critic's role and function at the black presses of that moment, at least from his self-interested position. First of all, there is some significance in the fact that Walton, Russell, and Adams were not mere cultural informants or detached discussants. Each was a participant-observer of the local theatrical scene. Walton also possessed impressive theatrical credentials as a member of New York's influential theatrical association

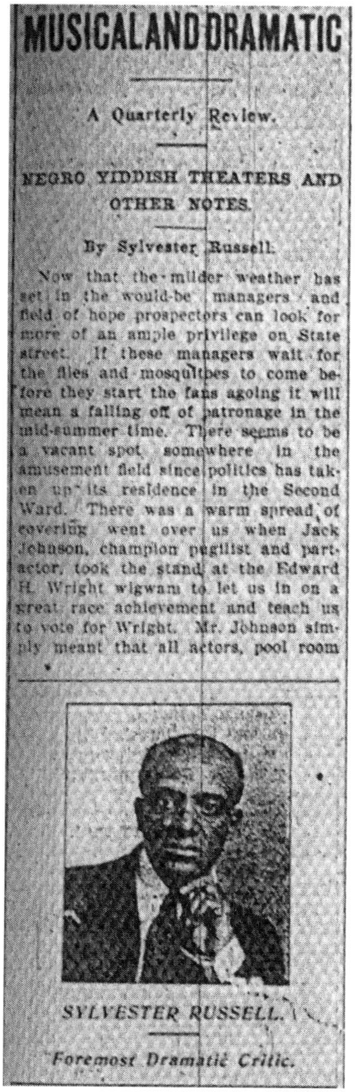

MUSICAL AND DRAMATIC

A Quarterly Review.

NEGRO YIDDISH THEATERS AND OTHER NOTES.

By Sylvester Russell.

Now that the milder weather has set in the would-be managers and field of hope prospectors can look for more of an ample privilege on State street. If these managers wait for the flies and mosquitoes to come before they start the fans agoing it will mean a falling off of patronage in the mid-summer time. There seems to be a vacant spot somewhere in the amusement field since politics has taken up its residence in the Second Ward. There was a warm spread of covering went over us when Jack Johnson, champion pugilist and part-actor, took the stand at the Edward H. Wright wigwam to let us in on a great race achievement and teach us to vote for Wright. Mr. Johnson simply meant that all actors, pool room

SYLVESTER RUSSELL.

Foremost Dramatic Critic.

Figure 7.6 Sylvester Russell, the *Chicago Defender*'s self-styled "foremost dramatic critic." 1910

of the 1900s called the Frogs (Hughes and Meltzer 1967, 60). In addition to their journalistic activities, Russell was a vocalist; Adams, a musician; and Bragg, a playwright. In one of his more candid moments, Russell makes this revelation:

> Negro stage criticism is now over ten years old and it takes a very capable man in these days to handle it. And it must be handled carefully and cautiously. And much depends upon who the man is who ventures to tell tales out of school. . . . But actors can't afford to trust the best of us; we are mean to the meager and [magnanimous] to the meritorious. We can't help it. That's our business.
>
> (1910a)

It is the case that Russell ignores the obvious fact that meritocracy too often attaches to a highly subjective set of perceptions and pronouncements, and he seems perfectly at ease with its economic determinants. The 30 December 1911 column discussing theatrical competition on State Street, Chicago's black theater district, continues Russell's informative disclosures on the symbiosis of theatrical production and the promotional agenda of critics:

> The most delicate point with managers is the box office, and no intelligent critic of honorable reputation, of long, reliable service has ever been known to criticize the box office system of any theater unless the public had complained and the critic himself had experienced the same unfair treatment and insult from the management. The days of ignorant managers who think they have the divine right to dictate to an intelligent newspaper representative of honest capability is past. . . . Unlawfully prohibiting a newspaper man from a theater . . . is generally the most disastrous thing a manager can do, even in a city where a manager has corrupt assurance of winning law suits by influence and money. . . . I have often been told that Colored newspapers are a joke. . . . The newspapers I represent are far from being a joke. . . . The power of public sentiment is great.
> (Russell 1911d)

Apart from drawing attention to the imbrication of the critical establishment in the system of mass entertainments, Russell's comments veer into even more intriguing cultural thickets, especially as they concern the racial problematic. First, in tandem with the previous quote, Russell's assertions serve to acquaint both theatrical consumers and producers with his importance as a cultural aesthete or middleman capable of arbitrating their respective desires. For the newly urbanized mass of untutored African American migrants from the South, Russell positions himself as the voice of experience to whom decisions regarding their hard-earned leisure time and money should be entrusted. With the increased competition for black patronage along the Stroll, as State Street was also known, it is not unreasonable to presume that Russell's position of influence grew accordingly. If Russell is attempting here to inspire confidence and loyalty in the hearts of his readers, on the one hand, on the other, he aims to instill a sense of fiduciary anxiety in the minds of bigoted theater operators regarding race matters and box office receipts. At bottom, Russell is reminding "ignorant managers" that, indeed, the new day has brought with it the New Negro, whose newfound socioeconomic status dictated a new approach in the area of public accommodations. One is also left with the distinct impression that Russell betrays his personal frustrations and anger at having suffered the indignities of second-class citizenship in these race theaters during the execution of his duties as theater and film critic. Furthermore, Russell makes it clear that his constituency is not unaware of the judiciary's complicity in perpetuating the theatrical managers' discriminatory cabals. The subtext of Russell's message, however, seems to be that though such treatment of the average Negro patron may go unpunished in a court of law, no such immunity would be granted in the court of Negro public opinion, especially when a respected newspaper man such as himself was victimized (Russell 1911d).

Russell's comment that "no intelligent critic of honorable reputation, of long, reliable service has ever been known to criticize the box office system" underscores E. Franklin Frazier's (1957) concern about black businesses' wholesale adoption of the capitalist ethos. Instead of challenging or opposing the "box office system," Frazier reminds us of the intoxicating nature of the profit motive. He observes that the "Negro professional men engage in the same 'rackets' as the successful Negroes in the underworld" (110) and their white counterparts. Thus Russell's own willful compliance with the "box office system," save the indignities of racism, suggests a sort of uncritical adherence to middle-class consumerist ideology.[6] Although class lines were drawn and blurred to a lesser extent among the second-class African

American community in its racial uplift quest, Russell's expectation of enjoying the privileges and prerogatives of an elite class of newspaper men as against those of the average Negro attest to his susceptibility to Lizabeth Cohen's embourgeoisement idea.

Over the course of the following year, the changes in Russell's column to accommodate "the motion picture craze" were minimal. Lacking the critical depth that we see in Walton, Russell's early, inauspicious film commentary appears as little more than footnotes wherein he simply catalogs the weekly film offerings at the neighborhood nickelodeons. These brief mentions of the cinema began with a subtle addition to his column as offset subheadings denoting the latest film schedules at the different theater houses on the Stroll. And thus began the budding commentary on the cinema as an autonomous topic in the high-profile entertainment page of the *Defender*. Accordingly, the first film commentary found in Russell's column stated, "The Phoenix Theatre Shows Good Pictures." Appearing on 1 July 1911, this subheading typified the manner in which the "Musical and Dramatic" column demarcated the boundaries of its theater and film commentary. Although the tone of the short paragraph, which primarily announced the Phoenix Theater's moving picture fare for the week, is uninspiring, it nevertheless carves out a narrative niche for the paper's later, more expanded versions. Generally, in Russell's discussions of films, the narrative tone is subjective, passionate, and suasive; for example, he writes that "the Phoenix theatre is the place for the children, and we are glad to see them go. The picture plays are moral and humorous" (1911b). Here, as before, Russell not only touts the merits of the cinema where children are concerned but also extols its benefits as a suitable and wholesome amusement for young adults.

In his 22 July 1911 column, Russell proclaimed that the Phoenix theater's films were of "high moral character." In his view, "the good class of young people who attended" these moral films should serve to reassure any skeptical parents concerned about the leisure activities of their impressionable youths. In stressing the high moral character of the films at the Phoenix, Russell sought to disabuse dubious parents of the notion that film theaters were equivalent to those other notoriously amoral dens of iniquity littering the crowded tenement districts of southside Chicago, the burlesque houses, saloons, and juke joints, for example. It is through such passages that the *Defender* and Russell's articles often divulge their strong assimilationist ideology (as Franklin and Cohen might argue), or their adherence to bourgeois norms of social progress that critics such as Russell then pass on to their readers. It is important to bear in mind that the *Defender*'s readers are both the dislocated black masses from the South and their slightly less downtrodden brethren hailing from the North, and that both classes were seeking useful clues to effect their respective sociopolitical transformations. Viewed from this vantage point, Russell's endorsement in the article of the songs accompanying the film, "Battle Hymn of the Republic" and "Wages and Wage Earners," which he says "were especially good" (1911c), is revealing. It reveals that conservative and patriotic values as conveyed through these songs were appealing to, and expressive of, African Americans' Americanness.

One noticeable change early on in the *Defender*'s entertainment column occurred with Russell's exit from the paper. During Russell's tenure as the "Musical and Dramatic" column's resident critic, his distinguished and pensive-looking photo gazed out at readers. At that time, Russell was the *Defender*'s only columnist identified by a photo in addition to a byline. On some level, it seemed that his photo and his theatrical credentials functioned to authorize and legitimize Russell's more grandiloquent journalistic prose, and to distinguish it from the sensational and everyday prose of the paper's "hard" news sections. With Russell's eventual departure, the removal of his photo, and the abandonment of his unique writing style, the more quotidian style of his immediate successor, Minnie Adams, became the column's narrative standard.

Adams's arrival on the entertainment column signaled the column's transitional shift in tone and mood. J. Hockley Smiley, of the *Defender*, notes that "as a critic, she [Adams] is plain but just, and concerns her own self more about whether her efforts are more clearly understood" (Smiley 1911). Whether Smiley's remarks amount to a direct imputation of Russell's more idiosyncratic style is unclear, but the inference seems fair. Ultimately, Russell's photo gave way to Adams's aphorism "All Passes, Art Alone Endures." This decidedly less personalized mode of address also marks the column's linguistic shift from Russell's author-centered, high-art aesthetic of theatrical reviews and critiques to Adams's more circumspect and reportorial prose style. Perhaps the decline of theatrical productions brought about by films, coupled with Russell's own apparent discomfiture with discoursing on the new medium, more an attraction than art, precipitated the increased prominence of film news, for a time, in the entertainment pages of the *Defender*. During her critical reign, the column moved away from discussions of theater syndicates, quarterly assessments, and the role of the critic to more parochial matters. The broader-based discussions of topics such as "The Advisability of a Colored and White Managers' Alliance," "Important Issues of the Negro Stage Profession," "The Duty of Colored Actor Organizations," and comparative analyses of Negro and Yiddish theaters clearly were Russell's domain. Adams's work, instead, is defined by a more localized sensibility. Her commentary most often was restricted to local reviews of African American vaudeville shows, dramatic plays, and musical concerts and rare discussions of film. However, the most notable contribution Adams made to the early corpus of African American film literature is her essay "In Union Is Strength." Published on 24 February 1912, this article, with its chastisement of Chicago's black community's lack of economic solidarity, was to become Adams's most substantive critique on the cinema. Here Adams holds up the tarnished mirror reflecting the community's failure to adequately patronize the black-owned Pekin Theater, the only such "race" establishment on the Stroll. In so doing, her aim to instill shame and foment a sense of business loyalty in her readers is paramount:

> It is a shame so great that we should blush when we realize how little we care for the welfare of our own. The efforts of individuals for the betterment and the pleasure of the race should be met by the hearty cooperation of every man and woman. . . . One might argue that the offerings at the above named house were not creditable, perhaps not at all times, but on whom can the blame be laid? By all means on the community. Give the [Pekin] theater your support and watch its policies improve. What other house has given our local talent as much consideration as the Pekin? And for that reason if no other, it should have our approval and patronage. . . . We wish to . . . entreat the people to wake up to the fact that they are not letting charity begin at home.
>
> (Adams 1912)

In voicing her scorn for this dereliction of group responsibility, Adams fails to recognize the incredible lure of the better-equipped venues for a downtrodden people anxious to experience the best their meager and hard-earned monies could procure. It would be unreasonable, after all, to expect black audiences not to be attracted by the luxury or elegance of theaters featuring decorated foyers, stairways, and ceilings. As Robert Sklar (1976) observes in another context, these amenities greatly enhanced the film experience for early spectators and the profit margins for theater owners who could afford the costly renovations (45). A *Defender* announcement for one of the Star Theater's weekly offerings illustrates the point. " 'The Mad Hermit,' in three reels, will be presented. . . . 'The Flash of Fate,' a two reel Bison picture, will be thrown on the screen. Both are first runs and well worth seeing. . . .

Mr. William Riley, the genial manager, spares no pains or expense in making this the coziest and most attractive movie house on The Stroll. Get the Habit" ("Jottings Theatrical" 1914). These important factors in the totality of the filmgoing experience seem lost on Adams, but apparently not on the film enthusiasts among her readership. Her self-help argument, nonetheless, is well-advised. It is striking that Adams makes it clear that she is not advocating wholesale abandonment of the other, white-owned theaters, but she insists that her readers be mindful of this disquieting reality:

> Many [white] theaters in the city we go to and are admitted on sufferance and more than apt to be relegated to the rear of the house, but we grin and bear it. . . . For those who only laugh in your face for your money and then are willing to lynch you if given half a chance, or, if they become prosperous after having bled you sufficiently they will turn you down. With all due respect for the theaters on State Street, and their managers . . . I feel they are of the opinion that a race is crazy who would not assist to upbuild its own. . . . There are sufficient of the race in Chicago to give to each of the theaters excellent box-office receipts, so that all might live and flourish.
>
> (Adams 1912)

Functioning here as a repository of cultural memory for readers expecting perhaps too much from their new urbanized existences, Adams refuses to let them lose sight of the ever present danger of black lynchings as a coercive force in assuring white power and dominance, even in the North. To militate against this formidable obstacle, it is her position, as well as that of most of the black elites, that successful black businesses and subsequent economic strength were the only real leverage against the repressions of white supremacy. In spite of it all, Adams states, "I approve of all the playhouses, the Grand and the Monogram are delightful places of amusement." Her point is not to foreclose the option blacks exercised in attending theaters better appointed than the Pekin along the Stroll. She simply believes that the community should occasionally sacrifice their temporary specular pleasures for a bit of permanent community "upbuilding."

Aside from this rare instance of protracted discourse on the black community's involvement with the cinema, Adams's critical reign displaced Russell's interpretive mode of engagement with the theatrical arts and featured instead description and précis. Occurring as they did before the advent of the feature-length film, Adams's modifications appear a somewhat fitting discursive move for what was largely regarded as the early cinema's passage through its mere recording function. In this light, it is easy to understand how the manifest content of the primitive cinema seemed to eschew critical depth and thorough interpretation (although Walton's lengthy exegeses trouble this proposition somewhat—Walton's case must be contextualized in terms of his consistent and autonomous reign as the *Age*'s solitary critic, and not as one among many). Unlike Russell, Adams would often not be the sole author of the column. Whereas Russell's authorship was never in question, during Adams's one-year or so tenure there were times when the "Musical and Dramatic" column displayed no byline whatsoever.

Eventually, Columbus Bragg and Tony Langston replaced her, each in his turn, as the durable column's critics-at-large. Both Langston and Bragg contribute something to our understanding of the cultural dynamics existing between the black press and its heteroglot readership, a readership speaking multiple regional dialects. This dialogism of the mass and the elite is a crucial intragroup dynamic suffusing the spoken and written languages in the diverse black community at this time. (Because African Americans tend to be regarded as a monolithic group, the complexity of their linguistic practices is too often essentialized and described unproblematically as "black English.") However, it is well worth noting the historical existence of marked language variations within the African diasporic community in America from the turn of the century onward, which are attributable to significant educational, regional, and even national differences in the case of West Indian immigrants. Before shifting our focus to the black press's treatment of the cinema as general rather than entertainment news, one particular column by *Defender* writer Columbus Bragg deserves mention.

By mid-1914, with the "Musical and Dramatic" column under the editorial control of Columbus Bragg, news and promotion of the cinema as an autonomous category becomes even less pronounced. When limited coverage of the cinema does occur, there is, however, an echo of Sylvester Russell's critical style. For example, Bragg begins his column, which he calls "On and off the Stroll," by announcing his arrival and by inserting himself into the narrative:

> Starting on my journey into the Holy Mount of Muses and reflections and close observations on the mental calisthenics of the gay white way or the stroll. . . . The saying that goodness draws children but beauty draws men, heroism draws women, accounts for the big crowds at [the Elite café] nightly.
>
> (Bragg 1914)

Here Bragg not only restructures the column to suit his own more figurative linguistic approach but also resuscitates the theater, music, and society news that for a time had become overshadowed by the passively descriptive and uncritically celebratory billboarding of the cinema house offerings. As with Russell before him, Bragg took advantage of the pedagogical possibilities of this entertainment column. In this 1 August 1914 article, Bragg educates readers about the subtleties of cinematic, as opposed to theatrical, performance techniques. In response to readers' inquiries about employment in films, Bragg articulated the distinctions between the two performative modes. In his "On and off the Stroll" section of the column, Bragg delves into the specificities of the cinematic art not broached by the other critics, including Walton. In response to "so many letters asking of [cinematic] work," Bragg sets out to explain a few distinguishing properties and specific requirements of the cinema. To assist aspiring thespians seeking to break into film work, Bragg writes:

> It is not necessarily actors or actresses that have worked on the stage, as they are seldom successful in motion picture work or photo-play productions. To act before a camera requires special qualities. The pantomime actor of 100 years ago who depended for effects solely upon actions and not words would have made an ideal motion picture actor today, who must necessarily rely upon facial expression and gesture for the interpretation of any scene or incident which he may desire to portray. Now an experienced motion picture actor or actress very rarely looks direct at the camera, but does his part as though it were non-existent.
>
> (Bragg 1914)

Such commentary written in 1914 is remarkable indeed, and it marks a foray into aspects of the cinema clearly separate from the usual concerns with the racial problematic. Bragg demonstrates a familiarity with the dictates of silent-film performance techniques that even predates the theories of cinema as art contained in Vachel Lindsay's 1915 book *The Art of the Motion Picture*, Hugo Munsterburg's 1916 seminal study *The Film: A Psychological Study*, and Rudolph Arnheim's anthology of writings from the 1930s, *Film as Art*. Although Bragg's reflections on these issues are not sustained and sophisticated treatises on the subject, his early albeit limited articulations of them do portend the eventual development along these aesthetic lines in both black and mainstream film criticism. It is impressive that Bragg addresses in this one essay such broad themes as techniques of performance, dialogue and rhetoric, lighting effects, and what he calls "the art of condensation." He makes the point that

> the beginner always has to be cautious that every action is not definitely recorded by the machine. I have noticed that in all big studios that I have visited you cannot depend on your makeup for facial expressions. Very little is used as the immense enlargement the film undergoes when thrown on the screen would intensify the paint and powder to such an extent you would look ridiculous. The light which is so strong from the arc lights that are used in the studio forms a striking contrast of lights and shade: Now the time of a play only takes a very short time, the rehearsal might be a day or a month. . . . A minute or two is sufficient to film a play, as all dialogues are cut out, as action is the important thing wanted. The successful film producer is a past master in the art of condensation, being capable of boiling down a four-act play into say 500 or 600 feet of concentrated actions.
>
> (Bragg 1914)

Here Bragg's apt explication of the cinematic codes that characterize what Nicholas Vardac (1949) calls the film "storyette," the one- to three-reelers that preceded feature films, demonstrates Bragg's prescience in concentrating on the cinema's visual aesthetics as well as its narrative themes. In this passage, he engages such issues as cinematic naturalism and photographic realism as conveyed through character direction, camera techniques, spatio-temporal manipulation, and both theater and film acting styles. It is obvious that Bragg's assessments of the specificities of the silent film form unquestionably are on target. His response to "questions that have been mailed me this week by readers of the *Defender*" exceeds our expectations. Later in the article, he highly recommends *The Fall of the Mighty*, a film by the Bartlett Film company: "the best Afro American picture for real clean comedy with a moral to it, well posed, well acted and the plot was clever." Now, these perfunctory comments on the film *The Fall of the Mighty* create a dissonance in comparison to his foregoing analysis, especially because both appeared in the same column.

Bragg's meager film reviews compared to his brilliant revelations about the unique demands of the silent cinema leave us quite disappointed, perplexed, and yearning for more. How does this film production, for instance, fulfill or abnegate Bragg's prior statements? We are left to ponder this obscure film's merits relative to Bragg's own fitting criteria for successful silent cinema techniques. This critical absence becomes all the more intriguing and elusive when we learn finally of Bragg's departure from journalistic criticism to pursue his successful theatrical production of *The Ahjah*, a "classic Ethiopic drama" featuring "the sacred songs of Solomon." Bragg's obvious training in the art and craft of the classical theater informs his brilliant assessment of the requisites of silent cinema and promises so much more than his anemic film review delivers. Bragg concludes his article by jokingly threatening to "tell on some people" in next week's issue, and after a Machiavellian confession that he is "talking out of school," he ends with "Nuff said." We, however, respectfully disagree and wish this able critic had said more about *The Fall of the Mighty*. As concerns Bragg's production of *The Ahjah*, it is important to note that owing to the lack of theatrical venues available to African American theatrical impresarios, the production was staged at a church, and according to Tony Langston, it was a major hit. Alas, there is no further information in the *Defender* about Bragg's subsequent activities along these lines.

Bragg's legacy was the column's return to privileging African American music and stage productions, too long overshadowed by the rush to embrace the new mainstream cinematic offerings. His reapportionment of the column's ratio of film commentary to reviews of other amusements is symbolized by the appearance of a new subheading, "Jottings Theatrical and Otherwise." Gone for a time is the billboarding of State Street's various nickelodeon offerings that had dominated the column previously. Bragg tended to incorporate his film commentary into the larger theater and society news, as Russell had done three years earlier. It is important to stress, however, that with the formal shift, the silent cinema news remained an important feature of the 1914 "Musical and Dramatic" column.

As Bragg's foregoing address to his readers indicates, the *Defender*'s readers did not suffer their media expectations and disappointments in silence. "Southern black men and women" especially, Vilma Raskin Potter (1993) points out, "wrote to editors as though they knew them personally," and they wrote about everything, including their opinions of, and desires for, balanced entertainment and amusement coverage. Under the subheading "Resents Criticism," a letter from a self-identified "constant reader" was printed on 18 July 1914 in the "Musical and Dramatic" column and placed directly adjacent to the weekly entry. The letter's content serves as a forceful example of the author-reader interaction that informed much of the black press's journalistic philosophy at the turn of the century. As early as the late 1840s, the black press understood well its mission "partly to relieve 'the inability of the colored people to bring their inflicted wrongs and injustices before the public.' . . . Any person of color asking for correction of an error in a white paper or for the chance to reply in kind to a story offensive to the Negro would be likely to get the runaround or an outright refusal" (Pride and Wilson 1997, 56). Addressing the editor, the author of the letter complains that "the dramatic critic overworked himself, and went way beyond the boundary line of the unwritten rules of criticizing talent and art," because "the great writer had a little too much time on his hands or lacked the material to fill the allowed space" ("Resents Criticism" 1914). This breach was wholly unacceptable to this particular reader for several reasons. Most unforgivable was the fact that the critic was disparaging in his comments about the one musician in all of Chicago responsible for black orchestras procuring work in State Street's film theaters. "Had the writer [critic] made any inquiries," the letter continues, he would have discovered that the piano player he panned was responsible for compelling "every house along State Street to put in orchestras." Although the "constant reader" concedes that "everybody in public life is open to criticism," he or she feels compelled to "read" the critic in this way: "No critic is beyond the opinion of his readers, but when a writer [especially this unidentified critic] dabs his pen to comment on a moving picture orchestra, the limit has been reached." As the unnamed, pilloried film critic who drew the ire of that "constant reader" soon learned, early-twentieth-century African American film spectators did love the early cinema, but once introduced, they loved equally well, if not more, the role their traditional music played alongside this technological marvel. Because early films were considered mere novelties, the letter writer seems reconciled to critics' need for dabbing their "pen to comment on a moving picture," but to have a critic's pen trifle with the reputations of black orchestras, which often were more of a draw for black spectators than the films they accompanied—that was "the limit."[7]

By the end of 1915, the *Defender*'s "Musical and Dramatic" column found a way to accommodate a regular film review section featuring synopses of the latest offerings at the movie theaters all along Chicago's State Street Stroll. Each theater, including the New Grand, the Lux, the Merit, and the States, had its name prominently featured and its weekly program separately discussed in the column. And as might be expected, the column's film space expanded to reflect the increasing popularity of this phenomenal urban pastime with routine news of black spectators' attendance patterns. The cinema's onslaught was now evident as its coverage had begun, once again, to eclipse that of music and the stage.

Extra! The Black Press Discovers the Newsworthiness of the Cinema

When we recall the trenchant legal and de facto prohibitions against black literacy in America from slavery and beyond, the fact that Lester Walton, Sylvester Russell, and their peers and a vibrant African American literary tradition even existed at all, to say nothing of its amazing flourishes, during this era is remarkable in and of itself. News of the cinema that tended to grab front-page headlines and other general news columns focused largely on racially explosive topics (like biased seating and pricing policies in local theaters, and defamatory themes), on the cinema's technological advances, on black filmmaking enterprises, and on African American responses to the new medium. "Discusses Fight Pictures" was the headline referring to the Johnson-Jeffries championship fight that grabbed black Harlemites' attention when it appeared on the front page of the *New York Age* in 1910. The language of its reportage on the efforts of the Washington, D.C., chief of police to get the pugilist film suppressed, owing to its potential to impassion racial animosities, hints at the *Age*'s cautious endorsement of the contested measure. But the *Age* betrays the conditional nature of its endorsement of this suppression measure by joining the controversy over this fight picture to that over Thomas Dixon's race-baiting play *The Clansman:* "If the fight pictures could be barred in theatres on the grounds that they incited race against race and inflamed the passions of those who attended . . . Then certainly on the same grounds such plays as Thomas Dixon's 'The Clansman' would be barred from the established theatres as being more harmful than beneficial" ("Discusses Fight" 1910).

While the tenor of cool reason and the expectation of civic fair play regarding this racial powder keg governs the *Age*'s coverage in the turbulent aftermath of the Johnson-Jeffries match (for this was the one social arena where a black and a white man were permitted to compete on relatively equal terms), prior coverage of the much anticipated event in the white trade journal *Moving Picture World* points up the futility of the *Age*'s reasoned approach to such an unreasonably motivated and promoted public spectacle. On 21 May 1910, *Moving Picture World* ran a near-full-page advertisement for the film footage of Jack Johnson training for his competition with James Jeffries. The ad featured in this white journal ran the following promotional copy:

> Moving pictures of Jack Johnson, *Champion of the World* in training for the Big Fight of July 4, 1910 with James J. Jeffries, consisting of 6 rounds with his sparring partners. . . . And the features incidental to training quarters—The Best Ever Seen—Approximate length 1,000 feet. Ready for delivery May 16, 1910. States Sold: Massachusetts, Connecticut, Rhode Island, Vermont, New Hampshire, Maine, Ohio, Indiana . . . Illinois, Nebraska, Colorado, Utah . . . Tennessee, Kentucky, Virginia, West Virginia . . . Balance of States Rights For Sale: Write or Wire at Once.
>
> ("Fight Film" 1910)

One month later, the same *Moving Picture World* printed a fascinating full-page story on the Johnson-Jeffries fight wherein speculations about the untold millions of dollars to be made on this fight film pending "the unmistakable victory of Jefferies" ran rampant. In contrast, the article states unequivocally that if Jeffries, the "Great White Hope," were to be defeated by Johnson, "*It is commonly believed that the pictures would then be of comparatively little value* [italics mine] especially amongst the white section of the community" ("Pictures" 1910).

Hanging in the balance, of course, were the already strained race relations of polarized communities across the nation. While the *World*'s article voiced its concern about the "racial pride" Johnson's victory would signify for African Americans and the subsequent elevation of Johnson's status to "demigod," it is revealing that no such corollary regarding white racial pride pending Jeffries's success was even entertained. Jack Johnson was the victor, and melees of violence did ensue ("Discusses Fight" 1910). Clearly, then, it is in the context of the fight's violent aftermath that the *Age*'s conciliatory position on suppressing the fight pictures must be adjudicated. More substantial, however, is the strategic use to which the *Age* puts the words of Major Sylvester, the D.C. chief of police and chief censor. Before printing Sylvester's personal appeal to the paper's readership, the *Age* frames his remarks in a legitimating discourse of sincerity: "Major Sylvester, some are willing to believe, is sincere in this matter. He has previously waged successful fights against billboards, which display criminal actions, on account of the influence these have upon children." Though the major's comments do specifically address the "fights" among children of both races that occurred in the wake of Johnson's victory, as with the *World*, no issue is made of the white adults' participation in the racially motivated discord. It is unlikely that white children were responsible for the injuries sustained by "the vice president of the Negro Business League, A. H. Underdown" ("Discusses Fight" 1910) during the riots that broke out after news of Johnson's victory was publicized. Instead of confronting the systemic racism responsible for such wanton displays of violence, both Sylvester and the *Age* were content to blame the "lower class of both races." Be that as it may, by taking the opportunity to conflate the racism surrounding the Jeffries-Johnson fight with the racism of *The Clansman* in this article, the *Age* must be seen as striking a strategic oppositional blow to the nation's racial status quo and its propagandistic perpetuation in the popular media.

A 1910 *Chicago Defender* front-page story apprised its readers of early efforts to develop talking pictures. Below the heading "Talking Pictures," which was typeset in big, bold print, a short article reported on a demonstration at the Edison laboratories in New Jersey. This news item briefly explains some basic principles of the new kinetophone while simultaneously tempering reader expectation of its imminence by cautioning that Edison "thinks he needs one year more to so improve the mechanism." The earliest news of, and commentary on, the cinema in the black press that I have located dates back to 1909 editions of both the *Baltimore Afro-American Ledger* and the *New York Age*. Judging from the profusion of theater, music, and sports news in these papers, it appears that racial segregation governing the public sphere, from which the moving picture theaters were by no means exempt, militated against the widespread access of African American audiences to the new medium at its founding. The national commitment to racial separation, and the consequent inability of African American writers to screen the bulk of the early film releases, no doubt greatly impeded the formation of a systematic and far-reaching black press foundation for early black film reviews and criticism. Still, it is possible to assess a typology of general trends in the nature and tone of the critical responses to the cinema forged by those black critics (as discussed earlier) fastidious enough to meet the challenge. Starting with the *Afro-American Ledger*, we can see one example of an early film story in which the sizable headline "Moving Pictures Doing Good Business" hardly merits the scant copy corresponding to it. The *Age*'s earliest film news, by comparison, manages a full column of information that continues beyond page 1 of its 21 July 1910 film story. As both these papers enjoyed national circulations (and in the case of the *Age*, limited international circulation), they were able to extend their interpretations of the early cinema outside their regional borders. Thus these earliest reports on the cinema in the black newspapers convincingly illustrate black publishers', editors', and writers' recognition of, and interest in, the growing fascination the African American masses were developing with the movies. The purpose of foregrounding these articles is not to overstate the merits of these early writings in terms of a cohesive or consistent body of work on the early cinema by African American journalists at the dawn of the century. The point is to cull this early material from 1909 onward so as to point the way to an emergent critical discourse in the black press on the cinema's inauguration that would expand significantly in the decades that followed. Our introduction of Walton's emergence as a film critic during the first decade of the 20th century clearly signals black newspapers' and periodicals' increasing interest in serving and influencing the black community's growing fascination with the then-promising new technology.

Obviously, fiscal concerns were another motive force driving the black press's interest in the early cinema. For editors of the black press, moving pictures were doubly newsworthy both as regularly scheduled entertainments with built-in advertising revenue and as a source of genuine headline news, as the front-page news of the Johnson-Jeffries "fight picture" discussed earlier amply conveys. Also, cinema news blended well with the established social and entertainment pages so important in the black press of this era. In fact, the *Age* and the *Defender* vigorously promoted their entertainment columns.

Typically, when the black press covered cinema news in the early years, they frequently engaged in a myopic celebration of what they saw as the medium's emancipatory potential, that is, the liberation of the black image from the damning iconography of what Donald Bogle (1989) has described as "Toms, coons, mulattos, mammies, and bucks." There are, however, many reasons for this seeming naïveté. For the organic intellectuals who founded and wrote for the black press, the cinema represented a break with the old representational arts (namely, literature and the stage) because of its mechanical ability to record or hold up a less biased mirror to the progressive reality of black life. Clearly, New Negro self-representations were anathema to the retrograde mythologies underlying the national belief system that reified black backwardness and pathology. The black press's optimism about the cinema might also be contextualized within its collective faith in the establishment of nationwide boards of censors coupled with an inverted sense of technological determinism.

Whereas much has been written about the antimachinery Luddite tendency among many white Americans,[8] who were anxious or hostile in the face of employment competition from machine technologies that impelled the modern industrial age, many black Americans, it seems, did not share that same anxiety about the machine technologies' usurpation of their employment opportunities. Perhaps this attitude can be explained by blacks' incredulity that technology could plunge them any lower than their present positions at the bottom of America's racially stratified civil society. Thus, after more than three hundred years in bondage, it is easy to imagine that news of technological progress would not necessarily represent the same threat for blacks as it might for working-class whites. A passage from the *Ledger*'s 1909 front-page article proclaiming "Moving Pictures Doing Good Business" convincingly demonstrates the black press's embrace of motion picture technology and the promise it suggests for African Americans: "The Hiawatha Theater is doing all the business it can handle. . . . An important member of the Hiawatha staff is Mr. Raymond Murray, who operates the moving picture apparatus in the machine room. . . . The Hiawatha is helping the proscribed Negro to solve their amusement problem" ("Moving Pictures" 1909). Immediately striking in this passage, besides the pro-machine apparatus statement, is the hopeful tone of the article, which is symptomatic of black America's desperation for any mechanism to alleviate the nation's repressive racial order at this historical juncture. One senses, in all probability, that the Mr. Murray identified here is a member of the race. On balance, then, it is likely that Murray is cited not so much for his singular ability to participate in this modern industry as a skilled projector in the age of Jim Crow but as material proof of African American socioeconomic uplift theory put into practice despite Jim Crow.

In proffering the cinema as the black entertainment remedy for the decades of discrimination holding sway on the Great White Way, for its part, the *Ledger*'s "Moving Pictures Doing Good Business" performs two acts of cultural intervention on behalf of its readers.

First, the paper serves notice to white theater owners that black entertainment dollars can no longer be ignored or taken for granted, especially with such a rival and democratizing medium as the cinema looming large on the horizon. Second, the paper reveals to its "textual community" of New Negroes that the modern cinema industry manifests America's latent capacity to do the right thing, particularly since Mr. Raymond Murray's achievement provided confirmation that even prestigious employment opportunities were available to the race in this modern and exciting medium. An essay by Bill Foster appearing under his professional pseudonym, Juli Jones, in the 9 October 1915 edition of the *Defender*, entitled "Moving Pictures Offer the Greatest Opportunity to the American Negro," reinforces the point:

> Thus hundreds and hundreds of talented colored ladies and gentlemen who would really join the ranks of the moving picture business, that would not entertain the idea of going on the stage, because the stage, with a few exceptions, never offers the Negro an opportunity to display any real talent as a playwriter. . . . In a moving picture the Negro would offset so many insults to the race. . . . The world is very anxious to know more of the setaside race, that has kept America in a political and social argument for the last two hundred and fifty years. . . . Any one can buy cameras and machines of all kinds in open market. A picture show can be turned into a church very profitably with a very little outlay of money to start with.
>
> (J. Jones 1915)

Jones's statements focus attention on several important matters. From him we begin to see that the purchase on the black press's faith in the cinema is attributable in part to expectations of its radical potential to manumit the black image from the shackles of blackface minstrelsy. Also, the popularity of the early cinema among the black masses represented a viable means for black entertainers, impresarios, and writers to avoid altogether the intractability of racist practices on the legitimate stage. As Jones attests, speaking from his enlightened position as founder of one of the first African American film production companies ("Foster Photoplay"), "any one can buy cameras and machines of all kinds in open market." The hour of black self-articulation in the mechanical arts clearly had arrived. Having himself produced such film shorts as *The Fall Guy, The Butler, The Grafter and the Girl*, "and that sensational comedy, *The Railroad Porter*," when Jones writes on 9 October 1915, "The time is now,"[9] his challenge that blacks should seize the moment is no mere hyperbole. Rather, his brash observations and bold recommendations issued from his insider knowledge and years of film production experience.

To better appreciate the transition early-twentieth-century black writers and editors made from covering cinema news as a novel but promising curiosity and as entertainment staple to treating it as a more legitimate and consistent source of real news, it is useful to consider, in a bit more detail, news of the cinema as it matured in the pages of both the *New York Age* and in the *Chicago Defender* from 1909 to 1916. On an empirical level, in the case of the *Defender*, we notice the shift occurring as the news of the cinema encroaches spatially on theatrical and music news, the traditional mainstays of the paper's social and entertainment page. Noticeably, the moving picture news's spatial gain often was inversely proportional to the music and theatrical news's loss. This logistical shift seems also to have contributed to, if not precipitated altogether, the marked decline in the cultural prominence of the black theater of this era, with its compromising links to both the racism of white minstrelsy and the ribaldry of burlesque. Both papers, but especially the *Age*, do engage in a bit of self-criticism when they lay blame for much of black theatrical loss squarely on the shoulders of black businessmen and black theater patrons because of their respective lack of vision and racial unity.[10]

In analyzing these entertainment columns over time, it is possible to map the cultural ascendancy of the white-dominated cinema in segregated black communities, an ascendancy, I might add, secured uneasily at the expense of black cultural workers, including writers, theatrical impresarios, drama critics, and thespians.

From 1914 on, we begin to see a modification in the rhetoric of the black press regarding news of the cinema. After having sold its readers on the virtues of the cinema, with such hyperbole as "solving the Negro's entertainment problem," and with such boosterism as "get the habit" and "join the crowd," the black press—especially the *Defender*—was now emboldened to rail against it. Repositioning itself as a media watchdog of sorts, the paper printed a blistering front-page denunciation of one particular film. In a big, bold headline stating " 'Hit the Nigger,' New Film Insult," the *Defender* uses the film *Levinsky's Holiday* to reproach the board of censors, the film's exhibitor, and the film's black spectators, although not in equal measure. Leading into the article is a subtitle: "Major Funkhouser and his board of censors fail to suppress moving pictures that breed race hatred and Afro-Americans keep silent." In a move that anticipates, by one year, the furor that was to follow *The Birth of a Nation*, this article takes aim at the institutional racism responsible for the circulation of such biased cultural productions as *Levinsky's Holiday* and others of its ilk.

> In its last issue, *The Chicago Defender* called attention to the fact that on the moving picture censor board every race was represented but the Afro-American. The ink was hardly dry before the New Grand Theater . . . put on a film "Levinsky's Holiday" which shows a Jew on a frolic. "Hit the Nigger" is Levinsky's delight and runs through the entire film. . . . And as usual the house was crowded with Afro-Americans evidently insult-proof for they laughed and applauded. . . . [Funkhauser's board allows] the race to be insulted and ridiculed for they know no complaint will be made. It used to be "Hit the Jew" or "Down with the Irish," but alert members of those races watch with hawk-like eyes any attempt to belittle their people. . . . However, all concerned must remember that *The Chicago Defender* never sleeps.
>
> ("Hit the Nigger" 1914)

Interestingly, the paper's front-page editorial bite does not exact the pound of flesh from the exhibitor as might be expected in this article. By resting the blame for this film's screening solely at the feet of an employee of the New Grand Theater, it is clear that the paper saves face even as it promotes regularly the same theater's weekly schedule, and it blunts its own criticism of the theater for "being unfair to the people to whom they cater." Whether the leniency shown to the proprietor, whom the article claims was too busy to have prior knowledge of the incident, was based on fiscal concerns remains uncertain. What is certain, however, is that the black press' stormy honeymoon with the white-dominated cinema was rapidly disintegrating. Just three months later, yet another front-page condemnation of the cinema appeared in the *Defender*. This time banner headlines alerted readers to a new cinematic offense.

On 30 May 1914, the *Defender's* readers saw "States Theater Shows Colored Men Stealing Chickens" emblazoned across the paper's front page. Contrasting this article to the prior one, it becomes obvious that the paper's editors are no longer willing to soft-pedal their criticism of a theater proprietor a second time around. Perhaps it was the States Theater's audacity to screen two racially offensive films that the paper and black spectators found particularly egregious. Another factor may have to do with the fact that the States Theater did not employ blacks as did the Grand. The two films in question are *The Tale of the Chicken* and *Mother of Men*. Whereas the *Defender*'s article chose to lay stress on the antiblack theme of the former title, I want to call attention to the eerie resonance of the latter film's theme with the anti-black sentiments that propelled a late-1990s national news story of a carjacking hoax in Union, South Carolina, to national prominence. Consider the 1914 *Defender*'s brief synopsis of the film *Mother of Men:*

> Another picture equally as bad was entitled "Mother of Men," by Warren. This was supposed to show a slave stealing a white child, the hunt for her, and other exciting things. In the first place, this picture is foolish. Slaves do not steal white children, and if they did they could not find a place to hide them. The Chicago *Defender* disapproves of such depraved pictures and brands the last one as a lie from start to finish.
>
> ("States Theater" 1914)

This passage suggests that it is the existence of America's irrational anti-black collective consciousness that licenses the manufacture of such "vile race pictures" (as the *Defender* terms them). To that I would add, very little seems to have changed in the eighty years since this article was published. At any rate, the article goes on to reiterate the culpability of the black audiences and the Board of Censors in the latest conflagration over race and representation in the new cinema. Unlike the previous article, here the paper indicts the theater owner explicitly for booking the "objectionable and insulting" pictures. Another sign of the paper's tried patience on this issue is the acknowledgment of the newspaper's conflict of interest. The *Defender* asserts that "this newspaper has no thought of advertisements when it makes this complaint, as it has done the same thing with its best advertisers."

It is interesting to speculate about how the paper's ideal readers are inscribed in the black newspapers' bipartite coverage of the cinema both on the front pages, as general important news, and inside the paper, as fodder for the community entertainment calendars. Can we assume, as perhaps did the editors, a schizophrenic reading subject who, on the one hand, can refuse the disparaged cinema of the front pages and, on the other, become wholly seduced by it a few pages later in the entertainment and promotions pages? Whatever the answer, it is apparent that theories of the mimetic versus creative nature of art and aesthetics confront a more thorny set of problems when the art form in question is the cinema, and when its thematic content is race and representation.

Notes

1 In *The Sermon and the African American Literary Imagination*, Hubbard (1994) describes the African American's preacherly voice in this way: "Through his magnificently wrought oral poetry, the unlettered and semi-literate black preacher . . . moves the people beyond the boundary of hierarchical social order to the creation of new forms of human consciousness" (5).

2 In major debates between ministers who were in favor of the nickelodeons and those who were not, the Reverend Adam Clayton Powell took the former position: "The Abyssinian Church is surrounded by theaters and nickelettes as is no other church in the city, but I do not believe that they have affected our attendance in the slightest degree" (quoted in Walton 1910).

3 In his book *Before the Nickelodeon: Edwin S. Porter and the Edison Manufacturing Company*, Charles Musser (1991) observed that black characters were typically cast in films such as *The Watermelon Patch* as an outcast group, whose happy-go-lucky thievery suggests that "eating watermelon is the only pleasure in the world" (312).

4 Significantly, Walton's critical thrust is consistent with Benjamin's point that film's technical structure, in effect, could be made to evacuate the physical and moral shock effect from otherwise disturbing photographic images (1909, 44). Illustrating the moral crisis such an evacuation precipitates is Georges Duhamel's confession from "Scenes of Life in the Future": "I can no longer think what I want to think. My thoughts have been replaced by moving images" (quoted in Benjamin 1986, 44).

To his credit, Walton is intent on disclosing, if not foreclosing altogether, the potential for psychological control and coercion inherent in the cinema's powerful imagery, alluded to by Duhamel. For our purposes, connecting these later observations by Benjamin and Duhamel is crucial because they evolve out of lessons learned as a result of the horrific encounter between art and the regime of fascism. And yet Walton comes to a similar realization about the overwhelming influence exerted by the cinema decades earlier.

5 Hans Magnus Enzensberger popularized this idea in the 1970s.

6 Lizabeth Cohen's (1989) study of mass culture among early-twentieth-century workers in Chicago was useful here. In her article "Encountering Mass Culture at the Grassroots," Cohen "credits hegemonic mass culture with blurring class lines" (6) to the extent that mobilizing class consciousness among working-class groups to challenge bourgeois structures of domination becomes nearly impossible.

7 The black press made it possible for its readers at once to read and to be read. Henry Louis Gates, among others, has written extensively on the intricacies of African American signifying practices, tropes, and functions. Following this tradition, I am troping, here, on the doubleness of the term "read" as it often circulates in black vernacular discourse. There is a phrase in the African American vernacular tradition of signifying that admonishes, "Don't make me have to 'read' you," or, if the admonition fails, then the concomitant boast "Child, I 'read' him/her like a book" is uttered; and it is to this kind of verbal jousting that black critics' point about the polysemy and indirection inherent in black signifying rituals refers. Thus it is according to this logic that we must understand and interpret the "reading" (or the "dressing-down") the letter's author levels against one of the "Musical and Dramatics" column's errant critics. Basically, this letter's author has "read" through or deciphered the rhetorical indirection of the newly evolving film crit-speak and has set pen to paper to write a notification that the errant film critics' "signifying" on the orchestra director providing music accompaniment to the film under discussion was not appreciated.

8 In his influential book *The Cult of Information* (1994), Theodore Roszak revisits the legend of the Luddites, those infamous machine destroyers of the early industrial revolution. Discussing the reality and the mythology of England's working-class response to the threat posed by machine technology to their livelihoods, Roszak believes that "the original Luddites may have taken a bad rap. . . . Though they were desperate men fighting to feed their families, their hostility was carefully targeted. They asked how the machines were being used, by whom, for whose benefit—and then normally tried negotiating a better deal with their employers. Only when that effort failed did they feel forced to resort to violence" (xviii).

9 In a *Defender* article entitled "Moving Pictures Offer the Greatest Opportunity to the American Negro in History of the Race from Every Point of View" (1915), Juli Jones discusses the financial and cultural incentives for African Americans to become more active in the production of films. In addition to the economic benefits, Jones points out the international dimensions of black-produced films. He asserts that international interest in the plight of African Americans is enormous and singles out Brazil and South America as being "crazy to know more of the American Negro, and wanting to see some of his redeeming points" (6).

10 Lester Walton (1909c) writes about the failure of blacks to take "advantage of the laws in force which guarantee . . . the same rights and privileges in theaters" to blacks as to any other group. See also Walton's *New York Age* article entitled "New Yorkers Have Gone 'Dippy' over the Movies" (1914b).

Works Cited

Adams, Minnie. 1912. "In Union Is Strength." *Chicago Defender*, 24 Feb.

Benjamin, Walter. 1986. "The Work of Art in the Age of Mechanical Reproduction." In *Video Culture: A Critical Investigation*, ed. John Hanhardt, 27–52. Rochester, N.Y.: Visual Studies Workshop.

Bogle, Donald. 1989. *Toms, Coons, Mulattoes, Mammies, and Bucks*. 1973. Reprint. New York: Continuum.

Bragg, Columbus. 1914. "On and off the Stroll." *Chicago Defender*, 1 Aug.

Carbine, Mary. 1990. "'The Finest outside the Loop': Motion Picture Exhibition in Chicago's Black Metropolis, 1905–1928." *Camera Obscura* 23: 9–42.

Cohen, Lizabeth. 1989. "Encountering Mass Culture at the Grassroots: The Experience of Chicago Workers in the 1920s." *American Quarterly* 41: 6–33.

"Discusses Fight Pictures." 1910. *New York Age*, 21 July.

Du Bois, W. E. B. 1926. "Criteria of Negro Art." *The Crisis*, Oct. 1995. Reprinted in *W. E. B. Du Bois: A Reader*. ed. David Levering Lewis, 509–15. New York: Henry Holt.

Dunbar, Paul Laurence. 1913. "To a Captious Critic." In *The Complete Poems of Paul Laurence Dunbar*. 1980. Reprint, New York: Dodd, Mead.

"Fight Film." 1910. Advertisement. *Moving Picture World*. 21 May.

Frazier, Franklin E. 1957. *Black Bourgeoisie*. 1970. Reprint, London: Collier.

"'Hit the Nigger' New Film Insult." 1914. *Chicago Defender*. 38 Feb.

hooks, bell. 1984. *Feminist Theory: From Margin to Center*. Boston: South End.

——. 1989. *Talking Back*. Boston: South End.

Hubbard, Dolan. 1994. *The Sermon and the African American Literary Imagination*. Columbia: University of Missouri Press.

Hughes, Langston, and Milton Meltzer. 1967. *Black Magic. A Pictorial History of the African American in the Performing Arts*. New York: Da Capo Press.

Janken, Kenneth Robert. 1993. *Rayford W. Logan and the Dilemma of the African American Intellectual*. Amherst: University of Massachusetts Press.

Johnson, James Weldon. 1968. *Black Manhattan*. New York: Atheneum.

Jones, Juli [pseud.]. 1915. "Moving Pictures Offer the Greatest Opportunity to the American Negro." *Chicago Defender*, 9 Oct.

"Jottings Theatrical and Otherwise." 1914. *Chicago Defender*, 28 Mar.

"Moving Pictures Doing Good Business." 1909. *Baltimore Afro-American Ledger*, 6 Nov.

Musser, Charles. 1991. *Before the Nickelodeon: Edwin S. Porter and the Edison Manufacturing Company*. Berkeley and Los Angeles: University of California Press.

"Pictures of the Jeffries-Johnson Fight." 1910. *Moving Picture World*, 18 June.

Potter, Vilma Raskin. 1993. *Afro-American Publications and Editors, 1827–1946*. Ames: Iowa State University Press.

Pride, Armistead S., and Clint C. Wilson II. 1997. *A History of the Black Press*. Washington, D.C.: Howard University Press.

"Resents Criticism." 1914. *Chicago Defender*, 18 July.

Roszak, Theodore. 1994. *The Cult of Information: A Neo-Luddice Treatise on High Tech, Artificial Intelligence, and the True Art of Thinking*. Berkeley: University of California Press.

Russell, Sylvester. 1910a. "A Quarterly Review." *Chicago Defender*, 12 Mar.

——. 1910b. "Negro, Yiddish Theaters and Other Notes." *Chicago Defender*, 9 Apr.

——. 1911b. "The Phoenix Theatre Shows Good Pictures." *Chicago Defender*, 1 July.

——. 1911c. "The Phoenix Theater Has Good Houses." *Chicago Defender*, 22 July.

——. 1911d. "New Year's Offerings." *Chicago Defender*, 30 Dec.

Sklar, Robert. 1976. *Movie Made America: A Cultural History of American Movies* New York: Vintage.

Sloan, Kay. 1988. *The Loud Silents: Origins of the Social Problem Film*. Urbana and Chicago: University of Illinois Press.

Smiley, J. Hockley. 1911. "Our Musical and Dramatic Critic." *Chicago Defender*, 23 Dec.

"States Theater Displays Vile Pictures." 1914. *Chicago Defender*, 5 May.

Toll, Robert C. 1974. *Blacking Up: The Minstrel Show in Nineteenth Century America*. New York: Oxford University Press.

Vardac, A. Nicholas. 1949. *Stage to Screen, Theatrical Origins of Early Film: David Garrick to D. W. Griffith*. New York: Da Capo.

Walker, George. 1906. "The Negro on the American Stage." *Colored American Magazine*, June, 242–46.

Walton, Lester A. 1909a. "The Degeneracy of the Moving Picture Theatre." *New York Age*. 5 Aug.

——. 1909b. "Moving Picture Paper Takes Up the Age Crusade." *New York Age*, 26 Aug.
——. 1909c. "Negroes in New York Theaters." *New York Age*, 18 Nov.
——. 1910. "The Moving Picture Theater." *New York Age*, 15 Dec.
——. 1911. "Change Wrought by Motion Picture Craze." *New York Age*, 23 Feb.
——. 1912a. "The Influence of Moving Picture Shows." *New York Age*, 21 Mar.
——. 1912b. "Ban on Titanic Moving Pictures." *New York Age*, 2 May.
——. 1913b. "The Motion Picture Industry and the Negro." *New York Age*, 5 June.
——. 1914a. "Want Representation on Film Censor Board." *New York Age*, 19 Mar.
——. 1914b. "New Yorkers Have Gone 'Dippy' over the Movies." *New York Age*, 4 May.
——. 1919a. "Stop German Opera; Un-American Film Allowed." *New York Age*, 15 Mar.
Winston, Brian. 1993. "The Documentary Film as Scientific Inscription." In *Theorizing Documentary*, ed. Michael Renov, 37–57. New York and London: Routledge.

Chapter 8

Kathryn H. Fuller-Seeley

DISH NIGHT AT THE MOVIES: EXHIBITOR PROMOTIONS AND FEMALE AUDIENCES DURING THE GREAT DEPRESSION (2007)

Editors' Introduction

At least since the early 1930s, historians have examined how the cinema dealt with the Great Depression in textual terms, so that we have any number of readings of films that concern themselves with the representation of economic collapse. But in the mid-1970s, scholars began to examine systematically the relationships between film practices more broadly and historical events and periods. Film studies aligned itself here with a growing interest in other historical fields to produce social histories of leisure activities and pursuits, with Kathy Peiss' work on Coney Island and Nan Enstad's investigation of turn-of-the-century working girls' engagement with fashion marking this trend. Kathryn Fuller-Seeley's essay is a model of this kind of scholarship applied to cinema. In this case, the films themselves have far less significance than the overall experience of Depression-era filmgoing. By looking at dish nights and other giveaways at theatres in the 1930s, Fuller-Seeley analyzes the film industry's responses to declining movie attendance, and also examines the links between cinema and other industries and institutions, for instance dishware manufacturing and also the legal system that had to rule on the viability of the giveaways. The dish give-aways also provide us with information about the gender of the period's movie audiences, with theatre managers clearly targeting female movie fans. More broadly, Fuller-Seeley charts the production of a kind of desire that drops out of more routine film analysis. In Fuller-Seeley's case study, the women in the audience were not attracted by the fantasies of the films, but by the fantasies of consumption supplied by the theatre and by the desire to keep coming back to the movies in order to acquire a full service of dishware. As Fuller-Seeley shows, this not only motivated women at the time to go to the movies, but became a fundamental aspect of their memories of the cinema years later.

Suggested Reading

Charles Eckert, "The Carole Lombard in Macy's Window," *Quarterly Review of Film and Video*, 3:1 (Winter, 1978), pp. 1–21; Nan Enstad, *Ladies of Labor, Girls of Adventure:*

Working Women, Popular Culture, and Labor Politics at the Turn of the Twentieth Century (New York: Columbia University Press, 1999); Lauren Rabinovitz, *Electric Dreamland: Amusement Parks, Movies, and American Modernity* (New York: Columbia University Press, 2012).

THE GREAT DEPRESSION, THE worst economic downturn ever experienced in the United States, began in October 1929 with the stock market crash. Conditions then continued to spiral downward to terrible lows in 1932 and 1933. To some panicked observers, it looked like the entire consumer economy was collapsing. With the unemployment rate over 25 percent and a further quarter of the country's labor force working only part-time, cash-strapped families cut their purchasing to the bone. One of the first nonessential expenses trimmed by working- and middle-class households was money spent on entertainment. Attendance at sporting events turned dismal—the National League saw baseball game receipts drop 40 percent, and the minor leagues were nearly wiped out. Two-thirds of all Broadway theaters closed, and federal tax revenue from theater and concert entertainments across the country plummeted by more than 65 percent. Seasonal hotels saw a 75 percent drop in business.[1] Instead of going out, families sat at home and listened to the radio, which at least was free after they had paid for the receiver.

Even America's favorite pastime, going to the movies, was gravely affected. In the kind of news story that appeared all over the nation in summer 1932, a headline in Virginia's *Richmond News Leader* stated, "100 Movie Houses in State Suspend Operations." The article further reported that fully one-third of the state's three hundred movie theaters had closed, and that "the number of theaters in the large cities of the state have been appreciably reduced in number . . . but the greatest reduction has been in the smaller towns, where a great many have closed down. In a number of the smaller places, as well, theaters which had formerly showed pictures two or three times a week have cut their programs to once a week. Motion picture addicts, who formerly took in a picture five or six nights a week in the cities, have cut their movie sprees to one or two nights."[2]

Small town and neighborhood movie theaters across America during the early Depression years faced a tremendous drop in ticket sales. Exhibitors had to find the means to stem their losses and find profit in difficult times or else face widespread bankruptcy. Theater managers, whose options were significantly limited by block-booking and other aspects of the studio control of film product, often focused their efforts less on which features they could play and more on the nonfilmic elements of their program—the advertising and promotional events that they could control on a local level.

Dish Night giveaway promotions were one of the most successful solutions to exhibitors' problem of bringing movie patrons back to the theater in the 1930s. Merchandise giveaways and cash-award contests filled movie theaters in the Depression with as much drama, elation, desire, disappointment, and anguish as anything that was shown on their silver screens. Yet while these promotions boosted box office receipts at a crucial time, critics feared that they also opened a Pandora's box of woes. The seemingly benign "one free to each lady" plates, cups, and bowls could become dangerous weapons in the hands of film exhibitors locked in lethal competition with each other to remain in business, let alone in the hands of rioting movie audiences.

In this essay I examine film exhibitors' use of "premiums" or free giveaway promotions directed at women. I focus especially on Dish Night, which we now look back on as a quintessential Depression-era movie theater event. By investigating the publicity material surrounding these giveaway programs, I note how the persuasive arguments that chinaware companies provided to exhibitors, and the discord that Dish Night provoked between exhibitors trying to rebuild box office business in tough times, reveals several aspects of the film exhibitors' contentious relationship with their patrons. In analyzing the variety of responses of exhibitors and the public to Dish Night and its even more volatile rival, Bank Night, I provide new insights into the fears of social mayhem that haunted American businessmen and authorities, as well as into the hopes they cherished that an expanded consumer economy would restore calm, order, and control.

The Sudden End of Prosperity

The film exhibition business had experienced an unprecedented boom in 1929, due to the astonishing popularity of the new talking pictures and the opening of sumptuous picture palaces in cities across the nation. Movie attendance had nearly doubled in four years, skyrocketing from 55 million admissions weekly in 1925 to 110 million in 1929, if industry estimates can be believed. Executives had a more utilitarian purpose than mere public relations puffery for inflating attendance totals, for optimistic attendance figures would help boost film companies' stock prices and reputations among investors during the massive studio merger deals that were taking place in 1929.[3]

Initially, the movie business was not greatly affected by the downturn that followed the October 1929 stock market crash, and film producers and exhibitors thought they would be immune to any ills of an economic down-turn. While small town and neighborhood theaters in the hard-hit textile centers in New England had seen box office declines since the beginning of the recession there in 1927, exhibitors elsewhere had assumed that this was merely a regional slump. By the end of 1930, however, movie theater weekly admissions across the country had declined by 28 percent to 80 million. A year and a half after the stock market crash, movie theater business began to tumble rapidly. Box office receipts fell from $732 million in 1930 to $482 million in 1933, a drop of nearly 34 percent. Weekly attendance plummeted from its 1929 high by 45 percent, down to only 50 million. "The winter of 1932–1933 was just about the toughest year in the history of the amusement business," recalled one reporter. When President Franklin Roosevelt closed the nation's banks for several weeks in March 1933 so that the financial system could be stabilized, cash became nonexistent. The film exhibitors' trade papers reported that movie attendance plummeted (albeit temporarily) by yet another 45 percent.[4]

It is probable that the actual declines were even more precipitous than these estimates, for, as Tom Doherty and Tino Balio point out, the film industry was known for inflating all of its statistics, from attendance figures and box office revenues to production costs. Doherty notes that the *Film Daily Yearbook* initially reported that weekly movie attendance had collapsed from 100 million to fewer than 40 million. But by 1939, the *Yearbook* editors had revised their story by boosting the Depression low figure by 50 percent; now they reported that theater attendance had only declined to 60 million at its lowest point. In 1939, the film industry trumpeted that attendance had risen to about 90 million a week, but again the numbers are suspect—Balio cites a Gallup Poll report in 1940 showing actual weekly movie attendance to be only about 54 million. The movie business had a lot at stake in these numbers—nearly all of the studios faced bankruptcy, and the disastrous box office figures might make financial support for their reorganization impossible to obtain. Flamboyantly boastful in good times but secretive in bad times, the film industry was loath to reveal exactly how low its attendance figures had sunk.[5]

While few hard numbers exist to chart the decline of business at movie houses in the Depression, evidence suggests that small town and neighborhood theaters were hit harder than urban picture palaces. One of the few tangible figures that show the Depression's impact on smaller theaters was the percentage of movie houses that were forced to close. The number of open movie theaters declined by 35 percent, from about 23,000 to fewer than 15,000.[6] In 1933, 30.5 percent of all theaters were still closed, and 25 percent remained shuttered in 1934. The number of theater employees dropped by one third, from 129,600 in 1929 to just 86,937 in 1932.[7] Contributing to the problem was the overabundance of older theaters in small towns, where exhibitors had far smaller populations to draw from than their urban counterparts.[8] It was difficult for the theaters in non-metropolitan areas to draw in new patrons or to achieve the economies of scale upon which the corporately owned urban theater chains and picture palaces could count. A great many small town and rural theaters could not withstand the one-two punch of the expense of switching to "talkies" and the loss of ticket sales. Thus they closed by the thousands.[9]

A *Motion Picture Herald* survey in January 1934 showed that the theater closings impacted some of the nation's thirty-one film distribution districts (which were roughly equal in population) far more severely than others. Large cities fared relatively well. Only 11 percent of the New York City district's movie houses were closed. Five other urban districts fared well, including Philadelphia with 6.8 percent closed, Detroit 9.4 percent, Seattle 10 percent, and New Haven 10.8 percent closed. Eight other districts, mainly in the South and Pacific West, saw only 15 to 20 percent of their movie houses closed, while seven districts in the mid-Atlantic and in the industrial Midwest had 22 to 32 percent of their theaters shuttered.

At the same time, other film distribution districts across the nation were hit disproportionately hard by Depression-era movie theater closings—the largely rural and small town Albany, New York, district saw 33.6 percent of its theaters closed; New Orleans and Indianapolis both lost 35 percent, Omaha 37.1 percent, Boston 37.7 percent, and Salt Lake City 43.2 percent. In the Cincinnati district, which included most of rural Kentucky, West Virginia, and southern Ohio, a shocking 47.7 percent of all movie houses were closed.[10]

Across the nation, even the movie theaters that already had been wired for sound took a beating—12.6 percent of them were shut down. But again, the decline was not distributed equally across the country. Despite the high unemployment in America's largest cities, eight major urban districts saw only 9 percent or fewer sound theaters closed in January 1934. The more rural areas experienced significantly higher closure percentages of their wired theaters: the Albany district had 20 percent shuttered, Boston 22 percent, Cincinnati 15 percent, Kansas City 20.7 percent, Memphis 18 percent, St. Louis 16.5 percent, and in Salt Lake City 21 percent of the wired theaters were closed.[11]

The less-affected film distribution districts not only tended to have more areas of urban concentration, they were also dominated by large theater chains, which could absorb the box-office losses of individual theaters. On the other hand, the hardest-hit districts tended to have larger numbers of rural areas and small towns, where independently owned theaters and smaller chains were more common—such as in New England, upstate New York, Appalachia, and the Mississippi Valley. The independently owned theaters accounted for only 40 percent of theaters in New York City, 65 percent in Philadelphia, and 73 percent in Detroit; however, independents represented 86 percent of theaters in Cincinnati and in Salt Lake City and 91 percent in Omaha. The seven healthiest film distribution districts in 1934 accounted for 26 percent of the national market, according to figures from the *Motion Picture Herald*, but the seven worst-off districts could not be easily dismissed, for they accounted for 21 percent of the national total. The full impact of the Depression on film exhibition, particularly on independently owned theaters in districts comprised of small towns and agricultural areas, may never be precisely known but it was devastating, indeed.[12]

Dish Night and Other Theater Promotional Plans

"The movies have been hit just like jewelry and other luxury trades," despaired an exhibitor in Muncie, Indiana, in 1933.[13] The decline of moviegoing from an inexpensive, thrice-weekly habit to an unaffordable luxury was a sudden, painful shock for audiences and exhibitors alike. The great fear among all film exhibitors, both urban and small town, was that Americans were permanently falling out of the moviegoing habit. Small exhibitors looked for any scheme to restore the flow of regular, twice-weekly patrons. Their focus shifted away from the screen toward nonfilmic ways to make a profit, for with block-booking they had very little control over which films they could schedule.[14] Even a few blockbuster films that drew large audiences, such as *King Kong* or *Grand Hotel*, could not significantly help theaters that changed programs every three days.[15]

Instead, exhibitors began playing double features, which offered their patrons more show for the money (even though the second film was often a mediocre B-grade picture). They cut ticket prices from a boom-time average of 50 cents for the best seats at evening shows back to 35 or 25 cents, or even as low as 10 cents for "bargain nights."[16] They slashed theater-operating expenses by laying off musicians, ushers, and projectionists. They increased their promotions and advertising, undertaking all manner of attention-getting stunts, contests, amateur nights, and local business booster and charity events to keep themselves in the public eye. They held SCREENO nights (a form of bingo), which offered prizes, groceries, or money to winning audience members. Theater owners also gave away everything from toys, postcards, pocket mirrors, and beauty aids to groceries and coal. Some exhibitors arranged "country store nights" in which patrons who had accumulated "dollars" by attending the theater regularly could "spend" or bid them for goods displayed on stage.

While most of these promotions addressed the movie audience as an undifferentiated mass that could be attracted back to the movies by rational appeals to economics, exhibitors moved further to tailor their promotional campaigns to reach target audiences. Teenage girls and adult women made up 55 to 60 percent or more of the small independent theater's audience; children under twelve represented about 20 to 25 percent, and teenage boys and adult males accounted for 20 to 25 percent. Women formed the core of the neighborhood theater market, whereas men represented a larger percentage of the audiences at downtown picture palaces and the "action houses" that specialized in cowboy and horror films. Savvy film exhibitors knew that women usually made the decisions for the whole family about what films they might see together and which neighborhood theater they might attend.[17]

Appealing to women was thus essential to luring audiences back to the small independent theaters in hard times. But what promotions might bring them in? As times got harder and housewives had little spare change left in the family budget to indulge in movie shows, exhibitors searched for a different type of free gift (or premium, as they were known in the retail trade) for their female patrons, something that was useful and practical yet attractive and appealing. The more that female patrons desired these products, the more necessary it would be for them to attend the theater each week in order to acquire them. Exhibitors thus found a solution in dishware, which was a perfect premium for Depression times.

The humorist Jean Shepherd, in his 1965 short story "Leopold Doppler and the Great Orpheum Theater Gravy Boat Riot," captured the bitter-sweet memories of his Depression-era childhood in Hohman (actually Hammond), Indiana. His stories detailed the thousand small absurdities that working- and middle-class families faced in hard times. He emphasized how the desire for consumer goods and sensual pleasures continued to gnaw at people, and how in a world of reduced means everyone was hungry to have something to call their own. Hohman's housewives stoked those acquisitive desires at the movie theater; as Shepherd describes:

> A spectacular display in a gleaming case appeared without warning in the Neo-Mosque lobby of the beloved Orpheum. Row on row of radiant, magnificent works of pure beauty lay displayed before them, cushioned on dark, blood-red velvet and setting each observer's soul on fire with instant desire. . . . "FREE! FREE! Beginning next Friday, one piece of this magnificent set of Artistic De-Luxe Pearleen Tableware, the Dinner Service of the Stars, will be presented FREE to each adult woman in attendance. . . ." The effect of the Orpheum's incredible offer was galvanic. The word spread like the bubonic plague. . . . Red, chapped, water-wrinkled hands paused on clothes wringers and washboards; bathrobe clad figures hunched over sinks nodded in amazement. . . . By the end of the week of waiting the air had become tense and fretful. It was as though the whole town was waiting for Christmas morning. . . . Dish Night had come to Hohman, Indiana.[18]

Dish Night was not a frivolous matter for Hohman's middle- and working-class housewives, for dishes were a tangible symbol of social status in the 1930s. A young woman engaged to be married eagerly selected a china pattern to register at the local department store; she and her mother collected dinnerware, utensils, and linens to "go to housekeeping" in the proper manner, just as surely as they assembled her trousseau. The young bride faced the social challenges of setting a dinner table that would be admired when her husband's boss—or the minister, or the in-laws—came to dinner. Mismatched, chipped, and cracked old plates could cause a woman as much shame in front of her guests as holes in her Sunday dress.[19]

Most entertaining was done in the home, and many women, like the wives of Middletown or Carol Kennicott and her Sauk Center neighbors in Sinclair Lewis's novel *Main Street*, invested much energy and pride in competing to throw the loveliest tea parties and the most stylish bridge club luncheons, Saturday night buffets, and Sunday dinners. The guests expected not only good food but also the elegant presentation of meals on delicate chinaware, and they leveled critical judgments on the hostess's skills.

How humiliating it was, then, for homemakers in the Depression to see their dishes wear and break and not be able to afford to replace them. What would the neighbors think if no two plates or cups matched? What if the family were reduced to drinking out of empty pickle jars, or if a woman owned neither casserole nor platter to take to the church covered-dish supper? The neighborhood's best serving dishes thus might be loaned from one woman to the next to keep up appearances at social gatherings.[20]

Cultural historians such as Studs Terkel, Robert McIlvaine, Steven Mintz, and Susan Kellogg have noted how personally most people took their losses in the Great Depression. People blamed themselves, not the collapsing capitalist system, for poverty and failure. Families suffered psychological blows from job layoffs and reduced economic status. For homemakers, the loss of status was painfully visible—in their children's worn clothing, in their own best overcoats, frayed and twenty years old, and even in the boiled vegetable suppers they had to serve when they could not pay the butcher's bill. Stung with humiliation that neighbors might see their distress, some women stopped entertaining, dropped out of clubs, and hid at home in their shabbiness.[21]

Under these circumstances, a shiny new dinner plate was a marvelous gift for a Depression-era housewife. Many women denied themselves pleasures and slighted their own needs during hard times in order to provide for their families. Not all women were selfless, by any means, but there are thousands of Depression family stories about mothers pinching pennies by refusing to buy anything new for themselves, and by making do or doing without so that their children could have shoes for school, a Christmas gift, or the rent could be paid.

With pretty dishes on the table, a woman could have at least a few new consumer items in the house. Further, she got to know them well as she washed them up every night. Plates, cups, and bowls were useful items, but they could also be beautiful objects, desirable enough to collect. For a poor woman, a matched set of new dishes could symbolize a return of the family's former prosperity, or a step up the ladder toward gentility. Although for some of the lucky middle-class families less affected by the Depression the free dishes might have held little value, the genteel status made visible in a well-set dinner table, was something that struggling working- and middle-class women, fearful of slipping further down the social ladder, might desperately desire to hang on to.[22]

Giving away gifts to female patrons was nothing new at movie theaters; since the days of nickelodeons, exhibitors had used premiums to build loyal patronage. Most giveaways were in the form of picture postcards of movie stars, but small gifts to women and children, like handkerchiefs, beauty aids, stuffed bears, booklets, and small toys also were popular. Yet these items were handed out only at occasional giveaway events, and many of the items were worth only a penny or two. In hard times, however, people were attracted to items with more utility and value, and giveaways of practical china and kitchenware filled the bill.[23]

Film exhibitors planned to hold Dish Nights to boost attendance on the slowest nights of the week, usually Mondays and Tuesdays, when they otherwise showed films to empty houses. On Dish Night, what film a theater played mattered little, so theater owners saved money by showing cheap "poverty row" features. Female movie patrons were sometimes even involved in selecting the night of the week for the program: a display placed in the lobby of the New Fruitvale Theater in Oakland, California, announced: "Ladies! You choose which night will be Dish Nite"; in that community, Tuesday, Wednesday, and Thursday split the vote for the favorite night.[24] Once established at a theater, Dish Night could seemingly go on forever, as exhibitors lured in women once or twice a week for a solid year to collect all of the pieces of a 54- or 104-piece china set.

On average, each "free" dish cost the exhibitor a dime, so how was the exhibitor able to make up this expense to gain profits at the box office? As a *Business Week* article on movie house premiums explained: "Prior to the giveaway, a certain house took in $50 on Monday. By distributing 1,000 pieces of china costing $110, Monday business increased to $300. Net boost from premiums, $140."[25]

The Salem China Company was one of dozens of potteries in the Ohio River Valley devastated by the downturn in retail product sales. Like other firms that survived the Great Depression, Salem sold inexpensive dinnerware in bulk as advertising stunts to thousands of banks, furniture stores, groceries, and food product marketers. Prior to the 1930s, consumers had saved box tops from products, or collected "points" at drug stores to purchase dishes at deep discount, while banks offered dishware with new accounts and furniture stores gave away dish sets with dining room purchases. As the Salem sales manager Floyd McKee noted in a company history, in the 1920s, "Peoples Drug used over 150,000 32-piece sets from Salem, the housewife playing $2.98 for a set costing about $2.72 at the factory." The American Stores grocery chain in Philadelphia used about 130 railroad car-loads of Salem dinnerware in another promotion.[26]

Salem quickly got on the Dish Night bandwagon; their sales literature even claims that they invented the movie theater program in 1927. Salem's Theater Sales Department offered exhibitors bulk prices on dishes such as their distinctively art deco triangular-patterned Tricorne dishware, which ranged from 14 cents for a nine-inch dinner plate to 10 cents for the tea-cup and 7 cents for the saucer. For a minimal investment of five cents per head, exhibitors could get ceramic coasters or ashtrays. As special event premiums, creamers and sugar bowls were available for 20 cents each and sandwich trays were 30 cents.[27]

Salem's theater sales department captured the opening night scenes of Dish Night promotions in advertising photographs, which show long lines of patrons passing under theater marquees announcing "Dish Night Tonight!" Other photos show auditoriums crammed with plain-clothed, worn-faced women brandishing dinner plates for the cameraman. The caption for one such photo states: "A Full House. Opening China Night June 2, 1932 Roosevelt Theater, San Francisco, California. Original contract 700-sets of Square Golden Pheasant China. Seating capacity 1,005. Attendance first China Night 1,230 paid admissions. Distributed first China Night 702 pieces. Second China Night 800 pieces. Now planning to hold China Night twice each week to accommodate the crowds." The 702 women in attendance that night had brought 528 men and boys along with them, further filling the Roosevelt Theater's coffers. The caption of the Salem publicity photograph showing the jam-packed interior of the Parkway Theater in Oakland, California, stated, "Showing 73rd consecutive China Nite."[28] The photographs of big crowds of happy movie theater patrons must have made very persuasive advertising for the Salem China Company.

As *Business Week* commented on 1933's Dish Night boom, "Here is a business worth the battle." The report estimated that on the national level, pottery sales to theaters topped $25 million. This success caused severe price cutting and competition among the potteries in attempts to secure Dish Night orders. Further, Dish Night's success at some theaters bred adverse reaction at others, for *Business Week* also noted that "part of the [theater] industry is trying to abolish them."[29]

Although many film exhibitors were using giveaway programs in the early 1930s, the trade journals *Motion Picture News, Exhibitors Herald*, and *Film Daily Yearbook* were adamantly opposed to the practice. They followed the lead of film producers who disliked any movie theater activity that diverted money normally spent for picture rental to go toward promotional expenses.[30] While reports of closed and failing theaters filled each issue, the trade journal columnists preached that what exhibitors needed to do was to increase their ballyhoo. They claimed that suffering local exhibitors just weren't trying hard enough, and that good showmanship would bring patrons back to the box office. "Study your situation!" a typical story instructed, "Are you posting enough paper? Is it the right kind? Is it going on the best location obtainable?" "Show is Lure, Not Premiums," warned *Motion Picture News*, "A theater sells entertainment. If the sales argument is proper, if your schedules, prices and programs are right—then you don't need premiums or prizes."[31] Yet the columnists' words rang more hollow with each more disastrous month, and soon few exhibitors could afford to listen only to trade journals' dictums.

Most large urban theater chains hated premium giveaways because they felt forced to participate to stay in competition at the box office. In 1934 neighborhood theaters gained a few percentage points over their dismal 1933 figures, and as such they were reported to be doing better than the picture palaces; in response, jealous picture palace exhibitors charged that Dish Nights were the reason why.[32] Small town exhibitors defended their use of premiums not as underhanded competition but as a service to the industry to revive America's moviegoing habit.[33] They argued that premiums (and the idea of value added to the movie ticket being sold) were a better sales stimulant than straight price cuts in Depression times, for angry consumers resented attempts to raise prices once they had been lowered.[34] Their explanations fell on deaf ears, for theater corporations wanted to abolish giveaways, and they looked to the new National Recovery Act (NRA) codes being drawn up by the federal government to give them the power to do it.

Film exhibition was just one of sixteen hundred industries that came under Roosevelt's sweeping plan to stabilize American business through the New Deal's National Recovery Act. Each industry had to create a "Code of Fair Conduct," prohibiting destructive competition and (supposedly) curtailing unfair labor practices in factories and stores. Critics complained that the major film producers, distributors, and exhibitors dominated the code-writing process to guarantee their advantage at the expense of independent exhibitors and studio and theater workers. Thus, if the big boys got their way, movie ticket prices were to be kept as high as possible and giveaways and prizes would be abolished.[35]

Much of the contentious debate at the film exhibitors' NRA code-writing hearings, held in Washington, D.C., in September 1933, revolved around labor issues—theater owners did not want to give projectionists guaranteed employment, higher wages, or better working conditions. However, Dish Night was also on the table in discussions of how the Code of Fair Conduct could prevent ruinous competition and unfair advertising. The seriousness of the Dish Night dilemma brought pottery manufacturers to testify before the NRA code-writing committee. As Terry Ramsaye reported the scene in the *Motion Picture Herald*:

> Manufacturers of chinaware and other premiums distributed in motion picture theaters registered vigorous protests against the code's prohibition of the practice. At the same time, it became known that RKO Theaters was the first large circuit to outlaw this form of merchandising. Charging they will be driven out of the business, therefore defeating the very purpose of the NRA, pleas were made on behalf of premiums and giveaways by Michael Flynn, National Brotherhood of Operating Potters, Charles Sebring, of Sebring Pottery Company [and Salem China Company], and W.E. Wells of the United States Potters' Association. . . . Mr. Sebring declared that 20 percent of his business comes from theaters, adding that this percentage applied to all others in his field.
>
> Sebring warned that 100 skilled potters would lose their own jobs if Dish Night was banned.[36]

The potters' pleas only slightly softened the hearts of the corporate theater powers. The final draft of the NRA code for film exhibitors stated that if 75 percent of a community's theater owners voted to ban Dish Night in their district, then it was illegal; each theater had one vote. In cities with a large chain-theater presence, small exhibitors wishing to hold Dish Nights were outmaneuvered, outvoted, and out of luck. The NRA administrators had their hands full from the moment the motion picture code went into effect, making sure that exhibitors properly followed the rules of allowable competition. The regional grievance boards were swamped in 1934 with 548 complaints by exhibitors against one another for giving away premiums, running cash prize contests, and reducing ticket prices in places where local exhibitor groups had decreed such practices illegal. In fact, 52 percent of all complaints filed in the first eight months were about giveaway programs.[37]

Dish Night remained popular with theater owners but unsanctioned by the film exhibition industry. The trade journals contained virtually no information for exhibitors on Dish Night, nor were there any advertisements from giveaway product distributors. Some dishware manufacturers like the Salem China and Homer Laughlin companies along with other premium product makers contacted theater owners directly through their own sales forces. Other middlemen, like Playhouse Premiums in New York and the Price Company in Chicago, set themselves up as distributors of giveaway merchandise to movie theaters; the Stetson Company, for example, sold through premium wholesalers almost all of the dinnerware it manufactured.[38] Both potteries and distributors promised to school novice theater managers in the art of the giveaway by providing Dish Night promotional kits complete with posters, banners, theater displays, handbills, newspaper advertising, and special "talkie" promotional film trailers.[39]

The Depression Appeals of Salem's Dishware Premiums

The Salem China Company attempted to associate its dishes with the allure of Hollywood glamour and celebrity; its sales and marketing department arranged for stars from Warner Bros. to pose for advertising and publicity photographs taking their tea with Salem's distinctive triangular-patterned Tricorne dishware. Glenda Farrell and Ruby Keeler, for example, were shown on the set between scenes of the First National/Warner Bros. 1935 feature *Go into Your Dance*. Another photo in the Salem Company files showed "Joan Blondell, William Gargan and Dick Powell between scenes of Warner Brothers forthcoming production *Broadway Gondolier*, 'enjoying a little bite.' "[40]

The cultural historian Roland Marchand uses the phrase "the democracy of goods" to explain the particular appeal that such promotions would have for Depression movie audiences. A poor woman could eat from the same elegant Salem china that the movie stars did, so she could share some essential part of their glamour. Richard deCordova and Charles Eckert have shown how widespread this hope was among manufacturers in the early 1930s—that is, that the notion of "tying up" or linking their goods to the movies would help boost their product sales in the Depression as well as enhance the consumption ideal's appeal for wary American families. Both authors show, however, that these appeals to Hollywood celebrity and style were only partially successful.[41]

The Salem China Company did not merely associate its dishes with the movies in the hope that film popularity would increase interest in its products; instead, the company slyly insinuated in its theater sales literature that the Salem dishware itself was superior to the movies and more reliable than star power to pull in the patrons to their movie theaters on a regular basis. In its advertising letters sent to exhibitors, Salem argued that "only occasionally can you feature a star that jams the aisles. But when you add Salem China Nites to your bill, you have a string of features week after week that draw the crowds in all seasons, all weathers."[42]

In sales fliers like "Salem China Nite Pleases the Ladies—Packs Your House," Salem's general manager Floyd McKee developed themes for selling Dish Night to exhibitors that centered on women and what they want, the question that so befuddled male film exhibitors. McKee's sales rhetoric touched on the Depression's humiliating impact on housewives: "Remember, they are always wanting new dishes in every home. . . . It gives them something they need and prize."[43] But the hard facts of hard times were not the key to the real appeal of dishes. Perhaps unconsciously, McKee and the Salem sales literature writers drew on imagery of addiction and uncontrollable desires. "Chinaware as premium has more appeal to the house wife than most articles. Since she never has the idea that she has enough chinaware already."[44] Salem further told exhibitors that, with the help of Dish Night products, they could condition their female patrons to keep returning to fetch another piece of the china set: "Salem Dinnerware has the color, the sparkle, the year-round usefulness that makes women glad to come and get it, and bring their men and children with them."[45] "Give them a chance to build up a dinner set by offering it as an attendance prize and you will see the crowds coming your way, and they will keep on coming week after week, steadily, surely, with big profit to you."[46] McKee also hinted at chinaware's potent symbolism of women's attachment to consumer goods and their homemaking ability: "The housewife can always remember where she secured each particular dish, much more so than with other items which she does not identify with the source."[47] Even a reply postcard that Salem sent to theater owners, which featured a smiling Mickey Mouse jauntily waving a greeting, offered a response that could be read as a hint about dishware's addictive power, "Sure Mickey, send me the dope on Salem's China Night plan for my theater!"[48]

Salem counseled exhibitors as one concerned man to another about their female problem: "Year in and year out, Salem China Nites have proved to be the most reliable attendance builders theater men have ever found."[49] The company also suggested it would deliver to the exhibitor an audience of women so mesmerized by the free dinnerware in their hands that they would be oblivious to the fact that the movie they paid to see was third rate, or that the theater had never reduced its ticket prices. "If you cut your retail price to move an over-stock, it is hard to go back to the original price, as the public have appraised the article at the reduced price. With a premium offer, you can set a date or fix a quantity limit and when that has been met, there is no criticism of the deal."[50]

Yet these spellbound female patrons were only partially under the exhibitor's control; if angered, they could turn and bite at any moment. To disappoint a woman was to make her unhappy, to earn her rancor and make her the enemy of the theater owner. "The ladies go for it because they do not need to guess or gamble to win. Every woman who attends goes home happy with a piece of high-grade dinnerware that she is proud to own and use." As McKee assured the exhibitors, "You take no risk" with Dish Nite's democratic handing out of prizes; with this type of promotion there was no chance to offend and anger the women.[51] Salem's marketing materials reassured women of their good intentions and reminded them of how other giveaway programs might infuriate them: as a sign on the Salem lobby display at the Lincoln Theater in Decatur, Illinois, announced, "Ladies Free! Free! Attend this theater every Tuesday and receive a piece of Mandarin Tricorne China! No raffles or drawing."

Salem even drew on the same arguments put forth by the exhibitor's trade journals. *Motion Picture News* had warned readers in 1930 of the smoldering anger that could build from audience members' disappointment in losing big prize contests: "One thing you must remember. For one person that benefits through a theater contest where prizes are given, there are many hundreds that get nothing for their effort. One person boosts for you, the others hold a grudge because they did not win."[52] Dish Night giveaways had a democratic inclusiveness based on plain jealousy—women hated a situation where other women got something they did not have. But the women's anger at losing games could be turned to the exhibitors' advantage when they offered Dish Night. As Salem stated: "Because every woman wins, it creates good will and steadily growing business."[53]

Although Salem's advertising rhetoric might at times seem amusing, McKee and the Salem Company marketing staff were familiar with the desires and preferences of their customers. They knew from firsthand experience about the emotional connections between women's consumer desires and the pleasures of pretty-but-utilitarian dinnerware. However, if women's consumer desires were as easily controlled as was claimed by Salem and other advertisers in the 1930s, then wouldn't the economy have improved much more quickly? As Marchand explains, consumer product advertisers in the 1930s had a love-hate relationship with female purchasers. No matter how much they cajoled or whipped women into a frenzy of desire, no matter how enticingly they presented their goods, no matter what horrible threats about the health of their children, rejection by potential mates or other judgmental women if the advertised products like Listerine were not used religiously, women might still not buy the product. Advertisers continually railed about the perfidy, inconstancy, stubbornness, and stupidity of the female consumer, but this disdainful attitude often masked how fearful they were. In despair, advertisers sometimes admitted that they did not really understand women and what women wanted.[54]

Film exhibitors were as frustrated as advertisers in 1936 when Dish Night ticket sales began to sag. Merchants groused about the success of movie theater Dish Night (Chicago retailers claimed to have lost $6 million in dish and kitchenware sales),[55] and the effectiveness of dishware's seductive appeal seemingly had worn off. The film exhibitor's trade press continued to warn theater owners away from Dish Night by asserting that premium programs would inevitably fail. Giveaway schemes that lasted twenty-six or fifty-two weeks dragged on so long that they bored the housewives; an extended dishware promotion offered little variety, little drama, and prizes of relatively low value. Trade journal columnists anticipated with growing trepidation, however, that Dish Night would be swept aside by a flood of new cash prize programs at theaters, and that a bad situation would be replaced with one that was infinitely worse.[56]

Bank Night and Disorder in the Theaters

Far more controversial and contentious than Dish Night was the Bank Night cash giveaway program, which swept through American movie theaters between 1935 and 1940. Charles Yaeger, a young entrepreneur who worked his way up through his father's movie theaters in small town New Mexico and Colorado, invented a simple yet highly effective scheme. In a Bank Night promotion, townspeople registered their names each week at the movie theater; on the same dead Monday or Tuesday evening that previously had been brightened with dinnerware, the theater manager held a drawing on stage for an enticingly large cash prize—often $100 to $500 or more, a sum that could make a great difference to most families in the Depression. The winner of the drawing had to rush to the stage to claim the money within sixty seconds or the prize was forfeited and the pot grew larger at the next drawing.[57] Unlike Dish Night, Bank Night allowed for only one lucky winner and many empty-handed losers.

Small towns across America came to a standstill on Bank Night because everyone was in the theater or was standing outside the packed house, straining to hear the winner announced over a loudspeaker attached to the marquee. It did not matter what picture was showing at the theater on Bank Night because people came for the drawing, not the film. A cartoon in *Esquire Magazine* (reprinted in the *Literary Digest*) depicts a movie theater draped with huge Bank Night banners; at the box office a man turning away remarks to his companion, "He says they've stopped having pictures." Ira Parkhill, who examined the Bank Nite frenzy in a lengthy *Saturday Evening Post* article, noted that the practice "has profoundly affected the social life of America, especially in the small town, although movie audiences of the largest cities have gone equally mad over it."[58]

Yaeger devised the program in 1931, and when he took Bank Night nationwide, a thousand theaters quickly joined up. The participating exhibitors paid Yaeger a license fee of $5 to $50 per week or a percentage of box office receipts, depending on seating capacity.[59] In September 1933 Bank Night was totally prohibited by the film exhibitors' NRA code, although Yaeger campaigned to have it reclassified from a lottery to a premium program.[60] The Supreme Court declared the NRA unconstitutional on June 1, 1935, however, and the Motion Picture Code's restrictions were voided.[61] Immediately, thousands of theaters plunged into the previously restricted giveaway schemes. Of the 15,000 operating movie theaters in 1935, an estimated 4,000 played Bank Night, a figure that swelled to 5,600 in late 1936, then to 6,000. Although an estimated 10,000 exhibitors (two-thirds of all theaters) had been hosting Dish Nights, the number of pottery giveaway programs dropped as theaters switched to the flashier cash games.[62] By 1937, Parkhill estimated that 10,000 of the nation's theaters were either playing Bank Night or one of its imitation games, and Yaeger was earning $30,000 to 65,000 per week in licensing fees.[63]

Many observers expressed concern about the frenzy of anticipation that Bank Night aroused in the crowds who jammed theaters and spilled outside onto the sidewalks. "It is a headache to the traffic squads," one commented.[64] The palpable excitement and frustration of the throngs anticipating a win or regretting their loss could lead, local authorities feared, to pushing and shoving or outright riots. *Time* magazine reported that, in Des Moines, "Bank Night has been so popular that police and fire departments had to be called out sometimes to control theater crowds."[65]

Bank Night was unsettling to some social critics because it disrupted traditional social activities. Choir rehearsals in one Long Island community, along with high school sporting events in Perryopolis, Pennsylvania, were canceled because so many people insisted on going to Bank Night instead. The *Literary Digest* reported that hoodlums in the Midwest had attended a Bank Night drawing and then mugged the winner on his way home.[66] As one civic leader complained, "It's got to the point where nobody can schedule a basketball game, a church social or a contract [bridge] party on Tuesday night, because everybody is down at the Gem hoping to cop a cash prize."[67] To stop the drawings, the town of Pittsfield, Massachusetts, threatened to withdraw the Sunday showing permits of any theater that ran Bank Night.[68] The four major newspapers in New Orleans banned movie theater advertising that made any mention of Bank Night.[69] The wildly popular cash promotion faced court hearings in Maine, New Hampshire, Texas, Massachusetts, New York, Illinois, and Iowa (where three hundred theaters had suspended Bank Night for five months waiting for the decision on its legality to be handed down).[70]

The appeal of Bank Night was significantly different from that of Dish Night. The game was not specifically geared toward women, for women may have preferred that everyone should share in the gift receiving. However, in hard times the attraction of large sums of money knew few gender restrictions. Both women and men would scramble for cash, and the competition could provoke disorder. Unrest lay just under the surface of Yaeger's giveaway scheme, as the *Literary Digest* hinted in a Bank Night report: "Mrs. Joseph Sebastian Phau, an adult white citizen of the United States, went to a motion picture theater last Monday night. She paid a desperate quarter for an admission ticket, squared her ample shoulders and began the violent task of thrusting her way through 2000 other citizens fired by a similar zeal. No portentous film was to be screened that night. Indeed, the picture to be shown was of inferior quality, But Mrs. Phau didn't mind. It is doubtful if she ever knew what the picture was about, or cared, what brought her there was a 200-to-1 chance of going home with $150. It was Bank Nite."[71]

The rivals of a game-playing theater feared Bank Night perhaps most of all. In Kansas City, where 68 percent of neighborhood theaters were said to be giving away premiums,[72] Mrs. Abe Baier, owner of the Lindbergh Theater, lobbied the U.S. Post Office (which banned lottery materials from traveling through the mail) to help exterminate Bank Night at her rival theaters. As her legal brief stated:

> At the present time, practically all suburban theaters in Kansas City are giving away dishes, silverware, running children's bargain shows, using trading stamps, etc. If Bank Night at the Prospect and Belmont Theaters is allowed to continue, it is reasonable to assume that at least 75 percent of the theaters in Kansas City will adopt the scheme. This will lead to a most disastrous condition not only for my theater and a few others which do not wish to cheapen their operation by running lotteries, but will grow until all first run theaters will be compelled to resort to similar tactics to protect their huge investments.[73]

The intense competition among film exhibitors over premium programs could even turn openly violent, as the *Motion Picture Herald* reported in September 1935: "Minneapolis recently was the scene of considerable excitement when the Northtown [theater], operated by Harry Dickerman, was bombed. Exhibitors have been protesting what they termed Mr. Dickerman's 'unethical' practices in giveaways, and it is understood he has agreed to discontinue a combined gift night plan at three of his houses." While this level of open warfare was rarely reached, the trade journals routinely described the struggle between exhibitors as a "Chance Games 'War.' "[74]

Historians have examined the potential for anger, violence, and revolt that the collapse of the consumer economy caused in the Great Depression. The Bonus Army's march on Washington in summer 1932, one of the most public episodes of protest and disorder, greatly alarmed authorities like President Herbert Hoover, FBI head J. Edgar Hoover, and General Douglas MacArthur, who saw too much potential for unrest in allowing the veterans and their families to remain camped in the city, despite the fact that participants and most observers saw the march and occupation as a peaceful gathering. Much of the nation worried that the intensity of the violence with which the U.S. army routed the veterans out of Washington, as well as the resulting chaos and fear, were harbingers of things to come across the nation.[75]

Social critics and local authorities in the 1930s were quite frightened by the potential for mob action. Film exhibitors were among the most worried of the Main Street merchants, for they feared that movie audiences could erupt into violence upon viewing incendiary films. A radical call to revolution, a long shot panning across a garbage-dump Hooverville, or even a picture of Hoover himself might generate an uproar in their auditoriums. Rioting audiences might first tear up the theater then surge out to rampage up and down Main Street, and theater owners could be held responsible. Tom Doherty's examination of newsreels and fiction films in the early years of the Depression finds that both producers and exhibitors strove to keep unvarnished reality off their screens and avoided showing anything that might upset their audience. Theater managers edited out anything questionable that had slipped unawares into their newsreels from the producers. Yet while exhibitors were keeping patrons distracted and amused with films that portrayed nothing of the Depression's suffering and disorder, with Bank Night drawings they were stirring up dangerous passions among their patrons in the theater. Jammed together inside a movie theater or overflowing the Main Street sidewalks after the prize announcement, angry groups of Bank Night losers were situated at the heart of commercial districts with the plate glass windows of nearby stores ready to smash.

As noted above, in the advertising fliers of the Salem China Company there was a sly appeal to exhibitors' worries—"Women hate to be disappointed . . . they hate lotteries. . . . They hate going away empty handed." Salem argued that women patrons would not like the intense competition and the slim chance of winning that Bank Night entailed. Was this part of the calculated appeal of Dish Night to movie theater managers—to avoid the potential for violence and social disorder that Bank Night's big jackpots could provoke? Many people assumed that white middle- and working-class women did not like gambling, and that they were less competitive and less given to anger than were men. Theater managers thus felt that the "equality" of dish night—something for every woman—would be much more congenial to the average female patron. There is no evidence, however, to suggest that women avoided or were significantly less attracted to Bank Nights; female names are mentioned as winners about half of the time in 1930s news articles on Bank Night games. Social critics knew that angry women could cause as much destruction as rioting men, but American culture assumed that women as a whole were less prone to violence and disorder.

As Marchand argues, the genius of the "Democracy of Goods" advertising appeal was that if producers could offer the public some minimally expensive items that were equally available to everyone (and everyone, including movie stars, smoked cigarettes and ate off dishes), then even the lowest people on the economic scale would feel they had something in common with the privileged. The less fortunate would be more likely to subordinate their differences rather than gather together in class conflict and revolt against the rich, or at least the advertisers hoped so.[76]

Despite this cultural assumption of women's controllability and even passivity that may have led authorities and movie theater managers to think that female movie patrons would be kept quiet by the present of a small consumer item, even the benign Dish Night could be a source of friction for audience members. Many women became impatient with the seemingly endless length of the promotion; Gussie Seidenberg recalls that "it took *forever* to assemble the whole set of dishes." Women could feel fiercely entitled to their "free" gifts, and once they had made a "contract" with a film exhibitor that they would get a whole set of china if they purchased weekly tickets to the movies, they could become agitated when that agreement was tampered with.

Jean Shepherd's short story "Leopold Doppler and the Great Orpheum Theater Gravy Boat Riot" explored women's anger over thwarted consumer desires in the Depression, as well as the eternal battle of the sexes. The moviegoing housewives of Hohman anxiously awaited the arrival of each lovely new plate and bowl so that they could complete the entire set of Dish Night free china. They attended every giveaway performance for months without fail in order to get their "due" promised to them by the manager of the Orpheum Theater.

In the story's climax, through a terrible turn of events a shipping mix-up with the dinnerware distributor meant that for several weeks in a row Mr. Doppler had only gravy boats to hand out to his increasingly agitated female patrons. One gravy boat might symbolize the elegance of a formal dinner, and a second boat still had usefulness for holding salad dressing, perhaps, but a third and a fourth were totally superfluous—worse, even, than getting nothing. Increasingly restless and hungry to consume, the frustrated women felt it was their right to have all the different pieces of the set. In response the nervous Doppler attempted to defuse his patrons' anger by promising to trade extra gravy boats for useful cups, saucers, and serving bowls if the women brought the extras back to the theater the next week. On the fifth week, however, the gangly teenaged ushers, with down-cast eyes, handed out yet another gravy boat to the furious homemakers:

> Each gravy boat was received in stony silence, quietly stuffed into shopping bag or hatbox completing a set of four carried hopelessly for exchange. The feature that night was "The Bride of Frankenstein," the story of a man-made monster that returned to pursue and crush his creator. . . . On this night no gay music played through the theater loudspeakers. No Coming Attractions. The candy counter was dark and untended, as though Mr. Doppler himself felt the impending end near. The mothers waited. A sudden blinding spotlight made a big circle on the maroon curtain next to the cold, silent screen, then out of the wings stepped Mr. Doppler to face his Moment of Truth.
>
> "Ladies," he began plaintively, "I have to apologize for tonight's Gravy Boat." A lone feminine laugh, mirthless and arid, mocking, punctuated his pause. He went on as though unhearing. "I give you my personal Guarantee that next week . . ." At this point a low, subdued hissing arose spontaneously. The sound of cold venom landing on boiling lava began to rise from the depths of the void. Doppler, his voice bravely raised, continued: "Next week I personally guarantee we will exchange ALL gravy boats for . . ."
>
> And then it happened. A dark shadow sliced through the hot beam of the spotlight, turning over and over and casting upon the screen an enormous magnified outline of a great Gravy Boat. Spinning over and over, it crashed with a startling suddenness on the stage at Doppler's feet. Instantly a blizzard of Gravy Boats filled the air. Doppler's voice rose to a wail. "Ladies! Please! We will Exchange . . .!" A great crash of Gravy Boats like the breaking of surf on an alien shore drowned out his words. And then, spreading to all corners of the house, shopping bags were emptied as the arms rose and fell in the darkness, maniacal female cackles and obscenities driving Doppler from the stage.[77]

Conclusion

The sociologist Jesse Steiner, studying the impact of the Depression on commercial amusements toward the end of the decade, found that the response by movie exhibitors to the economic crisis had been the key to the recovery of the film business from the disastrous situation of the early 1930s: "Equally if not more significant than the changes in attendance, are the steps taken by the moving picture industry to stimulate increased popular support."[78]

Dish Night and other premium promotions had been important elements of independent neighborhood and small town theaters' campaigns to bring patrons back to the theater in the 1930s. Merchandise giveaways and cash-award contests filled Depression-era movie theaters with patrons anxious for the winning number to be drawn, dreaming of what they could do with a sudden windfall of cash, a shiny bicycle, or a house full of new furniture, and then deflated when yet again their luck failed them. At least for women, their acquisitive desires could be mollified somewhat by the experience of seeming to get "something for nothing."

Yet while these promotions boosted movie theater box office receipts and propped up the business of American potteries at a crucial time, they also created numerous problems and concerns. Dish Nights and giveaways were used by rival film exhibitors to intensify local competition and to capture patrons from each other and from alternative forms of entertainment and leisure. The death of vaudeville, theatrical stock, and road show companies and concert groups across the nation was hastened by the public's turn to the movies and radio, both of which used technologies of mass production and mass communication to undercut the viability of the expensive performances of live performers in local theaters. The cutthroat competition between film exhibitors meant that thousands of small, independently owned theaters in the poorer, more rural portions of the country could not continue to eke out a profit, and a quarter to a third of small town silent theaters closed and never reopened.

Bank Night in particular also raised concerns among conservative social critics that traditional social habits were being pushed aside as theaters lured all the impressionable and penny-pinched townspeople to the movies with cruelly unrealistic hopes of winning sudden riches. Like their suspicions of New Deal relief payments to the poor and unemployed, some critics claimed that the dreams of "easy wealth" engendered by Bank Night made people lazy and too dependent on "handouts," and made them feel "entitled" to receive such largess permanently. Social critics feared that this sense of entitlement and dependency urged disappointed losers on toward disorder and mob violence. Thus the crowds of moviegoers filling theaters to the rafters in pursuit of big cash prizes, or brandishing their free plates and cups, looked very threatening to outside observers. Yet concurrently, other critics hoped that the further spread of inexpensive consumer products into the economy, a "democracy of goods" in practice, would do much to diffuse class antagonisms and social unrest among the poor. Thus presents of pretty dishes from sympathetic film exhibitors might bond working- and middle-class housewives more loyally to the movies, even in hard times.

Nevertheless, as the *Motion Picture News* had warned theater managers, "All the crockery, silverware and china ever made won't do you lasting good if your entertainment isn't what the people want."[79] It is doubtful that the small independent theaters, or the urban picture palaces for that matter, could have survived the Depression decade if the Hollywood studios had not been turning out good product. Indeed, it was only because of audiences' enduring interest in the movies that giveaway promotions could succeed. The resilience of movie theaters and the film industry in the face of the Depression crisis is significant. Although families cut back moviegoing from four or five times a week to once or twice, they increasingly considered the movies a necessary recreation, and they cut back much further on other amusements in order to afford an occasional movie. During the Depression the American people put a higher percentage of their amusement dollars into the movies than they had done in previous years.[80]

Dish Night and Bank Night did help movie theaters recover from the Depression's ravages. By propping up the moviegoing habit in the hardest times, these promotions ensured that the movies would become even more popular and further entrenched as America's favorite pastime. By the late 1930s, movie theaters would run in the black again and they had regained their former attendance figures. It would take World War II prosperity, however, to return theater income to a level as high as it had been in the late 1920s; during the war years, movie attendance would reach its highest levels ever. The practice of giving premiums at smaller neighborhood movie theaters would continue sporadically among theaters throughout the 1940s and 1950s. However, due to the movement of the population to the suburbs and the devastating competition from television, ultimately such attempts to stem the loss of patrons were unsuccessful.

Notes

1 Jesse Steiner, *Research Memorandum on Recreation in the Depression* (New York: Social Science Research Council, 1937), 94.

2 "100 Movie Houses in State Suspend Their Operations," *Richmond News Leader*, July 15, 1932.

3 On film exhibition in the 1930s, see Douglas Gomery, *Shared Pleasures: A History of Film Presentation in the United States* (Madison: University of Wisconsin Press, 1992); Tino Balio, *Grand Design: Hollywood as a Modern Business Enterprise, 1930–1939* (New York: Charles Scribner's Sons, 1993); Donald Crafton, *The Talkies: American Cinema's Transition to Sound, 1926–1931* (New York: Charles Scribner's Sons, 1997); and Thomas Doherty, *Pre-Code Hollywood: Sex, Immorality, and Insurrection in American Cinema, 1930–1934* (New York: Columbia University Press, 1999).

4 Balio, *Grand Design*, 15.

5 *Film Daily Yearbook*, 1939, 43; Doherty, *Pre-Code Hollywood*, 28–29.

6 Andrew Neff, "Slump-Proof? Not Films: Depression Figures on Profits, Payroll, Sites," *Variety*, April 2, 1980, 6; A. D. Murphy, "Trace Recession's Impact on Pix: Data Puts Sluggish B.O. in Perspective," *Variety*, August 6, 1980, 1.

7 "National Income in the United States, 1929–1935," Division of Economic Research, U.S. Department of Commerce, 1936, table 200, reprinted in Steiner, *Research Memorandum on Recreation in the Depression*, 107.

8 *International Motion Picture Almanac* 1934, 889.

9 Ibid.; Gomery, *Shared Pleasures*, 70. On rural and small town film exhibition, see Gregory Waller, *Main Street Amusements: Movies and Commercial Entertainment in a Southern City, 1896–1930* (Washington, D.C.: Smithsonian Institution Press, 1995); Kathryn Fuller, *At the Picture Show: Small Town Audiences and the Creation of Movie Fan Culture* (Charlottesville: University Press of Virginia, 2001 [1996]); George Potamianos, *Film Exhibition in Sacramento and Placerville* (Berkeley: University of California Press, forthcoming); and Fuller-Seeley, ed., *Movie-Going History in Small-Town America* (Berkeley: University of California Press, 2007).

10 "Theaters in the United States," *Motion Picture Herald*, January 20, 1934. Eight other districts that saw 15 to 20 percent of their movie houses closed were Atlanta, Charlotte, Denver, Memphis, Minneapolis, Portland, St. Louis, and San Francisco. A number of districts had between 22 and 32 percent of their theaters shut, including Buffalo, Chicago, Cleveland, Dallas, Milwaukee, Pittsburgh, and Washington, D.C.

11 "Theaters in the United States."

12 Ibid.

13 Robert Lynd and Helen Lynd, *Middletown in Transition: A Study in Cultural Conflicts* (New York: Harcourt Brace, 1937), 260–61.

14 Crafton, *The Talkies*, 256–65.

15 Doherty, *Pre-Code Hollywood*; Gomery, *Shared Pleasures*.

16 "Small Town Showmen Pruning Prices," *Motion Picture News*, June 28, 1930, 46; Steiner, *Research Memorandum on Recreation in the Depression*, 107; Crafton, *The Talkies*, 264.

17 On the history of the dishware industry, see Regina Blaszczyk, *Imagining Consumers: Design and Innovation from Wedgwood to Corning* (Baltimore, Md.: Johns Hopkins University Press, 2000). On the importance of women in the movie audience, see Shelly Stamp, *Movie-Struck Girls: Women and Motion Picture Culture after the Nickelodeon* (Princeton, N.J.: Princeton University Press, 2000); Miriam Hansen, *Babel and Babylon: Spectatorship in American Silent Film* (Cambridge, Mass.: Harvard University Press, 1991); Nan Enstad, *Ladies of Labor, Girls of Adventure: Working Women, Popular Culture, and Labor Politics at the Turn of the Twentieth Century* (New York: Columbia University Press, 1999); Fuller, *At the Picture Show*.

18 Jean Shepherd, "Leopold Doppler and the Great Orpheum Theater Gravy Boat Riot," in *In God We Trust, All Others Pay Cash* (New York: Doubleday, 1966), 252–53.

19 On women and their households in the 1920s and 1930s, see Blaszczyk, *Imagining Consumers*; Robert Lynd and Helen Lynd, *Middletown: A Study in Contemporary American Culture* (New York: Harcourt, Brace, 1929); Lynd and Lynd, *Middletown in Transition*; Ruth Schwartz Cowan, *More Work for Mother: The Ironies of Household Technology from the Open Hearth to the Microwave* (New York: Basic Books, 1983); Susan Strasser, *Never Done: A History of American Housework* (New York: Pantheon Books, 1982).

20 Shepherd, "Leopold Doppler and the Great Orpheum Theater Gravy Boat Riot."

21 On the impact of the Depression on American families, see Studs Terkel, *Hard Times: An Oral History of the Great Depression* (New York: Avon, 1970); Robert McElvaine, *The Great Depression: America, 1929–1941* (New York: Times Books, 1984); Robert McElvaine, ed., *Down and Out in the Great Depression: Letters from the "Forgotten Man"* (Chapel Hill: University of North Carolina Press, 1983); T. H. Watkins, *The Great Depression: America in the 1930s* (Boston: Little, Brown, 1993); Steven Mintz and Susan Kellogg, *Domestic Revolutions: A Social History of American Family Life* (New York: Free Press, 1988).

22 Blaszczyk, *Imagining Consumers*.

23 Stamp, *Movie-Struck Girls*; Fuller, *At the Picture Show*.

24 Photograph of lobby display at New Fruitvale Theater, Salem China Company papers, The National Museum of American History Archives, Washington, D.C. (hereafter, Salem China Company papers).

25 "Premium Thriller," *Business Week*, December 8, 1934, 24; Gomery, *Shared Pleasures*, 70–71.

26 Floyd McKee, "History of USA Pottery Industry," n.d., Salem China Company papers.

27 List prices for Tricorne ware for theaters, January 24, 1935, Salem China Company papers. The noted ceramics designer Don Schreckengost created the now-famous Tricorne pattern in 1934 when he was a nineteen-year-old local art college student on a summer internship at the firm (interview with Don Schreckengost, August 2001).

28 All photographs from Salem China Company papers.

29 "Premium Thriller"; "The Unconquerable Premium," *Business Week*, January 5, 1935, 16; "Give Aways—Premium Men Look Forward to 500 Million Sales of 'Free' Merchandise," *Literary Digest*, October 10, 1936, 44–46.

30 Forbes Parkhill, "Bank Night Tonight," *Saturday Evening Post*, December 4, 1937, 82.

31 "Danger to Theater in Prize Contests," *Motion Picture News*, June 7, 1930, 107.

32 "Neighborhood Theaters are Getting Most of the New Business," *Motion Picture Herald*, June 16, 1934, 9.

33 "Small Town Showmen Pruning Prices," *Motion Picture News*, June 28, 1930, 46.

34 "Something for Nothing," *Business Week*, March 1, 1933, 9.

35 On the NRA, see Watkins, *The Great Depression*; McElvaine, *The Great Depression*, Balio, *Grand Design*.

36 Terry Ramsaye, "Problem of Labor Leads Debate at Capital's Hearing on Code," *Motion Picture Herald*, September 16, 1933, 22.

37 Louis Nizer, "1934 and the Motion Picture Code," *Film Daily Yearbook* 1935, 618.

38 Some entrepreneurs even vertically integrated from distribution only to an integrated manufacturing-distribution arrangement. One well-known example was that of Beatrice Miller who, after working for a premium distributor, purchased the old E. H. Sebring dinnerware plant and created the Royal China Company. The company went on to become a prominent manufacturer and distributor of dinnerware in the 1940s and 1950s. Jo Cunningham, *Collector's Encyclopedia of American Dinnerware* (Paducah, KY: Collector Books, 1982), 246–47.

39 E-mail interview with Phil Stetson, April 2001; Cunningham, *Collector's Encyclopedia of American Dinnerware*, 272.

40 Photographs, Salem China Company papers. Salem's triangular Tricorne design, introduced in 1934, was used in movie theater premium sales between 1935 and 1937.

41 Roland Marchand, *Advertising the American Dream: Making Way for Modernity, 1920–1940* (Berkeley: University of California Press, 1985); Richard deCordova, "The Mickey in Macy's Window: Childhood, Consumerism and Disney Animation," in *Disney Discourse: Producing the Magic Kingdom*,

ed. Eric Smoodin (New York: Routledge, 1994), 203–13; Charles Eckert, "The Carole Lombard in Macy's Window," in *Fabrications*, ed. Jane Gaines and Charlotte Herzog (New York: Routledge 1990), 100–21.

42 DeCordova, "The Mickey in Macy's Window"; Eckert, "The Carole Lombard in Macy's Window"; "Salem China Nites Give Star Performances," n.d., Salem China Company papers.

43 "Salem China Nite Pleases the Ladies—Packs Your House," n.d., Salem China Company papers.

44 Floyd McKee, "Dinnerware as Premiums" n.d., Salem China Company papers.

45 "Salem China Nites Give Star Performances."

46 "Lovely Dinnerware," n.d., Salem China Company papers.

47 McKee, "Dinnerware as Premiums."

48 Mickey Mouse sales postcard design, July 17, 1934, Salem China Company papers.

49 "Lovely Dinnerware."

50 McKee, "Dinnerware as Premiums."

51 "Lovely Dinnerware."

52 "Danger to Theaters in Prize Contest," *Motion Picture News*, June 7, 1930, 107.

53 "Salem China Nite Pleases the Ladies."

54 Marchand, *Advertising the American Dream*.

55 "The Unconquerable Premium."

56 *Motion Picture Herald*, August 10, 1935, 59–60.

57 On the history of Bank Night, see Paige Reynolds, " 'Something for Nothing': Bank Night and the Refashioning of the American Dream," in Fuller-Seeley, ed., *Movie-Going History in Small-Town America*; and Gomery, *Shared Pleasures*, 70–71. "It evades most state lottery laws because the patron does not pay for his number and may conceivably win the prize without buying a ticket to the theater, by waiting outside while the winning number is announced by a loudspeaker in the lobby, then running in to claim his prize" ("Bank Night," *Time*, February 3, 1936, 56).

58 " 'Bingo!—Aw! Nuts!': Movie Temples Lure Monday, Tuesday Patrons with Prize-Money," *Literary Digest*, March 6, 1937, 36; Parkhill, "Bank Night Tonight," 20.

59 Parkhill, "Bank Night Tonight," 82.

60 James Cunningham, "The Code Question Box," *Motion Picture Herald*, October 6, 1934.

61 "Film Code Machine Jams at Collapse of the NRA," *Motion Picture Herald*, June 1, 1935, 9.

62 "Exhibitors Spend $13 Million Yearly on Chance Game Awards," *Motion Picture Herald*, September 21, 1935, 23. It noted that in the Chicago area, "since the inception of prize giveaways, free chinaware to patrons has fallen off sharply, more than 60 percent of the houses using the plan have abandoned it for the cash award idea, and the percentage is growing" ("Chicago Stores Fight $6 Million Chance Games," *Motion Picture Herald*, December 5, 1936, 13).

63 Parkhill, "Bank Night Tonight," 20–21.

64 Ibid., 20.

65 "Bank Night," *Time*, February 3, 1936, 57.

66 " 'Bingo!—Aw! Nuts!' "

67 Parkhill, "Bank Night Tonight," 20.

68 " 'Bingo!—Aw! Nuts!' "

69 "Bank Night," 57–58.

70 "Bank Night," 56–57; Parkhill, "Bank Night Tonight," 82; "Exhibition," *Film Daily Yearbook*, 1937, 755.

71 " 'Bingo!—Aw! Nuts!' "

72 "Exhibitors Spend $13 Million."

73 "US Mail Bars Ads on Bank Night 'Lottery,' " *Motion Picture Herald*, May 4, 1935, 9.

74 "Exhibitors Spend $13 Million"; "Chance Games 'War,' " *Motion Picture Herald*, September 14, 1935, 72.

75 Lynd and Lynd, *Middletown in Transition*. On the Bonus March, see McElvaine, *The Great Depression*; Terkel, *Hard Times*; and Watkins, *The Great Depression*.

76 Marchand, *Advertising the American Dream*.

77 Shepherd, "Leopold Doppler and the Great Orpheum Theater Gravy Boat Riot," 258–60.

78 Steiner, *Research Memorandum on Recreation in the Depression*, 99.

79 "Poor Losers Big Element in Stunts," *Motion Picture News*, June 7, 1930, 108.

80 Steiner, *Research Memorandum on Recreation in the Depression*, 92.

Chapter 9

Eric Smoodin

"THIS BUSINESS OF AMERICA": FAN MAIL, FILM RECEPTION, AND *MEET JOHN DOE* (1996)

Editors' Introduction

In his 1975 essay, "Notes on Columbia Pictures Corporation, 1926–41," reprinted in this volume, Edward Buscombe expressed his frustration with the text-based film studies of the previous fifteen years. "In the black and white footage" of classical era Hollywood films, Buscombe complained, "the social comments can simply be read off as if the films were so many sociologists' reports," and that all audiences understood all films in the same ways. Buscombe's essay appeared in the same issue of *Screen* that also featured Laura Mulvey's *Visual Pleasure and Narrative Cinema*, and while that latter piece produced a cottage industry of engaged scholarship, Buscombe's helped generate the historiography of the last forty years. Film scholars started to look for evidence of audience response and interpretation, and understood that viewers should be considered not as constituting a mass audience, but as a series of separate and overlapping groups, based on such categories as age or gender or race or location. Developments in the archive supported this kind of scholarship; the availability of censorship reports, industrial records, or State Department memoranda, for example, provided insight into viewers connected to the film studios, or to educational institutions, or who simply identified as private citizens. In the following case study, Eric Smoodin makes use of the fan mail that Frank Capra saved and deposited with the rest of his papers at Wesleyan University. Using Capra's *Meet John Doe* as an example, Smoodin tries to determine if we can understand what audiences wanted to see in movies during the late 1930s and early 1940s, what provided pleasure or displeasure, and how viewers negotiated the differences between escapism and engaged cinema. In the scholarship on reception from the last four decades, audiences emerge not as passive spectators with little interpretive capacity of their own, but as viewers who actively work to make sense of films and to understand the relations of cinema to events taking place outside the movie theatre.

Suggested Reading

Richard deCordova, "Ethnography and Exhibition: The Child Audience, The Hays Office and Saturday Matinees," *Camera Obscura* 23 (May, 1990), 91–107; Melvyn Stokes and Richard Maltby, eds., *American Movie Audiences: From the Turn of the Century to the Early Sound Era* (London: British Film Institute, 1999); Kristin Thompson, *Interpreting Films: Studies in the Historical Reception of American Cinema* (Princeton: Princeton University Press, 1992).

> Yesterday morning at 2 am we were seeing our eldest son Denny, with 45 others, off for an Army Camp somewhere. At 2 pm of the same day, we were seeing our first Frank Capra picture, *Meet John Doe*. My! What a picture, just what this old world needs.[1]

IN CONTEMPORARY FILM STUDIES, the voices of 'average' moviegoers like Mrs E. Coate, who wrote the above letter to Frank Capra in June 1941, typically have been lost. For Mrs Coate, seeing Capra's latest film marked an intense conflation of real-life problems – losing a son to military service and an almost certain war – with the fictional ones of the film. In addition, highly personal concerns combined with those that were, in fact, global. The film not only helped Mrs Coate through a difficult period, but was precisely 'what this old world needs'. This letter to Capra indicates a need to thank the film director, and to tell him that, rather than allowing Mrs Coate to forget about her difficulties for two hours, *Meet John Doe* helped her to contextualize them and to see them in relation to the issues that his film addressed.

We have little understanding of this kind of complex and deeply felt response to films from this period, largely because the study of the historical audience presents such serious problems, both methodologically and practically. It is impossible, for example, to produce any reasonable kind of 'ethnography' of the 1940s film audience to match the one that David Morley has constructed, through interviews and a careful process of selection, for the contemporary British television audience.[2] Moreover, the evidence of the historical audience's responses to films, probably ephemeral in the first place (preview cards, diary entries and so on), is exceedingly difficult to come by.

Although methodological constraints remain, film studies has begun the project of historicizing the film spectator. Among the most compelling work is that which indicates an interest, on the part of certain audiences, in a cinema that addressed concerns of 'political' importance. For instance, Janet Staiger has examined the mixture of spectatorial and political desire as it becomes apparent in a very specific group of viewers – film critics of the 1920s. Staiger has found that reviewers for ostensibly 'non-ideological' periodicals, such as the trade journal *Variety*, quite explicitly developed an aesthetic based as much upon a film's expression of hyperpatriotic nationalist positions as upon its manipulation of such formal categories as narrative development or visual style. In perhaps the most detailed analysis of an audience's political expectations and pleasures, Stephen Ross has shown that in the years leading up to World War I a wide audience existed, in New York and perhaps elsewhere, for labour union-produced feature films about unfair economic practices.[3]

Thus we have evidence that, at least during certain periods, the cinema came to be seen by many 'average' viewers as contributing directly to regional or national discussions about political issues. In this article, I want to examine film spectatorship from just such a period, the very early 1940s. My primary source of information will be the fan mail – and I use this term loosely to include both enthusiastic and critical letters – that Frank Capra received in

1941 just after the opening of *Meet John Doe*. Several significant questions arise from these fan-generated texts about the film: when, why, and in what manner did audiences perceive that a major Hollywood production spoke to national concerns or embodied a national consensus? What were viewers' expectations of a Capra film, and what pleasures did his work generate? Finally, what role did certain segments of the audience expect a film celebrity of Capra's status to play within the national political scene?

The letters about *Meet John Doe* indicate that for many film viewers the Hollywood cinema needed to engage more directly with issues of perceived importance. Even more broadly, for reasons that may have had something to do with the era's economic collapse but are not altogether self-evident, during this period there seems to have existed no necessary contradiction between consuming all manner of popular culture for entertainment and escape, and consuming it for at least a degree of political edification. By the time of *Doe*'s release, as Barbara Foley has pointed out, the proletarian novel had become an accepted (and occasionally best-selling) literary genre, one even occasionally spoken of admiringly by such arbiters of middle-class taste as the *New York Herald Tribune* and the *Saturday Review of Literature*.[4] During the same period, the populism of the previous century received its first serious scholarly attention with the 1931 publication of John D. Hicks's *The Populist Revolt*, and at least some limited popular success with C. Vann Woodward's 1938 biography of the populist hero, *Tom Watson: Agrarian Rebel*. This interest in a politicized popular culture came from both the Left and the Right, from those who made Upton Sinclair's *I, Governor of California* a best seller, to those who listened to Father Coughlin's weekly national radio broadsides against Jews and communists.

This is not to imply that the readers of proletarian novels, or those with an interest in nineteenth-century political history, or those who sympathized with the socialist Sinclair, formed the central audience for Capra's films. But by 1941, as I will show, there was a broad field of cultural production aligning not only literature, history and political tracts, but also school textbooks, radio music programmes, public assemblies and even the occasional gossip column with discussions of pressing national issues. My own work on the reception of other Capra films released before *Doe* indicates that by the end of the 1930s at least some fairly large segments of the motion picture audience hoped for Hollywood to deal more 'realistically' with pressing political issues, and celebrated Capra for standing out from the rank and file of film directors because of his willingness to interrogate issues of wealth, corporate power, and government corruption.[5]

The era's discourse on Capra himself demonstrates that a popular culture that stressed politics over pure escape, and that attempted a critique of capitalism and the fabulously rich, might attract any number of eager viewers. By the late 1930s, after three Academy Awards, a number of box-office hits, and concerted publicity efforts by his employer, Columbia Pictures, Capra was almost certainly one of the two most famous directors in the country (probably only Cecil B. De Mille was better known). He was also one of a very select group of filmmakers (besides De Mille, Walt Disney comes to mind, and perhaps some of the studio moguls) who could compete with major movie stars in terms of celebrity and media attention; this attention, in Capra's case, typically centring as much on his politics as on his filmmaking abilities.

In 1938, even the magazine of homespun Americana, *The Saturday Evening Post*, wrote admiringly of Capra's reception in the Soviet Union, and implied that a communist audience understood democratic values far better than government officials in the USA:

> For painting America as he sees it, [Capra] is regarded in Moscow as a Utopian dreamer. . . . Traveling in Russia after *Mr. Deeds [Goes to Town]* appeared, he was hailed as a comrade, a world improver and a Red propagandist. In their enthusiasm over Capra's portrait of an American philanthropist [in *Mr. Deeds*],

> the Soviet critics showed themselves far behind the advanced thinkers of Washington, who want to abolish the American philanthropist because his money is needed to buy votes with.[6]

While the *Post* certified the filmmaker's patriotism ('Capra likes American institutions'), the magazine posited him as a version of one of his own heroes, battling against institutional forces that have a knee-jerk response to all social criticism and political debate: 'Capra says the best thing he ever worked on was *Soviet*, an unborn photoplay. He was getting ready to shoot it for Metro-Goldwyn-Mayer, when the company decided it was full of controversial dynamite and put it on the shelf.'[7]

In 1940, *The New Yorker*, a magazine with a decidedly more intellectual and elitist approach than the *Post*, called a profile on Capra 'Thinker in Hollywood', and referred to him as 'the most thoughtful man in the industry'. The magazine also admiringly stressed the connection between Capra and communist ideology, saying that, 'in Russia, the point of view he had displayed in *Mr. Deeds* caused him to be well received by Soviet officials'.[8] Writers for mainstream magazines apparently saw no problem in constructing Capra as someone who embodied the best in the USA by incorporating that which was best about the Soviet Union. Almost certainly, part of the enthusiasm for Capra's films came from the audience's willingness to have their own political institutions criticized, and to have solutions posited that could, in some sense at least, be labeled 'communist', but that still posed no conflict with perceived basic US values, and that of course signalled no endorsement of Stalin or the Soviet Union.

Indeed, this position formed one of the defining, characteristics of the 1930s-style populism embodied not only by Capra, but by, among others, such disparate characters as Father Coughlin, old-person's advocate Francis Townsend, Louisiana governor Huey Long and even Franklin Roosevelt: that is, a serious critique of wealth and class inequality, and a concomitant belief in a mixture of egalitarianism and the kind of activist Christianity endorsed by Pope Pius XI's 1931 encyclical, 'On reconstructing the social order'. The fan mail for *Doe* exhibits the same kind of commitment, but beyond this, and beyond the conviction that the cinema should address significant issues, the letters show no necessary formal or ideological consistency, ranging from Mrs Coate's family melodrama to more overtly political tracts, from religious allegory to discussions of the problems of nosy neighbours in small towns.

Capra deposited at least one hundred *Meet John Doe* letters with his papers at Wesleyan University, and I have transcribed approximately two thirds of them.[9] The entire Capra collection is an interesting one, largely documenting the director's career and reputation from the early 1930s through the 1980s. The documents about his films – production records, press books, contracts, scripts, correspondence and so on – date from the early years of Capra's directing career, with materials covering such films as *Flight* (1930) and *Forbidden* (1931). For many of his films, Capra saved the correspondence that he received not only at the time of a production, but for many years after it, as new viewers were exposed to his movies on television, at retrospectives, in college classes or on video. It is impossible to tell how selective Capra may have been in maintaining his papers. For virtually all of his post 1934 films, however, there are ample numbers of unfavourable film reviews and critical fan letters, implying that the filmmaker, early on, was interested in being able to document his career fully and was also something of a pack rat, unable to throw much out.

In spite of this apparent inclusiveness, interpreting the letters about *Meet John Doe* raises the issue of typicality, both in terms of the general response to Capra's movies and to those made by other filmmakers. Because of his celebrity, Capra undoubtedly received more fan mail than most directors, and because his films were frequently so overdetermined as narratives of nationalism, fan mail about his movies probably differed significantly from the fan mail generated by the more typical Hollywood product. And, of course, most viewers, whatever they may have thought about the movies they saw, chose to write no fan mail at all. Despite these limitations on interpretation, it seems at least plausible to assume that the mail Capra received tells us something about a variety of the subgroups and subcultures, to use Morley's terms, that made up the film audience in 1941. The letters certainly provide information about segments of what might be called the 'Capra audience', those fans who took a special interest in such films as *Mr Deeds Goes to Town, Mr Smith Goes to Washington* and *Meet John Doe*. Further, given the widespread popularity of Capra's films during this period, and the general desire of so many consumers for a politicized popular culture, it figures that we can at least cautiously assume that the opinions expressed in the letters were shared by a great many movie fans.

The most extensive holdings in the Capra collection, including fan mail, begin around 1933 and 1934, with the production of *Lady For a Day* and *It Happened One Night*. At the same time, at least according to his autobiography, Capra became more and more concerned about his status as a filmmaker with a social consciousness, claiming that, in his post 1932 movies, 'I took a hard look at life from the eye level of the hard-pressed Smiths and Joneses'. Arguably, then, starting at about this time, Capra used his mail as something of a barometer, to determine whether he was in touch with what he called 'the real lot of American citizens'.[10] Thus, Capra himself may have believed in the reliability of a relatively small number of letters to indicate a more broadly experienced response to his movies.

There are several reasons for studying the reception of *Meet John Doe* in particular, and its relationship to the period's popular political discourses. Most obviously, the film comes from a period in US history perched precariously between domestic economic collapse and entrance into World War II. In the context of Capra's career, *Doe* was the director's first film as an independent producer, and it also appeared more or less in the middle of what generally is considered Capra's most productive period – 1934 to 1946. *Meet John Doe* also comes from that cycle of films – *Mr Deeds Goes to Town* (1936), *You Can't Take It With You* (1938), *Mr Smith Goes to Washington* (1939), the *Why We Fight* films (1942–5), and *It's a Wonderful Life* (1946) – that typically have been considered the most reflective of the US body politic. In film studies, however, in spite of a general acknowledgement of the social impact of the films, there has been very little effort made to examine just how that impact was felt, and, in fact, if it was felt at all, and by whom. As a result, we are left with little understanding of the tensions within the 'mass' audience, of the different kinds of pleasure that the Hollywood cinema could generate, and of the often intense interaction between viewers and the films they watched.

The experience of seeing Capra's film in 1941, at least as expressed on the conscious level of the fan letters, indicates a diverse range of interpretive possibilities. But the constant trope in the letters is the extent to which the film itself became something of a national document at a particularly crucial period in the country's history, when the effects of the Depression had hardly lessened, a war in Europe threatened to come to the USA, and Franklin Roosevelt's unprecedented election to a third term as president in 1940 raised concerns, at least among a significant minority of the electorate, about the possibilities of domestic dictatorship. Capra himself hoped that the film would depict 'the hard-nosed brutality' of the era, and reflect the manner in which 'Hitler's strong-arm success against democracy' was spreading, with 'little "führers" . . . springing up in America, to proclaim that freedom was weak, sterile, passé'.[11]

Meet John Doe depicts the production of a 'forgotten man' by journalist Ann Mitchell (Barbara Stanwyck). Washed-up baseball player John Willoughby (Gary Cooper) 'becomes' Doe, and with Ann as his coach he protests the condition of all the John Does in the country. As a sign of his seriousness, Doe pledges to commit suicide on Christmas Eve, after which he becomes a national celebrity. Newspaper magnate D. B. Norton (Edward Arnold), who commands a personal army of storm troopers, senses the possibility of using Doe and his followers to promote his own dictatorial ambitions, and actively promotes Doe's celebrity and the Doe Clubs being formed across the country. Doe finally finds out about Norton's machinations and tries to expose them, but Norton manipulates the crowd at a mass rally for Doe into turning on their hero. A despondent Doe tries to fulfil his promise to commit suicide, but Ann and a suddenly repentant Norton convince him not to.

A number of fans, in the manner of Mrs Coate, spoke of *Doe*, which so clearly narrativized concerns about poverty, leadership, democracy and the possibilities for collective action, in terms of its significant connection to major personal events, with at least three of the letter writers aligning the events in the film with their own graduation from high school. One recent graduate was up until three in the morning writing his letter, and told Capra that if he did not get to bed soon he would not be able to be at work by eight, and would certainly lose his job. The film made him realize 'that all this talk of pessimism that all high school graduates get must be wrong. . . . We are told that we go out to meet a cruel, hard, debasing world, of men that will cut your heart to sunders if they possibly can. There must be something else in the world.'[12] Yet another eighteen-year-old, who said she was graduating in a week, viewed the film as a statement directly from Capra, and took the occasion to admonish him. For her, spectatorship meant a kind of direct discussion with filmmakers, and implied contracts between Hollywood and filmgoers: 'I am very serious about this business of America', she wrote. 'I am hoping with all my heart that the message you gave *to me* . . . is sincere. I am hoping that you are not a D. B. Norton' (emphasis mine).[13]

Despite the emphasis on graduating from high school and the common denominator of the viewers' age, these examples represent differing experiences of *Meet John Doe*: one about the possibilities and problems confronting young people, and another that delineated an extraordinary kind of spectatorship that stressed a personal and very political conversation with Capra. Both letter writers, however, aligned the film with varying notions of the national – 'this business of America', in the words of the student – and about the responsibility of the cinema during times of perceived national crisis. For the first letter writer, motion pictures needed to provide an antidote to pessimism; for the second, movies had to offer both a serious message and a commitment to continuing to spread that message.

The high-school seniors or recent graduates who wrote to Capra (another told him 'I have often had ideas [like those in the movie], but never had the nerve to write them on paper for fear that someone would laugh at me')[14] may in fact have been responding to more texts than just Capra's film. On 3 March 1941, *Time* magazine put Gary Cooper as John Doe on its cover. In the same issue, *Time* devoted several columns to the current textbook controversy in which high-school social science texts were being challenged by such institutions as the New York State Economic Council for being 'New Dealish in tone . . . critical of big business . . . [and] against unequal distribution of wealth and unequal opportunities in the U.S.'. The National Association of Manufacturers decided to examine the texts, hiring 'a liberal, a conservative and a Marxist' to look for objectivity and bias, with particular concentration on the texts' views of the US government and 'free business enterprise'. In other words, a battle was being waged over the possible interpretations of 'historical' rather than motion-picture texts, but many of the issues were precisely the same. The textbooks themselves apparently engaged in the same kind of mildly progressive politics as Capra's film, which arguably equates big-time corporate capitalism with incipient fascism, and also tries to expose the plight of the 'forgotten men', the army of John Does. Moreover, the specific concerns about the textbooks centred on issues of representation, on the manner in which they depicted government and business and created a portrait of the nation.[15]

If even *Time* took notice, then the textbook controversy probably had some currency amongst Americans generally. Indeed, education leaders at this time seem to have been almost obsessively, and quite publically, interested in national, political projects. As just one example among many, in March 1941, a few days before *Doe* premiered in Los Angeles, a Pasadena, California school district official, speaking at a 'Youth and Democracy' rally, offered a five hundred dollar prize for the student who wrote the best essay on the topic, 'Why I Believe in America'.[16] It seems reasonable to argue, then, that the students watching *Doe* and writing to Capra were in fact responding to a textual field that, in 1941 at least, could contain both movies and school books. Their intense reaction to Capra's film, and their stress on the connection between the movie and their own high-school graduations, might well show that their experience as film viewers was deeply influenced by their experience as members of the classroom audience. For these students, *Meet John Doe*, if not other films, provoked a similar kind of national and political sensibility to the one being constructed in schools, and encouraged its teenage viewers to respond as if they were listening to a teacher or reading a class text. In this case, two kinds of spectatorship – in movie theatres and in schoolrooms – merged, particularly around issues of government and business and the best ways to represent each.

Most of the letters that Capra deposited in the Wesleyan Collection, however, came from people whose frame of reference was not contemporary educational practice in secondary schools. In fact, some letter writers, through their spelling or grammatical practice, or through their own descriptions of themselves, stressed their opposition to educational discourse but nevertheless read the film in relation to complex national problems, often critiquing *Doe* for not dealing with them in a sufficiently sophisticated fashion. As with the high-school graduates, these letter writers show that spectatorship, in 1941, constituted an extremely nuanced and varied relationship between viewer and film text, and also between consumer and film industry.

One such letter writer, indicating her difference from those fans who confidently philosophized for Capra, told the director that 'I am just a dum [sic] person in your estimation'. But she also provided information about her and her husband's filmgoing habits and attitudes, both of which problematize notions of an audience eager for escape and viewing motion pictures as the ideal instrument of that escape. 'We go to a movie once in awhile', she wrote, 'once a month or so that is at night when I can get a tired husband to go.' Then she added that typically, they 'come home dripping with disgust and so mad that we have wasted our time energy and money, the money is the last you notice'. If these sentiments were in any way common, perhaps among adult, working audiences, then the cinema of the period constructed, along with other kinds of viewers, a sort of anti-spectator, for whom the cinema provided displeasure (in fact, generated 'disgust'). This viewer hated what she/he saw and considered moviegoing a waste of time and money, but nevertheless, at least occasionally, went to the movies anyway.

Capra films, however, stood out from the routine Hollywood product and, for this dissatisfied audience at least, constituted a kind of special, quality, adult viewing experience, one worth the effort. The letter writer told Capra that despite her and her husband's low opinion of movies, 'we have always looked to you to do the right thing'. She proceeded to criticize the film, particularly for its ending (a constant complaint in the letters, and in much subsequent Capra literature). She wanted Doe to commit suicide and not to be saved by the repentant Norton. This final narrative failure particularly bothered her, because until then the film was 'just right for the times'. Then she told Capra something that had 'been smoldering in my heart for some time', and that his film had had the chance to address: 'why don't the Motion Pictures do something to help our country from the Hitlers within. The time is ripe for big things to be done.'

In other words, she interpreted *Meet John Doe* as detailing the possibility of a fascist takeover of the USA, from domestic enemies rather than foreign ones. By far the greatest number of letter writers in the Wesleyan collection interpreted Capra's film, with its corporate magnate plotting to take over the country, in just the same way, as a document detailing the USA's potential ruin from within, as a national allegory produced during perilous times. One viewer wrote that she 'was certainly made familiar by said picture with the unscrupulous political machines working in our country today to undermind [sic] American principles and ideals'. Another wrote that, until the problematic ending, the film showed him the possibility to 'beat the pants off all the crooked politicians and lick all the hard luck and "isms" in this cockeyed world of ours'. Yet another insisted that 'the spirit that is awakened in people through seeing *John Doe* must be related somehow to the need for national unity'. A viewer from New York wrote of the responsibility of the entire motion picture industry to uphold democratic institutions, and thus of the exemplary status of Capra's film: 'as one who regards democracy as the strongest theme the movie makers can use now and forever . . . I should like to congratulate you on your achievement'.[17]

For these viewers, then, the Hollywood cinema typically was not enough concerned with the national welfare, in that movies tended not to promote or embody the country's values or protect its institutions. As a result, *Meet John Doe* deserved special mention because of the way it ably reflected, at least according to these viewers, both spectatorial desire and political reality. At least twenty fans (almost one third of the sample that I have been able to study carefully) wrote to Capra to talk about the film's timeliness and its defence of democracy, implying that for many spectators, viewing pleasure by 1941 meant not being allowed to forget, even for two hours, a perceived threat to the USA from domestic fascism and political corruption. I do not intend to imply here that most viewers completely eschewed escapism – there were certainly plenty of movies made in 1941 that amply provided it. But the *Doe* letters indicate a desire for a kind of viewing practice that addressed the audience as a nation, and that audience members could apply outside the theatre, particularly in the development of the 'national unity' and regard for democracy that so many fans stressed should be the primary goal of motion pictures.

The concerns of these letter writers were not isolated ones. Their readings of the film, in fact, can be placed against numerous texts from different sources that emphasized the national implications of Capra's film. In her gossip column in the *Los Angeles Times*, for example, Hedda Hopper, hardly a defender of politicized cinema, wrote that people had been waiting for *Doe* ever since Capra's last film, *Mr Smith Goes to Washington*, had critiqued government so effectively. She was hardly disappointed in the follow-up effort, calling *Doe* 'a much-needed dose of optimism to lift us out of the slough of defeatism everyone's wallowing in'. In a more detailed analysis of the film's relation to current events, Edwin Schallert, in his *Los Angeles Times* review, praised the film's 'social significance', and insisted that the picture would 'give a new turn to the thoughts of a nation'. The communist newspaper *The Daily Worker* discussed throughout its review the connection between the film (and, indeed, Capra's entire oeuvre) and contemporary politics. Even some of the studio-generated publicity for the film sought to produce something of a nationalist response by stressing, for instance, the score by Dmitri Tiomkin, which 'will describe in musical terms the daily life of an average American family of four', and which 'blends the folk music of every section of the nation'.[18]

Of course, the texts surrounding any film are never so unanimous. While some of the advertising emphasized the romanticized, US folk tradition reflected in the score, other publicity stressed the film's relation to consumption practice rather than to issues of national unity or of any perceived urgency to the body politic. Exhibitors across the country concocted tie-ins between the movie and newspapers, department stores, transit systems and radio shows, thus using *Doe* to support the same mass media and economic practices that Capra's film ostensibly critiques.[19] Even the 'text' of the film's gala Los Angeles premiere exemplified a kind of fascist aesthetic that seems antithetical to the film's political project, at least as the letter writers interpreted it. Reporting on the premiere, the *Los Angeles Times* noted that the security staff that evening 'was augmented by . . . 40 members of the Vic McLaglen motorcycle troop', reprising their role as Norton's private storm troopers in the film, with the difference that these Hollywood vigilantes were viewed as keepers of the peace at the premiere rather than as threats to it, as in the film.[20]

Even the viewers, while concentrating on the political implications of the film, interpreted them in different ways. Rather than concentrating on the threat of domestic fascism and the erosion of democratic institutions, at least eight fans concentrated on the manner in which the film conflated national values with spiritual ones. One viewer wrote to Capra that 'I really had a feeling that I had seen a picture that was destined not only to make a name for itself . . . but a picture that actually would start the country in a movement toward the Golden Rule'. Another 'commended' Capra 'for the red-blooded patriotism and the spiritual atmosphere that permeates the entire picture', while a teenager who claimed that she was 'not a specially serious minded person' nevertheless told Capra that 'people know this picture stands for everything Christ stood for', and that 'America is a grand country, but it needs more of this'.[21]

In fact, several of these viewers seemed to seek these values and also find them in a range of films, indicating that for at least one group of filmgoers there might have been little difference between that which today we might consider typically escapist, and that which, like *Doe*, might seem like serious entertainment. One viewer asked Capra for a series of *Doe* films, saying that 'a continuity of pictures in this theme might be possible, just as the *Andy Hardy* series has been in its concept'. The letter went on that at 'the center of these [*Hardy*] pictures is the spiritual value, but in my estimation *Meet John Doe* was more penetrating and practical'.[22] If some of *Doe*'s viewers desired a cinema that refused to provide them with escape, others clearly went to the movies primarily to see a reflection of religious values, and did not make the distinction between films that were escapist or not, realistic or non-realistic, frivolous or high minded. Rather, there were only spiritual and non-spiritual films, so that *Meet John Doe* and an *Andy Hardy* film, despite the generic, production, authorial, political and other differences we might point out today, could be seen as providing virtually identical viewing experiences.

The fan mail about *Meet John Doe* indicates that many viewers believed in the possibility of a kind of participatory spectatorship, and looked to Hollywood to make films to promote civic action and even to create politically motivated audiences outside of the theatre. Capra received no less than a dozen letters telling him that his film had indeed started a John Doe movement, with Doe Clubs across the country trying to create a local and then national response to national problems (other than the testimony of the letters, however, I have found no evidence in newspapers and magazines from the period that Doe Clubs actually formed or, if they did, created much of a following).

Letter writers discussed the film as well as these attempts to create the clubs in relation to the perceived dangerous route that Depression-era democracy had taken. One person complained, for example, that there had been limited response to her clubs, and to her theory of a 'people's democracy', because 'the people have been doped for so long it's awfully hard for the poor devils to see the light'.[23] Another viewer, in a letter deeply critical of the end of the film, asserted nevertheless that *Doe* virtually formed the clubs spontaneously, and in describing this phenomenon the viewer alluded to the construction of a spectator motivated to political, collective action by the movie, but also virtually helpless against the workings of the film text: 'By the time you had the band play the Star Spangled Banner', he wrote, 'we were about ready to turn around and give away anything we had to anybody that needed it. You *had* a John Doe Club right there in the theater.'[24]

Of course, the viewer exaggerated; no John Doe Club actually formed during the movie that night. Nevertheless, despite the hyperbole, this statement stands out as an extraordinary assertion of a kind of spectatorship that has not been theorized fully, if at all: viewers who are simultaneously completely passive (apparently ready to do anything the film tells them) and absolutely active (seemingly mobilized to engage in collective action while still in the theatre). More broadly, the letter points up the astonishing political power that many audiences wanted the cinema to exercise, and the deep disappointment they felt when movies seemed to refuse this responsibility. Viewers of *Doe* typically extended this power to Capra himself, with the director emerging as a potential hero of national rehabilitation, as just the man to mobilize the masses.

Nine viewers told Capra he was a 'genius', or compared him to such disparate national heroes as General Pershing and Walter Winchell.[25] And at least another seven viewers expressed their admiration for Capra by urging him to continue, and take control of, the incipient John Doe movement. One letter writer, for instance, insisted that 'the responsibility falls on your shoulder, to you will come the plea to carry through that which you have started'. By fulfilling this responsibility, Capra would help 'raise the motion picture industry to the height which it deserves – that of being a bearer of the simple truth to all people who seek it'.[26] Capra's special status comes out in many of the letters, as well as the belief that the film industry had not nearly reached its potential as a political force, a potential that also, at least in part, was like a religious calling.

Echoing those viewers who conflated nationalism with spirituality and who viewed the film in deeply religious terms, one letter writer, for instance, implicitly looked to Capra as a kind of evangelical leader. 'This isn't a picture', the viewer insisted, 'it's one of the most powerful sermons since the one on the mount', and he continued that 'there are millions of more John Does who believe the same thing, but who are waiting for someone to bring it to their attention'. Indeed, Capra's leadership was necessary because of crushing national and even global problems. 'I'm just one of the millions of John Does', the letter continued, 'who are sick of wars . . . and the eventual taxes that are piled on us; of the cheap petty politics with their intrigue and selfishness'. Then, in a final assertion of Capra's influence and the power of the film text to mobilize people, the letter suggested a sequel to *Doe*, at the end of which Capra himself would appear and urge 'those in the audience to get together on the John Doe principle'.[27] In other words, this viewer proposed a direct address appeal by Capra as director/star/national leader, thereby invoking, while not mentioning, the model of Charles Chaplin at the end of *The Great Dictator*, when Chaplin steps out of character to address the audience about tolerance and world peace.

To his credit, it appears that Capra responded to many of the viewers who wrote to him (these responses are included in the Wesleyan collection). To those who virtually demanded his leadership he always demurred, citing his own limited organizational skills and the possibility for critics to detect a conflict of interest. Running the John Doe Clubs 'would be cynically taken in many places as a publicity stunt for the picture', he wrote to one fan, adding that 'my job and my talents and my hope is to continue to make pictures', rather than direct a national movement.[28]

The number of letter writers who so admired Capra, who requested his help and who asked him to be their leader, at least implies, without making any direct link between the fans who wrote and those who did not, that a significant portion of the audience wished to be spoken to by someone they could trust, to be addressed as a mass audience eager to implement the John Doe philosophy. In an invaluable discussion of the complexity of contextualizing Hollywood products, Nick Browne has pointed out that the discursive strategies of *Meet John Doe* – the use the narrative makes of mass rallies and radio networks, the constant invocations of 'the people' – work to address the audience 'as a congregation', as 'America'.[29]

Indeed, if the letters in the Wesleyan collection are any indication, the audiences of the film clearly wanted to be addressed in just this way, and felt the strongest identification not so much with any major characters in *Meet John Doe*, but with the audience within the film, the audience that Doe exhorts.

If the cinema can be read in terms of audience desire, then we must keep in mind, at least for the period covered by *Doe*'s release, the desire to be addressed as an audience, and indeed as a national audience needing to be called to action around national concerns. In fact, one of the perceived problems with the film had to do with the intensity of the identification with the audience-within-the-film. At least nine of the letter writers were harshly critical of the scene towards the end of the movie when the members of the John Doe Clubs turn on their leader, expressing a sense of personal betrayal at the portrait of themselves as mean spirited and unforgiving. A letter from 'six John and Jane Does' told Capra that 'You showed us that you *don't* believe in us', and insisted that 'You think we're a lot of silly sheep'. Yet another viewer complained to Capra that 'We John Does are made to look like Judases who would sell out their leader'.[30] Indeed, the most common criticism in the fan mail that Capra saved dealt with the representation of a featureless national audience, of a mass which, for many viewers, constituted the real star in the film, directly mirrored the audience in the theatre, and finally appeared as nothing more than a mob. Individual spectators clearly viewed the film as speaking to a national spectator, and their most intense reactions came from their understanding of how that national spectator was both depicted and addressed.

By so stressing their own status as members of a national audience, viewers showed themselves to be adopting a subject position that had seemingly come to be required by the growing number of entertainment activities that were overtly nationalist or political in nature, or by 1941 had come to be considered so. On network radio alone in 1941, for example, 'the time had come for U.S. writers to fill the air full of the cause of democracy', in the words of an article in *Time* magazine, with CBS broadcasting *The Free Company*, a weekly programme dwelling on those freedoms guaranteed by the Bill of Rights. Three times a week, the same network broadcast *Back Where I Come From*, devoted to US folk songs, while other shows, like *America's Town Meeting of the Air* and *MBS's American Forum of the Air*, broadcast discussions about the New Deal or the dangers of domestic communism. Even the popular media's discussion of cultural production, which typically had been spoken of aesthetically rather than in political terms, emphasized the political systems that might lead to certain forms. In the same issue of *Time* that discussed *The Free Company*, for example, an art critic reviewed a display of European sculpture in New York, and opined that 'under paternalistic governments, artists produce the kind of art the government likes', while 'under a democracy, artists produce the kind of art they themselves like'.[31]

By the time of the release of *Meet John Doe*, then, it had become difficult to read about popular culture or to 'experience' it without being made aware of being addressed as a spectator or listener whose primary identity had to be that of US citizen, or at least that of active participant in a political system. In an acknowledgement of this kind of audience, national leaders, before the widespread availability and use of television, frequently took their shows on the road, just as Doe does in Capra's film, and developed one of the significant forms of popular entertainment in the 1930s and 1940s, the mass rally, which self-consciously collapsed the distinctions between politics, patriotism, audience participation and spectatorial pleasure. In March 1941, for instance, Los Angeles alone hosted several of these rallies at the same time as it served as one of the sites of the initial, limited release of *Meet John Doe*. News analyst H. V. Kaltenborn, himself something of a Capra hero after appearing in a small part (as himself) in *Mr Smith Goes to Washington*, addressed a crowd of five thousand, despite a threatened demonstration by the isolationist America First Committee. Similarly, journalist and author Eve Curie spoke to a large audience about the war in Europe, while the same America First Committee that had challenged Kaltenborn's right to an audience sponsored a mass anti-war rally featuring the ex-governor of Wisconsin, Philip LaFollette. Demonstrating the era's easy slippage, at least publicly, between government and entertainment, a group of actors along with federal and Los Angeles city officials announced the formation of the 'I Am an American Foundation', with plans to organize a rally to 'welcome . . . and instruct new citizens before a Shrine of the Constitution'.[32]

In March of the same year, in New York, the Communist Party sponsored a rally for eighteen thousand people in Madison Square Garden to celebrate the birthday of party leader William Foster 'in song, pageant, banners and tributes', with the audience urged to 'rally and demonstrate for freedom and peace'.[33] Clearly, by 1941, politics, celebrity, entertainment, education and spectacle had coalesced in the mass rally, with audiences expected to take part in the proceedings by asserting, for instance, their status as citizens, as in the case of the 'I Am an American' extravaganza, or their commitment to non-intervention, as in the Communist rally, or, as in the case of the Kaltenborn or Curie addresses, their concern with national and world affairs. The audiences of *Meet John Doe* that were so critical of the representation of the audience-within-the-film were in fact acting like the mass rally audience, judging and then responding to the message Doe gives at his own rally, and then chastising Capra for misunderstanding that response.

I do not mean to romanticize a kind of politically motivated, now long-gone movie audience that tried to interact politically and collectively with a broad range of popular entertainments. Such an audience would provide no guarantee of progressive politics, as a few of the most enthusiastic fans of *Meet John Doe*, for instance, displayed an all too eager nativism, thanking Capra for making a film for 'real Americans'.[34] My point is that in 1941 there existed at least a significant section of the audience organized around issues of perceived national importance and ready to participate in debates about those issues, and that expected the popular culture industries to take their interests and desires into consideration. Even the federal government apparently recognized the significance of that audience and Capra's ability to reach out to it. Only a year after *Meet John Doe*, Army Chief of Staff General George Marshall made the newly enlisted Capra the director of a massive military propaganda project that resulted in the *Why We Fight* and *Know Your Ally* films, as well as lesser known documentaries that proselytized for the war effort, and that sought to create a national consensus among the millions of armed forces personnel who were compelled to watch those movies.

There is ample evidence in the fan mail that the 'nationalized' and 'politicized' audience for *Meet John Doe* definitely was not a monolithic one. Capra received a number of letters that had nothing to do with the connection between his film and any perceived national emergency. Some letter writers asked him for jobs, sent him ideas for movies, shared the poems or songs they had written or just made general gripes. There were also several letters that complained about Capra's commitment since 1936 to 'message' films, and implored him to return to the more escapist fantasies of *It Happened One Night* and *Broadway Bill* (both from 1934).[35] At a greater-than-fifty-year remove from the letters, and because writers tended to speak of themselves primarily as 'John Does', it is also extremely difficult to categorize responses to the film that might be class- or race-based. Finally, I know of no reliable method of determining whether the dominant sentiments expressed in the fan letters accurately represented the opinions of the millions of viewers who did not write to Capra.

What do emerge from the letters, however, are concerns both at odds with and sympathetic to much New Deal discourse. Rather than reflecting the need for economic reorganization, which so many Roosevelt bureaucrats stressed, the letters indicate a belief in a disjunction between 'traditional' US values of neighbourliness and participatory democracy, and an individualized, segmented modernity. In this, the letters closely followed the general findings of Robert and Helen Lynd's *Middletown*, a 1929 study of Muncie, Indiana, except that while the Lynds blamed developments in capitalism for the demise of long-held values, the letter writers cast a larger net, and worried about the effects of 'isms' in general.[36]

The issues relating to a politicized, nationalized popular culture, and the relations between 'the people' and their political systems, cannot be settled purely by an analysis of a sample of the fan mail sent to one director about just one of his films. But I would argue that such an analysis allows us to begin the process of studying the cinema at the point of consumption, that is, by looking at the varied reception strategies of movie audiences. This kind of project also forces us to complicate a tendency to consider Hollywood production from the studio era as unproblematically constituting a 'national' cinema. Evidence such as the Capra fan mail demonstrates that formations such as 'the nation' and 'the national audience' are never static or unchanging. Instead, the letters indicate the possibility for tracking the formation of and perceptions about the nation in particular periods through the interaction of audiences and the products of their popular culture. In doing so, we might, in fact, have to proceed on a case-by-case basis. *Meet John Doe*, then, may well stand out as a nationalist film and political tract produced by a cinema that many in the audience from the period believed to be derelict precisely in its production of national, politically significant artefacts.

Although the information can be difficult to locate, there exists a fair amount of evidence from the period of *Meet John Doe*'s release of the interactive nature of film production and film viewing, of the manner in which those making films solicited and made use of audience response – among other things, exhibitors' reports, preview cards, poll results, box-office figures and, of course, fan mail. Capra himself claimed in his autobiography that the mail he received about *Meet John Doe* after its initial, limited release helped him decide to modify the ending of the film for national distribution.[37] Thus we need to place any study of Hollywood production alongside an analysis of the reception texts produced by historically specific audiences. In particular, these texts help us understand not just the interpretations that some spectators made of the films that they saw, but also the charged, dynamic relationships between spectators and the film industry, the film celebrity and, perhaps most interestingly, other spectators.

I would like to thank Caren Kaplan for the intellectual, editorial and practical support she gave me during the preparation of several drafts of this essay; my thanks also to Richard de Cordova, for his invaluable comments on an earlier version of this essay.

Notes

1 26 June 1941, from Mrs Coate. All of the correspondence cited in this essay is from the Frank Capra Collection, housed at the Wesleyan University Cinema Archives in Middletown, Connecticut.

2 David Morley, *The 'Nationwide' Audience* (London: British Film Institute, 1980).

3 Janet Staiger, *Interpreting Films: Studies in the Historical Reception of American Cinema* (Princeton: Princeton University Press, 1992), ch. 6; Steven J. Ross, 'Struggles for the screen: workers, radicals, and the political uses of silent film', *American Historical Review*, vol. 96, no. 2 (1991), pp. 333–67.

4 Barbara Foley, *Radical Representations: Politics and Form in US Proletarian Fiction, 1929–1941* (Durham: Duke University Press, 1993).

5 See my article, ' "Compulsory" viewing for every citizen: *Mr Smith* and the rhetoric of reception', *Cinema Journal*, vol. 35, no. 2 (1996).

6 Alva Johnston, 'Capra shoots as he pleases', *The Saturday Evening Post*, 14 May 1938, p. 72.

7 Ibid.

8 Geoffrey T. Heltman, 'Profiles: thinker in Hollywood', *The New Yorker*, 24 February 1940, pp. 23–4.

9 I have read all of the *Meet John Doe* fan mail; those letters that I have not transcribed nevertheless correspond closely, in terms of concerns, interests and criticisms, to those that I have looked at most closely and that make up the letter sample used in this article. When I refer to the number of letters on a given topic. I mean the number that can be taken from the sample of letters that I have transcribed and studied the most carefully.

10 Frank Capra, *The Name Above the Title: an Autobiography* (New York: The MacMillan Company, 1971). Both quotes are taken from p. 136.

11 Ibid., pp. 303, 297.

12 13 June 1941, from David Stephens.

13 Undated, from Linda Schoen.

14 24 June 1941, from Joyce Eden.

15 'Textbooks brought to book', *Time*, 3 March 1941, pp. 39–40.

16 'Youth hear defense plea', *Los Angeles Times*, 7 March 1941, part 1 p. 12.

17 11 February 1941, from Mrs T. M. Cantwell; 29 March 1941, from Ezilda Marie Suton; 9 April 1941, from Mary Hagedorn; 17 March 1941, from Horace E. Levin.

18 'Hedda Hopper's Hollywood', *Los Angeles Times*, 2 March 1941, part III, p. 3; Edwin Schallert, '*Meet John Doe* hailed as Capra victory', *Los Angeles Times*, 13 March 1941, part 1, p. 16; David Platt, '*Meet John Doe* lets film audiences down', *The Daily Worker*, 15 March 1941, p. 7; *Hollywood News*, from the News and Feature Service, Warner Bros Studio, vol. VII, no. 13, 27 January 1941; 'Gary Cooper, Barbara Stanwyck star in Capra production *Meet John Doe*', in Warner Bros press book.

19 For promotional tie-in information, see, for example, '*John Doe* gets 4-city opening', *Motion Picture Herald*, 29 March 1941, p. 66.

20 Read Kendall, 'Stars, fans brave rain to attend gay film event', *Los Angeles Times*, 13 March 1941, part I, p. 16.

21 26 February 1941, from Howard V. C. Davis; 9 March 1941, from Maurine Robison; 19 August 1941, from Miss Grace Rasche.

22 13 June 1941, from E. C. Olson.

23 23 March 1941, from Ingeborg Tillisch.

24 13 March 1941, from M. Gluck.

25 14 May 1941, from Louis A. Meli; 9 April 1941, from Mary Hagedorn; 19 May 1941, from Mr and Mrs David Greenberg.

26 13 May 1941, from Charles H. Martin.

27 Undated, from George B. Nordman.

28 16 May 1941, Capra to Charles H. Martin.

29 Nick Browne, 'System of production/system of representation: industry context and ideological form in Capra's *Meet John Doe*', in Charles Wolfe (ed.), *Meet John Doe* (New Brunswick: Rutgers University Press, 1989), pp. 284–5.

30 13 March 1941, from M. Gluck: undated, from Keith Gordon.

31 All citations are from *Time* magazine: 'Of thee I sing', 24 February 1941, p. 55; 'Folk songs in the White House', 3 March 1941, p. 57; 'MBS Soapbox', 24 March 1941; 'Democracy on pedestals', 24 February 1941, p. 66.

32 All citations are from *Los Angeles Times*: 'Threatened demonstration at Kaltenborn talk fizzles', 5 March 1941, City News, p. 1; 'Eva [sic] Curie arrives in city', 7 March 1941, part II, pp. 1–2; 'Philip F. La Follette will speak Monday', 7 March 1941, part II, p. 2; ' "I Am an American" leaders selected', 7 March 1941, part II, p. 1.

33 'Get your tickets today for Foster mass meeting', *The Daily Worker*, 14 March 1941, p. 4.

34 See, for example, 27 February 1941, from Alida Ducker.

35 See, for example, 4 August 1941, from Bill McNutt.

36 For a discussion of the discourses of the New Deal, including both government policy and the work of the Lynds, see Gary Gerstle. 'The protean character of American liberalism', *American Historical Review*, vol. 99, no. 4 (1994), pp. 1043–73.

37 Capra, *The Name Above the Title*, p. 305.

PART IV

Films and Filmmakers

Chapter 10

Molly Haskell

HOWARD HAWKS (1980)

Editors' Introduction

For contemporary film scholars, *auteurism* is viewed as a quaint but necessary first step in the evolution of a proper, academic film history. Merging biography, textual analysis, and all too frequently a hefty dose of journalistic subjectivity, the initial practitioners of this method – François Truffaut, Jean-Luc Godard, Eric Rohmer, and Claude Chabrol in France; Ian Cameron and Robin Wood in the U.K.; and Andrew Sarris in the U.S. – firmly established authorship as a key to the argument for "film as art," which was a necessary battle to be won in the 1960s and 1970s.

In this essay on Howard Hawks, published in one of the seminal *auteurist* collections, Richard Roud's 1980 *Cinema: A Critical Dictionary,* Molly Haskell, the author of *From Reverence to Rape: The Treatment of Women in the Movies,* examines the work of a director whose career seems at once to defy and exemplify the strictures of *auteur* criticism; a director renowned for his ability to get along in studio Hollywood, a director whose *oeuvre* does not so clearly evince a stylistic signature and/or ideological/thematic preoccupation. Haskell acknowledges "the squeamishness we feel in applying to Hawks words like 'poet' and 'artist' " and yet upon close reading insists on the presence of a stylistic and thematic consistency: the preference for group shots, for example, "themes of male-female competition, sexual inversion and the struggle between adolescence and maturity. . . ." Providing a model for a more academic *auteur* scholarship – carefully surveying the available literature at the start of the essay and then closely examining specific moments in a broad range of films – Haskell profiles a film director whose peculiar genius was exemplified in an ability to maintain an artistic integrity despite a system rigged to undermine it.

Suggested Reading

Peter Wollen, "The Auteur Theory," in *Signs and Meaning in the Cinema* (Bloomington: University of Illinois Press, 1972); Robin Wood, *Howard Hawks* (London: BFI, 1981); and Andrew Sarris, *The American Cinema: 1929–1968* (NY: EP Dutton, 1968).

GODARD, IN ONE OF those oracular utterances which at first seem merely perverse but gradually sink in with the authority of truth, once referred to Howard Hawks (1896–1977), quite casually, as 'the greatest American artist'. 'Artist', of course, is precisely the word that we Hawksians, culturally on the defensive as we are accustomed to being, would hesitate to apply to him. Hawks is in the curious position of having attracted more buff attention in the last ten years than almost any American director (thus making it almost impossible to say anything new about him), while remaining outside the purview of official culture. As late as 1961, Andrew Sarris could write that Hawks was 'the least known and least appreciated giant in American cinema'. Although the neglect has been partially corrected by a number of books published since then (by Jean-Claude Missiaen and Jean A. Gili, respectively, in French, and, in English, Peter Bogdanovich's 1962 monograph, Robin Wood's critical study and Joseph McBride's anthology *Focus on Howard Hawks*) and by countless exegetical (and feminist!) essays in the little film magazines, Sarris' statement still holds true in the larger context of Anglo-American culture.

Generally placed third along with Ford and Hitchcock in the triumvirate of the classical Hollywood commercial directors (perhaps the Adler to their Jung and Freud), Hawks has lagged behind in garnering those laurels of official culture—American Film Institute dinners and honorary university degrees—with which their efforts have been crowned; and his parity with them has yet to be conceded by critics outside the premises of *auteur*ism. Many of the British fail to respond to the Hawks mystique at all, while those American critics like Manny Farber and Pauline Kael who love one or another of his films—and use them as a club to attack 'academics' who 'take the fun out of movies'—resist the attempt to analyse Hawks' work in terms of a consistent *oeuvre* that sets forth, in the alternating heroic and mock-heroic terms from which it is inseparable, a vision of man as a ramrod of courage and tenacity, a squiggle in the margin of the universe.

Certainly, once one has identified with the intuitively American quality of Hawks' films, as expressed in themes of male-female competition, sexual inversion and the struggle between adolescence and maturity for a grown man's soul, it is hard to resist the idea that the semaphore of our native body language is being transmitted in every maniacal, offensive-or-defensive gesture of his characters to get attention. And once one has realized that the same man directed *Scarface* (1932) and *I Was a Male War Bride* (U.K.: *You Can't Sleep Here*, 1949), *Ceiling Zero* (1936) and *Man's Favorite Sport?* (1964), in other words, once one has accepted the interdependence of comedy and tragedy in his work, it is hard to miss the deeper implications, the picture of man poised, comically or heroically, against an antagonistic nature, a nothingness as devoid of meaning as Samuel Beckett's, but determined none the less to act out his destiny, to assert mind against mindlessness.

The squeamishness we feel in applying to Hawks words like 'poet' and 'artist' which sit easily on the shoulders of his colleagues in the Pantheon has less, I think, to do with Hawks' status than with the connotations of the term (artist or poet) itself, particularly as it has come to be used in modern society. (Often what seems gnomic and perverse in Godard's paradoxes is the reverse: a return of a word to its purest classical meaning, in this case to a pre-Platonic wholeness.) Since the Socratic split between mind and body, the function of the artist, whether he himself was exalted or down-graded, has corresponded to the spiritual side of man, the contemplative function being, by implication, superior to the active mode of life. Christianity, with its emphasis on the individual and his own immortality, strengthened this view, and the 'death of God' in the twentieth century consolidated the artist's position as the high-priest of subjectivity in a world in which only the self could be known.

To the figure of the artist as mystic, madman, symbolist, solipsist, imagist or theologian, Hawks bears little resemblance, either physically (as a dapper, athletic, well-bred, gregarious man-about-Hollywood) or philosophically. Although Hawks' universe is a Godless one, his roots are more ancient: he harks back to a pre-Platonic, pre-Christian world in which man (even in his anthropomorphic gods) was the ultimate creation and measure of all things. In a world in which only nature was eternal, his activities on earth, as recounted by poets and historians, were his only claim to immortality. In this sense it is not Ford but Hawks who is the modern counterpart of Homer, or perhaps Herodotus, a teller of tales describing what men *are* through what they *do*. Performance counts for more than intention; performance *reveals* intention instead of—in the manner of works in the modern *Zeitgeist*—concealing or contradicting it. Through cinematic conventions that most directly connect appearance and action, and through his own ever more sophisticated use of gesture and voice as well as 'deeds', Hawks' characters define themselves psychologically while carrying forward the story from which their status is inseparable.

In Hawks, the pioneer hubris, and brashness and naïveté, of the American converges with the austere, man-centred morality of ancient Greece. There is no afterlife either beyond or within man, no spiritual dimension to excuse physical disability—although this is somewhat modified in the later films. Even conscience is external—it consists of the admiration and approval of one's peers, hence the preference for group shots over shots of individuals and the reluctance, contrary to the practice of Ford or Preminger, to isolate one member from the group by the use of an overhead angle or positioning within the frame. In his tales of man struggling against the environment, in his odysseys (for even when the locales are stationary, the films are journeys) of fraternal bands in remote places with only themselves to rely on, his is a vision of man (and woman) stripped of ecclesiastical significance, self-created (to the point where he omits not only God, but mothers) and evolved to a precarious ascendancy over nature and animals which he must struggle to maintain. But the hubris of the Hawks protagonist leads not to tragedy but to comedy: the pratfall is the equivalent of the fall from grace or from the gods' favour; the humiliation, in the behavioural idiom of one of the three or four best directors of comedy in the history of film, corresponds to the tragedian's retribution, and performs the same service of exposing the limits of man's powers. As critics have come more and more to realize, a separation of Hawks' films into comedies and tragedies (or melodramas) fails to suggest the degree to which the two veins are intermingled—e.g. Jacques Rivette has remarked on the theme of degeneration that makes *Monkey Business* (1952) so dark and disconcerting a comedy, and so difficult to laugh at. And their intermingling provides the depth of vision and the sense of proportion that are the essence of classical design and morality.

If, as Rivette has claimed, Hawks is concerned not with examining the truths of a particular society but with the 'adventure of the intellect', it is the intellect as expressed in men's actions which like those of the Greeks, in Hannah Arendt's words, 'interrupt the circular movement of daily life'. Hawks' eye-level camera and axial cuts are the most direct expression of the film-maker's loyalty to the men (or the characters) themselves and to their actions rather than to an artistic enterprise which subordinates them; nor is he concerned with his own idealization of the man of action in the Hemingway or Mailer mould. His is a fidelity to what the Greeks called *praxis* (actions or deeds) as opposed to *poesis* (fabrication). He shows, Godard wrote, 'a greater awareness than anyone else of what the cinema can glory in, and a refusal to profit from this (as I would accuse Orson Welles of doing in *Macbeth*, and Robert Bresson in *Journal d'un Curé de Campagne*) to create anti-cinema, but instead, through a more rigorous knowledge of its limits, fixing its basic laws'.

The ascertainment of these laws was more gradual in Hawks than we generally realize, a matter of growth, of greater and greater daring sustained by an accompanying maturity. Because of the remarkable consistency of Hawks' films even from the beginning, and the degree of artistic and stylistic control he exercised over almost all his projects, we are likely to underestimate the evolution in his work, particularly in his vision of women, and his mellowing attitude towards the (once all-male) group, marked by a relaxation of the criteria of admission to include freaks and outsiders, cripples and women.

From home to Hollywood, Hawks had less distance to travel than either Ford or Hitchcock. His family had moved from Indiana to California while he was a child, and after prep school (Exeter) and college (Cornell), with stints as a stock-car racer and airplane builder during vacations, and as a flight commander during the war, Hawks and his two brothers—the literal, real-life prototype of the Hawksian fraternity—went into the film industry. He worked as an independent producer for two years (from 1922 to 1924), then spent two years in the Paramount story department where among forty or fifty films he worked on the scripts of *Quicksands* (1927), *Tiger Love* (1924) and *The Dressmaker from Paris* (1925). When he went into directing, Hawks, often his own producer, continued to write part or all of his scripts, or submit story ideas. The correct apportionment of screenwriting credit is, as usual, difficult, not just because of the Screenwriters Guild ruling denying directors credit for anything less than fifty per cent of the script, but because of the casual informality of contributions in the early days. Hawks has told tales of the way he and Ben Hecht used to call each other up and confer on scripts—in a *Cahiers* interview some years ago he said he worked on the script of *Underworld* (1927) and actually invented the name 'Feathers' which, because it cropped up in *Rio Bravo* (1959), has generally been credited to Jules Furthman, co-author of both screenplays. In the same interview, Hawks also claimed to have contributed some dialogue to *Gone With the Wind* (as indeed, who did not?), during the phase in which it was being directed by his pal Victor Fleming.

Figure 10.1 Cary Grant and Katharine Hepburn in *Bringing Up Baby*: 'Hawks' genius consists of bipolar impulses; thus his ability to understand, and portray, in men, the temptation to regress, to succumb, to be passive, to be taken care of . . . and, in women, the opposing need to initiate, act, dominate'

At any rate, the sound of Hawks' voice—and he is a remarkably verbal man for an 'action' director—is unmistakable and pervasive, going beyond the obvious: the songs that provide unity and catharsis at a crucial time in the adventure films, the names and recurrent situations and gestures (the symbolic use of cigarettes, for example), to a feeling for character which, while rooted in sex-role expectations, goes beyond these to the reversals that are, as much as the mixed moods, the source of humour and peril in Hawks' view of a world precariously divided between the male and female principles. The masculine and feminine instincts are locked in perennial combat. A consummately Hawksian scene is the sexual duel that begins *His Girl Friday* (1940), a brilliantly choreographed and edited sequence in which the balance changes every second: between the characters, as first Cary Grant, then Rosalind Russell gains the upper hand; between the prevailing strategies, as each uses 'masculine' tactics (physical assault) and 'feminine' wiles (pleading and wheedling); and in the alternating tone of the scene, from emotional (close-ups) to comic (medium shots).

Beneath the vigorous and sometimes willed virility of the action pictures, Hawks' genius consists of bipolar impulses; thus his ability to understand, and portray, in men, the temptation to regress, to succumb, to be passive, to be taken care of (Cary Grant in *Bringing Up Baby*, 1938, and *I Was a Male War Bride*) and, in women, the opposing need to initiate, act, dominate. The perilousness of Hawks' world, the sense of a cosmic (and comic) disequilibrium, comes from the problematic nature of sexual differentiation, an issue which is never completely resolved. There is an evolution: the 'feminine' side that is viewed by the young man as dangerous or debilitating (the 'weakening' effect of the emotions) is gradually welcomed as a crucial element in adult men's lives; and the aggressive side of woman becomes less and less incompatible with femininity.

The 'Hawksian woman' does not really blossom until the late 30s. Though often found in Hawksian situations, the women of his 20s films are closer to the general stereotypes prevailing in silent film than to his own gutsy, deep-voiced (voice is important in Hawks' women), modern and very American heroines. His first film, *The Road to Glory* (made in 1926, and no relation to the 1936 war film), starred May McAvoy in a tragedy about a blind girl. Possibly Hawks' most downbeat film, it indicates something of his mood and bent before he determined that tragedy 'wasn't what audiences wanted to see [as he reported later to a *Cahiers* interviewer] so, in my next film, I changed the tone'. It happens that, in his own life, Hawks had both a sister and a brother who died young, the latter in a plane crash while making a film. Obviously these tragedies—particularly the death of the brother which is repeated in various forms and through various surrogates in film after film—had a tremendous effect on Hawks. We can see the influence on his work, beginning with the tendency, in the early melodramas, towards a maudlin, fatalistic self-pity, but gradually growing, through an objectification and sublimation of these emotions, into an acceptance, a wider world view in which the maudlin and the self-mocking are subtly balanced.

But the silent films, callow and occasionally charming, have none of the qualities we associate with the later Hawks. Although from a technical point of view he revealed a sure hand from the outset, it was a hand guided by the masters of the day, by Lubitsch (in *Paid to Love*, 1927), or Murnau (in *A Girl in Every Port*, 1928). *Fig Leaves* (1926) is thematically interesting in that it pits Adam against Eve, archetypal man against archetypal woman, in a parable that skips from Paradise to the present. In the timelessness of the central gag—Eve needing 'something to wear'—Hawks shows how little he believes in the progressive theory of human history. Hawks is concerned not with the manners or social customs of a contemporary present, but with his characters' relation to eternity. Here is the same time span that will be metaphorically retraced, through the 'youth potion', in his devolutionary comedy *Monkey Business* twenty-five years later, or in the regression to the Garden of Eden in *Man's Favorite Sport?*. History is more of a joke than a monument, a circle rather than a straight line, from which gravity's backward pull is a thousand times stronger than the forward pull of 'progress'.

Of all the silents, only *A Girl in Every Port* has sustained more than marginal interest. The plot, in which a beautiful circus entertainer (played by Louise Brooks) threatens to break up a beautiful male friendship, presents the prototype triangle of the Hawks male adventure film, but the movie's high reputation with the French seems based on the presence of Brooks rather than on any inherent virtues in the film itself. And Brooks is far less interesting here than in her films with Pabst, or even her non-Hawks Paramount films. Hawks was not really at home with the *femme fatale*; he was at ease with the overtly sensual woman only when, as with Lauren Bacall in *To Have and Have Not* (1944), or Angie Dickinson in *Rio Bravo*, he could play around with their sensuality, suggest a kind of gamesmanship that was the equivalent of a man's self-deprecating bravery.

The melodramas of the 30s present the ideal of male heroism and self-sufficiency in its purest form: men at war, facing death daily as fliers (*The Dawn Patrol*, 1930, *Ceiling Zero*), soldiers (*The Road to Glory*), torpedo boat pilots (*Today We Live*, 1933), lapsed heroes trying to redeem themselves or expiate guilt by taking a friend's place on a suicide mission; men engaged in high-risk commercial ventures like tuna fishing (*Tiger Shark*, 1932), commercial aviation (*Only Angels Have Wings*, 1939), auto racing (*The Crowd Roars*, 1932), organized crime (*Scarface*), taking outrageous risks without questioning the ground rules, attracted by what Robin Wood has called 'the lure of irresponsibility'; men ruined, separated, betrayed, goaded to their death by women. In the framework of the early action films, the woman who disrupts a man's friendship, or who precipitates his downfall, is more symbolic than real: a projection of the grown-up world—of civilization, home, family, adult responsibility—that is hateful to the adolescent and inhibiting to the free play of his fantasies of adventure and omnipotence.

But the women to whom Hawks eventually gravitates are not 'killjoys', not hearth-and-home types, but women who (for better or worse, and feminists are divided on this point) could get along in a man's world. Women at this early stage (and in this Hawks is no different from other male artists—Renoir, for example) are fantasy figures who conveniently bear the brunt of youth's disillusionment.

Significantly, the *femme fatale* in *The Dawn Patrol*, Hawks' first sound film, is not even present in person. Her malfeasance—a break in the friendship of flight commander Neil Hamilton and Richard Barthelmess, his second in command—has been accomplished off-screen. The 'woman problem' is introduced to intensify the conflict between the man in authority who must send fliers out to their death each day (the film takes place at an American base on the French front lines during the First World War), and the intermediary who pleads for mercy. The irony and the ambiguity come when Barthelmess replaces Hamilton upon the latter's promotion, and is obliged to send the kid brother of his best friend (Douglas Fairbanks, Jr) on a fatal mission.

The retreat to the all-male world, as well as the projection of woman as an evil force, suggests a fear of the feminine side of oneself—a side that is especially, and delightfully, prominent in Hawks. Manny Farber astutely commented on 'Hawks' uncelebrated female touch', and it is as much responsible for the mixed moods of his films as for the graceful movements of his actors.

If the dialogue is occasionally stilted and the sound crude, the flying sequences of *The Dawn Patrol* are tremendously exciting, and there is already the strong sense of contrast between the two worlds: the exhilaration and danger of the action world, and the comforting womblike enclosure of the base. But the relation between the two is paradoxical: for if the action world entails the greatest risk to life, it also provides, in the submergence of the self in a womanless world, a cathartic release; while in the interior world, for all its physical security, there is greater friction between people, in relationships which are complicated, explicitly or implicitly, by women. The two worlds are more deftly threaded together in *Tiger Shark*, where the extraordinary fishing sequences are directly related to the tragic Ahab-like character of Edward G. Robinson, and the rivalry over the woman (played by Zita Johann) culminating in Robinson's death coincides with that other Hawksian theme of the superiority of the 'whole' man over the mutilated one. Robinson, old, unattractive and without an arm, loses the girl to the young and handsome Richard Arlen (just as Robinson loses Miriam Hopkins to Joel McCrea in *Barbary Coast*, 1935) in a ruthless application of the law of survival in which, as Andrew Sarris has pointed out, woman is the equivalent of God and nature in arbitrating the process of natural selection. And yet, once again, Hawks seems to be projecting onto woman something that he himself feels—a distaste for the ugly, the maimed, the unfit. In *The Big Sky* (1952) the fingerless Kirk Douglas must lose the Indian princess (Elizabeth Threatt) to Dewey Martin, and yet it is not the girl who makes the decision but Douglas himself, sending Martin back in the end to remain with her on the reservation.

The bond between brothers or brother-surrogates is the bond of emotional or blood kinship (and thus the brother and sister in *Scarface* are analogous to the brothers in *The Crowd Roars*), a rapport between people who understand and are at ease with each other instinctively rather than by intellectual or emotional effort, who come together without the tension created by sexual attraction/antagonism. The girl in *Ceiling Zero* hugs her confederate Pat O'Brien, and shakes hands with her boy friend. Hawks directs scenes of action and robust affection with the utmost fluidity but is awkward in love scenes, like the culminating one in *Barbary Coast*, in which he cuts nervously between, and away from, Hopkins and McCrea. But when the sexual antagonism is confronted, or transmuted into the artful chaos of the comedies, it creates an emotional field that is in some ways richer and more dynamic than the relatively straightforward, simple and overt expression of love among 'likes'.

Like the Platonic (as opposed to physical) homosexuality that Robert Graves criticizes in *The White Goddess*, or the incestuous pull that D. H. Lawrence finds in Poe, it is ultimately a form of narcissism, the self-fixation of man unable or unwilling to acknowledge the Other, or take the necessary steps (ranging from an acknowledgment of dependency to a willingness to be *depended upon*) to understanding this creature who plays the moon to his sun. Both the glorification of the two brothers in *The Crowd Roars* and the shared doom of Paul Muni and Ann Dvorak in *Scarface* are means of isolating them from heterogeneous humanity. But perhaps this morbid fatalism is as necessary to the gangster film as it was to Poe's horror tales. At any rate, from cameraman Lee Garmes' long tracking shot that defines the underworld atmosphere of gangland Chicago, through Ben Hecht's tight script and the memorable ensemble acting of people like Karen Morley, Osgood Perkins, George Raft, Boris Karloff and Vince Barnett, *Scarface* still stands as the definitive gangster film, as violent (if not as bloody) as any made since. Paul Muni's Toni Camonte is an early model of the gangster as hero, and his ambition that of the American dream perverted (with scriptwriter Hecht carrying over the sign, 'The World is Yours', from *Underworld*) in what is essentially a Hawksian tragedy of a *hamartia* that is both intellectual (hubris) and physical (the scar), leading inevitably to doom.

In *Ceiling Zero*, his brilliant adaptation of the Frank Wead play—with James Cagney as the daredevil flier and Pat O'Brien as the boss enmeshed in bureaucracy—the worlds of action and enclosure, of women and men, of comedy and tragedy, are integrated to a degree unusual even for Hawks. This is partly in the nature of the property—*not* its origins as a play (what was to prevent Hawks from shooting aerial footage, as in *The Dawn Patrol?*), but the plot, which concerns a defection from responsibility. Cagney, cocksure and irresistible, a flier of the old order that Hawks admires, fakes illness to stay behind and date a cute girl flier named Tommy (June Travis). One of the first examples of the Hawksian woman, she generates an excitement that, as a bright and active woman as obsessed with her job as any man, is beyond the dimensions of her role. In an even smaller part, Isabel Jewell, as one of the fliers' wives, begins as a conventional nag and killjoy but turns, with her husband's death, into a figure out of Greek tragedy.

Ceiling Zero is consummately cinematic without ever 'going outside' in the usual misbegotten manner of adaptations or even of some of Hawks' movies. Here the momentum is achieved almost entirely through a contrast of personalities—the genial but phlegmatic O'Brien (whose minimal gestures correspond to his hamstrung position) and Cagney's non-stop motion as Dizzy Davin, one of his most beguilingly kinetic roles. (There is also an attention to instructional details like control panels that is more than ritualistic.)

Although *Ceiling Zero* is technically a tragedy and *Twentieth Century* (1934) technically a comedy, the mixture of the two veins in both of them—in Cagney's hell-raising personality and the horror it precipitates, in Carole Lombard's zaniness and the chaos on which it thrives—creates a similar duality of mood and suggests the kinship of disparate genres in Hawks. In the Hecht-MacArthur adaptation of Charles Bruce Milholland's Broadway play, Twentieth Century is the name of the train which carries the director (John Barrymore) and his star. But it is also the name of the force of unleashed energy—call it woman, man or modern society, call it a love, potion, sexual confusion or hallucinogenic drugs—that confounds, overwhelms, exasperates, humiliates, exalts Hawks' characters in their advance/retreat through the screwball comedies, through the madhouse worlds of the theatre (*Twentieth Century*), a suburban Connecticut jungle (*Bringing Up Baby*), a newspaper office (*His Girl Friday*), a sanctuary of lexicographers (*Ball of Fire*, 1942, and the musical remake, *A Song Is Born*, 1948), an army base in France (*I Was a Male War Bride*) and a science laboratory (*Monkey Business*). It is the force that bears Cary Grant aloft—on a rising drawbridge in *I Was a Male War Bride* or atop the scaffolding of a dinosaur in *Bringing Up Baby*—the force that hurls Rosalind Russell back into the dog-eat-dog jungle of the newspaper world in *His Girl Friday*. It is a force that, while remaining outside man and his control, is as vertiginous as anything in Hitchcock: life, seen comically, as a runaway roller coaster, rather than life, seen pessimistically, as a runaway *id*. And yet the two are not so far apart; and the external chaos in Hawks' films often seems to correspond to, or act as a catalyst for, some deep need of one of his characters.

As in Hitchcock, the bitterness, even the nastiness, is masked by the charm of the actors. Hawks' genius for casting and directing is nowhere more apparent than in the comedies, where the choice of performers and the comic framework permit him to show people guilty of the most infamous crimes against human sensitivity, who not only get away with it but actually enchant us in the process. But the zaniness—or so it seems in the women Hawks chooses—is something of a defence mechanism, a cover for an underlying vulnerability. Susan in *Bringing Up Baby* and Lily Garland in *Twentieth Century*, so headstrong and self-reliant, are socially and sexually insecure. (Ann Sheridan's Catherine Gates in *I Was a Male War Bride* is professionally competent, but a sexual dunce.) They don't know how to 'play games' and in allying themselves with the forces of nature, in hurling themselves at the opposite sex like hurricanes, they increase their chances of survival in a man's world. But the moment they turn into pure whimsical aggression their targets reveal themselves to be not male supremacists, stalwart and secure, but specimens of the opposite sex as faltering and insecure as they are. In the safari metaphors of the comedies—Paula Prentiss tracking down and exposing Rock Hudson's phony fisherman in a California hunting resort; Katharine Hepburn and Cary Grant ploughing up a lawn in search of a fossil (and Grant winding up in a net); the lexicographers in *Ball of Fire* entangling themselves in the briars and brambles of Sugarpuss O'Shea's slang underworld; Cary Grant and Ann Sheridan on their circuitous mission through

Germany—the bravado, fear and sexual uncertainty of the American dating ritual are comically exposed.

Grasping the principle that a fundamental sobriety is essential to comedy, Hawks intensifies his characters' seriousness until it becomes a kind of maniacal self-absorption, the obsessiveness that is the madness of the screwball characters. The normal person is someone who relates to others, who, like John Wayne in the later Westerns, can adjust his tempo to theirs without compromising himself. The breakneck pacing of the comedies comes from the fact that in a sense no one is sane. Cary Grant's palaeontologist in *Bringing Up Baby* is, in Hawks' view of the pure scientist, as abnormal as Hepburn's country-club playgirl. Rosalind Russell is headed for suffocation and slow death in her prospective marriage to Ralph Bellamy in *His Girl Friday*. Ginger Rogers' understanding wife, in *Monkey Business*, is full of hidden resentments which emerge, like truth in alcohol, once she has taken the drug. Two madnesses must collide to shake the male-female antagonists into some kind of awareness of each other, of themselves and of a mutual destiny that, though problematical, is defiantly not that of the average suburban couple.

The world and tone of *Ball of Fire*, largely because of the screenplay by Billy Wilder and Charles Brackett, is more 'normal' and less anguished; the invasion of the male sanctuary and the collision of the two worlds are gentle, almost quaintly comical, with none of the sharp antagonisms and embarrassments that colour the other comedies. Except for Gary Cooper, who is protected by his complete befuddlement, the men are all older, and their malehood less vulnerable, and Barbara Stanwyck herself is mellower and more womanly, according to a sophisticated European conception of women that is closer to Wilder than to Hawks. This, and the resonance of Gregg Toland's photography of the interiors of the Gingerbread-Victorian house, creates a more soothing and less disconcerting atmosphere, a humour that is never forced and is less abrasive than that of the other screwball comedies, but which lacks the quality of intellectual excitement and tension that makes them so audaciously exhilarating.

Another comparison which strikingly illuminates the uniquely Hawksian view is the difference in treatment between *Red River* (1948) and Raoul Walsh's version of what is basically the same story in *The Tall Men*. Not only is Walsh's visualization of the cattle drive itself superior to Hawks', in its breath-takingly lyrical shots of animals and a countryside which assume a life of their own apart from men, but some might find in Walsh's relaxed attitude towards women a more mature vision of the sexes. The Jane Russell character is more of a companion than a threat, and even the distracting influence she represents is treated with affection rather than resentment. She is bawdy, sexy and tough, and yet it is the women in *Red River*—Coleen Gray as Fen, the woman left behind by John Wayne, and Joanne Dru as Tess, the Fen-surrogate who falls in love with Matthew (Montgomery Clift)—who are crucial in the elaboration of the intense primal conflicts which make this a greater film. The fraternal relationship between Clark Gable and Cameron Mitchell in *The Tall Men* is almost too good to be true, whereas the conflict between Wayne and Clift allows Hawks to explore what is less an Oedipal problem than one of growing old, allowing him to experience simultaneously the dual identity of the younger and the older man, and ease the passage from one to the other.

In the 40s, there is a *détente* with women, prefigured, perhaps, in the reconciliation which concludes *Only Angels Have Wings*, in which Grant, having lost his closest friend (Thomas Mitchell), is united with Jean Arthur, and in the close mother–son relationship of *Sergeant York* (1941), with Margaret Wycherly as one of the few major mother figures in all of Hawks. There is still, in *Only Angels Have Wings*, a strong streak of self-pity disguised as tough indifference, but within the fogbound base of the civil aviators in South America, one of Hawks' moodiest and most romantic fantasies unfolds. Rita Hayworth is a more

Figure 10.2 Humphrey Bogart and Lauren Bacall in *The Big Sleep*: 'it was Hawks' idea to pair Bogart and Bacall, and although he must be credited as the originator of their best roles, they did bring something of their own to the films, a personal chemistry, to create the one truly and magically equal couple in all of Hawks' cinema'

sympathetic version of the *femme fatale*, but Jean Arthur, lacking the worldly independence of later heroines in the same situation, is too craven in her availability, and she makes one wince in embarrassment to the tune of woman as second fiddle. The use of woman is again symbolic—she is the 'emotional' element—so that although the film's cast and setting prove almost irresistible, one almost prefers the all-male world of *Air Force* (1943), in which Hawks takes the ethic of the group—and the submergence of individuals in a common purpose (the adventures of a B-17 crew during and after Pearl Harbor)—to an almost Fordian extreme, the point at which the fliers become one with their mission or, in this case, their machine.

It was Hawks' idea to pair Humphrey Bogart and Lauren Bacall in *To Have and Have Not* and *The Big Sleep* (1946), and although he must be credited as the originator of their best roles, they did bring something of their own to the films, a personal chemistry, to create the one truly and magically equal couple in all of Hawks' cinema—a rarity in any art form where the personality of one person, the artist, necessarily dominates his sexual opposite. This is not to say that Bacall somehow escapes being a male fantasy, but she pulls her own weight—verbally, professionally, sexually—to a much greater degree than most movie heroines; she's tough, smart, feminine, neither virgin nor whore, and if she makes no bones about loving Bogey, she somehow gains the upper hand by having the confidence to be open, funny and honest. She not only isn't a threat to male supremacy but, in *To Have and Have Not*, she represents the alternative—heterosexual pairing of equals—that is, finally and unequivocally, *both* adult *and* fun.

Like so many of those behind-the-scene accidents of chemistry whose effects on movies we can never fully know or measure, her success as a character can probably be attributed to

Hawks' *dislike* for Bogart, and his consequent identification with Bacall. 'You are about the most insolent man on the screen,' Hawks is quoted as having said to Bogart before *The Big Sleep*, 'and I'm going to make the girl a little more insolent than you are.' Thus whereas before the Bacall–Bogart movies, and even after them (in *The Big Sky, Rio Bravo* and the 1967 *El Dorado*), the woman would take a back seat in the friendship between two men, in *To Have and Have Not* they are completely on a par, her work corresponding to his. Although Walter Brennan, as the loyal but enfeebled sidekick, will reappear in the later films, the peer comrade whose counterpart will be Dean Martin or Robert Mitchum is here played by Bacall.

The interests of melodrama and comedy are perfectly fused in the sexual atmosphere of *The Big Sleep*, beginning with the initiation of Marlowe, the detective, into the hothouse/greenhouse world of General Sternwood, a scene which comes not out of Faulkner (who worked on the screenplay) but straight out of Chandler. To the assorted dames of the author, Hawks added a few, creating the sense of a world run and manipulated by women (the two Sternwood sisters run their father, Dorothy Malone runs a bookstore, Peggy Knudsen fronts for the gangsters, and an unbilled woman runs a taxi!) that would recur only in *Rio Lobo* (1970).

Hawks was ahead of his time, not only in a certain cavalier indifference to plot connections, but in his sophistication about drugs (in the spaced-out Martha Vickers character and in plot mysteries which a drug-based operation explains) and homosexuality (Bogart does a 'fairy' imitation in *The Big Sleep*; back in *Bringing Up Baby*, Grant actually used the word 'gay'). Such references, so apparently glib, are more central than their casual introduction would indicate to the themes of Hawks' work, to the sense of complex and conflicting character tendencies and the struggle to maintain an equilibrium which is felt less as a natural inclination than as a social and moral necessity. Thus, however simple Hawks' idea of maleness, or femaleness, may seem to a modern, liberated, technological society, it is a moral, existential view, and if the professionalism that becomes the 'solution' to character is simple, the urges behind it are not.

How much more heroic is Bogart's Marlowe, who turns into an avenger of a minor character (Elisha Cook, Jr), than Elliott Gould's Marlowe (in Altman's *The Long Goodbye*), who ignores the savage mutilation of a minor character to pursue his own virtue-enhancing quest. And whereas Altman's hero is set up as the one nearly pure knight in a corrupt world, the division between the pure and the impure, the attractive and the unattractive, is less clear in the Hawksian universe; Bogart's Marlowe never asks for special consideration the way the ironic, self-deprecating Gould's does; he is lost in the mist in his genuine 40s car. Hawks sticks closer to the level of his characters, closer to the studio back-lot dirt to which Altman feels so comfortably superior.

That Hawks feels at once the difficulty and the importance of heterosexual coupling becomes explicitly clear in *The Big Sky*, when after the trapping expedition Kirk Douglas sends Dewey Martin back to his Indian wife. The dialectic between emotions and obligations, between natural inclination and socially correct resolution, has never been expressed in quite such mutually exclusive terms. A situation which Lubitsch might have concluded with a triangular 'design for living' is resolved in a coercive either/or manner to signal a young man's coming of age, weaning himself from a father-figure who has exercised far too dominating an influence on him. The act of the will by which he fulfils both his conjugal and filial debts becomes, at least theoretically, a triumphant synthesis. The Indian princess, denied the power of (English) speech, is the most physical of Hawks' heroines and establishes (and secures) her identity not only by her expertise as a guide, but by keeping her husband on the reservation rather than following him as a chattel in *his* world.

From *The Big Sky* onward, including films like *Land of the Pharaohs* (1955) and *Hatari!* (1962), the group is mixed, and the struggle itself becomes communal rather than individual.

The youthful all-male platoons and patrols give way to heterodox collectives of widely varying ages, who are engaged in a primal struggle to assert themselves against an indifferent nature. Through his John Wayne surrogate, Hawks begins to delegate authority to the younger generation or (as in *Red Line 7000*, 1965) turns the film over to them. It's a long way from Toni Camonte's egocentric motto and the driving, jabbing, angular world of *Scarface* to the pastel, end-of-day (but no less violent) world of *Rio Lobo*, with a wounded John Wayne hobbling along, supported by a pretty but unmemorable ingénue. But before this dissemination of power, there is one last gunfighter duel, only the gunfighters are gold-diggers, and they aren't men, but women.

Gentlemen Prefer Blondes, which seemed completely immersed in 50s garishness when it appeared in 1953, looks somewhat more sceptical today—a musical that is as close to satire as Hawks' films ever get on the nature (and perversions) of sexual relations in America, particularly in the mammary-mad 50s. As the Dean Martin and John Wayne of the transatlantic liner (arrayed in the most violently clashing purples and reds that Technicolor could muster), Marilyn Monroe and Jane Russell have not only the biggest knockers in the West (a monumentality to which the ship's passengers pay hushed tribute as they pass by) but the best relationship in the film. Russell defends Monroe against her critics, and Monroe loves Russell in return. The men in their lives consist of a rich old sugar daddy (Charles Coburn, in a switch from his customary benevolent paternal roles), a precocious child (George Winslow), an effeminate fiancé (Tommy Noonan) and an ostensibly normal suitor (Eliott Reid) who turns out to be a spy. Hawks totally transforms the original—a Broadway musical adapted from the Anita Loos novel—by making a mythic link between greed and sexual freakishness, and creating a whole world which revolves on a principle of unnatural sexuality. There is the magnificent gag with the porthole in which Monroe's protruding head perches atop an elongated blanketed torso concealing little Winslow. He croaks complaints while Coburn caresses his extended hand and Monroe tries desperately to 'control' her body, in a hilarious three-way image of sexual short-circuitry. The other biting, brilliant commentary on sexual cross-purposes is, of course, the song number in which Russell, surrounded by a corps of body-building athletes too intent on toning themselves up to notice her, sings 'Is there anyone here for love?'

The question as to whether Russell represents 'normal' or excessive sexual drives is answered in the ambiguity with which Hawks perceives Monroe and Russell as filling their roles as sex goddesses. Hawks has pointed, in interviews, to the irony of Russell marrying her high-school boyfriend and settling into domesticity in private life and of Monroe being a wallflower at a party with no one to drive her home. This sense of incongruity is felt at the heart of the sexual exaggeration and masquerade. In a funny but truly pessimistic ending, Russell finally gives up on finding anything like a normal relationship and joins Monroe as a mock-blonde, opting for gold over diamonds, securing her future against a sexist tradition.

It is a tradition to which Hawks himself is not altogether immune, not just in the ethic of his films, but in his choice of actresses, who reflect the sexual taste of the man as much as the professional criteria of the director. Men like Grant and Wayne appeared over and over again, accumulating character lines, gaining resonance with familiarity, being allowed to grow old. But, with the exception of Bacall, his women appeared only once, carrying the implication that having once starred, a woman had had her day and, like the aftermath of a love affair, was now 'used'. Hawks gravitated to a certain kind of woman and coached her to conform to a taste, expressed once in a *Cahiers* interview, for a woman who would look young but *seem* older. Thus if Angie Dickinson, sensual and active, womanly and direct, is one of his most exciting heroines (in *Rio Bravo*), she is also the impossible male fantasy, being at once the blossom and the fruit, ripe and yet virginal, sexually aware and yet somehow newborn for the hero. An active woman, she is suddenly willing to wait as he works things

Figure 10.3 John Wayne and Angie Dickinson in *Rio Bravo*: 'deservedly, a favourite among Hawksians and a masterpiece among Westerns'

out with the men who occupy first place in his life. She brings her independence only as far as the threshold of a relationship, as a sort of gift, and no further.

The resonance and humour with which four unlikely friends (Wayne, Martin, Brennan and Ricky Nelson) raise their defence against villainy and effect a transformation in one another's character, make *Rio Bravo*, deservedly, a favourite among Hawksians and a masterpiece among Westerns. But if *Rio Bravo* is a movie one loves and returns to as to an old friend, isn't this partly because there is something clubby and reassuring in the male enclosure, where the dimension of risk (the real risk created by women rather than 'bad guys') has been artificially excluded?

Hatari! shows a commune of men and women engaged, under John Wayne's guidance, in big-game hunting. The youthful unknown cast of *Red Line 7000* works out its own definitions of professionalism and love in a world that seems devoid of most of the Hawksian graces. The later Westerns of the *Rio Bravo* trilogy—*El Dorado* and *Rio Lobo*—show Wayne ageing and edging towards the periphery of the action. (In *Rio Lobo*, the community itself, composed largely of females, becomes the protagonist, redefining itself as the film progresses.) But *Rio Bravo* presents Wayne as the apotheosis of the Hawksian hero, older, still strong but requiring help (and that need becoming the instrument of salvation for his weaker colleagues), generous, firm, a little foolish about women, but coming to terms with his prejudices by recognizing that a woman can act with the resolve and daring of a man, and thus accepting his 'weakness'—his need for her—through her own 'masculinization'.

The charge levelled by feminists that Hawks' women must model themselves after men to get their attention is largely true. For one thing, his men are somewhat retarded in the process of learning how to deal with women. But the behaviour of his tomboys and bachelor girls is also an explicit challenge to traditional stereotypes of what a woman is and should be. Their aggressiveness arises from a variety of motives and instincts, from ambition, energy, intelligence, and sexual insecurity, and from a frustration, perhaps, at being so long excluded from the world of action and camaraderie and non-sexual love that Hawks' cinema celebrates.

For better or worse, the maternal—child-bearing and nurturing—side of woman which has been so beautifully evoked in Ford and so blindly and exclusively honoured by most male artists is foreign to Hawks. Its loss is felt not in the most obvious area of character invention and the absence of older women, but in some subtler, more shadowy region of the sensibility. A mature acceptance of the dual principles of life in which woman is complementary to man would undoubtedly have given Hawks a more complete and stimulating vision, a richer and more mystical view of the world; but perhaps it would have removed the sexual tension and the tension with nature (as Mother Earth) which is at the heart of Hawks' work, and which activates the genius of an artist who has been at once the most knowing and naïve, the most elegant and awkward, the most male and female, the most American of directors.

Chapter 11

Judith Mayne

FEMALE AUTHORSHIP RECONSIDERED (1990)

Editors' Introduction

To fully appreciate and understand the film career of Dorothy Arzner, one of the classical era's most successful woman filmmakers, Judith Mayne asks us to consider first a fairly obvious, but nonetheless crucial point that "women have not had the same relationship to the institutions of cinema as men have." Any historical approach that privileges directorial authorship, Mayne contends, would by design diminish the contributions of women who, especially in the classical era, were seldom afforded such an authority. What makes Mayne's essay so interesting and important is that she asks us to consider how female authorship in this unusual, singular case might unsettle the critical notion in feminist film criticism of a "patriarchal gaze." Mayne theorizes what happens when women are on both sides of the camera eye, both sides of "the keyhole" to use her metaphor, looking and being looked at, voyeur and exhibitionist. This phenomenon, Mayne contends, fundamentally unsettles the articulation of women (as the subject and object of the gaze). Throughout the essay, Mayne explores work by Kaja Silverman, Lucy Fischer, and Claire Johnston to re-articulate a female gaze inherent to Arzner's work, a gaze complicated by Arzner's biography as a closeted lesbian in Hollywood, as a woman who nonetheless "favored a look and a style connoting lesbian identity." Arzner's look through the keyhole, so to speak, is thus complicated by female desire for the female object of the gaze. Such a theoretical reconsideration of Arzner's *auteur* signature allows Mayne to read Arzner's two best-known films, *Christopher Strong* (1933) and *Dance, Girl, Dance* (1940), films that otherwise fit neatly into the Hollywood heterosexist paradigm, as provocatively disruptive of the patriarchal status quo. In contrast to the Freudian paradigm of classical film theory and film narrative, for Mayne, Arzner's films, which bear "the marks of lesbian authorship," posit "a desire for another representation of desire."

Suggested Reading

Judith Mayne, *Directed by Dorothy Arzner* (Bloomington: Indiana University Press, 1995); Claire Johnston, *Notes on Women's Cinema* (London: BFI, 1975); Kaja

Silverman, *The Acoustic Mirror: The Female Voice in Psychoanalysis and Cinema* (Bloomington: Indiana University Press, 1988).

ALL OF THE FILMS discussed in the previous chapter* take as their central premise and plot the relationship between women and image-making, and may thus be read as explorations of female authorship in the cinema. The importance of female authorship is accentuated by the fact that, with the exception of Julie Dash, the filmmakers themselves appear in their films, from Helke Sander's role as protagonist of *Redupers*, to the more cameolike appearances of Yvonne Rainer (as a voice and briefly on screen) in *The Man Who Envied Women* and Patricia Rozema (in a window as Polly climbs up a building during one of her fantasies) in *I've Heard the Mermaids Singing*. In more general ways, of course, all of the films trace a relationship between women and cinematic production.

In this chapter, I will examine how female authorship has been theorized in feminist film studies, and I will focus in particular on the example of Dorothy Arzner, one of the few women to have been successful as a director in Hollywood in a career that spanned from the late 1920s to the early 1940s. Arzner was one of the early "rediscoveries" of feminist film theory, and she and her work remain to this day the most important case study of female authorship in the cinema. While the most significant work on Arzner's career was done in feminist film studies of the early to mid-1970s, I will suggest that important dimensions of her status as a female author have yet to be explored.

In contemporary feminist literary criticism, inquiries into the nature of female authorship have been shaped by responses to two somewhat obvious assumptions: first, that no matter how tenuous, fractured, or complicated, there is a connection between the writer's gender, her personhood, and her texts; and second, that there exists a female tradition in literature, whether defined in terms of models of mutual influence, shared themes, or common distances from the dominant culture. A wide range of critical practice is held within these assumptions. But insofar as a self-evident category of womanhood may be implicit in the female author defined as the source of a text and as a moment in a female-specific tradition, these seemingly obvious assumptions evoke what has become in contemporary theory a dreaded epithet: essentialism.

A decade or so ago, a friend of mine remarked sarcastically upon the prevalence of "oedipus detectors" at a Modern Language Association meeting, that is, critics eager to sniff out any remnants of oedipal scenarios in work that was ostensibly "progressive," "feminist," or "postoedipal." Contemporary feminist criticism—and feminist film studies in particular—is marked by a similar presence of "essentialist detectors." For virtually any mention of "real women" (especially insofar as authors are concerned) tends to inspire a by-now-familiar recitation of the "dangers" of essentialism—an affirmation of the difference between men and women as given, and an attendant belief in the positive value of female identity which, repressed by patriarchy, will be given its true voice by feminism. While there is obviously much to be said about the risks of essentialism, the contemporary practice of essentialism detection has avoided the complex relationship between "woman" and "women," usually by bracketing the category of "women" altogether.

Even though discussions of the works of women filmmakers have been central to the development of feminist film studies, theoretical discussions of female authorship in the cinema have been surprisingly sparse. While virtually all feminist critics would agree that the works of Germaine Dulac, Maya Deren, and Dorothy Arzner (to name the most frequently invoked "historical figures") are important, there has been considerable reluctance to use any of them as privileged examples to theorize female authorship in the cinema, unless, that is, such theorizing affirms the difficulty of women's relationship to the cinematic apparatus. This reluctance reflects the current association of "theory" with "antiessentialism." In the realm of feminist literary theory and criticism, however, antiessentialism has not had quite the same widespread effects of negation. In the works of critics such as Margaret Homans and Nancy K. Miller, for instance, female authorship is analyzed not in terms of simple categories of agency and authority, but rather in terms of complex textual and cultural processes which dramatize and foreground women's relationships to language, plot, and the institutions of literature.[1] My point is not that feminist film critics have the proverbial "much to learn" from feminist literary critics, but rather that the paradigm of female authorship in literature may provide a useful point of departure to examine the status of female authorship in the cinema.

For such a point of departure, I turn to two anecdotes, one "literary" and one "theoretical," both of which stage an encounter between women's writing and the cinema in similar ways. My first anecdote, the more "literary" one, concerns two contemporary novels by women concerned with the vicissitudes of female writing. In both novels, cinema becomes a persuasive metaphor for the difficult and sometimes impenetrable obstacles that confront the woman writer. Doris Lessing's novel *The Golden Notebook* explores the relations between female identity and artistic production, and a formulation of that relation is represented through the cinema. Woman is the viewer, man the projectionist, and the whole viewing process a form of control and domination. Writer Anna Wulf describes her vision of events from her own past as films shown to her by an invisible male projectionist. The films represent what Anna calls the "burden of recreating order out of the chaos that my life had become." Yet Anna is horrified by this vision of cinematic order:

> They were all, so I saw now, conventionally, well-made films, as if they had been done in a studio; then I saw the titles: these films, which were everything I hated most, had been directed by me. The projectionist kept running these films very fast, and then pausing on the credits, and I could hear his jeering laugh at *Directed by Anna Wulf*. Then he would run another few scenes, every scene glossy with untruth, false and stupid.[2]

Lessing's cinematic metaphor is informed by a relationship between viewer and image, and between projectionist and screen, that is profoundly patriarchal in the sense that separation, hierarchy, and power are here synonymous with sexual division. The conventionality and gloss of untruth of the films are complicit with Anna Wulf's alienation from her name that appears on them. If, for Lessing, the conditions of film viewing suggest patriarchal domination, then the most immediate terms of that metaphor are the simultaneous evocation and denial of female authorship. Cinema embodies distance from the self—or at least, distance from the *female* self, a distance produced by the mockery of female authorship in the titles of the film. As evoked in *The Golden Notebook* within the context of the female narrator's relationship to language and to experience, cinema functions as a particularly and peculiarly negative inflection of the female authorial signature.

In her novel *The Quest for Christa T.*, Christa Wolf evokes the cinema as a form of illusory presence, as a fantasy control of the past. The female narrator of *The Quest for Christa T.* describes her search for Christa, as well as for the very possibility of memory: "I even name her name, and now I'm quite certain of her. But all the time I know that it's a film of shadows being run off the reel, a film that was once projected in the real light of cities, landscapes, living rooms."[3] Film may create images of the past, but the images are contained by a reified memory. The cinema thus suggests a past that has been categorized, hierarchized, and neatly tucked away.[4] Like Lessing's Anna Wulf, the narrator of *The Quest for Christa T.* searches for the connections between female identity and language. While less explicit in its patriarchal configuration, Wolf's metaphor nonetheless posits cinema as resistant to the process of active searching generally, and female self-expression specifically. The female narrator in *The Quest for Christa T.* is engaged, in Wolf's words, in a search for "the secret of the third person, who is there without being tangible and who, when circumstances favor her, can bring down more reality upon herself than the first person: I." As in *The Golden Notebook*, cinema obstructs the writing of female self-representation, thus embodying what Wolf calls "the difficulty of saying 'I.' "[5]

If we are to take Lessing's and Wolf's metaphoric representations of the cinema at their word, then the difficulty of saying "I" for the woman filmmaker is far greater than for the woman writer. Feminist interrogations of the cinema have supported Lessing's and Wolf's metaphors, for the narrative and visual staging of cinematic desire relies, as most theoretical accounts would have it, on the massive disavowal of sexual difference and the subsequent alignment of cinematic representation with male-centered scenarios. To be sure, one could argue—with more than a touch of defensiveness—that such metaphoric renderings of the cinema suggest the strategic importance of the works of women filmmakers. For if the cinema is symptomatic of alienation (Lessing) and reification (Wolf), then the attempts by women directors to redefine, appropriate, or otherwise reinvent the cinema are crucial demonstrations that the boundaries of that supremely patriarchal form are more permeable, more open to feminist and female influence, than these film-inspired metaphors would suggest. At the same time, it could be argued that the works of women filmmakers offer reformulations of cinematic identification and desire, reformulations that posit cinematic metaphors quite different from those in the passages from Lessing and Wolf cited above. In other words, the "difficulty of saying 'I' " does not necessarily mean that female authorship is impossible in the cinema, but rather that it functions differently than in literature.

If Lessing's and Wolf's formulations reflect the spirit of much feminist writing about film, suggesting that the cinema is peculiarly and forcefully resistant to the female creator, yet another obstacle to the theorizing of female authorship in the cinema emerges when the literary comparison is pursued in another direction. My second, more properly "theoretical" anecdote of the relationship between female authorship in its literary and cinematic forms is drawn from the introduction to *Revision*, a collection of essays on feminist film theory and criticism. The editors of the volume note that feminist film critics have "reason to be envious" of those feminist critics working in literature who "were able to turn to a comparatively substantial canon of works by women writers." Unlike literature, the cinema has no such evidence of a female-authored cinema to which feminist critics might logically turn to begin to elaborate the components of women's cinema or of a feminist film aesthetic. "For where in the classic cinema," the editors ask, "do we encounter anything like an 'autonomous tradition,' with 'distinctive features' and 'lines of influence'? And if, with some difficulty, we can conceive of Lois Weber and Dorothy Arzner as the Jane Austen and George Eliot of Hollywood, to whom do they trace their own influence?"[6]

While feminist literary critics have their own disagreements about the validity of the concept of a "female tradition" (autonomous or not) or a female "canon" (substantial or not), it is true that feminist film critics simply do not have the body of evidence to suggest how and in what ways female-authored cinema would be substantially different from cinema directed and created by men. The absence of this body of evidence notwithstanding, however, it seems to me that the reluctance of many feminist critics to speak, as feminist literary critics do, of a "female tradition" in cinema had to do with a number of other factors, ranging from theoretical frameworks in which any discussions of "personhood" are suspect, to the peculiar status of authorship in the cinema. Particularly insofar as the classical Hollywood cinema is concerned, the conventional equation of authorship with the role of the film director can repress or negate the significant ways in which female signatures *do* appear on film. For instance, consideration of the role of the often-forgotten, often-female screenwriter might suggest more of a female imprint on the film text; and the role of the actress does not always conform to common feminist wisdom about the controlling male gaze located in the persona of the male director—witness Bette Davis as a case in point.[7]

The reluctance to speak of a "female tradition" has perhaps been most influenced, however, by the fear of essentialism—the fear, that is, that any discussion of "female texts" presumes the uniqueness and autonomy of female representation, thus validating rather than challenging the dualism of patriarchal hierarchy. However, the act of discarding the concept of female authorship and of an attendant female tradition in the cinema as necessarily compromised by essentialist definitions of woman can be equally dualistic, in assuming that the only models of connection and influence are unquestionably essentialist ones. Sometimes it is assumed that any discussion of authorship is a throwback to the era of biographical criticism, to the text as transparent and simple reflection of the author's life. While the limitations of such an approach are obvious, purely textual models of cinematic representation have their own limitations insofar as the narrative strategies of many contemporary women's films are concerned, for these strategies frequently involve an inscription of authorship in literal terms, with the director herself a performer in her film.

Any discussion of female authorship in the cinema must take into account the curious history of definitions of cinematic authorship in general.[8] It was not really until the 1950s that "auteurism" became a fixture of film theory and criticism. The French term did not connote then, as French terms have in the past two decades of film studies, a particularly complex entity. For *auteurism* refers to the view that the film director is the single force responsible for the final film, and that throughout the films of a given *auteur* a body of themes and preoccupations will be discernible.[9] The obviousness of these claims is complicated, rather, by the fact that the object of inquiry for auteurist critics was primarily the Hollywood cinema. To speak of a "Hitchcock" or a "John Ford" or a "Nicholas Ray" film as opposed to an "MGM" or a "John Wayne" film was, if not a necessarily radical enterprise, then at least a historically significant one, in that a shift was marked in the very ways in which one speaks of film. For the corporate industrial model of film production was being challenged by a liberal humanist one, and "Hitchcock" does not carry quite the same capitalist, industrial, or corporate baggage as "MGM."

Despite the opposition between the industry and the creative individual from which auteurism emerges, however, the terms do not differ all that much in their partiarchal connotations; "MGM" and "Hitchcock" may be patriarchal in different ways, but they share a common ground. The cinematic *auteur* was identified as a transcendental figure resistant to the leveling forces of the Hollywood industry; to use Roland Barthes's words, the *auteur* theory in cinema reinstated the "formidable paternity" of the individual creator threatened by the institutions of mass culture of which the cinema is a paradigmatic and even privileged example.[10] Thus it does not require too much imagination to see Alexandre Astruc's famous equation of the camera with a writer's pen, in his phrase "caméro-stylo," as informed by the same kind of metaphorical equivalence between pen and penis that has defined both the Western literary tradition (symptomatically) and feminist literary history (critically).[11] The phallic denominator can be read several ways, most obviously as a denial of the possibility of any female agency. Conversely, it can be argued that the privileging of female authorship risks appropriating, for women, an extremely patriarchal notion of cinematic creation. At stake, then, is whether the adjective *female* in female authorship inflects the noun *authorship* in a way significant enough to challenge or displace its patriarchal and proprietary implications.

Whether authorship constitutes a patriarchal and/or phallocentric notion in its own right raises the specter of the "Franco-American Disconnection" (to use Domna Stanton's phrase) that has been the source of much critical debate, or confusion, depending upon your point of view, in contemporary feminist theory.[12] The position usually described as "American"—and therefore empirical and historical—would claim female authorship as basic to the goals of a feminist appropriation of (cinematic) culture, and the position described as "French"—theoretical and deconstructive—would find "authorship" and "appropriation" equally complicitous in their mimicry of patriarchal definitions of self, expression, and representation.[13] Although it is a commonly held assumption that contemporary film studies, especially as they developed in England, are virtually synonymous with "French theory," the fate of auteurism, particularly in relationship to feminist film theory, has not followed such an easily charted or one-directional path. In a famous 1973 essay, for example, Claire Johnston argued against the dismissal of the *auteur* theory. While acknowledging that "some developments of the *auteur* theory have led to a tendency to deify the personality of the (male) director." Johnston argues nonetheless for the importance of auteurism for feminism. She notes that "the development of the *auteur* theory marked an important intervention in film criticism: its polemics challenged the entrenched view of Hollywood as monolithic, and stripped of its normative aspects the classification of films by director has proved an extremely productive way of ordering our experience of the cinema."[14]

Johnston's argument recalls Peter Wollen's writings on *auteur* theory, where the cinematic *auteur* is defined less as a creative individual and more as a figure whose imprint on a film is measured by the repetition of sets of oppositions and the network of preoccupations, including unconscious ones.[15] Her analysis needs to be seen in the context of a certain moment in feminist criticism, when notions of "good roles" for women (and therefore "positive" versus "negative" images) had much critical currency. Johnston turns that critical currency on its head in a comparison of Howard Hawks and John Ford. She argues that the apparently more "positive" and "liberated" heroines of Hawks's films are pure functions of male desire. For John Ford, women function in more ambivalent ways. Whereas in Hawks's films woman is "a traumatic presence which must be negated," in Ford's films woman "becomes a cipher onto which Ford projects his profoundly ambivalent attitude to the concepts of civilisation and psychological 'wholeness.' "[16] Defined as a narrative and visual system associated with a given director, Johnston's auteurism allows for a kind of analysis which goes beyond the categories of "good" and "bad" (images or roles) and into the far more productive critical territory of symptom and contradiction.

While Johnston's analysis seems to stress equally the importance of auteurism and of "symptomatic readings," her work is read today far more in the context of the latter. As with Peter Wollen's work on authorship, one senses that perhaps the auteurist part is a backdrop upon which more significant critical and theoretical assumptions are projected—those of structuralism and semiotics in the case of Wollen, and those of Althusserian-based critical readings in the case of Johnston. The kind of analysis for which Johnston argues—analysis of the position of "woman" within the narrative and visual structures of the cinema—has by and large been pursued without much direct consideration for the *auteur* theory, or for *auteurs*.[17] Despite the importance of auteurism in staking out what Johnston would call progressive claims for film criticism, the analysis of the kinds of structures to which Johnston alludes in the films of Hawks or Ford has been pursued within the framework of textual and ideological analyses of that ubiquitous entity, the classical Hollywood cinema, rather than within the scope of authorship.

By and large, the preferred mode of textual analysis, given its particular attention to unconscious resonances within narrative and visual structures, has had little room for an exploration of auteurism. One notable exception is Raymond Bellour's analyses of Hitchcock's role as "enunciator" in his films, which nonetheless define authorship in explicity literal and narrow textual terms—i.e., the fact that Hitchcock's famous cameo appearances in his films occur at crucial moments of the exposition and/or resolution of cinematic desire.[18] More frequently in contemporary film studies, one speaks of a "Hawks" film or a "Ford" film in the same way one would speak of a "horror" film or a "film noir"—as a convenient categorization of films with similar preoccupations and similar stylistic and narrative features. Such a demystification of authorship might well be more progressive than Johnston's defense of authorship. Conversely, authorship itself may have assumed a symptomatic status, in which case it has not been demystified so much as concealed within and displaced onto other concerns, evoking a process similar to what Nancy K. Miller has observed in the field of literary studies, where the concept of authorship has been not so much revised as it has been repressed "in favor of the (new) monolith of anonymous textuality."[19]

In film theory and criticism of the last decade, auteurism is rarely invoked, and when it is, it is more as a curiosity, as a historical development surely influential, but even more surely surpassed. In this context, Kaja Silverman has suggested that a curious slippage occurs in feminist discussions of the avant-garde works of women filmmakers, for the concept of authorship—largely bracketed in textual analysis—reappears, but in an extratextual way.

> The author often emerges . . . as a largely untheorized category, placed definitively "outside" the text, and assumed to be the punctual source of its sounds and images. A certain nostalgia for an unproblematic agency permeates much of the writing to which I refer. There is no sense in which the feminist author, like her phallic counterpart, might be constructed in and through discourse—that she might be inseparable from the desire that circulates within her texts, investing itself not only in their formal articulation, but in recurring diegetic elements.[20]

Silverman recommends a theorization of female authorship that would account for a diversity of authorial inscriptions, ranging from thematic preoccupations, to the designation of a character or group of characters as a stand-in for the author, to the various enunciative strategies (sonoric as well as visual) whereby the film *auteur's* presence is marked (whether explicitly or implicitly), to the "fantasmatic scene" that structures an author's work.[21]

The concept of female authorship in the cinema may well have a currency similar to categories of genre or of style. But can female authorship be so easily assimilated to the existing taxonomy of the cinema? Present categories of authorship are undoubtedly much more useful in analyzing the configurations of "woman" on screen than in coming to terms with the ways in which women directors inflect cinematic practice in new and challenging ways. The analysis of female authorship in the cinema raises somewhat different questions than does the analysis of male authorship, not only for the obvious reason that women have not had the same relationship to the institutions of the cinema as men have, but also because the articulation of female authorship threatens to upset the erasure of "women" which is central to the articulation of "woman" in the cinema. Virtually all feminist critics who argue in defense of female authorship as a useful and necessary category assume the political necessity for doing so. Hence, Kaja Silverman urges that the gendered positions of libidinal desire within the text be read "in relation to the biological gender of the biographical author, since it is clearly not the same thing, socially or politically, for a woman to speak with a female voice as it is for a man to do so, and vice versa."[22] The notion of female authorship is not simply a useful political strategy; it is crucial to the reinvention of the cinema that has been undertaken by women filmmakers and feminist spectators.

One of the most productive ironies of feminist theory may be that, if "woman" and "women" do *not* coincide (to borrow Teresa de Lauretis's formulation), they also connect in tenuous and often complex ways. It is customary in much feminist film theory to read "subject" to "object" as "male" is to "female." But a more productive exploration of female authorship insofar as "woman" and "women" are concerned may result when subject-object relationships are considered within and among women. Visions of "woman" that appear on screen may be largely the projections of patriarchal fantasies, and the "women" who make films and who see them may have problematic relations at best with those visions. While it is tempting to use de Lauretis's distinction as an opposition between traditional cinematic representations of "woman" and those "women" filmmakers who challenge and reinvent them, the gap, the noncoincidence are better defined by exploring the tensions within both "woman" and "women."[23]

One such strategy has been directed toward the "reading against the grain" of traditional cinematic representations of women, demonstrating how they can be read in ways that contradict or otherwise problematize their function within male-centered discourse.[24] Surprisingly little comparable attention has been paid, however, to the function and position of the woman director. Central to a theorizing of female authorship in the cinema is an expanded definition of textuality attentive to the complex network of intersections, distances, and resistances of "woman" to "women." The challenge of female authorship in the cinema for feminist theory is in the demonstration of *how* the divisions, overlaps, and distances between "woman" and "women" connect with the contradictory status of cinema as the embodiment of both omnipotent control and individual fantasy.

The feminist rediscovery of Dorothy Arzner in the 1970s remains the most important attempt to theorize female authorship in the cinema. Arzner may not be feminist film theory's answer to George Eliot, but her career as a woman director in Hollywood with a significant body of work (and in whose work—true to the most rudimentary definitions of film authorship—a number of preoccupations reappear) has posed issues most central to a feminist theory of female cinematic authorship. As one of the very small handful of women directors who were successful in Hollywood, particularly during the studio years, Arzner has served as an important example of a woman director working within the Hollywood system who managed, in however limited ways, to make films that disturb the conventions of Hollywood narrative.

The significance of this argument, advanced primarily by Claire Johnston and Pam Cook, in which Arzner is defined as a director "critical" of the Hollywood cinema, needs to be seen in the context of the development of the notion of the film *auteur*. Arzner was very definitely *not* one of the directors for whom auteurist claims were made in the heyday of auteurist criticism. For despite the core themes and preoccupations visible across her work, Arzner does not satisfy any of the specific requirements of cinematic authorship as they were advanced on either side of the Atlantic—there is little of the flourish of mise-en-scène that auteurists attributed to other directors, for instance, and the preoccupations visible from film to film that might identify a particular signature do not reflect the life-and-death, civilization-versus-the-wilderness struggles that tended to define the range of more "properly" auteurist themes.[25]

Given the extent to which feminist analysis of the cinema has relied on the distinction between dominant and alternative film, the claims that can be made for an alternative vision that exists within and alongside the dominant cinema will be crucial in gauging the specific ways in which women directors engage with "women's cinema" as divided between representations that perpetuate patriarchal definitions of femininity, and representations that challenge them and offer other modes of identification and pleasure. One can read in responses to Arzner's work reflections of larger assumptions concerning the Hollywood cinema. At one extreme is Andrew Britton's assessment of Arzner, in his study of Katharine Hepburn, as the *auteur* of *Christopher Strong* (1933), the film in which Hepburn appears as an aviatrix who falls in love with an older, married man.

That *Christopher Strong* functions as a "critique of the effect of patriarchal heterosexual relations on relations between women" suggests that the classical cinema lends itself quite readily to heterogeneity and conflicting ideological allegiances, whether the "critique" is the effect of the woman director or the female star.[26] At the opposite extreme, Jacquelyn Suter's analysis of *Christopher Strong* evolves from the assumption that whatever "female discourse" there is in the film is subsumed and neutralized by the patriarchal discourse on monogamy.[27] If the classical cinema described by Britton seems remarkably open to effects of subversion and criticism, the classical cinema described by Suter is just as remarkably closed to any meanings but patriarchal ones, and one is left to assume that female authorship is either a simple affirmation of agency, or virtually an impossibility as far as Hollywood cinema is concerned.

In contrast, Claire Johnston's analyses of Arzner are reminiscent of Roland Barthes's description of Balzac as representative of a "limited plurality" within classical discourse.[28] For Johnston suggests that the strategies of her films open up limited criticisms of the Hollywood cinema. Johnston's claims for female authorship in Arzner's films rely on notions of defamiliarization and dislocation, and more precisely on the assumption popularized within film studies, primarily by Jean-Louis Comolli and Jean Narboni, that there exists within the classical Hollywood cinema a category of films in which realist conventions are criticized from within, generating a kind of internal critique. Claims for this "progressive" text have been made from a variety of vantage points, virtually all of them concerned with ideological value—with, that is, the possibility of a Hollywood film that critiques the very values that are ostensibly promoted, from the literal dark underside of bourgeois ideology "exposed" in *Young Mr. Lincoln* to the impossibility of familial ties for women in *Mildred Pierce*.[29] For Johnston, female desire is the *auteurist* preoccupation that generates a critique of patriarchal ideology in Arzner's films.

Initially, Johnston's analysis of Arzner appears to rely on a definition of the classical cinema that allows for more heterogeneity and more articulation of contradiction than is the case in those analyses that posit a rigid distinction between the classical cinema and its alternatives. However, Arzner's films can be identified as "progressive" only in relationship to a norm that allows for no divergences from purely classical filmmaking. More problematical within the present context, there is nothing in this kind of analysis to suggest what these marks of dislocation and critique have to do with distinctly *female* authorship. Many "woman's films" are motivated by the representation of female desire, and feminist critics have shown how these films might also be read as driven by such an internal—if often unconscious—critique.[30] It is not clear, in other words, to what extent the fact of female authorship gives a particular or distinct inflection to the representation of female desire.

The "political" reasons for insisting on the relevance of the author's gender are not adequate in and of themselves, for they can easily harden into an idealized abstraction, and the name "Dorothy Arzner" would thus become just one more signature to add to the pantheon of (male) directors who critique the conventions of Hollywood cinema from within. While the importance of Arzner's signature in extratextual terms is undeniable, stressing that importance should not be a substitute for an examination of the textual ramifications of female authorship. Yet Johnston's approach to those textual ramifications in Arzner's work seems torn between female authorship understood ("politically") as agency and self-representation, on the one hand, and as a negative inflection of the norms of classical cinema, on the other.[31] This ambivalence—which could be read in terms of the conflicting claims of the so-called American and French positions—is not particularly productive, for the agency thus affirmed dissolves into negation and the impossibility of a female position, evoking Julia Kristéva's extremely limited hypothesis that "women's practice can only be negative, in opposition to that which exists, to say that 'this is not it' and 'it is not yet.' "[32]

Noting that structural coherence in Arzner's films comes from the discourse of the woman, Johnston relies on the notion of defamiliarization, derived from the Russian formalists' *priem ostranenie*, the "device of making strange," to assess the effects of the woman's discourse on patriarchal meaning: "the work of the woman's discourse renders the narrative strange, subverting and dislocating it at the level of meaning."[33] Johnston discusses in this context what has become the single most famous scene from any of Arzner's films, when Judy (Maureen O'Hara), who has played ballet stooge to the vaudeville performer Bubbles (Lucille Ball) in *Dance, Girl, Dance* (1940), confronts her audience and tells them how *she* sees *them*. This is, Johnston argues, the only real break between dominant discourse and the discourse of the woman in Arzner's work, and it is a break that is quickly recuperated within the film, for the audience applauds Judy, and she and Bubbles are quickly dispatched to center stage, where they engage in a catfight, to the delight of the audience. The moment in *Dance, Girl, Dance* when Judy faces her audience is a privileged moment in feminist film theory and criticism, foregrounding as it does the sexual hierarchy of the gaze, with female agency defined as the return of the look, thus "citing" the objectification of woman.[34]

The celebrity accorded this particular scene in Arzner's film needs to be evaluated in the context of feminist film theory in the mid-1970s. Confronted with the persuasive psychoanalytically based theoretical model according to which women either did not or could not exist on screen, the discovery of Arzner, and especially of Judy's "return of the gaze," offered some glimmer of historical hope as to the possibility of a female intervention in the cinema. To be sure, the scope of the intervention is limited, for as Johnston herself stresses, Judy's radical act is quickly recuperated within the film when the audience gets up to cheer her on, and she and Bubbles begin to fight on stage. But the need to revise Johnston's model of authorship is most apparent in this reading of recuperation, for it is informed by the assumption that such a "break" can be only a brief eruption, and can occur in classical cinema only if it is then immediately contained within the laws of male spectatorial desire.

Only one kind of look (Judy's return of the look to her audience) and one kind of spectacle (where men are the agents of the look and women its objects) have received attention in *Dance, Girl, Dance*. In other words, the disruptive force of female desire central to Arzner's work exists primarily within the symmetry of masculinity and femininity.[35] However, I would suggest that female authorship acquires its most significant contours in Arzner's work through relations between and among women. The female gaze is defined early on in the film as central to the aspirations of women as they are shaped within a community of women. Madame Basilova, the older woman who is in charge of the dancing troupe of which Judy and Bubbles are a part, is seen gazing through the rails of a stairway as Judy practices her ballet, and the gaze of Judy herself is isolated as she looks longingly at a rehearsal of the ballet company which she wishes to join. Even Judy's famous scolding of the audience is identified primarily as a communication, not between a female performer and a male audience (the audience is not, in any case, exclusively male) but between the performer and the female member of the audience (secretary to Steven Adams, the man who will eventually become Judy's love interest) who stands up to applaud her.[36] And the catfight that erupts between Judy and Bubbles on stage is less a recuperative move—i.e., transforming the potential threat of Judy's confrontation into an even more tantalizing spectacle—than the claiming by the two women of the stage as an extension of their conflicted friendship, rather than as the alienated site of performance.

To be sure, the men—promoters as well as onlookers—eagerly consume the spectacle of Judy and Bubbles in a catfight. But I see this response less as a sign of pure recuperation by the male-centered system of looks and spectacles, and more as the dramatization of the tension between performance and self-expression which the film attempts to resolve. Although Johnston is more concerned with the devices that give Arzner's films "structural coherence," it is tempting to conclude from her analysis that Judy functions as a metaphoric rendering of the woman filmmaker herself, thus establishing something of a homology between Arzner's position vis-à-vis the classical Hollywood cinema and Judy's position on stage.[37] The stage is, in other words, *both* the site of the objectification of the female body *and* the site for the theatricalizing of female friendship. This "both/and"—the stage (and, by metaphoric implication, the cinema itself) is an arena simultaneously of patriarchal exploitation and of female self-representation—stands in contrast to the more limited view of Arzner's films in Johnston's work, where more of a "neither/nor" logic is operative—neither patriarchal discourse nor the "discourse of the woman" allows women a vantage point from which to speak, represent, or imagine themselves.

Reading Arzner's films in terms of the "both/and" suggests an irony more far-reaching than that described by Johnston. Johnston's reading of Arzner is suggestive of Shoshana Felman's definition of irony as "dragging authority as such into a scene which it cannot master, of which it is *not aware* and which, for that very reason, is the scene of its own self-destruction. . . ."[38] The irony in *Dance, Girl, Dance*, however, does not just demonstrate how the patriarchal discourse of the cinema excludes women, but rather how the cinema functions in two radically different ways, both of which are "true," as it were, and totally incompatible. I am borrowing here from Donna Haraway's definition of irony: "Irony is about contradictions that do not resolve into larger wholes, even dialectically, about the tension of holding incompatible things together because both or all are necessary and true."[39] This insistence on two equally compelling and incompatible truths constitutes a form of irony far more complex than Johnston's analysis of defamiliarization.

Johnston's notion of Arzner's irony assumes a patriarchal form of representation which may have its gaps and its weak links, but which remains dominant in every sense of the word. For Johnston, Arzner's irony can be only the irony of negativity, of puncturing holes in patriarchal assumptions. Such a view of irony has less to do, I would argue, with the limitations of Arzner's career (e.g., as a woman director working within the inevitable limitations of the Hollywood system) than with the limitations of the film theory from which it grows. If the cinema is understood as a one-dimensional system of male subjects and female objects, then it is not difficult to understand how the irony in Arzner's films is limited, or at least would be *read* as limited. While rigid hierarchies of sexual difference are indeed characteristic of dominant cinema, they are not absolute, and Arzner's films represent other kinds of cinematic pleasure and desire.

An assessment of Arzner's importance within the framework of female authorship needs to account not only for how Arzner problematizes the pleasures of the cinematic institution as we understand it—e.g., in terms of the voyeurism and fetishism reenacted through the power of the male gaze and the objectification of the female body—but also for how, in her films, those pleasures are identified in ways that are not reducible to the theoretical clichés of the omnipotence of the male gaze. The irony of *Dance, Girl, Dance* emerges from the conflicting demands of performance and self-expression, which are linked in their turn to heterosexual romance and female friendship. Female friendship acquires a resistant function in the way that it exerts a pressure against the supposed "natural" laws of heterosexual romance. Relations between women and communities of women have a privileged status in Arzner's films. To be sure, Arzner's films offer plots—particularly insofar as resolutions are concerned—that are compatible with the romantic expectations of the classical Hollywood cinema; communities of women may be central, but boy still meets girl.

Claire Johnston claims that the conclusion of *Dance, Girl, Dance*, where Judy is embraced by Steven Adams, destined for a fusion of professional mentoring and romance, is marked by Judy's defeat. This strikes me more as wishful feminist thinking than as a convincing reading of the film's conclusion, which "works" within the conventions of Hollywood romance.

Noting Judy's final comment as she is in Steven's arms—"when I think how simple things could have been, I just have to laugh"—Johnston says that "this irony marks her defeat and final engulfment, but at the same time it is the final mark of subversion of the discourse of the male."[40] If the "discourse of the male" is subverted in *Dance, Girl, Dance*, it has less to do with the resolution of the film and more to do with the process of heterosexual initiation which the film has traced. Judy's attractions to men are shaped by substitutions for women and female rivalry—Steven Adams is a professional mentor to substitute for Basilova, and Jimmie Harris is an infantile man who is desirable mainly because Bubbles wants him too.[41] Therefore, the heterosexual romance provides the conclusion of the film, but only after it has been mediated by relationships between women.

A controversial area in feminist theory and criticism has been the connection between lesbianism and female friendship in those fictional worlds which, like Arzner's, take communities of women as their inspiration. Barbara Smith's suggestion that the relationship between Nel and Sula in Toni Morrison's novel *Sula* can be read in lesbian terms has been provocative to say the least, particularly given Toni Morrison's own assertion that "there is no homosexuality in *Sula*."[42] But the case of Arzner is somewhat different. What is known about Arzner implies that she herself was a lesbian.[43] But this assertion raises as many questions as it presumably answers, concerning both the responsibility of a critic vis-à-vis an individual who was presumably in the closet, and the compulsion to define lesbianism as something in need of proof.[44] Bonnie Zimmerman has suggested that "if a text lends itself to a lesbian reading, then no amount of biographical 'proof' ought to be necessary to establish it as a lesbian text."[45] The point is well taken, but in Arzner's case another "text" mediates the relationship between director, her films, and their reception. For Arzner's films are virtually no longer read independently of her persona—an issue to which I will return momentarily. Nonetheless, if relationships between and among women account for much more narrative and visual momentum than do the relations between men and women in Arzner's work, then one begins to wonder about the perspective that informs these preoccupations.

For all of the attention that has been given to Arzner's work, one striking aspect of her persona—and of her films—has been largely ignored. Although the photographs of Arzner that have accompanied feminist analyses of her work depict a woman who favored a look and a style connoting lesbian identity, discussions of her work always stop short of any recognition that sexual identity might have something to do with how her films function, particularly concerning the "discourse of the woman" and female communities, or that the contours of female authorship in her films might be defined in lesbian terms. This marginalization is all the more notable, given how *visible* Arzner has been as an image in feminist film theory. With the possible exception of Maya Deren, Arzner is more frequently represented visually than any other woman director central to contemporary feminist discussions of film. And unlike Deren, who appeared extensively in her own films, Arzner does not have the reputation of being a particularly self-promoting, visible, or "out" (in several senses of the term) woman director.

Sarah Halprin has suggested that the reason for this omission is, in part, the suspicion of any kind of biographical information in analysis of female authorship:

> most discussions of Dorothy Arzner's films, especially those by the English school, carefully avoid any mention of Arzner's appearance in relation to some of the images in her films. Lengthy analyses of *Dance, Girl, Dance* ignore the fact that while the "main" characters, Judy and Bubbles, are recurrently placed as immature within the context of the film, there are two "minor" characters who both dress and look remarkably similar to Arzner herself (i.e., tailored, "mannish," in the manner of Radclyffe Hall and other famous

> lesbians of the time) and are placed as mature, single, independent women who are crucial to the career of young Judy and who are clearly seen as oppressed by social stereotyping, of which they are contemptuous. Such a reading provides a whole new way of relating to the film and to other Arzner films, encouraging a discussion of lesbian stereotypes, relations between lesbians and heterosexual women as presented in various films and as perceived by any specific contemporary audience.[46]

Indeed, one of the most critical aspects of Arzner's work is the way in which heterosexuality is assumed equivocally, without necessarily violating many of the conventions of the Hollywood film.

In his book on gay sexuality and film, Vito Russo quotes another Hollywood director on Arzner: "an obviously lesbian director like Dorothy Arzner got away with her lifestyle because she was officially closeted and because 'it made her one of the boys.' "[47] An interview with Arzner by Karyn Kay and Gerald Peary gives some evidence of her status as "one of the boys," at least insofar as identification is concerned, for in discussing both *Christopher Strong* and *Craig's Wife*, Arzner insists that her sympathies lie with the male characters.[48] However, one has only to look at the photographs of Arzner that have accompanied essays about her work in recent years to see that this is not a director so easily assimilated to the boys' club of Hollywood. Arzner preferred masculine attire, in the manner, as Halprin says, of Radclyffe Hall. Two dominant tropes shape the photographic mise-en-scène of the Arzner persona. She is portrayed against the backdrop of the large-scale apparatus of the Hollywood cinema, or she is shown with other women, usually actresses, most of whom are most emphatically "feminine," creating a striking contrast indeed.

Both tropes appear in the photograph on the cover of the collection edited by Claire Johnston, *The Work of Dorothy Arzner: Towards a Feminist Cinema*. We see Arzner in profile, slouching directorially on a perch next to a very large camera; seated next to her is a man. They both look toward what initially appears to be the unidentified field of vision (Figure 11.2). When the pamphlet is opened, however, the photograph continues on the back cover: two young women, one holding packages, look at each other, their positions reflecting symmetrically those of Arzner and her male companion (Figure 11.3). It is difficult to read precisely the tenor of the scene (from *Working Girls* [1930]) between the two women: some hostility perhaps, or desperation. The camera occupies the center of the photograph, as a large, looming—and predictably phallic—presence (Figure 11.4). The look on the man's face suggests quite strongly the clichés of the male gaze that have been central to feminist film theory; from his perspective the two women exist as objects of voyeuristic pleasure. Arzner's look has quite another function, however, and one that has received very little critical attention, and that is to decenter the man's look, and to eroticize the exchange of looks between the two women.[49]

While virtually none of the feminist critics who analyze Arzner's work have discussed lesbianism, a curious syndrome is suggested by this use of "accompanying illustrations." The photograph on the covers of the pamphlet edited by Claire Johnston speaks rather literally what is unspoken in the written text, in a teasing kind of way. Johnston's and Cook's essays are reprinted in a recent collection of essays on feminist film theory, not one of which discusses erotic connections between women.[50] Yet on the cover of the book is a photograph of Arzner and Rosalind Russell exchanging a meaningful look with more than a hint of female homoeroticism. One begins to suspect that the simultaneous evocation and dispelling of an erotic bond between women in Arzner's work is a structuring absence in feminist film theory. Like any good symptom it rather obsessively draws attention to itself. Arzner's lesbian persona may not be theorized in relationship to her films, but her visibility in feminist

Figure 11.1 Dorothy Arzner. Credit: Paramount/The Kobal Collection

film criticism suggests that one of the mechanisms cited most frequently as central to male spectatorial desire informs feminist film theory, too. I am referring, of course, to fetishism.

To be sure, any parallel between a classical, male-centered trajectory such as fetishism and the dynamics of feminist theory can be made only tentatively.[51] But there is nonetheless a telling fit between Octave Mannoni's formula for disavowal ("I know very well, but all the same . . ."), adapted by Christian Metz to analyze cinematic fetishism, and the consistent and simultaneous evocation and disavowal of Arzner's lesbian persona.[52] A heterosexual master code, where any and all combinations of "masculinity," from the male gaze to Arzner's clothing, and "femininity," from conventional objectification of the female body to the female

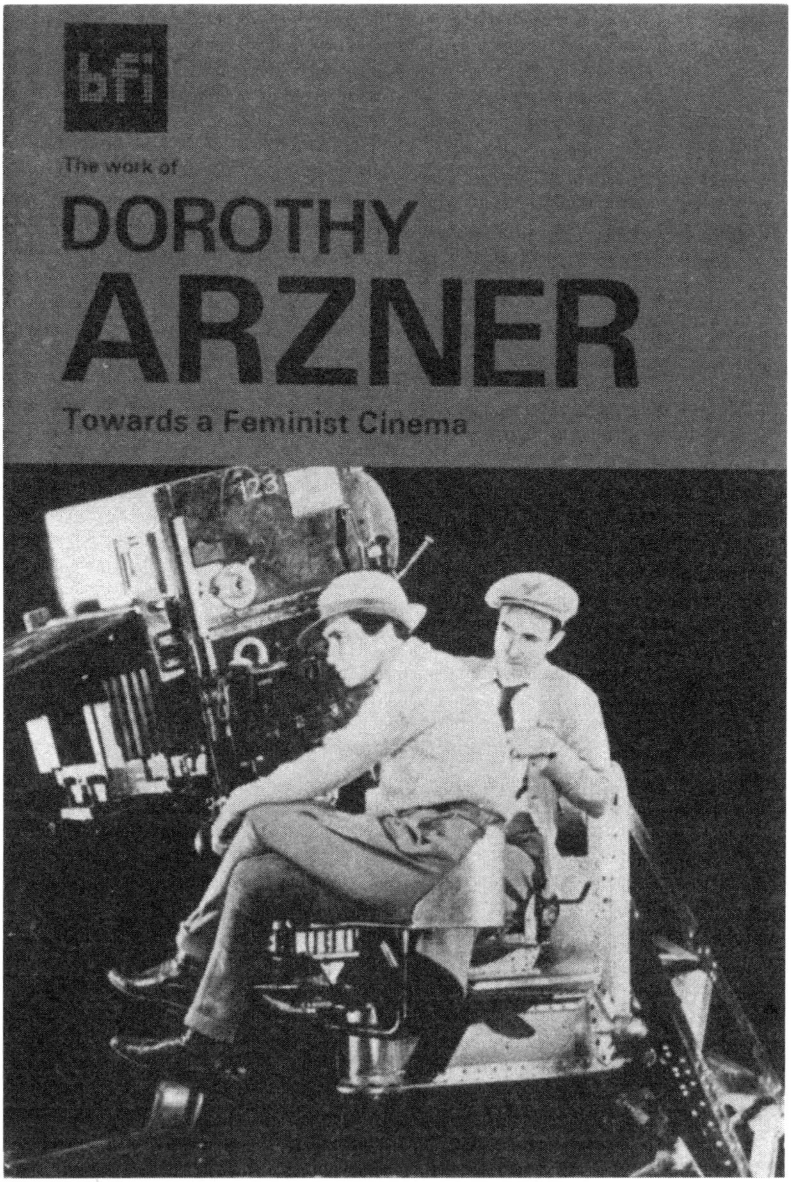

Figure 11.2 Front cover of Claire Johnston's *The Work of Dorothy Arzner: Towards a Feminist Cinema*

objects of Arzner's gaze, has shaped discussions of Arzner's work. The narrative and visual structures of her films are praised for their "critique" of the Hollywood system, but the critique is so limited as to only affirm the dominance of the object in question.

The photographs of Arzner are interesting not only in the biographical terms suggested by Sarah Halprin, but also in textual terms. For one of the most distinctive ways in which Arzner's authorial presence is felt in her films is in the emphasis placed on communities of women, to be sure, but also in the erotic charge identified within those communities. If heterosexual initiation is central to Arzner's films, it is precisely in its function as rite of passage (rather than natural destiny) that a marginal presence is felt—an authorial presence

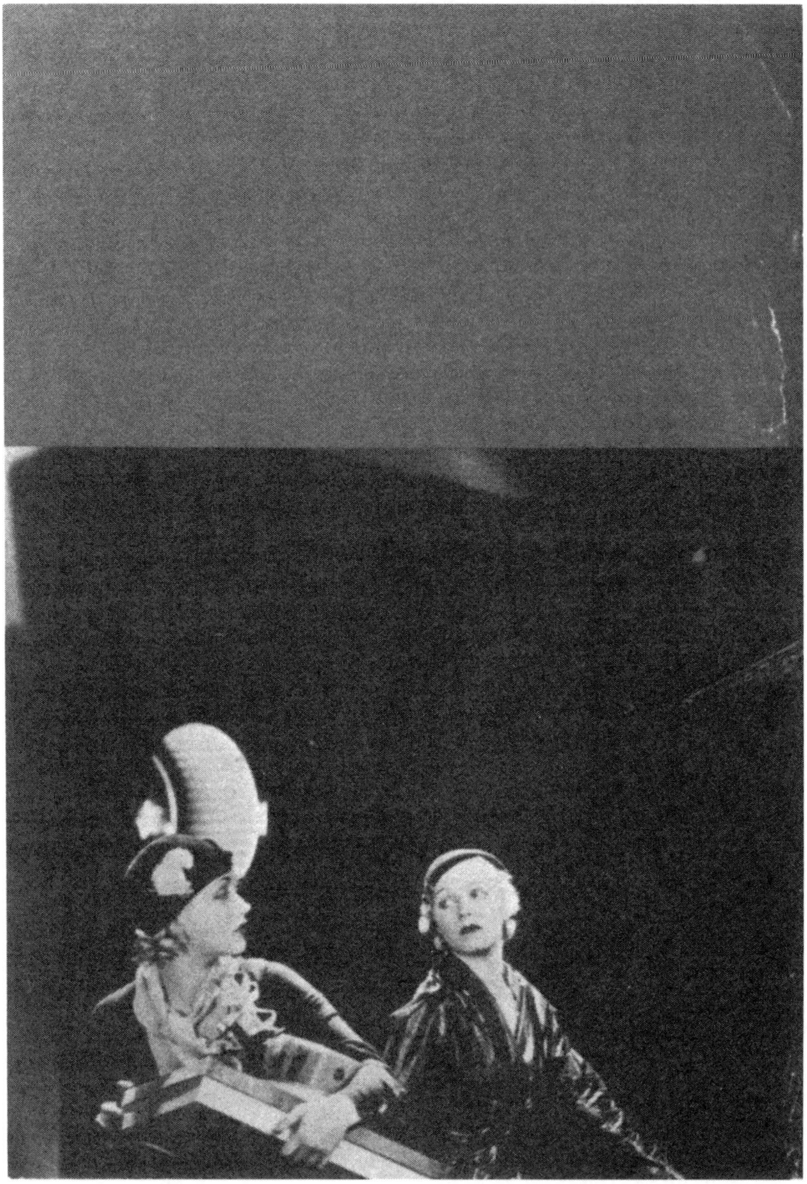

Figure 11.3 Back cover of Claire Johnston's *The Work of Dorothy Arzner: Towards a Feminist Cinema*

that is lesbian, as well as female. Consider, for instance, *Christopher Strong*. Katharine Hepburn first appears in the film as a prize-winning object in a scavenger hunt, for she can claim that she is over twenty-one and has never had a love affair. Christopher Strong, the man with whom she will eventually become involved, is the male version of this prize-winning object, for he has been married for more than five years and has always been faithful to his wife. As Cynthia Darrington, Hepburn dresses in decidedly unfeminine clothing and walks with a swagger that is masculine, or athletic, depending upon your point of view. Hepburn's jodhpurs and boots may well be, as Beverle Houston puts it, "that upper-class costume for a woman performing men's activities."[53] But this is also clothing that strongly denotes lesbian

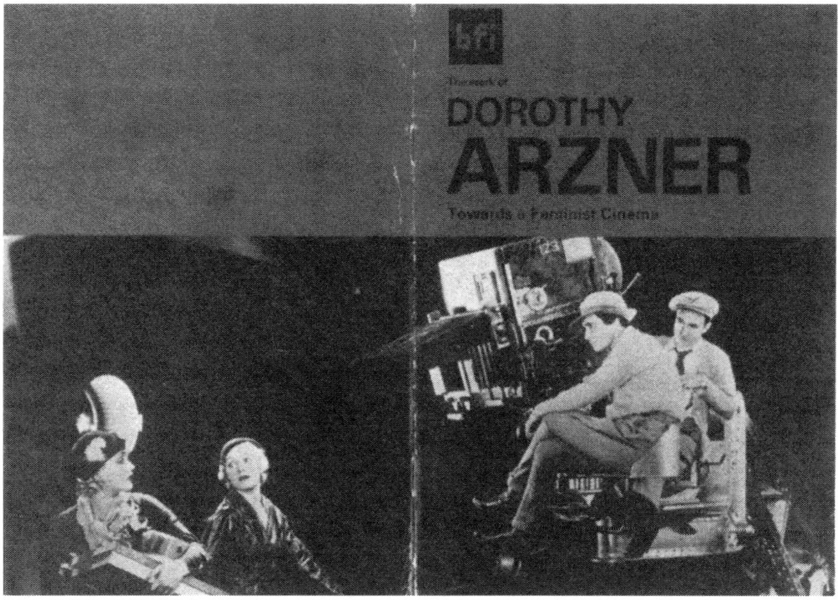

Figure 11.4 Complete cover of Claire Johnston's *The Work of Dorothy Arzner: Towards a Feminist Cinema* (BFI, 1975)

Figure 11.5 Katharine Hepburn as aviatrix Cynthia Darrington in Dorothy Arzner's *Christopher Strong*. Credit: RKO/The Kobal Collection

Figure 11.6 Katharine Hepburn and Colin Clive in *Christopher Strong*

Figure 11.7 Billie Burke and Rosalind Russell in Dorothy Arzner's *Craig's Wife*

identity, and which (to stress again Sarah Halprin's point) is evocative of the way Arzner herself, and other lesbians of the time, dressed.

Cynthia's "virginity" becomes a euphemistic catchall for a variety of margins in which she is situated, both as a woman devoted to her career and as a woman without a sexual identity. The film traces the acquisition of heterosexual identity, with some peculiar representations of femininity along the way, including Hepburn dressed as a moth. I am not arguing that *Christopher Strong*, like the dream which says one thing but ostensibly "really" means its mirror opposite, can be decoded as a coherent "lesbian film," or that the real subject of the film is the tension between gay and straight identities. The critical attitude toward heterosexuality takes the form of inflections, of bits and pieces of tone and gesture and emphasis, as a result of which the conventions of heterosexual behavior become loosened up, shaken free of some of their identifications with the patriarchal status quo.

Most important, perhaps, the acquisition of heterosexuality becomes the downfall of Cynthia Darrington. Suter has described *Christopher Strong* in terms of how the feminine discourse, represented by the various female characters in the film, is submerged by patriarchal discourse, the central term of which is monogamy. The proof offered for such a claim is, as is often the case in textual analysis, convincing on one level but quite tentative on another, for it is a proof which begins from and ends with the assumption of a patriarchal master code. Even the "feminine discourse" described by Suter is nothing but a pale reflection of that master code, with nonmonogamy its most radical expression. The possibility that "feminine discourse" in *Christopher Strong* might exceed heterosexual boundaries is not taken into account.[54] As should be obvious by now, I am arguing that it is precisely in its ironic inflection of heterosexual norms, whether by the mirroring gesture that suggests a reflection of Arzner herself or by the definition of the female community as resistant to, rather than complicitous with, heterosexual relations, that Arzner's signature is written on her films.

These two components central to female authorship in Arzner's work—female communities and the mirroring of Arzner herself—are not identical. The one, stressing the importance of female communities and friendship among women, may function as a pressure exerted against the rituals of heterosexual initiation, but is not necessarily opposed to them. This foregrounding of relationships among women disturbs the fit between female friendship and heterosexual romance, but the fit is still there, the compatibility with the conventions of the classical Hollywood cinema is still possible. The representation of lesbian codes, as in the mirroring of Arzner's—and other lesbians'—dress, constitutes the second strategy, which is more marginal and not integrated into narrative flow. These two authorial inscriptions—the emphasis on female communities, the citing of marginal lesbian gestures—are not situated on a "continuum," that model of continuity from female friendship to explicit lesbianism so favored in much contemporary lesbian-feminist writing.[55] Rather, these two strategies exist in tension with each other, constituting yet another level of irony in Arzner's work. Female communities are compatible with the classical Hollywood narrative; the lesbian gesture occupies no such position of compatibility, it does not mesh easily with narrative continuity in Arzner's film.

Thus, in *Dance, Girl, Dance*, Arzner accentuates not only the woman's desire as embodied in Judy and her relationships with other women, but also secondary female figures who never really become central, but who do not evaporate into the margins, either—such as the secretary (who leads the applause during Judy's "return of the gaze" number) and Basilova (the dance teacher and director of the troupe). That these figures do not simply "disappear" suggests even more strongly their impossible relationship to the Hollywood plot, a relationship that *is* possible insofar as Judy is concerned. In *Craig's Wife*, however, there is more of an immediate relationship between marginality and female communities, although in this case, the marginality has less of a lesbian inflection, both dress- and gesturewise. Julia Lesage has noted that in *Craig's Wife*, Arzner rereads George Kelley's play, the source of the film, so that the secondary women characters are treated much more fully than in the play.[56]

Craig's Wife—preoccupied with heterosexual demise rather than initiation—shows us a woman so obsessively concerned with her house that nothing else is of interest to her. Harriet Craig (Rosalind Russell) married as "a way towards emancipation. . . . I married to be independent." If marriage is a business contract, then Harriet Craig's capital is her house. Indeed, Harriet's sense of economy is pursued with a vengeance. And the men in the film are the victims, explicit or not, of her obsession. It is Harriet's husband who married for love, not money, and in a subplot of the film, a friend of Walter Craig is so obsessed by his wife's unfaithfulness that he kills her and then himself.

At the conclusion of the film, virtually everyone has cleared out of Harriet's house. Her niece has left with her fiancé, her servants have either quit or been fired, and Walter has finally packed up and left in disgust. Harriet seems pathetically neurotic and alone. The widow next door (Billie Burke) brings Harriet some roses. In Kelley's play, Harriet has become a mirror image of her neighbor, for both are portrayed as women alone, to be pitied. But in Arzner's film, the neighbor represents Harriet's one last chance for connection with another human being. Thus the figure who in Kelley's play is a pale echo of Harriet, becomes in the film the suggestion of another identity and of the possibility of a female community. The resolution of Arzner's *Craig's Wife* has little to do with the loss of a husband, and more to do with situating Harriet Craig's fantasy come horribly true alongside the possibility of connection with another woman. And while Billie Burke is hardly evocative of lesbianism (as Basilova is in *Dance, Girl, Dance*), she and Rosalind Russell make for a play of contrasts visually similar to those visible in photographs of Arzner with more "feminine" women.[57]

To be sure, Arzner's authorship extends to an ironic perspective on patriarchal institutions in general, and in this sense her films do not require or assume a lesbian audience, as if this was or is likely to happen within the institutions of the Hollywood cinema. At the same time that the irony of Arzner's films appeals to a wide range of female experiences, and is thus readable across a wide spectrum, ranging from lesbian to heterosexual and from female to feminist, the marks of female authorship in her work do not constitute a universal category of female authorship in the cinema. The female signature in Arzner's work is marked by that irony of equally compelling and incompatible discourses to which I have referred, and the lesbian inflection articulates the division between female communities which do function within a heterosexual universe, and the eruptions of lesbian marginality which do not. This lesbian irony taps differing and competing views of lesbianism within contemporary feminist and lesbian theory. Lesbianism has been defined as the most intense form of female and feminist bonding, on the one hand; and as distinctly opposed to heterosexuality (whether practiced by women or men), on the other. In Arzner's own time, these competing definitions were read as the conflict between a desexualized nineteenth-century ideal of romantic friendship among women, and the "mannish lesbian" (exemplified by Radclyffe Hall), defined by herself and her critics as a sexual being.[58] Arzner's continued "visibility" suggests not only that the tension is far from being resolved, but also that debates about lesbian identity inform, even (and especially!) in unconscious ways, the thinking of feminists who do not identify as lesbians.

I see, then, several points to draw from the example of Dorothy Arzner as far as female authorship in the cinema is concerned. The preoccupations with female communities and heterosexual initiation are visible and readable only if we are attentive to how the cinema, traditionally and historically, has offered pleasures other than those that have received the most sustained critical and theoretical attention in recent years. Female authorship finds an inadequate metaphor in the female gaze as it returns the ostensibly central and overriding force of the male gaze. Other forms of the female gaze—such as the exchange of looks between and among women—open up other possibilities for cinematic meaning and pleasure and identification. In addition, a female signature can take other forms besides the gaze—costume and gesture, and the strategies of reading "marginality" in the case of Arzner. Textually, the most pervasive sign of female authorship in Arzner's film is irony, and that irony is most appropriately described as the confrontation between two equally compelling, and incompatible, discourses.

I am suggesting, of course, that lesbian irony constitutes one of the pleasures in Arzner's films, and that irony is a desirable aim in women's cinema. Irony can misfire, however.[59] It has been argued that in Jackie Raynal's film *Deux Fois*, for instance, the ironic elaboration of woman-as-object-of-spectacle is rendered decidedly problematic by the fact that it is only in offering herself as an object of spectacle that the category of woman-as-object-of-spectacle can be criticized; it is only by affirming the validity of patriarchal representation that any critique is possible.[60] I have in mind here another kind of misfiring, when the ironic reading of patriarchal conventions collides with other coded forms of representation which may serve, quite disturbingly, as a support for that irony.

In *Dance, Girl, Dance*, for instance, racial stereotypes emerge at three key moments in the narrative of the film. In the opening scenes, at a nightclub in Akron, Ohio, the camera moves over the heads of the members of the audience as it approaches the stage where the female dance troupe is performing. Intercut is an image of the black members of the band, who are smiling like the proverbially happy musicians. While an equivalence seems to be established between women and blacks as objects of spectacle, I see little basis for any "critical" use of the racist stereotype. Later in the film, when Judy watches longingly the rehearsal of the ballet company, another stereotype emerges. The performance number portrays the encounter between ballet and other forms of dance and body language within the context of the city. At one point in the performance, the music switches suddenly to imitate a jazzy tune, and a white couple in blackface struts across the stage. During one of the concluding scenes of the film, when Judy and Bubbles resolve their friendship in a court of law, the ostensibly "amusing" conclusion to the scene occurs when the clerk announces the arrival of a black couple whose names are "Abraham Lincoln Johnson" and "Martha Washington Johnson."

However disparate these stereotypes, they do emerge at crucial moments in the deployment of irony and performance. In each case, the racial stereotype appears when the sexual hierarchy of the look is deflected or otherwise put into question. The black performers at the beginning of the film are defined securely within the parameters of objectification when it is apparent—much to Bubbles' irritation and eventual attendant desire—that Jimmie Harris, one of the spectators in the audience, is totally unengaged in the spectacle on stage. The appearance of the white couple in blackface occurs when the centrality of Judy's desire, as defined by her longing gaze at the performance, is affirmed. In the courtroom scene, Judy assumes aggressively and enthusiastically the court as her stage, and the racist stereotype of "Mr. and Mrs. Johnson" appears once the rivalry between the two women is on the verge of resolution.

In each of these instances, the stereotype affirms the distinction between white subject and black object just when the distinction between male subject and female object is being put into question. While there is nothing in *Dance, Girl, Dance* that approximates a sustained discourse on race, these brief allusions to racist stereotypes are eruptions that cannot be dismissed or disregarded as mere background or as unconscious reflections of a dominant cinematic practice that was racist. The marks of authorship in *Dance, Girl, Dance* include these racist clichés as well as the ironic inflection of the heterosexual contract. I want to stress that female irony is not just a function of sexual hierarchy, but that virtually all forms of narrative and visual opposition are potentially significant. To ignore, in Arzner's case, the intertwining of sexual and racial codes of performance is to claim female authorship as a white preserve.

The racist stereotypes which serve as an anchor of distinct otherness in *Dance, Girl, Dance* speak to a more general problem in female authorship. While Arzner's films suggest other forms of cinematic pleasure that have been relatively untheorized within film studies, these forms cannot be posited in any kind of simple way as "alternatives." I think it is a mistake to assume that the racist clichés are symptomatic of the compromises that inevitably occur with any attempt to create different visions within the classical Hollywood cinema. Such clichés are possible within virtually any kind of film practice.

Dorothy Arzner has come to represent both a textual practice (consciously) and an image (less consciously) in feminist film theory, and the relationship between the textual practice and the image suggests an area of fascination, if not love, that dares not speak its (her) name. The preferred term *sexual difference* in feminist film theory can slide from the tension between masculinity and femininity into a crude determinism whereby there is no representation without heterosexuality. Challenging that implicit homophobia would be reason enough to read the marks of lesbian authorship in Arzner's work. There are two other issues which the designation of lesbian authorship crystallizes in particularly important ways. First, female authorship cannot be a useful concept if it perpetuates the notion of a monolithic essentialist identity, with a feminist inflection, perhaps, but no less problematic for that. Feminists have said frequently enough that when unchallenged, the notion of the "human subject" refers inevitably to a subject that is white, male, and heterosexual.

Similarly, the unexamined female subject may not be male, but is usually assumed to be nonetheless white and heterosexual. To be sure, there is much "female bonding"—to use the preferred phrase whereby lesbianism is usually repressed—in Arzner's films, but that female bonding takes many forms, one of which is lesbian; and it is the lesbian inflection where Arzner's authorial signature is most in evidence. Second, lesbianism raises some crucial questions concerning identification and desire in the cinema, questions with particular relevance to female cinematic authorship. Cinema offers simultaneous affirmation and dissolution of the binary oppositions upon which our most fundamental notions of self and other are based. In feminist film theory, one of the most basic working assumptions has been that in the classical cinema, at least, there is a fit between the hierarchies of masculinity and femininity on the one hand, and activity and passivity on the other. If disrupting and disturbing that fit is a major task for filmmakers and theorists, then lesbianism would seem to have a strategically important function. For one of the "problems" that lesbianism poses, insofar as representation is concerned, is precisely the fit between the paradigms of sex and agency, the alignment of masculinity with activity and femininity with passivity.

It is perhaps "no coincidence" that one discourse in which the "problem" of lesbianism is thus posed most acutely is psychoanalysis. For reasons both historical and theoretical, the most persuasive as well as controversial accounts of cinematic identification and desire have been influenced by psychoanalysis. Laura Mulvey's classic account of sexual hierarchy in narrative cinema established the by-now-familiar refrain that the ideal spectator of the classical cinema, whatever his/her biological sex or cultural gender, is male. Many critics have challenged or extended the implications of Mulvey's account, most frequently arguing that for women (and sometimes for men as well), cinematic identification occurs at the very least across gender lines, whether in transvestite or bisexual terms.[61] However complex such accounts, they tend to leave unexamined another basic assumption common both to Mulvey's account and to contemporary psychoanalytic accounts of identification, and that is that cinematic identification not only functions to affirm heterosexual norms but finds its most basic condition of possibility in the heterosexual division of the universe.

While feminist film theory and criticism have devoted extensive attention to the function of the male gaze in film, the accompanying heterosexual scenario has not received much attention, except for the occasional nod to what seems to be more the realm of the obvious than the explorable or questionable. Even David Bordwell, Kristin Thompson, and Janet Staiger's *The Classical Hollywood Cinema*—a model of historical and formal precision—characterizes heterosexual love as a theme that links cinema with other historical forms in a very simple way. "Almost invariably," writes David Bordwell, one of the main lines of action in the classical Hollywood cinema "involves heterosexual romantic love. This is, of course, not startling news." Bordwell goes on to specify that in the sample of 100 films used in the study, "ninety-five involved romance in at least one line of action, while eighty-five made that the principal line of action."

Thus, Bordwell concludes, "in this emphasis upon heterosexual love, Hollywood continues traditions stemming from the chivalric romance, the bourgeois novel, and the American melodrama."[62] The unbroken narrative connecting chivalric romance and Hollywood plots suggests, quite accurately of course, that heterosexual love is common to both forms. But this is a bit like saying that the *Iliad* and *Citizen Kane* are alike in that they both explore the relationship between the individual and society—true, perhaps, but only in the most a-historical way. When feminists criticize heterosexual scenarios, or, to use Monique Wittig's phrase, the "heterosexual contract," it is rarely heterosexuality as a simple "attraction to the opposite sex" that is under scrutiny, but rather the absolute equation between one kind of heterosexuality, drawn as the norm against which all differences are measured as "perversions," and cultural meaning. Or as Wittig puts it, the heterosexual contract "produces the difference between the sexes as a political and philosophical dogma."[63]

An impressive body of feminist writing has been devoted to the exploration of how—following Luce Irigaray—heterosexuality functions as a ruse, a decoy relation to mask male homosocial and homosexual bonds. "Reigning everywhere, although prohibited in practice," Irigaray writes, "hom(m)o-sexuality is played out through the bodies of women, matter, or sign, and heterosexuality has been up to now just an alibi for the smooth workings of man's relations with himself."[64] Comparatively little attention has been paid to how heterosexual economies work to assure that any exchange between women remains firmly ensconced within that "hom(m)osexual" economy. To be sure, male and female homosexualities occupy quite different positions, and given the logic of the masculine "same" that dominates the patriarchal order, female homosexuality cannot be ascribed functions that are similar to male homosexuality. However, the two homosexualities share the potential to disrupt, in however different ways, the reign of the "hom(m)osexual." Irigaray speaks of the "fault, the infraction, the misconduct, and the challenge that female homosexuality entails." For lesbianism threatens to upset the alignment between masculinity and activity, and femininity and passivity. Hence, writes Irigaray, "the problem can be minimized if female homosexuality is regarded merely as an imitation of male behavior."[65]

Irigaray's discussion of the disruptive potential of female homosexuality emerges from her symptomatic reading and rewriting of Freud. In the Freudian text that occasions Irigaray's remarks on the "problem" of female homosexuality within psychoanalysis, "The Psychogenesis of a Case of Homosexuality in a Woman" (1920), questions of narration and identification, masculinity and femininity, and dominant and alternative practice are posed in ways that are particularly relevant to lesbian authorship in the cinema. Jacqueline Rose has said of the case history that here, Freud "is in a way at his most radical, rejecting the concept of cure, insisting that the most psychoanalysis can do is restore the original bisexual disposition of the patient, defining homosexuality as nonneurotic."[66]

In the case history, Freud describes the brief analysis of a young woman who was brought to him by her parents after her unsuccessful suicide attempt. This "beautiful and clever girl of eighteen" pursued with great enthusiasm her attraction to a woman ten years older than she, and her parents (and her father in particular) were particularly distressed by her simultaneous brazenness ("she did not scruple to appear in the most frequented streets in the company of her questionable friend") and deception ("she disdained no means of deception, no excuses and no lies that would make meetings with her possible and cover them").[67] The suicide attempt occurred when these two factors that so distressed her parents coincided in full view of her father. After the young woman and her female companion were greeted by the woman's father with extreme displeasure as his path crossed theirs on the street one day (as Freud notes, the scene had all the elements of a mise-en-scène planned by the young woman), the young woman threw herself in desperation over a railway fence.

Despite the apparent gravity of the suicide attempt, Freud saw little hope for successful analysis, for the woman—while not necessarily hostile to analysis, as was Dora, to whom this patient has frequently been compared—was nonetheless brought to analysis of a will other than her own.[68] In addition, Freud saw little actual illness in the young woman, at least as far as her sexuality was concerned; rather than resolving a neurotic conflict, Freud was being asked to assist in "converting one variety of the genital organization of sexuality into the other" (p. 137). As Freud proceeds to untangle the various threads of the young woman's lesbian attachment, a somewhat confusing and often contradictory portrait of homosexuality emerges.[69]

The woman's sexuality is read through a variety of oppositions which form the territory of psychoanalysis—body and mind ("in both sexes *the degree of physical hermaphroditism is to a great extent independent of the psychical hermaphroditism*" [p. 140]); masculine and feminine desire ("She had thus not only chosen a feminine love-object, but had also developed a masculine attitude towards this object" [p. 141]); maternal and paternal identification (written before Freud hypothesized more extensively about the importance of the preoedipal phase for women, the case history nonetheless acknowledges the maternal object as, if not on the same level of importance as the oedipal scenario, then at the very least constitutive of her sexual identity). The case history is written within the field of these opposing terms, but there are shades of a breakdown of opposition, and the subsequent interdependence of the opposing terms. Hence, Freud speculates that the woman to whom the analysand was so intensely attracted evoked two love objects, her mother and her brother.

> Her latest choice corresponded, therefore, not only with her feminine but also with her masculine ideal; it combined gratification of the homosexual tendency with that of the heterosexual one. It is well known that analysis of male homosexuals has in numerous cases revealed the same combination, which should warn us not to form too simple a conception of the nature and genesis of inversion, and to keep in mind the extensive influence of the bisexuality of mankind. (p. 143)

Indeed, this case history occasions some of Freud's most famous pronouncements on the importance of bisexuality. Speculating that rage toward her father caused the young woman to turn away from men altogether, Freud notes that "in all of us, throughout life, the libido normally oscillates between male and female objects; the bachelor gives up his men friends when he marries and returns to club-life when married life has lost its savour" (p. 144).

But the "bisexuality of mankind" posited in the case history takes two distinctly different forms. On the one hand, it is posited as an originary force, a kind of biological given from which a variety of factors—Freud sometimes privileges predisposition, and sometimes environment—will determine one's choice of sexual aim and sexual object. On the other, bisexuality emerges in a much more challenging and disturbing way as the violent play of warring forces, as evidenced most particularly in the young woman's suicide attempt. For the desperate jump over the railroad wall is no quivering oscillation, and it is far from the kind of serial bisexuality alluded to in the above quotation about bachelors, marriage, and club-life. Rather, in the suicide attempt the battle of maternal and paternal objects attains crisis proportions and provokes a parallel crisis in representation. There are two divergent conceptions of bisexuality in the case history—one that assures that the young woman is either really like a man (in her choice of role) or really like a heterosexual (in her choice of love object), and the other which suggests, rather, a deeper tension between the desire to be seen by the father and the desire to construct an alternative scenario of desire altogether.

Despite its reputation as a more successful exploration of questions posed in the case history of Dora, "The Psychogenesis of a Case of Homosexuality in a Woman" does not read as a particularly convincing narrative in its own right. The "problem" of the case history centers on the woman's self-representation, on her desire, not simply for the loved object but for a certain staging of that desire. In the event of the attempted suicide, it is not clear to what extent it was an unconscious attempt to put an end to parental—and particularly paternal—disapproval by literal self-annihilation, or rather an equally unconscious attempt to dramatize her conflicting allegiances by creating a scene where she is at once active subject and passive object (Freud notes frequently that the young woman's amorous feelings took a "masculine" form). The suicide attempt is best described as both of these simultaneously—one a desire for resolution, the other a desire for another language altogether whereby to represent her conflicted desires.[70] Put another way, the suicide attempt crystallizes the position of "homosexuality in a woman" as a problem of representation and of narrative.

Freud discusses the young woman's case in ways that suggest quite strongly the pressure of lesbianism against a system of explanation and representation. Throughout the case history, the young woman's "masculinity" is the inevitable frame of reference. Masculinity acquires a variety of definitions in the course of the essay, at times associated with the biological characteristics of men (the young woman favored her father in appearance), and at others equated with the mere fact of agency or activity (she displayed a preference for being "lover rather than beloved" [p. 141]). But "masculinity" never really "takes" as an explanation, since throughout the case history the woman remains an embodiment of conflicting desires. The suicide attempt turns upon what has become, in the cinema, a classic account of the activation of desire, the folding of spectacle into narrative. However, in the standard account, woman leans more toward the spectacle with man defined as the active agent. Here, the woman's desires to narrate and to be seen collide, leading her to make quite a spectacle of herself, but without a narrative of her own to contextualize that spectacle. As the young woman recounted the scene, the disapproving gaze from her father led her to tell her female companion of his disapproval, and her companion then adopted the opinion of the father and said that they should not see each other again. The sudden collapse, the identity between lover and father, the erasure of tension, seem to precipitate the woman's quite literal fall. The woman's desire for self-annihilation occurs, in other words, when her desire becomes fully representable within conventional terms.

What I am suggesting, then, is that the conditions of the representability of the lesbian scenario in this case history are simultaneously those of a tension, a conflict (which is "readable" in other than homosexual terms), *and* those of a pressure exerted against the overwhelmingly heterosexual assumptions of the language of psychoanalysis a desire for *another* representation of desire. Or as Wittig puts it, "Homosexuality is the desire for one's own sex. But it is also the desire for something else that is not connoted. This desire is resistance to the norm."[71] Expanding on Irigaray, de Lauretis writes: "Lesbian representation, or rather, its condition of possibility, depends on separating out the two contrary undertows that constitute the paradox of sexual (in)difference, on isolating but maintaining the two senses of homosexuality and hommo-sexuality."[72] The irony in Arzner's signature suggests the division to which de Lauretis refers, between a representation of female communities and an inscription of marginality. That irony stands in (ironic) contrast to feminist film theory's division of Arzner into a textual hommo-sexual (in print) and a visible homosexual (in pictures).

Given Arzner's career in Hollywood, and the realist plots central to her films, her influence would seem to be most apparent among those filmmakers who have appropriated the forms of Hollywood cinema to feminist or even lesbian ends—Susan Seidelman (*Desperately Seeking Susan*), Donna Deitch *(Desert Hearts)*. A more notable connection, however, exists with those contemporary women filmmakers whose films extend the possibilities of lesbian irony while revising the components of the classical cinema and inventing new cinematic forms simultaneously. I turn now to two films which are remarkable explorations of the desire, so succinctly expressed in the case history, to see and to be seen, to detach and to fuse, to narrate one's own desire and to exceed or otherwise complicate the very terms of that narration.

Notes

* This refers to "Screen Tests," in Judith Mayne, *The Woman at the Keyhole: Feminism, and Women's Cinema* (Bloomington: Indiana University Press, 1990).

1 See Margaret Homans, *Bearing the Word: Language and Female Experience in Nineteenth-Century Women's Writing* (Chicago: University of Chicago Press, 1986); and Nancy K. Miller, *Subject to Change: Reading Feminist Writing* (New York: Columbia University Press, 1988).

2 Doris Lessing, *The Golden Notebook* (1962; rpt. New York: Simon and Schuster, 1973), p. 619.

3 Christa Wolf, *The Quest for Christa T.* (1968; English trans. Christopher Middleton, New York: Delta, 1970), p. 4.

4 In her essay on the relation between feminism and Christa Wolf's work, Myra Love analyzes the status of film as an image "used to evoke the connections among domination, manipulation and experiential impoverishment." See "Christa Wolf and Feminism," *New German Critique* 16 (Winter 1979), 36.

5 Wolf, *The Quest for Christa T.*, p. 170.

6 Mary Ann Doane, Patricia Mellencamp, and Linda Williams, "Feminist Film Criticism: An Introduction," in Doane, Mellencamp, and Williams, eds., *Revision: Essays in Feminist Film Criticism* (Frederick, Md.: The American Film Institute/University Publications of America, 1984), p. 7. The editors are responding to a definition of feminist literary criticism by Elizabeth Abel, as the exploration of "distinctive features of female texts" and "lines of influence connecting women in a fertile and partially autonomous tradition." Abel's comments are drawn from "Editor's Introduction," *Critical Inquiry* 8, no. 2 (Winter 1981), 173.

7 Maria LaPlace argues for Bette Davis's significance as a creative force in her own right. See "Producing and Consuming the Woman's Film: Discursive Struggle in *Now, Voyager*," in Christine Gledhill, ed., *Home Is Where the Heart Is: Studies in Melodrama and the Woman's Film* (London: British Film Institute, 1987), pp. 138–66.

8 An excellent survey of the most significant texts on cinematic authorship is John Caughie, ed., *Theories of Authorship* (London: Routledge and Kegan Paul, 1981).

9 A useful survey and analysis of the different meanings that have been attached to the term *auteurism* can be found in Peter Wollen, *Signs and Meaning in the Cinema* (Bloomington: Indiana University Press, 1969), chapter 2.

10 Roland Barthes, *The Pleasure of the Text* (New York: Hill and Wang, 1975), trans. Richard Miller, p. 27.

11 Alexandre Astruc, "The Birth of a New Avant-Garde: *La caméra-stylo*," in P. Graham, ed., *The New Wave* (London: Secker and Warburg, 1968), pp. 17–23. Susan Gubar and Sandra Gilbert begin their analysis of women writers with a query into the equivalence between pen and penis; see *The Madwoman in the Attic* (New Haven: Yale University Press, 1979), p. 3.

12 See Domna Stanton, "Language and Revolution: The Franco-American Disconnection," in Hester Eisenstein and Alice Jardine, eds., *The Future of Difference* (1980; rpt. New Brunswick, N.J.: Rutgers University Press, 1985), pp. 73–87.

13 For particularly lucid expositions of these two positions, as well as the problems involved in defining the positions as opposing in the first place, see Peggy Kamuf, "Replacing Feminist Criticism," and Nancy Miller, "The Text's Heroine: A Feminist Critic and Her Fictions," *Diacritics* 12, no. 2 (Summer 1982), 42–53.

14 Claire Johnston, "Women's Cinema as Counter-cinema," in Claire Johnston, ed., *Notes on Women's Cinema* (1973; rpt. London: British Film Institute, 1975), p. 26.

15 See Wollen, *Signs and Meaning in the Cinema*, chapter 2.

16 Johnston, "Women's Cinema as Counter-cinema," p. 27. A comparison between Hawks and Ford as *auteurs* is also central in Wollen's discussion of auteurism (*Signs and Meaning in the Cinema*, chapter 2).

17 One notable exception is Tania Modleski's study of women and female spectatorship in the films of Alfred Hitchcock, although it is in no way a conventional "auteurist" study. See *The Women Who Knew Too Much* (New York: Methuen, 1988).

18 See Raymond Bellour, "Hitchcock the Enunciator," *Camera Obscura*, no. 2 (Fall 1977), 66–91.

19 Nancy K. Miller, "Changing the Subject: Authorship, Writing, and the Reader," in Teresa de Lauretis, ed., *Feminist Studies/Critical Studies* (Bloomington: Indiana University Press, 1986), p. 104.

20 Kaja Silverman, *The Acoustic Mirror: The Female Voice in Psychoanalysis and Cinema* (Bloomington: Indiana University Press, 1988), p. 209.

21 Ibid., pp. 212–17.

22 Ibid., p. 217.

23 This is suggested by de Lauretis herself: "the differences among women may be better understood as differences within women." See "Feminist Studies/Critical Studies: Issues, Terms, and Contexts," in de Lauretis, *Feminist Studies/Critical Studies*, p. 14.

24 Kaja Silverman refers to such a process as the "re-authoring" of a traditional text in feminist terms. See *The Acoustic Mirror*, p. 211.

25 For an insightful discussion of the ideology of auteurist critics in France, see John Hess, "La Politique des auteurs: Part One: World View as Aesthetic," *Jump Cut*, no. 1 (1974), 19–22; and "La Politique des auteurs: Part Two: Truffaut's Manifesto," *Jump Cut*, no. 2 (1974), 20–22.

26 Andrew Britton, *Katharine Hepburn: The Thirties and After* (Newcastle upon Tyne: Tyneside Cinema, 1984), p. 74.

27 Jacquelyn Suter, "Feminine Discourse in *Christopher Strong*," *Camera Obscura*, no. 3–4 (Summer 1979), 135–50.

28 Roland Barthes, *S/Z* (New York: Hill and Wang, 1974), trans. Richard Miller, p. 8.

29 See the editors of *Cahiers du cinéma's* collective text, "John Ford's *Young Mr. Lincoln*," *Screen* 13 (Autumn 1972), 5–44; on *Mildred Pierce*, see Joyce Nelson, "*Mildred Pierce* Reconsidered," *Film Reader*, no. 2 (1977), 65–70; Pam Cook, "Duplicity in *Mildred Pierce*," in E. Ann Kaplan, ed., *Women in Film Noir* (London: British Film Institute, 1978), pp. 68–82; Janet Walker, "Feminist Critical Practice; Female Discourse in *Mildred Pierce*," *Film Reader*, no. 5 (1982), 164–72; Judith Mayne, *Private Novels, Public Films* (Athens: University of Georgia Press, 1988), pp. 142–54; and Linda Williams, "Feminist Film Theory: *Mildred Pierce* and the Second World War," in Deidre Pribram, ed., *Female Spectators: Loking at Film and Television* (London and New York: Verso, 1988), pp. 12–30.

30 One of the best examples of this kind of analysis is Lea Jacobs, "*Now, Voyager:* Some Problems of Enunciation and Sexual Difference," *Camera Obscura*, no. 7 (1981), 89–109.

31 I am not arguing here, as Janet Bergstrom has done in her criticism of Johnston, that the problem is the ultimate recuperability of all forms of difference by the apparatus of the Hollywood cinema. Referring specifically to the work of Stephen Heath, and more generally to textual analyses by critics such as Raymond Bellour and Thierry Kuntzel, Bergstrom criticizes Johnston's proto-feminist claims for elements which, she says, fit quite readily into classical narrative cinema. Bergstrom speaks of the "seemingly unlimited capacity for classical narrative film to create gaps, fissures, ruptures, generated most of all by its difficulty in containing sexual difference, only to recover them ultimately and to efface the memory, or at least the paths, of this heterogeneity. It is just this rupturing activity that is said to be characteristic of the classical text, and which, moreover, is thought to be the condition of a large part of its pleasure." While I would agree with Bergstrom that Johnston makes somewhat extravagant claims for elements which may well be incorporated into the overall narrative and visual momentum of the individual film, the view of the Hollywood cinema put forth by those critics to whose work she points approvingly is no less monolithic in the articulation of oedipal scenarios and male heterosexual desire. And needless to say, if heterogeneity is effaced, then there is no room in which to speak of female authorship. See Janet Bergstrom, "Rereading the Work of Claire Johnston," *Camera Obscura*, no. 3–4 (1979), 27.

32 "Interview—1974: Julia Kristéva and Psychanalyse et politique," trans. Claire Pajaczkowska, *m/f*, no. 5–6 (1981), 166.

33 Claire Johnston, "Dorothy Arzner: Critical Strategies," in Claire Johnson, ed., *The Work of Dorothy Arzner: Towards a Feminist Cinema* (London: British Film Institute, 1975), p. 6.

34 Lucy Fischer reads *Dance, Girl, Dance* in terms of this "resistance to fetishism." See *Shot/Countershot* (Princeton: Princeton University Press, 1989), pp. 148–54.

35 Karyn Kay and Gerald Peary's reading of the film, however, focuses much more centrally on women's friendships and the rites of initiation. See "Dorothy Arzner's *Dance, Girl, Dance*," in Karyn Kay and Gerald Peary, eds., *Women and the Cinema: A Critical Anthology* (New York: Dutton, 1977), pp. 9–25.

36 Barbara Koenig Quart stresses the relationship between Judy and the secretary in her reading of the scene. See *Women Directors: The Emergence of a New Cinema* (New York and Westport, Conn.: Praeger, 1988), p. 25.

37 Barbara Quart (ibid.) suggests a connection between Arzner's career and the show-business world depicted in *Dance, Girl, Dance:* "Arzner is clearly ambivalent about the vital, glamorous vulgarity of Bubbles, the Lucille Ball showgirl—but the scorn for Hollywood implicit in the film, and for the need to be a flesh peddler to survive there, is doubtless something Arzner herself felt in no small part, in this next to last of her films, close to her retirement."

38 Shoshana Felman, "To Open the Question," *Yale French Studies*, no. 55–56 (1980), 8.

39 Donna Haraway, "A Manifesto for Cyborgs: Science, Technology, and Socialist Feminism in the 1980s," *Socialist Review*, no. 80 (1985), 65.

40 Johnston, "Dorothy Arzner: Critical Strategies," p. 7.

41 The relationships of desire between women in Arzner's films are developed at length in my book-length study of Arzner (forthcoming, Indiana University Press). For an analysis of the secondary roles men play in Arzner's films, see Melissa Sue Kort, " 'Spectacular Spinelessness': The Men in Dorothy Arzner's Films," in Janet Todd, ed., *Men by Women, Women and Literature* (New Series), vol. 2 (1982), pp. 189–205.

42 Barbara Smith, "Toward a Black Feminist Criticism," *Conditions*, no. 2 (October 1977), 25–44; Interview with Toni Morrison in Claudia Tate, ed., *Black Women Writers at Work* (New York: Continuum, 1983), p. 118.

43 See, for example, Vito Russo, *The Celluloid Closet: Homosexuality in the Movies* (New York: Harper and Row, 1981), p. 50.

44 Sharon O'Brien addresses these questions in her study of Willa Cather. Noting that the definition of "lesbianism" and "lesbian writer" has been important in recent feminist criticism, O'Brien says, "For good reason, genital sexual experience with women has been the least-used criterion. As several critics have observed, to adopt such a definition requires the unearthing of 'proof' we do not think necessary in defining writers as heterosexual—proof, moreover, that is usually unavailable. . . ." See *Willa Cather: The Emerging Voice* (New York and Oxford: Oxford University Press, 1987), p. 127.

45 Bonnie Zimmerman, "What Has Never Been: An Overview of Lesbian Feminist Criticism," *Feminist Studies* 7, no. 3 (Fall 1981), 457.

46 Sarah Halprin, "Writing in the Margins (Review of E. Ann Kaplan, *Women and Film: Both Sides of the Camera*)," *Jump Cut*, no. 29 (1984), 32.

47 Russo, *The Celluloid Closet*, p. 50.

48 Karyn Kay and Gerald Peary, "Interview with Dorothy Arzner," in Johnston, *The Work of Dorothy Arzner*, pp. 25–26.

49 Jackie Stacey discusses female sexual attraction as a principle of identification in *All about Eve* and *Desperately Seeking Susan;* see "Desperately Seeking Difference," *Screen* 28, no. 1 (Winter 1987), 48–61.

50 Constance Penley, ed., *Feminism and Film Theory* (New York and London: Routledge, 1988). In Mary Ann Doane's essay "*Caught* and *Rebecca:* The Inscription of Femininity as Absence," Julia Kristéva is cited on "female homosexuality" (p. 199), but in order to demonstrate the radical difference between male and female spectatorship.

51 For an excellent discussion of the very possibility of a feminist fetishism, see Jane Marcus, "The Asylums of Antaeus. Women, War, and Madness: Is There a Feminist Fetishism?" in Elizabeth Meese and Alice Parker, eds., *The Difference Within: Feminism and Critical Theory* (Amsterdam and Philadelphia: John Benjamins Publishing Co., 1989), pp. 49–83. Marcus examines how feminists in the suffrage movement oscillated "between denial and recognition of *rape* as the common denominator of female experience" (p. 76). Naomi Schor has examined the possibility of female fetishism in the writings of George Sand; see "Female Fetishism: The Case of George Sand," in Susan Suleiman, ed., *The Female Body in Western Culture* (Cambridge: Harvard University Press, 1986), pp. 363–72.

52 See Christian Metz, *The Imaginary Signifier* (Bloomington: Indiana University Press, 1982), trans. Ben Brewster, pp. 69–80. A chapter of Octave Mannoni's *Clefs pour l'imaginaire ou l'autre scène* (Paris: Editions du Seuil, 1969) is entitled "Je sais bien, mais quand même . . ." ("I know very well, but all the same . . .").

53 Beverle Houston, "Missing in Action: Notes on Dorothy Arzner," *Wide Angle* 6, no. 3 (1984), 27.

54 See Suter, "Feminine Discourse in *Christopher Strong*."

55 The phrase "lesbian continuum" comes from Adrienne Rich, "Compulsory Heterosexuality and Lesbian Existence," *Signs* 5, no. 4 (Summer 1980), 631–60.

56 Julia Lesage, "The Hegemonic Female Fantasy in *An Unmarried Woman* and *Craig's Wife*," *Film Reader*, no. 5 (1982), 91. In Karyn Kay and Gerald Peary's interview, Arzner states that Kelley was angry at the changes in emphasis that were made.

57 Melissa Sue Kort also discusses Arzner's reading of the Kelley play, noting that the "shift from play to film changes Harriet from villain to victim." See her discussion of the film in " 'Spectacular Spinelessness,' " pp. 196–200.

58 See Esther Newton, "The Mythic Mannish Lesbian: Radclyffe Hall and the New Woman," *Signs* 9, no. 4 (Summer 1984), 557–75. See also Lillian Faderman, *Surpassing the Love of Men: Romantic Friendship and Love between Women from the Renaissance to the Present* (New York: William Morrow and Co., 1981), esp. parts II and III.

59 Nancy K. Miller makes this observation about irony: "To the extent that the ethos (charcter, disposition) of feminism historically has refused the doubleness of 'saying one thing while it tries to do another' (the mark of classical femininity, one might argue), it may be that an ironic feminist discourse finds itself at odds both with itself (its identity to itself) and with the expectations its audience has of its position. If that is true, then irony, in the final analysis, may be a figure of limited effectiveness. On the other hand, since nonironic, single, sincere, hortatory feminism is becoming ineffectual, it may be worth the risk of trying out this kind of duplicity on the road." See "Changing the Subject: Authorship, Writing, and the Reader," in de Lauretis, *Feminist Studies/Critical Studies*, p. 119, n. 18.

60 See the Camera Obscura Collective, "An Interrogation of the Cinematic Sign: Woman as Sexual Signifier in Jackie Raynal's *Deux fois*," *Camera Obscura*, no. 1 (Fall 1976), 11–26.

61 See David Rodowick, "The Difficulty of Difference," *Wide Angle* 5, no. 1 (1982), 4–15; de Lauretis, *Alice Doesn't*, chapter 5; Miriam Hansen, "Pleasure, Ambivalence, Identification: Valentino and Female Spectatorship," *Cinema Journal* 25, no. 4 (Summer 1986), 6–32; Gaylyn Studlar, *In the Realm of Pleasure: Von Sternberg, Dietrich, and the Masochistic Aesthetic* (Urbana: University of Illinois Press, 1988). Mulvey herself has contributed to the discussion; see "Afterthoughts on 'Visual Pleasure and Narrative Cinema' Inspired by King Vidor's *Duel in the Sun* (1946)," in *Visual and Other Pleasures* (Bloomington: Indiana University Press, 1989), pp. 29–38.

62 David Bordwell, in David Bordwell, Janet Staiger, and Kristin Thompson, *The Classical Hollywood Cinema: Film Style and Mode of Production to 1960* (New York: Columbia University Press, 1985), p. 16.

63 Monique Wittig, "The Straight Mind," *Feminist Issues* 1, no. 1 (Summer 1980), 107.

64 Luce Irigaray, "Women on the Market," in *This Sex Which Is Not One*, trans. Catherine Porter (Ithaca: Cornell University Press, 1985), p. 172.

65 Irigaray, "Commodities among Themselves," in *This Sex Which Is Not One*, p. 194.

66 Jacqueline Rose, "Dora: Fragment of an Analysis," in Charles Bernheimer and Claire Kahane, eds., *In Dora's Case* (New York: Columbia University Press, 1985), p. 135.

67 Sigmund Freud, "The Psychogenesis of a Case of Homosexuality in a Woman (1920)," in *Sexuality and the Psychology of Love*, ed. Philip Rieff (New York: Collier Books, 1963), p. 134. Subsequent page numbers will be indicated in parentheses in the text.

68 See Rose, "Dora: Fragment of an Analysis"; and Suzanne Gearhart, "The Scene of Psychoanalysis: The Unanswered Questions of Dora," in *In Dora's Case*, pp. 105–127.

69 Mandy Merck discusses the peculiar portrait of homosexuality in the case history, and notes in particular that there is a sharp break between the young woman's homosexual and heterosexual pasts as described by Freud, suggesting that despite what Rose describes as a "nonneurotic" definition of homosexuality, there remains nonetheless the desire to read heterosexuality as the privileged source of all desire. See "The Train of Thought in Freud's 'Case of Homosexuality in a Woman,' " *m/f*, nos. 11–12 (1986), 37, 39.

70 I believe what I am describing as the desire for another representation of desire is quite close to Mandy Merck's discussion of the young woman's conflict about "masculine identification." See "The Train of Thought," p. 40.

71 Monique Wittig, "Paradigm," in George Stambolian and Elaine Marks, eds., *Homosexualities and French Literature: Cultural Contexts/Critical Texts* (Ithaca: Cornell University Press, 1979), p. 114.

72 Teresa de Lauretis, "Sexual Indifference and Lesbian Representation," *Theatre Journal* 40, no. 2 (May 1988), 159.

Chapter 12

Robin Wood

PAPERING THE CRACKS: FANTASY AND IDEOLOGY IN THE REAGAN ERA (1986)

Editors' Introduction

From the late 1950s through the early 1980s, the *auteur* theory enabled a straightforward aesthetic history of cinema. Primarily a study of exemplary films and film directors fashioned around textual analyses, it provided a film studies equivalent to the Great Books tradition in the heyday of the New Criticism. In "Papering the Cracks: Fantasy and Ideology in the Reagan Era," Robin Wood introduces a rather significant new direction for *auteurism*; one focusing on the ideological function of popular art in general. Borrowing freely from the philosophy of Roland Barthes, especially the notion of "inoculation" (in which works of popular mythology distract from the very real problems of the larger culture), and the formidable film historian Andrew Britton, whose essay "Blissing Out: The Politics of Reaganite Entertainment" foregrounds a Frankfort School approach to films and filmmaking in the 1980s, Wood's reading of George Lucas' and Steven Spielberg's intersecting *oeuvres* draws connections between "an era of sequels and repetition" in American filmmaking and "an era of recuperation and reaction" in American politics. The filmmakers under review here are characterized not as artists tilting against a system rigged against them, but as "extraordinarily efficient" company men producing works of "conservative reassurance," works sporting a timely symmetry with the "Reagan Revolution."

Wood examines the influence of Lucas and Spielberg's films on their legions of fans, contending that the films by and large prioritize "the reactionary over the progressive, the safe over the challenging, the childish over the adult, spectator passivity over spectator activity." While the majority of *auteur* histories feature a fair share of subjective analysis and evaluation, Wood takes that one step further, focusing here on directors whose work is, with regard to artistic achievement, (in his view) unaccountably over-rated, and with regard to ideological influence, profoundly under-estimated.

Suggested Reading

Andrew Britton, "Blissing Out: The Politics of Reaganite Entertainment," in *Britton on Film: The Complete Film Criticism of Andrew Britton* (Detroit: Wayne State University Press, 2009); Jon Lewis, "The Perfect Money Machines: George Lucas, Steven Spielberg, and Auteurism in the New Hollywood," in *Looking Past the Screen: Case Studies in American Film History and Method* (Duke University Press, 2007); and Lester Friedman, *Citizen Spielberg* (Bloomington: Illinois University Press, 2006).

The Lucas–Spielberg Syndrome

THE CRISIS IN IDEOLOGICAL confidence of the 70s visible on all levels of American culture and variously enacted in Hollywood's "incoherent texts," has not been resolved: within the system of patriarchal capitalism no resolution of the fundamental conflicts is possible. Instead, it has been *forgotten*, though its specter, masquerading as idealized nostalgia for lost radicalism, still intermittently haunts the cinema (*The Big Fix, The Big Chill, Return of the Secaucus Seven*). Remembering can be pleasant when it is accompanied by the sense that there is really nothing you can do any more ("Times have changed"). Vietnam ends, Watergate comes to seem an unfortunate aberration (with a film like *All The President's Men* actually feeling able, though ambiguously, to celebrate the democratic system that can expose and rectify such anomalies); the Carter administration, promising the sense of a decent and reassuring liberalism, makes possible a huge ideological sigh of relief in preparation for an era of recuperation and reaction, *Rocky* and *Star Wars*—the two seminal works of what Andrew Britton (in an article in *Movie* 31/32 to which the present chapter is heavily indebted) has termed "Reaganite entertainment"—appear a few years before Reagan's election, and are instant, overwhelming commercial successes. Their respective progenies are still very much with us.

Reassurance is the keynote, and one immediately reflects that this is the era of sequels and repetition. The success of *Raiders of the Lost Ark*, *E. T.*, and the *Star Wars* movies is dependent not only on the fact that so many people go to see them, but also that so many see them again and again. The phenomenon develops a certain irony in conjunction with Barthes' remarks on "rereading", in *S/Z*. "Rereading [is] an operation contrary to the commercial and ideological habits of our society, which would have us 'throw away' the story once it has been consumed ('devoured'), so that we can then move on to another story, buy another book, and which is tolerated only in certain marginal categories of readers (children, old people, and professors)."

Clearly, different kinds of rereading occur, (children and professors do not reread in quite the same way or for the same purpose): it is possible to "read" a film like *Letter from an Unknown Woman* or *Late Spring* twenty times and still discover new meanings, new complexities, ambiguities, possibilities of interpretation. It seems unlikely, however, that this is what takes people back, again and again, to *Star Wars*.

Young children require not-quite-endless repetition—the same game played over and over. When at last they begin to weary of exact repetition they demand slight variation: the game still easily recognizable, but not entirely predictable. It can be argued that this pattern forms the basis for much of our adult pleasure in traditional art. Stephen Neale, in one of the very few useful works on the subject (*Genre*, British Film Institute, 1980), discusses the Hollywood genres in such terms. The distinction between the great genre movies and the utterly uncreative hack work (between, say, *Rio Bravo* and *The Man Who Shot Liberty Valance* on the one hand, and the Roy Rogers or Hopalong Cassidy series on the other) lies very largely in the relationship between the familiar and the surprising—in the length of the leap the spectator is asked to make from generic expectations to specific transformations, the transformations being as much ideological as conventional. The repetition-and-sequel pattern of the 80s is obviously of a very different order: despite the expensiveness of the films and their status as "cultural event," it is closer to Roy Rogers than to Ford and Hawks. The satisfactions of *Star Wars* are repeated until a sequel is required: same formula, with variations. But instead of a leap, only an infant footstep is necessary, and never one that might demand an adjustment on the level of ideology.

Hence the ironic appositeness of Barthes' perception that rereading is tolerated in children. The category of children's films has of course always existed. The 80s variant is the curious and disturbing phenomenon of children's films conceived and marketed largely for adults—films that construct the adult spectator as a child, or, more precisely, as a childish adult, an adult who would like to be a child. The child loses him/herself in fantasy, accepting the illusion; the childish adult both does and does not, simultaneously. The characteristic response to *E. T.* (heard, with variations, over and over again) was "Wasn't it *wonderful?*" followed instantly by a nervously apologetic "But of course it's pure fantasy." In this way, the particular satisfactions the films offer—the lost breast repeatedly rediscovered—can be at once indulged and laughed off. That the apology (after all, the merest statement of the obvious) has to be made at all testifies to the completeness of the surrender on another level to the indulgence.

It remains to define just what those satisfactions are, the kinds of reassurance demanded and so profitably supplied. It will be scarcely surprising that they—as it were, incidentally and obliquely—diminish, defuse, and render safe all the major radical movements that gained so much impetus, became so threatening, in the 70s: radical feminism, black militancy, gay liberation, the assault on patriarchy. Before cataloguing them, however, it is as well to foreground certain problems that arise in discussing (and attacking) the films. It is, in fact, peculiarly difficult to discuss them seriously. The films themselves set up a deliberate resistance: they are so insistently not serious, so knowing about their own escapist fantasy/pure entertainment nature, and they consistently invite the audience's complicity in this. To raise serious objections to them is to run the risk of looking a fool (they're "just entertainment," after all) or, worse, a spoilsport (they're "such fun"). Pleasure is indeed an important issue. I had better confess at once that I enjoy the *Star Wars* films well enough: I get moderately excited, laugh a bit, even brush back a tear at the happy endings, all right on cue: they work, they are extremely efficient. But just what do we mean when we say "they work"? They work because their workings correspond to the workings of our own social construction. I claim no exemption from this: I enjoy being reconstructed as a child, surrendering to the reactivation of a set of values and structures my adult self has long since repudiated, I am not immune to the blandishments of reassurance. Pleasure itself, in fact, is patently ideological. We may be born with the desire for pleasure, but the actual gratifications of the desire are of necessity culturally determined, a product of our social conditioning. Pleasure, then, can never be taken for granted while we wish to remain adult; it isn't sacrosanct, purely natural and spontaneous, beyond analysis which spoils it (on many levels, it is imperative that our pleasure be spoiled). The pleasure offered by the *Star Wars* films corresponds very closely to our basic conditioning; it is extremely reactionary, as all mindless and automatic pleasure tends to be. The finer pleasures are those we have to work for.

I do not want to argue that the films are intrinsically and uniquely harmful: they are no more so than the vast majority of artifacts currently being produced by capitalist enterprise for popular consumption within a patriarchal culture. In many ways they resemble the old serials (Buck Rogers, Superman, Batman, etc.) that used to accompany feature films in weekly instalments as program fillers, or get shown at children's matinees. What I find worrying about the Spielberg–Lucas syndrome is the enormous importance our society has conferred upon the films, an importance not at all incompatible with their not being taken seriously ("But of course, it's pure fantasy"): indeed, the apparent contradiction is crucial to the phenomenon. The old serials were not taken seriously on *any* level (except perhaps by real children, and then only young ones); their role in popular culture was minor and marginal; they posed no threat to the co-existence of challenging, disturbing or genuinely distinguished Hollywood movies, which they often accompanied in their lowly capacity. Today it is becoming difficult for films that are not like *Star Wars* (at least in the general sense of dispensing reassurance, but increasingly in more specific and literal ways, too) to get made, and when they do get made, the public and often the critics reject them: witness the box office failure of *Heaven's Gate, Blade Runner*, and *King of Comedy*.

These, then, are what seem to me the major areas in which the films provide reassurance. I have centered the argument in the *Star Wars* films (*E. T.* is dealt with separately afterward), but it will be obvious that most of my points apply, to varying degrees, over a much wider field of contemporary Hollywood cinema.

1. *Childishness*. I cannot abandon this theme without somewhat fuller development. It is important to stress that I am not positing some diabolical Hollywood-capitalist-Reaganite conspiracy to impose mindlessness and mystification on a potentially revolutionary populace, nor does there seem much point in blaming the filmmakers for what they are doing (the critics are another matter). The success of the films is only comprehensible when one assumes a widespread *desire* for regression to infantilism, a populace who wants to be constructed as mock children. Crucial here, no doubt, is the urge to evade responsibility—responsibility for actions, decisions, thought, responsibility for changing things: children do not have to be responsible, there are older people to look after them. That is one reason why these films must be intellectually undemanding. It is not exactly that one doesn't have to think to enjoy *Star Wars*, but rather that thought is strictly limited to the most superficial narrative channels: "What will happen? How will they get out of this?" The films are obviously very skillful in their handling of narrative, their resourceful, ceaseless interweaving of actions and enigmas, their knowing deployment of the most familiar narrative patterns: don't worry, Uncle George (or Uncle Steven) will take you by the hand and lead you through Wonderland. Some dangers will appear on the way, but never fear, he'll also see you safely home; home being essentially those "good old values" that Sylvester Stallone told us *Rocky* was designed to reinstate: racism, sexism, "democratic" capitalism; the capitalist myths of freedom of choice and equality of opportunity, the individual hero whose achievements somehow "make everything all right", even for the millions who never make it to individual heroism (but every man can be a hero—even, such is the grudging generosity of contemporary liberalism, every woman).

2. *Special Effects*. These represent the essence of Wonderland Today (Alice never needed reassurance about technology) and the one really significant way in which the films differ from the old serials. Again, one must assume a kind of automatic doublethink in audience response: we both know and don't know that we are watching special effects, technological fakery. Only thus can we respond simultaneously to the two levels of "magic": the diegetic wonders within the narrative and the extra-diegetic magic of Hollywood (the best magic that money can buy), the technology on screen, the technology off. Spectacle—the sense of reckless, prodigal extravagance, no expense spared—is essential: the unemployment lines in the world outside may get longer and longer, we may even have to go out and join them, but if capitalism can still throw out entertainments like *Star Wars* (the films' very uselessness an aspect of the prodigality), the system must be basically OK, right? Hence, as capitalism approaches its ultimate breakdown, through that series of escalating economic crises prophesied by Marx well over a century ago, its entertainments must become more dazzling, more extravagant, more luxuriously unnecessary.

3. *Imagination/Originality*. A further seeming paradox (actually only the extension of the "But of course it's pure fantasy" syndrome) is that the audiences who wish to be constructed as children also wish to regard themselves as extremely sophisticated and "modern". The actual level of this sophistication can be gauged from the phenomenon (not unfamiliar to teachers of first-year film studies in universities) that the same young people who sit rapt through *Star Wars* find it necessary to laugh condescendingly at, say, a von Sternberg/Dietrich movie or a Ford western in order to establish their superiority to such passé simple-mindedness. "Of course it's pure fantasy—but what imagination!"—the flattering sense of one's own sophistication depends upon the ability to juggle such attitudes, an ability the films constantly nurture. If we are to continue using the term "imagination" to apply to a William Blake, we have no business using it of a George Lucas. Imagination and what is popularly referred to as pure fantasy (actually there is no such thing) are fundamentally incompatible. Imagination is a force that strives to grasp and transform the world, not restore "the good old values." What we can justly credit Lucas with (I use the name, be it understood, to stand for his whole production team) is facility of invention, especially on the level of special effects and makeup and the creation of a range of cute or sinister or grotesque fauna (human and non-human).

The "originality" of the films goes very precisely with their "imagination": window dressing to conceal—but not entirely—the extreme familiarity of plot, characterization, situation, and character relations. Again, doublethink operates: even while we relish the originality, we must also retain the sense of the familiar, the comforting nostalgia for the childish, repetitive pleasures of comic strip and serial (if we can't find the lost breast we can at least suck our thumbs). Here doublethink becomes almost a synonym for sophistication. The fanciful trimmings of the *Star Wars* saga enable us to indulge in satisfactions that would have us writhing in embarrassment if they were presented naked. The films have in fact largely replaced Hollywood genres that are no longer viable without careful "it's pure fantasy" disguise, but for whose basic impulses there survives a need created and sustained by the dominant ideology of imperialist capitalism. Consider their relation to the 40s war movie, of which Hawks' *Air Force* might stand as both representative and superior example: the group (bomber crew, infantry platoon, etc.) constructed as a microcosm of multiracial democracy. The war movie gave us various ethnic types (Jew, Polack, etc.) under the leadership of a WASP American; the Lucas films substitute fantasy figures (robots, Chewbacca) fulfilling precisely the same roles, surreptitiously permitting the same indulgence in WASP superiority. *Air Force* culminates in an all-out assault on the Japanese fleet, blasted out of the sea by "our boys": a faceless, inhuman enemy getting its just deserts. Today, the Japanese can no longer be called Japs ("One fried Jap going down"—*Air Force*'s most notorious line), and are no longer available for fulfilling that function (we are too "sophisticated"). However, dress the enemy in odd costumes (they remain faceless and inhuman, perhaps even totally metallic) and we can still cheer our boys when they blast them out of the sky as in the climax of *Star Wars*, etc.: the same indoctrinated values of patriotism, racism and militarism are being indulged and celebrated.

Consider also the exotic adventure movie: our white heroes, plus comic relief, encounter a potentially hostile tribe; but the natives turn out to be harmless, childlike, innocent—they have never seen a white man before, and they promptly worship our heroes as gods. You can't do that any more: such movies (mostly despised "B" movies anyway) don't get shown now, and if we saw one on late-night television we would have to laugh at it. But dress the natives as koala bears, displace the god identity on to a robot so that the natives appear even stupider, and you can still get away with it: the natives can still be childlike, lovable, and ready to help the heroes out of a fix; the nature of the laughter changes from repudiation to complicity.

4. *Nuclear Anxiety*. This is central to Andrew Britton's thesis, and for an adequately detailed treatment I refer readers to the article cited above. The fear of nuclear war—at least, of indescribable suffering, at most, of the end of the world, with the end of civilization somewhere between—is certainly one of the main sources of our desire to be constructed as children, to be reassured, to evade responsibility and thought. The characteristic and widespread sense of helplessness—that it's all out of our hands, beyond all hope of effective intervention, perhaps already predetermined—for which there is unfortunately a certain degree of rational justification, is continually fostered both by the media and by the cynicism of politicians: whether we *can* actually do anything (and to escape despair and insanity we must surely cling to any rational belief that we can), it is clearly in the interests of our political/ economic system for us to believe we can't. In terms of cinema, one side of this fear is the contemporary horror film, centered on the unkillable and ultimately inexplicable monster, the mysterious and terrible destructive force we can neither destroy, nor communicate with, nor understand. The Michael of *Halloween* and the Jason of the later *Friday the 13th* films are the obvious prototypes, but the indestructible psychopath of Michael Miller's *Silent Rage* is especially interesting because he is actually signified as the product of scientific experimentation with nuclear energy. The other side is the series of fantasy films centered on the struggle for possession of an ultimate weapon or power: the Ark of the Covenant of *Raiders of the Lost Ark*, the Genesis project of *Star Trek II*, "the Force" of *Star Wars*. The relationship of the two cycles (which developed simultaneously and are both extremely popular with, and aimed at, young audiences) might seem at first sight to be one of diametrical opposition (hopelessness vs. reassurance), yet their respective overall messages—"There's nothing you can do, anyway" and "Don't worry"—can be read as complements rather than opposites: both are deterrents to action. The pervasive, if surreptitious, implication of the fantasy films is that nuclear power is positive and justified as long as it is in the right, i.e., American, hands. *Raiders* is particularly blatant on the subject, offering a direct invitation to deliberate ignorance: you'll be all right, and all your enemies will be destroyed, as long as you "don't look"; nuclear power is synonymous with the power of God, who is, by definition, on our side. The film is also particularly blatant in its racism: non-Americans are in general either evil or stupid. The disguise of comic strip is somewhat more transparent than the disguise of pure fantasy. Nonetheless, it can scarcely escape notice that the arch-villain Khan of *Star Trek II* is heavily signified as foreign (and played by a foreign actor, Ricardo Montalban), as against the American-led crew of the spaceship (with its appropriate collection of fantasy-ethnic subordinates). The younger generation of *Star Wars* heroes is also conspicuously American.

The question has been raised as to whether the *Star Wars* films really fit this pattern: if they contain a fantasy embodiment of nuclear power it is surely not the Force but the Death Star, which the Force, primarily signified in terms of moral rectitude and discipline rather than physical or technological power, is used to destroy. Can't they then be read as *anti*-nuclear films? Perhaps an ambiguity can be conceded (I concede it without much conviction). But moral rectitude has always been an attribute of Americans in the Hollywood war movie; the Death Star was created by the Force (its "dark side," associated with the evil-non-Americans); and the use of the Force by Luke Skywalker in *Star Wars* is undeniably martial, violent, and destructive (though *Return of the Jedi* raises some belated qualms about this). Given the context—both generic and social-political—it seems to me that the same essential message, perhaps more covert and opaque, can be read from the *Star Wars* trilogy as from *Raiders* and *Star Trek II*.

5. *Fear of Fascism*. I refer here not to the possibility of a Fascist threat from outside but from *inside*: the fear, scarcely unfounded, that continually troubles the American (un-) consciousness that democratic capitalism may not be cleanly separable from Fascism and may carry within itself the potential to become Fascist, totalitarian, a police state. The theme has

been handled with varying degrees of intelligence and complexity in a number of overtly political films—supremely, *Meet John Doe;* but also a range of films from *All the King's Men* through *Advise and Consent* and *The Parallax View* to *The Dead Zone*, the theme particularly taking the form of the demagogue-who may-become-dictator by fooling enough of the people enough of the time. The fear haunts the work of Hitchcock: the U-Boat commander of *Lifeboat* is of course German and explicitly Fascist, but he is not clearly distinguishable in his ruthlessness, his assumption of superiority and his insidious charm from the American murderers of *Shadow of a Doubt* and *Rope*. More generally, how does one distinguish between the American individualist hero and the Fascist hero? Are the archetypes of westerner and gangster opposites or complements? The quandary becomes ever more pressing in the Reagan era, with the resurgence of an increasingly militant, vociferous and powerful Right, the Fascist potential forcing itself to recognition. It would be neither fair nor accurate to describe *Rocky* and *Raiders of the Lost Ark* as Fascist films; yet they are precisely the kinds of entertainment that a potentially Fascist culture would be expected to produce and enjoy (what exactly are we applauding as we cheer on the exploits of Indiana Jones?).

The most positively interesting aspect of the *Star Wars* films (their other interests being largely of the type we call symptomatic) seems to me their dramatization of this dilemma. There is the ambiguity of the Force itself, with its powerful, and powerfully seductive, dark side to which the all-American hero may succumb: the Force, Obi One informs Luke, "has a strong influence on the weak-minded," as had Nazism. There is also the question (introduced early in *Star Wars*, developed as the dominant enigma in *The Empire Strikes Back*, and only resolved in the latter part of *Return of the Jedi*) of Luke's parentage: is the father of our hero *really* the prototypical Fascist beast Darth Vader? By the end of the third film the dilemma has developed quasi-philosophical dimensions: as Darth Vader represents rule-by-force, if Luke resorts to force (*the* Force) to defeat him, doesn't he become Darth Vader? The film can extricate itself from this knot only by the extreme device of having Darth Vader abruptly redeem himself and destroy the unredeemable Emperor.

The trilogy's simple but absolutely systematic code of accents extends this theme in the wider terms of the American heritage. All the older generation Jedi knights, both good and evil, and their immediate underlings, e.g. Peter Cushing, have British accents, in marked contrast to the American accents of the young heroes. The contradictions in the origins of America are relevant here: a nation founded in the name of freedom by people fleeing oppression, the founding itself an act of oppression (the subjugation of the Indians), the result an extremely oppressive civilization based on the persecution of minorities (e.g., the Salem witch-hunts). Britain itself has of course markedly contradictory connotations—a democracy as well as an imperialist power ("the Empire"), which America inherited. It is therefore fitting that both Obi One and Darth Vader should be clearly signified as British, and that doubt should exist as to which of them is Luke Skywalker's father, whether literal or moral/political. Hence the films' unease and inability satisfactorily to deal with the problem of lineage: what will the rebels against the Empire create if not another empire? The unease is epitomized in the final sequence of *Star Wars*, with its visual reference (so often pointed out by critics) to *Triumph of the Will*. A film buff's joke? Perhaps. But Freud showed a long time ago that we are often most serious when we joke. From the triumph of the Force to the Triumph of the Will is but a step.

Parenthetically, it is worth drawing brief attention here to John Milius' *Conan the Barbarian*, perhaps the only one of these 80s fantasy films to dispense with a liberal cloak, parading its Fascism shamelessly in instantly recognizable popular signifiers: it opens with a quotation from Nietzsche, has the spirit of its dead heroine leap to the rescue at the climax as a Wagnerian Valkyrie, and in between unabashedly celebrates the Aryan male physique with a singlemindedness that would have delighted Leni Riefenstahl. Its token gay is dispatched with a kick in the groin, and its arch-villain is black. There is an attempt, it is true, to project Fascism on to *him* (so that he can be allotted the most gruesome of the film's many grisly deaths), but it is difficult to imagine a more transparent act of displacement.

6. *Restoration of the Father*. One might reasonably argue that this constitutes—and logically enough—the dominant project, ad infinitum and post nauseam, of the contemporary Hollywood cinema, a veritable thematic metasystem embracing all the available genres and all the current cycles, from realist drama to pure fantasy, taking in en route comedy and *film noir* and even in devious ways infiltrating the horror film. The Father must here be understood in all senses, symbolic, literal, potential: patriarchal authority (the Law), which assigns all other elements to their correct, subordinate, allotted roles; the actual heads of families, fathers of recalcitrant children, husbands of recalcitrant wives, who must either learn the virtue and justice of submission or pack their bags; the young heterosexual male, father of the future, whose eventual union with the "good woman" has always formed the archetypal happy ending of the American film, guarantee of the perpetuation of the nuclear family and social stability.

The restoration of the Father has many ramifications, one of the most important of which is of course the corresponding restoration of women, after a decade of feminism and "liberation." The 80s have seen the development (or, in many cases, the resurrection) of a number of strategies for coping with this project. There is the plot about the liberated woman who proves she's as good as the man but then discovers that this doesn't make her happy and that what she really wanted all the time was to serve him. Thus Debra Winger in *Urban Cowboy* proves that she can ride the mechanical bull as well as John Travolta but withdraws from competition in order to spend the future washing his socks. Or Sondra Locke in *Bronco Billy* demonstrates that she can shoot as well as Clint Eastwood but ends up spread out on a wheel as his target/object-for-the-gaze. (The grasp of feminist principle implicit in this—that what women want is to be able to do the same things men do because they envy them so much—is obviously somewhat limited). The corollary of this is the plot that suggests that men, if need arises, can fill the woman's role just as well if not better (*Kramer vs. Kramer, Author! Author!, Mr. Mom*). It's the father, anyway, who has all the real responsibility, women being by nature irresponsible, as in the despicable *Middle Age Crazy*, which asks us to shed tears over the burden of "being the daddy," the cross that our patriarchs must bear.

If the woman can't accept her subordination, she must be expelled from the narrative altogether, like Mary Tyler Moore in *Ordinary People* or Tuesday Weld and Dyan Cannon in *Author! Author!*, leaving the father to develop his beautiful relationship with his offspring untrammeled by female complications. *Ordinary People* makes particularly clear the brutality to the woman of the Oedipal trajectory our culture continues to construct: from the moment in the narrative when our young hero takes the decisive step of identification with the father/acquisition of his own woman, the mother becomes superfluous to Oedipal/patriarchal concerns, a mere burdensome redundancy. The father, on the other hand, must be loved, accepted and respected, even if he is initially inadequate (*Kramer vs. Kramer*) or generally deficient, unpleasant or monstrous (*Tribute, The Great Santini*). Even a non-family movie like *Body Heat* can be read as another variant on the same pattern. Its purpose in reviving the *film noir* woman of the 40s so long after (one had innocently supposed) her cultural significance had become obsolete seems to be to suggest that, if women are so perverse as to want power and autonomy, men are better off without them: at the end of the film, William Hurt is emotionally "with" his male buddies even though ruined and in prison, while Kathleen Turner is totally isolated and miserable even though rich and free on a Mexican beach. Clearly, what she really needed was the love of a good man, and as she willfully rejected it she must suffer the consequences. Seen like this, Body Heat is merely the *Ordinary People* of *film noir*.

Back in the world of pure fantasy (but we have scarcely left it), we find precisely the same patterns, the same ideological project, reiterated. Women are allowed minor feats of heroism and aggression (in deference to the theory that what they want is to be able to behave like men): thus Karen Allen can punch Harrison Ford in the face near the beginning of *Raiders*, and Princess Leia has intermittent outbursts of activity, usually in the earlier parts of the movies. Subsequently, the woman's main function is to be rescued by the men, involving her reduction to helplessness and dependency. Although Princess Leia is ultimately revealed to be Luke Skywalker's sister, there is never any suggestion that *she* might inherit the Force, or have the privilege of being trained and instructed by Obi One and Yoda. In fact, the strategy of making her Luke's sister seems largely a matter of narrative convenience: it renders romance with Luke automatically unthinkable and sets her free, without impediments, for union with Han Solo. Nowhere do the films invite us to take any interest in *her* parentage. They play continually on the necessity for Luke to confirm his allegiance to the "good father" (Obi One) and repudiate the "bad father" (Darth Vader), even if the latter proves to be his *real* father. With this set up and developed in the first two films, *Return of the Jedi* manages to cap it triumphantly with the redemption of Darth Vader. The trilogy can then culminate in a veritable Fourth of July of Fathericity: a grandiose firework display to celebrate Luke's coming through, as he stands backed by the ghostly figures of Obi One, Darth and Yoda, all smiling benevolently. The mother, here, is so superfluous that she doesn't figure in the narrative at all—except, perhaps, at some strange, deeply sinister, unconscious level, disguised as the unredeemably evil Emperor who, as so many people have remarked, seems modeled on the witch in *Snow White* (the heroine's stepmother). Her male disguise makes it permissible to subject her to the most violent expulsion from the narrative yet. Read like this, *Return of the Jedi* becomes the *Ordinary People* of outer space, with Darth Vader as Donald Sutherland and Obi One and Yoda in tandem as the psychiatrist.

If the *Star Wars* films—like the overwhelming majority of 80s Hollywood movies—put women back where they belong (subordinate or nowhere), they do the same, in a casual, incidental way, for blacks and gays. The token black (Billy Dee Williams) is given a certain token autonomy and self-assertiveness, but he has a mere supporting role, in all senses of the term, on the right side and raises no question of threat or revolution. Gays are handled more surreptitiously. Just as the 40s war movie generously included various ethnics in its platoon/bomber crew, so its 80s equivalent has its subordinate, subservient (and comic and timid) gay character, in the entirely unchallenging form of an asexual robot: CP-30, with his affected British accent, effeminate mannerisms, and harmlessly pedophile relationship with R2D2 (after all, what can robots do?). On the other hand, there is the *Star Wars* rendering of a gay bar, the clientele exclusively male, and all grotesque freaks.

Thus the project of the *Star Wars* films and related works is to put everyone back in his/her place, reconstruct us as dependent children, and reassure us that it will all come right in the end: trust Father.[1]

Spielberg and *E. T.*

While it is in many respects permissible to speak of a Lucas–Spielberg syndrome—films catering to the desire for regression to infantilism, the doublethink phenomenon of pure fantasy—Spielberg and, especially, *E. T.* also demand some separate consideration. The *Star Wars* films are knowing concoctions, the level of personal involvement (that facility of invention that I have granted them) superficial. *Raiders of the Lost Ark* belongs with them, but with *Close Encounters of the Third Kind* and *E. T.* there is a certain sense of pressure, of personal necessity. Semiologists would call this the inscription of the author in the film; the popular response is to applaud Spielberg's "sincerity." However one takes it—as evidence of a genuine creative drive, or as simply one further level of signification—I am not arguing that it necessarily makes the films better than the *Star Wars* movies. Sincerity is a difficult concept (Spielberg's, in conjunction with the films' extraordinary efficiency, makes him a lot of money) and in itself carries no connotations of value; popularly, it tends to get confused with "giving us a nice feeling," but logically there is no more reason to credit Spielberg with it than, say, Mickey Spillane, whose novels also carry a charge of personal investment. If the Spielberg films are in some ways more interesting than the *Star Wars* trilogy, it is because the personal investment has as its corollary, or perhaps its source, a certain disturbance; the sincerity seems in large part the need to cover over that disturbance, a *personal* need for reassurance (which the *Star Wars* films peddle as a commodity), the desire to "believe." Another way of saying this is to suggest that the patriarchal/Oedipal trajectory is never quite as simple, direct or untroubled, and takes more curious and deviant routes, in the Spielberg movies. That the films fail to be more interesting than they are testifies to the success of the fantasy: the disturbance is covered over very effectively, almost obliterated. Illuminating comparisons might be made with two of *E. T.*'s thematic antecedents: Lewton's *Curse of the Cat People* and Cohen's *It's Alive* movies.

One needs to distinguish carefully between the childlike and the childish (just as one needs to distinguish the true innocence of childhood from the sentimental, sanitized, desexualized version of bourgeois ideology). Peter Coveney's admirable *The Image of Childhood* undertakes just such a distinction, examining the differences between the Romantic concept of the child (Blake, Wordsworth) as symbol of new growth and regeneration (of ourselves, of civilization) and the regressive Victorian sentimentalization of children as identification figures for "childish adults," the use of the infantile as escape from an adult world perceived as irredeemably corrupt, or at least bewilderingly problematic.[2] Both models persist, intermittently, in our culture: within the modern cinema, one might take as an exemplary reference point the Madlyn of *Celine and Julie Go Boating* and the multiple suggestions of growth and renewal she develops in relation to the four women of the film. Spielberg in *E. T.* seems to hesitate between the two concepts (Elliott's freshness and energy are seen in relation to a generally oppressive civilization, though he is never Blake's "fiend hid in a cloud") before finally committing himself to the childish. If Spielberg is the ideal director for the 80s, it is because his "sincerity" (the one quality that the *Star Wars* films are vaguely felt to lack) expresses itself as an emotional investment in precisely that form of regression that appears to be so generally desired.

The attitude to the patriarchal family implicit in Spielberg's films is somewhat curious. In *Jaws* the family is tense and precarious; in *Close Encounters* it disintegrates; in *E. T.* it has already broken up before the film begins. The first part of *E. T.* quite vividly depicts the oppressiveness of life in the nuclear family: incessant bickering, mean-mindedness, one-upmanship. This state of affairs is the result of the father's defection, perhaps: the boys have no one to imitate, as Roy Scheider's son in *Jaws* had. But he has defected only recently, and the *Close Encounters* family is scarcely any better. Yet Spielberg seems quite incapable of thinking beyond this: all he can do is reassert the "essential" goodness of family life in the face of all the evidence he himself provides. Hence the end of *E. T.* surreptitiously reconstructs the image of the nuclear family. Spielberg is sufficiently sophisticated to realize that he can't bring Dad home from Mexico for a last-minute repentance and reunion (it would be too corny, not realistic, in a film that for all its status as pure fantasy has a great stake in the accumulated connotations of "real life"). But he produces a paternal scientist in Dad's place (an even better father who can explicitly identify himself with Elliott—"When I was ten I was just like you," or words to that effect). A climactic image groups him with mother and daughter in an archetypal family composition, like a posed photograph. For Spielberg it doesn't really matter that the scientist has no intimate relationship with the mother, as his imagination is essentially presexual: it is enough that he stands in for Elliott's missing father.

It follows that the position of women in Spielberg's work is fairly ignominious. Largely denied any sexual presence, they function exclusively as wives and mothers (especially mothers), with no suggestion that they might reasonably want anything beyond that. The two women in *Close Encounters* typify the extremely limited possibilities. On the one hand there is the wife of Richard Dreyfuss (Teri Garr), whom the film severely criticizes for not standing staunchly by her husband even when his behavior suggests that he is clearly certifiable: she has to be dismissed from the narrative to leave him free to depart in the spaceship. On the other hand there is the mother (Melinda Dillon) whose sole objective is to regain her child (a male child, inevitably). No suggestion is made that *she* might go off in the spaceship, or even that she might want to. The end of *E. T.* offers the precise complement to this: the extraterrestrial transmits his wisdom and powers to the male child, Elliott, by applying a finger to his forehead, then instructs the little girl to "be good": like Princess Leia, she will never inherit the Force.

As for men, Spielberg shows an intermittent desire to salute Mr. Middle America, which is not entirely incompatible with his basic project, given the way in which serious (read subversive) thought is repressed by the media: at the end of Jaws, Roy Scheider destroys the shark after both the proletarian and the intellectual have failed. By inclination, however, he gravitates toward the infantile, presexual male, a progression obviously completed by Elliott. (No one, of course, is really pre-sexual; yet the myth of the pre-sexuality of children remains dominant, and it is logical that the desire for regression to infantilism should incorporate this myth.) Roy Neary in *Close Encounters* is an interesting transitional figure. As he falls under the influence of the extraterrestrial forces his behavior becomes increasingly infantile (given the dirt he deposits all over the house, one might see him as regressing to the pre-toilet training period). Divested of the encumbrances of wife and family, he proceeds to erect a huge phallus in the living room; but, before he can achieve the actual revelation of its meaning, he must learn to slice off its top. As with the mother and the scientist of *E. T.* the film contradicts generic expectations by conspicuously not developing a sexual relationship, although Neary's alliance with Melinda Dillon makes this more than feasible—generically speaking, almost obligatory. Instead, the symbolic castration makes possible the desexualized sublimation of the ending: Neary led into the spaceship by frail, little, asexual, childlike figures, to fly off with a display of bright lights the Smiths of *Meet Me in St. Louis* never dreamed of. The logical next step (leaving aside the equally regressive comic strip inanities of *Raiders of the Lost Ark*) is to a literal, but still necessarily male, child as hero.

Spielberg's identification with Elliott (that there is virtually no distance whatever between character and director is clearly the source of the film's seductive, suspect charm) makes possible the precise nature of the fantasy *E. T.* offers: not so much a child's fantasy as an adult's fantasy about childhood. It is also essentially a male fantasy: apart from Pauline Kael (whose feminist consciousness is so undeveloped one could barely describe it as embryonic), I know of no women who respond to the film the way so many men do (though not without embarrassment), as, in Kael's term, a "bliss-out." The film caters to the wish—practically universal, within our culture—that what W. B. Yeats so evocatively called "the ignominy of boyhood" might have been a little less ignominious. It is the fulfillment of this wish that most male adults find so irresistible. It is, however, always worth examining what precisely it is that we have failed to resist. The film does for the problems of childhood exactly what Spielberg's contribution to *Twilight Zone* did for the problem of old age: it raises them in order to dissolve them in fantasy, so that we are lulled into feeling they never really existed. Meanwhile boyhood (not to mention girlhood) remains, within the patriarchal nuclear family, as ignominious as ever.

Such a view of family life, male/female relations, and compensatory fantasy is obviously quite curious and idiosyncratic, always verging on the exposure of contradictions that only the intensity of the commitment to fantasy conceals. The essential flimsiness and vulnerability of the fantasy are suggested by the instability of E. T. himself as a realized presence in the film. Were it not for Spielberg's sincerity (a sincerity unaccompanied by anything one might reasonably term intelligence, and in fact incompatible with it)—his evident investment in the fantasy—one might describe the use of E. T. as shamelessly opportunistic. From scene to scene, almost moment to moment, he represents whatever is convenient to Spielberg, and to Elliott: helpless/potent, mental defective/intellectual giant, child figure/father figure.

The film's central theme is clearly the acceptance of Otherness (that specter that haunts, and must continue to haunt, patriarchal bourgeois society)—by Elliott, initially, then by his siblings, eventually by his mother, by the benevolent scientist, by the schoolboys. On the surface level—"E. T." as an e. t.—this seems quite negligible, a nonissue. This is not to assert that there are no such things as extraterrestrials, but simply that, as yet, they haven't constituted a serious social problem. They have a habit of turning up at convenient moments in modern history: in the 50s, with the cold war and the fear of Communist infiltration, everyone saw hostile flying saucers, and Hollywood duly produced movies about them; at a period when (in the aftermath of Vietnam and Watergate, and with a new Vietnam in Central America hovering over American heads) we need reassurance, Hollywood produces *nice* extraterrestrials. (The 50s produced some benevolent ones, too—*It Came from Outer Space*, for example—but they proved less profitable; contrariwise, the hostile, totally intractable kind are still with us—witness Carpenter's *The Thing*, released almost simultaneously with *E. T.*—but the model is definitely not popular).

Unfortunately, on a less literal level, as a more general representation of Otherness, E. T. almost totally lacks resonance ("zero charisma," one might say). All the Others of white patriarchal bourgeois culture—workers, women, gays, blacks—are in various ways threatening, and their very existence represents a demand that society transform itself. E. T. isn't threatening at all: in fact, he's just about as cute as a little rubber Martian could be. This, it seems to me, is what makes the film (for all its charm, for all the sincerity) in the last resort irredeemably smug: a nation that was founded on the denial of Otherness now—after radical feminism, after gay liberation, after black militancy—complacently produces a film in which Otherness is something we can all love and cuddle and cry over, without unduly disturbing the nuclear family and the American Way of Life. E. T. is one of us; he just looks a bit funny.

Poltergeist requires a brief postscript here. It is tempting to dismiss it simply as Tobe Hooper's worst film, but it clearly belongs to the Spielberg *oeuvre* rather than to Hooper's. Its interest and the particular brand of reassurances it offers both lie in its relation to the 70s family horror film—in the way in which Spielberg enlists the genre's potential radicalism and perverts it into 80s conservatism. One can discern two parallel and closely related projects: First, the attempt (already familiar from *Jaws*) to separate the American family from "bad" capitalism, to pretend the two are without connection: there are a few greedy people, putting profit before human concerns, who bring on catastrophes, whether by keeping open dangerous beaches or not removing the bodies before converting cemeteries into housing developments. The project has a long history in the American cinema (its inherent tensions and contradictions wonderfully organized by Capra, for example, in *It's a Wonderful Life*). With Spielberg it becomes reduced merely to a blatant example of what Barthes calls "inoculation," where ideology acknowledges a minor, local, reformable evil in order to divert attention from the fundamental ones. Second, the attempt to absolve the American family from all responsibility for the horror. In short, a cleansing job: in the 70s, the monster was located within the family, perceived as its logical product. *Poltergeist* appears at first to be toying with this concept, before declaring the family innocent and locating the monstrous elsewhere: it is defined in terms of either meaningless superstition (corpses resent having swimming pools built over them) or some vague metaphysical concept of eternal evil ("the Beast"—superstition on a more grandiose scale), the two connected by the implication that the latter is evoked by, or is working through, the former. In any case, as in *E. T.*, the suburban bourgeois nuclear family remains the best of all possible worlds, if only because any other is beyond Spielberg's imagination. One might suggest that the overall development of the Hollywood cinema from the late 60s to the 80s is summed up in the movement from Romero's use of the Star Spangled Banner (the flag) at the beginning of *Night of the Living Dead* to Spielberg's use of it (the music) at the beginning of *Poltergeist*.

Blade Runner

Blade Runner was released in the United States simultaneously with *E. T.* and for one week was its serious challenger at the box office; then receipts for *Blade Runner* dropped disastrously while those for *E. T.* soared. The North American critical establishment was generally ecstatic about *E. T.* and cool or ambivalent about *Blade Runner. E. T.* was nominated for a great many Academy Awards and won a few; *Blade Runner* was nominated for a few and won none. I take these facts as representing a choice made in conjunction by critics and public, ratified by the Motion Picture Academy—a choice whose significance extends far beyond a mere preference for one film over another, expressing a preference for the reassuring over the disturbing, the reactionary over the progressive, the safe over the challenging, the childish over the adult, spectator passivity over spectator activity.

Admirers of the original novel (Philip Dick's *Do Androids Dream of Electric Sheep?*) tend to regard the film with some hostility. But *Blade Runner* is not really an adaptation: rather, the film is built upon certain ideas and motifs selected from the novel. Its aim, argument and tone are so different that it is best to regard it as an autonomous work. Gone or played down are most of the novel's major structuring premises: the nuclear war that has rendered the earth unsafe for the support of life and health; the use of animals as rare, expensive, coveted status symbols; the pseudoreligion of "Mercerism." One might define the fundamental difference thus: the concerns of the novel are predominantly metaphysical, those of the film predominantly social. Some of the features discussed here derive (in most cases rather loosely) from the book; others do not. They are so well integrated that it seems unnecessary to spell out the distinction in each individual case.

Fantasy, by and large, can be used in two ways—as a means of escaping from contemporary reality, or as a means of illuminating it. Against the Spielbergian complacency of *E. T.* can be set *Blade Runner's* vision of capitalism, which is projected into the future, yet intended to be clearly recognizable. It is important that the novel's explanation of the state of the world (the nuclear war) is withheld from the film: the effect is to lay the blame on capitalism directly. The society we see is our own writ large, its present excesses carried to their logical extremes: power and money controlled by even fewer, in even larger monopolies; worse poverty, squalor, degradation; racial oppression; a polluted planet, from which those who can emigrate to other worlds. The film opposes to Marx's view of inevitable collapse a chilling vision of capitalism hanging on, by the maintenance of power and oppression, in the midst of an essentially disintegrated civilization.

The depiction of the role played in this maintenance by the media is a masterly example of the kind of clarification—a complex idea compressed into a single image—advocated by Brecht: the mystified poor are mostly Asians; the ideal image they are given, therefore, dominating the city in neon lights, is that of a beautiful, richly dressed, exquisitely made-up female oriental, connected in the film (directly or indirectly) with emigration, Coca-Cola and pill-popping, various forms of consumption, pacification and flight.

The central interest of the film lies in the relationship between the hero, Deckard, and the "replicants"; the hero, one might add, is interesting *only* in relation to the replicants. The relationship is strange, elusive, multi-leveled, inadequately worked out (the failure of the film is as striking as its evident successes): the meeting of Raymond Chandler and William Blake is not exactly unproblematic. The private eye / *film noir* aspect of the movie is strongly underlined by Deckard's voice-over narration, demanded by the studio after the film's completion because someone felt that audiences would have difficulty in following the narrative (justifiably, alas: our own conditioning by the contemporary media is centered on, and continually reinforces, the assumption that we are either unable or unwilling to do any work). But that aspect is clearly there already in the film, which draws not only on the Chandler ethos but also on the rethinking of it in 70s cinema (Altman's *The Long Goodbye*, more impressively Penn's *Night Moves*): the moral position of Chandler's knight walking the "mean streets" can no longer be regarded as uncompromised. Deckard's position as hero is compromised, above all, by the way the film draws upon another figure of *film noir* (and much before it), the figure of the double—which brings us to the replicants.

If *Blade Runner's* attitude to American capitalism is at the opposite pole to Spielberg's, the logical corollary is that the film's representation of the Other is at the opposite pole to that of *E. T.*, though without falling into the alternative trap embodied by Carpenter's "Thing." The replicants (I am thinking especially of Roy and Pris) are dangerous but fascinating, frightening but beautiful, other but not totally and intractably alien; they gradually emerge as the film's true emotional center, and certainly represent its finest achievement. Their impressiveness depends partly on their striking visual presence, but more on the multiple connotations they accrue as the film proceeds, through processes of suggestion, association, and reference.

The central, defining one is that established by the near-quotation from Blake with which Roy Batty introduces himself (it has no equivalent in the novel):

> Fiery the angels fell; deep thunder rolled
> Around their shores, burning with the fires of Orc
>
> (*America: A Prophecy*, lines 115–16)

Blake's poem is a celebration of the American Revolution, a narrative about the founding of modern America, interpreted on a spiritual/symbolic plane. Orc leads the revolt against oppression; he is one of Blake's devil-angels, descendant of Milton's Lucifer as reinterpreted by Blake ("Milton was of the devil's party without knowing it"), the spirit of freedom, "Lover of wild rebellion and transgression of God's law," consistently associated with fire ("the fiery joy"). Roy, however, misquotes: Blake's original reads "Fiery the angels rose," the rising of the angels signifying the beginning of the revolt which is to found the free democratic state that, two hundred years ago, could be viewed idealistically as a step in humanity's progress toward the New Jerusalem. The change from "rose" to "fell" must be read, then, in terms of the end of the American democratic principle of freedom, its ultimate failure; the shot that introduces Roy, the rebel angel, links him in a single camera movement to the imagery of urban squalor and disintegration through which he is moving. Clearly, in the context of 80s Hollywood, such an implication could be suggested only in secret, concealed in a particularly esoteric reference. Subsequently, Roy's identification with the Blake revolutionary hero is rendered visually; stripped to the waist for the final combat with Deckard, he could have stepped straight out of one of Blake's visionary paintings.

The other connotations are less insistent, more a matter of suggestion, but (grouping themselves around the allusion to Blake) they add up to a remarkably complex and comprehensive definition of the Other. First, the replicants are identified as an oppressed and exploited proletariat: produced to serve their capitalist masters, they are discarded when their usefulness is over and "retired" (i.e., destroyed) when they rebel against such usage. Roy tells Deckard: "Quite an experience to live in fear. That's what it is to be a slave." They are also associated with racial minorities: when Deckard's boss refers to them by the slang term "skin-jobs," Deckard immediately connects this to the term "niggers." Retaining a certain sexual mystery, they carry suggestions of sexual ambiguity: Rachael's response to one of Deckard's questions in the interrogation scene is "Are you trying to find out if I'm a replicant or if I'm a lesbian?"; the climactic Roy/Deckard battle accumulates marked homoerotic overtones (made explicit in Roy's challenge "You'd better get it up"), culminating in his decision to save Deckard's life. The replicants have no families: they have not been through the bourgeois patriarchal process known euphemistically as socialization. They appear to be of two kinds—those who are not supposed to know they are replicants (Rachael) and have accordingly been supplied with "memory banks," false family photographs, etc., and who are therefore more amenable to socialization, and those who know they are other (Roy/Pris) and live by that knowledge. Roy and Pris are also associated with childhood, not only by the fact that they are literally only four years old, but by their juxtaposition with the toys in J. F. Sebastian's apartment, an environment in which they are so at home that Pris can be assimilated into it, becoming one of Sebastian's creations when she hides from Deckard. Pris, made up as a living doll, irresistibly evokes punk and the youth rebellion associated with it. As in Blake, the revolution is ultimately against the Father, the symbolic figure of authority, oppression and denial ("Thou shalt not"); it is therefore appropriate that the film should move toward Roy's murder of Tyrell, his creator, owner, and potential destroyer.

The parallels that seek to establish Roy as Deckard's double are fairly systematic but not entirely convincing, the problem lying partly in the incompatibility of the film's literary sources (Philip Marlowe can scarcely look into the mirror and see Orc as his reflection). Rachael's question (never answered) "Did you ever take that test yourself?" suggests that Deckard could be a replicant; Deckard's own line, "Replicants weren't supposed to have feelings, neither were blade runners," develops the parallel. The crosscutting in the battle with Roy repeatedly emphasizes the idea of the mirror image with the injured hands, the cries of pain. The relationship is above all suggested in Roy's contemptuously ironic "Aren't you 'the good man'?": hero and villain change places, all moral certainties based upon the status quo collapse.

The more often I see *Blade Runner* the more I am impressed by its achievement and the more convinced of its failure. The problem may be that the central thrust of the film, the source of its energy, is too revolutionary to be permissible: it *has* to be compromised. The unsatisfactoriness comes to a head in the ludicrous, bathetic ending, apparently tacked on in desperation at the last minute. But how should the film end? In the absence of any clear information, two possibilities come to mind, the choice depending, one might say, on whether Philip Marlowe or Orc is to have the last word. The first scenario involves the *film noir* ending in which Rachael is retired by Deckard's superior who is then killed in turn by Deckard (himself mortally wounded, perhaps) in a final gun battle. In the second, Deckard joins the replicant revolution. The former is probably too bleak for 80s Hollywood, the latter too explicitly subversive for any Hollywood. Either would, however, make some sense and would be the outcome of a logical progression within the film, whereas the ending we have makes no sense at all: Deckard and Rachael fly off to live happily ever after (where?—the film has clearly established that there is nowhere on earth to go). The problem partly lies in the added voice-over commentary, the only evidence we are given that Rachael has been constructed without a "determination date": were she about to die, the notion of a last desperate fling in the wilderness would make slightly more sense, and we would not be left with the awkward question of how they are going to survive.

The film's problems, however, are not confined to its last couple of minutes: just as its strengths are centered in the replicants, so too are its weaknesses. If Roy is the incarnation of the Blakean revolutionary hero, he also, especially in association with Pris, carries other connotations that are much more dubious, those of an Aryan master race. This is very strongly suggested by the characters' physical attributes (blondness, beauty, immense strength), but it is also, more worryingly, signified in their ruthlessness: the offscreen murder of J. F. Sebastian (not in the novel) seems completely arbitrary and unmotivated, put in simply to discredit the replicants so that they cannot be mistaken for the film's true heroes. The problem is rooted in the entire tradition of the Gothic, of horror literature and horror film: the problem of the positive monster, who, insofar as he becomes positive, ceases to be monstrous, hence no longer frightening. It is the problem that Cohen confronted in the *It's Alive* movies (and failed to resolve in the second) and that Badham confronted in *Dracula* (a film that, like *Blade Runner*, develops disturbing Fascist overtones in its movement toward the monster's rehabilitation).

The central problem, however, is Rachael and her progressive humanization. The notion of what is human is obviously very heavily weighted ideologically; here, it amounts to no more than becoming the traditional "good object," the passive woman who willingly submits to the dominant male. What are we to make of the moment when, to save Deckard's life, Rachael shoots a fellow replicant? Not, clearly, what other aspects of this confused movie might powerfully suggest: the tragic betrayal of her class and race.

The film is in fact defeated by the overwhelming legacy of classical narrative. It succumbs to one of its most firmly traditional and ideologically reactionary formulas: the elimination of the bad couple (Roy, Pris) in order to construct the good couple (Deckard, Rachael). The only important difference is that in classical narrative the good couple would then settle down ("I'll take you home now"), whereas here they merely fly away to nowhere. Long ago, *Stagecoach* had its couple drive off, "saved from the blessings of civilization," to start a farm over the border; *The Chase* was perhaps the first Hollywood film to acknowledge, ahead of its time, that there was no longer any home to go to. Seventeen years later, *Blade Runner* can manage no more than an empty repetition of this—with the added cynicism of presenting it as if it were a happy ending.

Blade Runner belongs with the incoherent texts of the 70s: it is either ten years behind its time or hopefully a few years ahead of it. If the human race survives, we may certainly hope to enter, soon, another era of militancy, protest, rage, disturbance, and radical questioning, in which context *Blade Runner* will appear quite at home.

Notes

1 It is striking that, since this chapter was written, the essential ugliness of the 80s science fiction/comic strip project—hitherto concealed beneath the sweetness-and-light of patriarchal morality—has risen to the surface: witness the obsessive violence of *Indiana Jones and the Temple of Doom* and the pervasively sick imagery of *Gremlins* (which Spielberg "presented"). *Dune* is the culmination of the exposure of rottenness. It is the most obscenely homophobic film I have ever seen, managing to associate with homosexuality in a single scene physical grossness, moral depravity, violence and disease. It shows no real interest in its bland young lovers or its last-minute divine revelation, all its energies being devoted to the expression of physical and sexual disgust. Much of the imagery strongly

recalls David Lynch's earlier *Eraserhead*, but the film seems only partly explicable in auteurist terms; the *choice* of Lynch as writer-director would also need to be explained, and the film must be seen in the wider context as a product of the 80s Hollywood machine.

2 It is peculiarly appropriate that a new version of *Peter Pan* should be among Spielberg's current projects.

PART V

Censorship and Regulation

Chapter 13

Lea Jacobs

THE CENSORSHIP OF *BLONDE VENUS*: TEXTUAL ANALYSIS AND HISTORICAL METHOD (1988)

Editors' Introduction

Lea Jacobs' exploration of the case files from the Motion Picture Producers and Distributors Association (MPPDA) chronicling the censorship history of Joseph von Sternberg's 1932 film *Blonde Venus* offers a model for archival historical research (especially her use of primary source material) just as it lays out a more nuanced notion of the film (as a text) and by extension any subsequent close readings of that text. The files provided Jacobs with a wealth of correspondence between the Production Code Administration (PCA) censor Lamar Trotti, the Paramount Pictures executive B.P. Schulberg, and von Sternberg, the film's director. Focusing on two key moments in the film – the night-club performer Helen's dalliance with Nick, a millionaire who falls in love with her; and at the end of the film the reconciliation of her marriage with Ned, a scientist suffering the effects of radium poisoning – Jacobs examines the complex interplay between Trotti, Schulberg, and von Sternberg, and ponders the likely rationale behind decisions that fundamentally affected the final cut of the film: the clever way in which Helen and Nick's liaison is negotiated in the shooting script and then complicated by the actors' performance (she sleeps with him for money to pay for her husband's medical treatment; though the exact reason for his "gift" is never stated, Marlene Dietrich and Cary Grant exchange looks that speak volumes) and the prescribed happy ending that jettisons Nick and restores Helen and Ned's marriage. Peculiar as the various changes made to suit the censors' notion of "compensating moral values" may strike us today – is it better to cheat on your husband for money than to do it for lust or love? – the point here is less to observe such a capricious process than to call for a more careful and comprehensive close reading, one that, Jacobs asserts, involves looking at a film from development (of its script and the various negotiations regarding that script with the PCA) through reception (by an audience savvy to the censorship guidelines that have been applied to the text at hand).

Suggested Reading

Controlling Hollywood: Censorship and Regulation in the Studio Era, edited by Matthew Bernstein (New Brunswick, NJ: Rutgers, 1999); Lea Jacobs, *The Wages of Sin: Censorship and the Fallen Woman Film, 1928–1942* (Berkeley: University of California Press, 1997); Leonard Leff and Jerrald Simmons, *The Dame in the Kimono: Hollywood, Censorship, and the Production Code from the 1920s to the 1960s* (NY: Grove Weidenfeld, 1990).

UNDER THE STUDIO SYSTEM, industry self-censorship worked at the service of quite obvious, often explicit, social and ideological imperatives. For example, the industry's Production Code states that films should maintain respect for the institutions of marriage and the law.[1] Less obvious, however, is how a historian might be able to prove that censorship had a given effect on film form and style or, in methodological terms, how to make use of the documents that industry self-regulation left in its wake. One problem with this project, clearly, is the concept of determination; that is, the logic and mechanisms by which the film industry as an institution can be said to mediate conventions of representation.[2] This theoretical problem is accompanied by a host of more narrowly methodological ones concerning the evidentiary status of documents such as censorship memos and correspondence, studio production records, and story files.

I would like to consider these problems via the example of Joseph von Sternberg's *Blonde Venus*. The film is of interest because it has been the subject of several textual analyses that take up the issue of its ideological function. In general, *Blonde Venus* has been interpreted as being relevatory of conflicts relating to the representation of female sexuality and the family. Bill Nichols argues that through visual style the film undermines the character of Ned, the heroine's priggish husband, and is thereby subversive of the ideals of female chastity and domesticity that Ned espouses.[3] E. Ann Kaplan also suggests that the film undercuts the ideal of female domesticity. Kaplan argues that in the terms of the male fantasy that dominates the film, the eroticized image of Dietrich as spectacle is incompatible with and ultimately comes to subsume the de-sexualized image of the woman as domestic, wife, and mother.[4] However, she does not see this as necessarily "subversive." Despite pronounced differences in their interpretations, both Nichols and Kaplan hold to a model of the text as at least symptomatic of tensions or conflicts that revolve around the figure of the woman. Moreover, they identify and explain these tensions through close analysis of narrative and film style. I will argue that attention to the production context of *Blonde Venus* allows us to be much more specific about the social conflicts that determine this text, and significantly alters the way in which we read or interpret its form.

The most important primary documents for the study of censorship are the case files of the Motion Picture Producers and Distributors Association (MPPDA), the industry trade association responsible for monitoring scripts before films went into production.[5] These files, which have only recently become available for research, contain a variety of sources that yield distinct kinds of evidence concerning the evaluation of films and the negotiations between industry censors and producers.[6] Most of the files contain correspondence between the MPPDA and the film's producer. In these letters, censors state their objections to a script, suggest revisions, and list lines of dialogue and bits of action likely to be deleted by external censorship agencies (state and foreign censorship boards). Along with this correspondence, some of the files hold what are called "inter-office memos" in which censors summarize the plot of a screenplay and note possible points of difficulty. Although not available in every case, these memos generally provide the most detailed assessments of scripts and are the best source of information we have on how censors went about the process of evaluating screenplays.

The files for the early thirties also sometimes contain correspondence between the censors in Hollywood and Will Hays in the New York office of the MPPDA. These are an invaluable source of information on policy decisions and matters relating to the Production Code as such. Finally, almost all of the files include data compiled by the MPPDA on the actions taken by external agencies after the film's release. There is generally a list of all the cuts made by state and foreign boards as well as letters of complaint from irate individuals or reform groups. For the MPPDA, the importance of this data was cumulative. Gauging the public response to films on a case-by-case basis, censors would constantly refine their sense of what would offend reform groups or make problems for distribution and exhibition.

The MPPDA case files provide the basis for a historical reconstruction of the process of self-regulation under the studio system. However, there are practical limitations on the kinds of inferences we can draw from these documents. One difficulty is that some of the most important decisions seem to have occurred in verbal negotiations. Often, the correspondence between industry censors and producers provides only tantalizing hints, preludes to or summaries of longer story conferences. The best way to make use of this evidence, then, is to attempt to correlate letters that were written by MPPDA personnel requesting revisions with the successive drafts of the screenplay. This obviates the need for relying on written summaries of verbal negotiations and provides much more direct evidence concerning the impact of negotiations on the script itself.

Even in the absence of extensive script or story files it is possible to make inferences about how censorship occurred by means of comparisons to other instances for which extensive documentation exists. Thus it is important to view individual cases in the larger context of the standardized patterns or routines of censorship—to know what was typically defined as a problem from the point of view of the MPPDA and what was typically proposed or accepted as a solution.

Within certain limits, one can empirically reconstruct the process of industry self-regulation. But how does this change the way in which films are read? How do the procedures and assumptions of film analysis alter when one tries to take account of this aspect of the production context?

In the case of *Blonde Venus*, I have used the documents in two basic ways to inform and delimit the work of analysis. First, censors' letters and memos serve as a justification for privileging certain passages within the text. They call attention to moments of difficulty or stress—marking out what was considered offensive, morally repugnant, politically dangerous. Second, by comparing the successive drafts of the script and the completed film, I have mapped out how material deemed unacceptable came to be represented. Thus, as a methodological principle, all of the extant written materials—drafts of screenplays, memos in which censors rewrote scenes or proposed readings of scripts—are placed at the same level of importance as the film itself. The boundaries of the text are, in effect, expanded so that the object of study becomes not the film in isolation, but the process of revision as such.

By examining the range of narrative possibilities articulated during the process of revision, we can infer what was deviant or unusual within the completed film in relation to a clearly specified norm; that is, the forms of the script approved by censors. In this context, textual analysis, and particularly a discussion of film style, provides a means of examining how the film exceeds or bypasses the ideological impetus of censorship.

Industry self-censorship was complicated in the case of *Blonde Venus* by a dispute which Lamar Trotti, an industry censor, described between "Von Sternberg and Marlene Dietrich on one side and the studio officials on the other."[7] Arising from this conflict were three drafts of the screenplay. The first was written by Sternberg. The second was prepared according to the directions of B. P. Schulberg, the film's producer at Paramount. In it the final act of the screenplay was drastically altered. The third was prepared when Sternberg and Schulberg were reconciled. It reinstated much of the director's original script including the ending.[8] Lamar Trotti, the censor in charge of this project, found the first draft, written by Sternberg, "utterly impossible," but did not comment on this draft because the producer was already planning to ask for drastic revisions.[9] Trotti found the second draft (the studio's) better than the first,[10] but he was still extremely concerned about how to represent the adulterous love affair (which is present in all three versions of the script)[11] and the studio's version of the ending. Censors considered Sternberg's third draft an improvement upon the studio's version and approved it after some minor revisions.[12]

Rather than discussing the film in sequence then, I will focus my analysis on the prominent points of censorship, those scenes that were contested in the rewriting of the script. The ending is the most important of these because the course of the debate clarifies the differences between the director, producer, and censors. In Sternberg's version of the script, Helen (Marlene Dietrich) gives up a glamorous career on the stage in Paris, and also her engagement to a millionaire, Nick (Cary Grant), in order to return to her relatively impoverished husband, Ned (Herbert Marshall), and son, Johnny. It should be noted that recent commentary on the film often takes up the question of the strained quality of this putatively happy ending. Ann Kaplan, for example, notes that Ned is a particularly harsh and unsympathetic character and describes the reconciliation as "unbelievable."[13]

The studio's version of the ending is quite different because it pairs off Helen and Nick rather than Helen and Ned. Upon Helen's return from Paris, Nick reveals that Ned has been having an affair with his housekeeper. Nick threatens to expose this sordid affair in the course of a trial for custody of Johnny whereupon Ned abandons the boy to his mother, and Helen and Nick make plans to marry. Although the studio's plot is more convoluted than that of the film, it seems to me to be motivated in a more compelling way at the level of character. I surmise that the studio found Ned's harshness toward his wife unsympathetic and, therefore, sought to reconstitute the couple around the more agreeable romantic lead. Another effect of the change in ending is that Helen remains a success as star and as wife of a millionaire. The film is thus made to conform to a general trajectory of class rise that was conventionalized and extremely popular in this period.[14]

Industry censors, however, object vociferously to the studio's ending. Lamar Trotti writes: "It does not seem proper to have that [Helen's] affair justified in the minds of the audience by tearing down the character of the husband, who, up to this point, has been a decent man who was deceived by his wife."[15] Trotti complains about the way in which the studio's version undermines Ned, a character who, for him, represents a moral position or point of view. This kind of reasoning is quite typical of industry censors, who routinely sought to justify what they deemed offensive material within a script on the basis of a moral that could be attributed to the ending. According to what was known as the rule of "compensating moral values," censors generally advocated the final punishment and suffering of "bad" characters or their regeneration. The problem with the studio's ending of *Blonde Venus*, then, for Trotti, is that the compensatory logic has gone askew. One act of adultery is balanced, "justified," by something still worse. That is, Helen's affair, which is motivated at the beginning of the film in terms of financial need, as a sacrifice to save her ailing husband, is made to look good in relation to Ned's illicit liaison.

The correspondence indicates that industry censors preferred Sternberg's third draft of the script because, in their view, it followed the rule of compensating moral values. I infer this on the basis of two letters written by Jason Joy.[16] As was routine in cases in which he anticipated problems with external (state) censorship boards, Joy prepared a statement for studio personnel explaining why he considered the film unacceptable (studio personnel could then mount a campaign to get the film past the state censor boards with a minimum of cuts). The letters cover every point in the plot that might plausibly have been found offensive—not only adultery, but also the idea of prostitution, which is suggested at several points in the film. This material is defended in terms of the moral logic that Joy ascribes to the narrative as a whole: Helen remains a loyal mother, she suffers for her adulterous love affair and undergoes a moral regeneration. Thus, although she seems to enter upon a life of prostitution, this is only to provide for her son. Further, she gives up custody of her child when she realizes she cannot care for him, "thereby sacrificing her own happiness for his good." And, although she becomes rich in Paris, she is not happy there and gives up her luxurious life, "to return to her husband and child on the same economic level which she had left. . . ."[17]

The strategy of Joy's reading, then, is to recuperate Helen's adultery and her deviations from the maternal role in terms of her "underlying" motives and desires as a mother. This is a very powerful logic because even the worst transgressions can be made to reinforce the woman's position within the family. No matter how far she appears to stray, the fallen woman never really leaves home.

The sophisticated and wickedly perverse irony of Sternberg's rendering of this story becomes apparent if we situate it between the Scylla and Charybdis of the studio's "happy ending" and the censor's tale of maternal sacrifice and regeneration. Sternberg's ending destabilizes the romantic idea of courtship, the precondition of the classical happy end. At the same time I would argue that the completed film exceeds the interpretation that the censors offer.

The director's insistence on pairing Helen and Ned for the ending can be explained in terms of a change he made in the third draft of the script (a difference between the first and third versions). Walking with his comrades in a forest, Ned encounters Helen, with a group of actresses, bathing in a pool. This event is retold, in the form of a bedtime story for the child, Johnny, near the opening of the film. The story is repeated yet again, at the boy's insistence, when Helen returns home, and it constitutes the primary device by which husband and wife are reconciled. Thus, the director's choice for the ending is consistent with the establishment of a pattern of repetition. It is usually argued that repetition works at various levels within the classical text to reduce ambiguity and promote closure.[18] However, in this instance, repetition undermines the formation of the couple and renders the ending highly ambiguous. This effect is due to the contrast between the first and last scenes. There is a striking disparity between Ned's attitude in the opening sequence in which he lives out his attraction for Helen, as it were, and the final sequence in which he appears disenchanted with his wife and must be persuaded to play his part in a story for Johnny. The contrast between these scenes is heightened through the motif of performance. The very fact that the reiteration of the story of falling in love is presented as a fairy tale for Johnny underscores, precisely, its status as fiction. Thus, although the repetition establishes a parallel between the beginning and ending, the differences between the scenes are so marked that the final reconciliation has a hollow and rather dissonant quality, and the expectation of closure is not entirely fulfilled.

By comparing the various versions of the ending of *Blonde Venus*, we can infer something about the complex network of constraints which were placed on representation under the studio system. Not only did industry self-regulation impose explicit, prescriptive rules, such as the rule of compensating moral values, but also, implicitly, it served to reenforce certain narrative conventions. Thus, the studio advocated the formation of the romantic couple, a highly conventionalized means of achieving narrative closure within the classical cinema. And building upon this logic, censors sought to superimpose a moral upon the moment of resolution—the couple formed must be the "legitimate" one, purged of the taint of adultery through the narrative logic of punishment and redemption. Sternberg's use of repetition and his emphasis upon performance vitiates these forms of closure, and thereby the rules that circumscribed the representation of adultery.

This mode of analysis does not obviate the problem of intepretation, however. For example, I cannot prove that the film's spectators in 1933 necessarily found the ending ironic. But clearly, the conventions about endings that the studio and the censors sought to maintain also partly determined the audience's expectations about narrative. To this extent, it seems plausible to argue that the film frustrated their expectations and could have been experienced as disruptive or aberrant.

Aside from the ending, there are several other moments in which *Blonde Venus* seems to defy the censor's rule of compensating moral values. This is a function of visual style and also of the way in which character is represented within the film. In justifying this story, the censor Jason Joy emphasizes the disjuncture between motive and action—Helen's actions are rendered inoffensive, he argues, because at the level of intention she remains a loyal wife and mother.

I would argue, however, that the film pushes this disjuncture between motive and action to an extreme. Helen's good intentions are often made incongruous with the postures she assumes. For example, she proves her devotion to her son by kidnapping him and taking to the streets. Her status as outlaw/prostitute contrasts oddly with her maternal aims, a juxtaposition that is often pointed up through visual style. For example, in one sequence, Helen approaches the detective who has been pursuing her and Johnny and accompanies him to a bar. Without revealing her identity, she engages in an argument concerning the woman he is pursuing, thus defending her own actions in terms of mother love. As she flirts with him, she is photographed in a series of tight close-ups in which shadow plays across her face, and the brim of her hat alternately obscures and reveals her features. The beauty of such close-ups, at once alluring and elusive, works against the sense of punishment and degradation suggested by the censor's reading. Indeed, the use of Dietrich's image is quite difficult to reconcile with the role of suffering mother that Helen claims for herself in the dialogue in this scene. The mise-en-scène of the ending evokes a similar sense of incongruity with regard to Helen's domestic role. She returns from Paris wearing an elegant coat trimmed in fur, which is entirely out of keeping with Faraday's dirty and cramped apartment. She takes off her coat to give Johnny a bath, only to reveal a long-sleeved, backless evening gown that is even more inappropriate for this task. Thus, through visual style, the character's role as a mother becomes increasingly ironic, hovering on the absurd. And this questioning of the definition of the maternal role was possible, I would argue, because industry censors did not routinely take full account of the visual register of the text.

The censor's analysis of *Blonde Venus* is also dependent upon a certain conception of character, his interpretation of Helen's "real" feelings and interior states. However, the film is quite difficult to interpret at this level. For example, in Paris, Helen tells Nick she does not want to return to New York. She announces that she is through with men, and even speaks disparagingly of mother love. This stance is reversed abruptly in the following scene, in which a newspaper article relates that Helen and Nick are engaged and have embarked for New York. The break in continuity and the impersonality of the newspaper account de-emphasizes the character's interior state just when the story hinges upon the question of the heroine's sentiments (or lack thereof). One might assume that Helen returns out of longing for her family, but equally, that she is in love with Nick. Thus, the use of ellipsis makes it difficult to specify Helen's relation to Ned and Johnny. Ambiguity, at this level, works against the aims of censorship by making it difficult to establish a stable motivation for the heroine's action.

There are a number of other instances in which the motivation of the action in *Blonde Venus* seems to make the terms of Joy's reading problematic. One point, of particular concern to censors, was Sternberg's treatment of the initiation of the love affair between Helen and Nick. In their review of the final version of the script, censors complain about scenes that make the exchange between Helen and Nick explicit:[19] she sleeps with him for $300 (to help her ailing husband) and then falls in love with him. In response to the suggestions of the MPPDA, the film as it stands has been rendered much more opaque at this point in the plot. Nick witnesses Helen as "The Blonde Venus" performing in a nightclub and, following her act, writes her a check for reasons that are not made explicit in dialogue. But while the exchange of sex for money is never directly stated by the characters, it is implicit at the level of the performance. Nick is photographed as the most important spectator of Helen's act, and there are several point-of-view shots in which he watches, and comments on, the performance. Thus, the dynamic of the exchange between these two—her invitation, his desire—is established before any dialogue between them, through the alternation between the performance and the look of the male character. By interpolating the registers of narrative and spectacle in this way, it becomes possible for the film to suggest a whole range of motivations for Helen's actions that lie outside the scenario of wifely sacrifice and devotion.

The nightclub act Helen performs for Nick, "Hot Voodoo," verges on self-parody through the sheer weight of accumulated metaphor. Sexuality is constructed as exotic, allied with cannibals, the jungle, Voodoo. In performance, this set of associations is accentuated by the costumes—the chorus wears body-length primitive masks—and the music, which is decidedly percussive. Dietrich, who first appears in a gorilla suit, is thereby associated with the primitive, at the center of a symbolic constellation that links female sexuality, animals, and blacks. For several reasons, the connection between this spectacle and the narrative—the melodrama of the couple—is not immediately apparent. First, the performance introduces a certain floating of identity. In going on the stage, Helen disguises her connection to Ned and Johnny. Helen's agent changes her name from Faraday to Jones, and this designation, a state of virtual anonymity, gives way to another devised by the club manager for the purposes of the act: the Blonde Venus. Moreover, the extreme stylization of her costume—for example, she wears a tall wig pierced by an arrow—heightens the motif of disguise. Along with the assumption of a persona indicated within the diegesis, there is also a play upon the persona of the star. This becomes apparent if we consider the various stages of her appearance in the opening segments of the film. Dietrich's appearance in New York as Ned's wife runs counter to the style of the opening and more generally the conventions of glamour photography. The space of the apartment is dark and confined. Dietrich wears an apron, her hair obscured by a kerchief. While there are some flattering close-ups in this segment, Dietrich tends to be shown in long shot performing a variety of mundane tasks: bathing the baby, cooking dinner. Her body is not overtly fixed or positioned for the camera. The "Hot Voodoo" number provides the return, and with a vengeance, of the image of the star, alluring, glamorous. In a sense then, it is not *Helen* but *Dietrich* who is the Blonde Venus.

The film exploits this division between character and star to introduce material relating to female sexuality that would otherwise have been taboo. The lyrics connect dancing and transgression ("Hot Voodoo—dance of sin") and take exhibition as the accomplishment of desire ("I want to start dancing in cannibal style . . . burn my clothes"). Indeed, the moment in which the Blonde Venus reveals her costume beneath the ape disguise echoes the line about shedding ("burning") her clothes and points to her active participation in the display. And this emphasis upon the dancer's pleasure redoubles, and is re-enforced by, the return of Dietrich's star image and the spectator's pleasure in the spectacle. Of course, given the floating of her identity, the film avoids positing any direct relation between Helen's motives and those we might impute to the "I" of the lyrics. Still, there are hints that Helen returns to the stage for her own reasons, apart from Ned's illness (she tells her husband that she had been planning to return to work even before his illness). More important, the film uses spectacle to destabilize the unity or identity of character. Thus, through the vehicle of performance, the sexuality that Helen must hold back, that cannot achieve expression in the domestic space, is displaced to the space of the stage and image of the star. This has important consequences for the way in which the initiation of the affair between Helen and Nick can be interpreted. In effect, it superimposes upon the impetus for Helen's affair (she needs money for Ned) the transgressive stance of the Blonde Venus ("I don't know the right from the wrong. . . . I'm going to blazes, I want to be bad").

In evaluating this film, then, industry censors proposed a rather delimited splitting or division of character between the heroine's feelings as a mother and her external actions. Although this reading is not entirely implausible, it presupposes narrative conventions such as unambiguous motivation of the action and unified constructions of character that do not hold in the case of this film. Thus, through the use of ellipsis *Blonde Venus* consistently downplays the moments of high melodrama in which the heroine's sentiments or attitude toward her family would be emphasized; for example, the decison to return home from Paris, but also, her decision to betray Ned in the first place. And, through the division between character and star, the film introduces a motivation for infidelity that would have been unacceptable if directly attributed to Helen. Finally, the visual style of the film emphasizes incongruities of class and sexual status that undermine any straightforward definition of the heroine's role as mother. Although this does not entirely foreclose the possibility of the reading that Jason Joy offers, it opens up an alternate path of interpretation, in which the heroine's transgressions are not recuperated as maternal sacrifice.

I would argue then, that *Blonde Venus* is an example of a subversive text, one that transgresses and transforms the social norms concerning female sexuality and the family that censorship sought to reenforce.[20] The category of the subversive text must be approached with some caution, however, having been recently criticized as anachronistic and historically untenable. For example, alluding to the example of *Blonde Venus*, Richard Maltby argues that the process of finding subversive meanings is unbounded, "restrained only by the subjectivity of the critic," and thus, necessarily ahistorical.[21] The problem here is the status of textual analysis as evidence; that is, of finding viable ways to delimit and contextualize the process of interpretation.

In the case of *Blonde Venus*, I have sought to ground my reading in an account of the procedures of self-regulation under the studio system. I have defined the object of study as the entire process of revision rather than the film as such. This approach provides a sense of the *mechanisms* by which social conflicts impinged on a given text—through the protracted negotiations and disputes between the studio, censors, and the director. Further, through sources such as studio production files and the MPPDA case files, it becomes possible to document, with some precision, the way these conflicts surfaced in representation—that is, as choices among various versions of the script. Analyzing the differences between these versions permits us to reconstruct the complex network of explicit rules and implicit narrative conventions that determined what was deemed aberrant or acceptable. Further, analysis of the completed film suggests some of the ways in which these conventions could be circumvented or displaced. Thus, the possibilities of resistance can be measured against a sense of the constraints placed on narrative. Although this approach does not explain how contemporary audiences read the film, it does indicate how texts were received and interpreted at the level of the production. Thus, the work of analysis is delimited by the specific conflicts that gave form to the contradictory text.

Notes

1 The Production Code is reprinted in Garth Jowett, *Film the Democratic Art* (Boston: Little, Brown, 1976), 468–72. The relevant sections of the Code are: "Law, natural or human, shall not be

ridiculed, nor shall sympathy be created for its violation," and, "The sanctity of the institution of marriage and the home shall be upheld."

2 For a discussion of the problem of determination within the context of the studio system, see David Bordwell, Janet Staiger, and Kristin Thompson, *The Classical Hollywood Cinema: Film Style and Mode of Production to 1960* (New York: Columbia University Press, 1985), 85–113, 241–62.

3 Bill Nichols, *Ideology and the Image* (Bloomington: Indiana University Press, 1981), 115–18.

4 E. Ann Kaplan, *Women and Film: Both Sides of the Camera* (New York: Methuen, 1983), 49–60.

5 The West Coast division of the MPPDA responsible for monitoring production was initially called the Studio Relations Committee. In 1934, following the Legion of Decency Campaign, its name was changed to the Production Code Administration, and Joseph Breen assumed control of the office.

6 The MPPDA Case Files, Special Collections, Herrick Library, Academy of Motion Picture Arts and Sciences, Los Angeles, are organized by title beginning in 1928 and continuing until the early sixties.

7 Letter to Hays, 22 April 1932, *Blonde Venus*, MPPDA Case Files (hereafter Academy Library).

8 The three versions of the script are dated 18 March, 23 April, and 11 May 1932, in *Blonde Venus*, Paramount Story File, Academy Library. Please note that the Paramount Story Files are housed in a collection distinct from the MPPDA Case Files.

9 Lamar Trotti, Memo, 28 March 1932; Jason Joy to Hays, 1 April 1932, *Blonde Venus*, MPPDA Case Files, Academy Library.

10 Lamar Trotti to B. P. Schulberg, 20 April 1932, and to Hays, 22 April 1932, *Blonde Venus*, MPPDA Case Files, Academy Library.

11 Jason Joy (head MPPDA censor) to B. P. Schulberg, 26 May 1932, *Blonde Venus*, MPPDA Case Files, Academy Library.

12 Jason Joy to B. P. Schulberg, 26 April 1932, *Blonde Venus*, MPPDA Case Files, Academy Library.

13 Kaplan, *Women and Film*, 56 and 59. The problem with this kind of analysis, in my view, is that the description of Ned's character does not take account of the ways the film distorts conventional modes of characterization, both by refusing to motivate the story at this level and by setting up structural parallels between scenes (for example, the opening and closing versions of Helen and Ned's first meeting).

14 The motif of class rise is pervasive in thirties cinema; it is associated with a male character in the case of the gangster film and with a female character in both melodramas and comedies in which a show-girl or goldigger pursues a rich man. Examples of the latter category include *Gold Diggers of 1933* (Mervyn LeRoy and Busby Berkeley, 1933), *Baby Face* (Alfred Green, 1933), and *Red-Headed Woman* (Jack Conway, 1932).

15 Lamar Trotti to B. P. Schulberg, 20 April 1932, *Blonde Venus*, MPPDA Case Files, Academy Library.

16 Jason Joy to Harold Hurley (Paramount Legal Department), 1 September 1932, and to John Hammel (Paramount Distribution), 16 September 1932, *Blonde Venus*, MPPDA Case Files, MPPDA.

17 Jason Joy to John Hammel, 16 September 1932, *Blonde Venus*, MPPDA Case Files, MPPDA.

18 See, for example, Raymond Bellour, *L'analyse du film* (Paris: Editions Albatros, 1979); Stephen Heath, "Film, System, Narrative," in *Questions of Cinema* (London: Macmillan, 1981). Also, see Janet Bergstrom's discussion of textual analysis in "Enunciation and Sexual Difference," *Camera Obscura* 3/4 (Summer 1979): 33–65.

19 Jason Joy writes that he is "very much perturbed about the situation in which Helen deliberately accepts Nick's invitation to go away for two weeks and to a less extent about the prostitution of herself and frank confession of the fact to her husband." Joy to B. P. Schulberg, 26 May 1932, *Blonde Venus*, MPPDA Case Files, Academy Library.

20 The notion of the contradictory or subversive text derives from the collective associated with the *Cahiers du Cinéma*. See Jean-Louis Comolli and Jean Narboni, "Cinema/Ideology/Criticism," *Cahiers du Cinéma* (October 1969), translated in *Screen* 12 (Spring 1971); "John Ford's *Young Mr. Lincoln*," translated in *Movies and Methods*, ed. Bill Nichols (Berkeley: University of California Press, 1976) and "*Morocco*," translated in *Sternberg*, ed. Peter Baxter (London: BFI Publishing, 1980). The argument is that certain films rupture the transparency and closure typical of the classical text, thereby revealing the ideological presuppositions that underlie them. Formal analysis is privileged as a technique for locating such instances of contradiction or rupture.

21 " 'Baby Face' or How Joe Breen Made Barbara Stanwyck Atone for Causing the Wall Street Crash," *Screen* 27 (March/April 1986): 24. Barbara Klinger makes a similar critique of the category, arguing that it is necessary to take account of the multiplicty of discourses that determine the consumption of the supposedly subversive or progressive text. See "Cinema/Ideology/Criticism Revisited: The Progressive Text," *Screen* 25 (January/February, 1984).

Chapter 14

Thomas Doherty

CLASSICAL HOLLYWOOD CINEMA: THE WORLD ACCORDING TO JOSEPH I. BREEN (1999)

Editors' Introduction

In *Pre-Code Hollywood: Sex, Immorality, and Insurrection in American Cinema 1930–1934*, Thomas Doherty focuses on a liminal period in American moviemaking, the half-decade between the advent of the Production Code and its formal enforcement. In this essay, the final chapter in that book, Doherty tracks the transition into PCA-era Hollywood by focusing on a single industry player, the "supreme pontiff of picture morals," Joseph I. Breen. Counter to widely held assumptions about Breen as a religious zealot and intransigent bully, Doherty depicts him as a "true player who relished his role as a creative collaborator in the filmmaking process." So when Breen boasted "I am the Code," Doherty contends, he was merely pointing out that among all of the players in the moviemaking process, he had a unique and unparalleled degree of influence and power.

Using a wealth of primary documents (trade and newspaper accounts, mostly), Doherty presents a picture of Hollywood at a crossroads in which Breen's enforcement of the Code managed delicate relationships between the federal government, state and local censorship offices, religious organizations (like the Catholic Legion of Decency) and the Hollywood Studios (themselves composed of Los Angeles and New York offices that often found themselves at odds with each other). What Breen's PCA brought, then, was stability. The artistic cost to film content may indeed have been considerable – note the changes made to W.S. van Dyke's *Forsaking All Others*, 1934, discussed by Doherty, for example – but it is hard to ignore the coincidence of the industry's fiscal rebound at the end of that year and the appointment of Breen atop the PCA just a few months earlier. Though Breen may not have had his eye on the bottom line, his tenure proved once again the public relations value – a value that could be measured in dollars and cents – of content regulation in Hollywood.

Suggested Reading

Thomas Doherty, *Hollywood's Censor: Joseph I. Breen and the Production Code Administration* (NY: Columbia University Press, 2009); Jon Lewis, *Hollywood v. Hard*

Core: How the Struggle over Censorship Saved the Motion Picture Industry (NY: NYU Press, 2002); and Gregory Black, *Hollywood Censored: Morality Codes, the Catholics and the Movies* (NY: Cambridge University Press, 1996).

AFTER FOUR YEARS OF gun-toting gangsters and smart-mouthed convicts, adulterous wives and promiscuous chorines, irreverence from the lower orders and incompetence from above, the immoral and insurrectionist impulses on the Hollywood screen were beaten back by forces dedicated to public restraint and social control. Though other media were more sexually explicit and politically incendiary, the domain of American cinema was panoramic and resonant, accessible to all, resisted by few. It was to Hollywood that politicians, clerics, and reformers looked when they detected a shredding of the moral fiber of the nation and a sickness in the body politic.

Toward the end of 1933, a cluster of political and cultural pressures brewing throughout the pre-Code era gathered momentum and, by mid-1934, had converged to transform the moral landscape of American cinema. The events leading to the curtailment of pre-Code license and the enshrinement of the Production Code were at once fixed and certain (a classic case of special interest groups hitting sensitive nerves for maximum impact) and hazy and atmospheric (a shift in zeitgeist intangible in outline but decisive in impact). The currents that flowed together in 1933–34 have identifiable names—the National Legion of Decency, the Motion Picture Research Council, and the New Deal—but what they represented was part of a stronger centrifugal force. Where pre-Code Hollywood vented the disorientations and despair of America in the nadir of the Great Depression, Hollywood after 1934 reflected the restoration of cultural equilibrium under FDR.

In December 1933, a front-page article in the *Hollywood Reporter* summarized the religious-political confluence. "The picture industry is going to be made to clean up or else—and that 'else' will be Federal censorship with no less a power than President Roosevelt ready to sponsor its passage through Congress." Reviewing the past few years, the trade paper asserted that "an important factor is also the attitude of the Catholic Church, which saved the industry from Federal censorship three years ago by listening to the promises of censorship [from] within the industry. The Hays Code of practice was largely the work of Father Daniel Lord, S.J.—and if producers had lived up to it, they would still have a strong ally." More than anything else, the alignment of church and state—the righteous opposition of a Roman Catholic hierarchy sternly admonishing parishioners to shun Hollywood combined with the threat of federal censorship under a new administration vigorously consolidating power in Washington, D.C.—forced the motion picture industry in 1934 to adopt in fact what in 1930 was adopted in name.

"The Storm of '34"

The Roman Catholic Church entered the fray first and most fiercely. After suffering years of noncompliance with Father Lord's Code, prelates felt duped by the Hollywood hustlers. "We believed we were dealing with moral gentleman," lamented George Cardinal Mundelein of Chicago in a letter to his flock. "We were mistaken. To them it was just another scrap of paper." Indignant, the Catholic leadership embarked upon a nationwide crusade to lead parishioners away from Hollywood's temptations.

In 1933 the Church hierarchy announced formation of the National Legion of Decency to spearhead a renewed and more aggressive crusade to clean up "the pest hole that infects the entire country with its obscene and lascivious moving pictures." During Sunday masses in cathedrals across America, Catholics took an oath to avoid objectionable movies as "occasions for sin." With the solemnity of an Act of Contrition, upwards of eleven million communicants recited the Legion pledge:

> I wish to join the Legion of Decency, which condemns vile and unwholesome moving pictures. I unite with all who protest against them as a grave menace to youth, to home life, to country, and to religion.
>
> I condemn absolutely those salacious motion pictures which, with other degrading agencies, are corrupting public morals and promoting a sex mania in our land.
>
> I shall do all that I can to arouse public opinion against the portrayal of vice as a normal condition of affairs, and against depicting criminals of any class as heroes and heroines, presenting their filthy philosophy of life as something acceptable to decent men and women.
>
> I unite with all who condemn the display of suggestive advertisements on billboards at theater entrances and the favorable notices given to immoral motion pictures.
>
> Considering these evils, I hereby promise to remain away from all motion pictures except those which do not offend decency and Christian morality. I promise further to secure as many members as possible for the Legion of Decency.
>
> I make this protest in a spirit of self-respect and with the conviction that the American public does not demand filthy pictures, but clean entertainment and educational features.

To assure that the covenant was kept, parish priests stationed themselves outside box office windows to eyeball wayward communicants contemplating a date with Mae West.

On June 8, 1934, Denis Cardinal Dougherty of Philadelphia raised the stakes by ordering good Catholics to avoid *all* motion pictures. "A vicious and insidious attack is being made on the very foundation of our Christian civilization," Dougherty wrote in a letter to parishes. "Perhaps the greatest menace to faith and morals in America today is the motion picture theater. Nothing is left for us except the boycott." The admonition to stay away, His Eminence concluded sternly, was "not merely a counsel, but a positive command binding all in conscience under pain of sin."

Although American Catholics were the best organized and most vocal of the religious groups condemning the movies, the crusade was very much an ecumenical movement. In fact, a shared hatred of Hollywood seemed to imbue Christians of all denominations with the spirit of brotherly love. "We feel that this move by our Catholic friends is one of the finest we have heard recently and we pledge them our unqualified support," said a Protestant spokesman for the Washington Federation of Churches. "We mean business in this thing. We have made up our minds to put an end to disgraceful and indecent motion pictures and I believe that with such a splendid start made by the Catholics, and with the Protestants joining hands, we shall be able to get results."

As Protestant clergy urged their congregations "to unite with Catholics in their campaign to raise the moral standards of pictures," the Central Conference of American Rabbis called for cooperation "with other religious and civic bodies in bringing home to the picture producers their responsibility for taking immediate steps to elevate the standards of pictures." American Jews had special reason to work shoulder to shoulder with Christian America. An antisemitism that was never too thinly veiled lay behind at least some of the attacks on Hollywood as the Sodom on the Pacific. Largely ruled and disproportionately populated by

American Jews, the motion picture industry was a conspicuous national stage for a people whose every historical instinct counseled against conspicuous displays. Perhaps noting the significant omission of the "Judeo" from the possessive "our Christian civilization" in Cardinal Dougherty's pastoral letter, Rabbi Sidney E. Goldstein of the Central Conference of American Rabbis averred that Jews should be more concerned than other religious groups in making sure movies were wholesome "for if the screen is not kept clean, the disgrace will fall on the shoulders of the Jews."

As clerics of all stripes fulminated against Hollywood impiety, sociology unexpectedly allied itself with religion. In 1933 the Motion Picture Research Council, under the auspices of the Payne Fund, issued the first results of a five-year investigation into the corrosive effects of motion pictures on the young. The study was summarized in an alarmist tome by Henry James Forman entitled *Our Movie-Made Children*. An immediate bestseller, it accused Hollywood of being "subversive to the best interests of society . . . nothing less than an *agent provocateur*, a treacherous and costly enemy let loose at the public expense." Couched in the jargon of white-coated researchers who had monitored sleeping children with a device called the "hypnograph" (a "sleep recorder" placed under the mattress to measure nocturnal jitters after exposure to horror movies) and ladled throughout with statistical precision (while 26 percent of delinquent boys reported "that pictures had taught them to act 'tough,' or to act like a 'big guy,' " no less than 72 percent of delinquent girls admitted to "having improved their attractiveness by imitating the movies"), the Payne Fund studies seemed to quantify what the matrons and clerics knew in their hearts. To editorial writers and city councilors for whom Catholic theology was but hearsay evidence, the authority of social science clinched the case.

Meanwhile, another quite different code was asserting itself over Hollywood. Like other businesses, the motion picture industry found itself subject to the elaborate guidelines and intrusive bureaucracy of the National Recovery Act, the New Deal legislation overseeing what had mainly been unfettered business practices in a laissez-faire economy. The arrival of the New Deal in Washington prompted no little panic about what kind of hand Hollywood would be left holding. On December 20, 1933, after months of wrangling between the motion picture industry and the federal government, the NRA promulgated a Code Authority for the Motion Picture Industry. It loomed to regulate not only business operations, everything from hourly wages for projectionists to ticket prices, but film content as well. The appointment to the NRA Code Authority of Dr. A. Lawrence Lowell, president emeritus of Harvard University and active president of the Motion Picture Research Council, was perceived as Washington's way of telling Hollywood to clean up its act.

Unlike the Production Code, the NRA Code was vague on matters of morality and, moreover, the legal status of its regulatory authority over film content was uncertain. But studios were leery of defying FDR's New Deal initiatives and running the risk of drawing fines or having their films banned. To motion picture executives who wondered what defined "off-color pix" or "dirt" in the eyes of federal regulators, an industry observer warned, "If they don't know [what dirt is], President Roosevelt will soon let them know." Or maybe President Roosevelt's mother would first let him know: Mrs. Sarah Delano Roosevelt served as honorary vice president of the Motion Picture Research Council.

In one sense, the prospect of New Deal censors was but the latest permutation on an old story. After all, the specter of federal censorship had shadowed the motion picture industry from its inception, or at least since 1915, when the Supreme Court disabused a consortium of producers of the notion that film possessed the same First Amendment rights as the press. Ruling in *Mutual Film Corporation v. Industrial Commission of Ohio*, the Court decreed that the upstart medium was "a business pure and simple, originated and conducted for profit, like other spectacles, not to be regarded . . . as part of the press of the country or as organs of public opinion." For blow-hard congressmen, the introduction of bills to set up federal censorship boards had long been a reliable path to publicity and reelection. In 1932 a weary headline in *Variety* evoked the clockwork predictability of the harassment from Capitol Hill: "Congress Has 11 Legislative Film Bills Including Usual Nut Stuff."

The atmospherics of 1934 turned the empty threat into a dread possibility. The bills were not just grandstanding gestures, but ominous likelihoods. That summer a "drastic and far-reaching bill" introduced by Congressman Raymond Cannon (D-Wis.) was being weighed by the Committee on Interstate and Foreign Commerce, a measure that provided that "whosoever shall transport or cause to be transported in interstate or foreign commerce any moving picture film in which (a) any of the persons taking part in the film have ever been arrested and convicted of an offense involving moral turpitude; or (b) the actions of the persons taking part in the film are suggestive, unwholesome and or morally objectionable, shall be punished by a fine of not more than $5,000 or by imprisonment for not more than five years, or both." With the New Deal drawing governmental power once vested to the states into the hands of Washington bureaucrats, the stark threat of federal fines and imprisonment concentrated studio minds powerfully. Moreover, unlike most pending legislation in the Democratic Congress, the censorship bills claimed strong bipartisan support. "Steadily the stream of pollution which has flowed forth from Hollywood has become wilder and more turbulent," declared Francis D. Culkin (R-N.Y.), who estimated that 70 percent of Hollywood output was "salacious, criminal, or indecent" and protested "hectic stories of sex appeal, white slavery, and criminalistic vice."

As church, academe, and government pressed in upon the industry from the outside, internal differences prevented a united defense against the three-front war. The vertical integration of production, distribution, and exhibition worked in harmony as economics, but as social practice the exhibition end of the business took the hardest hit when Hollywood came under attack. The neighborhood theater manager functioned as the nearest available representative of all that was vile in American cinema and served as the face-to-face "squawk absorber" for brickbats from a disapproving public. Small town exhibitors faced community pressures big city exhibitors were insulated from; angry calls from customers they knew on a first-name basis, sharp lectures from lodge brothers and Chamber of Commerce associates, or a parish priest planting himself outside the theater front.

A small town exhibitor in Michigan complained about the personal grief he faced over *The Life of Vergie Winters* (1934), a women's weepie about the lifelong travails of a politician's mistress ["We took a terrible licking on the picture as it is one of the blacklisted and, believe me, these small town [clerics] are telling their congregations what pictures to not hop and see. If they don't clean them up, it will be curtains for us guys out in the sticks." Another Midwest theater manager agreed. "It may be okay for the large cities [but] out here in this small town and in all others it's bad medicine for our business and is going to bring down a lot of blue-nosed ladies before the local city council wanting something done about the matter." Of the risqué wisecracks in *Hot Pepper* (1933), a third manager complained: "Too 'hot' for small town patronage catering to respectable people and family trade. Every town has some people who like them 'hot,' but they won't keep you in business." The sophisticated diet of the urban crowd was deemed anathema to the guileless moviegoer from the heartland who preferred his film fare hearty and simple. "Producers are building their own funeral pyre by making films for the theater man and New York," said Cecil B. DeMille, the reigning expert on pagan rituals. From the hinterlands, the word came back that the sticks nixed sexed-up flicks.

By mid-1934, the sense of siege and impending crisis around Hollywood was palpable. "The cumulative effect of this movement is dangerous," warned one of a series of frightened front-page stories in the *Hollywood Reporter*. "The matter is beyond the annoyance stage; it is inflicting wounds at the box office." The trade press dubbed the uproar "the storm of '34," the sense that blasts from all sides were buffeting the motion picture industry in a whirlwind of destructive force. "The whole world has gotten the idea that Hollywood is Hell's home office and Hays is the District Manager," a flustered theater manager blurted out.

Desperate to stop box office boycotts by the Catholics, to forestall the controversy incited by the Motion Picture Research Council, and to preempt the imposition of federal censorship, the MPPDA reorganized the enforcement mechanism of the 1930 Code to give it coercive power over member producers. In an amendment proposed on June 13, 1934, and formally adopted by the MPPDA's Board of Directors on July 12, 1934, two key alterations in the 1930 Code changed the way Hollywood did business. First, the Producers Appeal Board, the Hollywood-based group of studio chiefs empowered to reverse decisions by the Studio Relations Committee, was abolished. Second, the Studio Relations Committee was itself supplanted by the Production Code Administration, an office whose decisions could be reversed only by a remote court of appeals back in New York, the full board of directors of the MPPDA. By redrawing the lines of authority away from the Hollywood moguls and toward their New York financiers, the MPPDA granted the PCA autonomy and power. Bank of America president A. P. Giannini, one of Hollywood's most powerful financial backers, cemented the new arrangements by stating flatly that no film would receive financing without prior clearance from the PCA.

Figure 14.1 "The Storm of '34": Hollywood slime merchants scoff at demands for a cleaner screen, May 17, 1934. Courtesy of the *Chicago Tribune*:

The watchword was "self-regulation," the promise that Hollywood itself would do what churchmen and politicians demanded, provided the former let up and the latter butt out. "Self regulation in the industry is the answer to clean pictures. It was evident in March 1934 that the place to do any cleaning up was at the source of the trouble—where the pictures were made and at the time they were made," declared Sol A. Rosenblatt, NRA division administrator in charge of amusement and transportation codes, putting the federal stamp of approval on the Code. "I myself do not believe in [government censorship]. Self regulation and education, under powerful and virile leadership, are the only effective mediums."

The powerful and virile leader appointed to head the Production Code Administration was Joseph I. Breen. In December 1931, Hays had brought Breen to Hollywood to work on public relations, and by January 1934 he had succeeded Dr. James Wingate as head of the Studio Relations Committee. Breen had immediately demonstrated a passionate and personal commitment to upholding the letter of the Code. Yet prior to July 1934, he had been stymied by having to answer to the very men he was trying to regulate. With the elimination of the Producers Appeal Board and the creation of the PCA, Breen's authority henceforth flowed not from a council of Hollywood-based executives but from the MPPDA board back in New York, the same men the studio moguls served. He could confront Jack L. Warner, Louis B. Mayer, or Sam Goldwyn on a plane of equality or maybe even a higher perch: as long as New York was happy, his position in Hollywood was secure.

Besides, as a prominent Roman Catholic himself, Breen was a human bulwark against the Legion of Decency. Jesuit-educated and studio wise, he acted as both mediator and missionary, a kind of Vatican envoy to the Hollywood heathen (to the Catholics) and a participant-observer conversant in the ways of gentile America (to the moguls). He could be a double agent, injecting Catholicism into the movies at the same time he instructed studio executives in the distinctions between venal and mortal, sins of omission and sins of commission. "I am the Code," Breen later said, not because the Code was whatever he said it was—it wasn't, everyone could read it—but because he enforced and embodied it.

If Breen's severe brand of Irish-Catholicism motivated his desire to fumigate Hollywood, his intricate knowledge of film grammar and the production process allowed him to enforce his dictates. Unlike most censors, Breen knew the art he bowdlerized. From story treatments and shooting scripts he spotted early warning signs of trouble and resolved difficulties before more expensive stages of production had proceeded. He made useful suggestions to producers on how to circumvent problem areas, permitting them to abide by the letter of the Code while keeping the spirit of their script. Breen may have been at the table by edict, but he was true player who relished his role as a creative collaborator in the filmmaking process. Moreover, he was a tireless and efficient bureaucrat who brought managerial order to the office and predictability to the review process.

In 1930, when the MPPDA first voted to abide by the Code, the decision was made as a placating gesture, an act taken seriously neither by the studio signatories nor the trade press. The Code, *Variety* quipped at the time, "prohibits or minimizes the use of all ingredients that have actually proven sure fire. If actually followed in a single feature release, said picture, it is officially observed, would bore in Rome, irritate in Palestine, and cause a riot in Moscow." Cynics on all sides viewed the revamped 1934 Code as another stalling maneuver, a tactical concession to violate as soon as the heat cooled. Four years later, however, the pressures to keep in line had become heavier and the penalties for noncompliance higher.

Having put in place the process and the person to make the 1934 Code in reality what the 1930 Code was in theory, the industry launched an advertising campaign to persuade the public of its sincere commitment to moral conduct. Breen went on radio and appeared before the newsreels to explain the Code and to assure Americans that Hollywood was putting its house in order. Shown by Pathé cameras visiting the set of RKO's *Dangerous Corner* (1934),

Breen met with director Phil Rosen and actor Conrad Nagel and told the cast and crew, "I want you people really to understand what we are doing in the way of making clean pictures." On his feet and looking square into the camera in a clip released to all the newsreels, Breen clarified why "all of the motion picture companies of the United States have joined hands in adopting what has come to be known as a Production Code of ethics." An accomplished public speaker, he delivers his lines forcefully in an uninterrupted long take:

> Its broad general purpose is to insure screen entertainment which will be reasonably acceptable to our patrons everywhere—entertainment which is definitely free from offense. Now, of course, this does not mean that we are to impose upon you any unreasonable restrictions in the development of the art which is the motion picture. This does not mean that motion pictures are not to deal with live and vital subjects, stories based upon drama which is vigorous and stimulating as well as entertaining. Neither does it mean that we are to make pictures only for children.

As Breen winds up, he warms to his point:

> But it *does* mean *quite definitely* that the vulgar, the cheap, and the tawdry is out! There is no room on the screen at any time for pictures which offend against common decency—and these the industry will not allow.

A sure sign of the new order came in the form of a title card inserted before the credits of the first Code-approved releases of 1934. Superimposed over the oval seal of the MPPDA, the announcement read:

> This Picture Approved by the Production Code Administration of the Motion Picture Producers & Distributors of America.
>
> *Certificate Number ###.*

The message was underscored by Breen's force of personality, a polite way of saying he could be as obnoxious and intransigent as the producers he dealt with. Early on, the designated censor drew lines in the sand to assert his authority and to signal that he was no compliant Colonel Joy or befuddled Dr. Wingate, that a new regime with an alert sentinel had come to power. As Jack Vizzard recalled in *See No Evil: Life Inside a Hollywood Censor*, a witty memoir of his days as a Production Code official, "The mainspring of [Breen's] vitality was the fact that he nurtured not the slightest seed of self-doubt regarding his mission or his rectitude. He was right, the moviemakers were wrong, and that was that." Gradually, it dawned on studio executives that however insincerely they had pledged renewed fidelity to the Code, this time they really had meant it.

The first showdown between Breen and a studio came about over a small matter. MGM's *Forsaking All Others* (1934) was a zesty comedy of manners with Clark Gable, Joan Crawford, and Robert Montgomery entwined in a fairly standard romantic triangle. In Breen's view, however, the film treated the sacrament of marriage too lightly, an offense that dozens of pre-Code films had committed with impunity. The most troublesome scene involved a night in a mountain lodge spent together by single girl Crawford and married man Montgomery. Discovered the next morning by Gable, Crawford walks back into the lodge and says, "I forgot something," and Gable answers, "Well, it's in there, dressing," referring to Montgomery.

Though any adulterous conduct from the night before occurred only in the mind and not on the screen, Breen demanded dialogue that underscored the upright behavior of the heroine. Detailing his objections in a seven-page letter to Louis B. Mayer, Breen asserted that "in its present form the picture is definitely and specifically a violation of our Code because of its general low moral tone and specifically because of its very definite wrong reflection upon the institution of marriage." Trapped between the immovable enforcement mechanisms of the PCA and the invincible opposition of Joseph Breen, MGM caved. "[Studio manager Eddie] Mannix agreed today to make all cuts insisted upon by us in *Forsaking All Others*," Breen gloated in a telegram to Hays. "Peace Reigns Supreme." Director W. S. Van Dyke swallowed hard and shot the required retakes. "I shouldn't have seen you no matter how much I wanted to," Crawford says in a blatant editorial insert during her love scene with Montgomery. Later, referring to Gable's lectures on the sanctity of marriage, she confesses, "I was wrong yesterday. I thought I could knock the rules over, but I guess I'm not the type." Afterwards, Van Dyke penned a kiss-and-make-up letter to Breen but he couldn't resist a defiant postscript: "I still think I'm right!"

Besides saving MGM $100,000 on the cost of retakes with his uncredited dialogue contributions, Breen's successful intrusion into the process of motion picture editing marked a turning point in the balance of power. "Of course that censorship of *Forsaking All Others* will go down in the history of the picture business as something or other," predicted trade reporter W.R. Wilkerson, giving the devil his due. "We have heard Breen called everything in the world since he became the purifier of the screen, but not one person has accused him of doing other than what he honestly believes to be right." Moreover, Breen "will not weaken under fire" and when he issues an order, he "*makes it stick*." Around Hollywood, Breen's very name soon entered the vernacular as an ironic verb meaning "to purify" or "to whitewash." "Meticulous Breening" from "Purity Headquarters" was said to be hamstringing producers and creating films that must be "pure and simple at all costs." When MGM repainted their studios a bright new shade of alabaster, a sly headline in the *Hollywood Reporter* read: "MGM 'Breens' Plant."

Concerned that his profile as the "supreme pontiff of picture morals" had become too prominent too quickly, Breen filmed another newsreel spot in 1934 to assure moviegoers that "our Production Code Administration" was *not* an exercise in "one-man censorship." Rather "it represents the considered judgement of many persons of wide experience and a sincere interest in motion pictures." Shown sitting at the head of a table with three subordinates on either side, Breen invites moviegoers to "sit in with us at a meeting of the Production Code Administration in Hollywood, where we are working for finer and better motion pictures." He makes tactical use of the first-person plural as he explains something of the process: "From the very beginning of the picture we work with producers, authors, scenario writers, directors, and all who are connected with the production to the end that the finished product may be free from reasonable objection and that our pictures may be the vital and wholesome entertainment we all want them to be."

Now truly under the Code, the landscape of American cinema underwent a tectonic shift. In a matter of months, the genres, tones, and textures of pre-Code Hollywood were erased from the screen. The Breen Office refused passage to films bearing the stamp of the old epoch and called back from release those already in circulation. "Eliminate views of dancer wiggling her posterior at audience" and "re-edit the scene between George Raft and Carole Lombard so as definitely to remove present inference that they spent the night together," Breen demanded when Paramount applied to reissue *Bolero* (1934). Only after clearance from the Breen Office was a pre-Code Hollywood film let loose again: but of course then it was no longer pre-Code.

The toned-down quality of motion picture advertising reflected the modesty of the new regime. Advertising had always been a flash point because salacious taglines and lush illustrations were incandescent signs of vice. No matter that the films themselves were far tamer

Figure 14.2 The "supreme pontiff of picture morals": Joseph I. Breen, head of the Production Code Administration and guardian of Hollywood's moral universe.

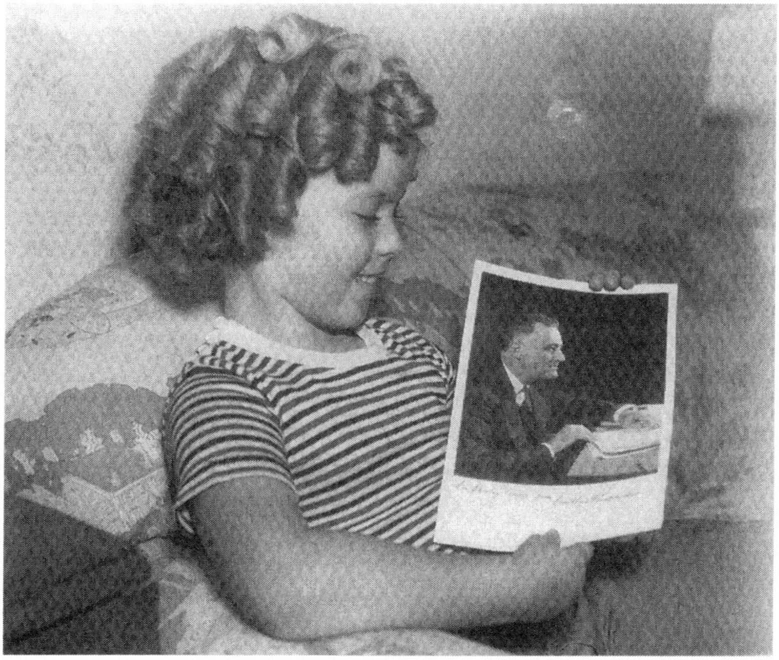

Figure 14.3 A New Deal in motion pictures: Shirley Temple, mascot of the new morality, cradles the patriarch of the New Deal. Credit: Consent to the use of Shirley Temple's likeness courtesy of Shirley's World, L.P.

than the poster art and exclamatory blurbs; Hollywood sold the promise of immorality and insurrection. An unintended consequence, however, was that influential people who never went to the movies got their main impressions of the screen from the false advertising, the prime example being Cardinal Dougherty, provoked by a billboard to launch his boycott in Philadelphia.

Committed to "raising the standards of exploitation, promotion, and advertising copy," the Advertising Advisory Council of the MPPDA stanched the leering taglines, fleshy illustrations, and come-on trailers. The title of the next Jean Harlow vehicle underwent symbolic changes of heart, from the pre-Code *Born to Be Kissed* to the Code-approved *It Pays to Be Good*, before becoming the bland *The Girl from Missouri* (1934). Likewise, what was *Broadway Virgin* in preproduction crystallized into *Manhattan Butterfly* (1934) upon release. Before publication, studio advertising henceforth needed to be submitted and stamped with approval from the Hays Office. In the Warner Brothers publicity department, a sign was put up: "Did the Hays Office See It?" Caught in the gap between pre-Code production and post-Code advertising regulations, the publicity for *Tarzan and His Mate* (1934) is actually *less* titillating than the film. In billboards and one-sheets, Maureen O'Sullivan wears an outfit containing a yard more cloth than the skimpy outfit she models in the film.

More than taglines and ad mattes, however, the new product line showed that the studios had made good on their promise to "say it with pictures." Historical and biographical films of a kind that warmed the hearts of librarians were exhibit A for the reformed Hollywood. The 1934–35 season, promised Hays, would see "a very large increase in the number of films being made from the great classics of literature and the stage and from books that have already won a place in the hearts of millions of readers." Fox took out nationwide ads trumpeting the commitment to family fare and literary excellence. "Thanks to [Will Rogers'] *David Harum* (1934) and *Little Women* (1933) for setting a new fashion in motion pictures—the extraordinary success of these two fine, wholesome movies was a mandate to the producers from the American public starting a new trend in motion picture entertainment and launching the screen on what promises to be its most worthwhile season." Moreover, the cycle of novels-into-films could be exploited with commercial tie-ins to elementary and junior high schools, helping at once to pump up box office and win over skeptical educators.

Six-year-old Shirley Temple rocketed to superstardom that year in *Stand Up and Cheer* (1934), *Little Miss Marker* (1934), and *Bright Eyes* (1934), the former Baby Burlesk toddler coming to personify the purity and wholesomeness of the new family-friendly fare. She was billed as "the perfect entertainment for every family in the land" and, not incidentally, "an attraction that will serve as an answer to many of the attacks that are being hurled at pictures." Temple's extraordinary success—she was by far the most lucrative human asset held by Hollywood throughout the 1930s—went a long way in proving that Code-approved films meant not just less trouble but more profit. No wonder Fox chief Winfield Sheehan trumpeted his product line for 1935 as "good music, clean comedy, and dramas of modern life built on strong simple stories."

Other studio heads spouted the same rhetoric. RKO-Radio president B. B. Kahane warned producers that "there is no need and no excuse whatsoever for productions which scoff at chastity and the sanctity of marriage, present criminals and wrong doers as heroes and heroines, or in which smut and salaciousness are deliberately injected for the appeal they may have to coarse and unrefined minds. The Production Code is comprehensive and clear. If we honestly carry out the spirit of the provisions, our productions will be unobjectionable." "Pictures for the entire family" was the keynote theme of Jack Warner's 1934–35 production schedule, "the absence of sophisticated and sex problem type features" being conspicuous in a program built around "adventure pictures jammed with action, musicals, dramas, romances, comedy dramas, and straight comedies." Adolph Zukor also pledged his wholehearted cooperation. "Paramount does not and will not make dirty pictures. Producers who make indecent pictures, who inject dirt into pictures, without excuse, should be driven out of the business." Chastened after straying into unsanctified realms, the motion picture industry adopted the guise of a prodigal medium, repentant and now ready to be welcomed back into the fold of hallowed American entertainment.

Not everyone praised the cleaner sheen of American cinema. Independent producers, seeing the Code as but another device to cut them out of the action, were defiant at first. "If the majors have not got the guts, if they are afraid of a few churchmen and a handful of professional reformers, we are not," said a spokesman for the Independent Motion Picture Producers Association. "We do not recognize and will give no thought to Mr. Joe Breen or anything he represents." After a month of inveighing against the "psalm singing politicians and professional reformers," however, the bluster turned to accommodation when the indies pledged to adhere to the Code and arranged cooperative oversight from the Breen Office.

Select cadres of critics and exhibitors also complained. "Breen can give the Church a picture that will be acceptable to the Legion of Decency, but not one that will be bought by the legions of movie fans," objected Fred Pasley in the *New York Daily News*. After tallying up the diminished returns for Mae West's misfiring in *The Belle of the Nineties* (1934), a rueful exhibitor sneered that "the Legion of Decency gummed things up—if I may be allowed that expression." A like-minded studio executive grumbled that under the Code "the leading woman must start out good, stay good, and be whitewashed for the finish." On Broadway and in Los Angeles, some audiences hissed when the Production Code seal appeared on the screen, a response that only laid bare the corrupt desires of the denizens of the big city against the homespun decency of small town folk.

But the recalcitrants were outnumbered by the accommodationists. By the end of 1934, three hard facts had created a consensus around the virtues of self-censorship.

First, the Code saved Hollywood huge sums on the editing and distribution of prints. Postproduction alterations demanded by the myriad of state and local censorship boards—groups with varying, shifting, and conflicting standards—cost plenty in money, hassle, and good will. Censorship boards in seven states and fifty-five cities bedeviled the industry, and no two seemed to have the same or even a consistent set of standards. In some regions, the town sheriff or the mayor's wife wielded mogul-like power to slice objectionable scenes before a film was permitted a local playdate. Moreover, an enormous amount of revenue was lost on films cut jagged beyond repair by the pruning sheers of local amateurs. In 1931 lost income on films "so drastically cut that the entertainment was washed out, with the resultant loss of patronage" was estimated at between $8,000,000 and $10,000,000. Worse, the rate of local censorship and its costs to the industry had actually *increased* since 1930, when the Code was adopted to forestall just such interference and expense. In achieving one of its central goals—placating the state and local censorship boards—the pre-Code experiment had been a woeful failure. Only with the Code as fortress and Breen as sentinel did the influence of the censorship boards wane. By the end of 1934, the studios calculated that over a million dollars on film alterations *alone* had already been saved via the expedient of the Code, a figure that did not estimate the box office revenues recouped on films that earlier would have been rendered unplayable by local interference.

Second, the wholesome family pictures took off at the box office. Shirley Temple was the preeminent example of virtue rewarded, but other stars and film cycles confirmed the profit in rectitude. Beginning with RKO's *Little Women* in November 1933, a pre-Code film in date only, a high school reading list's worth of literary classics was sanitized for a series of high-prestige and generally high-profit motion pictures: *Treasure Island* (1934), *Alice Adams* (1935), *Becky Sharp* (1935), *David Copperfield* (1935), *A Midsummer Night's Dream* (1935), and

A Tale of Two Cities (1935). Guaranteed to be honored on Academy Awards night, the novels-into-films put Hollywood's best face forward and showcased its ideal sense of self to America. "Pictures based on great works of literature and drama are being presented without violating the screen's primary function of entertainment," declared a contented Will Hays, looking forward to 1935. "The screen is transforming class entertainment into mass entertainment." Hays didn't mention that in transferring the Anglo-American literary canon to the screen, the dark undertones of the classic texts were brightened and the supple ambiguities flattened out. A few proved incorrigible to the core. A contemplated version of Mark Twain's *Pudd'nhead Wilson* was suspended because the "miscegenation angle" was judged too integral to the plot line, "meticulous Breening" or not.

Third, and most persuasive, was the astonishing financial rebound of the motion picture industry by the close of 1934, the beginning of a rising arc of prosperity that Hollywood enjoyed until television ended the sweet ride in the late 1940s. The streamlining and belt-tightening forced upon the industry after 1929 had finally paid off. Fox endured a net loss of $226,346 in 1933; it earned profits of $2.4 million in 1934. Warner Brothers ended 1933 with losses of some $6.3 million; it closed out 1934 with earnings of nearly $3.8 million. Always the strongest of the big studios, even MGM-Loews weathered a slump in 1933; it rebounded strongly in 1934 with a net profit of $7.5 million. Most remarkably, Paramount, recently in bankruptcy, earned in excess of $5 million in 1934. Other studios were similarly flush. Hollywood, if not the rest of the nation, had turned the prosperity corner.

Whether because of the Code or not, the economic revival occurred immediately after the establishment of the Production Code Administration. Proponents noted the precipitous upswing and insisted upon a direct causal relationship between the new morality and the new prosperity. Audiences offended by the licentiousness of 1930–1934 had forgiven the industry and embraced it anew. "The Production Code Administration in its short period of functioning has eliminated at least two thirds of the costs of outside censorship and in the same movement reduced a loss at the ticket window," claimed a smug *Motion Picture Herald*. No one denied the motion picture industry was back in the black with the Code, and *post hoc ergo propter hoc*, the Code must have caused it.

Why quibble? The Code kept the Catholics happy, restored Hollywood to public respectability, greased the production machinery, and pumped up profits in the midst of a crippling Depression. Before the motion picture medium was granted First Amendment protection, before the temperamental "auteur" supplanted the job-of-work contract director, censorship was a basic assumption of moviemaking, a necessary item on the balance sheet, factored into the cost of doing business. As such, it had best be done in a businesslike manner, and the Production Code Administration under Joseph I. Breen was nothing if not businesslike.

Hollywood Under the Code

With the inauguration of President Franklin Delano Roosevelt on March 4, 1933, a fever burning in American culture since October 29, 1929, seemed suddenly to break. "I will never forget the electrifying effect of the phrase 'we have nothing to fear but fear itself,' " recalled CBS radio's H. V. Kaltenborn. "Here was a speech that seemed to lift a nation's spirit and change its mood." To scan the newspapers, to read the memoirs of artists and politicians, or to consult the memories of anyone alive during the Great Depression is to sense how indispensable FDR was as a unifying force and political lifeline. "The Houdini of Hyde Park," Will Rogers dubbed him. "That bird has done more for us in seven weeks than we've done for ourselves in seven years." Prosperity remained elusive, still tantalizingly out of sight behind that corner, but with the good father reigning in Washington and the New Deal reining in discontent, the crisis of American democracy had passed.

Admiring historians of the early days of FDR's first term of office speak of how the new president "saved capitalism in eight days," a lurch into hyperbole but not by much. "Roosevelt saved the system," recalled Sidney J. Weinberg, an industrial adviser during FDR's first two terms. "We were on the verge of something. You could have had a rebellion. You could have had a civil war." If not quite the avenging Gabriel over the White House barking out orders to solve every problem, the "fighting president" in the White House was working wonders with morale. By 1935, under orders from Moscow, even American communists had embraced the New Deal order in the coalition of liberals and progressives known as the Popular Front. No longer did cartoons in the *New Masses* picture the unholy trinity of Mussolini, Hitler, and FDR or label the president "a puppet of the monopolists" who would "bridge the gap to fascism" in America.

The motion picture industry colluded in the return to restraint and decorum, tradition and control. However unruly the streets of Great Depression America, however dire conditions remained for one-third of the nation, precious little of it worked its way onto the American screen after 1934. Hollywood undertook a wholesale depoliticizing of its subject matter and a desexualization of its atmosphere, language, and bodies. Political currents still welled up, but more calmly, with less radical force. Erotic sparks still flew but less visibly, with lower voltage.

The new political equilibrium in American cinema was official MPPDA policy. "It is suggested in important places that the riots between police and the public in *Manhattan Melodrama* [1934] do harm," Will Hays confided in a communication to Joseph Breen, assuming a meaningful passive voice. "It is not suggested they be taken out of this picture since it is in and gone, but that we give some thought and time to the advisability of showing any riots at this time. You know the care which is exercised in the newsreels in this regard by the editors of the newsreels. I think the whole matter of care in this regard should be definitely in our minds from the angle of law and order." Breen agreed with his chief. "We shall endeavor in the future to persuade our people to delete all such scenes from their pictures," he assured Hays.

On the erotic front, the concealment of skin was the most visible sign of the new order. Maureen O'Sullivan's jungle outfit in *Tarzan and His Mate* (1934)—mere pieces of strategically placed leather—was cut to Mr. Breen's fashion in *Tarzan Escapes* (1936)—a modest, knee-length skirt. The chorus girls orchestrated for parade drill in Busby Berkeley's *Gold Diggers of 1935* (1935) are less carnal and more clothed than their sisters in *Gold Diggers of 1933* (1933). Jean Harlow covered her breasts, Clark Gable kept his shirt on, and even the cartoon gamin Betty Boop wore a longer hemline, sans garter.

Just as the conversion to talkies had doomed silent stars, the conversion to morality struck down actors incapable of a Code-approved personality transplant. Mae West took the hardest hit, the Code nearly doing to her what the microphone had done to John Gilbert. Her first Code-approved film was to be titled *It Ain't No Sin*, but Breen objected—not to the word "sin" but to the possible antecedents for the word "it." Only half facetiously, West suggested Paramount release the project with no title, just her name emblazoned on the credits. *The Belle of the Nineties* (1934), as it was eventually called, was a tepid imitation of earlier Mae West films. "It ain't no sin to see Mae West in *Belle of the Nineties*," assured ads, which was part of the problem. "Mae West is through, I'm afraid," reported a disappointed exhibitor. "The 'kick' audiences expected wasn't there" nor were the "expected 'cracks.' The Decency Campaign took the edge off Mae." West required rigid corsetting because most anything she said oozed sexual desire, any line reading packed with double meaning. Neutered without a free range of libidinous wisecracks, her film career sputtered and finally ended with the sadly titled *The Heat's On* (1943).

Gangsters were eliminated with deliberate speed on screen and off. In *G-Men* (1935) James Cagney himself switched allegiances from public enemy to government agent. For the balance of the 1930s, gangsters were magnetic intruders, as in *The Petrified Forest* (1936) and *Dead End* (1937), not centers of attraction whose rise and fall dictated the trajectory of the narrative. By the time of *The Roaring Twenties* (1939), when Cagney returned to type to revive a second wave of gangster films, the retrospective title signaled that the political dimension of the criminal threat had been safely relegated to the distant past.

The bloody deaths of real-life outlaws punctuated the terminus of the genre they had inspired. Almost on cue, the bullet-riddled bodies of colorful desperadoes began turning up in the newsreels. Within days of the creation of the Production Code Administration, John Dillinger was shot outside Chicago's Biograph Theater after watching the pre-Code gangster film *Manhattan Melodrama* ("Dillinger Died to See This Picture!" blared ads the next day). That November, Dillinger's successor as Public Enemy Number One, Baby Face Nelson, died in a hail of bullets outside Niles Center, Illinois, after a fierce gun battle in which two federal agents lost their lives. The newsreels need not protest that crime didn't pay when the death tableaux featured the contorted remains of Bonnie and Clyde in a stolen car honey-combed with bullet holes, the waxen corpse of Dillinger on a slab, or the perforated body of Baby Face Nelson in a wayside ditch. "1934 proved to be a bad year for the nation's public enemies, with John Dillinger heading the list the government swore to get," declared Hearst Metrotone News, concluding its year-end wrap-up on the FBI's war on crime with a montage of morgue shots of Dillinger and Baby Face Nelson ("the inevitable end of the killer—a grim warning indeed") and images of Al Capone and Machine Gun Kelly being transported to Alcatraz ("America's Devil's Island").

In the prison genre, the stoic stance of hardened convicts facing their final moment crumpled in *Angels with Dirty Faces* (1937) when Rocky Sullivan (James Cagney) is strapped to the electric chair screaming and slobbering in terror. His final act of sacrifice for his boyhood friend Father Connolly (Pat O'Brien) is to give up his reputation for stone courage, so the boys in the parish will not admire his criminal élan and follow his career path. The priest smiles when he sees the mocking obituary in the newspaper. Like Joseph Breen, he knows the facts of the matter, but he also knows he gets final edit when the medium prints the legend in a tabloid headline: "Rocky Dies Yellow!"

Turning away from racial and ethnic diversity, the Breen Office smoothed out the multi-colored rawness of pre-Code Hollywood into a monochromatic monotony. In practice, the Code's injunction to respect non-Anglo-Americans generally meant to ignore them. The guiltless play of stereotypes in the central casting melting pots of *The Mayor of Hell* (1933), *This Day and Age* (1933), and *Wild Boys of the Road* (1933) was leavened out, the swarthy made white, the rough smoothed over. Trading on their kinship with the chief censor, the Irish alone were granted pride of place, free to drink, fight, and spout blarney.

Not until the assimilationist requirements of the Second World War did a full complement of warm-blooded Americans gain admission into screen ensembles molded into military platoons. Still later, the postwar social problem film, the spiritual descendent of the preachment yarns of the Great Depression, began to depict antisemitism and racism with a modicum of verisimilitude. In *Gentleman's Agreement* (1947), when gentile reporter Gregory Peck decides to go undercover ethnically, he blurts out a word barely whispered in a Hollywood film since 1934. "I'll be a Jew!"

African-Americans continued to endure wide-eyed stereotypes throughout a racially unbalanced program of newsreels, shorts, cartoons, and A features. "Negroes can expect little from this crusade because the moralists themselves define 'cleanliness' in traditional

Figure 14.4 Self-reflexive censorship: Father Connolly (Pat O'Brien) beams from backscreen as the Dead End Kids read the official version in *Angels with Dirty Faces* (1937)

terms," *The Crisis*, the official voice of the NAACP, observed bitterly and correctly in the wake of the storm of '34. "Hardly an organization in the present purity drive is opposed to Jim Crow and all that it means." The newsreels deemed African-American affairs worthy of note only when the camera caught a stereotype: ecstatic baptismal rituals, rhythmic boot-blacks, and stuttering interviewees. If venomous racism imbued the portraits of servants and sidekicks, the main rule remained condescension and indifference. Among the black press and the civil rights community, *Gone with the Wind* (1939) was the most despised example of the status of African-Americans in classical Hollywood cinema, but one-tenth of the nation was more often just plain missing in action. Again, only after a world war against two racist empires did Hollywood initiate a slow, incremental change in an unquestioned racial hierarchy.

In political terms, the distance between pre-Code Hollywood and Hollywood under the Code is well registered in the gulf between *Gabriel Over the White House* (1933) and a like-themed film, Frank Capra's *Mr. Smith Goes to Washington* (1939). Both play out in the nation's capital, both indict congressional inaction and corruption, and both tackle the milestone crisis of the moment, one economic (the Great Depression) and one political (the totalitarian threat to democracy). The differences, however, mark the transition from an America that requires radical surgery to one that needs therapeutic rehabilitation.

Gabriel Over the White House has no faith in the tenets of American constitutional democracy. The film calls for a total redefinition of the government, institutionally and ideologically. The president must become a benevolent dictator because the solution to the present crisis cannot, in pre-FDR 1933, be envisioned from within the present system. The film is authentically radical in its utter contempt for the nation's economic and political underpinnings. Capitalism, the Congress, and the courts are tossed aside. Only the president remains as a vestige of the old constitutional machine, and he is no longer a president the Founding Fathers would recognize.

A reaffirmation not a rebuke, *Mr. Smith Goes to Washington* is a civics lesson in American values. "The more uncertain are people of the world, the more their hard-won freedoms are scattered and lost in the winds of chance, the more they need a ringing statement of America's democratic ideals," proclaimed director Frank Capra. Jefferson Smith is a common man who comes to reinvigorate the system not overthrow it: the foundation is solid and good; the men charged with preserving the structure are weak and corrupt. Like President Jud Hammond in *Gabriel Over the White House*, Jefferson Smith derives spiritual sustenance from Lincoln, but Smith's inspiration is the Lincoln of the better angels of our nature, the martyr for the Republic, not a demonic archangel of vengeance. Rogue elements temporarily betray their custodial duties as the people's representatives—governors pinned under the thumb of party bosses, senators selling their votes to special interests, newspapermen boozed up and up for sale—but in *Mr. Smith* it is men who fail the system; in *Gabriel* it is the system that fails the men. In *Mr. Smith*, the polis is set right by a reinfusion of common decency and traditional American values; in *Gabriel* nothing less than divine intervention can resurrect the terminal case that is America in the nadir of the Great Depression.

Mr. Smith Goes to Washington lives in American memory in a way *Gabriel Over the White House* never will because *Gabriel* has nothing to do with American culture after 1933 and everything to do with its terrifying historical moment, a moment so traumatic that Americans, or at least MGM and William Randolph Hearst, were willing to entertain seriously the prospect of a radical overthrow of constitutional democracy. Its unhinged like would not be seen again in Hollywood cinema until the turbulent 1960s, after the Code, when *Wild in the Streets* (1968) fantasized a futureworld where a rock star president puts everyone over thirty into concentration camps and spikes the drinking water with LSD. *Wild in the Streets* is a drug-addled satire; *Gabriel Over the White House* is dead serious.

Post-Code Hollywood Cinema

In 1934, with financial health restored, sound technology seamlessly woven into the grammar of cinema, and quality control of the product assured by Joseph Breen, the American motion picture began a high renaissance of artistic achievement and commercial good fortune. Until the cracking and eventual breakup of the Code's moral universe in the late 1950s, an explicit obeisance to Code authority influenced the nature of Hollywood cinema as much as its economic structure and aesthetic conventions.

From 1934 until 1954, save for a short interregnum at RKO in 1940–41, Breen oversaw the bureaucracy known to the public as the Hays Office and around Hollywood by his name. The causes célèbres and challenges to the Code that erupted on his watch—notably the case of *The Outlaw* (1943), where billboards pinpointing Jane Russell's breasts gave Breen two good reasons to deny the film a Production Code seal of approval—are anomalies, exceptions to the rule of studio compliance and smoothly operating censorship. During Breen's tenure, to go to the movies meant to see the world through Breen's eyes. In 1946, when Will Hays left his job as head of the newly renamed Motion Picture Association of America and turned over the reins to Eric Johnston, the effect on the content of Hollywood cinema was imperceptible.

The retirement of Breen in 1954 had more of an impact—not just because the founder and guardian of the moral universe was no longer at the helm, but because by then American culture too had changed. The social and cultural forces that transformed the nation in the postwar era, above all the cornucopia of earthly delights that survivors of the Great Depression never quite embraced as their birthright, broke up the old centers of moral authority. The greater personal freedom and private satisfactions that went hand in hand with economic prosperity offered Americans a wider selection of moral options no less than consumer items.

Throughout the 1950s, the Code was questioned, challenged, and ignored. Imports from overseas and a vibrant art house market applied pressure from the edges, but it was television, the new mass medium of the moving image, that pushed Hollywood to transgress its own laws. Having broken up the monopoly on moving image entertainment, television also precipitated the collapse of Hollywood's moral hegemony. At the same time, a series of idiotic decisions by the Legion of Decency and the Production Code turned motion picture censorship from a fair barometer of widely shared opinion into a laughing stock. In postwar America, the very notion of official morality, officially regulated, came to seem antiquated and intrusive. National security and economic prosperity, the obsessions of the 1930s and 1940s, now shared cultural space with freedom of expression and civil rights, the obsessions of the 1950s and 1960s.

The nicks and bruises the Production Code weathered in the 1950s, the creeping incursions of vulgar language, sexually explicit content, and violent imagery, were preludes to a mortal blow, a final brutal bloodletting. If classical Hollywood cinema was born in 1934, it was killed off in 1960 by a man nurtured in its bosom. The film was *Psycho* (1960), and the apostate in the ranks was director Alfred Hitchcock.

The notorious montage of murder in the bathroom of the Bates Motel is the scene of the crime, the place where Joseph Breen's moral universe went swirling down the drain. A naked woman steps into a shower and, as violins screech on the soundtrack, she is stabbed in a jump-cut danse macabre. At the end of the deed, the camera pulls back, absent a center of identification, Janet Leigh, the name-above-the-title star, being indisputably and shockingly dead. A surrogate for the suddenly unmoored spectator, the camera's gaze tracks sideways in search of a human to identify with until, finally, the tension is relieved with the screechy pitch of an offscreen voice: "Mother! Oh God! Mother, mother! Blood, blood!" The pyscho bursts into the hotel room and the film world will now be seen from his point of view.

The impact of *Psycho* on Hollywood cinema is difficult to overstate. Hardened film critics, men who had championed Italian Neo-Realism, Swedish existentialism, and the French New Wave, who had inveighed for years against the puritanical hypocrisy of Production Code censorship, began having second thoughts about sex and violence and the linkage of the two unleashed on the American screen. "A nasty little film," Dwight Macdonald wrote, "a reflection of a most unpleasant mind, a mean, sly, sadistic little mind." Macdonald was not alone in seeing *Psycho* as the prototype and harbinger of a full-blown "sado-masochistic genre" nor was he the only liberal film critic who came to think, "I am against censorship on principle but this killing in the shower makes me wonder." The shock of the new Hollywood universe in *Psycho* remains a primal movie memory for generations of Code-bred Americans, a tribute to how well Joseph Breen had done his work and how completely Alfred Hitchcock had demolished it.

After *Psycho*, the Code was walking dead. Incrementally, cumulatively, the likes of *Lolita* (1962), *Kiss Me, Stupid* (1964), *Dr. Strangelove, or How I Learned to Stop Worrying and Love the Bomb* (1964), *The Pawnbroker* (1965), and *Who's Afraid of Virginia Woolf?* (1966) vied to deliver the coup de grâce. Finally, facing the obvious in 1968, the Motion Picture Association of America adopted a new strategy, not a system of self-censorship but of ratings. Henceforth, American cinema would come with warning labels, for mature audiences, for children under seventeen, for parents and guardians "Viewer beware," Hollywood now said, no longer, "Viewer be assured."

Today, scanning an entertainment bazaar with minimal limits on violence, sex, and end-reel nihilism, the world according to Joseph I. Breen may seem less a golden age of Hollywood

Figure 14.5 Down the drain: Alfred Hitchcock and Janet Leigh plot the end of the moral universe of classical Hollywood cinema in a publicity still from *Psycho* (1960). Credit: Paramount/The Kobal Collection.

cinema than a paleolithic interlude in American popular culture. In the family emporiums of the multiplex mall, on network television and cable channels, and across the World Wide Web of a wired planet, the images screened and the meanings affirmed abide no commandments and know no Codes. Some of the material that can be rented at the local video store or downloaded on the Internet is so appallingly graphic, so soul-deadeningly vicious, that, like Dwight Macdonald in post-traumatic shock from a screening of *Psycho*, it makes one, though against censorship on principle, wonder. Confronted with the right, or wrong, set of images, few spectators will not flinch and find a bit of Breen in themselves, itching to grasp final cut away from the hands of less moral sensibilities.

The story of pre-Code Hollywood traces the movement of that impulse from inchoate desire to operative reality. Defying expectations about the permissive forward trajectory of freedom of expression, films made *after* 1934 were censored with more rigor than films made before 1934. For those who deem censorship a word more profane than any of the utterances forbidden by the Production Code, the clampdown warns that repressive forces are always willing to restrain the free flow of information and images. Contrary to cliché, the genie can be put back in the bottle.

In comparing the relative value of the product lines, it would be tempting to sing a lament for the brief four-year flowering of a vital and liberating motion picture art in pre-Code Hollywood, to disdain Hollywood under the Code as a torrent of mindless dreck afraid to speak truth to power, and to celebrate the extinction of the Code as the aborning of a modern motion picture renaissance. The inconvenient truth is that Hollywood's output on the other side of the Code reveals no ready correlation between freedom of expression and aesthetic worth. To take an even longer view, and to look back over the first full century of the moving image, is to suspect that the most vivid and compelling motion pictures—glorious as art, momentous as texts—were created under the most severe and narrow-minded censorship ever inflicted upon American cinema.

Whatever the aesthetic rankings, motion pictures enjoy a rough equality as sites for historical investigation. Undeniably, though, the search for history in film tends to be more exciting when the territory has yet to be mined for cultural meaning. The world of pre-Code Hollywood is no virgin landscape, but it remains relatively uncharted and open to exploration, best so when the inhabitants are understood on their own terms. Throughout the early 1930s, long after it really needed to, Hollywood ballyhooed the breathless promise that the movies were now "all talking!" We know better: they speak their meanings selectively, sometimes inarticulately. Sometimes we have to strain to hear, and sometimes we hear what we want to hear, but sometimes too American cinema speaks loud and clear, expressing the worst fears and best hopes of its moments in time.

Chapter 15

Jon Lewis

WE DO NOT ASK YOU TO CONDONE THIS: HOW THE BLACKLIST SAVED HOLLYWOOD (2000)

Editors' Introduction

In 2000, when Jon Lewis' provocatively titled essay on the Hollywood blacklist was first published, there was already a wealth of quality historical work written on the subject. Most of this work focused on a fundamental ideological struggle in Hollywood – a struggle rooted in the history of the American Left and in the larger political history of the Cold War. Lewis' essay, "We Do Not Ask You to Condone This: How the Blacklist Saved Hollywood," focuses on the blacklist as instead something of a public relations strategy, motivated (much as other forms of movie industry self-regulation are) by Hollywood executives who routinely lend far more weight to a fiscal bottom line than to any political or moral imperative. The industry adage, "When they say it's not about the money; it's about the money," is the key here as Lewis observes and analyzes why the studio members of the Motion Picture Association of America (MPAA) cooperated with the House Committee on Un-American Activities and how the studios implemented the blacklist to subdue the unions and counter popular assumptions about Hollywood's essential Jewishness. Of primary interest are twelve days in the fall of 1947 – the time between MPAA President Eric Johnston's promise that "There'll never be a blacklist" and his about-face less than two weeks later: "We did not defend them. We do not defend them now." Lewis' cynical notion that such a dark moment in Hollywood's history became the key to the industry's successful economic transition in the aftershock of the Paramount Decision, hinges upon what in those twelve days changed Johnston's and the MPAA's position on the Hollywood Ten, and what then led the industry to indulge for over a decade a politically motivated regulation of the moviemaking workforce and a coincident chilling of political speech in commercial film content.

Suggested Reading

Victor Navasky, *Naming Names* (NY: Hill and Wang, 2003); Larry Ceplair and Steven Englund, *The Inquisition in Hollywood: Politics in the Film Community, 1930–60*

(Champaign: University of Illinois Press, 2003); *Tender Comrades: A Backstory of the Hollywood Blacklist,* edited by Patrick McGilligan and Paul Buhle (Minneapolis: University of Minnesota Press, 2012).

THE BLACKLIST WAS BACK in the news again recently. The March 21, 1999, Academy Awards telecast saw to that. On that night, Elia Kazan, a director who named names in the early fifties, received his Lifetime Achievement Award, and a huge international audience got a quick glance at the still-evolving legacy of Hollywood's Cold War.

When Kazan took the stage, the television cameras panned the audience. Warren Beatty stood up and applauded. Nick Nolte and Ed Harris sat on their hands. Martin Scorsese and Robert DeNiro—both of whom appeared nervous—accepted Kazan's embrace on stage. These new Hollywood players will all have to live with what they did in those few minutes. Fifty years after the fact, the blacklist continues to force the Hollywood community to take sides. And it continues to take names.

This essay may well strike some readers as subjective, even polemical. That's fine with me. I have gone where the story, where the evidence, has taken me. The documents one comes across when studying the blacklist appeal so successfully and so intentionally to the emotions that objectivity—the supposed hallmark of historical inquiry—is, frankly, inappropriate. Much of the history of the blacklist is cast in the first person, and many of the stories are tragic. History, these texts remind us, consists of stories told by survivors. I see no reason to cheapen these stories by pretending to be unmoved.

My project here involves (re)contextualizing the blacklist as it evolved out of and affected economic conditions. I am interested in the ways in which the blacklist helped foreground the new Hollywood, the ways in which collusive strategies put in place to control the industry workforce in 1947 enabled the studios to regain control over the entertainment marketplace after the Second World War. It is a complex story and one that at times results in a subjective account of the material. To signal *my* stake in this in advance, let me point out that I come to this subject with a certain amount of baggage, a predisposition to find sympathy for those who were blacklisted. For those readers who like to know such things, I am Jewish. My father, who is now retired, worked with and then for the Teamsters. My mother's brother is a union man as well, an electrician who worked on skyscrapers in New York. And although no one in my family ever worked in the film business, my mother's cousin, the first in our family to get a college education, was fired by Columbia University in the late 1940s for refusing to sign a loyalty oath and subsequently was blacklisted out of academia. Perhaps these details help explain my personal bias.

But my bias is not really the issue. How much it guides my account I leave up to the reader. My scholarly contention—and I am convinced that the evidence bears this out—is that the blacklist saved Hollywood. My essay details how and why.

HUAC. The U.S. House Committee on Un-American Activities (HUAC) first convened in the fall of 1947 and served most of its subpoenas on September 23, 1947.[1] At the time, the film industry was on the verge of some very big changes. Three coincident events—the shift in population out of the big cities (prompting a decrease in revenues at the studios' first-run deluxe theaters), the Justice Department's rekindled interest in breaking up the studio trusts,[2] and the development of a competitive audiovisual pop culture on television—severely threatened the stability and profitability of theatrical motion picture exhibition. In addition, the business of producing and distributing motion pictures was becoming increasingly expensive and complicated as talent agents exploited movie stars' growing independence from the contract system and various industry guilds and unions threatened job actions. Relationships between the studios and exhibitors and between the studios and the industry workforce had become profoundly unstable and adversarial.

Beginning in 1947, HUAC provided the studios with lists of unionized writers, actors, and directors who, despite National Labor Relations Board (NLRB) protections, could be fired without cause, without severance, and, in a number of cases, without concern for previously earned wages or option fees. In doing so, HUAC helped the studios better manage the uncertain labor situation and, moreover, helped them cut expenses and payrolls in preparation for a widely predicted postwar box-office decline. The so-called free market got much less free during the blacklist era as the studios discovered that if they just learned to work better together, they could circumvent the various antitrust decrees, keep production costs down, and control the industry guilds. The new Hollywood we see in place today—a new Hollywood that rates and censors its own and everyone else's films and flaunts its disregard for antitrust legislation and federal communications and trade guidelines—is very much the product and the still-evolving legacy of the blacklist.

To fully understand its complex history, it is necessary to stop viewing the blacklist as primarily an ideological struggle. Of course, the Red Scare was political, but in Hollywood it is difficult to separate the ideological from the industrial. The studios' cooperation with HUAC featured ample anti-Communist rhetoric. At the same time, the industry blacklist was designed as, or evolved into, a complex and collusive business strategy that diminished the threat of further federal regulation of the movie business and of film censorship. The blacklist may well have reflected shifting political alliances among studio ownership, management, and the industry's celebrity workforce, but it also enabled the studios to establish a new way of doing business that solved several larger long-term problems.

As we begin to look at the blacklist as a first move toward a new Hollywood, two parallel dramas emerge. The first involves a residual, pervasive, postwar anti-Semitism that got HUAC interested in (Jewish) Hollywood in the first place. The committee's efforts to clean up the film business focused in large part on the industry's workforce, in which American Jews were well represented at the time. That the committee also set in motion larger changes in the management of the industry—in which Jews were also well represented—was a bonus. The New York corporate offices of the studios exploited postwar anti-Semitism not only to combat the unions but also to force out the first-generation Jewish studio moguls. In so doing, they put an end to an entrepreneurial system run by charismatic but inefficient self-made businessmen, a system that seemed suddenly out of step with postwar American capitalism.

Thus, the blacklist was a first step in a larger transformation of the film industry from its roots in entrepreneurial capital to a more corporatist, conglomerate mode. Impending deregulation—and what can only be characterized as industry-wide panic in response—prompted change that the Red Scare made not only possible but easy. In the final analysis, the blacklist did not save America from films promoting Communism, liberalism, or humanitarianism. Instead, it encouraged studio owners to develop and adopt a corporate model more suited to a future new Hollywood, one in which, despite market deregulation and stricter self-regulation of film content, studio owners would maintain profitability and control.

The shift from the entrepreneurial model of the moguls to the more anonymous conglomerate model that is in evidence today involved a complex assimilation. The Paramount decision put an end to the contract system that supported the entrepreneurial model. The blacklist enabled the Motion Picture Association of America (MPAA) to establish in its place a system far better suited for business in postindustrial, postwar America and far more suitable ethnically and politically for doing business with the federal government in the 1940s and 1950s.

A second story involves the MPAA, which allied with the Thomas Committee seemingly against its own best interests, only to emerge from the fray as a powerful industry gatekeeper. In 1947, the MPAA was little more than a new name for the old and fraying Motion Pictures Producers and Distributors Association (MPPDA). The MPAA got its charter in 1945, at the very moment the Justice Department resumed its antitrust suit against the studios. The studio membership of the MPAA used the 1947 Waldorf Statement (which made public its intention to cooperate with HUAC) to establish an identity and, moreover, to assert studio unity in the face of a seeming ideological and very real fiscal crisis. Over the years, the MPAA has downplayed its roots in the Red Scare, but its power today owes much to right-wing congressional support at its inception and the collusive strategies it developed during the late 1940s and 1950s.

The Hollywood guilds and unions that gained so much power and influence in the thirties and forties lost their momentum during the blacklist and never recovered. In the new Hollywood, the guilds are so weak that strikes afford little hope for even celebrity talent. For example, in 1980, a strike by the Screen Actors Guild (SAG) was organized to establish residual pay scales for films exhibited in the home box-office market, including videocassette sales/rentals and cable television. The studios responded by locking out the entire union workforce. Universal announced in the trades that it intended to invoke the force majeure clause in its contracts with talent, effectively suspending all film and television projects. Other studios were likely to follow suit. SAG leadership, which had timed the strike to coincide with the beginning of the fall television season, underestimated the extent of studio collusion and also misunderstood how little filmmaking mattered in the new Hollywood.[3] What the guild members discovered in 1980 was that the studios no longer needed to make movies or TV shows to make money; such is the legacy of the Red Scare in Hollywood.

Concurrent with the decline in the effectiveness of the industry guilds, there has been dramatic growth at the MPAA. The very antitrust regulations that promised to break up the studios in the midforties are no longer enforced: witness Time/Warner/Turner, Disney/Capital Cities/ABC, and Viacom/Paramount. The regulation of film content, formerly complicated by grassroots organizations (like the Catholic Legion of Decency), state and local censorship boards, and, during the blacklist, the House Committee, is now wholly supervised by the MPAA. Through its ratings system (G, PG, PG-13, R, and NC-17), first adopted in 1968, the MPAA not only self-regulates its various product lines but also monitors any and all participation in the theatrical and home box-office markets.

The operative roots of the MPAA ratings system lay in the various industry codes of self-regulation that preceded it. The Production Code Administration (PCA), its industry predecessor, was, like the blacklist, rooted in anti-Semitic assumptions about (the dangers of) movies and the men who made them. Joseph Breen, one of the cofounders of the PCA and its chief censor for much of its existence, was a Catholic procensorship activist before he became an industry player. His mission to regulate Hollywood cinema can be traced in large part to his dislike and distrust of the Jews who seemed to run the business. "These Jews seem to think of nothing but money making and sexual indulgence," Breen wrote in a letter to a fellow Catholic activist. "They are, probably, the scum of the scum of the earth."[4]

As a business practice, the ratings system dates most directly to 1947, when the studio membership of the MPAA began to understand and exploit the complex relationship between censorship and other forms of industrial regulation. What the studios discovered was that self-regulation in compliance with HUAC and grassroots pressure to make less political, less meaningful films enabled them to better control the industry workforce and to exploit the increasingly international postwar theatrical marketplace.

The Hollywood Ten. When HUAC made its recommendation to indict Alvah Bessie, Herbert Biberman, Lester Cole, Edward Dmytryk, Ring Lardner, Jr., John Howard Lawson, Albert Maltz, Samuel Ornitz, Adrian Scott, and Dalton Trumbo (the so-called Hollywood Ten) for contempt of Congress, the MPAA assured those under investigation that it would oppose government regulation.[5] "Tell the boys not to worry," MPAA president Eric Johnston remarked on October 18, 1947. "There'll never be a blacklist. We're not going to go totalitarian to please this committee."[6]

But just twelve days later—five days before the full House was scheduled to vote on the contempt citations—Johnston issued a stunning public reversal: "We did not defend them. We do not defend them now. On the contrary, we believe they have done a tremendous disservice to the industry which has given them so much material rewards and an opportunity to exercise their talents."[7] Indictments, incarcerations, and an industry-wide blacklist followed, all with the cooperation and under the supervision of the MPAA.

The sudden change in policy at the MPAA was a source of considerable speculation at the time.[8] The hearings were a public relations nightmare, but capitulation was neither the only nor the most fiscally prudent way for the studios to deal with the situation. Reliable polls revealed that public opinion was split, especially about the way the committee treated the unfriendly witnesses. The results of a Gallup Poll were released on November 29, 1947. The poll highlighted two questions, the first of which focused on the conduct of the committee: "What is your opinion of the investigation—do you approve or disapprove of the way it was handled?" Thirty-seven percent approved, 36 percent disapproved, and 27 percent had no opinion. The second question was: "Do you think the Hollywood writers who refused to say whether or not they were members of the Communist Party should be punished or not?" Forty-seven percent said that they should be punished, 39 percent that they should not be punished, and 14 percent had no opinion.

Gallup's Audience Research Institute (ARI), a unit formed to perform market research for the studios, produced data that complicated matters further. It too revealed that the moviegoing public was evenly split over the conduct of HUAC and found that only 10 percent of those polled believed that there were all that many Communists in the film business. The majority of those who believed the committee's contention that Communism posed a significant threat were older than thirty and stridently anti-Communist. They were also, as the ARI survey revealed, not regular moviegoers before or during the Red Scare.[9]

Several big-city newspapers, including the *New York Times* and the *Washington Post*, openly criticized the way the committee conducted the hearings.[10] While skirting the central ideological issues (anti-Communism, patriotism, anti-Semitism, anti-unionism), editorials in major newspapers across the nation highlighted HUAC's disregard for due process and apparent disinterest in the civil rights of the unfriendly witnesses.

Gordon Kahn, one of the original nineteen, attempted to explain the MPAA reversal by alleging that the Ten were sacrificed as part of a complicated deal between the Feds and studio owners.[11] "[The MPAA's] surrender was the result of a deal," Kahn wrote in 1948 in *Hollywood on Trial*. "They would immolate on the altar of hysteria and reaction. . . . They would purge other writers, directors, producers and actors from the industry . . . In return for all of this, Thomas would promise to call off any further investigation of Hollywood."[12] Attractive as Kahn's theory was at the time, no such conspiracy ever existed, and no such bargain was ever struck. Thomas and others continued to investigate and terrorize the liberal and radical Left in Hollywood until the end of the 1950s,[13] but Kahn was right about the industry-wide panic, the roots of which lay not, as is commonly assumed, solely or even primarily in the politics of patriotism.

In the fall of 1947, studio executives had something bigger than the Thomas Committee to worry about: *U.S. v. Paramount Pictures, Inc.*, the antitrust case before the Supreme Court. The government's eventual victory in the case in 1948 put an end to the distribution/exhibition guarantees that supported the old studio system. The Thomas Committee benefited from and capitalized on studio panic over the impending and inevitable decision by offering a means by which the studios could continue to control their workforce (despite divestiture and the unions). The working relationship between the MPAA and the committee was less a concession vis-à-vis control of a product line than a strategy on the part of the studio establishment to regain control over the marketplace, itself in the process of postwar privatization.

When HUAC began its investigation of the movie industry, a new Hollywood seemed imminent. In concert with the forthcoming Paramount decision, this new Hollywood promised (or threatened) to be a place where talent, suddenly organized, seemingly radicalized, and soon to be further empowered by the free market engendered by divestiture, held significant power. It was therefore in the best interests of studio managers to find a way to control the industry workforce before it controlled them.

The Jews. The hearings revealed a tendency on the part of HUAC and those who shared its politics to conflate Communism with unionism and antiracism. Since the union and civil rights movements were, in the committee's view of things, Jewish causes, they further conflated Communism with Jewishness. The Thomas Committee steadfastly refused to view films or review screenplays, claiming that Communists (and, by association, Jews) were smart and insidious and that the political messages they inserted into films were thus very difficult (for non-Jews and non-Communists) to discern.[14] The logical extension of such an argument—that the mass audience would be unable to recognize such subtle political content and were thus unlikely to be poisoned by such propaganda—never seemed to cross their minds. Or maybe it did. The committee could not explicitly set out to ban films with civil libertarian leanings; it could not legally prohibit or call for the censorship of films about unions, Jews, or African Americans. What made the blacklist so effective was that it offered a means by which the government (or, by proxy, the MPAA) could censor film content without ever reading a script or viewing a movie.

Six of the Hollywood Ten were Jewish: Lawson, Maltz, Bessie, Ornitz, Biberman, and Cole. Of the four who were not, two (Scott and Dmytryk) were responsible (as producer and director) for *Crossfire* (1947), an antiracist, anti-anti-Semitic film nominated for Best Picture, Best Director, and Best Screenplay Oscars. *Crossfire* was an important Hollywood film for a number of reasons: it was a provocative and political movie, and it struck a lot of people on the right as a harbinger of things to come.

Crossfire proved to be the film that most interested HUAC, but its development was quick and untroubled, and its production posed few problems for the industry censors. RKO production chief Dore Schary took the screenplay to Joe Breen, head of the PCA, which censored films at the time. Breen, a political conservative and an anti-Semite, did not express a single concern about the picture's politics. In a memo to Schary, he requested the usual changes: minimize the drinking, be careful not to condone prostitution (Ginny, a principal character in the screenplay, is the prototypical whore with a heart of gold), and insert a speech by an army major noting that the killer (a serviceman named Monty) is not typical of army personnel. Otherwise, Breen gave the film his okay.

Crossfire tells the story of a vicious, racist serviceman who murders a Jew in what today would be termed a hate crime. In a 1946 memo to RKO studio executives William Dozier and Charles Korner, Adrian Scott pitched *The Brick Foxhole*, later retitled *Crossfire*, as a modest-budget suspense picture prepackaged with "A" talent (screenwriter John Paxton and director Edward Dmytryk). After presenting the package to Dozier and Korner, Scott moved on to describe some key changes from story to screenplay: "This is a story of personal fascism as opposed to organized fascism. . . . In the book Monty hates fairies, Negroes, Jews and foreigners. In the book Monty murders a fairy. He could have murdered a foreigner or a Jew. It would have been the same thing. In the picture he murders a Jew."[15]

A number of those blacklisted who actually belonged to the Communist Party (CP) in the forties have since remarked that they first turned to the party because it seemed to support the civil rights movement to a degree that the Democrats and Republicans did not at the time.[16] With *Crossfire*, such a civil rights (if not explicitly CP) agenda was at stake from the start, as Scott reveals in his memo: "Dmytryk, Paxton and I want to make this picture for two reasons. First, we are ambitious. We want to make fine pictures. This will make a fine picture. Secondly, and more important, is this: anti-Semitism is not declining as a result of Hitler's defeat. . . . Anti-Semitism and anti-Negroism will grow unless heroic measures can be undertaken to stop them. This picture is one such measure."[17]

Dozier and a third RKO executive, Peter Rathvon, responded positively to the film's anti-anti-Semitic message—perhaps cynically, since Hollywood was abuzz with news about Fox's production of a similarly themed picture, *Gentleman's Agreement* (1947). Rathvon concluded his response to Scott's memo by lamenting "the sterility" of "general motion picture production," implying an impatience with the usual Hollywood escapist fare and, by extension, the PCA's tendency to censor controversial political content, RKO production chief Dore Schary, himself a former member of the Screenwriters Guild, expressed interest in financing the film *because* it was politically meaningful.[18]

Schary was an interesting Cold War Hollywood player.[19] In testimony before the Thomas Committee, Schary (who was called because of his role in *Crossfire*) conceded that RKO had no standing policy concerning the hiring of Communists and that so long as CP membership was not against the law, he saw no reason to develop one: "Up until the time it is proved that a Communist is a man dedicated to the overthrow of the government by force or violence, or by any illegal methods, I cannot make any determination of his employment on any basis except whether he is qualified best to do the job I want him to do." Asked if he'd employ Scott and Dmytryk again, Schary stunned the committee by responding "yes." So long as they did not prove to be foreign agents, Schary concluded, they would be welcome to pitch their work to him again.

After the Waldorf Statement was issued, the MPAA held a meeting to bring the bad news about the blacklist officially to the membership of the Screenwriters Guild. To soften the blow, Johnston chose Schary to speak on behalf of management. Schary's first words that night provide the title for this essay: "We do not ask you to condone this." No doubt Schary felt sympathy for his former guild members, but he could afford to be sentimental; for their role in the production of *Crossfire*, Scott and Dmytryk were jailed and blacklisted, while Schary continued to work at the top levels of studio management. Even after his testimony before the committee, Schary remained in charge of production at RKO. A massive cost-cutting shake-up at the studio in 1948, set in motion by RKO's new owner, Howard Hughes, forced Schary to exit. But Schary had little trouble finding another top executive position at a healthier studio, MGM, which was run at the time by Nicholas Schenck, who, like Hughes, was an anti-Communist and a staunch supporter of the blacklist.[20]

The "propaganda hearings" of 1941, convened at the urging of two conservative, isolationist senators, Burton Wheeler of Montana and Gerald Nye of North Dakota, revealed the trenchant anti-Semitism that lay at the root of much of the government's interest in regulating the film industry in the 1940s.[21] Encouraged by the Justice Department's early successes in challenging the studio trusts, Wheeler and Nye railed against the Hollywood "propaganda machine" and studios "operated by a central agency." Senate hearings were convened on September 9, 1941, with attention focused on seventeen "war-mongering features," including Charles Chaplin's *The Great Dictator* (1940) and *Foreign Correspondent* (1940), directed by Alfred Hitchcock and produced by Walter Wanger.[22] Liberal Republican Wendell Willkie was hired by the studios to speak for the MPPDA. Willkie quickly lured Nye into an embarrassing diatribe against the industry's Jews. Nye claimed that the seventeen pictures at issue served the agenda of the Hollywood elite, which consisted, he claimed, exclusively of foreign-born Jews. When Nye added, "If anti-Semitism exists in America, the Jews have themselves to blame," Willkie took the offensive. He convincingly argued that Nye and Wheeler had planned to exploit the hearings to discourage "accurate and factual pictures on Nazism" and to "divide the American people in discordant racial and religious groups in order to disunite them over foreign policy."[23]

Willkie successfully embarrassed Nye and Wheeler and in doing so put off further federal scrutiny of Hollywood. But although Nye's and Wheeler's anti-Semitism was poorly concealed and ill timed (the Japanese attacked Pearl Harbor during the hearings' extended Thanksgiving recess, and the United States was at war with Germany before the anti-Semitic senators could regroup and respond), the "propaganda hearings" foreshadowed and foregrounded HUAC's far more successful disruption of studio production and its Jewish workforce after the war.

Nye and Wheeler focused specifically on the apparent political messages in leftist, politically progressive movies. Their concerns about the ideological and economic ramifications of social realist films were shared by the Thomas Committee as well as by such grassroots organizations as the Legion of Decency, the Knights of Columbus, and the American Legion.

As the fight to clean up Hollywood took off again after the war, the PCA took much of the heat. Unfortunately for the MPAA, the PCA's vague charter—"to uphold the larger moral responsibility of the motion pictures"—sounded good but was restricted to fairly narrow issues about film content. As an administrative body, the PCA had no authority over the workforce, the unacknowledged target of Cold War film regulation.

As the war took shape in Europe in the late 1930s, conservative and isolationist politicians began to complain that the PCA, the industry's principal self-regulatory agency, had become unable to enforce even the narrowest interpretation of its charter, especially with regard to politically sensitive material. For example, *Confessions of a Nazi Spy* (1939, Warner Bros.), a potent antifascist melodrama, was developed, produced, and released *despite* PCA opposition.[24] Breen and his fellow censors viewed the project as "a portentous departure" because it was so unlike the usual spy picture and because the talent behind the project was notoriously left-wing: director Anatole Litvak, screenwriter John Wexley, and actors Paul Lukas and Edward G. Robinson.[25] The PCA finally capitulated to Warner Bros, and gave the film its production seal only to have their worst fears realized as a wave of anti-Nazi, antifascist films found their way into the marketplace: *The Great Dictator, Pastor Hall, The Mortal Storm*, and *I Married a Nazi* (all 1940).

Breen had little sympathy for the politics of these films and disliked the men who made them, many of whom were active in the Hollywood anti-Nazi movement.[26] But his opposition to these films did not end (or perhaps even begin) there. Breen was concerned about the impact these antifascist films would have in the worldwide marketplace. A film like *Confessions of a Nazi Spy* could not play in Germany, Spain, or Italy in 1939, and it complicated matters for other, less political studio films in those same markets. The official Hays Office memo to Jack and Harry Warner concerning the original script read as follows: "Hitler and his government are unfairly represented in this story in violation of the Code. . . . To represent Hitler

ONLY as a screaming madman and a bloodthirsty persecutor and *nothing else* is manifestly unfair. . . . Are we ready to depart from the pleasant and profitable course of entertainment to engage in propaganda, to produce screen portrayals arousing controversy? . . . Where's the line to be drawn? Why not make [pictures about] the Stalin purges, the Japanese rape of China, the Terror of Spain, etc.?"[27]

While Breen concerned himself with doing a better job policing politically sensitive material in films (to keep the Feds out of the censorship business and protect the studios' stake in international markets), several prominent Hollywood producers and directors broke ranks and went public with their dissatisfaction with the PCA's political censorship. For example, in a 1939 letter to the *New York Times*, producer Walter Wanger complained that the PCA's "formulated theory of pure entertainment [made] impossible the honest handling of important truths and ideas." On behalf of the MPPDA, Will Hays responded to Wanger's letter in terms oddly suggestive of Dye's and Wheeler's. Indeed, we can see the roots of MPAA cooperation with HUAC in Hays's insistence on maintaining the moral imperative of the production code and his validation of entertainment as an end in itself: "The screen has handled successfully themes of contemporary thought in dramatic and vivid form and presented the subject matter in a splendid entertainment, rather than propaganda."[28] Eight years later, just weeks after the Waldorf Statement was issued, Eric Johnston echoed Hays's sentiments in support of apolitical film entertainment. Fully embracing the leverage the PCA attained as a consequence of MPAA cooperation with the Feds, Johnston boldly announced, "There will be no more *Grapes of Wrath*, we'll have no more *Tobacco Roads*."[29]

Nye and Wheeler targeted management but lost in large part because their timing was bad and because the moguls had the support of the workforce in a common defense of free expression in motion pictures. The Jews targeted by HUAC and its various incarnations after 1947 were not able to depend on management to watch their backs. As a result, the assumptions that characterized Dye's and Wheeler's failed confrontation with industry management, the conflation of anti-Nazism with anti-Americanism and pro-Communism, reemerged in the peculiar logic that underscored the postwar blacklist.

Blacklisted playwright and screenwriter Edward Chodorov recently characterized the rift between the Jewish workforce and Jewish management as a matter of conscience: "I became angry at my studio [MGM] and all the studios who insisted that business as usual must go on in Europe [in the 1930s] and that it was none of our business. It was unthinkable to me that Louis B. Mayer, who was a Jew, knew what was happening in Germany . . . unthinkable to me that he would insist nothing was wrong."[30] Such a frustration prompted Chodorov to join the Anti-Nazi League in the 1930s, an affiliation that was enough for HUAC and the MPAA to brand him a Communist ten years later.

For the most part, the Jewish moguls and studio executives were careful not to make their ethnicity an issue in their films or in their public lives. In 1939, a group of Jewish film actors and actresses, writers, and directors held a press conference and spoke out against Hitler. The only mogul to sign their manifesto was Carl Laemmle, who was very ill and did not live out the year. U.S. ambassador to Great Britain Joseph Kennedy had warned the other moguls to keep their politics (and ethnicity) private. The executives' decision not to sign petitions brought to them by talent active in the various anti-Nazi organizations revealed the extent of their fear of anti-Semitism, but it also evidenced their growing distrust of the industry labor force, which was by then in the early stages of organizing. The membership of these newly formed guilds included many of the Jews who spoke out against Hitler. Many of these film actors and actresses, writers, and directors were—as the Thomas Committee would later contend—either members of or had interests in common with those of the Communist Party.

The blacklist engaged the subject of patriotism in a number of different ways. For the assimilated first-generation American Jewish moguls, many of whom no longer practiced the rituals of their faith, there was no question in *their* minds at least that they were Americans first and foremost. A 1998 cable television special based on Neil Gabler's history of the Jews in Hollywood examined how easily that patriotism was undermined in the late 1940s.[31] The show ends with a sentimental vignette about the last days of the legendary movie mogul Louis B. Mayer, who, after his ouster from MGM, aimlessly paced the floor in his house, with no studio to run and no idea how it had all happened. Although it is hard to feel sorry for Mayer, who was a hard man to work for and who never wavered in his support of the House Committee, the TV show's parting gesture is apt: once Mayer's ethnicity became an issue, he became a liability to the New York moneymen who controlled the studio's access to production and distribution financing.[32] All Mayer wanted was to be an American, but, in the end, the WASP establishment in New York and the American public at large insisted he was just a Jew.[33]

The year 1947 proved to be a watershed not only because of the HUAC hearings but because the 1947 Oscars seemed to celebrate politically themed, serious, antiracist filmmaking: *Gentleman's Agreement* won Best Picture and Best Director, beating out *Crossfire* for the two top awards. The production of Jewish-themed films called attention to Hollywood's Jewishness, and such an affirmation of creative Hollywood's politics and ethnicity prompted swift and firm federal regulation of the studio product.

All ten of the unfriendly witnesses called to appear before the Thomas Committee in 1947 requested permission to read a statement into the record, but only two were actually admitted into evidence, those of Alvah Bessie and Albert Maltz. Of the eight statements that were suppressed, five explicitly identified anti-Semitism as a motive behind the inquisition. Virtually all the suppressed statements cited similarities between the committee and (anti-Semitic) fascists in 1930s and 1940s Europe.[34]

Ornitz made anti-Semitism an issue in his opening sentence:

> I wish to address the committee as a Jew because one of its leading members [Rankin] is the outstanding anti-Semite in the congress and revels in this fact. . . . I am struck forcibly by the fact that this committee has subpoenaed the men who made *Crossfire*. . . . Is it a mere coincidence that you chose to subpoena and characterize as *unfriendly* the men who produced, wrote, directed or acted in the following feature length pictures and short subjects, which attacked anti-Semitism or treated Jews and Negroes sympathetically: *Pride of the Marines, The House I Live In, Don't Be a Sucker, None Shall Escape, Of Mice and Men, The Brotherhood of Man, The Commington Story*, *Freedom Road, Body and Soul, New Orleans, The Master Race*, and *The Al Jolson Story*. . . . Therefore, I ask as a Jew, based on the record, is bigotry this committee's yardstick of Americanism and its definition of subversive?[35]

When Lawson, the first to testify, took the stand, a heckler audibly grumbled, "Jew." It was an uncomfortable but apt prelude. Lawson's statement, which was suppressed, included the following: "What are J. Parnell Thomas and the Un-American interests he serves, afraid of? They want to cut living standards, introduce an economy of poverty, wipe out labor rights, attack Negroes, Jews, and other minorities."[36]

When Thomas perused Scott's opening statement in front of the newsreel cameras, it left him momentarily speechless; it was, as Thomas himself would describe it, from start to finish a vilification. Scott's statement began:

> I would like to speak about the cold war now being waged by the committee of [*sic*] Unamerican Activities against the Jewish and Negro people. Individually a

> member of this committee may protest that he is not anti-Semitic. He may say some of his best friends are Jews. . . . Let the committeeman say he is not anti-Semitic. But let the record show he does the work of anti-Semites. . . . This is a cold war being waged by the Committee on Unamerican Activities against minorities. The next phase—total war against minorities—needs no elaboration. History has recorded what has happened in Nazi Germany.[37]

Attorney Robert Stripling, who conducted most of the interrogations, opened his questioning of Scott by referring to him as Mr. Dmytryk, a slip that suggests that *Crossfire* was more at issue than the precise identity of the two Hollywood players who produced and directed it.

The analogy to Nazi Germany and to the anti-Semitic political platform that supported the Holocaust appears in several of the suppressed statements, most powerfully and memorably in the closing paragraph of Trumbo's prepared (and suppressed) remarks:

> Already the gentlemen of this Committee and others of like disposition have produced in this capital city a political atmosphere which is acrid with fear and repression; a community in which anti-Semitism finds safe refuge behind secret tests of loyalty; a city in which no union leader can trust his telephone; a city in which old friends hesitate to recognize one another in public places; a city in which men and women who dissent even slightly from the orthodoxy you seek to impose speak with confidence only in moving cars and in the open air. You have produced a capital city on the eve of its Reichstag fire. For those who remember German history in the autumn of 1932 there is the smell of smoke in this very room.[38]

When the committee moved unanimously to seek indictments for contempt of Congress against all ten unfriendly witnesses and brought the issue to the House floor, Mississippi representative John Rankin, who had been on the campaign trail in an unsuccessful bid for reelection and had not attended the interrogations, spoke on behalf of the committee. He opened his remarks by referring to the few congressmen who spoke in defense of the Ten as "traitor[s] to the government of the United States." He segued into a brief speech on Hollywood's "attempt to smear and discredit the white people of the Southern States" and then produced a petition signed by a number of Hollywood luminaries, condemning the committee. Rankin announced:

> They sent this petition to Congress, and I want to read some of the names. One of the names is June Havoc. We found from the motion picture almanac that her real name is Joan Hovick. Another one was Danny Kaye, and we found out that his real name was David Daniel Kaminsky. . . . Another one is Eddie Cantor, whose real name is Edward Iskowitz. There is one who calls himself Edward Robinson. His real name is Emmanuel Goldberg. There is another one here who calls himself Melvyn Douglas, whose real name is Melvyn Hesselberg. There are others too numerous to mention. They are attacking the Committee for doing its duty in trying to protect this country and save the American people from the horrible fate the Communists have meted out on the unfortunate Christian people of Europe.[39]

The Congress voted 346 to 17 to indict.

"Only Victims." In January 1946, President Truman appointed six Americans to the joint Anglo-American Committee of Inquiry into Palestine, one of whom was a prominent Catholic liberal-Republican attorney named Bart Crum, who a year later would appear at the Thomas Committee hearings representing Scott and Dmytryk. A veteran of the Committee against Nazi Persecution (founded by Henry Wallace), the Joint Anti-Fascist Refugees Committee, Citizens for Harry Bridges, the Scottsboro Boys Fund, and the Independent Citizens Committee of the Arts and Sciences and a founding member and one-time president of the National Lawyers Guild (all Communist front organizations, according to the Thomas Committee), Crum, like the unfriendly witnesses brought before HUAC, had a long and complex history of joining political organizations.

Crum offers a sobering reminder that what mattered at the time was the public perception of one's private beliefs and values. And the most dangerous perception—the most dangerous accusation—regarded Jewishness, actual Jewishness (by blood, birth, ethnicity, or belief) as well as membership in organizations that fronted for Jewish tendencies or sympathies (membership in the CP and/or the Screenwriters Guild, practicing law, supporting Zionism, or having liberal humanist politics). Although he became a target of the same repressive tactics (the blacklist, surveillance, and so forth), Crum, like his two Hollywood Ten clients, Scott and Dmytryk, was, by all available evidence, not only not Jewish but not a fellow traveler either.[40] As liberal activists but not CP members, Crum and his clients were conspicuously absent at the party-members-only evening sessions when Ben Margolis and other CP attorneys decided that the Ten (or at least the eight in attendance) should refuse to answer questions about party and union membership.[41]

Crum opposed Margolis's legal strategy because he believed that the unfriendly witnesses' refusal to answer questions raised rather than allayed suspicions about alleged conspiracies. Moreover, Crum was suspicious of the CP's motives, especially since Margolis seemed content to martyr the Hollywood Ten. Crum correctly concluded that Margolis's strategy guaranteed contempt citations, and it left Scott and Dmytryk with a difficult choice: they could either tell the committee that they were not members of the CP (and thereby affirm indirectly HUAC's right to demand an answer to their questions about CP affiliation) or go along with a legal strategy that hardly served their interests.

Ironically, neither Dmytryk nor Scott had time to say much of anything on the stand, and their statements were suppressed and never entered into the congressional record. When Dmytryk tried to explain his position, Thomas interrupted him; the chairman systematically interrupted any testimony that seemed to him to be unresponsive or ideological. When Dmytryk persisted, he was shouted down and cited for contempt.

After serving his prison sentence, Dmytryk broke ranks and testified, the only one of the Ten to do so. Both he and Crum were vilified by the CP. Just before his death, Crum also (secretly) named names in a final, desperate attempt to get the FBI off his back and to ingratiate himself with Robert Kennedy, for whom he did some secret business. Dmytryk, who appeared again before the committee on April 25, 1951, named twenty-six names. Included were fellow Hollywood *Nineteen* defendants Scott, Bessie, Biberman, Cole, Kahn, Lawson, and Maltz, director Jules Dassin (*Naked City*), and writer John Wexley (*Angels with Dirty Faces* and, in collaboration with Bertolt Brecht, *Hangmen Also Die*). Crum named just two names, both CP attorneys: Martin Popper and Ben Margolis, the architect of the legal strategy for the Hollywood Ten.

To the committee, liberal sentiments and CP membership were crimes distinguished mostly by degree.[42] The CP exploited this point of view, often at the expense of the liberal Hollywood Left. Trumbo's legendary "Only Victims" speech, delivered to the Writers Guild of America in 1970, contended that the blacklisted artist and the informer alike "reacted as his nature, his needs, his convictions, and his particular circumstances compelled him to, . . .

[that there was] bad faith and good, honesty and dishonesty, courage and cowardice, selflessness and opportunism, wisdom and stupidity, good and bad on both sides." In the spirit of Christian forgiveness, Trumbo concluded that "in the final tally we were all victims because almost without exception each of us was compelled to say things he did not want to say, to do things he did not want to do, to deliver and receive wounds he did not want to exchange. None emerged from that long nightmare without sin."[43]

Trumbo's speech was meant to be conciliatory, but the implication that the CP had to answer for its role in the wholesale scuttling of the Hollywood Left prompted an immediate reaction from, among others, Albert Maltz. Maltz attacked Trumbo: "To say, None of us emerged from that long nightmare without sin is to me ridiculous . . . What did people suffer for?"[44] While the question Maltz posed was meant to be rhetorical, it begged an answer several blacklisted Hollywood artists are now eager to provide. As Paul Jarrico, second in command to Lawson in the Hollywood section of the CP when the committee first convened, reflected in 1987:

> There was a fundamental mistake made in the defense of the Ten. Their stand that they were defending the constitution was justified. But their failure to identify themselves as Communists—those of them who were—certainly let the liberals who had been led to believe that they would identify themselves if they were Communists, off the hook. It gave them a rationale for deserting the ship. But it was a ship they were sailing on too. . . . The liberals suffered as much under McCarthyism as the Communists did, in that they lost their freedom to write liberal scripts, even though they themselves were not blacklisted.[45]

The MPAA. The selection of Eric Johnston to run the postwar MPAA revealed just how much the studios were concerned about federal regulation. Like his successor, Jack Valenti, Johnston was a Washington player—a four-time president of the U.S. Chamber of Commerce. When Johnston was hired to replace Will Hays in 1945, he promised not only to continue Hays's policy of endorsing American business and the capitalist interests that supported and profited from that business, but he publicly took the initiative in the evolving Cold War. During a well-publicized visit to the U.S.S.R. as a member of the Economic Policy Subcommittee of the State Department, Johnston told his hosts that "in economic ideology and practice my country is not only different from yours . . . it is more different from yours than any other country in the world. . . . We are determined to remain so—and even to become more so."[46]

With the European theatrical market ripe for the taking in the immediate aftermath of the war, with the ideological Cold War for the hearts and minds of free Europe in the balance, Johnston encouraged the studios to develop products that might capture the interest of film-starved audiences across the Atlantic. Johnston believed that film was "the greatest conveyor of ideas—the most revolutionary force in the world" and sought to match a corporate strategy of "dynamic capitalism" to an ideological agenda promoting the American way of life.[47]

In his first year in charge of the MPAA, Johnston established the Motion Picture Export Association (MPEA), a trade organization that merged industry interests in foreign film distribution with the federal government's overseas branch of the Office of War Information (OWI). While the studios had come to expect few easy alliances with the Feds at home, the MPEA enjoyed full cooperation from the OWI because it so clearly served the agency's Cold War political agenda. The effectiveness of the PCA, a subsidiary organization of the MPAA that censored politically unacceptable content in films, was paramount to this relationship.

The social problem films that raised the ire of the Thomas Committee after the war—*Crossfire, Gentleman's Agreement*, and *The Best Years of Our Lives*—were also the sort of films that were bad for business and public relations abroad. Efforts to curb production of these films and to focus instead on more entertaining and less disturbing and meaningful pictures conceded ground to the committee and the grassroots organizations that demanded that the studios regulate their product more effectively, but it also served the studios' financial interests.

In the first years after the war, studio profits declined from $119 billion in 1946 to $30.8 billion in 1950. Studio revenues decreased by 21 percent, reflecting declining attendance, especially for "A" features in first-run houses, the postwar studios' principal product on the market.[48] Over the same time period, Hollywood films dominated the world theatrical market. By 1949, studio income abroad exceeded $100 million. Despite widespread protectionism, especially in Europe, 38 percent of the studios' gross revenues for that year came from overseas.[49]

It is no wonder, then, that Johnston embraced the ideological war waged during the blacklist era; simply put, it was good for business. Sold out in the process of waging that war was a workforce exceedingly well represented by Jews; Hollywood in the forties was indeed managed (but not owned or controlled) by Jews, and the creative workforce, especially the Screenwriters Guild (the primary target of HUAC), included an inordinately large percentage of Jewish members. The battle lines were drawn between the Feds (fronted by a committee comprised of at least two anti-Semites, Rankin and Nixon)[50] and the Hollywood creative community and, more important, between the WASP/New York/Wall Street establishment, which for all practical economic purposes ran Hollywood at the time, and a frightened, self-loathing Jewish managerial class afraid of losing its jobs, six-figure salaries, women, and tables at posh restaurants.[51]

What was at stake in the blacklist era was control over a very lucrative industry. That seemed clear enough at the time, but the press (even newspapers that were critical of HUAC) tended to focus on the notion that the government (fronted by the committee) actually wanted to censor films.[52] Maybe it did in theory, but the Feds never had to because Johnston and the MPAA (through the PCA) were all too happy to do it for them.

In 1947, the MPAA was farsighted enough to understand that its cooperation in the Thomas Committee's ideological witch hunt was a means toward an end. As the Waldorf Statement so clearly reveals, battle lines were never drawn between the MPAA and HUAC. Instead, HUAC afforded the means by which the MPAA could deal with its problems with talent and, by extension, the guilds, agents, and lawyers who represented talent and thus set the stage for a confrontation between the New York offices (which supported the MPAA and its hand-picked president, Eric Johnston) and the erstwhile moguls who no longer could be trusted with control over an industry with so much potential but so many problems (with the Justice Department, competing popular audiovisual media, and the industry's notoriously politicized workforce).

Those under investigation in 1947 appreciated the relationship between Johnston's decision to turn his back on the Hollywood Ten and the growing acrimony between the ownership offices in New York and L.A.-based management. In *Hollywood on Trial*, the first book-length account of the Thomas Committee hearings, Gordon Kahn, one of the original Hollywood Nineteen, acknowledged the L.A./N.Y. story by deferring to the nation's best-known film reviewer, Bosley Crowther of the *New York Times:* "It should be fully realized that this action [the MPAA's capitulation to the Thomas Committee] was engineered by the major New York executives, the industry's overlords, and not the Hollywood producers, who form a different and subordinate group."[53]

The studios' complicity and collusion with the committee and with each other in the late 1940s seem a first and important affirmation of an increasingly conglomeratized and multinationalized new Hollywood. *Moody's Index* (of corporate holdings) reveals that in 1947 the studios were in partnership with and ostensibly answerable to big business.[54] Paramount ran on money supplied in part by Coca-Cola, RKO on funds from United Fruit, and Fox on capital from General Foods. The Hollywood Ten were sacrificed because they were bad for business—a business that was no longer (just) about making movies.

The Unions. In 1945, a tense and ultimately violent conflict between the Hollywood workforce and management took place at the Warner Bros. studio. Two years later, Jack Warner testified (albeit incoherently) as a friendly witness before the Thomas Committee. Lawson, Trumbo, Maltz, and Scott—four of the Hollywood Ten—all publicly supported the striking workers in the confrontation at Warners. Lawson so infuriated Jack Warner that when the executive testified before the committee, he introduced into evidence a picture of Lawson talking to strikers on the line.

During the 1930s, labor disputes were largely handled in-house; contracts were subject to "a basic agreement" overseen by the Motion Picture Academy.[55] If an actor, for example, filed a grievance for breach of contract, the Actors Adjustment Committee (staffed by four prominent actors and one industry executive) or an actor-producer relations representative mediated the case. The system was set up less to protect either side from the other than to protect the industry from poor public relations. As Academy president William C. DeMille remarked in 1930, the balance of the committee—a four-to-one split in favor of labor—was maintained in order to show support for and confidence in the mostly equitable labor-management relationship. The studios were willing to live with the arrangement because they believed few actors, directors, and writers would ever want or need to seek contract arbitration. The unions and guilds that emerged in the 1930s changed labor relations in Hollywood and rendered such self-regulation untenable.

Critics of the Hollywood Ten and of the CP in Hollywood in the thirties are quick to point out that the CP was first attracted to the movie business not so much because it was interested in using films for propaganda purposes but because it had failed to exert its influence virtually everywhere else. The relatively late emergence of unions in such a high-profile and lucrative industry was something of a last stand for the CP, which ended once and for all with the Thomas Committee hearings in 1947. As Richard Schickel, who produced the highlight reel of Kazan's films screened on Oscar night 1999, argues in a scathing review of Victor Navasky's blacklist study, *Naming Names:*

> In those days, when the economy was smaller—when Hollywood was, compared to other industrial complexes, larger and perhaps more significant than it is now (in the Thirties it was always in the top ten, from the point of view of sales, right up there with steel, autos and other heavyweights)—its unions were a great prize. If, through a strike, you could bring so rich and visible an industry to its knees, then a faction like the Communists could look to be more powerful than it actually was.[56]

Schickel argues that work on the blacklist tends to be politically myopic and that historians tend to focus on two oversimplified images: the heroic martyr and the self-serving fink. He agrees with Trumbo that there were "only victims," then adds that there were also victimizers on both sides. Schickel contends that the CP undermined the Hollywood Left through its insistence on secrecy: "If a group is open about its membership, it is damned difficult to persuade people it is conspiratorial, let alone subversive. . . . [The CP's] insistence on inviolable secrecy about their activities had as much to do with creating the blacklist (lending credence to the argument that they must have been up to something nasty) as the Committee itself did."[57]

Movie executives understood that organized labor posed a distinct threat to the basic agreement and system of self-regulation the Academy had managed so quietly and effectively. That someone, or some political party, from *outside* the industry might want to disrupt labor relations significantly complicated an already complex moment for the studios. In the late forties, management was so desperate to hang on that it was willing to deal, even though it seemed to invite federal censorship of its product and even though dealing forced the moguls into complicity with an anti-Semitic congressional committee.

Several of the "friendly witnesses" who testified before the Thomas Committee expressed concern about "outside agitators" stirring things up.[58] Like Schickel and other blacklist apologists, these so-called friendly witnesses blamed the blacklist on its primary victims. But it wasn't the CP, union activists, or outside agitators who precipitated the abandonment of the basic agreement and thus created the very unsettled labor situation that so complicated the blacklist.

The Academy system first showed signs of vulnerability in 1933 during the Bank Moratorium declared by President Roosevelt.[59] The Great Depression made even routine banking a difficult enterprise, particularly bad news for an industry so dependent on credit. The Bank Moratorium seemed to foreshadow an even more desperate crisis, the possibility that the studios would, for an indeterminate period of time, be unable to secure short-term loans to finance production and distribution. Beyond that, film executives had reason to believe that the Bank Moratorium was just a first step toward increased federal regulation by the Roosevelt administration. After all, Roosevelt was hardly shy about interfering with other lucrative industries and had displayed an interest in using the media to hawk the ideology of the New Deal.

Supporters of Roosevelt administration policies and members of political organizations who supported or were sympathetic to that administration were the first and easiest targets of HUAC. Studio executives encouraged such a payback. They supported the Thomas Committee's attack on FDR's legacy because they believed that the New Deal had been bad for business: it made banking more complex and difficult, supported the breakup of trusts, and protected workers' rights to collective action and unionization.

When Roosevelt introduced the moratorium, the Academy instituted an arrangement between management and labor by which, from March 4 to April 30, 1933, fees and salaries were deferred or reduced.[60] The agreement required the studios to resume full pay for full-time work after the eight-week moratorium expired, but just as SAG's leadership had suspected, once the moratorium went into effect, executives began to hedge on the time line. An unidentified executive admitted to the trades that "there is little chance of any of the slashed salary percentages being returned until the country's box offices reflect a decided up movement."[61]

Between 1931 and 1933, studio payrolls were cut by 60 percent, from $156 million to $50 million, and approximately ninety thousand employees lost their jobs.[62] The moratorium was designed to give ailing businesses time to develop new strategies. The studios used the time-out to breach existing employment, option, and development agreements with actors, directors, and writers. Studio employees appreciated that in the absence of enforceable contracts, they would be unable to recover fees in the event that studio management continued to cut payrolls and costs. To protect labor against such a likely management strategy, the Academy empowered its Emergency Committee to compel a studio, if a survey of its books warranted it, to resume full payment of salaries and fees before the moratorium was up. The accounting firm of Price, Waterhouse and Company was retained to audit the studios' books. But when Price, Waterhouse recommended to the Emergency Committee that Warners should resume full payments in advance of the eight-week moratorium date, studio *ownership*, in direct opposition to studio *management*, refused to comply with the committee's decision.

Conrad Nagel, the Academy president at the time, appreciated the ramifications of Warners' refusal and sought a compromise. He prevailed upon Will Hays, himself a veteran of studio deals involving self-regulation, to intervene. But the appeasement strategy backfired: the labor force at Warners resisted any deal that diminished the power of the Academy Emergency Committee. Neagle resigned in disgrace, and Darryl Zanuck, the production chief at Warners, quit and withdrew his membership from the Academy.[63] Zanuck recognized that the studios were powerful and profitable primarily because competition within the industry was so carefully and completely (self-)regulated. The contract system worked only because *all* the studios agreed to participate and follow a mutually advantageous set of rules.

When Warners refused to pay up after an impartial audit suggested it should, the studio undermined the Academy and the collusive industry the basic agreement protected. When the Academy proved too weak to protect its interests, industry labor sought alternatives, many of which leaned way to the left or, once and for all, redefined talent as labor and industry relations between labor and management as adversarial.

The lone exception to Hollywood labor's move to the left in the early 1930s was the Screen Actors Guild. From its very beginnings, SAG was a very different sort of movie industry union. Unlike the Screenwriters Guild, which included mostly anonymous screenwriters, SAG's leadership was made up of movie stars—larger-than-life celebrities who made astronomically high salaries. Early on, SAG benefited from its celebrity leadership. By 1937, SAG had gotten the studios to agree to a 90 percent closed shop and established employment standards designed to protect lower-paid actors. A few years later, SAG established a fully closed shop; all studio features were cast entirely with union actors.[64]

From the start, SAG's success with studio management was tied directly to the box office clout of its celebrity leadership. The rank and file—actors who had little bargaining power on their own—was therefore dependent on stars to bargain on their behalf. After the war, as box-office problems loomed, star actors became even more indispensable to studio production, and star agents emerged to exploit the situation for their star clients. These agents replaced SAG as the primary means of protecting the interests of the most powerful, productive, and influential screen actors.

As SAG became less and less useful to star actors in their negotiations with studio management, star actors used SAG to promote better public relations, joining management in an effort to protect the industry from outside regulation. They did so for pragmatic and selfish reasons. Like the studio executives who paid them, star actors had a lot riding on box-office revenues. By the late forties, agents had begun tying star compensation to box-office grosses. The first in a series of sellouts by SAG's postwar leadership involved an alliance with the pro-management and (at that time) Mob-run International Alliance of Theatrical and Stage Employees (IATSE). The alliance put SAG at odds with the other independent film unions, all of which had allied with the Conference of Studio Unions (CSU). It also placed SAG leadership at odds with its rank and file.

From 1945 to 1947, a period beginning with the Armistice and ending with the Thomas Committee hearings, IATSE was purged, or at least appeared to purge itself, of Mob influence. By the time Thomas convened the hearings, the leadership of IATSE was much like SAG's: devoutly anti-Communist, antistrike (IATSE members signed a no-strike pledge in 1945), and pro-management.

SAG President Ronald Reagan, along with SAG board members Robert Montgomery, George Murphy, and Leon Ames, complied with HUAC from the start because they shared its ideology and also because they accepted the larger argument that cooperation with the committee was good for business. As SAG board member Leon Ames so glibly put it at the time, "I believe we must approve [the termination of studio contracts with the Hollywood Ten, as elaborated in the Waldorf Statement] from a public relations standpoint, if nothing else." For Ames, it was up to the guild's celebrity actors to "protect the economic welfare of the industry."[65]

Reagan was less glib but no less cognizant of the public relations crisis that the Thomas Committee had set in motion. When he took the stand as a friendly witness at the HUAC hearings, Reagan extolled the virtues of the anti-Communist "majority" in the industry and cast the problem posed by Hollywood Communists and leftists as a threat to democracy and the free enterprise of the movie business: "Within the bounds of democratic rights, we have done a pretty good job in our business of keeping those [Communist] activities curtailed. . . . We have exposed their lies when we came across them, we have exposed their propaganda, and I can certainly testify that in the case of the Screen Actors Guild we have been eminently successful in preventing them from, with their usual tactics, trying to run a majority organization [SAG] with a well organized minority."[66]

The 1945 strike at Warners highlighted the increasingly bitter struggle between the two powerful industry "unions": the CSU (run by Herb Sorrell, a much-named name during the HUAC hearings) and IATSE (led from its inception by gangsters like Willie Bioff; in 1945, IATSE was managed by Roy Brewer, a Reagan compadre and avid anti-Communist). When the CSU organized the strike at the Warner Bros. studio, IATSE helped management hire scabs and then supported the studio's use of tear gas and high-powered water hoses on picketing strikers. The strike dragged on for eight months. As the strike fund was depleted, some CSU members joined IATSE in order to get back to work. The strike not only pitted labor against management but worker against worker. Two years later, when the MPAA established the blacklist, it did so with the support and organizational help of Roy Brewer and IATSE.[67] The larger political legacy of the blacklist can be found first in the so-called silent majority of the Nixon era and again in the steady move to the right during the Reagan-Bush years.

When Jack Warner appeared as a friendly witness before the Thomas Committee, his presence seemed to suggest sympathy with the investigators; however, his testimony was pretty hard to follow. (It is worth a look anyway because it includes a hilarious digression about the Warner Bros. film *Mission to Moscow* [1943], the development of which Jack Warner blamed on his brother, Harry.)[68] A far more useful witness was Walt Disney, himself the victim of a bitter strike in the early 1940s. After a long review of Disney's résumé (as if anyone in America at the time needed to know about their Uncle Walt), HUAC co-counsel H. A. Smith cut to the chase: "As a matter of fact, Mr. Disney, you experienced a strike at your studio." Following Smith's cue, Disney named names: Herbert Sorrell and animator Dave Hilberman, the two men who organized Disney animators.

For six months in 1922, Hilberman attended the prestigious Leningrad Art Theater (which Disney vaguely remembered as the Moscow Art Theater). That educational experience, along with his membership in the union and professional meetings with Sorrell, proved enough to get Hilberman fired at Disney, blacklisted in the industry, and hounded by the FBI into the early 1960s. Disney used his testimony not only to get back at Hilberman[69] but also to offer commentary on the labor movement: "[The Communists] have been hiding behind this labor set up, they get themselves closely tied up in the labor thing, so that if you try to get rid of them they make a labor case out of it."[70] Arthur Babbitt, a senior animator and pro-unionist, did just that. When Disney attempted to fire him for his union activity, Babbitt took his case to the NLRB. Disney was ultimately forced to pay Babbitt back wages plus a hefty penalty.

The nine-week strike at Disney was a turning point for the company.[71] The negative publicity attending the strike militated against long-held notions of amiable relations between supposedly dedicated animators and their Uncle Walt. It also marked the end of the studio's golden age; the animation unit never regained its prominence, at least during Walt's lifetime. Walt Disney's subsequent moves into theme park operations and television—a harbinger of things to come in the entertainment industry—were driven as much by necessity as creative vision. Once he was forced to capitulate to the Cartoonists Guild, Disney lost interest in making movies.[72]

For those who participated in the strike and for those who knew Disney during the war years, his testimony at HUAC came as no surprise. As biographer Marc Eliot depicts him, Disney was a vindictive boss with decidedly reactionary political beliefs. Throughout the 1930s, Disney attended meetings held at the houses of American Nazi Party members and appeared at rallies for America First, posing for photographs alongside the group's figurehead, Charles Lindbergh. In her memoirs, Leni Riefenstahl claims that Disney told her he admired her work and briefly considered hiring her. Eliot reports on a meeting between Henry Ford and Disney at which the automobile executive praised Disney for his success in a business otherwise dominated by Jews. According to Eliot, Ford advised Disney to sell his company outright before considering a public offering of stock, because, Ford contended, Wall Street was controlled by Jewish investment interests. During the war years, Disney made animated films in support of the war effort. And although Disney would later exaggerate his contribution to the cause, Eliot maintains that Disney resented every second he had to deal with "that Jew," Secretary of the Treasury Henry Morgenthau, whose job it was to oversee the budgets on films made for the War Department.[73] At a time when affiliations, memberships, friendships, and even casual conversations defined who you were in important ways, Disney's record in the 1930s and 1940s speaks volumes.

Less than two months after the Disney strike was settled in labor's favor, the California State Legislature mounted the so-called Little HUAC hearings. When the hearings were convened by California state senator Jack Tenney in July 1941, the first witness called to testify was CSU president Herbert Sorrell, the man responsible for unionizing the Disney Studio workers.

A New Hollywood. The unfair labor practices at the Disney studios resulted from a paternalistic system in which rewards and punishments were distributed according to the personal whims of Walt Disney. When more senior and, in some cases, fairly well-paid animators like Babbitt and Hilberman joined the strike force, Disney failed to understand the significance of their actions and instead viewed their support of the union as a personal betrayal. It is important to understand that Disney viewed his workers as children not only because he felt he knew what was best for them but also because, like the Jewish moguls who managed the other studios, he was an entrepreneurial capitalist. The unions ushered in a new way of doing business that at once professionalized labor relations and rendered obsolete the more personal, entrepreneurial, and paternalistic style that characterized management at virtually all the studios. Like that of the other moguls, most of whom Disney despised, Disney's way of doing business came to an abrupt end in the 1940s.[74]

It is important to note that the Red Scare did not mark the beginning of increased federal regulation of Hollywood. To the contrary, during the last four decades there has been a systematic erosion of antitrust regulation and enforcement in the entertainment business and the evolution of a film-rating system, supervised by the MPAA, that, with little concern for free trade, regulates participation in the various markets now routinely exploited by the conglomerate-owned studios.[75] The blacklist taught the membership of the MPAA that when they worked together they could turn a sow's ear—like the Thomas hearings—into a silk purse. And they have never for a moment looked back since.

The brief Waldorf Statement delivered on behalf of the MPAA on November 24, 1947, the very day the House voted to approve contempt indictments for the Hollywood Ten, revealed the economic bottom line of the blacklist: "We will forthwith suspend without compensation those in our employ and we will not re-employ any of the ten until such time as he is acquitted or has purged himself of contempt and declares under oath that he is not a Communist."[76] MGM immediately suspended Trumbo and refused to pay him $60,000 in fees (per his contract). Fox fired Lardner, and RKO dumped Dmytryk and Scott.

The breaking of contracts and the refusal to pay fees for scripts that were optioned, developed, and/or produced before the fall of 1947 prompted a number of civil litigations that dragged on well into the 1950s and 1960s and helped establish the acrimonious relationship between Hollywood management and talent that continues to today. Hollywood is an industry run by agents and lawyers; it's a common lament these days. It's true. One need only review the events of 1947 to understand why.

Notes

1 The subpoena commanded the person named at the top of the document to "appear before the Un-American Activities Committee of the House of Representatives of the United States, of which the Hon. J. Parnell Thomas is chairman, in their chamber in the city of Washington on [a specified date in late October 1947] then and there to testify touching matters of inquiry committed to said Committee; and he is not to depart without leave of said Committee. Herein fail not, and make return of this summons." The House Committee included Congressmen J. Parnell Thomas (chairman), John McDowell of Pennsylvania, Richard Vail of Illinois, Richard Nixon of California, and, though absent from the proceedings, John Rankin of Mississippi.

2 The Justice Department was particularly eager to resume its efforts to break up the studio trusts after the war because the studios had proven particularly unresponsive to previous consent decrees. Blind bidding and block booking continued despite prewar agreements between the studios and the Justice Department.

3 By 1980, all of the majors except Twentieth Century-Fox were owned and/or controlled by multinational conglomerates. These companies generated revenues and profits from a diverse array of industries, including insurance, real estate, and publishing. United Artists, owned at the time by Transamerica, an insurance conglomerate, provides a useful example. In 1979, United Artists' profits were down, and the company was beset by a management conflict (which culminated in the exodus of its executive team to Orion Pictures) and bad press attending the company's disastrous handling of Francis Coppola's *Apocalypse Now*. Despite hard times at the UA film division, Transamerica garnered $4.04 billion in revenue, a record for the insurance giant at the time. Two years later, when UA's *Heaven's Gate* lost over $40 million, Transamerica stock took an inconsequential and temporary dip of only three-eighths of a point. For more on conglomerate ownership in the industry in the 1980s, see Janet Wasko, *Hollywood in the Information Age* (Austin: University of Texas Press, 1994).

4 Thomas Schatz, *Boom and Bust: The American Cinema in the 1940s* (New York: Scribner's, 1997), 265.

5 Johnston took out a full-page ad in the *New York Times* affirming his and the studios' support of the Ten. *New York Times*, October 27, 1947, 17.

6 Gordon Kahn, *Hollywood on Trial* (New York: Boni and Gaer, 1948), 26.

7 Ibid., 191–92. This stunning reversal came three days after Johnston's full-page ad appeared in the *New York Times* (see note 5 above).

8 We no longer need to speculate because we now know more about the MPAA meeting that preceded the drafting of the Waldorf Statement. When Hollywood studio executives met with Johnston to decide how to respond to the committee's charges against the Ten, the MPAA chief advised his colleagues that they had two options: they could retain the Ten and make a public statement promising to keep subversive material offscreen or fire and refuse to reemploy the Ten (until they recanted). Johnston pointed out that if the executives decided to oppose the committee they could face boycotts targeting films written and/or produced by the Ten, as well as films featuring supposed sympathizers (including high-profile members of the Committee for the First Amendment such as Humphrey Bogart, Katharine Hepburn, and Fredric March). Spain, Chile, and Argentina threatened action against studios that refused to discipline the Ten—a prospect that proved daunting, given the importance of foreign markets after the war. Only Samuel Goldwyn voted for the first option, and

Johnston carried the day. See Larry Ceplair and Steven England, *The Inquisition in Hollywood: Politics in the Film Community, 1930–1960* (New York: Anchor Press, 1980), 328–29.

9 The ARI Report can be found in Dory Schary's papers at the University of Wisconsin, Madison. The Gallup Poll results have been reprinted in a number of places, including Kahn, *Hollywood on Trial*, 177–78, and Schatz, *Boom and Bust*, 312–13.

10 A *New York Times* editorial, for example, included the following: "We do not believe the Committee is conducting a fair investigation. We think the course on which it is embarked threatens to lead to greater dangers than those with which it is presently concerned." "Congress and Hollywood," *New York Times*, October 23, 1947, 24.

11 The Thomas Committee at first expressed interest in nineteen Hollywood artists, but in the first round of hearings only ten were required to appear and testify. In addition to the Hollywood Ten, the committee publicly expressed interest in Bertolt Brecht (who, after confusing testimony in closed session, left the United States), Richard Collins, Gordon Kahn, Howard Koch, Lewis Milestone, Larry Parks, Irving Pichel, Robert Rossen, and Waldo Salt.

12 Kahn, *Hollywood on Trial*, 189.

13 Thomas was, within a year of the celebrated hearings, found guilty of embezzling government funds and sentenced to three years in federal prison at Danbury, Connecticut. Among his fellow inmates were Ring Lardner, Jr., and Lester Cole. Though he hardly afforded the Ten the courtesy, let alone the right, to Fifth Amendment protection, Thomas pleaded nolo contendere and declined to take the stand at his trial. Although all ten were denied parole, both Thomas and fellow Red-baiter (ex-) Congressman Andrew May (who was convicted on bribery charges and served time in federal prison with Dalton Trumbo in Ashland, Kentucky) were paroled after serving less than a year behind bars.

14 See the well-orchestrated testimony of friendly witnesses like Jack Warner and especially Adolphe Menjou, which is reprinted in Kahn, *Hollywood on Trial*, 9–26 (Warner) and 47–51 (Menjou).

15 Scott's memo to Dozier and Korner is reprinted in its entirety in Ceplair and Englund, *The Inquisition in Hollywood*, 441–44.

16 While the committee contended that CP membership amounted to treason, a number of formerly blacklisted writers, directors, actors, and producers were first attracted to the CP in the 1930s, when the Soviet Union was a U.S. ally. Many cite as a principal reason for their party interest domestic concerns regarding civil rights. In his memoir, *Inside Out* (New York: Knopf, 1996), Walter Bernstein makes explicit the connection between CP affiliation/membership and the civil rights movement—and then between the civil rights movement and Jewishness: "We were all urban, middle-class intellectuals shaped by the Depression and the war. About half of us were Jews, which did not seem to me to be disproportionate. This was where Jews belonged, wherever there was a struggle for human rights. This was what being a Jew meant" (134–35). Blacklisted screenwriter Guy Endore shared Bernstein's sentiments: "I wasn't really a Communist. I didn't agree with [all of the party's doctrines]. [What] united me with it was simply the fact that they represented the most extreme protest against what I saw going on in the world . . . I was a Communist only in the sense that I felt it would stop war and it would stop racist feelings, that it would help Jews, Negroes and so on. I wasn't a Communist in wanting the Communist Party to run the world or in wanting the ideas of Karl Marx to govern everything." Guy Endore, *Reflections of Guy Endore* [Los Angeles: UCLA Oral History Project, 1964], 132, 140.

17 Ceplair and Englund, *The Inquisition in Hollywood*, 441–44.

18 Ibid., 318.

19 My account of Schary's testimony is based in large part on Schatz, *The Genius of the System*, 442–49.

20 One of the victims of Hughes's cost-cutting shake-up at RKO was studio president Peter Rathvon, one of the executives responsible for greenlighting *Crossfire*. Whether or not Rathvon was fired because he produced that film and whether Schary was dumped or forced to resign for political reasons is anybody's guess these days. Although Hughes was an anti-Communist, he proved to be an unpredictable, even illogical boss at RKO. Both Rathvon and Schary were expensive managers, and Hughes's treatment of them in the spring of 1948 may well have been the product of a misguided fiscal, as opposed to political, strategy.

21 This discussion of the propaganda hearings is based in large part on Schatz, *Boom and Bust*, 38–40.

22 *Foreign Correspondent* was based on Vincent Shean's nonfiction best-seller, *Personal History*, which chronicles the journalist's political awakening in fascist Spain and Germany and his role in the rescue of several Jews from Nazi tyranny. Joseph Breen, the anti-Semitic chief of the PCA, dismissed *Personal History* as "pro-Loyalist propaganda . . . pro-Jewish propaganda, and anti-Nazi propaganda." To get the film made, Wanger and Hitchcock reduced Shean's personal, political story into an entertaining but relatively apolitical espionage thriller. See Schatz, *Boom or Bust*, 265–66.

23 Ibid., 39–40.

24 Ibid., 267–68.

25 An anonymous letter sent to Jack Warner after the studio announced plans to produce *Confessions of a Nazi Spy* suggests just what sort of portent: "I would suggest that after you finish the picture it would be suitable to follow with *I Am a Communist* starring Eddie Cantor and a few other Communist Jews. . . . Mr. Warner, please don't think the American people are as dumb as you think they are." The letter can be found in the Hays Office file on *Confessions of a Nazi Spy* and is reprinted in Colin Schindler's *Hollywood in Crisis: Cinema and American Society, 1929–1939* (London: Routledge, 1996), 208–9.

26 Rumors that Chaplin was (part) Jewish only increased after the release of *The Great Dictator*. The comedian did little to quiet these rumors, though they hardly helped his career or his personal security. Chaplin was only the most famous creative artist to be labeled a Jew because of his (perceived) leftist politics.

27 Hays Office document, cited in Schindler, *Hollywood in Crisis*, 208.

28 Schatz, *Boom or Bust*, 36–37.

29 Ibid., 382.

30 Pat McGilligan, "Tender Comrades," *Film Comment* 24, no. 6 (December 1987): 43.

31 Neil Gabler, *An Empire of Their Own: How the Jews Invented Hollywood* (Garden City, N.Y.: Doubleday, 1989).

32 Jews continued and continue to be well represented in Hollywood management. The ouster of first-generation moguls like Mayer during the blacklist era did not put an end to Jewish management or influence. A very different sort of Jewish manager—former agent Lew Wasserman was the prototype—emerged in the post-blacklist era. These second-generation Jewish managers, such as Gerald Levin and Edgar Bronfman, were at first entertainment industry players, then later money industry players.

33 Mayer was ousted by Nicholas Schenck after years of acrimony between Mayer and production chief Dore Schary. It takes a leap of faith simply to blame the blacklist for Mayer's exit from MGM, but the business climate created by HUAC and the Paramount decision exaggerated the impression that Mayer, after twenty-seven years with the studio, had outlived his usefulness. That Schenck was willing to terminate Mayer's employment at a studio that still bore his family's name displayed a growing anxiety throughout the industry in the aftershock of the Thomas Committee hearings and the Paramount decision to, as Thomas Schatz so aptly puts it, "recolonize" the motion picture marketplace. Schatz, *The Genius of the System*, 440–81.

34 The suppressed statements were published verbatim in Kahn, *Hollywood on Trial*. It is the first place I know of where these statements were reprinted in their entirety.

35 Kahn, *Hollywood on Trial*, 98–99.

36 Ibid., 76.

37 Ibid., 106–8.

38 Ibid., 84.

39 Ibid., 176–77.

40 Patricia Bosworth, *Anything Your Little Heart Desires: An American Family Story* (New York: Simon and Schuster, 1997).

41 The CP/Margolis strategy is discussed at length in ibid., 227–33, 238, 244–45, 376, and Edward Dmytryk, *Odd Man Out* (Carbondale: Southern Illinois University Press, 1996), 36–38, 113, 167.

42 This is discussed at length in Richard Schickel, "Return of the Hollywood Ten," *Film Comment* 18, no. 2 (March–April 1981): 11–17, and by a number of those interviewed in Patrick McGilligan and Paul Buhle, *Tender Comrades: A Backstory of the Hollywood Blacklist* (New York: St. Martin's, 1997), 118, 312–13, 329, 345, 347, 490, 558, 592.

43 Dalton Trumbo, in Helen Manfill, ed., *Additional Dialogue: Letters of Dalton Trumbo* (New York: M. Evans, 1970), 569–70. The speech was delivered on March 13, 1970. One of the most widely read studies of the era is television and film actor Robert Vaughn's *Only Victims: A Study of Show Business Blacklisting* (New York: Putnam, 1972). Vaughn takes his title from Dalton Trumbo's conciliatory speech.

44 Maltz, cited in Schickel, "Return of the Hollywood Ten," 12.

45 McGilligan and Buhle, *Tender Comrades*, 345.

46 Stephen Vaughn, "Political Censorship during the Cold War," in Francis G. Couvares, ed., *Movie Censorship and American Culture* (Washington, D.C.: Smithsonian Institution Press, 1996), 250.

47 Ibid., 250–51.

48 Schatz, *Boom or Bust*, 293–95.

49 Ibid., 303.

50 Rankin made his anti-Semitism public with astonishing regularity in the forties. Nixon was more careful, but a quick listen to the infamous Nixon tapes leaves little doubt about his dislike and distrust of Jews. During the 1972 presidential campaign, for example, he made the following request to his dirty-tricks squad: "Please get me the names of the Jews. You know, the big Jewish contributors . . . Could we please investigate some of those cocksuckers."

51 This is perhaps more a conclusion than an observation, and the language I use is provocative or at the very least colorful. Of course, I don't know what was in the hearts and minds of the first-generation moguls, but their refusal to sign anti-Nazi petitions in the thirties and their abandonment of mostly Jewish writers, directors, actors, and producers during the Red Scare certainly suggest a repudiation of ethnicity and faith. As for the WASP/Wall Street establishment, the moguls did answer to the New York offices, and those New York offices had one eye on the stock market and the other on the banks that provided capital for studio/industry operations. Johnston's sudden turn-around in the fall of 1947—his decision on behalf of the MPAA and the industry to abandon the Hollywood Ten just days after vowing to protect them—certainly *suggests* that those higher up on the food chain told him to do so. (See note 47.)

52 While the suppressed statements were never read into the congressional record, they were submitted and reprinted in a number of newspapers at the time.

53 Kahn, *Hollywood on Trial*, 195.

54 See John Sherman Porter, ed., *Moody's Manual of Investments* (New York: Moody's Investment Service, 1947), 1880–83, 2247–53, 2907–13.

55 The analogy between the two entertainment businesses, sports and movies, is an important one. "Free agency" came to Hollywood in the late 1940s as an indirect result of divestiture, and it empowered star celebrities and their agents. Even a quick look at contemporary sports, all of which now have some form of free agency, reveals much the same result: star athletes, represented by agents, make outrageous salaries and, in the process, have changed the stakes and nature of the business and its product. Of course, as in the film business, since free agency, team owners make much more money than they ever did before.

56 Schickel, "Return of the Hollywood Ten," 12.

57 Ibid., 14.

58 Adolphe Menjou and Walt Disney, to name two.

59 This argument is made at some length in Murray Ross, *Stars and Strikes: Unionization of Hollywood* (New York: Columbia University Press, 1941), 23–47.

60 For a more detailed account, see Danae Clark, *Negotiating Hollywood: The Cultural Politics of Actors' Labor* (Minneapolis: University of Minnesota Press, 1995), 41–44.

61 Ibid., 43.

62 Ibid., 42.

63 Ross, *Stars and Strikes*, 44–46.

64 Gorham A. Kindem, "SAG, HUAC, and Postwar Hollywood," in Schatz, *Boom or Bust*, 314.

65 Ibid., 317–18.

66 Ibid., 317.

67 Ross, *Stars and Strikes*, 188. Brewer and Ronald Reagan became close friends and political allies during the blacklist era. In 1984, despite (or because of) Brewer's history of complicity with industry blacklisting and strike-breaking, then U.S. president Reagan appointed the former IATSE president chairman of the Federal Service Impasse Panel, which arbitrated disputes between federal agencies and unions representing federal workers.

68 Warner told Congressman Vail that his brother, Harry, "made the deal with [former U.S. ambassador] Davies" and that he, Jack, had nothing to do with the development or production of the film.

69 Hilberman has since returned the favor, generously affording damaging and embarrassing material about Disney's anti-union and Red-baiting activities to Marc Eliot, whose biography, *Walt Disney: Hollywood's Dark Prince* (New York: Birch Lane, 1993), ably refutes the mythos of the kindly Uncle Walt.

70 Taken verbatim from Disney's testimony before HUAC.

71 This argument is made at greater length and detail in Holly Allen and Michael Denning, "The Cartoonists' Front," *South Atlantic Quarterly* 92, no. 1 (winter 1993): 89–117.

72 Disney himself supported the theory that the strike broke the back of his animation unit. Both *Pinocchio* (1940) and *Fantasia* (1940), ambitious and arguably terrific films, took years to make and lost money at the box office. The strike held up production, and the interest on the short-term loans supporting these productions crippled the studio. That the two films failed to capture the interest of the American public seems another issue altogether.

73 Eliot, *Walt Disney*, 120, 121, 135, 136, 166.

74 Ibid., 47–51.

75 I discuss regulation in the new Hollywood at length elsewhere. See Jon Lewis, *Whom God Wishes to Destroy: Francis Coppola and the New Hollywood* (Durham, N.C.: Duke University Press, 1995), 21–40; "Trust and Antitrust in the New New Hollywood," *Michigan Quarterly Review* 35, no. 1 (winter 1996): 85–105; and "Money Matters: Hollywood in the Corporate Era," in Jon Lewis, ed., *The New American Cinema* (Durham, N.C.: Duke University Press, 1998), 87–124.

76 Ceplair and Englund, *The Inquisition in Hollywood*, 445.

PART VI

Stardom

Chapter 16

Daisuke Miyao

A STAR IS BORN: THE TRANSNATIONAL SUCCESS OF *THE CHEAT* AND ITS RACE AND GENDER POLITICS (2007)

Editors' Introduction

Fans and film historians alike frequently have considered stardom in purely national terms. Beginning at least in the early 1980s with the work of Richard Dyer, star studies has provided us with a sophisticated understanding of the film celebrity as perhaps the most significant commodity of the American film industry, as a worker in a vast industrial system, and as a signifier of viewer pleasure and desire. But it is only recently that scholars have understood American film stardom in international terms, and the American film star as a globally valuable "product." This modern work on the star has come as scholars also have begun to assess the American cinema as an international rather than just national leisure technology. Daisuke Miyao's analysis of Sessue Hayakawa combines both of these trends, and complicates them. With Hayakawa, we have the phenomenon of a Japanese actor becoming one of the biggest stars in the United States during the World War One era, and also one of the biggest stars in the world. This fame came largely from one film, Cecil B. DeMille's astonishing *The Cheat*, from 1915, which stunned both American and European audiences. But while Miyao's work makes us understand the international significance of American cinema and celebrity, it also reminds us that movies as well as movie stardom must also be considered in local terms. Audiences in Europe and America adored Hayakawa. But this broad acclaim was matched by distrust in smaller, Japanese and Japanese-American communities in the United States that criticized Hayakawa's roles in clearly racist films. Miyao's scholarship not only advances star studies, but also encapsulates two of the significant trends in film studies, the study of the international and at the same time the close examination of the local, of the neighborhood, and of small and distinct audiences.

Suggested Reading

Richard Dyer, *Heavenly Bodies: Film Stars and Society* (British Film Institute, 1986); Christine Gledhill, ed., *Stardom: Industry of Desire* (Routledge, 1991); Adrienne McLean, *Being Rita Hayworth: Labor, Identity, and Hollywood Stardom* (Rutgers, 2004).

ON DECEMBER 13, 1915, a film titled *The Cheat*, produced at the Jesse L. Lasky Feature Play Company, directed by Cecil B. DeMille, and starring Fannie Ward, a renowned stage actress in New York and London, was released in the United States.[1] *The Cheat* soon achieved big box office success[2] and opened a gate for the Japanese actor Sessue Hayakawa to become a "full-fledged star."[3] Before the success of *The Cheat*, Hayakawa had already appeared in many films, but it was *The Cheat* that paved the way for him to achieve superstardom.

In *The Cheat*, a rich Japanese art dealer on Long Island, Hishuru Tori (Sessue Hayakawa), offers money to Edith Hardy (Fannie Ward), a white middle-class woman, who has invested money from the Red Cross Fund and eventually lost it, in exchange for her body. When Edith tries to return his money after her husband's success in the stock market. Tori assaults her and brutally brands his mark on her shoulder. However, Edith fights back and shoots Tori in the shoulder. Knowing everything, Edith's husband decides to be arrested on a charge of attempted murder in order to save her name. During the trial, Edith confesses the truth, and the excited court audience attacks Tori in the end.

Not very many reviewers and audiences were impressed by the film's leading actress. What fascinated them most was the supporting Japanese actor, Sessue Hayakawa. The *New York Times* insisted, "Miss Ward might learn something to help her fulfill her destiny as a great tragedienne of the screen by observing the man who acted the Japanese villain in her picture."[4] *Variety* agreed: "The work of Sessue Hayakawa is so far above the acting of Miss Ward and Jack Dean that he really should be the star in the billing for the film."[5] *Moving Picture World* (*MPW*) noted that Hayakawa had "a prominent role" in *The Cheat* and added, "It is rumored he is soon to be starred by the Lasky Company in a big feature production."[6] Sessue Hayakawa thus became an overnight sensation to the moviegoers in America.

Cecil B. DeMille, the director of the film, recalled later that *The Cheat* was "Sessue Hayakawa's first giant stride on the road that made him within two years the peer of such contemporary bright stars as Douglas Fairbanks, William S. Hart, and Mary Pickford."[7] The *New Orleans Times* in February 1916 reported how prominent Hayakawa was after the release of *The Cheat*: "Undoubtedly the greatest success ever scored by a Japanese actor on [*sic*] American moving pictures was that of Sessue Hayakawa in the Lasky-Paramount production of "The Cheat," and so strong an impression thot [*sic*] make on New Orleans spectators that when the Japanese appeared for the moment on the screen in the part of a valet in "Temptation," at the Crescent, a murmur of recognition such as we have never known to greet any other player went through the audience—a most sincere tribute."[8] Similarly, *Wid's Films and Film Folk Independent Criticisms of Features* pointed out that Hayakawa was used in an inappropriate way in a minor role in *Temptation* (Cecil B. DeMille, 30 December 1915), the film that was released right after *The Cheat*: "Our Jap friend, of 'The Cheat' fame, is brought in for a very small 'valet' part at the finish. I think this is wrong. That boy is too big and too clever to be shoved into such films to do a small bit. It hits you in the eye like it would be to see Blanche Sweet come into the film as a maid."[9]

The Lasky Company dared not miss this opportunity. Right before the release of *The Cheat*, the studio head, Jesse L. Lasky, praised *The Cheat* as "one of the very best" films ever made, even though his claim should have contained a promotional intention. He said he was "so impressed by his [Hayakawa's] performance" that he "immediately signed him for a long term" contract.[10] After the box office success of *The Cheat*, the company came to recognize Hayakawa as its new potential moneymaker and to undertake a specific strategy to establish, publicize, and promote his star image.

Motion Picture News (*MPN*) reported on 15 April 1916: "Partly in response to the hundreds of requests from exhibitors and photoplay goers all over the United States, the Jesse L. Lasky

Feature Play Company announces that it will present as a star early in May the well-known Japanese screen player, Sessue Hayakawa, in a photoplay production entitled 'Alien Souls.' Hayakawa's work in 'The Cheat,' in which he appeared in leading support of Fannie Ward, stamped him immediately as a proficient figure in motion pictures."[11] Lasky spent five months before releasing the first star vehicle for Hayakawa, *Alien Souls* (Frank Reicher, 3 May 1916). This long five-month gap indicates the extent of Lasky's well-prepared publicity for the company's new star. When *Alien Souls* was finally released, reviews of the film appeared in various local papers such as the *New York Sun, Philadelphia Telegraph, Detroit News, Evening Wisconsin, Louisville Times, Springfield Mirror, Cleveland Daily, Atlanta Constitution, Los Angeles Examiner, Chicago Tribune, Toledo Blade*, and *Washington Star*, and they unanimously called Hayakawa a "star." After *Alien Souls*, Hayakawa's star vehicles were released in approximately two-month cycles.

But stardom has more than a national perspective, and Hayakawa, like Charlie Chaplin, was one of the first stars whose international reputation forms an essential part of his story. American spectators were not the only ones who were immensely impressed by Hayakawa in *The Cheat*. Hayakawa's performance was sensationally received in Europe and in Japan.[12] In France, when *The Cheat* opened at the Omnia Pathé Cinema in Paris in the summer of 1916, French intellectuals were "dumbfounded" by Hayakawa and the innovative aesthetics of *The Cheat*.[13] On 3 June 1918, the drama critic Louis Delluc claimed, "No one actually wanted to see anything in it [*The Cheat*] except the Japanese. . . . [The film] inspired nothing but pro-Japanese polemic."[14] In *Excelsior*, on 7 August 1916, the renowned poet, novelist, and essayist Colette reported, in an excited tone, on the impact of Hayakawa's performance in *The Cheat* on many artists:

> In Paris this week, a movie theater has become an art school. A film and two of its principal actors are showing us what surprising innovations, what emotion, what natural and well-designed lighting can add to cinematic fiction. Every evening, writers, painters, composers, and dramatists come and come again to sit, contemplate, and comment in low voices, like pupils. To the genius of an oriental actor is added that of a director probably without equal. . . . We cry "Miracle!" . . . Is it only a combination of felicitous effects that brings us to this film and keeps us there? Or is it the more profound and less clear pleasure of seeing the crude ciné groping toward perfection, the pleasure of divining what the future of the cinema must be when its makers will want that future . . .? . . . This Asiatic artist whose powerful immobility is eloquence itself. Let our aspiring ciné-actors go to see how, when his face is mute, his hand carries on the flow of his thought. Let them take to heart the menace and disdain in a motion of his eyebrow and how, in that his life is running out with his blood, without shuddering, without convulsively grimacing, with merely the progressive petrifaction of his Buddha's mask and the ecstatic darkening of his eyes.[15]

As mentioned in the introduction, Hayakawa's acting, which Delluc and Colette fervently described, inspired certain French intellectuals to generate a concept, *photogenie*, the unique aesthetic qualities that motion picture photography brings to the subject it films. For them, the concept of *photogenie* was the basis of a new idea of film as a unique art form, thus Hayakawa of a new form of acting. According to Delluc, using the camera and the screen, *photogenie* changes "real" into something else without eliminating the "realness" and makes people "see ordinary things as they had never been before."[16] It is a mystical and theoretically incoherent concept due to the fact that *photogenie* is "designed to account for that which is inarticulable, that which exceeds language and hence points to the very essence of cinematic specificity."[17] Yet, such a theorist as Delluc believed that the cinema would give viewers access to a realm beyond everyday experience and show them the souls of people and the essence of objects. The concept of *photogenie* later became a significant theoretical basis of the French impressionist film movement, filmmaking that "displayed a fascination with pictorial beauty and an interest in intense psychological exploration."[18] As a result, by 1921, French intellectuals achieved a consensus that *The Cheat*'s "revelation actually initiated the greater French public's education about the cinema."[19]

This enthusiastic reception of Hayakawa in France had a certain connection to the popularity of Madame Sadayakko, a Japanese actress. Sadayakko, who was in fact the aunt of Hayakawa's wife, Tsuru Aoki, was sponsored by the popular dancer Loie Fuller in the 1900 Exposition in Paris, together with her husband Kawakami Otojiro, who tried to modernize Japanese theater by dissociating it from the dominant world of kabuki and pleasure quarters. Sadayakko's geisha dance and act of dying and Kawakami's act of hara-kiri, which were in fact added at the request of Fuller, were sensationally received not only by the popular audience, but by some intellectuals and artists, including the renowned sculptor Auguste Rodin. Moreover, their acts were captured by a motion picture camera, which was another sensational form of entertainment at the Paris Exposition. After the Kawakami troupe returned to Japan, even Japanese-style dresses became fashionable in Paris. They were called "Yacco" style because Sadayakko always wore a kimono at parties. Sadayakko's fame was such that Guerlain introduced a perfume called "Yacco."[20]

Without Sadayakko, Kawakami, and Aoki, Hayakawa would never have entered the film business. In 1899, when Aoki was eleven, she went to the United States as a part of the Kawakami troupe. It was the first time a Japanese theater troupe had toured in the United States.[21] Aoki stayed in the United States as an adopted daughter of Aoki Toshio (Hyosai), an artist in San Francisco, and later, after Aoki Toshio died, of Louise Scher, a journalist at the *Los Angeles Examiner*. Aoki started her film career much earlier than Hayakawa and quite possibly introduced him to an influential producer in early Hollywood, Thomas H. Ince.

In 1925, the filmmakers Henri Fescourt and Jean-Louis Bouquet dated "the origins of the cinema around 1915–1916, with the appearance of the first good American films," and stated that "the most striking was *The Cheat*."[22] In 1937, Marcel L'Herbier remade *The Cheat*, entitled *Forfaiture*, using Hayakawa in the role of a Mongolian prince who attracts a French engineer's wife and entraps her using her gambling debts.[23] The images behind the opening credits of *Forfaiture*, a compilation of notable scenes with Hayakawa from *The Cheat*, clearly indicate the immense popularity of Hayakawa and *The Cheat* in France. *Forfaiture* thus presupposed the viewers' knowledge of the original.

Moreover, *Excelsior*, on 28 August 1917, reported that *The Cheat* was about to be staged as an opera. André de Lorde of the Théatre du Grand Guignol and Paul Milliet wrote a music drama based on *The Cheat*, for which Camille Erlanger wrote the music. The opera, entitled *La Forfaiture*, was in fact produced by the Opéra-Comique in 1921, after Erlanger's death, and became the first opera to be based on a motion picture scenario, even though the opera was not successful and played only three times.[24] Colette's reaction to this announcement of the stage production of *The Cheat*, written in a conversation style, indicates how highly she valued Hayakawa's eloquent performance. Colette's insight even predicts Hayakawa's future, his loss of popularity after talking pictures arrived:

> "And who will play it? Have they already found people worthy of taking over for Hayakawa and Fannie Ward?"
>
> "Ah . . . that's the difficulty. What do you think of Mary Garden for the role played by Fannie Ward?"

"Mary Garden would be fine. And the Japanese?"

The friend of film leaned forward, with an anxious face: "The Japanese, the Japanese . . ."

He looked at me steadily.

"It's strange," he said, "the Japanese . . . I don't conceive of that role, you understand, as being sung. Or, let's say there'd be very little singing. One would need a great artist capable of mime. Gesture, stage presence . . . Very little voice. No vocal effects, no melodic phrases. Everything in *recitative*. But silence, you understand, above all, silence. Jean Périer, perhaps . . ."

"Of course. Besides"—I insinuated with a poisonous sweetness—"really, the Japanese has nothing to say in the story."

"That's quite right. My opinion exactly. He has nothing to say. The first, the glare, that's the whole role. I see so clearly what's needed. I can see it as if I were there."

"I think you were there. Wait, one moment, I have an idea. Supposing that the Japanese, in your opera, were made evil, seductive, and . . . mute?"

"Mute?"

"Mute. As mute as a screen. He could, by mime, make himself understood just as easily—perhaps better—and then . . ."

"I've got it, I've got it!" the friend of film cried. "We'll get Hayakawa to create the role in the opera!"

"I hoped you'd say that."

"Magnificent! Magnificent! That takes a weight off me . . . It's foolish, perhaps, but the idea of hearing the role of the Japanese sung . . . and even that of the woman, if it comes to that, in the great scene, the struggle between Fannie Ward and Hayakawa, I can't yet imagine how they would exchange the lines 'Be Mine!' 'No, never!' 'You swore it!' 'Pity, pity! Oh, the villain—!' and so on."

"I share your apprehension. One could, though, get around the difficulty with those cries . . ."

"How?"

"One could arrange, for example, a silent scene, very rapid, in the style of that lovely scene in the film . . ."

"Of course . . ."

". . . and since the scene would be silent, there wouldn't be any difficulty in having it played by Fannie Ward . . ."[25]

Hayakawa's performance in *The Cheat* was sensationally received by Japanese spectators, too. However, the tone of the Japanese reception was not as favorable as that of the American and French ones. Japanese communities in the United States severely protested *The Cheat*, insisting that the Japanese character in the film was depicted unfavorably. On 23 December 1915, right after *The Cheat* was released at the Tally Theater in Los Angeles, the *Rafu Shimpo*, a Japanese newspaper in Los Angeles, started a campaign against the film. Hayakawa wrote in his autobiography, "Recalling my experiences in making this picture [*The Cheat*] brings to mind the opposition my playing the role of the villainous Japanese stirred among those of my nationality in Los Angeles and throughout the country after the film was released. For portraying the heavy, as screen villains are called, as a Japanese, I was indignantly accused of casting a slur on my nationality."[26]

The *Rafu Shimpo* criticized *The Cheat* by insisting that the film "distorted the truth of Japanese people" and would "cause anti-Japanese movements." A report in the *Rafu Shimpo* noted, "The film depicts Japanese people as outrageously evil. . . . This film would have a bad influence on people, living in places where there are not so many Japanese. They would come to think that the Japanese people are extremely savage. The film destroys the truth of the Japanese race. It is unforgivable for Japanese actors to appear in such a film, even for money."[27]

Another report in the paper similarly stated,

> The issue of Japanese exclusion is a big problem not just between the U.S. and Japan, but in the world. The intellectuals in both the U.S. and in Japan have made every effort to solve this problem. Our people in the U.S. have experienced many troubles and hardships, and 60 million Japanese people have been extremely patient in order to solve this problem. Under such conditions, how could Hayakawa, despite his blood of Japanese race, shamelessly appear in an anti-Japanese film, which leaves an impression of extremely evil Japanese? You, traitor to your country!! . . . The Japanese Embassy should do something to prevent this film from being exhibited.[28]

The *Rafu Shimpo* reported many incidents in which Japanese people were attacked by "white bad boys" after the release of *The Cheat.* A report noted, "Bad boys, who were crowded in front of the Tally Theater [where *The Cheat* was being played] and crying out anti-Japanese words, lynched a Japanese noodle shop owner, who came out of the theater, as Hayakawa was lynched in the courtroom scene." The report concluded, "the influence of the anti-Japanese film is doubtless."[29]

As a response to these serious criticisms against his character, Hayakawa had to quickly publish a note of apology in the *Rafu Shimpo* on 29 December. He wrote, "Sincere Notice: It is regrettable that the film *The Cheat*, which was exhibited at the Tally Theater on Broadway in Los Angeles, unintentionally offended the feelings of the Japanese people in the U.S. From now on, I will be very careful not to do harm to Japanese communities."[30]

Yet, the campaign against *The Cheat* continued after Hayakawa's apology. In February 1916, members of the Japanese Association of Southern California filed a protest against the showing of *The Cheat* with the Los Angeles City Council. The *Rafu Shimpo* reported almost every day until March 1916 the news about the Japanese Association's effort to ban *The Cheat* from playing in theaters. As a result, when *The Cheat* was re-released in 1918 because of popular demand, Hayakawa's character's nationality was changed from Japanese to Burmese in order not to excite anti-Japanese sentiment because Japan and the United States were allies during World War I. In the re-release version, which is the only version now extant, Hayakawa's Japanese character became a Burmese ivory king, Haka Arakau, by a change in intertitles.

Across the Pacific, in Japan, after *The Cheat* caused the anti-exhibition campaign in Japanese communities in the United States, Hayakawa's name was widely reported in newspapers and magazines for the first time. Hayakawa was scandalously introduced to Japanese spectators as a person who was recklessly enhancing anti-Japanese sentiment in the United States. Hayakawa was called "a cooperator in anti-Japanese propaganda films like *The Typhoon* and *The Cheat*." He was labeled as a "traitor" for appearing in such "insults to the nation."[31] The Japanese film magazine *Katsudo no Sekai* criticized Hayakawa's Japanese character in *The Cheat* as "a slave of carnal desire" and called Hayakawa an "unforgivable national traitor."[32] *The Cheat* was not released in Japan in the 1910s. It was imported in 1923 but never had a chance to be released.[33] Lasky and Paramount, the producer and the distributor of *The Cheat* in the United States, did not have a distribution branch in Japan at that time, which was the direct reason that most of Hayakawa's films did not come to Japan until 1918, when Hayakawa established Haworth Pictures Corporation, his own production company.[34] Yet, at the same time, there was no enthusiastic request for Hayakawa's films in Japan because they were considered too shameful to Japanese audiences.[35] As a result, for several years, Hayakawa had an extremely notorious reputation among Japanese spectators who knew him in name only. Okina Kyuin, a novelist and journalist who spent eighteen years in the United States, from 1907–24, wrote in 1930, "He [Hayakawa] made his way into the world with the success of *The Cheat*, but at the same time, he was cursed by the Japanese people with the success of *The Cheat*."[36] Thus, the success of *The Cheat* and Hayakawa's performance in the film had a huge transnational impact, positive and negative, in the history of cinema, and in the history of the sociopolitical relationship between the United States and Japan as well.

Hayakawa had appeared in many films with Japanese subject matter before *The Cheat* at the New York Motion Picture Company (NYMPC) and some others at Lasky. Yet, these films did not provide Hayakawa with as tremendous and sensational a success as *The Cheat*. Thomas H. Ince, the managing director at the NYMPC, never publicized Hayakawa as his star. What was different about *The Cheat?* What made Hayakawa stand out as a potential American star?

Thematically, most of the films in which Hayakawa appeared before *The Cheat* were set in faraway lands. In these films, Japanese people were objects to be looked at, but not people for American audiences to encounter in everyday life. Japan existed outside of the American domestic sphere. This image of Japan as a faraway land to be looked at in these early films was rooted in the nineteenth-century illustrated travel lecture, which was "a predominant form of magic lantern entertainment in America."[37] Such popular lecturers as John L. Stoddard and E. Burton Holmes, who actually spent five months in Japan in 1892, often talked about Japan and its people and drew mainly middle-class audiences. In contrast, in *The Cheat*, the Japanese man actually lives among white middle-class Americans.

There were actual human encounters between Japanese men and white American women in the middle-class domestic sphere in the Pacific states by the 1910s. Many male Japanese immigrants, who had entered the United States since the 1830s, were hired as domestic servants or valets. In contrast to Japanese art, which had been brought into the middle-class domestic sphere for the purpose of refining the home, Japanese immigrants, working as helping hands in the houses of white families, were often seen as a threat. The historian Robert G. Lee claims that the employment of the male Japanese servant to do "women's work" destabilized the gendered nature of labor. According to Lee, Japanese domestic servants were often regarded as a "third sex," which is "an alternative or imagined sexuality that was potentially subversive and disruptive to the emergent heterosexual and monoracial orthodoxy."[38] Japanese people, as opposed to Japanese art, could create threatening desires across race (multiracial), sex (homoerotic), and class and disturb conventional gender roles. Japanese in the middle-class American domestic sphere thus occupied an ambiguous middle-ground position between refined objects and threatening (human) subjects.

In fact, many tragic incidents were reported as a result of encounters between white women and Japanese men in the American domestic sphere. According to a report in the *Rafu Shimpo*, a married white woman named Mabel Smith shot to death Iguchi Eitaro, her Japanese lover, in July 1915.[39] The report noted, "Smith's husband knew the Japanese man as a nice guy. . . . During their three-year love affair, the Japanese man bought her clothes, and so forth. . . . The white woman got jealous when she heard that the Japanese man dated another woman. . . . The woman shot Iguchi when she thought he attacked her. . . . She said she killed Iguchi out of jealousy first, but she testified that she shot Iguchi to defend herself from him, who attacked her and her husband."[40] As in *The Cheat*, the white woman was declared not guilty on the grounds of self-defense.

In another case, a Japanese employee, Matsuno Shinkichi, was arrested because it was said that he threatened a white housewife with a pistol in order to rape her. The *Rafu Shimpo* reported, "The truth was . . . the housewife liked Matsuno very much and gave him extra money and her handkerchief, etc. Matsuno behaved carefully for a year because he had decided to marry a Japanese woman from Japan as soon as possible. One day, she woke up Matsuno in the middle of the night and took his hand and led him to the front door to check whether it was locked. The same thing happened the next day, and it is impossible to report here what kind of relationship they began to have then."[41]

The cases of Iguchi and Matsuno resembled that in *The Cheat*. They were tragic love affairs between married white women and rich Japanese men or Japanese servants. The white women were attracted to Japanese men and eventually destroyed them. Since these cases were reported when the *Rafu Shimpo* was conducting its campaign against *The Cheat*, the affinities of the situations stood out. *The Cheat* surely exploited such encounters between white American middle-class women and Japanese immigrants in the domestic sphere.

Hayakawa's rise as a prominent figure in *The Cheat* and the formation of his star image after *The Cheat* had a close relationship to these encounters. When the popular American cultural and racial imagination of Japan was connected to the discourse of the American middle-class domestic sphere, especially to that of gender politics, a strong momentum for Hayakawa's stardom was born.

More specifically, a white woman's sexual and economic transgression is metaphorically and metonymically expressed in the form of Japanese Taste and the yellow peril in *The Cheat*. The film historian Sumiko Higashi argues, "The threat of sexual difference, represented by the demands of the 'new woman' . . . in a materialistic consumer culture, is displaced onto ethnic difference" in *The Cheat*.[42] Japanese objets d'art and the Japanese art dealer played by Hayakawa function as racialized rhetoric of consumption and the New Woman.

Historically, Japanese Taste and the yellow peril co-existed and formed ambivalent popular discourses on Japan in the early twentieth century. They were not simply antithetical but intersected in a complicated manner, especially in the middle-class domestic sphere. Japanese Taste in the middle-class home symbolized the fact that the gendered construction of the middle-class domestic sphere was extended to the turn-of-the-century racial paradigm.

Japanese Taste was the use of Japanese motifs, decorative style, and objects in the Western home with "congeries of attributes: physical, philosophical, moral, and educational" from the late 1870s.[43] Japan was first articulated in the American imagination through its arts, goods, and culture that were accepted favorably in accordance with the middle-class discourse on arts and the home.

After the forceful "opening" of Japan to the West in 1853 following the arrival of a U.S. naval squadron under the command of Commodore Matthew Perry, commerce between the United States and Japan was established. In the exchange, American male intellectuals, who were hired by the Japanese government to teach and consult in many areas, became the first "Japanologists," introducing Japanese culture to Americans. Many Japanologists were upper-class men from New England, such as Edward Sylvester Morse, who collected thousands of Japanese vernacular tools and daily objects, and Ernest F. Fenollosa, who became a curator at the Boston Museum of Fine Arts, who brought their knowledge about Japan to Americans as high culture.[44] In the 1870s Japanese goods penetrated American markets, following the European vogue of *Japonisme* in art and style. Because Japanese culture, art, and design were introduced by upper-class men or imported as European vogue, they were considered high art in the beginning.

After the Centennial Exhibition of 1876, when many middle-class Americans encountered Japanese art for the first time, upscale Japanese Taste became gradually popularized. The first height of Japanese Taste came in the 1885–89 period, when the number of publications on the social trend was peaking in popular magazines. Lafcadio Hearn, the most influential writer to interpret Japanese culture for genteel society, published a number of works in *Harper's Magazine* and others and introduced Japanese culture in the form of artifacts, architecture, natural scenery, religious beliefs, folk tales, and so forth, to middle-class female readers.

In this middle-class notion of Japanese Taste, Japanese art, design, and culture were nostalgically regarded as premodern and primitive and highly valued as an alternative or an antithesis to the modernity that was threatening the concept of Victorian morality.[45] Compared with Western "progress" in art, the painter John La Farge claimed in 1893, the "simplicity of attitude" of Japanese painters was that of "children."[46] Their childlike simplicity was an attribute of inherent sincerity, and, in terms of the Christian desire to reach heaven, was more expedient than extreme erudition and modern, scientific technique.

More specifically, Japanese Taste came to reflect "an exemplum of middle-class women's desire to carry out moral reforms in their own households and to present their families and themselves favorably to the public," and Japanese art was considered to incorporate "a number of moral and spiritual qualities."[47] In the industrialization, mechanization, urbanization, and the development of materialism in the 1880s, a wide range of magazines mainly targeted for women discussed the roles of both home and women in terms of their moral influence on the family. The cult of domesticity, or the idea of home as an agent of "Christian nurture," was propounded in such magazine articles. Home became regarded as a place that would provide physical shelter and artistic and general education for the whole family in order to contain the deepening contradictions between the new urban life and the older ideals of community, family, and social order.[48]

Japanese art was used in Christian homes to enhance morality, purity, and good taste, but the use was only justifiable by its evocative relationship between nature and religion in the imagination of the American middle class. That is, in the American domestic sphere, Japan was located in a middle-ground position in a cultural hierarchy: morally and artistically refined on the one hand, and premodern and primitive on the other.

Together with Japanese Taste, there was another discourse on Japan in the popular American imagination in the early twentieth century: the one that viewed Japan as a modernizing nation, often with the image of a political and economic threat. In such a view, Japan's modernization was a fanatical ultra-nationalistic patriotism in service to its emperor, and the Japanese were thus ultimately different from other Western modernized nations. Alfred T. Mahan, a captain of the U.S. Navy and an influential writer on American foreign policy, had a high estimation of Japan's "remarkable capacity and diligence in the appropriation and application of European ways." At the same time, Mahan insisted that ultimately Japan is "Asiatic," and "it must . . . be recognized and candidly accepted that difference of race characteristics . . . entails corresponding temporary divergence of ideal and of action, with consequent liability to misunderstanding, or even collision."[49]

American people largely admired Japan's fast-paced modernization, which had occurred since its "opening" to the West. However, especially after the Russo-Japanese War of 1904–5, when Japan's military power became obvious, anti-Japanese sentiment developed in the Pacific states, where the number of Japanese immigrants was steadily increasing.[50] Japanese immigrants became regarded as a threat because Japanese immigration was seen in the light of Japanese military power. Together with the specter of Japanese immigration, the fear of Japanese expansion into China, where the U.S. government had substantial interests, or a Japanese invasion of the mainland United States or the Philippines and Hawaii, which had come under American control, appeared.

Yellow journalism spread the discourse of the yellow peril in sensational articles and books.[51] In February 1905, a series of articles that regarded Japanese immigration as the "problem of the day" appeared in the *San Francisco Chronicle*. The *Chronicle* stated that

Japanese immigrants would pose "a threat to American working men, American women, schoolchildren and the white race in general" because they were unable or unwilling to assimilate to the Anglo-American way of life.[52] Valentine Stuart McClatchy, an anti-Japanese agitator in San Francisco, called Japanese immigrants an "incoming yellow tide."[53] Jack London, who went to Asia as a journalist during the Russo-Japanese War, expressed his fear of Japan's expansion in his essay "Yellow Peril" (1904). The laboring classes in the Pacific states came to believe that Japanese immigrants achieved their working opportunities unfairly or dishonorably and formed the Asiatic Exclusion League in May 1905.

Except for those who were living in the Pacific states and facing immigrants from Asia in their daily lives, Japan's threat was still an ambiguous issue, not yet seen as a serious "peril." The number of Japanese residents in the United States was still limited, and the economic threat from Japanese immigrants was not yet a nationally perceived problem. Even President Theodore Roosevelt, although he recognized the potential conflict between Japan and the United States over control of the Pacific, was irritated by the activities of the anti-Japanese agitators on the West Coast. Yet, the term "yellow peril" gradually came to appear in such magazines for middle-class readers as the *Nation, Outlook*, and the *North American Review*.

In accordance with such popular discourses of the period, the narrative of *The Cheat* emphasizes the double-edged images of Japan, Japanese Taste, and the yellow peril from the very beginning and connects them to the ambivalent conception of consumerism in the middle-class American home, refinement and over-consumption. The first two scenes introduce the twofold image of the Japanese art dealer, Hishuru Tori. While the first scene implies Tori's threatening and primitive characteristics, the second scene shows how the same Japanese man looks Americanized and assimilated to American high society on the surface. The second scene also emphasizes that the Japanese man attracts a white woman by his refined and luxurious lifestyle.

The first shot of *The Cheat* after the title and credits is a medium shot of Tori in extremely low-key lighting. He is wearing a black Japanesque robe and a serious facial expression. Seated at his desk against a completely black backdrop, he brands a small objet d'art with his symbol mark (*torii*, a Japanese word meaning a shrine gate), using an iron poker from an Asian-style brass brazier. A line of smoke ominously rises from the brazier. He turns off the light with a satisfied expression and puts a lattice cover on the brazier. The glow of the brazier casts shadows of cross stripes on his face as though horrifying makeup has created a sinister mask.

The Cheat is famous for its innovative Rembrandt-like extreme low-key lighting effects that bathe characters in darkness but for a single source of illumination from the side. The film historian Lea Jacobs argues that in the DeMille films in 1915–16 "lighting is quite baldly used to create striking pictures which punctuate and heighten dramatic situations" and those films were "actually much *more* careful to motivate and integrate effects lighting than later classical filmmakers would be and than DeMille himself would be by the late teens."[54] In the opening shot in *The Cheat*, these lighting effects clearly enhance Tori's ominous and possibly villainous characteristics. Since this scene is directly followed by a medium shot of Richard Hardy (Jack Dean), a New York stockbroker, similarly seated at his desk but in uniform lighting, the effect of the low-key lighting in the first shot is emphasized. This scene clearly visualizes the ethnic and personality differences between Tori and the ordinary American gentleman.

While the introductory shot of Richard has a direct diegetic relationship with the following scene, the temporal connection between the shot of Tori in this opening and the next scene remains ambiguous. In the next scene Richard calls his wife, Edith, from the same office of the opening scene to scold her about her overconsumption. In contrast, the opening shot of Tori branding an object remains outside of the linear temporality of the narrative. It is unclear when this act of Tori's happens: Did it happen long before the actual story of *The Cheat* takes place? Does it happen in the middle of the story? Or is this simply Tori's habit? In either case, the temporal relationship between the first shot of Tori and the incidents in the narrative of *The Cheat* stays unclear. As a result, the major function of the first shot becomes to provide Tori with an innate ominous characteristic.

In the original script, however, Tori is located in the actual narrative temporality. In this script, Tori is first introduced as "One of Long Island's Smart Set in smart American flannels" just "reading magazine or newspaper, and smoking."[55] When his servant in Japanese kimono comes in and hands him a hat, he "looks at watch—smiles—and rises to go" to pick up Edith. Yet, there is a handwritten note in pencil, added in a margin, that reads "Scene dyed Red, Black Drop, brazier of branding" and "his face shown in light from coals."[56] Because of the change in the script, Tori's mysterious foreign nature is located in an atemporal and archetypal space in the film version.

In contrast, the following scene adopts an entirely different lighting technique and a costume strategy in order to emphasize the other characteristics of Tori: his apparent Americanized quality. In this scene, Tori is depicted as a person who has been assimilated into Long Island high society. Wearing a white duster cap, casual tweed suit, and bow tie, Tori comes into the frame driving an expensive high-powered roadster in the flat high-key lighting of daytime. He is about to escort Richard's wife, Edith, to the Red Cross Fund Bazaar. He jauntily runs up the steps. When he enters Edith's room, he shakes hands with her and gives her a relaxed smile. In the script, in this scene, Tori gets angry when Edith tells him that Richard objects to her extravagance and to her seeing him. According to the script, Tori thinks he "would like to wring [Edith's] husband's neck." However, in the film, Tori's anger is not displayed on the screen. A handwritten note in the script crosses out this display of Tori's anger in order to emphasize Tori's cheerful, gentle, and restrained nature in this particular scene.

On their way back from the Red Cross Bazaar, Tori opens the door of his car for Edith, and when Edith stumbles, he gently helps her to get up. In the script, "for just a second he holds her close—Edith is confused," and "Tori abruptly lets Edith go—as if coming to himself and bows—deeply respectful—Edith holds out her hand to Tori, striving to be at ease." However, on the screen Edith does not show any confusion. With his gentle behavior, Tori looks well assimilated into the American way of life.

In addition to their differences of ethnicity and personality, another significant difference between the two gentlemen, Tori and Richard, is implied in this second scene. Tori does not have to work during the day, while Edith's husband, a typical middle-class American, is working in the stock market. Tori appears in the main narrative right after Richard blames Edith for her expenditure on luxuries. As soon as Tori hears Edith say "He's [Richard is] forcing me to give up everything," he replies, "Can't I help? No one need know." This line, which tempts Edith to the forbidden pleasure of overconsumption, is the first line spoken by Tori in *The Cheat*. The rich Japanese art collector is the man who can satisfy her desire for leisure and luxuries. Thus, the narrative of *The Cheat* connects a white woman and a Japanese man within the American domestic sphere via the transgressive attraction of leisure and consumption.

In reality, both consumerism and Japanese Taste had twofold meanings and functions in middle-class families. Therein lay a paradoxical situation of American modernization. On the one hand, there was an economic structure based on consumerism, and on the other hand, there were social values based on traditional Puritan ethics about productive and restrained behavior, which were linked with Victorian morality. In order to satisfy both of these imperatives, middle-class women had to spend money in order to display genteel status but to spend within reason and on appropriate objects for their families and for the consumerist economy. According to the film scholar Janet Staiger, "Women were important in the expansion of consumption into the realm of pleasure and leisure," and, simultaneously, a woman was "articulating the status of her family" by her dress, belongings, and furniture in the home; this became considered to be part of a woman's job.[57] During the period of the popularity of Japanese Taste among middle-class Americans, the collection of Asian art was an integral part of these women's assertions of their social positions both as cultural leaders and as New Women.[58] Japanese art and culture were recognized as having refined standards and high moral values that could be incorporated by Western civilizations and into the domestic sphere, while at the same time they should be financially and spatially contained in order not to threaten the image of Western gentility they projected.

Edith's words to Richard, when she is criticized for her expenditures, appropriately summarize middle-class women's new role of "conspicuous consumption," purchasing expensive clothes and exotic Asian objects to express her family's social status to other people. She says, "I must have new gowns for the Red Cross affairs." As a treasurer of the Red Cross Fund, Edith's voluntary charity work also symbolizes the "conspicuous leisure" of her upper middle-class life. In 1899 Thorstein Veblen published *The Theory of the Leisure Class*, based on his observation of late-nineteenth-century American society. Veblen argued that the wealthier an individual the more able he is—and the more necessary it is—to adopt an affluent lifestyle, with a strong emphasis on waste, to demonstrate to others an ability to consume time and goods in nonproductive ways ("conspicuous leisure" and "conspicuous consumption"). This is because the ostentatious display of goods and services that are both expensive and highly valued by others provides the individual with a path to social prestige in any society, which recognizes wealth as a major determinant by which status is conferred. Furthermore, according to Veblen there comes a point on the economic scale, as the social order descends, where the husband must work to support his family and so he passes the responsibility for conspicuous leisure to his wife. Similarly, if the husband is obliged to forego conspicuous expenditure then the responsibility for maintaining a socially "decent" level of conspicuous consumption to maintain an "expected" standard of living falls on the wife.[59]

Despite the fact that his assumptions and conclusions were empirically unfounded or unproven, Veblen's views on conspicuous consumption in American society went largely unchallenged and were accepted as the basis to condemn ostentatious economic display as a social evil in the United States in the years leading up to World War I.[60] *The Cheat*'s characterization of Edith as a conspicuous consumer and the eventual restriction of her behavior should be located in this context of the theorization and condemnation of conspicuous consumption. Edith, as a wealthy middle-class wife, is required to have conspicuous leisure and consumption, of Japanese Taste, in particular, in order to display the expected standard of living, but to have them at a socially decent level. Edith, as a New Woman, is expected to reconcile her consumer desire and sexual freedom with traditional obligations to her family and society.[61]

Richard himself understands the necessity of his wife's "conspicuous" behavior for generating and maintaining the appearance of the appropriate middle-class family life. Therefore, he cannot respond to Edith's words, "If you want me to give up my friends and social position—well—I won't." Richard is not mad at her spending itself. He is irritated because Edith is on the verge of overconsumption and about to lose the respectability of their middle-class family life.

Throughout its narrative, *The Cheat* substitutes and enhances a fear of overconsumption with a fear of racial hybrids.[62] The film's melodramatic binary structure attributes the cause of Edith's overconsumption to the racially and culturally inassimilable and threatening Japanese man. Edith's words to Tori, "My husband objects to my extravagance—and you," not only explicitly indicate that Japanese Taste is an integral part of her behaviors of consumption but also imply Edith's possible sexual transgression. The Japanese man is not only the rich art collector who brings refined products of Japanese Taste to her home but is also a consumable object himself in her domestic space. Tori's luxurious costume and belongings, including his beautiful car, and his words "Can't I help? No one need know," function in the narrative as a tempting but threatening voice of overconsumption and implicit miscegenation. Eventually, the white American man controls the white woman's overconsumption by regulating the nonwhite man's economic and sexual transgression.

The scene at Tori's low-key lighted Japanesque shoji room during the evening of the Red Cross Ball clearly connects the threat of overconsumption and the fear of miscegenation. The shoji room, with its proliferation of Japanese objects, not only represents Tori's luxurious lifestyle, which Edith appreciates, but also functions to reinforce Tori's ultimately inassimilable Japanese cultural and racial traits.

The contrast between the shoji room where Tori and Edith enjoy looking at Japanese objects and the main room where the ball is held is particularly emphasized in the script. While the main room is a "gorgeous combination of modern luxury and oriental beauty—*Not* typically Japanese as is the *Shoji* Room," the shoji room is "the typically Japanese room" with "Shoji Doors," "The Shrine of Buddha," a "gold screen," a "tall black vase full of cherry blossoms," and a "brazier of coals with small branding iron."[63] When Edith finds a brand of Tori's seal on the bottom of a small wooden statue of Buddha in the room, Tori demonstrates how to brand and explains to Edith, "That means it belongs to me." Edith gets "confused," according to the script, or even looks frightened on the screen and retreats back into the rear of the room toward the shrine of Buddha. She "tries to throw confusion off by laughing lightly." Yet, Tori remains at the table for a while with a poker in his hands and his expression shows he has something on his mind. Here, for the first time since the introductory shot, the strong Rembrandt-like sidelight emphasizes the contrast of light and shadow on Tori's face, even though, at this point, Tori does not obviously show his villainous characteristics in his gestures or in his facial expressions.

Right after this, Edith's friend tells her that her stock investment using the Red Cross money has failed. When Edith faints, Tori kneels beside her, turns off the light, carries her out of the room, and hides in a dark corridor behind a shoji. In the off-screen light and the blue toning that imitate the moonlight, Edith's skin looks strikingly white. There, Tori steals a kiss. The sense of stealing is more emphasized on the screen, especially in the low-key lighting effects, than in the script and makes the scene more threatening.[64] The scene is much more romantically described in the script than on the screen. In the script, Tori brings the unconscious Edith to a bench in the garden, and "struck with her beauty and helplessness," he kisses her.

When Edith becomes conscious, she is scared by the thought of a newspaper headline, "EXTRA! SOCIETY WOMAN STEALS RED CROSS FUND," which is visually shown on the screen in double exposure. Tori leans closer to Edith and offers her money "if she will come to him," as the script is written, even though the intertitles on the screen never clearly state the line nor the details of their agreement. An intertitle states, "Do you agree?" before Tori signs his ten thousand dollar check for Edith and adds, "Tomorrow" after Tori hands the check to her. Here, *The Cheat* becomes a horrifying narrative of a fallen woman becoming a white slave under Asian despotism (see fig. 16.1).

The horror of miscegenation as a result of transgressive consumption reaches its height in the following scene after the intertitle declares, "The Cheat." The day after the ball, Edith comes back to Tori's place to return the money. Declaring that "You can't buy me off," Tori tries to assault her. He tears her clothes, grabs her hair, and throws her face forward onto the desk. In a close-up, Tori with the branding iron comes closer and closer to Edith's bare shoulder, and the iron almost reaches the white flesh. The lighting from the brazier casts ominous shadows on Tori's face and creates a horrifying expression. The branding itself is completed off screen, but the smoke comes up from off screen in front of Tori, who is grimacing with a tightly closed mouth.[65] His expression looks like a kabuki actor's exaggerated

Figure 16.1 A still from *The Cheat*

and temporally static face before entering his climactic violent act, *mie*, circling his head once, opening his eyes wide, raising his eyebrows, and glaring fiercely. The strongly contrastive makeup that emphasizes Tori's black eyebrows, slanted eyes, and red lips reminds viewers of a special makeup technique of kabuki actors who play violent acts (*kumadori*) that suggests extremes of hatred or anger.

Moreover, in this scene, Tori wears a Japanese-style dressing gown over his Western-style evening dress, white tie, and tuxedo shirt. Even though he wears the gown over his shirt, it serves to represent his Japanese traits that are hidden behind the Westernized surface. The script emphasizes the "oriental" atmosphere surrounding Tori in this scene. Tori is "standing under big oriental light over table" and "another lantern remains lighted over shoji door leading outside." Tori's property—the gown, the poker, the brazier, the shoji, the Japanese garden that Edith has to pass through, and the Japanese servants—all change from attractive consumable objets d'art of Japanese Taste into dangerous weapons and an ominous backdrop for the eruption of Tori's hidden threat. Thus, the horrifying action of this scene is achieved by emphasizing the Japanese traits that exploit the makeup and the facial expression of kabuki and the "oriental" costume and objects. In this sense, Tori is the "cheat" who has hidden his Japaneseness under his disguise of a Westernized gentleman.

Yet, Edith is also the "cheat." She breaks her promise with him. Economically speaking, she should keep the promise, even if the promise is that she will be Tori's mistress. At the same time, Edith is about to deceive her husband. Morally speaking, Edith should stay faithful to her husband.

Eventually, the narrative of *The Cheat* represses the two "cheats," the heroine and the villainous Asian male, simultaneously under white American patriarchal control. First, Tori is a vehicle for white male desire. In their relationships with Edith, Richard and Tori become juxtaposed as masculine counterparts. When Tori attacks Edith, he is a victimizer. Tori's brutal way of treating Edith may be seen as the repressed desire of white men who have apparently become too civilized. With the contract and the branding, Edith is even treated as an object by Tori.

However, by the end of the film, Tori also turns into a victim of white male dominant society. Throughout the narrative of *The Cheat*, Tori is juxtaposed with Edith, the white woman, both visually and thematically, and portrayed as an effeminate character.[66] Even though Tori is a man, he does not find his place among men but among women. In the scene at the Red Cross Bazaar, Tori mingles only with women. The extreme long establishing shot of the bazaar and the following long shots show that Tori is introduced to other Red Cross women, surrounded by them, and chats cheerfully with them.

The pursuit of consumption connects Edith and Tori more fully. First, their elaborate costumes indicate the similarities between them. Edith appears in a striped coat, and Tori wears a striped shirt. The striped design may imply their twofold characteristics, refinement on the surface and hidden desire beneath. Then the two flirt in Tori's Japanesque shoji room, sharing the experience of admiring a woman's gorgeous kimono and looking at exquisite small objects on a table and a statue of Buddha seated before an incense burner releasing puffs of smoke into the air. Edith does not hide her happy excitement when she sees those objects. Tori offers the kimono to Edith, even though Edith refuses it after some hesitation. Tori playfully shakes a potted cherry and its blossom petals rain down on Edith. As Sumiko Higashi points out, this scene in the shoji room juxtaposes Edith and Tori as if they were two window shoppers at "a site replicating exotic displays in department stores," or two New Women, playing around in consumer culture.[67]

The branding sequence in the shoji room clearly emphasizes the visual equivalence between Tori and Edith. As Higashi points out, Edith is branded off screen and Edith shoots Tori off screen after his branding of her. Both lie diagonally on the tatami mat clutching their left shoulders in high angle shots.[68] We see the brand on Edith's left shoulder, and the shot wound on Tori's left shoulder. Each leans on the shoji while staggering with pain.

Eventually, both Tori and Edith come under white American patriarchal control. At the beginning of the twentieth century, with the increased participation of the New Woman in the suffrage, reform, and anti-imperialist movements and the increased presence of women and immigrants in the workplace and the spheres of commercialized leisure, white masculinity's privileged grip on political legitimacy, cultural authority, and social control appeared to loosen. *The Cheat* participated in "the discursive construction of a rejuvenated white masculinity that was manufactured in response to, and at the expense of . . . the new woman" and Japanese masculinity.[69] This is symbolically displayed in the final courtroom scene of the film. After Edith confesses what really happened at Tori's shoji room to the all-white male jury, the excited crowd, which previously included both men and women, becomes all white male.[70] Tori is arrested in the courtroom, surrounded by the mostly white male spectators. At the end of the scene, the white middle-class American husband embraces his penitent wife. The final shot of the film symbolizes the white woman's reintegration into the white male patriarchy. In a symbolical remarriage, Edith walks down the aisle of the courtroom, tightly embraced and protected by Richard. Edith's sexual and consumerist desires become "contained within the institutional framework of middle-class marriage and the family" and "the Victorian ideal of womanhood."[71]

Yet, as the courtroom scene indicates, no matter how similar Edith and Tori are, the narrative of *The Cheat* eventually makes an invidious distinction between the white woman and the Japanese man. The problem of female overconsumption in a white middle-class family is cleverly replaced in the end by the threat of the inassimilable Japanese. The morality tale of the attraction and threat of overconsumption is concluded in the form of the protection of the white middle-class family from transgressive foreignness by the white male. In order to defend the white woman and incorporate her into the American patriarchal system, the narrative of *The Cheat* puts all the blame on the Japanese man and excludes him from American society. An intertitle, "East is East and West is West and never the Twain shall meet," which is placed right before the final courtroom scene, clearly indicates the difference between the white woman and the Japanese man. At the climax of *The Cheat* the discourse of consumerism is finally differentiated from that of Japanese Taste, and the latter is overridden by the discourse of the yellow peril.

The largest difference between Tori and Edith is that Tori has almost no opportunity to speak out in court while Edith can speak out to make up for her mistake. In melodrama, in which muteness is a signal feature according to the literary critic Peter Brooks, the breaking of silence is a climactic declaration of personal identity and the confrontation of villainy.[72] Moreover, Janet Staiger argues, "For the middle class talk was becoming vital to protect the class from infringements upon its boundaries and to regulate the behavior of the New Woman and the New Man."[73] Edith experiences a conversion from an inappropriate New Woman, who has indulged in overconsumption, to a proper middle-class wife when she chooses to talk in the courtroom. Speaking up in the courtroom, she declares her personal identity and confronts the villain who embodies the peril of overconsumption and sexual transgression. Her expenditure, her overconsumption, and her improper entry into the world of men are forgiven because of her devoted public act of speech in the interest of her family.

In contrast, Tori is not allowed to speak up about what happened; he cannot tell the court about Edith's immoral conduct, which was tantamount to prostitution. No one questions why Edith was attacked. Edith does not take the heat for assault charges despite Tori's actions. Literally, the already concluded case is dismissed after Edith's nonofficial testimony without even a cross-examination of Tori.

Tori is not even permitted to express his emotion. The script gives eloquent expression to Tori's feelings, such that he smiles "with satisfaction" when Richard testifies that he shot Tori and that he "registers pleasure" at the verdict. Additionally, he shows "surprise and dissatisfaction" when Edith starts to talk. However, on the screen, Tori remains a speechless and emotionless object, despite several close-ups—sometimes irised—being inserted during the courtroom scene. Since there are no intertitles following those close-ups, Tori's emotion stays unexplained and much more ambiguous than Edith's. Tori sneers slightly only once during the trial when Richard testifies that he shot Tori and Edith. Also, he changes his expression slightly when Edith starts her desperate confession. Both of these changes in Tori's expression are so slight that they are not eloquent gestures that convey his entire thought or emotion, whereas Edith speaks out loudly with her exaggerated gestures: running to the judge with extended arms, wide open mouth, and eyes full of tears. Tori's emotionless facial expression and sardonic slight smile restrict him to the mere stereotypical image of Japanese despotism, rather than allow him to be a human being with psychological depth. Tori is given no opportunity to talk and no chance to deviate from an evil persona of a melodramatic villain.

In comparison, a film dealing archetypally with an all-American identity, such as Frank Capra's *Mr. Deeds Goes to Town* (1936), relies on the hero finally breaking his silence and speaking in public. Deeds's (Gary Cooper) willingness to speak, to express desire, comes in response to the woman's (Jean Arthur) courtroom declaration of her thought under cross-examination. Stanley Cavell calls the film "the comedy of equality and reciprocity" because Arthur's character grants Deeds "his wish to rescue, to be active, to take deeds upon himself, earning his name; as he grants her wish to her."[74] In contrast, we can call *The Cheat* a tragedy of inequality and non-mutuality because Edith never grants Tori his desperate wish to be active and to regain his reputation.

In the end, Tori is attacked by the dominantly male audience in the courtroom and bleeds from his mouth. The crowd yells, "Lynch him! Lynch him!" Historically, lynching was a punishment meted out to Negro men who had or were believed to have had sexual relations with white women. Tori turns into a stereotypical representation of the oversexualized nonwhite (racialized) male, a unidimensional villain because of his skin color, and a mere tool for the reunification of a white American patriarchal family. *The Cheat* thus integrated middle-class American discourses on family, gender, and race with American people's popular and stereotypical views of Japan. *Photoplay* called *The Cheat* "a melodrama so rational, so full of incisive character touches, racial truths."[75] Hayakawa's character embodied the popular twofold cultural and ethnic images of Japan, the refinement of Japanese Taste and the threat of the yellow peril, within a domestic melodrama that eventually supported white American patriarchy.

Contradictorily, although Hayakawa's lack of affect may silence him as a character in *The Cheat*, it opens up big potentiality for him to become a star. With his refined and villainous, apparently Americanized and ultimately inassimilable, role in *The Cheat*, Hayakawa vividly impressed the public consciousness. This ambivalent coexistence of refinement (Japanese Taste) and threat (the yellow peril), Americanization and Japaneseness, which is eventually controlled under the white patriarchy, became an essential core of Hayakawa's star image. Even in 1920, a review of *An Arabian Knight* (Charles Swickard, 22 August 1920), a Hayakawa star vehicle, noted, "Whenever we hear of Sessue Hayakawa we think of 'The Cheat,' a five-reel production made about five years ago and to this day considered as the best example of photodramatic work ever presented on any screen. . . . And whenever we think of 'The Cheat' we think of Sessue Hayakawa because he was, in a big measure, instrumental in making 'The Cheat' the excellent production that it was."[76]

No matter how sensational Hayakawa's role in *The Cheat* was, it was not a result of Lasky's careful star-making plan. It was rather an accident. Hayakawa was only one of the supporting actors for Lasky. Hayakawa was originally engaged by Lasky in March 1915 to support Ina Claire with an "important" role.[77] Yet, Claire ended up making her debut on screen in a comedy, *The Wild Goose Chase* (June 1915), in which there was no role for Hayakawa. Instead, Hayakawa appeared in several supporting roles for Blanche Sweet before being chosen to support Ward in *The Cheat*.

Lasky was recruiting such renowned theatrical figures as David Belasco, a Broadway producer, and William DeMille, Cecil's brother and a celebrated playwright, and such famous stage actors as Claire, Ward, and the opera singer Geraldine Farrar to "upgrade" cinema for respectable middle-class audiences.[78] According to Higashi, Lasky was "prescient in developing a strategy to legitimate cinema for 'better' audiences and to appeal as well to the aspiring masses by demonstrating the intertextuality of cultural forms as spectacle in genteel society."[79] Lasky modeled films after stage productions already deemed part of so-called highbrow culture for middle- and upper-class consumption and exploited "the affinity between stage and screen in order to acquire cultural legitimacy during an era of progressive reform."[80]

Lasky cast Hayakawa to support these famous stage actresses for a specific reason. The company was particularly interested in Japanese Taste in cinema for its prestigious value to middle-class audiences. Lasky planned to produce a film of *The Darling of the Gods*, which originally opened on Broadway on 3 December 1902, and became a hit.[81] Lasky also wanted Belasco to come to California to supervise the filming of his plays, including "probably *Madame Butterfly*."[82] To Lasky, the Japanese actor Hayakawa was the perfect fit for these productions with Japanese subjects. Hayakawa and his image of embodying Japanese Taste were to enhance the legitimate quality of the company's films. The NYMPC, which first used Hayakawa and other Japanese people to make films with Japanese subjects, had publicized that Hayakawa had a background in the Japanese theatrical arts. In reality, Hayakawa did not have any theatrical career in Japan, but the promotional biography made by the NYMPC was persuasive enough for the studio producers at Lasky to hire him to support renowned stage actresses.

Not only Lasky, but also Paramount Pictures Corporation, which distributed the Lasky films, was interested in films with Japanese subjects for their prestige status for middle-class audiences. One article in Paramount's own promotional magazine stated, "Lafcadio Hearn's wonderful word-paintings are like memorial pictures done with the golden brush of a master on panels of ivory, and he is only one of many who have contributed to our joy and interest in that Land of the Lotus Flower. Prominent among the ceremonies, feasts and celebrations which have become known to us through books and the drama and lately through motion pictures, in the Japanese play 'The Typhoon,' as representative of the social and religious habits of that people of the distant Empire of the Northern Pacific, none is more appealing and beautiful than the feast of Nobori No Sekku."[83] Paramount even distributed a NYPMC film with Japanese subjects, *The Typhoon* (Reginald Barker, 8 October 1914), even though the Mutual Film Corporation usually distributed NYMPC films.[84]

However strongly Lasky and Paramount were interested in the prestige status of the films with Japanese subjects, they did not consider making a star out of Hayakawa before the success of *The Cheat*. Before *The Cheat*, Hayakawa only played small roles like those of Japanese spies disguised as valets waiting for an opportunity to lay hands on valuable documents and to violently murder people in *After Five* (Oscar Apfel and Cecil B. DeMille, 28 January 1915) and *The Clue* (James Neill and Frank Reicher [credited as Frank Reichert], 8 July 1915). He also played a villainous Chinese "hop joint proprietor" who lures the innocent Blanche Sweet into opium addiction in a labyrinth-like den in San Francisco's Chinatown that is filled with stereotypically vicious Chinese faces in *The Secret Sin* (Frank Reicher, 21 October 1915). The *New York Dramatic Mirror* (*NYDM*) juxtaposed Hayakawa with other "Celestial actors."[85] *Variety* even spelled his name incorrectly, "Succo Hayakawa," and possibly considered his ethnicity to be Italian in its review of *After Five*.[86] These mistakes in trade journals indicate that Hayakawa was regarded as just another nonwhite supporting actor even in his early work with Lasky.

The Cheat was merely another film for Hayakawa to play a supporting Japanese character. Not only does the opening title of *The Cheat* feature Fannie Ward as the star of the film, but

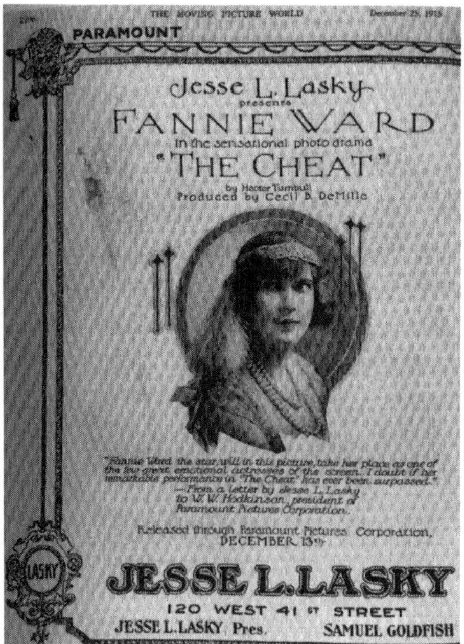

Figure 16.2 An advert for *The Cheat*. *Moving Picture World* 26.14 (25 December 1915): 2296

all of the advertisements of the film in trade journals before the film's release also treated Ward as the star, while they almost completely neglected Hayakawa (see fig. 16.2).

In spite of the fact that Jesse L. Lasky praised Hayakawa's performance in *The Cheat* before its release, he did not think of Hayakawa's potentiality of becoming a star at that point. Lasky did not say that he would produce star vehicles for Hayakawa.[87] When another film with Hayakawa in a supporting role as a Japanese valet, *Temptation*, starring the famous opera singer Geraldine Farrar, was released right after *The Cheat*, there was almost no publicity about his minor appearance in it.[88] Lasky and Paramount recognized Hayakawa as their potential star only when *The Cheat* achieved a huge box office success and the popular

Figure 16.3 Portraits of Sessue Hayakawa and other popular film stars of 1916.
Motion Picture News 14.16 (21 October 1916): 2545

recognition of Hayakawa became sensational; at this point their attempts to make Hayakawa their star finally started (see fig. 16.3).

As the forerunners of the star system in early Hollywood, Lasky and Paramount carefully prepared for Hayakawa's first star vehicle and planned how they should promote Hayakawa as a star. When *Alien Souls* (Frank Reicher, 11 May 1916) was finally released after a five-month gap, Hayakawa was no longer simply a capable supporting performer with a Japanese cultural stereotype. He became a star of the Famous Players-Lasky Corporation and Paramount Pictures Corporation.[89] After *Alien Souls*, fifteen star vehicles were made for Hayakawa at Famous Players-Lasky and distributed by Paramount between 1916 and 1918.[90] When *The Cheat* was re-released in 1918, not Ward but Hayakawa was publicized in trade journals as the star of the film.

In order to establish Hayakawa's star status, Lasky attempted to distinguish Hayakawa's own screen persona from the more pedestrian cultural stereotype roles accorded to Japanese people. Lasky also needed to carefully adjust his star image from the sensationally villainous one in *The Cheat* to a more appropriate but equally attractive one for middle-class audiences. Yet, before discussing Lasky's strategy in detail, I would like to go back in time a little and examine Hayakawa's film career before *The Cheat*. Before the success of *The Cheat* and before contracting with Lasky, Hayakawa appeared in many films at the NYMPC that stereotypically depicted Japan and its people. Hayakawa also played similarly stereotypical non-Japanese roles. What kind of stereotypes did the cinematic images of Japan, and other nonwhite cultures, contain, from which Lasky drew to distinguish Hayakawa's star image?

Notes

1 "Lasky and DeMille Enter Picture Field," *Motion Picture News* (*MPN*) (20 December 1913): 15; "Fannie Ward to Star for Lasky," *Moving Picture World* (*MPW*) 23.9 (6 March 1915): 1455; Holland, "Fannie Ward," 590–95.

2 *Wid's Daily* noted in 1918, " 'The Cheat,' in which this talented star [Hayakawa] began to acquire an individual following, proved an unusual box-office attraction at that time." *Wid's Daily* 5.66 (14 July 1918): 29.

3 "Lasky May Releases," *MPW* 28.6 (6 May 1916): 959.

4 "Fannie Ward as a Movie Tragedienne," in *The New York Times Film Reviews 1913–1968*, vol. 1, 1913–1931 (New York: Arno, 1970), 8.

5 *Variety* (17 December 1915): 18.

6 "Sessue Hayakawa," *MPW* 26.10 (4 December 1915): 1810.

7 Hayne, *The Autobiography of Cecil B. DeMille*, 150.

8 *New Orleans Times* (26 February 1916): n.p., in *SHE*.

9 *Wid's Films and Film Folk Independent Criticisms of Features* 1.17 (30 December 1915): 4.

10 *Exhibitor's Herald* (*EH*) 1.4 (4 December 1915): 18; *MPN* 12.23 (11 December 1915): 76; *Motography* 14.24 (11 December 1915): 1223.

11 *MPN* 13.15 (15 April 1916): 2209. As early as January 1916, *MPN* published a list of actors and actresses, and Hayakawa was listed under the category of "leads," not "supports." *MPN* 13.4 (29 January 1916): 44.

12 Numerous articles and books on Hayakawa were published in Europe, including "Sessue Hayakawa," *Invicta Cine* (Portugal) 3 (1 June 1923): 4–5, and "Um morto vivo: Sessue Hayakawa," *Cinefilo* (Portugal) 24 (2 February 1929): 11, 22. Leaflet magazines entirely dedicated to Hayakawa were published in Spain (Ferry and Moreno, "Sessue Hayakawa") and Russia (Ovanesov, *Sessue Hayakawa*).

13 Hammond and Ford, "French End Games," 330.

14 Colette, *Colette at the Movies*, 18.

15 Colette, *Colette at the Movies*, 19–20.

16 Abel, *French Film Theory and Criticism*, 110.

17 Doane, "The Close-Up," 89.

18 Thompson and Bordwell, *Film History*, 89, 92.

19 Léon Moussinac, "Cinématographie," 229–35. In 1932, Germaine Dullac emphasized the importance of *The Cheat* as the first American film that used the editing style based on "a psychological, emotive, and rhythmical logic." Before *The Cheat*, according to Dullac, "the pictures (tableaux) follow one after another independently from each other, bundled by one subtitle." Dullac, *Écrits sur le cinéma (1919–1937)*, 184, translation by Chika Kinoshita.

20 The Kawakami troupe started as "a purveyor of bitingly satirical antigovernment burlesques," which was called *oppekepe*. With his politically satirical dramas (*soshi shibai*), Kawakami supported *jiyu minken undo*, the people's rights movement, which was aimed at prevailing Western-style liberalism in Japan. The Kawakami troupe is often considered as a part of the *shingeki* movement, Japan's response to Ibsen and his contemporaries' realist reforms in Europe. Kawakami tried to modernize Japanese theaters with his original dramas that depicted the everyday lives of ordinary people and with his adopted European dramas, including *Othello* and *Hamlet*. In Kawakami's theater, Sadayakko, an actress, appeared on stage while female roles were played by an *onnagata*, a male impersonator, in most of the theaters in Japan. Y. Hayakawa, "Tsuru Aoki," 3–5, 16–18; Downer, *Madame Sadayakko*, 94–96, 113–14; Muramatsu, *Kawakami Otojiro (Jo)*, 160–61, 251–347; Muramatsu, *Kawakami Otojiro (Ge)*, 48–95; R. Yamaguchi, *Joyu Sadayakko* [The actress Sadayakko], 121–28.

21 In the United States, however, their tour was not financially successful. There was a strict regulation that prohibited a child from appearing on stage. Consequently, it became difficult for Kawakami to take Tsuru with them.

22 Fescourt and Bouquet, *L'Idée et l'écran*, 374.

23 Crisp, *Genre, Myth, and Convention in the French Cinema, 1929–1939*, 42. *The Cheat* was also remade in America in 1923, starring Pola Negri, and in 1931, starring Tallulah Bankhead. Hayakawa did not appear in either.

24 Stanley, *The New Grove Dictionary of Opera*, 68.

25 Colette, *Colette at the Movies, 35–36*. Later, Hayakawa produced his own play based on *The Cheat* in France in 1944. He did not play the role as mute, though.

26 Sessue Hayakawa, *Zen Showed Me the Way*, 136.

27 "Hainichi no tane o maku katsudo shashin" [Motion pictures that will cause anti-Japanese sentiment], *Rafu Shimpo* 3694 (23 December 1915): 3.

28 "Kyo ka oroka hainichi haiyu Hayakawa Sesshu" [Crazy or stupid, anti-Japanese actor Sessue Hayakawa], *Rafu Shimpo* 3695 (24 December 1915): 3.

29 "Nihon jin ashiki ka keisatsu muno ka" [Are the Japanese people bad, or the police incapable?], *Rafu Shimpo* 3698 (28 December 1915): 3; "Akudo no hainichi bodo" [Anti-Japanese riot by bad boys], *Rafu Shimpo* 3697 (26 December 1915): 1.

30 *Rafu Shimpo* 3699 (29 December 1915): 3.

31 *Osaka Mainichi Shinbun*, 23 February 1916, in *Shinbun shusei Taisho hennenshi*, 1916, vol. 1, (1980): 346.

32 *Katsudo no Sekai* 1.4 (April 1916): 41; SZO, "Katsudo omochabako" [Toy box of motion picture], 48.

33 *Katsudo Zasshi* 9.4 (April 1923): 147.

34 Aoyama, "Aren kun no Nihon kan" [Mr. Allen's view on Japan], 88.

35 Several Hayakawa films made at Lasky were released in Japan, including *Each to His Kind* (Edward Le Saint, 5 February 1917), *The Bottle Imp* (Marshall Neilan, 26 March 1917), *The Jaguar's Claws* (Neilan, 11 June 1917) in 1919, and *Forbidden Paths* (Robert T. Thornby, 5 July 1917), *The Victoria Cross* (William C. DeMille, 14 December 1916), and *The Hidden Pearls* (George H. Melford, 18 February 1918) in 1920. Most of them were the films in which Hayakawa did not play Japanese roles, except *Forbidden Paths*.

36 Okina, "Hayakawa Sesshu to Kamiyama Sojin" [Sessue Hayakawa and Sojin Kamiyama], 225.

37 Barber, "The Roots of Travel Cinema," 68–84.

38 Lee, *Orientals*, 88, 99–105.

39 "Shiro bijin Nihon jin koibito o jusatsu su" [A white beautiful woman shot a Japanese lover to death], *Rafu Shimpo* 3564 (20 July 1915): 3.

40 "Shiro bijin doho jofu goroshi zokkou kohan 4" [A white beautiful woman who killed her Japanese lover in court 4], *Rafu Shimpo* 3723 (28 January 1916): 3.

41 "Nihon jin no shufu gokan jiken shinso" [Truth about the rape of a housewife by Japanese], *Rafu Shimpo* 3725 (30 January 1916): 3.

42 S. Higashi, "Ethnicity, Class, and Gender in Film," 130.

43 J. Brown, "The 'Japanese Taste,' " 134.

44 See Notehelер, *Japan through American Eyes*.

45 J. Brown, " 'Fine Arts and Fine People,' " 123.

46 La Farge, "Bric-a-Brac," 427–29.

47 J. Brown, "The 'Japanese Taste,' " 1, 155; Lears, *No Place of Grace*, 42–43.

48 J. Brown, "The 'Japanese Taste,' " 337; Coontz, *The Social Origins of Private Life*, 224–36; Lee, *Orientals*, 86.

49 Mahan, *The Problem of Asia and Its Effect upon International Policies*, 108, 110.

50 Niiya, *Japanese American History*, 362. Beginning in 1900, the number of Japanese immigrants to the United States rose to more than ten thousand a year. Until 1906, the numbers were under 15,000 (except 1903), but in 1907 the number increased to 30,226. Commissioner General of Immigration, *Annual Report*, quoted in Iino, "Beikoku niokeru hainichi undo to 1924 nen iminho seitei katei" [Anti-Japanese movement in the U.S. and the enactment process of the 1924 immigration law], 32. In 1920, Japanese people owned approximately 16 percent of cultivated land for agriculture, which was obtained between 1910 and 1920. In 1910, the amount was only 0.4 percent, when the *San Francisco Chronicle* criticized Japanese immigrants by insisting that they were "not earnest" and "buying lands." State Board of Control of California, *California and the Oriental*, 8; U.S. Bureau of the Census, *Chinese and Japanese in the United States*, 43–44; Tupper and McReynolds, *Japan in American Public Opinion*, 22.

51 The term "yellow peril" was originally used by Kaiser Wilhelm II of Germany in 1898.

52 Quoted in Daniels, *The Politics of Prejudice*, 25. See also Daniels, *Asian America*, 109.

53 McClatchy, *Four Anti-Japanese Pamphlets*, 45.

54 Jacobs, "Belasco, DeMille and the Development of Lasky Lighting," 416. These lighting effects were marketed as "Lasky lighting" and associated with the work of DeMille, his cameraman Alvin Wyckoff, and the art director Wilfred Buckland, in the trade press.

55 Script of *The Cheat*, University of Southern California, Cine-TV Library, Special Collection.

56 According to Sumiko Higashi, this handwriting was DeMille's. S. Higashi, *Cecil B. DeMille and American Culture*, 108.

57 Staiger, *Bad Women*, 164, 179.

58 Yoshihara, *Embracing the East*, 15–43.

59 Veblen, *The Theory of the Leisure Class*; Mason, *Conspicuous Consumption*, 8–10.

60 Mason, *Conspicuous Consumption*, 12.

61 Trimberger, "The New Woman and the New Sexuality," 98–115.

62 Staiger, *Bad Women*, 170.

63 Emphasis in the original.

64 Tori in a tuxedo looks like a vampire figure in a black coat that approaches the white woman from the back. Diane Negra argues, "*Dracula* and other vampire myths represent the vampire first and foremost as a liminal figure, caught between an old world and a new one, at first a welcomed visitor but ultimately a new arrival who comes to be seen as a menace." Negra, "Immigrant Stardom in Imperial America," 168. Tori as a "liminal figure" from Japan can be located in this context of the vampire myths. In fact, the Canadian filmmaker Guy Muddin's film, *Dracula: Pages from a Virgin's Diary* (2002) depicts vampires as "immigrants" from "the East" and an Asian dancer and actor, Zhang WeiQiang, plays Count Dracula. Several "vampire" films had been released in the United States by the time *The Cheat* was released. *The Vampire* (Kalem, 1910) and *The Vampire* (Selig, 1913) were inspired by the "Vampire Dance" popularized in the early teens by Alice Eis and Bert French. Staiger, *Bad Women*, 151. In 1915, *A Fool There Was*, the film that made Theda Bara a sensational "vamp" star, was released. The vamp's iconography was characterized by her "pale skin and heavily made-up lips and eyes." Negra, "Immigrant Stardom in Imperial America," 183. Hayakawa's character, with "heavily made-up" eyebrows and pale skin, is similar to the vamp. The vampire image of Tori may enhance the fear of mixing blood and the destructive influence that he brings into America despite his superficially assimilated image.

65 For feminist film critics, these scenes in the shoji room "can be looked at as a fulfillment of secret, forbidden desires for the pleasures and freedoms [of women] promised by a love affair with a man of another race." Marchetti, *Romance and the "Yellow Peril,"* 22: S. Higashi, *Cecil B. DeMille and American Culture*, 107.

66 The ambiguous sexuality of Tori refers to that of Dr. Fu Manchu, the universally recognized early Oriental villain in pulp fiction created by Sax Rohmer (Arthur Sarsfield Ward). The first three novels, *The Insidious Dr. Fu Manchu* (1913). *The Return of Fu Manchu* (1916), and *The Hand of Fu Manchu* (1917), became popular in the United States in almost the same period when Hayakawa's stardom was being created. Fu Manchu's threat comes partly from his ability to shift his Chinese appearance to that of other nationalities. Also, Fu Manchu's power to incite the fevered imagination lies in his ambiguous sexuality, which combines a masochistic vulnerability marked as feminine and a sadistic aggressiveness marked as masculine.

67 S. Higashi, *Cecil B. DeMille and American Culture*, 104.

68 S. Higashi, *Cecil B. DeMille and American Culture*, 107.

69 Whissel, "The Gender of Empire," 141–42.
70 The script indicates that after Richard confirms that he shot Tori, a close-up of a group of three women in the audience, "who gossip pointing toward Edith," is to be inserted.
71 S. Higashi, *Virgins, Vamps, and Flappers*, 58.
72 Brooks, *The Melodramatic Imagination*, 56–80.
73 Staiger, *Bad Women*, 173.
74 Cavell, "What Photography Calls Thinking," 20–21.
75 *Photoplay* 9.4 (March 1916): n.p., in *SHE*.
76 *MPN* 22.10 (28 August 1920): 1755.
77 "Sessue Hayakawa to Support Ina Claire," *MPW* 23.11 (20 March 1915): 1779.
78 S. Higashi, "Cecil B. DeMille and the Lasky Company," 184–85. Cecil did not have a spectacular stage career, but the DeMilles are a distinguished Broadway family. S. Higashi, *Cecil B. DeMille and American Culture*, 1.
79 S. Higashi, "Touring the Orient with Lafcadio Hearn and Cecil B. DeMille," 332.
80 S. Higashi, "Cecil B. DeMille and the Lasky Company," 182–83.
81 *MPN* 9.22 (6 June 1914): 30.
82 *MPW* 23.3 (16 January 1915): 353.
83 "Japanese Customs in Motion Pictures," *Paramount Magazine* (March 1915): 7.
84 The conditions under which *The Typhoon* was made were complicated and unclear. The Paramount ad in *MPN* noted that the producer of *The Typhoon* was Paramount. *MPN* 10.13 (3 October 1914): 12. The review of *The Typhoon* in *Variety* ignored NYMPC and wrote that this film was "released by the Paramount, with no name of the manufacturing company given." *Variety* 36.13 (28 November 1914): 24. *Reel Life*, the promotional magazine of the Mutual, did not mention *The Typhoon* as its film at all. Yet, the NYMPC put an ad in *MPW* on 25 April 1914 announcing that the company would present the film "in the very near future, under the direction of Thomas H. Ince, The Imperial Japanese Company in Charles Swickard's version of The Typhoon." *MPW* 20.4 (25 April 1914): 549. According to Hayakawa, Paramount "bought" *The Typhoon*. "Popular Arts Project," Hayakawa-13. Paramount was adopting the Hodkinson system, which provided cash advances for production costs and guaranteed a minimum return to the producer. In exchange, Paramount received 35 percent of the proceeds for the right to distribute.
85 "Celestial" is an outdated slang for a Chinese person. *New York Dramatic Mirror* (*NYDM*) 73.1911 (21 July 1915): 27.
86 *Variety* 37.10 (6 February 1915): 23.
87 *EH* 1.4 (4 December 1915): 18; *MPN* 12.23 (11 December 1915): 76; *Motography* 14.24 (11 December 1915): 1223.
88 *MPN* 13.18 (6 May 1916): 2705. According to the dates written on the original scripts, the filming of *Temptation* started on 27 July 1915 and finished on 10 August 1915. It was released on 2 January 1916. The filming of *The Cheat* started on 20 October 1915 and finished on 10 November 1915, but it was released on 4 December 1915, earlier than *Temptation*. Script of *Temptation*, University of Southern California, Cine-TV Library, Special Collection.
89 91 *MPW* 28.15 (15 July 1916): 357; *MPN* 14.9 (2 September 1916): 1349. Famous Players and Lasky merged into Famous Players-Lasky Corporation in June 1916. Paramount Pictures Corporation had been a distributor of the productions of Lasky, the Famous Players Film Company, the Oliver Morosco Photo Play Company, and Pallas Pictures since 1914.
90 Sixteen films starring Hayakawa were made at Lasky starting with *Alien Souls*, but I do not consider *The Victoria Cross* (William C. DeMille, 14 December 1916) as a Hayakawa star vehicle. *The Victoria Cross* features Lou Telligan as the star, and Hayakawa as an Indian conspirator in a supporting role.

Bibliography

Abel, Richard. *French Film Theory and Criticism: A History/Anthology 1907–1939*. Volume 1, *1907–1929*. Princeton, N.J.: Princeton University Press, 1988.

Aoyama, Yukio. "Aren kun no Nihon kan" [Mr. Allen's view on Japan]. *Katsudo Shashin Zasshi* 3.12 (December 1917): 88–89.

Barber, X. Theodore. "The Roots of Travel Cinema: John L. Stoddard, E. Burton Holmes and the Nineteenth-Century Illustrated Travel Lecture." *Film History* 5.1 (1993): 68–84.

Brooks, Peter. *The Melodramatic Imagination: Balzac, Henry James, Melodruma, and the Mode of Excess.* 1976. Reprint, New Haven: Yale University Press, 1995.

Brown, Jane Converse. "'Fine Arts and Fine People': The Japanese Taste in the American Home, 1876–1916." *Making the American Home: Middle-Class Women and Domestic Material Culture 1840–1940*, ed. Marilyn Ferris Motz and Pat Browne, 121–39. Bowling Green, Ohio: Bowling Green State University Popular Press, 1988.

——. "The 'Japanese Taste': Its Role in the Mission of the American Home and in the Family's Presentation of Itself to the Public as Expressed in Published Sources: 1876–1916." Ph.D. diss., University of Wisconsin, Madison, 1987.

Cavell, Stanley. "What Photography Calls Thinking." *Raritan: A Quarterly Review* 4.4 (spring 1985): 1–21.

Colette. *Colette at the Movies: Criticism and Screenplays.* Trans. Sarah W. R. Smith. Ed. Alain Virmaux and Odette Virmaux. 1970. Reprint, New York: Frederick Ungar, 1980.

Coontz, Stephanie. *The Social Origins of Private Life: A History of American Families.* London: Verso, 1988.

Crisp, Colin. *Genre, Myth, and Convention in the French Cinema, 1929–1939.* Bloomington: Indiana University Press, 2002.

Daniels, Roger. *Asian America: Chinese and Japanese in the United States since 1850.* Seattle: University of Washington Press, 1988.

——. *The Politics of Prejudice: The Anti-Japanese Movement in California and the Struggle for Exclusion.* Berkeley: University of California Press, 1962.

Doane, Mary Ann. "The Close-Up: Scale and Detail in the Cinema." *Differences: A Journal of Feminist Cultural Studies* 14.3 (2003): 89–111.

Downer, Lesley. *Madame Sadayakko: The Geisha Who Seduced the West.* London: Review, 2003.

Dullac, Germaine. *Écrits sur le cinéma (1919–1937).* Paris: Paris Experimental, 1994.

Fescourt, Henri, and Jean-Louis Bouquet. *L'Idée et l'écran: Opinions sur le cinéma*, vol. 1. Paris: Haberschill and Sergent, 1925.

Hammond, Robert M., and Charles Ford. "French End Games: For Some American Silent Stars a Trip Abroad Was a Tonic for Ailing Careers." *Films in Review* 34.6 (June–July 1983): 329–33.

Hayakawa, Sessue. *Zen Showed Me the Way . . . to Peace, Happiness and Tranquility.* Indianapolis: Bobbs-Merrill, 1960.

Hayakawa, Yukio. "Tsuru Aoki: A Flower of Japan." *The Rafu Magazine* 1.4 (19 June 1998): 3–5, 16–18.

Hayne, Donald, ed. *The Autobiography of Cecil B. DeMille.* Englewood Cliffs, N.J.: Prentice-Hall, 1959.

Higashi, Sumiko. *Cecil B. DeMille and American Culture: The Silent Era.* Berkeley: University of California Press, 1994.

——. "Cecil B. DeMille and the Lasky Company: Legitimating Feature Film as Art." *Film History* 4.3 (1990): 181–97.

——. "Ethnicity, Class, and Gender in Film: DeMille's *The Cheat.*" In *Unspeakable Images: Ethnicity and the American Cinema*, ed. Lester D. Friedman, 112–39. Urbana: University of Illinois Press, 1991.

——. "Touring the Orient with Lafcadio Hearn and Cecil B. DeMille: Highbrow versus Lowbrow in a Consumer Culture." In *The Birth of Whiteness: Race and the Emergence of U.S. Cinema*, ed. Daniel Bernardi. 329–53. New Brunswick, N.J.: Rutgers University Press, 1996.

——. *Virgins, Vamps, and Flappers: The American Silent Movie Heroine.* St. Albans, Vt.: Eden Press Women's Publications, 1978.

Holland, Larry Lee. "Fannie Ward." *Films in Review* 36.12 (December 1985): 590–95.

Iino, Masako. "Beikoku niokeru hainichi undo to 1924 nen iminho seitei katei" [Anti-Japanese movement in the U.S. and the enactment process of the 1924 immigration law]. *Tsudajuku Daigaku Kiyo* 10 (1978): 1–41.

Jacobs, Lea. "Belasco, DeMille and the Development of Lasky Lighting." *Film History* 5.4 (1993): 405–18.

La Farge, John. "Bric-a-Brac: An Artist's Letters from Japan." *Century* 46.24 (1893): 427–29.

Lears, T. J. Jackson. *No Place of Grace: Antimodernism and the Transformation of American Culture, 1880–1920*. Chicago: University of Chicago Press, 1981.

Lee, Robert G. *Orientals: Asian Americans in Popular Culture*. Philadelphia: Temple University Press, 1999.

Mahan, A. T. *The Problem of Asia and Its Effect upon International Policies*. Boston: Little, Brown, 1900.

Marchetti, Gina. *Romance and the "Yellow Peril": Race, Sex, and Discursive Strategies in Hollywood Fiction*. Berkeley: University of California Press, 1993.

Mason, Roger S. *Conspicuous Consumption: A Study of Exceptional Consumer Behaviour*. Westmead, England: Gower, 1981.

McClatchy, Valentine Stuart. *Four Anti-Japanese Pamphlets*. 1919, 1921, 1921, 1925. Reprint, New York: Arno, 1978.

Moussinac, Léon. "Cinématographie: Le Lys brisé." *Mercurr de France* (1 February 1921): 797–804. Translated and reprinted in Richard Abel, *French Film Theory and Criticism: A History/Anthology 1907–1939*. Vol. 1, *1907–1929*, 229–35. Princeton, N.J.: Princeton University Press, 1988.

Muramatsu, Shofu, *Kawakami Otojiro (Jo)*. Tokyo: Taiheiyo shuppan, 1952.

———. *Kawakami Otojiro (Ge)*. Tokyo: Taiheiyo shuppan, 1952.

Negra, Diane. "Immigrant Stardom in Imperial America: Pola Negri and the Problem of Typology." *Camera Obscura* 48 (2001): 159–95.

Niiya, Brian, ed. *Japanese American History: An A-to-Z Reference from 1868 to the Present*. New York: Facts on File, 1993.

Noteheler, F.G., ed. *Japan through American Eyes: The Journal of Francis Hall Kanagawa and Yokohama 1859–1866*. Princeton, N.J.: Princeton University Press, 1992.

Okina, Kyuin. "Hayakawa Sesshu to Kamiyama Sojin" [Sessue Hayakawa and Sojin Kamiyama]. *Chuo Koron* 45.5 (May 1930): 223–31.

Staiger, Janet. *Bad Women: Regulating Sexuality in Early American Cinema*. Minneapolis: University of Minnesota Press, 1995.

Stanley, Sadie, ed., *The New Grove Dictionary of Opera*. Vol. 2, *E-Lom*. New York: Macmillan, 1992.

State Board of Control of California. *California and the Oriental*. Sacramento: State Board of Control of California, 1920.

SZO. "Katsudo omochabako" [Toy box of motion picture]. *Katsudo no Sekai* 1.7 (July 1916): 42–48.

Thompson, Kristin, and David Bordwell. *Film History: An Introduction*. New York: McGraw-Hill, 1994.

Trimberger, Ellen Kay. "The New Woman and the New Sexuality: Conflict and Contradiction in the Writings and Lives of Mabel Dodge and Neith Boyce." In *1915, the Cultural Moment: The New Politics, the New Women, the New Psychology, the New Art, and the New Theatre in America*, ed. Adele Heller and Lois Rudnick, 98–115. New Brunswick, N.J.: Rutgers University Press, 1991.

Tupper, Eleanor, and George E. McReynolds, *Japan in American Public Opinion*. New York: Macmillan, 1937.

U.S. Bureau of the Census. *Chinese and Japanese in the United States*. 13th Census Bulletin 127. Washington: Government Printing Office, 1914.

Veblen, Thorstein. *The Theory of the Leisure Class*. New York: Macmillan, 1899.

Whissel, Kristen. "The Gender of Empire: American Modernity, Masculinity, and Edison's War Actualities." In *A Feminist Reader in Early Cinema*, ed. Jennifer M. Bean and Diane Negra, 141–65. Durham, N.C.: Duke University Press, 2002.
Yamaguchi, Reiko. *Joyu Sadayakko* [The actress Sadayakko]. Tokyo: Asahi shinbun sha, 1993.
Yoshihara, Mari. *Embracing the East: White Women and American Orientalism*. New York: Oxford University Press.

Chapter 17

Miriam Hansen

PLEASURE, AMBIVALENCE, IDENTIFICATION: VALENTINO AND FEMALE SPECTATORSHIP (1986)

Editors' Introduction

Laura Mulvey's "Visual Pleasure and Narrative Cinema," from 1975, probably has generated more response than any other essay about film from the last forty years. In particular, feminist film scholars have worked with the Mulvey essay to refine its apparent theoretical binarism – between male spectators and the female subject of the gaze – and an ahistoricism that depends on Hitchcock and Sternberg films to count for all of Hollywood cinema. Miriam Hansen, along with Linda Williams, Mary Ann Doane, E. Ann Kaplan and others, is among the most important scholars to deal with Mulvey's essay. Hansen's project, as it appears in her work on Rudolph Valentino, has been to pose questions about the gaze in cinema, and to ask how we understand visual pleasure, how we might acknowledge it in varied ways in various eras, and how we might differentiate between viewers at the time of a film's production and viewers, like Hansen herself, watching a Valentino film some sixty years later. In addition, Hansen raises the problem of the "actual" viewer, sitting in a theatre watching a movie, and the spectator who is constructed by the film itself. Valentino functions as a significant test case in modes of gendered pleasure and identification. He became a star at the beginning of what we refer to as the classical period, but before all of the rules of that classicism had solidified. He became a star, as well, during an era of shifting American notions about gender, when the movie theatre itself served as a major site of female public presence. And he quickly became an object of fascination to male and female viewers alike, a fascination, as Hansen points out, that extended to his corpse, and he continues to be an object of great scholarly interest. This essay, then, that so prefigures Jackie Stacey's, reprinted here, about female identification with stars, assumes the theoretical truism of Mulvey's work, about the pleasure of looking and the ways that the gaze is gendered, but then seeks to examine its history, its connection to other historical phenomena, and its place in contemporary film studies.

Suggested Reading

Laura Mulvey, "Visual Pleasure and Narrative Cinema," *Screen*, 16:3 (Autumn 1975), pp. 6–18; Mary Ann Doane, Patricia Mellencamp, Linda Williams, eds., *Re-Vision: Essays in Feminist Film Criticism* (AFI, 1983); Jennifer Bean and Diane Negra, eds., *A Feminist Reader in Early Cinema* (Duke, 2002).

> Occasionally the movies go mad. They have terrifying visions; they erupt in images that show the true face of society. Fortunately, however, they are healthy at the core. Their schizophrenic outbursts last only a few moments, then the curtain is lowered again and everything returns to normal.
>
> (Kracauer, "The Little Salesgirls Go to the Movies", 1927)[1]

IN THE CONTEXT OF discussions on cinematic spectatorship, the case of Rudolph Valentino demands attention, on historical as well as theoretical grounds. For the first time in film history, women spectators were perceived as a socially and economically significant group; female spectatorship was recognized as a mass phenomenon; and the films were explicitly addressed to a female spectator, regardless of the actual composition of the audience. As Hollywood manufactured the Valentino legend, promoting the fusion of real life and screen persona that makes a star, Valentino's female admirers in effect became part of that legend. Never before was the discourse on fan behavior so strongly marked by the terms of sexual difference, and never again was spectatorship so explicitly linked to the discourse on female desire. This conjunction was to inform Valentinian mythology for decades to come—as the following cover prose from various biographies illustrates:

> Lean, hot-eyed and Latin, Valentino was every woman's dream. . . .
>
> On screen and off, his smoldering glance ignited fierce sexual fires in millions of hearts. . . .
>
> They breathed the words "The Sheik" like a prayer on their lips. They tried to tear his clothes off when he left the theater. . . .
>
> The studio telephones could not handle the thousands of calls from women. They begged for any job that would permit even a momentary glimpse of Valentino. Gladly they offered to work without pay.[2]

While these biographies rarely agree on any facts concerning Valentino's life, they stereotypically relate his personal success and suffering to the ongoing crisis of American cultural and social values.[3] Valentino's body, in more than one sense, became the site of contradictions that had erupted with World War I. His problematic centrality and violence of impact unprecedented for a film star are inextricably linked to the particular historical constellation that made him as well as destoyed him. This constellation I see delineated, tentatively, by developments partly caused by, partly in response to the upheaval of gender relations during the war, such as the massive integration of women into the work force and their emergence as a primary target in the shift to consumer economy; the partial breakdown of gender-specific divisions of labor and a blurring of traditional delimitations of public and private; the need to redefine notions of femininity in terms other than domesticity and motherhood; the image of the New Woman promoted along with a demonstrative liberalization of sexual behavior and life-styles; the emergence of the companionate marriage.[4]

However one may interpret the dialectics of women's so-called emancipation and their integration into a consumer culture, women did gain a considerable degree of public visibility in those years, and the cinema was one of the places in which this increased social and economic significance was acknowledged, in whatever distorted manner. The orientation of the market towards a female spectator/consumer opened up a potential gap between traditional patriarchal ideology on the one hand and the recognition of female experience, needs, fantasies on the other, albeit for purposes of immediate commercial exploitation and eventual containment.[5] It is in this gap that the Valentino phenomenon deserves to be read, as a significant yet precarious moment in the changing discourse on femininity and sexuality. Precarious, not least, because it sidetracked that discourse to question standards of masculinity, destabilizing them with connotations of sexual ambiguity, social marginality, and ethnic/racial otherness.

Valentino also presents a challenge to feminist film theory, in particular as it developed during the 1970s within the framework of psychoanalysis and semiology. This debate inescapably returns to Laura Mulvey's essay on "Visual Pleasure and Narrative Cinema" (1975) which first spelled out the implications of Lacanian-Althusserian models of spectatorship (Metz, Baudry) for a critique of patriarchal cinema. Whatever its limitations and blind spots, the significance of Mulvey's argument lies in her description of the ways in which the classical Hollywood film perpetuates sexual imbalance in the very conventions through which it engages its viewer as subject—its modes of organizing vision and structuring narratives. These conventions, drawing on psychic mechanisms of voyeurism, fetishism, and narcissism, depend upon and reproduce the conventional polarity of the male as the agent of the "look" and the image of woman as object of both spectacle and narrative. In aligning spectatorial pleasure with a hierarchical system of sexual difference, classical American cinema inevitably entails what Mulvey calls "a 'masculinization' of the spectator position, regardless of the actual sex (or possible deviance) of any real live movie-goer."[6]

Besides its somewhat monolithic notion of classical cinema and provocatively Manichean stance on visual pleasure, Mulvey's argument has been criticized frequently for the difficulty of conceptualizing a female spectator other than in terms of an absence.[7] In the decade since Mulvey's essay was published, however, feminist critics have attempted to rescue female spectatorship from its "locus of impossibility," in particular in areas elided by the focus on women's systematic exclusion. One such area is the body of films within the Hollywood tradition which are addressed to female audiences and marketed as such; for example, the "woman's film" of the 1940s and other variants of melodrama centering on female protagonists and their world. Another area of feminist investigation, less clearly delineated, is the question of pleasure and attendant processes of identification experienced by women spectators (including feminist critics) in the actual reception of mainstream films, even with genres devoted to male heroes and activities, such as the Western or the gangster film.

With regard to the latter, Mulvey, reconsidering her earlier argument, suggests that the female spectator, "enjoying the freedom of action and control over the diegetic world that identification with the male hero provides," takes recourse to the repressed residues of her own phallic phase. This type of identification, however, requires putting on transvestite clothes, which confirms the dominant polarity of vision by exchanging the terms of opposition for those of similarity. Like Pearl in Mulvey's reading of *Duel in the Sun*, the female spectator ends up being caught in a conflict "between the deep blue sea of passive femininity and the devil of regressive masculinity."[8]

While Mulvey's analysis of spectatorial cross-dressing ultimately upholds the notion of patriarchal cinema as a system of binary opposites, it also demonstrates the necessity to complicate such terms. The female viewer of "masculine" genres does not fit the mold of the spectator/subject anticipated by these films, and in many of them narcissistic identification with female characters is of marginal interest at best, especially when the spectacle is more dispersed (over landscape and action scenes) than in genres like the musical or romantic comedy which concentrate pleasure around the image of the female body. But neither is reception on the woman's part merely accidental, arbitrary, or individual—failing with regard to the meaning-potential of the film. Rather, one might say that the oscillation and instability which Mulvey and others have observed in female spectatorship constitutes a meaningful deviation—a deviation that has its historical basis in the spectator's experience of belonging to a socially differentiated group called women. As a subdominant and relatively indeterminate collective formation, female spectatorship is certainly contingent upon dominant subject positions, and thus not outside or above ideology, but it cannot be reduced to an either/or modality.

The very figure of the transvestite suggests that the difference of female spectatorship involves more than the opposition of activity and passivity, that it has to be conceptualized in terms of a greater degree of mobility and heterogeneity, including a sense of theatricality and selectivity.[9] As I will argue in the case of Valentino, sexual mobility, the temporary slippage between gender definitions, is crucial to an understanding of his historical impact; that sexual mobility is also "a distinguishing feature of femininity in its cultural construction" and that hence transvestism "*would be* fully recuperable"[10] does not seem a sufficient reason for simply dismissing it from the arsenal of a feminist countertradition. The heterogeneity of the female spectator position, moreover, extends not only to spatial registers (proximity/distance in relation to the screen as Mary Ann Doane proposes) but to registers of temporality as well. For the figure of the transvestite connotes a discrepancy, a simultaneity of unequal psychic developments. Phallic identification, while officially—in the present tense of the film text, as propelled by the linear flow of the narrative—aligned with positions of masculine agency and control, for the woman spectator depends upon a memory (on whatever level of consciousness), and thus may reactivate repressed layers of her own psychic history and socialization.[11]

The structural instability of the female spectator position in mainstream cinema surfaces as a textual instability in films specifically addressed to women, as an effect of the collision between immediate market interests and institutional structures of vision. In her work on the "woman's film" of the 1940s, Doane shows how the ideological crisis precipitated by a female address is contained in turn by scenarios of masochism which work to distance and de-eroticize the woman's gaze, thus restricting the space of a female reading. Linda Williams and Tania Modleski, on the other hand, emphasize the multiplicity of identificatory positions in female-addressed mainstream films (or, as in Modleski's case, TV soap opera), a textual multiplicity which they relate to the problematic constitution of female identity under patriarchy, from patterns of psychic development to a gender-specific division of labor. This difference in emphasis may partly be due to the choice of films—for example, maternal melodrama as opposed to the films analyzed by Doane which overlap with the gothic or horror genre—but it is also, and perhaps most important, a question of reading.[12]

The analysis of positions of identification available to female spectators is inseparable from positions of critical reading, as the recent debate between Linda Williams and E. Ann Kaplan exemplifies.[13] Does the ending of a film like *Stella Dallas* unify the variety of conflicting subject positions mapped out to this point, as Kaplan argues? Does it close off the contradictions in terms of a patriarchal discourse on motherhood, asking the spectator to accept desexualization, sacrifice, and powerlessness? Or do we, as Williams suggests, grant some degree of alterity to the preceding 108 minutes? Are processes of identification necessarily synchronous with the temporal structures of classical narrative, and to what extent is closure effective? How do films construct what we remember of them? How does this memory change over time in relation to the immediate effects of identification?

These questions urge us to reconsider the hermeneutics involved in the critical enterprise. Who is the subject of reading? Ann Kaplan points out the necessity of distinguishing between the historical spectator, the hypothetical spectator constructed through the film's strategies, and the contemporary female spectator with a feminist consciousness. But the textually constructed spectator/subject does not have any objective existence apart from our reading of the film, which is always partial and, if we choose, partisan. Therefore, the question of hermeneutics is not only one of measuring historical scopes of reception against each other, but also one of the politics of reading,[14] a question of how to establish a usable past for an alternative film practice. If all the time, desire, and money spent by women watching mainstream films should be of any consequence whatsoever for a feminist countertradition, then this activity has to be made available through readings, in full awareness of its complicity and contingency upon the dominant structures of the apparatus, but nonetheless as a potential of resistance to be reappropriated.[15]

The Valentino films add yet another angle to these arguments on female spectatorship and a feminist re-writing of film history. While participating in the general problematic of female-addressed Hollywood films, their distinction lies in focusing spectatorial pleasure on the image of a male hero/performer. If a man is made to occupy the place of erotic object, how does this affect the organization of vision? If the desiring look is aligned with the position of a female viewer, does this open up a space for female subjectivity and, by the same token, an alternative conception of visual pleasure?

Feminist theorists like Doane and Kaplan have cautioned against premature enthusiasm regarding such films, arguing that they merely present an instance of role reversal which allows women the appropriation of the gaze only to confirm the patriarchal logic of vision. "The male striptease, the gigolo—both inevitably signify the mechanism of reversal itself, constituting themselves as aberrations whose acknowledgment simply reinforces the dominant system of aligning sexual difference with a subject/object dichotomy. And an essential attribute of that dominant system is the matching of male subjectivity with the agency of the look."[16] Undeniably, the figure of the male as erotic object sets into play fetishistic and voyeuristic mechanisms, accompanied—most strikingly in the case of Valentino—by a feminization of the actor's persona. These mechanisms, however, are not naturalized as they are in the representation of a female body. Rather, they are foregrounded as aspects of a theatricality that encompasses both viewer and performer. The reversal thus constitutes a *textual* difference which has to be considered from case to case and cannot be reduced *a priori* to its symbolic content within a phallocentric economy of signification. It seems more promising, tentatively, to approach the textual difference of a male erotic object as a figure of overdetermination, an unstable composite figure that connotes "the simultaneous presence of two positionalities of desire" (Teresa de Lauretis)[17] and thus calls into question the very idea of polarity rather than simply reversing its terms.

Moreover, as even a cursory comparison of Valentino with more recent stars such as John Travolta and Robert Redford makes obvious, we need to observe historical differences as well. Figures like Travolta and Redford—not to mention performers like Mick Jagger, David Bowie, or Michael Jackson—emerge at the end of an era, if not already in the midst of an altogether different one. Valentino appears at the threshold of what has been termed, for better or for worse, Hollywood's "classical" period. The process by which American cinema became identified with particular conventions of editing and narrative was well under way during the 1920s. But not all of its crucial codes developed simultaneously; some were lagging behind while others were practiced obsessively and promiscuously.[18] This uneven development might account for a certain quality of excess often attributed to films of the 1920s, a quality which could be described more specifically as an unstable relationship between spectacle and narrative, falling back behind an economy already achieved during the mid and late 1910s. Whether a trace of primitive cinema or a mark of contemporary decadence, the peculiar inscription of the spectator in the Valentino films suggests a dissociation of pleasure and meaning which potentially undermines the classical imbrication of the gaze with masculine control and mastery.

From a theoretical perspective, then, this essay on Valentino is motivated by an interest in forms of visual pleasure that are not totally claimed, absorbed, or functionalized by the conventions of classical narrative. The redemption of scopophilia may require a return to Freud without the detour through Lacan, since in Lacanian models of spectatorship scopic desire is conceptually inseparable from voyeurism, fetishism and, thus, the regime of castration. Not that these are unrelated or free of determinism in Freud. The Freudian speculation, however, does not posit earlier stages of psychic development as always already negated by later ones, in a Hegelian sense of "*Aufhebung*" which Lacan assimilated to psychoanalysis. I would argue that Freud's writings still hold a more radical potential of interpretation,[19] in particular a more dialectical concept of regression and subjectivity. The latter might allow feminist film theory to rearticulate the question of aesthetic experience, in conjunction with the question of the erotic, neither of which we can afford to ignore if a feminist countercinema is to go beyond the abstract opposition of patriarchal mainstream film and feminist avantgarde.

Valentino. At first sight, Valentino's films seem to rehearse the classical choreography of the look almost to the point of parody, offering point-of-view constructions that affirm the cultural hierarchy of gender in the visual field. Between 1921 (*The Four Horsemen of the Apocalypse*) and 1926, the year of his premature death, Valentino starred in 14 films, produced by different studios and under different directors.[20] Illustrating the significance of the star as *auteur* as much as the economic viability of vehicles, each of these films reiterates a familiar pattern in staging the exchange of looks between Valentino and the female characters. Whenever Valentino lays eyes on a woman first, we can be sure that she will turn out to be the woman of his dreams, the legitimate partner in the romantic relationship; whenever a woman initiates the look, she is invariably marked as a vamp, to be condemned and defeated in the course of the narrative.

In the opening sequence of *The Eagle* (1925; based on Pushkin's novella *Dubrovsky*), the czarina (Louise Dresser) is about to inspect her favorite regiment, "the handsomest in all Russia," when a run-away carriage nearby prompts the hero into a Fairbanks-style rescue action. The first shot of Valentino shows him from a rear angle, looking through a pocket-size telescope; the first time we see his face, it is framed, medium close-up, within the windowframe of the coach, directing a curious gaze inside. The reverse shot completing the point of view, however, is illegible, hiding the object under a bundle of fur; only his repeated look makes the image readable, distinguishing the female figure from the setting, literally producing her for the spectator. As the young woman (Vilma Banky) returns the glance, she enters the romantic pact, acknowledging the power of his look(s). Her negative counterpart is the czarina, a stout, elderly woman who is shown catching sight of Valentino independently of his look, her face momentarily transfigured in desire. While she is masculinized by a military outfit and at the same time ridiculed for her lack of masculine physical skills, desire on her part is most crucially discredited through its association with political power. As she continues the inspection of Valentino's body in the privacy of the imperial suite, encircling and immobilizing him (no point of view), the expression of horror in his eyes pinpoints the scandal of the situation, the reversal of gender positions in the visual field, unilaterally enforced by the monarch. As soon as Valentino understands the sexual implications of his position, he decides to restore the traditional (im)balance, risking death as a deserter yet regaining the mastery of the look.

A similar pattern can be observed in *Blood and Sand* (1922): Doña Sol (Nita Naldi), the president's niece, is shown admiring the victorious torero through binoculars before he looks at her; thus, she is syntactically marked as a vamp. His future wife Carmen (Lila Lee), on the other hand, is singled out by the camera within his point of view, similar to the coach sequence in *The Eagle*. A close-up of his face signals the awakening desire, alternating with an indecipherable long shot of a crowd. The repetition of the desiring look, provoking a dissolve that extricates her from the crowd, resolves the picture puzzle for the spectator and, by the same logic of vision, establishes her as the legitimate companion (further sanctioned by the inclusion of his mother in the point-of-view construction that follows). Thus the legitimate female figure is deprived of the initiative of the erotic look and relegated to the position of scopic object within the diegesis. In relation to the spectator, however, *she shares this position of scopic object with Valentino himself*.

Valentino's appeal depends, to a large degree, on the manner in which he combines masculine control of the look with the feminine quality of "to-be-looked-at-ness," to use Mulvey's rather awkward term. When Valentino falls in love—usually at first sight—the close-up of his face clearly surpasses that of the female character in its value as spectacle. In a narcissistic doubling, the subject of the look constitutes itself as object, graphically illustrating Freud's formulation of the autoerotic dilemma: "Too bad that I cannot kiss myself."[21] Moreover, in their radiant pictorial quality, such shots temporarily arrest the metonymic drive of the narrative, similar in effect to the visual presence of the woman which, as Mulvey observes, tends "to freeze the flow of action in moments of erotic contemplation."[22] In Valentino's case, however, erotic contemplation governs an active as well passive mode, making both spectator and character the subject of a double game of vision.

To the extent that Valentino occupies the position of primary object of spectacle, this entails a systematic feminization of his persona. Many of the films try to motivate this effect by casting him as a performer (torero, dancer) or by situating him in a historically removed or exotic mise-en-scène; in either case, the connotation of femininity persists through the use of costumes—in particular flared coats and headdress reminiscent of a bridal wardrobe, as well as a general emphasis on dressing and disguises. *Monsieur Beaucaire*, a 1924 Paramount costume drama based on the Booth Tarkington novel, combines both the effect and its disavowal in a delightfully self-reflective manner. Valentino, playing the Duke of Chartres, alias Monsieur Beaucaire, is introduced on a stage playing the lute in an attempt to entertain the jaded king, Louis XV. The courtly mise-en-scène ostensibly legitimizes the desiring female gaze, contained in the alternation of relatively close shots of Valentino and the female members of the audience within the film. Unfailingly, however, this sequence thematizes the paradox of female spectatorship. Seeing one woman *not* focusing her eyes upon him in rapture, he stops midway in indignation and a title redundantly explains: "the shock of his life: a woman not looking at him"—sure enough, this refers to the leading romantic lady.[23] The partial reversal of the gender economy of vision is prepared by the film's opening shot, a close-up of hands doing needlepoint work. As the camera pulls back, those hands are revealed to be the king's. In the effeminate universe of the French court, Valentino succeeds in asserting his masculinity only by comparison, staging it as a difference which ultimately fails to make a difference.

Before considering the possibilities of identification implied in this peculiar choreography of vision, I wish to recapitulate some thoughts on female visual pleasure and its fate under the patriarchal taboo. Particularly interesting in this context are certain aspects of scopophilia that Freud analyzes through its development in infantile sexuality, a period in which the child is still far from having a stable sense of gender identity. Stimulated in the process of mutual gazing between mother and child, the female scopic drive is constituted with a *bisexual* as well as an *autoerotic* component. While these components subsequently succumb to cultural hierarchies of looking which tend to fixate the woman in a passive, narcissistic-exhibitionist role, there remains a basic ambivalence in the structure of vision as a component drive. As Freud argues in "Instincts and their Vicissitudes" (1915), the passive component of a drive represents a reversal of the active drive into its opposite, redirecting itself to the subject. Such a contradictory constitution of libidinal components may account for the coexistence, in their later fixation as perversion, of diametrically opposed drives within one and the same person, even if one tendency usually predominates. Thus a voyeur is always to some degree an exhibitionist and vice versa, just as the sadist shares the pleasures of masochism.[24]

The notion of ambivalence appears crucial to a theory of female spectatorship, precisely because the cinema, while enforcing patriarchal hierarchies in its organization of the look, also offers women an institutional opportunity to violate the taboo on female scopophilia. The success of a figure like Valentino, himself overdetermined as both object and subject of the look, urges us to insist upon the ambivalent constitution of scopic pleasure. Moreover, as one among a number of the more archaic partial drives whose integration is always and at best precarious, scopophilia could be distinguished from a socially more complicit voyeurism, as defined by the one-sided regime of the keyhole and the norms of genitality.[25]

Equally pertinent to an alternative conception of visual pleasure appears the potential dissociation of sexual and survival instincts, which is implicit already in Freud's notion of "anaclisis" but explicitly discussed with reference to the scopic drive in Freud's analysis of cases of psychogenic disturbance of vision. The eye serves both a practical function for the individual's orientation in the external world and the function of an erotogenic zone. If the latter takes over, if it refuses to accept its subservient role in forepleasure, the balance between sexual and survival instincts is threatened and the ego may react by repressing the dangerous component drive. The psychogenic disturbance of vision in turn represents the revenge of the repressed instinct, retrospectively interpreted by the individual as the voice of punishment which seems to be saying: "Because you sought to misuse your organ of sight for evil sensual pleasure, it is fitting that you should not see anything at all any more."[26]

While the psychogenic disturbance of vision, in the context of psychoanalytic theory, clearly functions as a metaphor of castration,[27] the potentially antithetical relationship of sexual and survival instincts could also be taken to describe the cultural and historical differentiation of male and female forms of vision. Although the neurotic dissociation may occur in patients of both sexes, the balance effected in so-called normal vision appears more typical of the psychic disposition by means of which the male subject controls the external world as well as the sexual field. Suffice it here to allude to the historical construction of monocular vision in Western art since the Renaissance, the instrumental standards imposed upon looking in technical and scientific observation and other disciplines, areas of cultural activity from which women were barred for centuries; on the flip-side of this coin, we find a variety of social codes enforcing the taboo on female scopophilia, ranging from makeup fashions like belladonna through the once popular injunction not to "make passes at girls who wear glasses."

The construction of femininity within patriarchal society, however, contains the promise of being incomplete. Women's exclusion from the mastery of the visual field may have diminished the pressure of the ego instincts towards the component drives, which are probably insufficiently subordinated to begin with. Thus the potential dissociation of the scopic drive from its function for survival may not be that threatening to the female subject, may not necessarily provoke the force of repression that Freud holds responsible for certain cases of psychogenic blindness. If such generalization is at all permissible, women might be more likely to indulge—without immediately repressing—in a sensuality of vision which contrasts with the goal-oriented discipline of the one-eyed masculine look. Christa Karpenstein speaks in this context of "an unrestrained scopic drive, a swerving and sliding gaze which disregards the meanings and messages of signs and images that socially determine the subject, a gaze that defies the limitations and fixations of the merely visible."[28]

If I seem to belabor this notion of an undomesticated gaze as a historical aspect of female subjectivity, I certainly don't intend to propose yet another variant of essentialism. To the extent that sexual difference is culturally constructed to begin with, the subversive qualities of a female gaze may just as well be shared by a male character. This is precisely what I want to suggest for the case of Valentino, contrary to the official legend which never ceased to assert the power of his look in terms of aggressive mastery. Hollywood publicity persistently advertised the state of bliss in store for the woman who would be discovered by his magical gaze—in the measure that he himself was becoming an erotic commodity of irrestible cash value for the studios.[29]

The feminine connotation of Valentino's "to-be-looked-at-ness," however, destabilizes his own glance in its very origin, makes him vulnerable to temptations that jeopardize the sovereignty of the male subject. When Valentino's eyes become riveted on the woman of his choice, he seems paralyzed rather than aggressive or menacing, occupying the position of the rabbit rather than that of the snake. Struck by the beauty of Carmen, in *Blood and Sand*, his activity seems blocked, suspended; it devolves upon Carmen throwing him a flower to get the narrative back into gear. Later in the film, at the height of his career as a torero, Valentino raises his eyes to the president's box, an individual centered under the benevolent eye of the State, when his gaze is side-tracked, literally decentered, by the sight of Doña Sol in the box to the right. The power of Valentino's gaze depends upon its weakness—enhanced by the fact that he was actually nearsighted and cross-eyed—upon its oscillating between active and passive, between object and ego libido. The erotic appeal of the Valentinian gaze, staged as a look within the look, is one of reciprocity and ambivalence, rather than mastery and objectification.

The peculiar organization of the Valentinian gaze corresponds, on the level of narrative, to conflicts between the pleasure and the reality principle. Whenever the hero's amorous interests collide with the standards of male social identity—career, family, paternal authority, or a vow of revenge—the spectator can hope that passion will triumph over pragmatism to the point of self-destruction.[30] As the generating vortex of such narratives, the Valentinian gaze far exceeds its formal functions of providing diegetic coherence and continuity; it assumes an almost figural independence. Thus the films advance an identification with the gaze itself; not with either source or object, but with the gaze as erotic medium which promises to transport the spectator out of the world of means and ends into the realm of passion.

The discussion of gendered patterns of vision inevitably opens up into the larger question of identification as the linchpin between film and spectator, the process that organizes subjectivity in visual and narrative terms. It seems useful at this point to invoke Mary Ann Doane's distinction of at least three instances of identification operating in the viewing process: (1) identification *with* the representation of a person (character/star); (2) recognition of particular objects, persons, or action *as* such (stars, narrative images); (3) identification with the "look," with oneself as the condition of perception, which Metz, in analogy with Lacan's concept of the mirror phase, has termed "primary."[31] These psychical mechanisms and their effects can be traced through the various levels of enunciation which structure cinematic identification, interlacing textual units such as shot, sequence, strategies of narrative, and mise-en-scène.[32]

Most productively, feminist film theorists have taken up the debate by insisting on the centrality of sexual difference, questioning the assumption of a single or neutral spectator position constructed in hierarchically ordered, linear processes of identification. While Mulvey initially reduced cinematic identification to a basically active relationship with a protagonist of the same sex (i.e., male), she subsequently modified this notion with regard to the female viewer who may not only cross but also be divided by gender lines (which in turn deflects identification from the fictive telos of a stable identity). As outlined above, the difficulty of conceptualizing a female spectator has led feminists to recast the problem of identification in terms of instability, mobility, multiplicity, and, I would add, temporality. Likewise, a number of feminist critics are trying to complicate the role of sexual difference in identification with the differences of class and race, with cultural and historical specificity. This might make it possible to rethink the concept of subjectivity implied, beyond the commonplace that subjects are constructed by and within ideology. The question of who is the subject of identification (so eloquently posed by Tonto) is also and not least a question concerning which part of the spectator is engaged and how: which layers of conscious or unconscious memory and fantasy are activated, and how we, both as viewers and as critics, choose to interpret this experience.[33]

I am not claiming that Valentino will answer all or any of these questions, but he might help articulate some of them a little more clearly. The first form of identification discussed by Doane, identification with the integral person filmed (Metz's "secondary" mode of identification), engages the female viewer transsexually insofar as it extends to the Valentino character; thus, it raises the problem of spectatorial cross-dressing—unless we consider other possibilities of transsexual identification beside the transvestite one. The alternative option for the woman spectator, passive-narcissistic identification with the female star as erotic object, appears to have been a position primarily advertised by the industry,[34] but it appears rather more problematic in view of the specular organization of the films.

If we can isolate an instance of "primary" identification at all—which is dubious on theoretical grounds[35]—the Valentino films challenge the assumption of perceptual mastery implied in such a concept by their foregrounding of the gaze as an erotic medium, a gaze that fascinates precisely because it transcends the socially imposed subject/object hierarchy of sexual difference. Moreover, the contradictions of the female address are located in the very space where the registers of the look and those of narrative and mise-en-scène intersect. In offering the woman spectator a position which is structurally analogous to that of the vamp within the diegesis (looking at Valentino independently of his initiating of the look) identification with the desiring gaze is both granted and incriminated, or, one might say, granted on the condition of its illegitimacy. This may be why the vamp figures in Valentino films (with the exception of *Blood and Sand*) are never totally condemned, inasmuch as they acknowledge a subliminal complicity between Valentino and the actively desiring female gaze. In *The Eagle*, for instance, the czarina is redeemed by her general's ruse of letting Valentino escape execution under an assumed identity; the closing shot shows Valentino and the czarina waving each other a never-ending farewell, much to the concern of the respective legitimate partners.

The least equivocal instance of identification operating in the Valentino films is that which feeds on recognition, the memory-spectacle rehearsed with each appearance of the overvalued erotic object, the star.[36] The pleasure of recognition involved in the identification of and with a star is dramatized, in many Valentino films, through a recurrent narrative pattern, which in turn revolves around the precarious cultural construction of the persona of the Latin Lover. Often, the Valentino character combines two sides of a melodramatic dualism, which he acts out in a series of disguises and anonymous identities. Thus, in *The Sheik* (1921), the barbaric son of the desert turns out to be of British descent; in *Moran of the Lady Letty* (1922), the San Francisco dandy proves himself a hearty sailor and authentic lover; the Duke of Chartres in exile becomes Monsieur Beaucaire; and the Black Eagle pursues courtship instead of revenge under the assumed identity of Monsieur LeBlanc.[37] The spectator recognizes her star in all his masks and disguises—unlike the female protagonist whose trial of love consists of "knowing" him regardless of narrative misfortune or social status.

Like most star vehicles, Valentino films have notoriously weak narratives and would probably fail to engage any viewer if it weren't for their hero's charisma. Many of his films are adapted from well-known popular novels, preferably costume dramas.[38] While there is some delight in action, in the sense of activity, physical movement, and gesture, there is very little suspense, very little of the game of concealing and revealing, of the dialectic of desire, knowledge, and power that has led theorists like Barthes, Bellour, and Heath to define all narrative as predicated on Oedipus. Identification in terms of narrative movement is likely to fall short of the plot in its totality, while closure tends to reside in smaller units, cutting across visual and narrative registers, defined by the succession of masks, disguises, milieus, and scenarios.

The emphasis on costumes, disguises, on rituals of dressing and undressing, undermines, in tendency, the voyeuristic structure of spectatorship in that it acknowledges the spectator as part of the theatrical display. This is emblematic in the famous dressing scene in *Monsieur Beaucaire*, during which Valentino punctuates the exercise in procrastination with occasional asides in the direction of the camera.[39] Such mutual recognition, in conjunction with the viewer's epistemological superiority over the female protagonist, encourages identification via a fantasy in which the spectator herself authorizes the masquerade; the publication, as late as 1979, of a Valentino paper-doll book would testify to the persistence of this phantasy in popular iconography. If there is any prototype for such a fantasy—and this is merely autobiographical speculation—it might be the penchant of prepubescent girls to dress up their younger brother as a little sister.[40]

But this is not the only type of scenario which organizes identification in the Valentino films. Pervasively, in these films, spectatorial pleasure is imbricated with self-consciously sadomasochistic rituals.[41] It may still be within the parameters of the vamp cliché when Doña Sol, holding on to the torero by the muscles of his arms, expresses the desire, according to the intertitle, one day to be beaten by these strong hands—and nearly bites off his thumb in the following shot. Here the sadomasochistic proclivity underlines the general perversity of a woman who dares to appropriate the privilege of the first look. The more interesting instances of sadomasochistic role-playing, however, take place in the context of the legitimate, romantic relationship. In *The Eagle*, Mascha, the young woman from the first sequence, turns out to be the daughter of the odious landowner against whom Valentino, in his persona as the Black Eagle, has pledged revenge on his father's deathbed. At one point, his men kidnap her and proudly present the catch to their leader. As he gets off his horse and steps toward her with a whip ready to lash out, the genre seems to slide into porn: the masks, the whip, phallic hats—insignia of anonymous lust, traces of the search for nonidentity in eros.[42] That Valentino actually directs the whip against his own men is the alibi the narrative provides for a kinky shot, the *défilement* into propriety; yet it does not diminish the subliminal effect. Valentino recognizes Mascha and, protected by his unilateral anonymity, continues the game in a more or less playful manner. As she rejects his horse and proudly embarks on her journey on foot, he follows her, mounted on the high horse—a constellation the camera exploits in straight-on backtracking shots. When she finally gives in, forced down by the obligatory fainting spell, Valentino reverses the spatial hierarchy by installing her on the horse, thus making her an involuntary accomplice in the dominance/submission game. This game is accomplished within the legitimate relationship only by means of the mask which temporarily suspends the mutuality of the romantic gaze in Valentino's favor.

The emphasis on the sadistic aspects of the Valentino persona echoes the publicity pitch advertising him to female audiences as the "he-man," the "menace," reiterated, as late as 1977, by one of his biographers: "Women were to find in *The Sheik* a symbol of the omnipotent male who could dominate them as the men in their own lives could not."[43] And, when in the film of that title the son of the desert forces the blue-eyed Lady Diana on his horse, ostensibly for her own pleasure ("lie still you little fool"), millions of women's hearts were said to have quivered at the prospect of being humiliated by the British-bred barbarian. Despite the display of virility in *The Sheik* (1922; based on the novel by Edith Maude Hull), however, this film initiated the much publicized rejection of Valentino by male moviegoers, which had more to do with the threat he presented to traditional norms of masculinity than with the actual composition of audience.[44] Not only the stigma of effeminacy but also, equally threatening, a masochistic aura was to haunt Valentino to his death and beyond. There were widespread rumors about his private life—homosexuality, impotence, unconsummated marriages with lesbians, dependency on domineering women, the platinum "slave bracelet" given to him by his second wife, Natasha Rambova. More systematically, the masochistic elements in the Valentino persona were enforced by the sadistic placement of the spectator in the films themselves. There is hardly a Valentino film that does not display a whip, in whatever marginal function, and most of them feature seemingly insignificant subplots in which the spectator is offered a position that entails enjoying the tortures inflicted on Valentino or others.[45]

The oscillation of the Valentino persona between sadistic and masochistic positions is yet another expression of the ambivalence that governs the specular organization of the films. As Freud asserts in the "Three Essays on the Theory of Sexuality," "a sadist is always at the same time a masochist, although in one case the active and in another case the passive aspect of the perversion may be more pronounced and may represent the predominant sexual activity."[46] But the question of the origin and economy of masochism troubled Freud over decades and led him to revise his views at least once.[47] Among post-Freudian attempts to theorize masochism, that of Gilles Deleuze has recently been put forward as an alternative model of spectatorship.[48] Deleuze challenges the conceptual linkage of masochism with sadism and the Oedipal regime; instead he proposes a distinct origin and aesthetics of masochism located in the relationship with the "oral mother." While the revisionist impulse to emphasize pregenital sexuality in spectatorship can only be welcomed, Deleuze's model seems somewhat limited by the parameters of his literary source—the writings of Leopold von Sacher-Masoch—and thus to an elaboration of the masochistic scenario within a basically male fantasy.[49] Therefore, I wish to return to Freud's essay, "A Child Is Being Beaten" (1919), not only for its focus on female instances of sadomasochistic fantasy, but also because it elucidates a particular aspect of the Valentino figure as fantasmatic object.[50]

The formula, "a child is being beaten," which, regardless of any actually experienced corporal punishment, may dominate masturbation fantasies of the latency period, is remarkable in that it stereotypically reiterates the mere description of the event, while subject, object, and the role of the person fantasizing remain indeterminate. On the basis of jealousy feelings aroused by the Oedipal constellation, Freud proceeds to reconstruct three different phases with explicit reference to female adolescents: (1) "My father is beating the child that I hate" (presumably a younger sibling); therefore, "he loves only me"; (2) "I am being beaten [therefore loved] by my father" (the regressive substitute for the incestuous relationship); (3) "a child is being beaten." While the second, sexually most threatening phase succumbs to repression, the first phase is reduced to its merely descriptive part and thus results in the third, in which the father is usually replaced by a more distant male authority figure. Thus the fantasy is sadistic only in its form—but grants masochistic gratification by way of identification with the anonymous children who are being beaten. This series of transformations reduces the sexual participation of the girl to the status of spectator, desexualizing both content and bearer of the fantasy (which, as Freud remarks, is not the case in male variants of the beating fantasy). Just as important in the present context, however, is the observation that in both male and female versions of the sadomasochistic fantasy the children who are being beaten generally turn out to be male. In the case of the female fantasy, Freud employs the concept of the "masculinity complex," which makes the girl imagine herself as male and thus allows her to be represented, in her daydreams, by these anonymous whipping boys.

The deepest, most effective layer of the Valentino persona is that of the whipping boy—in which he resembles so many other heroes of popular fiction devoured by adolescent girls (one of the examples Freud cites is *Uncle Tom's Cabin*). Freud's analysis of the sadomasochistic fantasy suggests that we distinguish between the sadistic appeal articulated in point-of-view structures on the one hand, and the masochistic pleasure in the identification with the object on the other. Transsexual identification, instead of being confined to simple cross-dressing, relies here as much on the feminine qualities of the male protagonist as it does on residual ambiguity in the female spectator. This simultaneity of identificatory positions is enabled by an interactional structure, a scenario whose libidinal force, protected by a series of repressive/rhetorical transformations, can be traced back to the nursery. (Given the amount of detail that Freud devotes to reconstructing the various stages of this scenario, it is indeed curious—and here one might concur with Deleuze's critique—how briefly he dismisses the role of the mother, especially in view of his emphasis on sibling rivalry.)[51]

Unlike the one-sided masochistic identification with a female protagonist encouraged by the "woman's film," female identification in Valentino films could be construed to entail the full range of transformations proposed by Freud. As Valentino slips into and out of the part of the whipping boy, intermittently relegating the woman to the position of both victim and perpetrator, he may succeed in recuperating the middle phase of the female fantasy from repression ("I am being beaten—and therefore loved—by my father") and thus in resexualizing it. This possibility is suggested above all by the unmistakable incestuous aura surrounding the Valentino persona; however, the appeal here is less that of a relationship between father and daughter than one between brother and sister, which turns on the desire of both for an inaccessible mother.[52]

The interchangeability of sadistic and masochistic positions within the diegesis potentially undercuts the a priori masochism ascribed by current film theory to the female spectator of classical cinema. In making sadomasochistic rituals an explicit component of the erotic relationship, Valentino's films subvert the socially imposed dominance/submission hierarchy of gender roles, dissolving subject/object dichotomies into erotic reciprocity. The vulnerability Valentino displays in his films, the traces of feminine masochism in his persona, may partly account for the threat he posed to prevalent standards of masculinity—the sublimation of masochistic inclinations after all being the token of the male subject's sexual mastery, his control over pleasure.

Sadomasochistic role-playing most strikingly intersects with the choreography of vision in *The Son of the Sheik* (1926; based on another novel by E. M. Hull), Valentino's last and probably most perverse film. Due to a misunderstanding that propels the narrative, Yasmin (Vilma Banky) represents a combination of both female types, vamp and romantic companion. Although transparent to the spectator, the misunderstanding on Ahmed/Valentino's part—that Yasmin lured him into a trap, thus causing him to be captured and whipped by her father's gang—has carefully been planted early on in the film by means of an editing device. The film's first close-up shows the face of Yasmin, lost in erotic yearning, which dissolves into a matching close-up of Valentino; a somewhat mismatched cut in turn reveals him to be looking at her legs as she is dancing for a crowd. A dissolve back to Yasmin's face eventually confirms the status of the sequence as a flashback which stages the usual discovery of the woman through Valentino's look; the objectification here is compounded by the demeaning situation, the fragmentation of Yasmin's body as well as the emphasis on money in the deployment of the romantic gaze. The potential misreading of the flashback as a point-of-view shot on the part of the woman falsely implicates Yasmin as a transgressor, thus supporting her double inscription as victim later on in the film, as both scopic and masochistic object. Herself ignorant of her lover's misunderstanding, Yasmin is kidnapped by him and imprisoned in his tent. His revenge accordingly consists in refusing her the mutuality of the erotic look and culminates in a veritable one-eyed stare with which he transfixes her to the point of rape. Valentino's unilateral transgression of the romantic pact is supposedly vindicated by the powerful image of him crucified, humiliated, and whipped earlier on in the film. This image of Valentino as victim, however, erroneously ascribed to Yasmin's authorship and not even witnessed by her, is primarily designed for the benefit of the spectator. No doubt there remains an asymmetry in the sadomasochistic role reversal on the diegetic level: a female character can assume an active part only at the price of being marked as a vamp; sadistic pleasure is specularized, reserved for the woman in front of the screen.

The multiple ambiguities articulated on the specular level of *The Son of the Sheik* contrast with the more flatly patriarchal discourse of the narrative, not to mention the simple-minded sexist and racist title prose. As if to conceal—and thus inofficially to acknowledge and exploit—this gap between narrative and visual pleasure, the Oedipal scenario is overinscribed to the point of parody. Valentino's private love/revenge affair meets with strong resistance on the part of his father who bends an iron rod with his mere hands in order to demonstrate his paternal power; Valentino, a chip off the old block, responds by straightening it out again. Only when his understanding mother, Lady Diana (Agnes Ayres), invokes a flashback to her own kidnapping in *The Sheik* does the father recognize and accept his successor. They reconcile in the course of yet another kidnapping scene, this time rescuing Yasmin from her father's gang: in the midst of tumultuous swashbuckling father and son shake hands, temporarily losing sight of the woman, the object of their endeavor.

Beneath this Oedipal pretext, as it were, the film offers a connotative wealth of deviations which radiate in a dialectic of repression and excess from the Valentino character to all levels of mise-en-scène and cinematography. Exotic costumes, oriental decor, and desert landscape provoke a sensuality of vision which constantly undermines the interest in the development of the narrative. Extreme long shots show Valentino riding through a sea of sand shaped like breasts and buttocks; he prefers the skin-folds of his tent to the parental palace, and he experiences in the allegorical moonlit ruin the pitfalls of adult sexuality, the threat of castration. Though concealing dangerous abysses, the eroticized landscape becomes a playground of polymorphous desire, in which the signs of virility—sables, pistols, cigarettes—remain phallic toys at best. The screen itself becomes a maternal body, inviting the component drives to revolt against their subordination. These textured surfaces do not project a realistic space which the hero, traversing it, would be obligated to subject. Rather, they construct an oneiric stage which cannot be bothered with perspective and verisimilitude. With a degree of irreality of which the silent screen was yet capable, Valentino's last film admits to the reality of a fantasy that assimilates the Oedipal scenario for its own purposes. Not only does it force the father to identify with the phallic caprices of his youth, but it even more thoroughly subverts the Oedipal script in its casting: Valentino himself plays the role of the father in whose mirror image the son achieves a presumably adult male identity which inevitably—and barely masked—reveals itself as both narcissistic and incestuous.

The appeal of the Valentino fantasy is certainly regressive, beckoning the female spectator (to revise Mulvey) beyond the devil of phallic identification into the deep blue sea of polymorphous perversity. Such an appeal cannot but provoke the connotation of monstrosity—which the films displace onto figures like the vamp or the sadomasochistic dwarf in *The Son of the Sheik*, a vicious caricature of Orientalism. The threat posed by Valentino's complicity with the woman who looks, like the affinity of monster and woman in Linda Williams's reading of the horror film, is not a threat merely of sexual difference but of a different *kind* of sexuality, different from the norm of heterosexual, genital sexuality.[53] While playing along with narrative conventions that assert the latter (e.g., the figure of couple formation), the Valentino films allow their spectators to repeat and acknowledge the more archaic component drives, reminders of the precarious constructedness of sexual identity. Moreover, in locating pleasure in the tension—if not excess—of partial libido in relation to genitality, they project a realm of the erotic as distinct from the socially cultivated ideal of a "healthy sex life."[54]

To claim a subversive function for polymorphous perversity as such is highly problematic, as Foucault asserts, given the degree to which disparate sexualities themselves have been appropriated by a discourse binding pleasure and power. It is therefore all the more important to reconsider the historical moment at which Valentino enters that discourse, marking its conjunction with other discourses, in particular those of social mobility and racial otherness. In a liberal gesture, Alexander Walker ponders the paradox of the Valentino craze; that is, that it took place alongside the progressive liberation of American women from traditional roles: "It was a perverse way of celebrating your sex's emancipation."[55] Perverse, yes, but not so paradoxical. As revisionist historians have argued, the New Woman was usually not as emancipated as her image suggested, and her access to consumer culture often entailed an underpaid job, loneliness, and social insecurity or, in the case of married women, the multiple burdens of wage labor, housework, and childrearing.[56] The period's demonstrative obsession with sexual reform may well confirm Foucault's argument on sexuality as discourse at large; still, this discourse must have had different implications for women than for men, or for single working women as compared, for instance, to upper-middle-class housewives.

However complicit and recuperable in the long run, the Valentino films articulated the possibility of female desire outside of motherhood and family, absolving it from Victorian double standards;[57] instead, they offered a morality of passion, an ideal of erotic reciprocity. Moreover, unlike the feminine reaction to sexual liberation in the shape of Elinor Glyn (the Edwardian novelist who invented the "it" girl), Valentino did not render the erotic a matter of social etiquette to be rehearsed by the aspiring female subject.[58] Rather, in focusing pleasure on a male protagonist of ambiguous and deviant identity, he appealed to those who most strongly felt the effects—freedom as well as frustration—of transition and liminality, the precariousness of a social mobility predicated on consumerist ideology.

If the Valentino films had no other critical function, they did present, by way of negation, a powerful challenge to myths of masculinity in American culture between the wars. The heroes of the American screen were men of action, like Douglas Fairbanks or William S. Hart, whose energy and determination was only enhanced by a certain lack of social graces, especially toward women. Even the more romantic stars, like Richard Barthelmess or John Barrymore, seemed to owe their good looks to a transcendent spirituality rather than anything related to their bodies and sexuality. Valentino not only inaugurated an explicitly sexual discourse on male beauty, but he also undercut standards of instrumental rationality that were culturally associated with masculine behavior; his resistance to expectations of everyday pragmatism, his swerving from the matter-of-fact and reasonable, may after all account for his subterranean popularity with male moviegoers, whether homosexual or heterosexual.

But Valentino's otherness cannot be explained exclusively in terms of masculinity and its discontents. Beyond the feminine connotations of his persona, his appeal was that of a "stranger." Whatever distinguished previous and contemporary male stars from each other, they were all Americans; that is, they did not display any distinct ethnic features other than those that were already naturalized as American. Valentino, however, bore the stigma of the first-generation, non-Anglo-Saxon immigrant—and was cast accordingly. He began his career as a seducer/villain of dark complexion, male counterpart of the figure of the vamp. When female audiences adopted him, despite the moral/racist injunction, he developed the persona of the Latin Lover, marketed as a blend of sexual vitality and romantic courtship. It is not surprising, then, that the paragons of virility responded to the threat he posed in a strongly nativist tone.[59] Yet more systematically, the films themselves both thematized and contained the scandal of his otherness through a recurrent pattern of the double identity mentioned earlier—a pattern which has to be read as a textual symptom of the repression of racial difference.

Valentino's darker self is ostensibly Southern European, somewhat redeemed by a veneer of French manners; in the context of American cinema and American culture, however, he could not have escaped the discursive economy of race and sex, encapsulated in the fear and repressed desire of miscegenation.[60] Sexual paranoia toward black men, rampant since the mid-1890s, reached a new pitch during the 1920s, precipitated by the imagined effects of women's sexual liberation. In terms of this economy, Valentino would have thrived on the fascination with the mulatto, a figure notoriously inscribed with sexual excess (cf. *The Birth of a Nation*), while historically inseparable from the white masters' abuse of black women. Whether or not Valentino touched upon that particular nerve, the connotation of racial otherness was masked by a discourse of exoticism—the Arab sheik, the Indian rajah, the Latin-American gaucho—allowing the female spectator to indulge in the fantasy at a safe distance. Sure enough, the respective narratives reveal the passionate Arab to be of British descent, like Tarzan, just as the lascivious gaucho in *The Four Horsemen* proves himself worthy of his French blood by dying on the field of honor. In such operations of fascination and disavowal, the Valentino films illustrate the ambivalence and fetishism characteristic of all racial stereotypes, the interdependence of racial and sexual difference.[61] At the same time, they mark a historical shift—if not, considering the force of repression provoked, an accidental leap or lapse—which enforced a transvaluation of the taboo and thus its partial recognition, albeit under the guise of the exotic.

Postscript. Some afterthoughts on the psycho-social enigma posed by the cult of Valentino seem appropriate here. While we may speculate on the appeal of the Valentino persona for both a textually and historically constructed female spectator, the massive impact of this appeal and the social forms it assumed remain quite mysterious. Roland Barthes speaks of the cult of the Valentinian face: "truly feminine Bacchanalia which all over the world were dedicated to the memory of a collectively revealed beauty."[62] Inevitably, however, such Dionysian rites are contaminated by the mechanisms of the mass media; the voyeuristic and fetishistic aspects of the Valentino excesses cannot be explained away. How could millions of women have indulged in such specifically male perversions? Barthes may ascribe the cult of Valentino to the aura of his face (*"visage"* vs *"figure"*); yet for Valentino himself and his female admirers it was certainly no less a cult of his body. In scores of publicity stills Valentino posed working out seminude, and in *Blood and Sand* and *Monsieur Beaucaire* he insisted on dressing scenes that would display individual parts of his body (note the close-up of his foot in *Blood and Sand*). Such exhibitionism, given the mechanisms of the apparatus, cannot escape fetishization: the male body, in its entire beauty, assumes the function of a phallic substitute. The more desperately Valentino himself emphasized attributes of physical prowess and virility, the more perfectly he played the part of the male impersonator, brilliant counterpart to the female "female" impersonators of the American screen such as Mae West or the vamps of his own films.

For the history of American cinema, on the threshold of its classical period, Valentino represents a unique instance of subversive irony—in that the commodity marketed as an idol of virility should have proven its success in the shape of a phallic fetish, a symbol of the missing penis. Valentino's miraculous career as a male impersonator illuminates the basic discrepancy between the penis and its symbolic representation, the phallus, thus revealing the male subject's position within the symbolic order as based upon a misreading of anatomy.[63] If women's fascination with Valentino, on whatever level of consciousness, expressed a recognition of that discrepancy, their massive and collective identification with this peculiar fetish also, and not least, asserted the claim to share in the reputation and representation of phallic power.

In the interaction with female audiences, moreover, the fetishization of Valentino's body assumed forms of theatricality which tended to subvert the mechanisms of separation intrinsic to cinematic voyeurism and fetishism. His female fans actively assailed the barriers that classical cinema was engaged in reaffirming, taking the star system more literally than the institution might have intended, while the media on their part shortcircuited the dialectics of public and private for the narrative of Valentino's life. Once women had found a fetish of their own, they were not content with merely gazing at it, but strove actually to touch it. Moreover, they expected him to reciprocate their fetishistic devotion: Valentino received intimate garments in the mail with the request to kiss and return them (which he did). The cult of Valentino's body finally extended to his corpse and led to the notorious necrophilic excesses: Valentino's last will specifying that his body be exhibited to his fans provoked a fetishistic run for buttons of his suit, or at least candles and flowers from the funeral home.[64] The collective mise-en-scène of fainting spells, hysterical grief, and, to be accurate, a few suicides, cannot be reduced to a mere spectacle of mass-cultural manipulation. It may be read, among other things, as a kind of rebellion, a desperate protest against the passivity and one-sidedness with which patriarchal cinema supports the subordinate position of women in the gender hierarchy. In such a reading, even the commercially distorted manifestation of female desire might articulate a utopian claim—to have the hollow promises of screen happiness be released into the mutuality of erotic practice.

Notes

1 Siegfried Kracauer, "Die kleinen Ladenmädchen gehen ins Kino," in *Das Ornament der Masse* (Frankfurt: Suhrkamp, 1977), 293. The following essay is a revised and expanded version of "S. M. Rodolfo," *Frauen und Film*, no. 33 (Oct. 1982): 19–33. For critical comments and shared enthusiasm, I would like to thank Serafina Bathrick, Atina Grossman, Gertrud Koch, Sally Stein, Maureen Turim, and, above all, Sandy Flitterman. All translations mine, unless otherwise indicated.

2 Brad Steiger and Chaw Mank, *Valentino: An Intimate and Shocking Exposé* (New York: MacFadden, 1966); Vincent Tajiri, *Valentino: The True Life Story* (New York: Bantam, 1977); Irving Shulman, *Valentino* (1967; New York: Pocket Books, 1968); also see Noel Botham and Peter Donnelly, *Valentino: The Love God* (New York: Ace Books, 1977). Tajiri's book contains a relatively detailed filmography and bibliography.

3 Valentino came to symbolize the failure of the American Dream, especially to more highbrow critics of culture like H. L. Mencken (*Prejudices, Sixth Series*, 1927) and John Dos Passos (*The Big Money*, 1936). Ken Russell's film, *Valentino* (1977), based on the Steiger/Mank biography and starring Rudolf Nureyev in the title role, articulates this theme through its pervasive references to *Citizen Kane*, such as the use of *post mortem* multiple flashback narration and other corny allusions.

4 Among the many reassessments of the period, see Estelle B. Freedman, "The New Woman: Changing Views of Women in the 1920s," *Journal of American History* 56, no. 2 (Sept. 1974): 372–93; Mary P. Ryan, *Womanhood in America*, second ed. (New York: New Viewpoints, 1979), ch. 5; Julie Matthaei, *An Economic History of Women in America* (New York: Schocken, 1982), especially chaps. 7–9.

5 This hypothesis implies a concept of the public sphere, in particular that of an alternative or counter public sphere as developed by Oskar Negt and Alexander Kluge in *Öffentlichkeit und Erfahrung/Public Sphere and Experience* (Frankfurt: Suhrkamp, 1972). For a review in English, see Eberhard Knödler-Bunte, "The Proletarian Public Sphere and Political Organization," *New German Critique*, no. 4 (Winter 1975): 51–75; and my own paraphrase of Negt and Kluge in "Early Silent Cinema: Whose Public Sphere," *New German Critique*, no. 29 (Spring/Summer 1983): 155–59. The role of the cinema for women during this period of transition is discussed in Judith Mayne, "Immigrants and Spectators," *Wide Angle* 5, no. 2 (1982): 32–41; Elizabeth Ewen, "City Lights: Immigrant Women and the Rise of the Movies," *Signs* 5, no. 3 (1980): S45–S65; Mary Ryan, "The Projection of a New Womanhood:

The Movie Moderns in the 1920s," in *Our American Sisters: Women in American Life and Thought*, second ed., Jean E. Friedman and William G. Shade, eds. (Boston: Allyn and Bacon, 1976): 366–84.

6 Laura Mulvey, "Afterthoughts . . . Inspired by *Duel in the Sun," Framework*, nos. 15–17 (1981): 12; "Visual Pleasure and Narrative Cinema" originally appeared in *Screen* 16, no. 3 (Autumn 1975): 6–18.

7 For a still useful discussion of Mulvey in a larger context of directions of recent theory, see Christine Gledhill, "Developments in Feminist Film Criticism" (1978), rpt. in *Re-Vision: Essays in Feminist Film Criticism*, Mary Ann Doane, Patricia Mellencamp, Linda Williams, eds. (Los Angeles: AFI monograph Series, 1983), 18–48. Among articles devoted primarily to a critique of Mulvey, see David Rodowick, "The Difficulty of Difference," *Wide Angle* 5, no. 1 (1982): 4–15; Janet Walker, "Psychoanalysis and Feminist Film Theory," *Wide Angle* 6, no. 3 (1984): 16–23. For discussions challenging the Metzian/ Mulveyan paradigm of spectatorship altogether, see Gaylyn Studlar, "Masochism and the Perverse Pleasures of the Cinema," *Quarterly Review of Film Studies* 9, no. 4 (Fall 1984): 267–82; Gertrud Koch, "Exchanging the Gaze: Re-Visioning Feminist Film Theory," *New German Critique*, no. 34 (Winter 1985): 139–53.

8 Mulvey, "Afterthoughts," 12.

9 This theoretical endeavor would greatly benefit from a more historical perspective taking into account the discourse on female reception during the formative decades of the institution, in particular the rejection of mass culture in terms of femininity. For German cinema, see Heide Schlüpmann's suggestive essay, "Kinosucht [Cinema Addiction]," *Frauen und Film*, no. 33 (Oct. 1982): 45–52; and my own "Early Silent Cinema": 173–84. Patrice Petro draws an impressive parallel between the German debates on "distraction" and American discourse on television in "Mass Culture and the Feminine: The 'Place' of Television in Film Studies," *Cinema Journal* 25, no. 2 (Spring 1986): 5–21. Significantly, in both American as well as German sources of the 1910s and 1920s, "distraction" and "absorption" are more often perceived in a relationship of affinity and simultaneity, than in one of opposition (as Brechtian film theory of the 1970s would have it). On the trope of transvestism, in particular its different uses by male and female writers, see Sandra M. Gilbert, "Costumes of the Mind: Transvestism as Metaphor in Modern Literature," *Critical Inquiry* 7, no. 2 (Winter 1980): 391–417, especially 404ff.

10 Mary Ann Doane, "Film and the Masquerade: Theorising the Female Spectator," *Screen* 23, nos. 3–4 (Sept./Oct. 1982): 81 (emphasis added).

11 The question of temporality has been raised as a crucial aspect of female spectatorship by Teresa de Lauretis, *Alice Doesn't: Feminism, Semiotics, Cinema* (Bloomington: Indiana University Press, 1984), 96ff.; also see Tania Modleski, "Time and Desire in the Woman's Film," *Cinema Journal* 23, no. 3 (Spring 1984): 19–30. Modleski refers to Julia Kristeva, "Women's Time," trans. Alice Jardine and Harry Blake, *Signs* 7, no. 1 (Fall 1981): 13–35. For a discussion of the conflicting temporal registers of individual life history and social experience, see Negt/Kluge, *Public Sphere and Experience*, 45–74.

12 Doane, "The 'Woman's Film': Possession and Address," in *Re-Vision*, 67–82; Linda Williams, " 'Something Else Besides a Mother': *Stella Dallas* and the Maternal Melodrama," *Cinema Journal* 24, no. 1 (Fall 1984): 2–27; Tania Modleski, *Loving with a Vengeance: Mass Produced Fantasies for Women* (1982; New York: Methuen, 1984).

13 Williams's " 'Something Else' " in part responds to E. Ann Kaplan, "The Case of the Missing Mother: Maternal Issues in Vidor's *Stella Dallas," Heresies* 16 (1983): 81–85; Kaplan's reply appeared in *Cinema Journal* 24, no. 2 (Winter 1985): 40–43.

14 See Jürgen Habermas's critique of Gadamer, *Zur Logik der Sozialwissenschaften* (Frankfurt: Suhrkamp, 1970), 174ff.; "Der Universalitätsanspruch der Hermeneutik," *Kultur und Kritik* (Frankfurt: Suhrkamp, 1973), 264–301.

15 This project obviously involves some "reading against the grain" but ultimately has a different objective: rather than merely to expose, from film to film, the textual contradictions symptomatic of the repression of female subjectivity under patriarchy, a rewriting of film history in a feminist sense seeks to discover traces of female subjectivity even in the most repressive and alienated forms of consumer culture. The paradigm I have in mind is Benjamin's huge work on the Paris Arcades which Susan Buck-Morss (in a forthcoming book) reads as a dialectical *Ur*-history of mass culture. Also see Habermas, "Consciousness-Raising or Redemptive Criticism: The Contemporaneity of Walter Benjamin" (1972), *New German Critique*, no. 17 (Spring 1979): 30–59.

16 Doane, "Masquerade," 77; Kaplan, *Women and Film: Both Sides of the Camera* (New York and London: Methuen, 1983), 29. In the context of this problem, a number of critics have recently focused on the representation of the male body and the question of masculinity, among them Pam Cook, "Masculinity in Crisis?" (on *Raging Bull*), *Screen* 23, nos. 3–4 (Sept.–Oct. 1982): 39–53; Richard Dyer, "Don't

Look Now: The Male Pin-Up," ibid., 61–73; Steve Neale, "Masculinity as Spectacle," *Screen* 24, no. 6 (Nov.–Dec. 1983): 2–16.

17 Teresa de Lauretis, *Alice Doesn't*, 83.

18 David Bordwell, Janet Staiger, Kristin Thompson, *The Classical Hollywood Cinema: Film Style and Mode of Production to 1960* (New York: Columbia University Press, 1985). Thompson, chap. 18, sees the basic narrative and stylistic premises of the classical system in place by 1917; the technological changes that gave 1920s films their distinct visual texture are described in chap. 21.

19 I feel supported in this contention by Teresa de Lauretis, *Alice Doesn't*, 125, 162; she also shares my skepticism concerning the Hegelian premises of Lacan, 128ff., 189 (n. 31), 205 (n. 32). By the same author, see "Aesthetic and Feminist Theory," *New German Critique*, no. 34 (Winter 1985): 154–75.

20 A more consistent trait in Valentino's history with the industry is the high number of women in the production of his films, although this was generally more often the case before 1930. His most important films had scripts written by women, in particular June Mathis who "discovered" him, but also Frances Marion; *Blood and Sand* was brilliantly edited by Dorothy Arzner; Alla Nazimova and Natacha Rambova, a designer and also his second wife, exerted their artistic and spiritual(ist) influence on many productions, with or without credit.

21 Sigmund Freud, "Three Essays on the Theory of Sexuality" (1905), *Standard Edition* 7: 182.

22 Mulvey, "Visual Pleasure," 11.

23 A more misogynist version of the same pattern occurs in *Cobra* (1925) when a friend advises the unhappily courting but as usual much pursued Valentino, "look at the woman with the torch: she is safe!"—cut to the Statue of Liberty. For an excellent reading of these "duels" and "ballets" of the gaze, see Karsten Witte, "Rudolph Valentino: Erotoman des Augenblicks," in *Die Unsterblichen des Kinos* 1, ed. Adolf Heinzlmeier et al. (Frankfurt: Fischer, 1982), 29–35.

24 "Instincts and their Vicissitudes," *Standard Edition* 14: 128ff.; "Three Essays," *SE* 7: 156ff., 199f. and passim.

25 I am much endebted here to the work of Gertrud Koch; for essays available in translation, see "Why Women Go to the Movies," *Jump Cut*, no. 27 (July 1982); and "Female Sensuality: Past Joys and Future Hopes," *Jump Cut*, no. 30 (March 1985). Also see Christian Metz's distinction between cinematic and theatrical voyeurism, in *The Imaginary Signifier* (Bloomington: Indiana University Press, 1982), 64–66, 91–98.

26 Freud, "The Psycho-Analytic View of Psychogenic Disturbance of Vision" (1910), *Standard Edition* 11: 216f.

27 For an elaboration of this aspect of Freud's essay, see Stephen Heath, "Difference," *Screen* 19, no. 3 (Autumn 1978): 86–87.

28 Christa Karpenstein, "Bald führt der Blick das Wort ein, bald leitet das Wort den Blick," *Kursbuch*, no. 49 (1977): 62. Also see Jutta Brückner's important essay on pornography, "Der Blutfleck im Auge der Kamera," *Frauen und Film*, no. 30 (Dec. 1981): 13–23; Brückner links the historical "underdevelopment" of women's vision with the modality of dreams, as a more archaic form of consciousness: "This female gaze, which is so precise precisely because it is not too precise, because it also has this inward turn, opening itself to fantasy images which it melts with the more literal images on the screen, this gaze is the basis for a kind of identification which women in particular tend to seek in the cinema" (19).

29 The discrepancy between advertising pitch and Valentino's actual lack of orientation and focus is obvious in the promotional short, *Rudolph Valentino and His Eighty-Eight American Beauties* (1923), which shows him as a somewhat half-hearted arbiter in a beauty contest. Even in Roland Barthes's compelling reading of the Valentinian face, the emphasis is on the aggressive aspect of his gaze: "The face is mysterious, full of exotic splendor, of an inaccessible, Baudelairean beauty, undoubtedly made of exquisite dough; but one knows all too well that this cold glistening of make-up, this delicate, dark line under the animal eye, the black mouth—all this betrays a mineral substance, a cruel statue which comes to life only to thrust forth." "Visages et figures," *Esprit*, no. 204 (July 1953): 7. ["Le visage est arcane, splendeur exotique, beauté baudelairienne, inaccessible, d'une pâte exquise sans doute, mais on sait bien que cette froid luisance du fard, ce mince trait sombre sous l'oeil d'animal, cette bouche noire, tout cela est d'un être minéral, d'une statue cruelle qui ne s'anime que pour percer."] The metaphor of piercing or thrusting, however, would only confirm the suspicion that the Valentinian gaze is ultimately a substitute for phallic potency, hence the fetishistic cult surrounding it.

30 Two of Valentino's most popular films, *The Four Horsemen* and *Blood and Sand*, actually culminate in the protagonist's death, bringing into play the deep affinity of eros and death drive which Freud observes in his fascinating paper on "The Theme of the Three Caskets" (1913), *SE* 12: 289–301.

According to Enno Patalas, Valentino himself identified much more strongly with these two roles than with the superficial heroism of the Sheik, *Sozialgeschichte der Stars* (Hamburg: Marion von Schröder Verlag, 1963), 96f.

31 Doane, "Misrecognition and Identity," *Ciné-Tracts* 3, no. 3 (Fall 1980): 25; Metz, *The Imaginary Signifier*, 46ff., 56ff and passim.

32 For example, the work of Stephen Heath, Raymond Bellour, and Thierry Kuntzel; also see the section on point of view in *Film Reader*, no. 4 (1979).

33 See Janet Walker, "Psychoanalysis and Feminist Film Theory" (note 7), 20ff.; de Lauretis, "Aesthetic and Feminist Theory" (note 19), 164ff.

34 This option actually prevails in contemporary statements of female spectators; see Herbert Blumer, *Movies and Conduct* (New York: Macmillan, 1933), 69–70. In retrospect, however, as I frequently found in conversations with women who were in their teens at the time, the female star has faded into oblivion as much as the narrative, whereas Valentino himself is remembered with great enthusiasm and vividness of detail.

35 Doane, "Misrecognition and Identity," 28ff.; Doane's major objection to Metz's concept of primary identification is that, based as it is on the analogy with the Lacanian mirror stage and thus the hypothetical constitution of the male subject, the concept perpetuates, on a theoretical level, the patriarchal exclusion of female spectatorship.

36 See Richard Dyer, *Stars* (London: BFI, 1979).

37 This pattern of combining dark and light oppositions in one and the same character must have been perceived as typical of the Valentino text; see the change of Dubrovsky's alias in *The Eagle* from Pushkin's Monsieur Deforge to Valentino's Monsieur LeBlanc.

38 Alexander Walker, *Rudolph Valentino* (Harmondsworth: Penguin, 1977), 54f.

39 As Tom Gunning points out, such instances of direct address were rather common in erotic films before 1908, but thereafter persist only in the pornographic tradition—"the seeming acknowledgment of the presence of the spectator-voyeur gives these films much of their erotic power." "An Unseen Energy Swallows Space: The Space in Early Film and Its Relation to American Avant-Garde Film," in *Film Before Griffith*, John Fell, ed. (Berkeley: University of California Press, 1983), 359.

40 Dressing up Valentino is a major theme in *Rudy: An Intimate Portrait of Rudolph Valentino by his Wife Natacha Rambova* (London: Hutchinson, 1926). Given his own sartorial extravagance as well as his being himself a phenomenon of fashion, it is actually curious how little the films participated in the promotion of contemporary clothing styles; only three of his major films, as far as I can tell, cast him in modern dress. In this context, without presuming too preposterous a parallel, one might remember the link between transsexual and trans-historical changes of costumes in Virginia Woolf's *Orlando* (1928); also see Gilbert, "Costumes of the Mind" (note 9, above), 406.

41 A number of critics have recently commented upon the role of sadomasochistic structures in cinematic identification: Rodowick, "The Difficulty of Difference" (note 7, above); Doane, "The Woman's Film" (note 12, above); Kaja Silverman, "Masochism and Subjectivity" (on Cavani's *Portiere di Notte*), *Framework*, no. 12 (1980): 2–9. Also see Jessica Benjamin, "Master and Slave: The Fantasy of Erotic Domination," in *Powers of Desire: The Politics of Sexuality*, ed. Ann Snitow et al. (New York: Monthly Review Press, 1983), 280–99.

42 Koch, "Schattenreich der Körper: Zum pornographischen Kino," in *Lust und Elend: Das erotische Kino* (München: Bucher, 1981), 35; English trans. forthcoming in *Jump Cut*. The investment in eros as a negation of the principle of social identity is, of course, a topos of the Frankfurt School, especially in the work of Adorno; see his and Horkheimer's critique of the subject under patriarchy and monopoly capitalism in *Dialectic of Enlightenment* (Amsterdam: Querido, 1947), his aphorisms and fragments, dating back to the period of exile, in *Minima Moralia* (Frankfurt: Suhrkamp, 1951), as well as later essays in cultural criticism such as "Sexualtabus und Recht heute," *Eingriffe* (Frankfurt: Suhrkamp, 1963): 104.

43 Tajiri (note 2), 63.

44 The male contingent among Valentino fans is not to be underestimated, including Elvis Presley, Kenneth Anger, and other luminaries; see Kenneth Anger, "Rudy's Rep," in *Hollywood Babylon* (1975; New York: Dell, 1981); and his contribution to a catalogue of the Berlin Film Festival retrospective of Valentino's work, "Sich an Valentino erinnern heisst Valentino entdecken," discussed by Karsten Witte, in "Fetisch-Messen," *Frauen und Film*, no. 38 (May 1985): 72–78. Ken Russell's film (see note 3) both exploits and disavows Valentino's place in the homosexual tradition. More important than biographical fact is the question of how Valentino challenged dominant standards of masculinity, which is also a question of their social and historical variability and changeability.

45 The sadistic spicing of cinematic pleasure (far from being the exclusive domain of Von Stroheim) is still rather common in pre-Code films, though seldom with such strong effects on the sexual persona

of the protagonist. Consider, for instance, a sequence early on in the Pickford vehicle *Sparrows* (1926) in which the villain (Gustav von Seyffertitz) crushes a doll sent, by an absent mother, to one of the children he keeps as slaves; the camera lingers, close-up, on the remnants of the doll as it slowly disappears in the swamp. The fascination deployed in such a shot far exceeds narrative motivation; i.e., its function for establishing Mr. Grimes as irredeemably evil.

46 Freud, "Three Essays," *SE* 7: 160; also "Instincts," *SE* 14: 126.

47 Most notably in "The Economic Problem of Masochism" (1924), *SE* 19: 155–70, where Freud develops the notion of a "primary" masochism linked to the death instinct; this notion is already present though rejected in "Instincts and Their Vicissitudes" (1915), 127, but resumed as early as 1920 in *Beyond the Pleasure Principle, SE* 18: 55.

48 Studlar, "Masochism and the Perverse Pleasures of the Cinema" (note 7); Deleuze, *Masochism: An Interpretation of Coldness and Cruelty* (French orig. 1967; New York: George Braziller, 1971).

49 Deleuze, *Masochism*, 21, 37f. Studlar acknowledges this problem in passing, "Masochism and Perverse Pleasures," 270 and her note 27. The reason why Deleuze's model seems to work so surprisingly well for the Sternberg/Dietrich films might have less to do with the validity of the model than with Sternberg's indebtedness to the same cultural background that gave us *Venus in Furs*.

50 The essay has been much discussed in recent film theory; for example, Rodowick, "The Difficulty of Difference," and Doane, "The Woman's Film."

51 Freud, "A Child Is Being Beaten," *Standard Edition* 17: 186.

52 This incestuous-narcissistic aura is encapsulated in a portrait showing Valentino and Rambova in profile and, obviously, in the nude; rpt. in Walker, 73; and Anger, *Hollywood Babylon*, 160–61.

53 Williams, "When the Woman Looks," *Re-Vision*, 83–96. The point Williams makes with regard to a number of classic horror films also elucidates the function of the dark/light split in the Valentino character: "the power and potency of the monster body . . . should not be interpreted as an eruption of the normally repressed animal sexuality of the civilized male (the monster as double for the male viewer and characters in the film), but as feared power and potency of a different kind of sexuality (the monster as double for the woman)" (87).

54 Adorno, "Sexualtabus" (note 42), 104–5; the phrase is used in English and without quotation marks; also see "This Side of the Pleasure Principle," *Minima Moralia: Reflections from Damaged Life* (London: New Left Books, 1974). Marcuse's plea for polymorphous perversity in *Eros and Civilization* (1955: Boston: Beacon Press, 1966) is more problematic, especially in light of the Foucauldian analysis of the "perverse implantation" (*The History of Sexuality* 1), but Marcuse himself takes a more pessimistic view in his "Political Preface 1966," while maintaining a utopian distinction between sexual liberty and erotic/political freedom (xiv–xv). Already during the 1920s, the prophets of a "healthy sex life" were numerous, drawing on the essentialist sexual psychology of Havelock Ellis, on the newly discovered "doctrine" of psychoanalysis, as well as libertarian positions developed among the Greenwich Village boheme although not necessarily all that liberating for women; see writings by Hutchins Hapgood, Max Eastman, V. F. Calverton and—probably the single most repressive instance of sexual hygiene—Floyd Dell, *Love in the Machine Age: A Psychological Study of the Transition from Patriarchal Society* (New York: Farrar & Rinehart, 1930).

55 Walker, *Rudolph Valentino*, 8, 47 and passim.

56 See works cited above, note 4.

57 *Blood and Sand*, closest to the melodramatic matrix, is the only film that makes Valentino's mate a mother; by contrast, most other female characters opposite Valentino have tomboyish qualities (especially Moran in *Moran of the Lady Letty*), an air of independence, owing to either a superior social status or work, and, above all, a certain "mischievous vivacity" (Ryan) that was associated with the New Woman.

58 Glyn actually endorsed Valentino's sex appeal, and he starred in *Beyond the Rocks* (1922), based on one of her novels. Still, the focus on a male star distinguishes the Valentino films from films that more immediately functioned to train their audiences in "fashionable femininity"; Ryan, "Projection" (note 5), 370f.

59 See the notorious "Pink Powder Puff" attack in the *Chicago Tribune*, July 18, 1926, reported in *Hollywood Babylon*, 156–58.

60 For this aspect of the Valentino persona I am indebted to Virginia Wright Wexman as well as to Richard Dyer's work on Paul Robeson; Winifred Stewart and Jane Hady, who remember the Valentino cult during their teenage years in Martinsburg, West Virginia, further encouraged the following speculations. Also see Jacqueline Hall, " 'The Mind that Burns in Each Body': Women, Rape, and Racial Violence," in *Powers of Desire* (note 41), 337.

61 Homi K. Bhabha, "The Other Question: The Stereotype and Colonial Discourse," *Screen* 24, no. 6 (Nov.–Dec. 1983): 18–36.

62 Barthes, "Visages et figures" (note 29), 6.

63 Richard Dyer suggests that all representations of the male body, especially however, of male nudity, share this fate, since the actual sight of the penis, whether limp or erect, is bound to be awkward, thus revealing the discrepancy between it and the symbolic claims made in its name, the hopeless assertion of phallic mastery; "Don't Look Now" (note 16), 71–72.

64 Any Valentino biography will elaborate on these events with great gusto. For the most detailed account, including an astonishing chapter on Valentino's afterlife ("Act V: Cuckooland"), see Shulman's book (note 2).

Chapter 18

Jackie Stacey

HOLLYWOOD MEMORIES (1994)

Editors' Introduction

At least since the 1970s, feminist uses of psychoanalysis have presented film studies with a powerful theoretical model. Following the groundbreaking work of Laura Mulvey and others, film scholars came to understand the significance of how women-in-films functioned as objects of the male gaze, from men within the film narrative and from a theoretical male spectator in the theatre. By the 1990s, feminists and other film scholars understood some of the limitations of the project of studying the gaze. Most notably, women themselves, as viewers, had been left out, and so too had any consideration of their varying degrees of agency, pleasure, and desire when they watched movies. With her work on "Hollywood Memories," Jackie Stacey bridged the feminism of the 1970s with a newer brand of feminist historiography and sociology, and developed a method for interpreting women's experiences at the movies, and in particular their experiences of female stars. These experiences could only be filtered through memory, however, with Stacey asking her subjects to write about going to the movies, and watching movie stars, in the 1940s, 1950s, and 1960s. Thus Stacey's work bridges the more purely ethnographic studies of audiences that began as early as the World War One period (see, for example, Emilie Altenloh's *A Sociology of the Cinema*, from 1914) and the more recent and theoretically informed work on movies and their contemporary audiences, by Richard Maltby and Melvyn Stokes, for example, and on movies and memory, typified in Annette Kuhn's *Dreaming of Fred and Ginger*. This scholarship, by Stacey and others, has helped move film studies away from a fixation on representation and towards a much more nuanced understanding of the practices of viewing films and the methodologies for studying viewers.

Suggested Reading

Emilie Altenloh, "A Sociology of the Cinema: The Audience," (1914), trans. Kathleen Cross, *Screen*, 42:3 (Autumn, 2001), pp. 249–93; Annette Kuhn, *Dreaming of Fred and Ginger: Cinema and Cultural Memory* (New York: New York University Press, 2002);

Gregory Waller, *Main Street Amusements: Movies and Commercial Entertainment in a Southern City, 1896–1930* (Washington, DC: Smithsonian Institution Press, 1995).

THE ABSENCE OF 'WOMAN' from Hollywood cinema has been a central concern within feminist film criticism for many years now; and I want to continue the investigation of this case of 'the missing woman'. My struggle, however, is not with the absence of certain screen images, but with the absence of the audience from both cinema history and feminist film criticism. The missing woman in the context of this article, then, is that slippery category 'the female spectator'.[1] How can we go about trying to trace this missing woman, and what methodological issues might such a search raise? After twenty years of feminist film theories preoccupied mainly with textual spectatorship, there is now an increasing interest in actual cinema audiences. Work by women such as Helen Taylor, Jacqueline Bobo, Angela Partington, Janet Thumim and Annette Kuhn has begun to investigate how texts might be read by particular audiences at particular times.[2]

My interest in questions of historical methodology[3] arises out of my own research with the memories of a particular group of female spectators of 1940s and 1950s Hollywood cinema. The women whose memories are used in this study are all white British women, mostly in their sixties and seventies (though ranging in age from forty-plus to over ninety), and are readers of the two leading women's magazines *Woman's Weekly* and *Woman's Realm*, through which I initially contacted them. The focus of this research is the relationships between female film stars of this period and their female spectators. Letters and questionnaires from over 350 women containing their memories of favourite Hollywood stars form the basis of the study, though I also draw on other historical sources in the longer version of this study.[4] My concern here is with how female spectators' memories might be used as a source for historical studies of cinema and the methodological issues raised by their use.

The focus is obviously on *past* cinema audiences, though many of the methodological issues raised pertain to all kinds of audience research. For just as we cannot view history as a straightforward retrieval of past time, neither can audience research ever capture that 'pure' moment of reception, what Valerie Walkerdine has called the 'magic convergence'.[5] The methodological complexities of audience research are merely amplified when we begin to investigate audiences from previous decades. After all, in one sense, the 'audiences' of the 1940s and the 1950s no longer exist: that originary moment of spectatorship is lost and can never be recaptured. However, the fact that audiences' accounts of their experiences are inevitably retrospective representations is a methodological issue for any 'ethnographic' audience research. A critical analysis of the forms and processes of memory, then, is pertinent to all ethnographic studies of audiences. However, in historical research, the length of the gap between the events and their recollection (in my own research, some forty or fifty years) highlights especially sharply the question of processes of memory formation.

The memories produced by these female spectators in the letters and questionnaires they sent me are structured through certain codes and conventions. Like other kinds of texts, these memories present an identifiable set of generic features. In this part of my article, I want to discuss briefly two of these genres of memory formation, before going on to analyze the dialogic exchange through which they are produced.

The first genre I call *iconic memory*. Memories of 1940s and 1950s Hollywood frequently take the form of a particular 'frozen moment', a moment removed from its temporal context and captured as 'pure image': be it of Bette Davis's flashing eyes, Rita Hayworth's flowing hair, or Doris Day's 'fun' outfits. A memory of 'love at first sight' is typical of this genre. Here religious signifiers articulate the special status of the star and the intensity of this moment:

> I'll never forget the first I saw her, it was in *My Gal Sal* in 1942, and her name was Rita Hayworth. I couldn't take my eyes off her, she was the most perfect woman I had ever seen. The old cliche of 'screen goddess' was used about many stars, but those are truly the only words that define that divine creature. . . . I was stunned and amazed that any human being could be that lovely.
>
> (Violette Holland)

Iconic memories are not only produced as memories of the stars: they can also be spectators' memories of themselves in such 'frozen moments':

> Our favourite cinema was the Ritz – with its deep pile carpet and double sweeping staircase. Coming down one always felt like a Hollywood heroine descending into the ballroom.
>
> (Anon)

The frequent recurrence of this form of memory might be explained by the centrality of the idea of 'image' in the definition of 'successful' femininity in patriarchal culture. Given the extent to which female stars function in Hollywood cinema through their status as objects of visual pleasure, it is hardly surprising that iconic memory features so centrally in these accounts.[6]

The second genre of memory which occurs most frequently is *narrative memory*. Narrative memories present temporally located sequential stories of cinemagoing in the 1940s and 1950s. As well as remembering particular narratives featuring their favourite screen idols, these spectators also recreate their own relationships to the stars through narrative forms of memory. These memories of Hollywood stars are often specific forms of self-narrativization in relation to cultural ideals of femininity. These spectators construct themselves as heroines of their remembered narratives, which in turn deal with their own cinema heroines of that time. Memories of Hollywood stars are thus represented through the narrative structures which connect the self to the ideal. This next memory reworks the conventions of the romance narrative, for example, giving a homoerotic charge to the pleasures of female spectatorship:

> In the late 1930s, when I was about nine or ten, I began to be aware of a young girl's face appearing in magazines and newspapers. I was fascinated. The large eyes, full mouth, sometimes the wonderful smile, showing the slightly prominent but perfect teeth. I feel rather irritated that I don't recall the moment when I realised that the face belonged to a lovely singing voice beginning to be heard on the radio record programmes. . . . The face and the voice belonged to Deanna Durbin. . . . In the 1940s at the age of twelve I was evacuated from my house in South London to Looe in Cornwall, and it was there I was first taken to the pictures for a special treat. There at last I saw her. The film, a sequel to her first, was *Three Smart Girls Grow Up*. The effect she had on me can only be described as electrifying. I had never felt such a surge of adoration before. . . . My feeling for her was no passing fancy. . . .
>
> (Patricia Robinson)

The structure of this first 'meeting' or, rather, first sighting is built around a series of enigmas, or absences, typical of the romance genre:[7] the anonymous face whose details are 'unforgettable', the voice on the radio, the lost moment when face and voice are matched together, and the gradual buildup to the culmination when 'there at last I saw her'. The star's screen appearance signifies closure, and yet, true to generic conventions, this moment of ending simultaneously suggests the beginning of a lifetime's devotion.

Several memories combine narrative and iconic elements. These two genres frequently construct each other: iconic memories may be of a narrative image from a particular film, for example; and many of the iconic memories, such as the fantasy of being a Hollywood heroine descending the cinema staircase, are also narrativized. Visual display is the common current running through many of these memory formations. Significantly, each of the processes of memory formation and selection I have discussed so far replicates, and is replicated by, distinguishing features of Hollywood cinema. Popular memories of Hollywood cinema in these accounts thus take cinematic forms. Memories are typically constructed through key icons, significant moments, narrative structures and heroic subject positions. These examples demonstrate how the past is produced in the present through visual and narrative conventions replicating their historical object: cinema.

> . . . *the life of any text – case history or otherwise – is not generated by itself, but through the act of being read.*[8]

> . . . *the intervention of the historian . . . is of crucial significance . . . as a catalyst for whole process of structured remembrance.*[9]

Having identified some of the formations of memory in my study, I want now to consider the role of the research process, and indeed the researcher, in their production. I would suggest that this type of audience research involves 'a dialogic exchange' in which the fantasies researcher and respondents have about each other have a determining effect on the accounts produced. The 'imagined reader' structures the forms of memory offered and, to a greater or lesser extent, is present within the texts themselves. Integral to an understanding of the textuality of these memories, then, is a recognition of the dialogicality of textual production. Here, audience researchers might usefully draw upon insights from dialogic theory which emphasize the ways in which texts are always produced *for readers*; indeed the imagined reader can be seen as written into particular textual modes of address.[10] This process might be summed up in what Lynne Pearce has recently identified as Voloshinov's most eloquent expression of addressivity:

> Orientation of the word toward the addressee has an extremely high significance. In point of fact, *word is a two-sided act*. It is determined equally by *whose* word it is and *for whom* it is meant. As word, it is precisely *the product of the reciprocal relationship between speaker and listener, addresser and addressee*. Each and every word expresses 'one' in relation to the 'other'. I give myself verbal shape from another's point of view of the community to which I belong. A word is a bridge thrown between myself and another. If one end of the bridge belongs to me, then the other depends on my addressee. A word is a territory shared by both addresser and addressee, by the speaker and his [sic] interlocutor.
>
> (Voloshinov's emphasis)[11]

In her comprehensive account of dialogic theory, Lynne Pearce outlines the significance of Bakhtin's work on the role of the addressee in characterizing various 'speech genres' in which the relationship between speaker and addressee is of crucial significance in understanding meaning:

> An essential (constitutive) marker of the utterance is its quality of being directed to someone, its *addressivity*. . . . Both the composition and, particularly, the

> style of the utterance depend on those to whom the utterance is addressed, how the speaker (or writer) senses and imagines his addressee, and the force of their effect on the utterance. Each speech genre in each area of speech communication has its own typical conception of the addressee, and this defines it as a genre.
>
> (Voloshinov's emphasis)[12]

Although this theory is derived from speech communication, it has been widely developed in relation to written texts.[13] Dialogic theory then highlights the subjective, yet social, relations of textual production: the role of the imagined reader in meaning production. It is important here to approach the text as a dialogic form in which the addressee is part of its structure and mode of communication. In audience research the relationship between the academic researcher and interviewees or respondents necessarily shapes which accounts are told and which are not, and indeed how they are told. This mutual (though, importantly, not equal) relationship has been paralleled with that between analyst and analysand in psychoanalysis.[14] For audience research such as this, a more textual model of exchange and interpretation might be appropriate: in either case, though, audiences and researchers may be seen as in a dialogic relationship – one in which the imagined other proves integral to the forms of knowledge produced. Dialogic theories of the reader imagined through the function of addressivity might be used to investigate this textual relationship between audiences and researchers. This model would operate in any kind of audience–researcher exchange. However, in retrospective representations of the past, it functions as a way for respondents to reconstruct their pasts in the present for another who is outside their worlds, but also (and as we shall see, importantly) outside their generation. Here, as work on popular memory has highlighted, the 'centrality of generation . . . [is] a fundamental impulse to remember'.[15] Thus, in this dialogic exchange, some of the processes of memory formation become visible as respondents negotiate their constructions of the past in relation to an imagined reader in the present.

Dialogic practices of writing are integral both to my initial invitations to produce a remembered past, which posit an imagined addressee, and also, in turn, to the written responses I received – which embody the projection of an imagined reader: the researcher. In my first communication with respondents, I imagined female fans who had stories to tell about their relationships to Hollywood stars of the past. My advertisement addressed them directly using the second person: 'Were you a keen cinemagoer of the 1940s and 1950s?' The ways in which I requested information encouraged women to use narrative forms to construct their memories. My request for letters from women who were keen cinemagoers in the 1940s and 1950s invited retrospective self-narrativizations in the retelling of past events so characteristic of the conventions of letter-writing more generally. Even in the followup questionnaire, a less personal mode of communication, and one associated with 'scientific' information-giving rather than with storytelling, the kinds of questions I asked inevitably produced, or at least delimited, the forms of responses. I invited a kind of narrativization of the past, for example, when I asked respondents to 'describe a favourite cinema experience of the 1940s/1950s'. Finally, I allowed maximum space for the central question in the questionnaire in which respondents were asked to 'write about your favourite star from the 1940s and then the 1950s, explaining what you liked about them and what they meant to you: what made these stars more appealing than others?'[16] This clearly requested narrativizations of the past and invited a commentary on respondents' own tastes and preferences.

Similarly, respondents signal my presence in their imaginations through a number of textual enunciations. Some use my name to effect a personal mode of address in order to emphasize a specific feeling: 'Oh Jackie, what lovely memories are being recalled – I do hope you are going to ask for lots more information as a trip down memory lane of this nature is most enjoyable'. (Barbara Forshaw) This example is taken from a letter; the use of my name suggests a familiarity which easily accompanies the letter form, but is normally absent from the relationship of researcher and researched. It also adds a note of authenticity to the exchange which is lacking in more formal types of address, suggesting a personal sharing of experiences 'between friends'. The depth of the emotion felt about the research project is given wistful exclamation here in the 'oh' as well as in the use of my name. My role in this dialogic exchange is thus included in the text itself as this respondent pauses to reflect upon the pleasures of remembering the 'Golden Age of Hollywood'. My obviously 'younger' generation name, in contrast to many of the respondents' names (such as 'Vera', 'Mabel' or 'Betty') which connote a very different generation, placed me outside the experience of 'Hollywood at its best': this produced a further imperative to convey to me the importance of Hollywood stars in their lives at that time, the significance of changes in the cinema since then, and the depth of the loss they mourn. Several respondents used stereotyped or cliched language to describe Hollywood stars of this era: 'stars of yesteryear', 'screen goddesses' and 'a trip down memory lane'. These and many other similar examples construct a special relationship to the past (through a direct knowledge of it, and use of dated language about it) for an imagined reader of a different generation.

In the role of 'invisible other' outside the memories, yet as the person for whom they are being produced, my position might be seen as equivalent to Bakhtin's 'superaddressee': 'the hypothetical presence who fully comprehends the speaker's words and hence allows his or her utterance to be made despite doubt about whether the "actual" addressee will understand and/or respond'.[17] As 'superaddressee' the researcher (by requesting them and then reading them) brings these memories into being, as it were. However, an ambivalence towards my role in this respect is also articulated; there is a feared mismatch between the ideal reader's and my actual position, for many respondents expressed anxiety about my not understanding the full significance of these memories (because I had not been there). The question of power imbalances between researcher and researched is central here. Straddling the roles of superaddressee and imagined addressee, I am expected to exercise authority over these memories (by representing them for publication, for example) – and indeed, this authority is seen in turn to 'authorize' these memories. However, my relationship to the material is also constantly under negotiation within the texts, as respondents establish their own authority about the Hollywood stars of the past over and above my own, and try to ensure that I make the correct readings of their memories.

In offering narrative accounts of the past, many respondents tell their stories and then add their own reflections upon them, as if anticipating the reader's response. This 'anticipatory mode' functions as a mediating voice which moves between the subject positions of 'self' and 'imagined other', producing a particular type of dialogicality in which reflexivity foregrounds the role of the addressee. The 'love at first sight' story about Deanna Durbin quoted above, for instance, ends with a shift of register in which the respondent comments directly on a possible (and within contemporary critical debates, virtually inevitable) interpretation of her love of Deanna Durbin. Continuing directly from the quotation above, she writes:

> I might just add that the members of our society [the Deanna Durbin Society] seem to be about equal in number male and female. I think perhaps it would be considered a bit of a giggle today, if a large number of women confessed to feeling love for a girl. Nobody seemed to question it then. Just in case: I have been married since 1948! Have two sons and a daughter, one grandchild.
>
> (Patricia Robinson)

In writing about her devotion to a star of the same sex, this respondent feels the need to guard against possible interpretations of homoeroticism in this charged connection.

Heterosexuality and reproduction are thus invoked to counter such speculations: a grandchild is even mentioned as if to stress the 'purity' and 'normality' not just of the respondent's desires, but also the next generation's. In the retelling, then, the presence of a (younger) imagined reader produces an anxiety about the story's significance today which needs to be defended against. A contrast is constructed between the 'innocence' of such an attachment in the past, and the embarrassment of 'confessing' it in today's culture in which homosexual interpretations might be more freely applied to such a declaration. Externalizing this memory of the 1930s and 1940s for a researcher in the 1980s, this respondent is brought up against a clash between present knowledge and past self: the former suggesting a different interpretation of the latter. If such a reading has occurred to the respondent's present self, she (quite correctly) anticipates its coincidence with my response to her story. Appealing against today's sexualization of such desires, she articulates concern that her memory may be spoiled or 'corrupted' by such discourses. Thus the reflection upon the account is produced in direct dialogue with the addressee, whose different values, or indeed desires, are imagined and incorporated into the account, and function to mediate between past and present discourses of sexuality and fandom.

An even more explicit extension of this anticipatory mode of addressivity occurs in the following example. Here, another respondent's account seems to be in dialogue not only with me, but also with herself, or rather with a version of her 'former selves'. Initially, an account is offered of how female stars functioned as role models for new fashions: 'We were quick to notice any change in fashion and whether it had arrived this side of the Atlantic. We were pleased to see younger stars without gloves and hats – we soon copied them'. However, this is followed by a self-conscious autocritique of the cultural construction of such feminine desirability:

> In retrospect, it's easy to see Hollywood stars for what they really were. This was pretty packaged commodities . . . the property of a particular studio. At the time I did most of my filmgoing, while I was always aware that stars were really too good to be true, I fell as completely under the spell of the Hollywood 'Dream Factory' as any other girl of my age. . . . Looking back, I can see much of what I took as authenticity was really technical skill. . . . Later on I realised just how much money and expertise went into creating the 'natural' beauties the female stars appeared to be.
>
> (Kathleen Lucas)

Throughout a long and very detailed reflection in answer to the central question about the appeal of particular stars in the 1940s and 1950s, this respondent shifts between a past self who was 'under the spell of Hollywood' and a present 'critical' self, producing an important contrast which might be seen to be in dialogue, as it were, with the reader/researcher. This example is exceptional rather than typical, and its particular form of dialogicality is due in part to the respondent's experience of similar research with the Mass-Observation Archive at Sussex University, to which she herself draws my attention in a covering letter. The self-commentary is offered here in response to an expected, even previously experienced, authoritative interpretation which might be imposed on these memories: the feminist critique is thus successfully anticipated and given voice in dialogue with the imagined researcher reading this account. As part of the same account she writes: 'Make-up artists were clever enough not to show the female stars as too artificial. The servicemen didn't want to see anything but a parade of glamour queens, so the make-up men aimed for a naturally perfect, or perfectly natural look'. Drawing attention to the power imbalances between researcher and researched, she correctly anticipates certain contemporary feminist critiques of stardom, glamour and 'the male gaze', and yet insists upon the pleasures for female spectators nevertheless: 'Really we were conned, but in the nicest possible way', she concludes.

Both these accounts might be seen as examples of what Bakhtin calls 'double-voiced discourse': this includes all speech 'which not only refers to something in the world but which also refers to another speech act by another addressee'.[18] The most obvious types of double-voiced discourse operating in these examples are what Bakhtin calls 'hidden dialogue' or 'hidden polemic' in which the narrator actively engages with an 'interlocutor not named in the text, but whose presence may be inferred'.[19] This inferred other outside the text may be a discourse as well as a known, or unknown, subject. In the case of hidden polemic, the inferred subject or discourse is seen as potentially antagonistic or hostile, which is not the case in hidden dialogue. Both the above examples present interesting dialogues with inferred others: each might be characterized as in dialogue with a discourse via my imagined subject position. Interestingly, despite never having met me, each narrator anticipates my concern with contemporary discourses of sexuality. In the Deanna Durbin example, for instance, the respondent both positions herself as the imagined reader of her own account, and comments upon the nature of her passion for this female star, whilst simultaneously defending against my also making such a comment and so constructing her desires within what she would consider a 'perverse' reading of her memories.

Similarly, in the last example, the respondent both produces an account of the 'mindless escapism of Hollywood of the past'; and yet, not wanting to be constructed as naive, also draws attention to the critique of such pleasures. In this case, the hidden polemic is not only with a potential feminist critique of Hollywood cinema, but also with a form of 'high culture' scorn for popular pleasures: her own ambivalence articulates precisely the complexity of the relationship between these two discourses. To offer one final example from this same account, which illustrates this exchange perfectly:

> Everything was rationed and shabby, then along came the glamour and expertise of Hollywood and we soaked it up like a sponge. It 'took people out of themselves' and transported them to a plane where they didn't need to think or worry. All they had to do was sit and stare. And the top Hollywood studios knew exactly what people wanted to see and they gave it to them. In a word, people needed 'escapism'.
>
> (Kathleen Lucas)

The repeated use of inverted commas, and the third, as well as the first person plural, produce a critical distance from the experience (this is something other people felt) whilst also including herself in it. The earlier reference to Hollywood as a 'Dream Factory' further reinforces this distance by invoking (knowingly?) a well-known sociological study of the American film industry.[20]

Thus, a contrast and mediation between past and present selves represented in these accounts is constructed through forms of dialogue with the researcher: it is, in part, my imagined presence in their texts which facilitates respondents' commentary and reflection upon their 'past selves' from the point of view of their present knowledges. In both the above examples, this anticipatory mode of addressivity not only incorporates me into the text as an imagined reader from another generation, but my anticipated construction of respondents' own identity is also projected into the text. Thus, not only is there a dialogue here between self and imagined other, but what might more accurately be described as a 'trialogic' relationship between self, imagined other and imagined other's fantasy of the self: in other words, the respondents, their projection of me and, finally completing this 'trialogic circuit', how they imagine my reading of their texts will in turn produce a version of their identities.

Indeed this 'third person presence' might be seen to characterize certain '*dynamics* of the dialogic context' if, as Pearce suggests, 'dialogues can be between more than two persons'.[21]

One of the 'inferred presences' of these hidden polemics is an evaluative discourse about popular culture and female pleasure in it. These negotiations of the researcher's anticipated responses, then, highlight particularly sharply the question of the value placed on female pleasures in these forms of popular culture: how should my 'invitation to remember' such pleasures be received – as a promise of their validation or as a threat of their condemnation? Either way, an anxiety about this question is clearly present in many of the responses I received, since, after all, I have the power to interpret and comment upon these texts and to represent them to (another) public. Kathleen Lucas is unusual in offering an autocritique of 'female fandom', but typical in so far as her memories are produced in relation to the *idea* of a judgement of such pleasures. For many respondents, my anticipated response is assumed to be an acknowledgment of the importance of their memories through their inclusion in 'cinema history', contradicting the usual derision they receive within patriarchal culture. Indeed, many offer accounts of how such attachments have been trivialized and not considered suitable for a 'mature' woman. Commenting on her brother's response to her collection of photographs of British and Hollywood stars, one woman writes:

> I had pictures of Patricia Roc, Margaret Lockwood, Petula Clarke, Jeanette McDonald, Dulcie Gray and my favourite, best loved of all – Margaret O'Brien! We used to send for photographs to MGM and RKO. . . . I'm afraid my brother cleared all 'that sort of rubbish' (his words, not mine) from my late mother's house before I was able to get there.
>
> (Cynthia Mulliner)

This respondent is keen to distance herself from the masculine trivialization of her much-loved collection by highlighting the gulf between his use of derisive language and her attachment to her belongings. Furthermore, her sense of regret is emphasized in the final phrase, 'before I was able to get there', suggesting the possibility of retrieval had the timing been different.

For others, the loss of such valued collections is attributed to World War II, *the* key event associated with loss during this period:

> I had a wonderful collection of personally autographed photos, mostly with my name written on them. Unfortunately, they went when my home was bombed during the war and I have been sad about this ever since. No personal loss has had so much effect on me as the loss of this collection (started when I was a schoolgirl).
>
> (Mrs M. Caplin)

> I wish I still had some of my magazines. My copies of *Photoplay* were immaculate – they were *never* loaned to *anybody*. I kept most of them for years, but unfortunately when the war came, they were discarded during my absence in the forces – much to my rage and frustration.
>
> (Mrs J. Kemp) (emphasis in original)

The most common explanation for change in spectators' attachments to the cinema at this time, however, is marriage – which marked the end of many female spectators' devotion to female stars. These accounts represent a shift in acceptability of such feelings for Hollywood stars:

> It amazes me to think of what choice of Picture Houses we had. I can remember at least twelve. You could go every night and see a different picture. And they were always full, with queues outside. We spent most of our Bank Holiday afternoons queuing to see Doris Day. But after I was married, we were rationed to once a week.
>
> (Jean Shepherd)

> At the time (1945) there was a film magazine called *Picturegoer* and I loved this book, but it was also a time of shortages, so one could only get this magazine from under the counter and also if you were a regular customer of that particular shop. When I discovered I could obtain this item I used to cycle like crazy from my work in the dinner time, just to obtain this film star book. I drove my poor Mum potty with all the cuttings plastered all over my bedroom walls and my masses of scrapbooks. I even dreamed of being an usherette. . . . I stopped going to the pictures after I was married and had a family.
>
> (Mrs M. Russell)

In a few examples, mothers are blamed for not recognizing the significance of such collections (thought perhaps they were thrown away precisely because such significance seemed inappropriate):

> I left home in 1953 on marriage and lived in a minute flat in London. By the time we could afford more space, my mother had dumped the things she thought a married woman didn't need. I found it hard to forgive her.
>
> (Anon)

All these stories point to respondents' feelings of a previous lack of recognition of the importance of film stars in their lives. Anger, betrayal and regret are expressed at the discrepancy between female spectators' high valuation of these photos and scrapbooks and other people's ridicule of them. Furthermore, marriage functions as a key boundary between 'girlhood' in which such attachments might be permissible and 'adulthood' in which such devotions might conflict with more 'appropriate' ones: 'When the time came to distinguish between "Childhood" and "Growing-Up", I must have destroyed as many as fifty books full'. (Avril Feltham) This construction of attachments to Hollywood stars of the same sex as immature, naive, foolish or even perverse, draws on a number of discourses of femininity and feminine sexuality in which the adoption of a man as the central love object signifies heterosexual maturity. In all these accounts, respondents articulate an ambivalent desire for recognition of the significance of these same-sex attachments as more than simply schoolgirl crushes or regressive narcissism, whilst simultaneously guarding against my criticism of their Hollywood passions: this they half-expect because they are so familiar with contempt from external critics, be these family, friends, husbands or researchers. Thus, running throughout many of these accounts is a dialogue with the imagined reader about the validity of indulging in such reminiscences of these 'silly' feminine pleasures.[22] Indeed, many express their own anxieties about the worth of their memories for cinema history, echoing the remembered questionability of their validity as a cultural experience at the time: several accounts finish with comments such as 'I can't imagine this is of much use to you' or 'I hope I have been of some help' and 'I can't see that my ramblings will be of great significance'.

Some respondents, however, took my research request for their memories to be a guarantee of recognition of previously low-status or stigmatized feelings about female stars. For example, an account of a previously discredited attachment to Doris Day implies a welcome contrast between past ridicule and my anticipated response. The direct address ('I wanted to write and tell you') suggests a sharing of a confidence with the expectation of an understanding reader:

> I wanted to write and tell you of my devotion to Doris Day. I thought she was fantastic, and joined her fan club, collected all the photos and info I could. I saw *Calamity Jane* 45 times in a fortnight and still watch all her films avidly. My sisters all thought I was mad going silly on a woman, but I just thought she was wonderful. . . . My sisters were all mad about Elvis, but my devotion was to Doris Day.
>
> (Veronica Mills)

The contrast to her sisters' attachments to Elvis, the epitome of smouldering heterosexual masculinity, suggests the unacceptability of the homoerotic connotations of this respondents' devotion. Previously dismissed as immature and trivial (she was considered 'mad' to be going 'silly' on a woman), these feelings towards a female star have not been recognized as significant since they lack the seriousness of mature heterosexual love. The dialogicality of this text is not just in relation to my position as imagined reader, then, but also in a 'hidden polemic' with her sisters; contesting her sisters' definition of her attachment to Doris Day as 'mad', the narrator defines it instead as 'devotion' and uses the (interestingly ambiguous) former term to refer to their love of Elvis.

These memories of cinematic spectatorship are thus constructed through forms of private storytelling which are given public recognition in the research process. Like many confessional acts, although utilizing so-called private forms, they are nevertheless written for another: for a kind of public consumption, first by me, the researcher; and secondly, once in print, by a wider audience. Indeed, perhaps the desire for recognition or validation of these previously low-status feelings is one reason why some of these female spectators offered their memories in a rather confessional mode. The disclosure of secret loves, private collections and lifetime devotions suggests that for some respondents the research process might function as a kind of 'secular confessional'. Perhaps my initial invitation to remember feelings towards female stars of the past belongs to a more general cultural imperative which encourages 'confession'. As Foucault has pointed out:

> We have become a singularly confessing society. The confession has spread far and wide. It plays a part in justice, medicine, education, family relationships, and love relations, in most ordinary affairs of everyday life, and in the most solemn rites; one confesses one's crimes, one's sins, one's thoughts and desires, one's illnesses and troubles; one goes about telling whatever is most difficult to tell. One confesses in public and in private, to one's parents, one's educators, one's doctor, to those one loves; one admits to oneself, in pleasure and in pain, the things people write books about.[23]

In describing some of these accounts as confessional, I do not mean to criticize the self-disclosures offered in this research process, but rather to comment on one particular form of articulation in the dialogic exchange between researcher and researched. As Rita Felski has pointed out, the use of the term 'confession' has sometimes 'acquired slightly dismissive overtones in recent years'; however, for her the confessional text is simply a subgenre of women's autobiography which 'makes public that which has been private'.[24] In the context of this research the making public of that which has been private is effected through producing written memories for someone else, someone invested with a certain amount of power and credibility. As a 'researcher', my academic status might in turn invest these memories with a weight and importance they are felt to lack. Confession might be understood here as a form of dialogics, for confession hinges on the idea of an addressee. According to Foucault we always confess to someone else, usually someone who represents authority:

> The confession is a ritual of discourse in which the speaking subject is also the subject of the statement; it is also a ritual that unfolds within a power relationship, for one does not confess without the presence (or virtual presence) of a partner who is not simply the interlocutor but the authority who requires the confession, prescribes and appreciates it and intervenes in order to judge, punish, forgive, console, and reconcile; a ritual in which truth is corroborated by the obstacles and resistances it has to surmount in order to be formulated; and finally, a ritual in which the expression alone, independently of its external consequences, produces intrinsic modifications in the person who articulates it: it exonerates, redeems, and purifies him [sic]; it unburdens him of his wrongs, liberates him and promises him salvation.[25]

The invitation to tell one's story to a researcher may offer the promise of being heard, recognized, and taken seriously. What makes this study particularly appealing as a 'confessional opportunity' is the way in which the act of confession itself elevates the material into significance. It thus offers the chance to (re)gain the (lost) status of certain emotions from the past. For what surfaces repeatedly in these narratives is the desire to recapture past pleasures which were either 'laughable' to begin with (as in the Doris Day example), or which have since lost their status (with marriage or maturity). The subsequent discrediting of attachments to female stars, then, seems to cast doubt on their original validity. In addition to changes in the film industry and the star system through which stars are perceived to have lost their earlier idol status, life history changes also mean the loss of status of earlier attachments to stars. These are combined in the desire to return to past moments and revalue them through the external recognition anticipated in the research process. This dialogical exchange thus promises an imagined transformation in the cultural status of emotional connections to Hollywood stars, resolving the discrepancy between respondents' own valuation, and others' trivialization, of these feminine popular pleasures.

> *For memory is, by definition, a term which directs our attention not to the past but to the past-present relation.*[26]

> *Memory alone cannot resurrect past time, because it is memory itself that shapes it, long after historical time has passed.*[27]

The dialogic analysis in the previous section highlights especially sharply the processes of memory in reworking past identities in relation to the present, and vice versa. Through these multiple dialogues, respondents are able to shift between past and present identities in their imaginations, and use my inferred presence to facilitate such temporal shifts. The dialogic exchanges function to produce both a dialogue with an imagined reader in the present, and also numerous other dialogues with discourses and interlocutors from the remembered past. These, it is argued, can only be understood in terms of 'the way in which popular memories are constructed and reconstructed as part of a *contemporary* consciousness'.[28] Popular memory theory therefore stresses the significance of the present as the standpoint from which remembered accounts are produced.

Why, then, do certain memories figure repeatedly in some people's accounts of the past, and how do such memories function as touchstones in their self-narrativizations? Certain memories, it has been suggested, have a particular function in processes of identity formation. Memories in which we have an enduring and recurring personal investment in terms of our identities have been called *treasured memories*.[29] Many respondents in my research wrote of such treasured memories and of their continuing significance: 'I have memories I shall always treasure. Other things in life take over, visiting the cinema is nil these days, but I shall always remember my favourite films and those wonderful stars of yesteryear'. (Mrs B. Morgan) Such treasured memories might be likened to a valued personal possession: an object of vast sentimental significance to the self, but a worthless trinket to others; that is, until the audience researcher revalues it, as it were. Here memories of Hollywood stars are a kind of personal cinema memorabilia. These fantasy objects are not only treasured by respondents, but also anticipated to be valuable proof of their own credentials as cinema historians:

> The major film stars of my major film-going period made a big impact on me. I can see a short clip from a film and know instantly whether I've seen it before or not – and as like or not, be able to add – 'then she moves off down the staircase' or 'the next dress she appears in is white with puffy net sleeves'.
>
> (M. Palin)

Indeed, it has been argued that treasured memories are particularly significant in conserving a fantasy of a past self and thereby guarding against loss.[30] Treasured memories may thus signify past selves or imagined selves which have also become important retrospectively. The notion of the treasured memory also suggests a place which can be regularly revisited. One woman writes:

> My grandfather's boss was kind enough to, every Christmas of my childhood, give me a present of a film annual. I enjoyed them then, but never dreamt what a treasure trove they'd prove to be. Now in my 50's, I pore over them from time to time and it's like opening Pandora's Box [sic]. Stars of yesteryear, long forgotten. Films I saw, but had forgotten all about. Hollywood at its height, the glitz and glamour. . . .
>
> (Barbara McWinter)

How might these treasured memories be understood as investments in particular versions of the past? One explanation might be that these memories represent particular 'transformative moments' in the spectator's life history.[31] Such moments are especially pertinent to the film star–spectator relationship because Hollywood stars embody cultural ideals of femininity and represent to spectators the possibility of transforming the self. Indeed, many memories pinpoint the role of Hollywood stars in the changes in spectators' own identities. This is partly due to the power of the discourse of transformation in the feminine life history, in which adolescence prefigures a fundamental change. Many respondents' memories are of a transitional period: their 'teenage' years, in which change and self-transformation were central to their desires and aspirations; and cinema is remembered as a transitional space in which the fantasy of possible futures is played out.

> The moment I took my seat it was a different world, plush and exciting, the world outside was forgotten. I felt grown up and sophisticated.
>
> (Betty Cruse)

It has been suggested that the pleasure of such memories derives from the ways they work as 'personal utopias', offering escape from the present. This is particularly pertinent with regard to spectators' memories of Hollywood stars, who seem to offer the most utopian fantasies to *female* spectators.[32] In this context, femininity itself might be seen as the ultimate utopian identity: an impossible ideal, predicated upon loss through its very embodiment in the *visual* image. The kinds of personal utopias produced depend upon past expectations and the extent to which these expectations have been met: some memories, in other words, retain a central emotional importance because of frustrations, disappointments and unfulfilled hopes. Furthermore, certain memories perhaps assume especial significance because they are 'stories of unfinished business'.[33] The degree of emotional investment in a memory may have to do with the extent to which the narrativization of a past self represents an aspect of identity with continuing significance in the present. Indeed, femininity might itself be regarded as 'unfinished business', since its production is quite literally never-ending.

Female spectators' youthful expectations and subsequent experiences of romance, motherhood or paid work, for example, may shape their reconstructions of past attachments to Hollywood ideals of femininity. Given the 'impossibility of femininity', such feelings may be especially pertinent to an understanding of these memories.[34] Feminine ideals are unrealizable, not only because of the fragility of the image, but also because they are often fundamentally contradictory (as, for example, ideals of motherhood and of sexual desirability). Furthermore, as Carolyn Steedman has shown, material constraints in certain periods in women's lives may shape investments in particular memories. This is especially pertinent in the context of 1950s consumerism and the 'age of affluence'.[35] Memories of Hollywood stars, as retrospective constructions of past time in which feminine identity still seemed realizable in the future, may have particular significance for female spectators as representations of a fantasy self never realized.

> *These occasions offer opportunities to* reassess *the past, in the light of subsequent experience and new information, in both personal terms ('when I was') and a past–present relation, and involve a constant process of reworking and transforming remembered experience.*[36]

Dialogic negotiations between past and present discourses and subjects are far from neutral. They are often shot through with wistful longing for remembered times, and with desire to recapture a lost sense of possibility: such memories, in other words, are deeply nostalgic. A yearning for an irretrievable lost time characterizes many of the memories in my study. The invitation to produce a remembered past promises the pleasure of an imagined retrieval, but simultaneously reminds respondents of the impossibility of reliving that past. In producing memories, 'people do *relive* certain past events imaginarily, often with peculiar vividness. This may be especially the case for those (for example, the elderly) who have been forced into a marginal position in the economic, cultural and social life of a society, and, fearful of absolute oblivion, have little to lose but their memories.'[37]

A typical version of the remembered past constructed in many of these Hollywood memories might be understood in relation to what Graham Dawson has referred to as a kind of 'mythic past': 'myth is always in the process of being alluded to, recycled, even controverted . . . yet there is never a moment when it appears *as itself* in pure form'.[38] In this respect, nostalgic yearnings for a lost Hollywood and for the 'truly great' stars of the 'Silver Screen' reinforce its mythic status during a 'Golden Age' of cinema which can never be recaptured. The 'genuine' star system is marked off from what came after, the demise of the studio era of Hollywood, in a remembered past in which stars were distant and still functioned as impossible ideals: 'I think in those eras we were more inclined to put stars on a pedestal. They were so far removed from everyday life, they were magical. These days are so ordinary – the magic has gone. Hollywood will never be the same again!' (Kathleen Sines)

This nostalgic pleasure of remembering Hollywood stars of the past has a particular appeal for female spectators because of the ways it connects with cultural constructions of femininity. Feminists using psychoanalytic theory have argued that nostalgia does indeed have a particular gendered appeal and that this is attributable to the significance of early feelings and beliefs about loss in relation to sexual difference.[39] However, the gendering of nostalgic desire in these memories hinges on the extent to which femininity is constructed in patriarchal culture as an unattainable visual image of desirability. To present oneself to the world for approval in terms of visible physical attractiveness is the fundamental and the ultimate demand made of femininity. Few women ever overcome the sense of mismatch between self-image and the feminine ideals of physical appearance. Feminine ideals are youthful ones and, being ephemeral, contain loss even in their rare attainment. The sense of loss evoked by nostalgic desire in these memories is partly bound up with the predication of femininity-as-image upon loss. The feelings of loss, often experienced in the gap between self-image and the currently fashionable ideal image, are deepened and extended as the ideal becomes ever-increasingly an impossibility. For these female spectators, then, nostalgic desire may be bound up with a particular sense of loss rooted in the unattainability of feminine ideals: perhaps it is its particular designation of femininity as image which gives cinematic nostalgia such potency.

Nostalgia is articulated here in relation to several 'lost objects': for a Hollywood of the past when cinema meant so much more than it does today; for a time when star status kept femininity a distant ideal image on the screen; for a former self – younger, more glamorous – who still maintained a fantasy connection to such ideals; for a past in which the future seemed to offer a promise of fulfilment. Nostalgia here is expressed as a yearning for a past in which the remembered self yearned for the future. The missing woman of cinema history and feminist film criticism has multiple references here: she is lost in history; lost in the demise of Hollywood and the star system; lost in the inevitable failure of femininity as desirable image; lost in personal narratives in which youth and feminine ideals no longer offer a promise of fulfilment. This sense of loss is bound up with femininity's cultural construction as an unattainable visual image of desirability, an image which is youthful and so doomed to transience. Memories of Hollywood stars in the 1940s and 1950s evoke nostalgic desire for a lost past, for imagined former identities, and for a time 'when stars were really stars'. Remembering these stars is an acknowledgement of the loss of that time, and yet also a way of guarding against complete loss by recreating the feeling of a past in which the future still held out promise.

Notes

1 For a comprehensive debate about the multiple meanings of the category 'the female spectator', see *Camera Obscura*, nos 20/21 (1989).

2 Helen Taylor, *Scarlett's Women: 'Gone With The Wind' and its Female Fans* (London: Virago, 1989); Jacqueline Bobo, '*The Color Purple*: Black women as cultural readers', in E. Deidre Pribram (ed.), *Female Spectators: Looking at Film and Television* (London: Verso, 1988); Angela Partington, 'Consumption practices as the production and articulation of differences: rethinking working-class femininity in 1950s Britain' (unpublished PhD: University of Birmingham, 1990); Janet Thumim, *Celluloid Sisters: Women and Popular Cinema* (London: Macmillan, 1992); Annette Kuhn, 'Researching popular film fan culture in 1930s Britain', in *Historical Studies of Film Reception* (Oslo: Norwegian Universities Press, 1994 forthcoming).

3 'Historical Methodologies' was the title of the opening plenary panel at the Screen Studies Conference 1993, at which an earlier version of this essay was presented. For discussions of this subject within film studies, see Janet Staiger, *Interpreting Films: Studies in the Historical Reception of American Cinema* (Princeton, NJ: Princeton University Press, 1992); and Thumim, *Celluloid Sisters*.

4 Jackie Stacey, *Star Gazing: Hollywood Cinema and Female Spectatorship* (London: Routledge, 1994).

5 Valerie Walkerdine, 'Video replay: families, films and fantasy', in Victor Burgin, James Donald and Cora Kaplan (eds), *Formations of Fantasy* (London: Methuen, 1986), p. 171.
6 Laura Mulvey, *Visual and Other Pleasures* (London and Basingstoke: Macmillan, 1989).
7 Jackie Stacey, entry on 'Romance', in Annette Kuhn (ed.), with Susannah Radstone, *The Women's Companion to International Film* (London: Virago, 1990), pp. 345–6; and Jackie Stacey and Lynne Pearce, 'The heart of the matter', in Lynne Pearce and Jackie Stacey (eds), *Romance Revisited* (London: Lawrence and Wishart, 1994 forthcoming).
8 History Workshop Journal, 'Review discussion: *In Search of a Past*: a dialogue with Ronald Fraser', *History Workshop Journal*, no. 20 (1985), pp. 175–88 (p. 182).
9 Popular Memory Group, 'Popular memory: theory, politics, method', in Centre for Contemporary Cultural Studies, *Making Histories* (London: Hutchinson, 1982), p. 243.
10 For a discussion of memory forms in oral history, see Luisa Passerini, *Fascism in Popular Memory: The Cultural Experience of the Turin Working Class*, trans. Robert Lumley and Jude Bloomfield (Cambridge: Cambridge University Press, 1987).
11 V. N. Voloshinov, quoted in Lynne Pearce, *Reading Dialogics* (London: Edward Arnold, 1994), p. 43. I am indebted to Lynne Pearce for my understanding and use of dialogic theory in this section.
12 M. Bakhtin, quoted in ibid., p. 74.
13 See, for example, Pearce's own textual readings in this light, ibid.
14 For a discussion of the uses of psychoanalysis in oral history, see Karl Figlio, 'Oral history and the unconscious', *History Workshop Journal*, no. 26 (1988), pp. 120–32: T. G. Ashplant, 'Psychoanalysis in historical writing', *History Workshop Journal*, no. 26 (1988), pp. 102–19; and responding to this work, Jacqueline Rose, 'A comment', *History Workshop Journal*, no. 28 (1989), pp. 149–54.
15 Popular Memory Group, 'Popular memory', p. 246.
16 For the full questionnaire see Stacey, *Star Gazing*, pp. 245–51.
17 Pearce, *Reading Dialogics*, p. 76.
18 David Lodge, quoted in ibid., p. 51.
19 Pearce, ibid., p. 53.
20 Hortense Powdermaker, *Hollywood, the Dream Factory* (Boston, MA: Little Brown, 1950).
21 Pearce, *Reading Dialogics*, pp. 202–3.
22 Taylor, *Scarlett's Women*, p. 204.
23 Michel Foucault, *The History of Sexuality: An Introduction*, trans. Robert Hurley (Harmondsworth: Penguin, 1981), p. 59.
24 Rita Felski, *Beyond Feminist Aesthetics: Feminist Literature and Social Change* (London: Hutchinson Radius, 1989), pp. 87–8.
25 Foucault, *History of Sexuality*. p. 62. I am grateful to Hilary Hinds for drawing my attention to these passages on confession.
26 Popular Memory Group, 'Popular memory', p. 211.
27 Carolyn Steedman, *Landscape for a Good Woman: A Story of Two Lives* (London: Virago, 1986), p. 29.
28 Popular Memory Group, 'Popular memory', p. 219.
29 Popular Memory Group, unpublished papers on popular memory (University of Birmingham: Centre for Contemporary Cultural Studies, n.d.).
30 Ibid., p. 26.
31 Ibid., p. 161.
32 Richard Dyer, 'Entertainment and utopia', in Bill Nichols (ed.), *Movies and Methods*, Volume II (Berkeley. CA: University of California Press, 1985), pp. 220–32; see also Stacey, *Star Gazing*, pp. 80–125.
33 Popular Memory Group, unpublished papers, p. 30.
34 Stacey, *Star Gazing*, pp. 212–7.
35 Steedman, *Landscape for a Good Woman*.
36 Graham Dawson and Bob West, 'Our finest hour?': the popular memory of World War II and the struggle over national identity', in Geoff Hurd (ed.), *National Fictions: World War Two in British Films and Television* (London: British Film Institute, 1984), pp. 10–11.
37 Popular Memory Group, 'Popular memory', p. 243.
38 Graham Dawson, 'History-writing on World War II', in Hurd, *National Fictions*.
39 For an account of the psychoanalytic arguments about gender and nostalgia, see Susannah Radstone, 'Remembering Medea: the uses of nostalgia', *Critical Quarterly*, vol. 35, no. 3 (1993), pp. 54–63; 'Remembering ourselves: memory, writing and the female self', in Penny Florence and Deidre Reynolds (eds), *Feminist Subjects, Multi-Media: New Approaches to Criticism and Creativity* (Manchester: Manchester University Press, 1994 forthcoming).

Index

Page references in *italics* denote figures; references in bold denote tables.

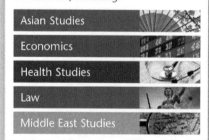